GREAT ISSUES
IN WESTERN CIVILIZATION

VOLUME II

Edited by BRIAN TIERNEY,

DONALD KAGAN,

and L. PEARCE WILLIAMS

CORNELL UNIVERSITY

CONSULTING EDITOR: *Eugene Rice*

COLUMBIA UNIVERSITY

Random House New York

GREAT ISSUES

IN WESTERN

CIVILIZATION

VOLUME II

TS-8630   Proof 1   5-31-67

To Frederick G. Marcham

TEACHER—SCHOLAR—COLLEAGUE—FRIEND

Preface

A major purpose of this two-volume work is to convince students in Western civilization courses that the essential task of a historian is not to collect dead facts but to confront live issues. The issues are alive because they arise out of the tensions that men have to face in every generation—tensions between freedom and authority, between reason and faith, between human free will and all the impersonal circumstances that help to shape our lives.

In order to achieve any sophisticated understanding of such matters a student needs to read the views of great modern historians as they are set out in their own words. He needs to develop a measure of critical historical insight by comparing these often conflicting views with the source material on which they are based. He needs above all to concern himself with the great issues that have shaped the course of Western civilization and not with historical "problems" that are mere artificially contrived conundrums.

This volume is divided into eleven sections. Each of them presents both original source material and a variety of modern interpretations; and each deals with a truly great issue in Western history.

We believe that there are three major themes whose development and interplay have shaped the distinctive characteristics that set Western civilization apart from the other great historic cultures. They are the growth of a tradition of rational scientific inquiry, the persistence of a tension between Judaeo-Christian religious ideals and social realities, the emergence of constitutional forms of government. These three themes are introduced in the first sections of Volume I. The reader will find them recurring in new forms and changing contexts throughout the rest of the two-volume work. We hope that in studying them he will come to a richer understanding of the heritage of Western civilization—and of the historian's approach to it.

Ithaca, 1967   BRIAN TIERNEY

DONALD KAGAN

L. PEARCE WILLIAMS

Contents

The Scientific Revolution—

Factual or Metaphysical?

CONTENTS

QUESTIONS FOR STUDY

1   How do the methods proposed by Bacon and Descartes for the study of nature differ?

2   What practical problems could the new science actually solve?

3   Compare Galileo's view of ultimate reality ("The Assayer") with Newton's view (Third Rule of Reasoning).

4   In what ways do Merton and Bernal agree? Disagree?

5   What would Koyré insist is the weakness in Bernal's interpretation? How would Bernal defend himself?

Between the publication of Nicolas Copernicus' On the Revolutions of the Heavenly Spheres *in 1543 and the beginning of the eighteenth century, a revolution in thought took place in Europe. The dimensions of this revolution are only now being fully revealed—no one can deny it transformed the world. It all started 400 years ago—but precisely* what *started and how the speculations of a Polish cathedral canon became the foundations for the structure of modern science is not at all clear. Did science arise naturally out of the new needs of European society? Or is science essentially a philosophical pursuit dealing with questions of ultimate reality that have fascinated Western man since the Greeks?*

1 The Dimensions of the Scientific Revolution

J. D. Bernal is one of England's leading scientists, who has, for many years, concerned himself with the mutual interactions of science and society. To Bernal, science is essentially an intellectual response to changing social and economic needs. In the following selection he maps out the ways in which this response led to the Scientific Revolution in the seventeenth century.

FROM *Science in History* BY J. D. BERNAL

T HE PERIOD roughly from 1540 to 1650 has no convenient name in history. It has been called the Counter-Renaissance, but this would indicate a far greater degree of reaction to the earlier phase than actually took place. It includes the Counter-Reformation, with the Baroque style that was its visible expression, the Wars of Religion that raged in turn in France (1560–98), in the Low Countries (1572–1609), and in Germany (1618–48), and the establishment of the States General of Holland in 1576 and the Commonwealth of England in 1649. Of these events it was the last two that were to have the greatest ultimate significance. They point to the political triumph of the new bourgeoisie in the two countries in which was concentrated the bulk of the world's trade and manufacture.

In science the period includes the first great triumphs of the new observational, experimental approach. It opens fresh from the first exposition of the solar system by Copernicus and closes with its firm establishment—despite the condemnation of the Church—through the work of Galileo. It includes in its scope Gilbert's description in 1600 of the earth as a magnet and Harvey's discovery in 1628 of the circulation of the blood. It witnesses the first use of the two great extenders of visible Nature, the telescope and the microscope.

J. D. Bernal, *Science in History*, 2nd ed. (1957), pp. 281–2, 287–8, 291–3, 295–8, 304–5, 307, 334–42. Reprinted by permission of C. A. Watts & Co. Ltd., London.

Economically the century was dominated by the cumulative effects of the navigations, which by then involved a trade comparable with the old internal trade of Europe. It was specially marked by the great increase in prices brought about by the influx of American silver. The breakdown of feudal land-holding in western Europe, especially in Holland and England, had thrown on the market landless people, and, at the same time, the real wages of hired workers were seriously depressed. This had the effect of lowering the cost of products in a period of rising prices and increasing markets, and at the same time of providing an abundant labour force for manufacturers. The result was an unprecedented increase in the wealth of those traders and manufacturers who were on the new oceanic trade routes and could draw on new resources and supply new markets.

*   *   *

THE NEW EXPERIMENTAL PHILOSOPHERS

It was in this atmosphere that the new, half-awakened science of Europe was to grow to maturity. Despite widespread privilege and corruption it was not by any means an unfavourable one. Even the movement of the Counter-Reformation, which successfully checked and turned back the advance of Protestantism in Europe, had not the same effect on science. The Jesuits who directed it had the intelligence to realize that they were more likely to win souls by fostering science than by blindly opposing it. They accordingly entered fully into the scientific movement, particularly the new astronomy, and were even the agents for spreading it and setting up observatories in India, China, and Japan. At the same time they acted as watchdogs inside science to guard against any damaging effect it might have on true religion, and thus unintentionally gave an advantage to scientists in Protestant countries out of their control.

*   *   *

The new experimental philosophers, or scientists as we would now call them . . . , no longer formed part of the intense city life of the Renaissance; they appeared more as individual members of the new bourgeoisie, largely lawyers, like Vieta, Fermat, Bacon; doctors—Copernicus, Gilbert, Harvey; a few minor nobles—Tycho Brahe, Descartes, von Guericke, and van Helmont; churchmen, like Mersenne and Gassendi; and even one or two brilliant recruits from the lower orders, like Kepler. In history they are made to figure as being isolated; but in reality they were, because of their very small numbers, always in far easier and quicker contact with each other than scientists of today, with their vast numbers and the pressure, publication delays, and increasing military and political restrictions to which they are subjected.

*   *   *

. . . Kepler tried to find the best way of representing planetary motions by a single curve. Copernicus had still stuck to circles and epicycles, but not only were these clumsy but they could not be made to fit the new accurate observations. Kepler found, after many failures, that the only explanation of the observed movement of the planet Mars was that its orbit was an ellipse with the sun as focus. The idea of elliptical orbits was not completely new; it had been suggested by Arzachel (1029–87) of Toledo in the eleventh century, but on quite inadequate data. Kepler succeeded because he came at a time when the data were exact enough to show that no circle or combination of circles would do, and not so late for them to be so exact that it was apparent that the orbits were not true ellipses but more complicated curves, which were to be explained only by Einstein.

The hypothesis of elliptical orbits, and the two other laws by which Kepler explained the speed of a planet in its orbit, not only removed the main astronomical objection to the hypothesis of Copernicus, but they also struck a mortal blow at the Pythagorean-Platonic view of the necessity of the heavens showing perfect—that is, circular—motions only, which even Copernicus had retained. . . .

THE TELESCOPE

The step that was to prove decisive in securing the acceptance of the new view of the heavens was not to be any further extension of astronomical calculation, appreciated only by experts, but a direct physical means available to all of bringing the heavens down to earth so that sun, moon, and stars could be more closely examined; in other words the invention of a telescope or far-seer.

*   *   *

GALILEO GALILEI

The telescope was to prove the greatest scientific instrument of the age. The bare news of it reaching the ears of the professor of physics and military engineering at Padua, Galileo Galilei (1564–1642), determined him to make one himself and turn it on the heavens. Galileo was already a convinced Copernican, as well as being deeply interested in the movements of pendulums and the related problems of the fall of bodies. In the first few nights of observation of the heavens he saw enough to shatter the whole of the Aristotelian picture of that serene element. For the moon, instead of being a perfect sphere, was found to be covered with seas and mountains; the planet Venus showed phases like the moon; while the planet Saturn seemed to be divided into three. Most important of all, he observed that around Jupiter there circled three stars or moons, a small-scale model of the Copernican system, which anyone who looked through a telescope could see for himself.

With his keen sense of publicity and of the material value of his discoveries, which he found in no way incompatible with the pure joy of discovery, Galileo immediately tried to sell the titles of these stars in succession to the Duke of Florence (a Medici), to the King of France, and to the Pope, but the celestial honours seemed too expensive to all of them. Later, when the more practical end of using their motion to determine longitude at sea occurred to him, he tried to sell the secret to the King of Spain and the States General of Holland, who had both offered prizes for the discovery of the longitude, but still found no takers.

These attempts, however, were to Galileo mere side-shows. He sensed at once the really revolutionary character of the new observations. Here he had for everyone to see the very model of Copernicus' system in the sky. This was knowledge not to keep but to broadcast. Within a month, in 1610, he had published what was clearly a scientific best seller, *Siderius Nuntius*, i.e. "Messenger from the Stars," in which his observations were set out briefly and plainly. . . .

THE FALL OF BODIES: DYNAMICS

But Galileo felt it was not sufficient to have verified by observation the aesthetic preference of Copernicus. It was also necessary to justify it by explaining how such a system could exist, and by removing the objections which both philosophy and good sense had raised to it in the past. It was necessary to explain how the rotation of the earth could occur without a mighty wind blowing in the opposite direction and how bodies projected through the air would not be left behind. This meant a serious study of bodies in free motion, a problem which had already become of great practical importance in relation to the aiming of projectiles.

*   *   *

EXPERIMENTAL PHYSICS

Galileo succeeded, where others had failed, in formulating a mathematical description of the motion of bodies. This was to be the major work of his life, expressed fully only in his *Dialogues on Two New Sciences,* published after his condemnation but implicit in the *Dialogue Concerning the Two Chief Systems of the World,* which was to be the immediate cause of his conflict with the Church. Galileo proceeded to question all the accepted views and to do so by the new method, the method of experiment. Whether or not in fact he dropped weights from the top of the tower of Pisa is not the essential point; we know that he used both the pendulum and the inclined plane to make accurate measurements of the fall of bodies.

These were almost but not quite the first experiments of the modern science. They differed from the experiments of the thirteenth-century scholars mainly in being exploratory rather than illustrative, and even more by their quantitative character, which could be fitted into mathematical theory. Galileo himself showed a transitional attitude towards his own experiments. He once stated that he carried them out not to convince himself but to convince others. He was superbly confident in his power to interpret Nature by reason. In this sense they were rather demonstrations than experiments. Nevertheless he really did carry them out, unlike the ideal, paper experiments which befog modern physics; and what is more, when they gave results he did not expect, he did not reject them but turned back to question his own arguments, thereby showing the essential humility before fact that is the hall-mark of experimental science.

The mathematical interpretation of Galileo's experiments on falling bodies here proved to be far more difficult than the experiments themselves. The idea that had to be grasped was that a body that was changing its speed all the time could have any particular speed at a given moment. As a matter of fact Galileo went wrong to start with and assumed that speed was gained in proportion to the distance gone through by the body, whereas, as he himself was later to conclude, it depended directly on the *time* the body was falling. To understand the falling of bodies, and consequently both the motions of cannon balls in the air and of the moon in the sky, it was essential to grasp the very difficult physical idea of the velocity at a moment of time. This corresponds to the mathematical idea of a differential, dx/dt: the ratio of two quantities that remains constant even if the quantities themselves become vanishingly small. Galileo used these ideas without precisely formulating them. By combining exact experiment and mathematical analysis, he solved the relatively simple problem of the fall of bodies, showing that in the absence of air they followed a parabolic path. In doing so he provided the first clear example of the methods of modern physics, which were to have such an extraordinarily successful development in succeeding centuries. Indeed the exact physical method he initiated has, until very recently, been taken as *the* basic method of science, one to which all other science may in the end be reduced.

*　　*　　*

To complete the chain of argument it was necessary for Galileo to link mathematics with mechanics. How to do this was a major preoccupation throughout his whole scientific life. Leonardo was groping after a quantitative approach to mechanics; Galileo, with the advantages of better experiments and a more applicable mathematics, fully grasped it. He became one of the founders of scientific engineering. Another was the same Simon Stevin of Bruges, the first great engineer of the new Holland, who took a large part in the war of liberation. He was responsible for the laws of composition of forces and for the foundations of quantitative hydraulics.

STATICS AND DYNAMICS: PRIMARY AND SECONDARY QUANTITIES

A full understanding of the movement of massive bodies requires a treatment of forces first in equilibrium, as in *statics,* then out of equilibrium, as in *dynamics*. These were the "Two new Sciences" in which Galileo laid the foundations not only of the laws of motion but also of the mathematical theory of the strength of materials, which he based on discussions with master shipwrights.

Galileo stated more clearly than anyone before him that the necessary and intrinsic properties of matter—the only ones in fact that could be dealt with mathematically, and therefore with any certainty—were extension, position, and density. All others, "tastes, smells, colours, in regard to the object in which they appear to reside are nothing more than mere names. They exist only in the sensitive body. . . ." This was not understood by the advocates of the new science as a limitation, but as a programme of reduction of all experiments to the primary qualities of "size, shape, quantity, and motion."

THE DESTRUCTION OF ANCIENT COSMOLOGY

To win general recognition for his new mathematical-mechanical science Galileo had first to destroy the Ptolemaic system of the heavenly spheres and with it, as he himself saw clearly, the whole Aristotelian philosophy which for nearly 2,000 years had been the foundation not only of the natural but also of the social sciences. He was particularly suited for the task, as he had seen Aristotelian philosophy at its best in Padua. He was no outsider, but was able to refute the master by his own logic in the way in which scholars could not ignore, however much they might disapprove. Implicitly all his work was a protest against Aristotelians, but his first explicit blast came in 1632 in his polemical book *Dialogue concerning the Two Chief Systems of the World, the Ptolemaic and the Copernican,* which he dedicated to the Pope. Here, not in learned Latin but in Italian for all to read, he mercilessly criticized and ridiculed the officially held views on the most important of subjects. This was the first great manifesto of the new science.

*   *   *

The first intellectual object of the scientific revolution had been achieved: the classical world-picture had been destroyed, though only the bare outlines of a new one had been put in its place. In doing so new means for understanding and conquering Nature had been found, but little had as yet emerged that could be claimed to be of general practical use. The telescope itself was a technical rather than a scientific invention. Before the effects of the revolution in thought could make themselves felt in practice, it was necessary that the possibilities the new science offered should be brought home not only to the learned but to the new class of enterprising people that were making their own political revolution—merchants, navigators, manufacturers, statesmen, and the early and progressive capitalists. Galileo had started to do this, but he was living in a country that had already lost its *élan* and that was rapidly being frozen into reaction by the Counter-Reformation.

THE PROPHETS: BACON AND DESCARTES

Two men from the less cultured but far more active northern countries were to take on the task—Bacon and Descartes. These two major figures stood at the turning point between medieval and modern science. Both were essentially prophets and publicists, men who had seen a vision of the possibility of knowledge and were making it their business to show it to the world. Both were universal in scope, though their approaches to knowledge were very different. Temperamentally, too, it would be difficult to find two more different people than the shrewd, self-seeking, and afterwards rather pompous lawyer, always at the centre of public affairs, and the intensely introspective, solitary ex-soldier of fortune. Each too is characteristic of the nature of the scientific revolution in his own country.

* * *

THE *Novum Organum* AND THE *Discours de la Méthode*

Both thinkers were preoccupied with methods, though their ideas of scientific method were very different. Bacon's was that of collecting materials, carrying out experiments on a large scale, and finding the results from a sheer mass of evidence—an essentially *inductive* method. Descartes, on the other hand, believed in the rapier thrust of pure intuition. He held that with clarity of thought it should be possible to discover everything rationally knowable, experiment coming in essentially as an auxiliary to *deductive* thought. The major difference, however, was that while Descartes used his science to construct a *system* of the world, a system which, though now almost forgotten, was able in its time completely to supersede that of the medieval schoolmen, Bacon put forward no system of his own but was content to propose an *organization* to act as a collective builder of new systems. His function as he saw it was only to provide the builders with the new tool—the logic of the *Novum Organum*—with which to do it.

In this sense they were strictly complementary. Bacon's concept of organization led directly to the formation of the first effective scientific society, the Royal Society. Descartes' system, by breaking definitely with the past, put up a set of concepts which could be the basis of argument about the material world in a strictly quantitative and geometric manner.

Bacon was taken to be, and rightly, the first great man who had given a new direction to science and who had linked it definitely once more to the progress of material industry.

With his empirical bent Bacon was inevitably an opponent of all predetermined systems in Nature; he believed that, given a well-organized and well-equipped body of research workers, the weight of facts would ultimately lead to truth. Descartes' method, on the other hand, was a more direct successor of that of the schools, with this absolute difference: that it was not *their* system that he wanted to establish but *his own.* In this he exhibited that individual arrogance which was one of the great liberating features of the Renaissance, the same arrogance that expressed itself in the great navigators, in the *conquistadores,* in all the defiances of authority that characterized the end of the feudal period and the beginning of one of individual enterprise.

Unconsciously, Descartes' system incorporated very much of the system which he wished to destroy. There was the same insistence on deductive logic and self-evident propositions, but starting with these he used the *mathematics,* of which he was a master, to arrive at conclusions far beyond the reach of his medieval or even of his classical predecessors. His major mathematical contribution was the use of co-ordinate geometry, by which a curve could be completely represented by an equation relating the values of the co-ordinates of its points referred to fixed axes. This was more than the mapping of geometry. It broke down the old distinction between the Greek science of the continuum—*geometry*—and the Babylonian-Indian-Arabic calculus of numbers—*algebra.* Henceforth their two powers would be joined to attack problems never before attempted.

*   *   *

CELESTIAL MECHANICS: THE NEWTONIAN SYNTHESIS

While all these achievements bear witness to the great flowering of scientific activity in many fields, the central interest and the greatest scientific triumph of the seventeenth century was undoubtedly the completion of a general system of *mechanics* capable of accounting for the motion of the stars in terms of the observable behaviour of matter on earth. Here the moderns were in effect settling their accounts once and for all with the ancient Greeks. Ancients and moderns were both agreed on the importance of the study of the heavens. But because the interests of the latter were now more practical than philosophic, they required a very different kind of answer. . . .

The intrinsic interest of the problem of the movements of the solar system was still very great, though, in fact, its philosophical and theological significance had already vanished with the destruction of the cosmology of the Ancients. The trial of Galileo was indeed in the nature of a futile parting shot by clerical Aristotelianism. But the new edifice that was to take its place would not be complete unless an acceptable physical explanation of the system of Copernicus and Kepler could be found. That was one reason why almost every natural philosopher speculated, experimented, and calculated with the aim of finding this explanation. Some got very close to it, particularly Hooke, until Newton's success ended the chase.

FINDING THE LONGITUDE

The astronomers had another and even more compelling reason for discovering the laws of motion of the solar system. This was the need for astronomical tables far more accurate than had sufficed in the days when astronomy was required mainly for astrological prediction. The needs of navigation were far more stringent. The determination of a ship's position at sea, and particularly the more difficult part of the position, the longitude, was a recurring problem. It became more and more urgent as a larger and larger share of the economic and military effort of countries was spent in overseas ventures, especially of those countries that were themselves the centres of scientific advance: England, France, and Holland. The finding of the longitude was a question that was to occupy both the learned astronomers and the practical sailors for many decades, even centuries. It was for the purpose of assisting in the solution of this practical problem that the first nationally financed scientific institutions were set up—the Observatoire Royal at Paris in 1672 and the Royal Observatory at Greenwich in 1675.

The question of the determination of longitude is essentially one of determining absolute time—or, as we now would call it, Greenwich time—at any place. This, compared with the local times, gives the time interval which is directly convertible to longitude. At any place there are, or were before the invention of radio, only two methods of determining the Greenwich time: one by observing the movements of the moon among the stars—a clock already fixed in the sky; and the other by carrying around an accurate clock originally set at that time. The first required extremely accurate tables for the prediction of the place of heavenly bodies, the second absolutely reliable clock mechanisms. All through the seventeenth and a large part of the eighteenth centuries both lines of attack were pursued without definite advantage falling to either. There was an immediate stimulus to thought, observation, and experiment in both directions, a stimulus in part simply mercenary but also one of national and individual prestige.

*   *   *

PLANETARY MOTIONS: THE DOCTRINE
OF ATTRACTION

It was, however, the purely astronomical approach that, though it failed to provide the practical solution, was to prove far the more valuable to the science of the future. This was because of the stimulus it gave to the finding of a mathematical and dynamical solution to the problem of planetary motion. Many people had speculated as to why the planets should move round the sun in the orbits which Kepler had first shown were elliptical; they had even guessed that they might be held there by some force of attraction. In fact the idea of attraction had been a common one ever since Gilbert's study of the magnet, and even before. The magnet showed that attraction was possible at a distance and Gilbert himself had suggested that what held the planets in their position and indeed drove them round their orbits might just be magnetism.

Borelli in 1666 introduced the important idea that the movements of planets implied the existence of the need to balance the centrifugal force, such as that exerted by a stone in a sling, by some other force which he characterized as the force of gravity extending beyond the immediate neighbourhood of the earth to the moon and from the sun to the planets. To account for an elliptical orbit, with the planet moving faster as it nears the sun, the force of gravity must increase to balance the increased centrifugal force. The force of gravity is therefore some function of the power of the distance. The question now became: What function? Hooke, who had already suspected that gravity diminished with the distance, tried to confirm it by looking, though in vain, for the variation of weight in a body on the ground, in a mine-shaft, and at the top of a steeple.

The prevailing theory of gravity remained that of Descartes: namely, that heavy bodies were sucked down to their centres of attraction by "some secret principle of unsociableness of the ethers of their vortices," to quote Newton, who adhered to this theory as late as 1679.

Things could go no further until these general ideas could be reduced to a mathematical form and checked with observations. The first step to this was taken by Huygens in 1673, when in connection with his work on pendulum clocks he enunciated the law of centrifugal force, showing that it varied as the radius and inversely as the square of the period. Now the square of the period, according to Kepler's third law, was proportional to the cube of the radius, and it follows therefore that the gravitational pull or centripetal force to balance the centrifugal force must depend on the radius divided by its cube, that is on the inverse square of the radius. Hooke, Halley, and Wren had made this deduction by 1679. Two problems remained: that of the explanation of elliptic orbits; and the mode of action of large attractive bodies. Hooke wrote to Newton, putting these problems, but received no reply, and in 1684 Halley offered a prize for their solution. It was clear that the answer was very near, but, though many men had led up to it, only one had the mathematical ability to find it and to draw the revolutionary conclusions that followed from it.

ISAAC NEWTON

That man was Isaac Newton, one of the younger generation of Fellows—born in 1642, the year Galileo died—but already well known for his mathematical and optical researches. Newton came from the new rural middle class that had already produced Cromwell and the parliamentary officers. He was the posthumous son of a small Lincolnshire farmer with connections good enough to send him to Cambridge, where he studied with no particular distinction.

*   *   *

Newton's public entry into the discussions of gravitation came late. . . . [His] contribution was, nevertheless, the decisive one. It lay in finding the mathematical method for converting physical principles into quantitatively calculable results confirmable by observation, and conversely to arrive at the physical principles from such observations. In his own words from the preface of *Principia:*

> I offer this work as the mathematical principles of philosophy, for the whole burden of philosophy seems to consist in this—from the phenomena of motions to investigate the forces of Nature, and then from these forces to demonstrate the other phenomena; . . . I wish we could derive the rest of the phenomena of Nature by the same kind of reasoning from mechanical principles, for I am induced by many reasons to suspect that they may all depend upon certain forces by which the particles of bodies, by some causes hitherto unknown, are either mutually impelled towards one another, and cohere in regular figures, or are repelled and recede from one another. These forces being unknown, philosophers have hitherto attempted the search of Nature in vain; but I hope the principles here laid down will afford some light either to this or some truer method of philosophy.

THE INFINITESIMAL CALCULUS

The instrument by which he did this was the infinitesimal calculus or, as he called it, the method of fluxions (the even flowing of a continuous function). . . .

By its use it is possible to find the position of a body at any time by a knowledge of the relations between that position and its velocity or rate of change of velocity at any other time. In other words, once the law of force is known, the path can be calculated. Applied inversely, Newton's law of gravitational force follows directly from Kepler's law of motion. Mathematically they are two different ways of saying the same thing; but whereas the laws of planetary motion seem abstract, the idea of a planet held in its course by a powerful attraction is a graspable image, even if the gravitational force itself remains a complete mystery.

The calculus, as developed by Newton, could be used and was used by him for the solving of a great variety of mechanical and hydrodynamic problems. It immediately became the mathematical instrument for all understanding of variables and motion, and hence of all mechanical engineering, and remained almost the exclusive one until well into the present century. In a very real sense it was as much an instrument of the new science as the telescope.

THE ''PRINCIPIA''

It must have required all Halley's persuasiveness to make Newton, in the two years 1685–86, embody his solution of planetary motions in his *Philosophiae Naturalis Principia Mathematica*. It was printed for the Royal Society and bears the imprint of its President, who was rather surprisingly Samuel

Pepys, but the Society was short of money and Halley had to pay for its production out of his own pocket. This book, in sustained development of physical argument, is unequalled in the whole history of science. Mathematically it can only be compared to Euclid's *Elements;* in its physical insight and its effect on ideas only to Darwin's *Origin of Species.* It immediately became the bible of the new science, not so much as a revered source of doctrine—though there was some danger of this, especially in England—but of further extensions of the methods there exemplified.

*   *   *

A great deal of the *Principia* is taken up with a careful and quantitative refutation of the system most in vogue and with which he himself had flirted, that of Descartes with its set of whirlpools in which each planet was held. This was a genial intuitive idea but one totally incapable, as Newton showed, of giving accurate quantitative results. In doing so, he was led into founding the science of *hydrodynamics,* discussing and refining the ideas of *viscosity* and the resistance of the air, and indeed laying the basis for a mechanics of fluids that was to come into its own only in the day of the aeroplane.

Though Newton used the calculus in arriving at his results, he was careful in the *Principia* to recast all the work in the form of classical Greek geometry understandable by other mathematicians and astronomers. The immediate practical consequence of its publication was to provide a system of calculation enabling the positions of the moon and planets to be determined far more accurately, on the basis of a minimum of observations, than his predecessors could by their empirical extension of long series. Three observations, for instance, were sufficient to fix the position of a celestial object for an indefinite future.

The proof of this was furnished soon after Newton's time by his friend Halley in his famous comet, whose return he successfully predicted on the basis of Newton's theories. As a result of using Newtonian theories nautical tables became far more accurate. Unfortunately, the most suitable celestial object to observe for the purpose of finding the longitude is the moon, and the moon's motion is quite the most complicated in the solar system. It was never reduced to good enough order to be a reliable guide to sailors, and in the end it was the scientifically minded clockmakers who took the prize—or as much of it as they could persuade the Admiralty to part with—from the mechanically minded astronomers.

NEWTON REPLACES ARISTOTLE: AN ESTABLISHED UNIVERSE AGAINST A MAINTAINED ONE

Newton's theory of gravitation and his contribution to astronomy mark the final stage of the transformation of the Aristotelian world-picture begun by

Copernicus. For a vision of spheres, operated by a first mover or by angels on God's order, Newton had effectively substituted that of a mechanism operating according to a simple natural law, requiring no continuous application of force, and only needing divine intervention to create it and set it in motion.

Newton himself was not quite sure about this, and left a loophole for divine intervention to maintain the stability of the system. But this loophole was closed by Laplace and God's intervention dispensed with. Newton's solution, which contains all the quantities necessary for the practical prediction of the positions of the moon and the planets, stops short of any fundamental questioning of the existence of a divine plan. Indeed Newton felt he had revealed this plan and wished to ask no further questions.

He got over the awkward assumption he had made on the existence of absolute motion by saying, following his Platonist friends, that space was the sensorium—awareness or brain—of God, and must therefore be absolute. In this way he avoided confusing himself in relativistic theories. His own theory gave no reasons why the planets should all be more or less in a plane and all go round the same way—for which Descartes' whirlpool had given a facile explanation. Newton honestly disguised his ignorance of origins by postulating that this was the will of God at the beginning of creation.

By this time the destructive phase of the Renaissance and Reformation was over; a new compromise between religion and science was needed just as much as those between monarchy and republic and between the upper bourgeoisie and the nobility. Newton's system of the universe did represent a considerable concession on the part of religious orthodoxy, for by it the hand of God could no longer be clearly seen in every celestial or terrestrial event but only in the general creation and organization of the whole. God had, in fact, like his anointed ones on earth, become a constitutional monarch. On their side the scientists undertook not to trespass into the proper field of religion—the world of man's life with its aspirations and responsibilities. This compromise, wisely advocated by Bishop Sprat, and preached by the redoubtable Dr Bentley in his Boyle sermons of 1692, was to last until Darwin upset it in the nineteenth century.

Although the system of universal gravitation appeared to be at the time, and still remains, Newton's greatest work, his influence on science and outside it was even more effective through the methods he employed in achieving his results. His calculus provided a universal way of passing from the changes of quantities to the quantities themselves, and vice versa. He provided the mathematical key adequate for the solution of physical problems for another 200 years. By setting out his laws of motion, which linked force not with motion itself but with change of motion, he broke definitely with the old commonsense view that force was needed to maintain motion, and relegated the friction, which makes this necessary in all practical mechanisms, to a secondary role which it was the object of the good engineer to abolish. In one word Newton established, once and for all, the *dynamic* view of the universe instead of the *static* one that had satisfied the Ancients. This transformation, combined with his atomism, showed that Newton was in unconscious harmony with the economic and social world of his time, in which individual enterprise, where each man paid his way, was replacing the fixed hierarchical order of the late classical and feudal period where each man knew his place.

2 What Is the Proper Scientific Method?

> *René Descartes (1596–1650) was one of the foremost "revolutionaries" in the Scientific Revolution. He not only contributed such fundamental instruments to the advance of science as analytical geometry, but also laid down what he considered to be the only proper method for the pursuit of scientific truth. His* Discourse on Method *was intended to lay out the future course of the Scientific Revolution.*

FROM *A Discourse on Method* BY RENÉ DESCARTES

AMONG THE BRANCHES of Philosophy, I had, at an earlier period, given some attention to Logic, and among those of the Mathematics of Geometrical Analysis and Algebra,—three Arts or Sciences which ought, as I conceived, to contribute something to my design. But, on examination, I found that, as for Logic, its syllogisms and the majority of its other precepts are of avail rather in the communication of what we already know, or even as the Art of Lully, in speaking without judgment of things of which we are ignorant, than in the investigation of the unknown; and although this Science contains indeed a number of correct and very excellent precepts, there are, nevertheless, so many others, and these either injurious or superfluous, mingled with the former, that it is almost quite as difficult to effect a severance of the true from the false as it is to extract a Diana or a Minerva from a rough block of marble. Then as to the Analysis of the ancients and the Algebra of the moderns, besides that they embrace only matters highly abstract, and, to appearance, of no use, the former is so exclusively restricted to the consideration of figures, that it can exercise the Understanding only on

René Descartes, *A Discourse on the Method of Rightly Conducting the Reason*, in *The Philosophy of Descartes* (1901), pp. 60–4, 74–6, 102–6, translated by John Veitch. Reprinted by permission of Tudor Publishing Company.

condition of greatly fatiguing the Imagination; and, in the latter, there is so complete a subjection to certain rules and formulas, that there results an art full of confusion and obscurity calculated to embarrass, instead of a science fitted to cultivate the mind. By these considerations I was induced to seek some other Method which would comprise the advantages of the three and be exempt from their defects. And as a multitude of laws often only hampers justice, so that a state is best governed when, with few laws, these are rigidly administered; in like manner, instead of the great number of precepts of which Logic is composed, I believed that the four following would prove perfectly sufficient for me, provided I took the firm and unwavering resolution never in a single instance to fail in observing them.

The *first* was never to accept anything for true which I did not clearly know to be such; that is to say, carefully to avoid precipitancy and prejudice, and to comprise nothing more in my judgment than what was presented to my mind so clearly and distinctly as to exclude all ground of doubt.

The *second,* to divide each of the difficulties under examination into as many parts as possible, and as might be necessary for its adequate solution.

The *third,* to conduct my thoughts in such order that, by commencing with objects the simplest and easiest to know, I might ascend by little and little, and, as it were, step by step, to the knowledge of the more complex; assigning in thought a certain order even to those objects which in their own nature do not stand in a relation of antecedence and sequence.

And the *last,* in every case to make enumerations so complete, and reviews so general, that I might be assured that nothing was omitted.

The long chains of simple and easy reasonings by means of which geometers are accustomed to reach the conclusions of their most difficult demonstrations, had led me to imagine that all things, to the knowledge of which man is competent, are mutually connected in the same way, and that there is nothing so far removed from us as to be beyond our reach, or so hidden that we cannot discover it, provided only we abstain from accepting the false for the true, and always preserve in our thoughts the order necessary for the deduction of one truth from another. And I had little difficulty in determining the objects with which it was necessary to commence, for I was already persuaded that it must be with the simplest and easiest to know, and, considering that of all those who have hitherto sought truth in the Sciences, the mathematicians alone have been able to find any demonstrations, that is, any certain and evident reasons, I did not doubt but that such must have been the rule of their investigations. I resolved to commence, therefore, with the examination of the simplest objects, not anticipating, however, from this any other advantage than that to be found in accustoming my mind to the love and nourishment of truth, and to a distaste for all such reasonings as were unsound. But I had no intention on that account of attempting to master all the particular Sciences commonly denominated Mathematics: but observing that, however different their objects they all agree in considering only the various relations or proportions subsisting among those objects, I thought it best for my purpose to consider these proportions in the most general form possible, without referring them to any objects in particular, except such as would most facilitate the knowledge of them, and without by any means restricting them to these, that afterwards I might thus be the better able to apply them to every other class of objects to which they are legitimately applicable. Perceiving further, that in order to understand these relations I should sometimes have to consider them one by one, and sometimes only to bear them in mind, or embrace them in the aggregate, I thought that, in order the better to consider them individually, I should view them as subsisting between straight lines, than which I could find no objects more simple, or capable of being more distinctly represented to my imagination and senses; and on the other hand, that in order to retain them in the memory, or embrace an aggregate of many, I should express them by certain characters the briefest possible. In this way I believed that I could borrow all that was best both in Geometrical Analysis and in Algebra, and correct all the defects of the one by help of the other.

And, in point of fact, the accurate observance of these few precepts gave me, I take the liberty of saying, such ease in unravelling all the questions embraced in these two sciences, that in the two or three months I devoted to their examination, not only did I reach solutions of questions I had formerly deemed exceedingly difficult, but even as regards questions of the solution of which I continued ignorant, I was enabled, as it appeared to me, to determine the means whereby, and the extent to which, a solution was possible; results attributable to the circumstance that I commenced with the simplest and most general truths, and that thus each truth discovered was a rule available in the discovery of subsequent ones. Nor in this perhaps shall I appear too vain, if it be considered that, as the truth on any particular point is one, whoever apprehends the truth, knows all that on that point can be known. The child, for example, who has been instructed in the elements of Arithmetic, and has made a particular addition, according to rule, may be assured that he has found, with respect to the sum of the numbers before him, all that in this instance is within the reach of human genius. Now, in conclusion, the Method which teaches adherence to the true order, and an exact enumeration of all the conditions of the thing sought includes all that gives certitude to the rules of Arithmetic.

But the chief ground of my satisfaction with this Method, was the assurance I had of thereby exercising my reason in all matters, if not with absolute perfection, at least with the greatest attainable by me: besides, I was conscious that by its use my mind was becoming gradually habituated to clearer and more distinct conceptions of its objects; and I hoped also, from not having restricted this Method to any particular matter, to apply it to the difficulties of the other Sciences, with not less success than to those of Algebra. I should not, however, on this account have ventured at once on the examination of all the difficulties of the Sciences which presented themselves to me, for this would have been contrary to the order prescribed in the Method, but observing that the knowledge of such is dependent on principles borrowed from Philosophy, in which I found nothing certain, I thought it necessary first of all to endeavour to establish its principles. And because I observed, besides, that an inquiry of this kind was of all others of the greatest moment, and one in which precipitancy and anticipation in judgment were most to be dreaded, I thought that I ought not to approach it till I had reached a more mature age, (being at that time but twenty-three,) and had first of all employed much of my time in preparation for the work, as well by eradicating from my mind all the erroneous opinions I had up to that moment accepted, as by amassing variety of experience to afford materials for my reasonings, and by continually exercising myself in my chosen Method with a view to increased skill in its application.

*   *   *

I am in doubt as to the propriety of making my first meditations in the place above mentioned matter of discourse; for these are so metaphysical, and so uncommon, as not, perhaps, to be acceptable to every one. And yet, that it may be determined whether the foundations that I have laid are sufficiently secure, I find myself in a measure constrained to advert to them. I had long before remarked that, in relation to practice, it is sometimes necessary to adopt, as if above doubt, opinions which we discern to be highly uncertain, as has been already said; but as I then desired to give my attention solely to the search after truth, I thought that a procedure exactly the opposite was called for, and that I ought to reject as absolutely false all opinions in regard to which I could suppose the least ground for doubt, in order to ascertain whether after that there remained aught in my belief that was wholly indubitable. Accordingly, seeing that our senses sometimes deceive us, I was willing to suppose that there existed nothing really such as they presented to us; and because some men err in reasoning, and fall into paralogisms, even on the simplest matters of Geometry, I, convinced that I was as open to error as any other, rejected as false all the reasonings I had hitherto taken for demonstrations; and finally, when I considered that the very same thoughts (presentations) which we experience when awake may also be experienced when we are asleep, while there is at that time not one of them true, I supposed that all the objects (presentations) that had ever entered into my mind when awake, had in them no more truth than the illusions of my dreams. But immediately upon this I observed that, whilst I thus wished to think that all was false, it was absolutely necessary that I, who thus thought, should be somewhat; and as I observed that this truth, *I think, hence I am,* was so certain and of such evidence, that no ground of doubt, however extravagant, could be alleged by the Sceptics capable of shaking it, I concluded that I might, without scruple, accept it as the first principle of the Philosophy of which I was in search.

In the next place, I attentively examined what I was, and as I observed that I could suppose that I had no body, and that there was no world nor any place in which I might be; but that I could not therefore suppose that I was not; and that, on the contrary, from the very circumstance that I thought to doubt of the truth of other things, it most clearly and certainly followed that I was; while, on the other hand, if I had only ceased to think, although all the other objects which I had ever imagined had been in reality existent, I would have had no reason to believe that I existed; I thence concluded that I was a substance whose whole essence or nature consists only in thinking, and which, that it may exist, has need of no place, nor is dependent on any material thing; so that "I," that is to say, the mind by which I am what I am, is wholly distinct from the body, and is even more easily known than the latter, and is such, that although the latter were not, it would still continue to be all that it is.

After this I inquired in general into what is essential to the truth and certainty of a proposition; for since I had discovered one which I knew to be true, I thought that I must likewise be able to discover the ground of this certitude. And as I observed that in the words *I think, hence I am,* there is nothing at all which gives me assurance of their truth beyond this, that I see very clearly that in order to think it is necessary to exist, I concluded that I might take, as a general rule, the principle, that all the things which we very clearly and distinctly conceive are true, only observing, however, that there is some difficulty in rightly determining the objects which we distinctly conceive.

*   *   *

I have never made much account of what has proceeded from my own mind; and so long as I gathered no other advantage from the Method I employ beyond satisfying myself on some difficulties belonging to the speculative sciences, or endeavouring to regulate my actions according to the principles it taught me, I never thought myself bound to publish anything respecting it. For in what regards manners, every one is so full of his own wisdom, that there might be found as many reformers as heads, if any were allowed to take upon themselves the task of mending them, except those whom God has constituted the supreme rulers of his people, or to whom he has given sufficient grace and zeal to be prophets; and although my speculations greatly pleased myself, I believed that others had theirs, which perhaps pleased them still more. But as soon as I had acquired some general notions respecting Physics, and beginning to make trial of them in various particular difficulties, had observed how far they can carry us, and how much they differ from the principles that have been employed up to the present time, I believed that I could not keep them concealed without sinning grievously against the law by which we are bound to promote, as far as in us lies, the general good of mankind. For by them I perceived it to be possible to arrive at knowledge highly useful in life; and in room of the Speculative Philosophy usually taught in the Schools, to discover a Practical, by means of which, knowing the force and action of fire, water, air, the stars, the heavens, and all the other bodies that surround us, as distinctly as we know the various crafts of our artizans, we might also apply them in the same way to all the uses to which they are adapted, and thus render ourselves the lords and possessors of nature. And this is a result to be desired, not only in order to the invention of an infinity of arts, by which we might be enabled to enjoy without any trouble the fruits of the earth, and all its comforts, but also and especially for the preservation of health, which is without doubt, of all the blessings of this life, the first and fundamental one; for the mind is so intimately dependent upon the condition and relation of the organs of the body, that if any means can ever be found to render men wiser and more ingenious than hitherto, I believe that it is in Medicine they must be sought for. It is true that the science of Medicine, as it now exists, contains few things whose utility is very remarkable: but without any wish to depreciate it, I am confident that there is no one, even among those whose profession it is, who does not admit that all at present known in it is almost nothing in comparison of what remains to be discovered; and that we could free ourselves from an infinity of maladies of body as well as of mind, and perhaps also even from the debility of age, if we had sufficiently ample knowledge of their causes, and of all the remedies provided for us by Nature. But since I designed to employ my whole life in the search after so necessary a Science, and since I had fallen in with a path which seems to me such, that if any one follow it he must inevitably reach the end desired, unless he be hindered either by the shortness of life or the want of experiments, I judged that there could be no more effectual provision against these two impediments than if I were faithfully to communicate to the public all the little I might myself have found, and incite men of superior genius to strive to proceed farther, by contributing, each according to his inclination and ability, to the experiments which it would be necessary to make, and also by informing the public of all they might discover, so that, by the last beginning where those before them had left off, and thus connecting the lives and labours of many, we might collectively proceed much farther than each by himself could do.

I remarked, moreover, with respect to experiments, that they become always more necessary the more one is advanced in knowledge; for, at the commencement, it is better to make use only of what is spontaneously presented to our senses, and of which we cannot remain ignorant, provided we bestow on it any reflection, however slight, than to concern ourselves about more uncommon and recondite phaenomena: the reason of which is, that the more uncommon often only mislead us so long as the causes of the more ordinary are still unknown; and the circumstances upon which they depend are almost always so special and minute as to be highly difficult to detect. But in this I have adopted the following order: first, I have essayed to find in general the principles, or first causes of all that is or can be in the world, without taking into consideration for this end anything but God himself who has created it, and without educing them from any other source than from certain germs of truths naturally existing in our minds. In the second place, I examined what were the first and most ordinary effects that could be deduced from these causes; and it appears to me that, in this way, I have found heavens, stars, and earth, and even on the earth, water, air, fire, minerals, and some other things of this kind, which of all others are the most common and simple, and hence the easiest to know. Afterwards, when I wished to descend to the more particular, so many diverse objects presented themselves to me, that I believe it to be impossible for the human mind to distinguish the forms or species of bodies that are upon the earth, from an infinity of others which might have been, if it had pleased God to place them there, or consequently to apply them to our use, unless we rise to causes through their effects, and avail ourselves of many particular experiments. Thereupon, turning over in my mind all the objects that had ever been presented to my senses, I freely venture to state that I have never observed any which I could not satisfactorily explain by the principles I had discovered. But it is necessary also to confess that the power of nature is so ample and vast, and these principles so simple and general, that I have hardly observed a single particular effect which I cannot at once recognise as capable of being deduced in many different modes from the principles, and that my greatest difficulty usually is to discover in which of these modes the effect is dependent upon them; for out of this difficulty I cannot otherwise extricate myself than by again seeking certain experiments, which may be such that their result is not the same, if it is in the one of these modes that we must explain it, as it would be if it were to be explained in the other. As to what remains, I am now in a position to discern, as I think, with sufficient clearness what course must be taken to make the majority of those experiments which may conduce to this end: but I perceive likewise that they are such and so numerous, that neither my hands nor my income, though it were a thousand times larger than it is, would be sufficient for them all; so that, according as henceforward I shall have the means of making more or fewer experiments, I shall in the same proportion make greater or less progress in the knowledge of nature. This was what I had hoped to make known by the Treatise I had written, and so clearly to exhibit the advantage that would thence accrue to the public, as to induce all who have the common good of man at heart, that is, all who are virtuous in truth, and not merely in appearance, or according to opinion, as well to communicate to me the experiments they had already made, as to assist me in those that remain to be made.

Sir Francis Bacon (1561–1626) was a lawyer who rose to be Lord Chancellor of England under James I. As a "practical" man, he had little patience with what he considered to be the hair-splitting of academic philosophers. To him, the only way to know Nature was to look at her, not to argue about her. In his "science-fiction" essay, The New Atlantis, *he pointed out what might be accomplished if men only organized their assault on Nature properly.*

FROM *The New Atlantis* BY FRANCIS BACON

THIS FABLE MY LORD DEVISED, to the end that he might exhibit therein a model or description of a college instituted for the interpreting of nature and the producing of great and marvellous works for the benefit of men, under the name of Salomon's House, or the College of the Six Days' Works. And even so far his Lordship hath proceeded, as to finish that part. Certainly the model is more vast and high than can possibly be imitated in all things; notwithstanding most things therein are within men's power to effect. His Lordship thought also in this present fable to have composed a frame of Laws, or of the best state or mould of a commonwealth; but foreseeing it would be a long work, his desire of collecting the Natural History diverted him, which he preferred many degrees before it.

*   *   *

"God bless thee, my son; I will give thee the greatest jewel I have. For I will impart unto thee, for the love of God and men, a relation of the true state of Salomon's House. Son, to make you know the true state of Salomon's House, I will keep this order. First, I will set forth unto you the end of our foundation. Secondly, the preparations and instruments we have for our works. Thirdly, the several employments and functions whereto our fellows are assigned. And fourthly, the ordinances and rites which we observe.

"The End of our Foundation is the knowledge of Causes, and secret motions of things; and the enlarging of the bounds of Human Empire, to the effecting of all things possible.

"The Preparations and Instruments are these. We have large and deep caves of several depths: the deepest are sunk six hundred fathom; and some of them are digged and made under great hills and mountains: so that if you reckon together the depth of the hill and the depth of the cave, they are

Sir Francis Bacon, *The New Atlantis* (1936), pp. 544, 574–84.

(some of them) above three miles deep. For we find that the depth of a hill, and the depth of a cave from the flat, is the same thing; both remote alike from the sun and heaven's beams, and from the open air. These caves we call the Lower Region. And we use them for all coagulations, indurations, refrigerations, and conservations of bodies. We use them likewise for the imitation of natural mines; and the producing also of new artificial metals, by compositions and materials which we use, and lay there for many years. We use them also sometimes, (which may seem strange,) for curing of some diseases, and for prolongation of life in some hermits that choose to live there, well accommodated of all things necessary; and indeed live very long; by whom also we learn many things.

"We have burials in several earths, where we put divers cements, as the Chineses do their porcellain. But we have them in greater variety, and some of them more fine. We have also great variety of composts, and soils, for the making of the earth fruitful.

"We have high towers; the highest about half a mile in height; and some of them likewise set upon high mountains; so that the vantage of the hill with the tower is in the highest of them three miles at least. And these places we call the Upper Region: accounting the air between the high places and the low, as a Middle Region. We use these towers, according to their several heights and situations, for insolation, refrigeration, conservation; and for the view of divers meteors; as winds, rain, snow, hail; and some of the fiery meteors also. And upon them, in some places, are dwellings of hermits, whom we visit sometimes, and instruct what to observe.

"We have great lakes both salt and fresh, whereof we have use for the fish and fowl. We use them also for burials of some natural bodies: for we find a difference in things buried in earth or in air below the earth, and things buried in water. We have also pools, of which some do strain fresh water out of salt; and others by art do turn fresh water into salt. We have also some rocks in the midst of the sea, and some bays upon the shore, for some works wherein is required the air and vapour of the sea. We have likewise violent streams and cataracts, which serve us for many motions: and likewise engines for multiplying and enforcing of winds, to set also on going divers motions.

"We have also a number of artificial wells and fountains, made in imitation of the natural sources and baths; as tincted upon vitriol, sulphur, steel, brass, lead, nitre, and other minerals. And again we have little wells for infusions of many things, where the waters take the virtue quicker and better than in vessels or basins. And amongst them we have a water which we call Water of Paradise, being, by that we do to it, made very sovereign for health, and prolongation of life.

"We have also great and spacious houses, where we imitate and demonstrate meteors; as snow, hail, rain, some artificial rains of bodies and not of water, thunders, lightnings; also generations of bodies in air; as frogs, flies, and divers others.

"We have also certain chambers, which we call Chambers of Health, where we qualify the air as we think good and proper for the cure of divers diseases, and preservation of health.

"We have also fair and large baths, of several mixtures, for the cure of diseases, and the restoring of man's body from arefaction: and others for the confirming of it in strength of sinews, vital parts, and the very juice and substance of the body.

"We have also large and various orchards and gardens, wherein we do not so much respect beauty, as variety of ground and soil, proper for divers trees and herbs: and some very spacious, where trees and berries are set whereof we make divers kinds of drinks, besides the vineyards. In these we practise likewise all conclusions of grafting and inoculating, as well of wild-trees as fruit-trees, which produceth many effects. And we make (by art) in the same orchards and gardens, trees and flowers to come earlier or later than their seasons; and to come up and bear more speedily than by their natural course they do. We make them also by art greater much than their nature; and their fruit greater and sweeter and of differing taste, smell, colour, and figure, from their nature. And many of them we so order, as they become of medicinal use.

"We have also means to make divers plants rise by mixtures of earths without seeds; and likewise to make divers new plants, differing from the vulgar; and to make one tree or plant turn into another.

"We have also parks and inclosures of all sorts of beasts and birds, which we use not only for view or rareness, but likewise for dissections and trials; that thereby we may take light what may be wrought upon the body of man. Wherein we find many strange effects; as continuing life in them, though divers parts, which you account vital, be perished and taken forth; resuscitating of some that seem dead in appearance; and the like. We try also all poisons and other medicines upon them, as well of chirurgery as physic. By art likewise, we make them greater or taller than their kind is; and contrariwise dwarf them, and stay their growth: we make them more fruitful and bearing than their kind is; and contrariwise barren and not generative. Also we make them differ in colour, shape, activity, many ways. We find means to make commixtures and copulations of different kinds; which have produced many new kinds, and them not barren, as the general opinion is. We make a number of kinds of serpents, worms, flies, fishes, of putrefaction; whereof some are advanced (in effect) to be perfect creatures, like beasts or birds; and have sexes, and do propagate. Neither do we this by chance, but we know beforehand of what matter and commixture what kind of those creatures will arise.

"We have also particular pools, where we make trials upon fishes, as we have said before of beasts and birds.

"We have also places for breed and generation of those kinds of worms and flies which are of special use; such as are with you your silk-worms and bees.

"I will not hold you long with recounting of our brew-houses, bake-houses, and kitchens, where are made divers drinks, breads, and meats, rare and of special effects. Wines we have of grapes; and drinks of other juice of fruits, of grains, and of roots: and of mixtures with honey, sugar, manna, and fruits dried and decocted. Also of the tears or woundings of trees, and of the pulp of canes. And these drinks are of several ages, some to the age or last of forty years. We have drinks also brewed with several herbs, and roots, and spices; yea with several fleshes, and white meats; whereof some of the drinks are such, as they are in effect meat and drink both: so that divers, especially in age, do desire to live with them, with little or no meat or bread. And above all, we strive to have drinks of extreme thin parts, to insinuate into the body, and yet without all biting, sharpness, or fretting; insomuch as some of them put upon the back of your hand will, with a little stay, pass through to the palm, and yet taste mild to the mouth. We have also waters which we ripen in that fashion, as they become nourishing; so that they are indeed excellent drink; and many will use no other. Breads we have of several grains, roots, and kernels: yea and some of flesh and fish dried; with divers kinds of leavenings and seasonings: so that some do extremely move appetites; some do nourish so, as divers do live of them, without any other meat; who live very long. So for meats, we have some of them so beaten and made tender and mortified, yet without all corrupting, as a weak heat of the stomach will turn them into good chylus, as well as a strong heat would meat otherwise prepared. We have some meats also and breads and drinks, which taken by men enable them to fast long after; and some other, that used make the very flesh of men's bodies sensibly more hard and tough, and their strength far greater than otherwise it would be.

"We have dispensatories, or shops of medicines. Wherein you may easily think, if we have such variety of plants and living creatures more than you have in Europe, (for we know what you have,) the simples, drugs, and ingredients of medicines, must likewise be in so much the greater variety. We have them likewise of divers ages, and long fermentations. And for their preparations, we have not only all manner of exquisite distillations and separations, and especially by gentle heats and percolations through divers strainers, yea and substances; but also exact forms of composition, whereby they incorporate almost, as they were natural simples.

"We have also divers mechanical arts, which you have not; and stuffs made by them; as papers, linen, silks, tissues; dainty works of feathers of wonderful lustre; excellent dyes, and many others; and shops likewise, as well for such as are not brought into vulgar use amongst us as for those that are. For you must know that of the things before recited, many of them are grown into use throughout the kingdom; but yet if they did flow from our invention, we have of them also for patterns and principals.

"We have also furnaces of great diversities, and that keep great diversity of heats; fierce and quick; strong and constant; soft and mild; blown, quiet; dry, moist; and the like. But above all, we have heats in imitation of the sun's and heavenly bodies' heats, that pass divers inequalities and (as it were) orbs, progresses, and returns, whereby we produce admirable effects. Besides, we have heats of dungs, and of bellies and maws of living creatures, and of their bloods and bodies; and of hays and herbs laid up moist; of lime unquenched; and such like. Instruments also which generate heat only by motion. And farther, places for strong insolations; and again, places under the earth, which by nature or art yield heat. These divers heats we use, as the nature of the operation which we intend requireth.

"We have also perspective-houses, where we make demonstrations of all lights and radiations; and of all colours; and out of things uncoloured and transparent, we can represent unto you all several colours; not in rain-bows, as it is in gems and prisms, but of themselves single. We represent also all multiplications of light, which we carry to great distance, and make so sharp as to discern small points and lines; also all colorations of light: all delusions and deceits of the sight in figures, magnitudes, motions, colours: all demonstrations of shadows. We find also divers means, yet unknown to you, of producing of light originally from divers bodies. We procure means of seeing objects afar off; as in the heaven and remote places; and represent things near as afar off, and things afar off as near; making feigned distances. We have also helps for the sight, far above spectacles and glasses in use. We have also glasses and means to see small and minute bodies perfectly and distinctly; as the shapes and colours of small flies and worms, grains and flaws in gems, which cannot otherwise be seen; observations in urine and blood, not otherwise to be seen. We make artificial rain-bows, halos, and circles about light. We represent also all manner of reflexions, refractions and multiplications of visual beams of objects.

"We have also precious stones of all kinds, many of them of great beauty, and to you unknown; crystals likewise; and glasses of divers kinds; and amongst them some of metals vitrificated, and other materials besides those of which you make glass. Also a number of fossils, and imperfect minerals, which you have not. Likewise loadstones of prodigious virtue; and other rare stones, both natural and artificial.

"We have also sound-houses, where we practice and demonstrate all sounds, and their generation. We have harmonies which you have not, of quarter-sounds, and lesser slides of sounds. Divers instruments of music likewise to you unknown, some sweeter than any you have; together with bells and rings that are dainty and sweet. We represent small sounds as great and deep; likewise great sounds extenuate and sharp; we make divers tremblings and warblings of sounds, which in their original are entire. We represent and imitate all articulate sounds and letters, and the voices and notes of beasts and birds. We have certain helps which set to the ear do further the hearing greatly. We have also divers strange and artificial echoes, reflecting the voice many times, and as it were tossing it: and some that give back the voice louder than it came; some shriller, and some deeper; yea, some rendering the voice differing in the letters or articulate sound from that they receive. We have also means to convey sounds in trunks and pipes, in strange lines and distances.

"We have also perfume-houses; wherewith we join also practices of taste. We multiply smells, which may seem strange. We imitate smells, making all smells to breathe out of other mixtures than those that give them. We make divers imitations of taste likewise, so that they will deceive any man's taste. And in this house we contain also a confiture house; where we make all sweet-meats, dry and moist, and divers pleasant wines, milks, broths, and sallets, far in greater variety than you have.

"We have also engine-houses, where are prepared engines and instruments for all sorts of motions. There we imitate and practise to make swifter motions than any you have, either out of your muskets or any engine that you have; and to make them and multiply them more easily, and with small force, by wheels and other means: and to make them stronger, and more violent than yours are; exceeding your greatest cannons and basilisks. We represent also ordnance and instruments of war, and engines of all kinds: and likewise new mixtures and compositions of gun-powder, wildfires burning in water, and unquenchable. Also fireworks of all variety both for pleasure and use. We imitate also flights of birds; we have some degrees of flying in the air; we have ships and boats for going under water, and brooking of seas; also swimming-girdles and supporters. We have divers curious clocks, and other like motions of return, and some perpetual motions. We imitate also motions of living creatures, by images of men, beasts, birds, fishes, and serpents. We have also a great number of other various motions, strange for equality, fineness, and subtilty.

"We have also a mathematical house, where are represented all instruments, as well of geometry as astronomy, exquisitely made.

"We have also houses of deceits of the senses; where we represent all manner of feats of juggling, false apparitions, impostures, and illusions; and their fallacies. And surely you will easily believe that we that have so many things truly natural which induce admiration, could in a world of particulars deceive the senses, if we would disguise those things and labour to make them seem more miraculous. But we do hate all impostures and lies: insomuch as we have severely forbidden it to all our fellows, under pain of ignominy and fines, that they do not shew any natural work or thing, adorned or swelling; but only pure as it is, and without all affectation of strangeness.

"These are (my son) the riches of Salomon's House.

"For the several employments and offices of our fellows; we have twelve that sail into foreign countries, under the names of other nations, (for our own we conceal;) who bring us the books, and abstracts, and patterns of experiments of all other parts. These we call Merchants of Light.

"We have three that collect the experiments which are in all books. These we call Depredators.

"We have three that collect the experiments of all mechanical arts; and also of liberal sciences; and also of practices which are not brought into arts. These we call Mystery-men.

"We have three that try new experiments, such as themselves think good. These we call Pioneers or Miners.

"We have three that draw the experiments of the former four into titles and tables, to give the better light for the drawing of observations and axioms out of them. These we call Compilers.

"We have three that bend themselves, looking into the experiments of their fellows, and cast about how to draw out of them things of use and practice for man's life, and knowledge as well for works as for plain demonstration of causes, means of natural divinations, and the easy and clear discovery of the virtues and parts of bodies. These we call Dowry-men or Benefactors.

"Then after divers meetings and consults of our whole number, to consider of the former labours and collections, we have three that take care, out of them, to direct new experiments, of a higher light, more penetrating into nature than the former. These we call Lamps.

"We have three others that do execute the experiments so directed, and report them. These we call Inoculators.

"Lastly, we have three that raise the former discoveries by experiments into greater observations, axioms, and aphorisms. These we call Interpreters of Nature.

"We have also, as you must think, novices and apprentices, that the succession of the former employed men do not fail; besides a great number of servants and attendants, men and women. And this we do also: we have consultations, which of the inventions and experiences which we have discovered shall be published, and which not: and take all an oath of secrecy, for the concealing of those which we think fit to keep secret: though some of those we do reveal sometimes to the state, and some not.

"For our ordinances and rites: we have two very long and fair galleries: in one of these we place patterns and samples of all manner of the more rare and excellent inventions: in the other we place the statua's of all principal inventors. There we have the statua of your Columbus, that discovered the West Indies: also the inventor of ships: your monk that was the inventor of ordnance and of gunpowder: the inventor of music: the inventor of letters: the inventor of printing: the inventor of observations of astronomy: the inventor of works in metal: the inventor of glass: the inventor of silk of the worm: the inventor of wine: the inventor of corn and bread: the inventor of sugars: and all these by more certain tradition than you have. Then have we divers inventors of our own, of excellent works; which since you have not seen, it were too long to make descriptions of them; and besides, in the right understanding of those descriptions you might easily err. For upon every invention of value, we erect a statua to the inventor, and give him a liberal and honourable reward. These statua's are some of brass; some of marble and touch-stone; some of cedar and other special woods gilt and adorned: some of iron; some of silver; some of gold.

"We have certain hymns and services, which we say daily of laud and thanks to God for his marvellous works: and forms of prayers, imploring his aid and blessing for the illumination of our labours, and the turning of them into good and holy uses.

"Lastly, we have circuits or visits of divers principal cities of the kingdom; where, as it cometh to pass, we do publish such new profitable inventions as we think good. And we do also declare natural divinations of diseases, plagues, swarms of hurtful creatures, scarcity, tempests, earthquakes, great inundations, comets, temperature of the year, and divers other things; and we give counsel thereupon what the people shall do for the prevention and remedy of them."

And when he had said this, he stood up; and I, as I had been taught, kneeled down; and he laid his right hand upon my head, and said; "God bless thee, my son, and God bless this relation which I have made. I give thee leave to publish it for the good of other nations; for we here are in God's bosom, a land unknown." And so he left me; having assigned a value of about two thousand ducats, for a bounty to me and my fellows. For they give great largesses where they come upon all occasions.

3 The Search for Truth

Galileo Galilei (1564-1642) was one of the principal archi-
tects of the Scientific Revolution. His observations of the
surface of the moon and of sunspots and his discovery of
the moons of Jupiter did much to destroy faith in the old
Aristotelian cosmology. His laws of motion were funda-
mental in creating a new picture of the physical universe.
In "The Assayer," Galileo defends himself from the attacks
of an Aristotelian, Sarsi, who felt that Galileo's way could
lead only to confusion and error.

FROM *The Assayer* BY GALILEO GALILEI

IN SARSI I seem to discern the firm belief that in philosophizing one must support oneself upon the opinion of some celebrated author, as if our minds ought to remain completely sterile and barren unless wedded to the reasoning of some other person. Possibly he thinks that philosophy is a book of fiction by some writer, like the *Iliad* or *Orlando Furioso,* productions in which the least important thing is whether what is written there is true. Well, Sarsi, that is not how matters stand. Philosophy is written in this grand book, the universe, which stands continually open to our eyes.

Perhaps Sarsi believes that all the host of good philosophers may be enclosed within four walls. I believe that they fly, and that they fly alone, like eagles, and not in flocks like starlings. It is true that because eagles are rare birds they are little seen and less heard, while birds that fly like starlings fill the sky with shrieks and cries, and wherever they settle befoul the earth beneath them. Yet if true philosophers are like eagles they are not [unique] like the phoenix. The crowd of fools who know nothing, Sarsi, is infinite. Those who know very little of philosophy are numerous. Few indeed are they who really know some part of it, and only One knows all.

To put aside hints and speak plainly, and dealing with science as a

From *Discoveries and Opinions of Galileo*, pp. 237, 239–41, 270–1, 273–8, translated by Stillman Drake. Copyright © 1957 by Stillman Drake. Reprinted by permission of Doubleday & Company, Inc.

method of demonstration and reasoning capable of human pursuit, I hold that the more this partakes of perfection the smaller the number of propositions it will promise to teach, and fewer yet will it conclusively prove. Consequently the more perfect it is the less attractive it will be, and the fewer its followers. On the other hand magnificent titles and many grandiose promises attract the natural curiosity of men and hold them forever involved in fallacies and chimeras, without ever offering them one single sample of that sharpness of true proof by which the taste may be awakened to know how insipid is the ordinary fare of philosophy. Such things will keep an infinite number of men occupied, and that man will indeed be fortunate who, led by some unusual inner light, can turn from dark and confused labyrinths in which he might have gone perpetually winding with the crowd and becoming ever more entangled.

Hence I consider it not very sound to judge a man's philosophical opinions by the number of his followers. Yet though I believe the number of disciples of the best philosophy may be quite small, I do not conclude conversely that those opinions and doctrines are necessarily perfect which have few followers, for I know well enough that some men hold opinions so erroneous as to be rejected by everyone else. But from which of those sources the two authors mentioned by Sarsi derive the scarcity of their followers I do not know, for I have not studied their works sufficiently to judge.

Guiducci has written, "Many stars completely invisible to the naked eye are made easily visible by the telescope; hence their magnification should be called infinite rather than nonexistent." Here Sarsi rises up and, in a series of long attacks, does his best to show me to be a very poor logician for calling this enlargement "infinite." At my age these altercations simply make me sick, though I myself used to plunge into them with delight when I too was under a schoolmaster. So to all this I answer briefly and simply that it appears to me Sarsi is showing himself to be just what he wants to prove me; that is, little cognizant of logic, for he takes as absolute that which was spoken relatively.

*   *   *

Sarsi goes on to say that since this experience of Aristotle's has failed to convince us, many other great men also have written things of the same sort. To this I reply that if in order to refute Aristotle's statement we are obliged to represent that no other men have believed it, then nobody on earth can ever refute it, since nothing can make those who have believed it not believe it. But it is news to me that any man would actually put the testimony of writers ahead of what experience shows him. To adduce more witnesses serves no purpose, Sarsi, for we have never denied that such things have been written and believed. We did say they are false, but so far as authority is concerned yours alone is as effective as an army's in rendering the events true or false. You take your stand on the authority of many poets against our experiments. I reply that if those poets could be present at our experiments they would change their views, and without disgrace they could say they had been writing hyperbolically—or even admit they had been wrong.

I cannot but be astonished that Sarsi should persist in trying to prove by means of witnesses something that I may see for myself at any time by means of experiment. Witnesses are examined in doubtful matters which are past and transient, not in those which are actual and present. A judge must seek by means of witnesses to determine whether Peter injured John last night, but not whether John was injured, since the judge can see that for himself. But even in conclusions which can be known only by reasoning, I say that the testimony of many has little more value than that of few, since the number of people who reason well in complicated matters is much smaller than that of those who reason badly. If reasoning were like hauling I should agree that several reasoners would be worth more than one, just as several horses can haul more sacks of grain than one can. But reasoning is like racing and not like hauling, and a single Arabian steed can outrun a hundred plowhorses. So when Sarsi brings in this multitude of authors it appears to me that instead of strengthening his conclusion he merely ennobles our case by showing that we have outreasoned many men of great reputation.

*   *   *

It now remains for me to tell Your Excellency, as I promised, some thoughts of mine about the proposition "motion is the cause of heat," and to show in what sense this may be true. But first I must consider what it is that we call heat, as I suspect that people in general have a concept of this which is very remote from the truth. For they believe that heat is a real phenomenon, or property, or quality, which actually resides in the material by which we feel ourselves warmed. Now I say that whenever I conceive any material or corporeal substance, I immediately feel the need to think of it as bounded, and as having this or that shape; as being large or small in relation to other things, and in some specific place at any given time; as being in motion or at rest; as touching or not touching some other body; and as being one in number, or few, or many. From these conditions I cannot separate such a substance by any stretch of my imagination. But that it must be white or red, bitter or sweet, noisy or silent, and of sweet or foul odor, my mind does not feel compelled to bring in as necessary accompaniments. Without the senses as our guides, reason or imagination unaided would probably never arrive at qualities like these. Hence I think that tastes, odors, colors, and so on are no more than mere names so far as the object in which we place them is concerned, and that they reside only in the consciousness. Hence if the living creature were removed, all these qualities would be wiped away and annihilated. But since we have imposed upon them special names, distinct from those of the other and real qualities mentioned previously, we wish to believe that they really exist as actually different from those.

I may be able to make my notion clearer by means of some examples. I

move my hand first over a marble statue and then over a living man. As to
the effect flowing from my hand, this is the same with regard to both objects
and my hand; it consists of the primary phenomena of motion and touch, for
which we have no further names. But the live body which receives these
operations feels different sensations according to the various places touched.
When touched upon the soles of the feet, for example, or under the knee or
armpit, it feels in addition to the common sensation of touch a sensation on
which we have imposed a special name, "tickling." This sensation belongs to
us and not to the hand. Anyone would make a serious error if he said that
the hand, in addition to the properties of moving and touching, possessed
another faculty of "tickling," as if tickling were a phenomenon that resided
in the hand that tickled. A piece of paper or a feather drawn lightly over any
part of our bodies performs intrinsically the same operations of moving and
touching, but by touching the eye, the nose, or the upper lip it excites in us
an almost intolerable titillation, even though elsewhere it is scarcely felt. This
titillation belongs entirely to us and not to the feather; if the live and sensitive
body were removed it would remain no more than a mere word. I believe
that no more solid an existence belongs to many qualities which we have
come to attribute to physical bodies—tastes, odors, colors, and many more.

A body which is solid and, so to speak, quite material, when moved in
contact with any part of my person produces in me the sensation we call
touch. This, though it exists over my entire body, seems to reside principally
in the palms of the hands and in the finger tips, by whose means we sense the
most minute differences in texture that are not easily distinguished by other
parts of our bodies. Some of these sensations are more pleasant to us than
others. . . . The sense of touch is more material than the other sense; and, as
it arises from the solidity of matter, it seems to be related to the earthly
element.

Perhaps the origin of two other senses lies in the fact that there are
bodies which constantly dissolve into minute particles, some of which are
heavier than air and descend, while others are lighter and rise up. The
former may strike upon a certain part of our bodies that is much more
sensitive than the skin, which does not feel the invasion of such subtle
matter. This is the upper surface of the tongue; here the tiny particles are
received, and mixing with and penetrating its moisture, they give rise to
tastes, which are sweet or unsavory according to the various shapes, numbers,
and speeds of the particles. And those minute particles which rise up may
enter by our nostrils and strike upon some small protuberances which are the
instrument of smelling; here likewise their touch and passage is received to
our like or dislike according as they have this or that shape, are fast or slow,
and are numerous or few. The tongue and nasal passages are providently
arranged for these things, as the one extends from below to receive descending particles, and the other is adapted to those which ascend. Perhaps the
excitation of tastes may be given a certain analogy to fluids, which descend
through air, and odors to fires, which ascend.

Then there remains the air itself, an element available for sounds, which come to us indifferently from below, above, and all sides—for we reside in the air and its movements displace it equally in all directions. The location of the ear is most fittingly accommodated to all positions in space. Sounds are made and heard by us when the air—without any special property of "sonority" or "transonority"—is ruffled by a rapid tremor into very minute waves and moves certain cartilages of a tympanum in our ear. External means capable of thus ruffling the air are very numerous, but for the most part they may be reduced to the trembling of some body which pushes the air and disturbs it. Waves are propagated very rapidly in this way, and high tones are produced by frequent waves and low tones by sparse ones.

To excite in us tastes, odors, and sounds I believe that nothing is required in external bodies except shapes, numbers, and slow or rapid movements. I think that if ears, tongues, and noses were removed, shapes and numbers and motions would remain, but not odors or tastes or sounds. The latter, I believe, are nothing more than names when separated from living beings, just as tickling and titillation are nothing but names in the absence of such things as noses and armpits. And as these four senses are related to the four elements, so I believe that vision, the sense eminent above all others in the proportion of the finite to the infinite, the temporal to the instantaneous, the quantitative to the indivisible, the illuminated to the obscure—that vision, I say, is related to light itself. But of this sensation and the things pertaining to it I pretend to understand but little; and since even a long time would not suffice to explain that trifle, or even to hint at an explanation, I pass this over in silence.

Having shown that many sensations which are supposed to be qualities residing in external objects have no real existence save in us, and outside ourselves are mere names, I now say that I am inclined to believe heat to be of this character. Those materials which produce heat in us and make us feel warmth, which are known by the general name of "fire," would then be a multitude of minute particles having certain shapes and moving with certain velocities. Meeting with our bodies, they penetrate by means of their extreme subtlety, and their touch as felt by us when they pass through our substance is the sensation we call "heat." This is pleasant or unpleasant according to the greater or smaller speed of these particles as they go pricking and penetrating; pleasant when this assists our necessary transpiration, and obnoxious when it causes too great a separation and dissolution of our substance. The operation of fire by means of its particles is merely that in moving it penetrates all bodies, causing their speedy or slow dissolution in proportion to the number and velocity of the fire-corpuscles and the density or tenuity of the bodies. Many materials are such that in their decomposition the greater part of them passes over into additional tiny corpuscles, and this dissolution continues so long as these continue to meet with further matter capable of being so resolved. I do not believe that in addition to shape, number, motion, penetration, and touch there is any other quality in fire corresponding to "heat"; this belongs so intimately to us that when the live body is taken away, heat becomes no more than a simple name. . . .

Since the presence of fire-corpuscles alone does not suffice to excite heat, but their motion is needed also, it seems to me that one may very reasonably say that motion is the cause of heat. . . . But I hold it to be silly to accept that proposition in the ordinary way, as if a stone or piece of iron or a stick must heat up when moved. The rubbing together and friction of two hard bodies, either by resolving their parts into very subtle flying particles or by opening an exit for the tiny fire-corpuscles within, ultimately sets these in motion; and when they meet our bodies and penetrate them, our conscious mind feels those pleasant or unpleasant sensations which we have named heat, burning, and scalding. And perhaps when such attrition stops at or is confined to the smallest quanta, their motion is temporal and their action calorific only; but when their ultimate and highest resolution into truly indivisible atoms is arrived at, light is created. This may have an instantaneous motion, or rather an instantaneous expansion and diffusion, rendering it capable of occupying immense spaces by its—I know not whether to say its subtlety, its rarity, its immateriality, or some other property which differs from all these and is nameless.

The last great treatise by Galileo was his Dialogues Concerning Two New Sciences. *It was in these dialogues that Galileo laid the foundations for the two sciences of the strength of materials and dynamics.*

FROM *Dialogues Concerning Two New Sciences*
BY GALILEO GALILEI

SALV. The constant activity which you Venetians display in your famous arsenal suggests to the studious mind a large field for investigation, especially that part of the work which involves mechanics; for in this department all types of instruments and machines are constantly being constructed by many artisans, among whom there must be some who, partly by inherited experience and partly by their own observations, have become highly expert and clever in explanation.

Galileo Galilei, *Dialogues Concerning Two New Sciences* (1914), pp. 1–6, translated by Henry Crew and Alfonso de Salvio. Reprinted by permission of Northwestern University Press.

s a g r. You are quite right. Indeed, I myself, being curious by nature, frequently visit this place for the mere pleasure of observing the work of those who, on account of their superiority over other artisans, we call "first rank men." Conference with them has often helped me in the investigation of certain effects including not only those which are striking, but also those which are recondite and almost incredible. At times also I have been put to confusion and driven to despair of ever explaining something for which I could not account, but which my senses told me to be true. And notwithstanding the fact that what the old man told us a little while ago is proverbial and commonly accepted, yet it seemed to me altogether false, like many another saying which is current among the ignorant; for I think they introduce these expressions in order to give the appearance of knowing something about matters which they do not understand.

s a l v. You refer, perhaps, to that last remark of his when we asked the reason why they employed stocks, scaffolding and bracing of larger dimensions for launching a big vessel than they do for a small one; and he answered that they did this in order to avoid the danger of the ship parting under its own heavy weight [*vasta mole*], a danger to which small boats are not subject?

s a g r. Yes, that is what I mean; and I refer especially to his last assertion which I have always regarded as a false, though current, opinion; namely, that in speaking of these and other similar machines one cannot argue from the small to the large, because many devices which succeed on a small scale do not work on a large scale. Now, since mechanics has its foundation in geometry, where mere size cuts no figure, I do not see that the properties of circles, triangles, cylinders, cones and other solid figures will change with their size. If, therefore, a large machine be constructed in such a way that its parts bear to one another the same ratio as in a smaller one, and if the smaller is sufficiently strong for the purpose for which it was designed, I do not see why the larger also should not be able to withstand any severe and destructive tests to which it may be subjected.

s a l v. The common opinion is here absolutely wrong. Indeed, it is so far wrong that precisely the opposite is true, namely, that many machines can be constructed even more perfectly on a large scale than on a small; thus, for instance, a clock which indicates and strikes the hour can be made more accurate on a large scale than on a small. There are some intelligent people who maintain this same opinion, but on more reasonable grounds, when they cut loose from geometry and argue that the better performance of the large machine is owing to the imperfections and variations of the material. Here I trust you will not charge me with arrogance if I say that imperfections in the material, even those which are great enough to invalidate the clearest mathematical proof, are not sufficient to explain the deviations observed between machines in the concrete and in the abstract. Yet I shall say it and will affirm that, even if the imperfections did not exist and matter were absolutely perfect, unalterable and free from all accidental variations, still the mere fact that it is matter makes the larger machine, built of the same material and in the same proportion as the smaller, correspond with exactness to the smaller in every respect except that it will not be so strong or so resistant against violent treatment; the larger the machine, the greater its weakness. Since I assume matter to be unchangeable and always the same, it is clear that we are no less able to treat this constant and invariable property in a rigid manner than if it belonged to simple and pure mathematics. Therefore, Sagredo, you would do well to change the opinion which you, and perhaps also many other students of mechanics, have entertained concerning the ability of machines and structures to resist external disturbances, thinking that when they are built of the same material and maintain the same ratio between parts, they are able equally, or rather proportionally, to resist or yield to such external disturbances and blows. For we can demonstrate by geometry that the large machine is not proportionately stronger than the small. Finally, we may say that, for every machine and structure, whether artificial or natural, there is set a necessary limit beyond which neither art nor nature can pass; it is here understood, of course, that the material is the same and the proportion preserved.

SAGR. My brain already reels. My mind, like a cloud momentarily illuminated by a lightning-flash, is for an instant filled with an unusual light, which now beckons to me and which now suddenly mingles and obscures strange, crude ideas. From what you have said it appears to me impossible to build two similar structures of the same material, but of different sizes and have them proportionately strong; and if this were so, it would not be possible to find two single poles made of the same wood which shall be alike in strength and resistance but unlike in size.

SALV. So it is, Sagredo. And to make sure that we understand each other, I say that if we take a wooden rod of a certain length and size, fitted, say, into a wall at right angles, i.e., parallel to the horizon, it may be reduced to such a length that it will just support itself; so that if a hair's breadth be added to its length it will break under its own weight and will be the only rod of the kind in the world.[1] Thus if, for instance, its length be a hundred times its breadth, you will not be able to find another rod whose length is also a hundred times its breadth and which, like the former, is just able to sustain its own weight and no more: all the larger ones will break while all the shorter ones will be strong enough to support something more than their own weight. And this which I have said about the ability to support itself must be understood to apply also to other tests; so that if a piece of scantling

---

[1] The author here apparently means that the solution is unique. [Trans.]

[corrente] will carry the weight of ten similar to itself, a beam [trave] having the same proportions will not be able to support ten similar beams.

Please observe, gentlemen, how facts which at first seem improbable will, even on scant explanation, drop the cloak which has hidden them and stand forth in naked and simple beauty. Who does not know that a horse falling from a height of three or four cubits will break his bones, while a dog falling from the same height or a cat from a height of eight or ten cubits will suffer no injury? Equally harmless would be the fall of a grasshopper from a tower or the fall of an ant from the distance of the moon. Do not children fall with impunity from heights which would cost their elders a broken leg or perhaps a fractured skull? And just as smaller animals are proportionately stronger and more robust than the larger, so also smaller plants are able to stand up better than larger. I am certain you both know that an oak two hundred cubits [braccia] high would not be able to sustain its own branches if they were distributed as in a tree of ordinary size; and that nature cannot produce a horse as large as twenty ordinary horses or a giant ten times taller than an ordinary man unless by miracle or by greatly altering the proportions of his limbs and especially of his bones, which would have to be considerably enlarged over the ordinary. Likewise the current belief that, in the case of artificial machines the very large and the small are equally feasible and lasting is a manifest error. Thus, for example, a small obelisk or column or other solid figure can certainly be laid down or set up without danger of breaking, while the very large ones will go to pieces under the slightest provocation, and that purely on account of their own weight. And here I must relate a circumstance which is worthy of your attention as indeed are all events which happen contrary to expectation, especially when a precautionary measure turns out to be a cause of disaster. A large marble column was laid out so that its two ends rested each upon a piece of beam; a little later it occurred to a mechanic that, in order to be doubly sure of its not breaking in the middle by its own weight, it would be wise to lay a third support midway; this seemed to all an excellent idea; but the sequel showed that it was quite the opposite, for not many months passed before the column was found cracked and broken exactly above the new middle support.

s i m p. A very remarkable and thoroughly unexpected accident, especially if caused by placing that new support in the middle.

s a l v. Surely this is the explanation, and the moment the cause is known our surprise vanishes; for when the two pieces of the column were placed on level ground it was observed that one of the end beams had, after a long while, become decayed and sunken, but that the middle one remained hard and strong, thus causing one half of the column to project in the air without any support. Under these circumstances the body therefore behaved differently from what it would have done if supported only upon the first beams; because no matter how much they might have sunken the column would have gone with them. This is an accident which could not possibly have happened to a small column, even though made of the same stone and having a length corresponding to its thickness, i.e., preserving the ratio between thickness and length found in the large pillar.

S A G R. I am quite convinced of the facts of the case, but I do not understand why the strength and resistance are not multiplied in the same proportion as the material; and I am the more puzzled because, on the contrary, I have noticed in other cases that the strength and resistance against breaking increase in a larger ratio than the amount of material. Thus, for instance, if two nails be driven into a wall, the one which is twice as big as the other will support not only twice as much weight as the other, but three or four times as much.

S A L V. Indeed you will not be far wrong if you say eight times as much; nor does this phenomenon contradict the other even though in appearance they seem so different.

S A G R. Will you not then, Salviati, remove these difficulties and clear away these obscurities if possible: for I imagine that this problem of resistance opens up a field of beautiful and useful ideas; and if you are pleased to make this the subject of to-day's discourse you will place Simplicio and me under many obligations.

> *The greatest scientist of the Scientific Revolution, and perhaps of all time, was Isaac Newton (1642–1727). In his letter to his friend Francis Aston, Newton pointed out what might be learned by Aston in his travels.*

Isaac Newton's Letter to Francis Aston

Trin. Coll. Cambr. May 18. 1669.

Fr.

S I N C E I N Y O U R L E T T E R you give mee so much liberty of spending my Judgment about wt may bee to your advantage in travelling, I shall doe it more freely then perhaps would otherwise have beene decent. First therefore I will lay down some generall rules most of wch I beleve you have considered

---

H. W. Turnbull, ed., *The Correspondence of Isaac Newton,* I (Cambridge University Press, 1959), 9–11. Reprinted by permission of the copyright holder.

already; but if any of them bee new to you they may excuse ye rest, if none at all yet tis my punisment more in writing them then yours in reading ym.

When you come into any fresh company, 1, observe their humours; 2, suit your own carriage thereto, by wch insinuation you will make their converse more free & open: 3, let your discours bee more in Quaerys & doubtings yn peremptory assertions or disputings, it being ye designe of Travellers to learne not teach; besides it will persuade your acquaintance yt you have the greater esteem of them & soe make ym more ready to communicate wt they know to you; whereas nothing sooner occasions disrespect & quarrells yn peremptorinesse. You will find little or noe advantage in seeming wiser or much more ignorant yn your company. 4, seldome discommend any thing though never so bad, or doe it but moderatly, least you bee unexpectedly forced to an unhansom retraction. Tis safer to commend any thing more then it deserves yn to discommend a thing so much as it deserves. For commendantions [*sic*] meet not soe often wth oppositions or at least are not usually so ill resented by men that think otherwise as discommendations. And you will insinuate into mens favour by nothing sooner then seeming to approve & commend wt they like; but beware of doing it by a comparison. 5 If you bee affronted, tis better in a forrain Country to passe it by in silence or wth a jest though wth some dishonour then to endeavour revenge; For in the first case your credit's ne're the wors when you return into England or come into other company yt have not heard of the quarrell, but in the second case you may beare ye marks of ye quarrell while you live, if you out live it att all. But if you find your self unavoydably engaged tis best, I think, if you can command your passion & language, to keep them pretty eavenly at some certain moderate pitch, not much heightning them to exasperate ye adversary or provoke his freinds nor letting them grow overmuch dejected to make him insult. In a word if you can keep reason above passion, yt & watchfulnesse will bee your best defendants. To wch purpose you may consider yt though such excuses as this [He provok't mee so much I could not forbeare] may passe amongst freinds yet amongst strangers they are insignificant & only argue a Travellers weaknesse.

To these I may ad some generall heads for inquirys or observations such as at present I can think on. As 1 to observe ye policys wealth & state affaires of nations so far as a solitary Traveller may conveniently doe. 2 Their impositions upon all sorts of People Trades or commoditys yt are remarkeable. 3 Their Laws & Customes how far they differ from ours. 4 Their Trades & Arts wherin they excell or come short of us in England. 5 Such fortifications as you shall meet wth, their fashion strength & advantages for defence; & other such military affaires as are considerable. 6 The power & respect belonging to their degrees of nobility or Magistracy. 7 It will not bee time mispent to make a Catalogue of the names & excellencys of those men that are most wise learned or esteemed in any nation. 8 Observe ye Mechanisme & manner of guiding ships. 9 Observe the products of nature in severall places especially in mines wth ye circumstances of mining & of extracting metalls or mineralls out of their oare and refining them and if you meet wth any transmutations out of one species into another (as out of Iron into Copper, out of any metall into quicksilver, out of one salt into another or into an insipid body &c) those above all others will bee worth your noting being ye most luciferous & many times lucriferous experiments too in Philosophy. 10 The prizes of diet & other things. 11 And the staple commoditys of Places.

These Generalls (such as at present I could think of) if they will serve for nothing else yet they may assist you in drawing up a Modell to regulate your Travels by.

As for particulars these yt follow are all yt I can now think of, viz: Whither at Schemnitium in Hungary (where there are Mines of Gold, copper, Iron, vitrioll, Antimony, &c) they change Iron into Copper by dissolving it in a Vitriolate water wch they find in cavitys of rocks in the mines & then melting the slymy solution in a strong fire wch in ye cooling proves copper. The like is said to bee done in other places wch I cannot now remember. Perhaps too it may bee done in Italy; For about 20 or 30 years agone there was a certain Vitriol came from thence (called Roman Vitrioll, but of a nobler vertue yn yt wch is now called by yt name) wch Vitrioll is not now to bee gotten becaus perhaps they make a greater gain by some such trick as turning Iron into Copper wth it then by selling it. 2 Whither in Hungary, Sclavonia, Bohemia neare the town Eila, or at ye Mountains of Bohemia neare Silesia there be rivers whose waters are impregnated wth gold; perhaps ye Gold being dissolved by som corrosive waters like *Aqua Regis* & ye solution carried along wth ye streame that runs through ye mines. And whither ye practise of laying mercury in the rivers till it be tinged wth gold & then straining ye mercury through leather yt ye gold may stay behind, bee a secret yet or openly practised. 3 There is newly contrived in Holland a mill to grind glasses plane wthall & I think polishing them too, perhaps it will bee worth ye while to see it. 4 There is in Holland one—Bory, who some yeares since was imprisoned by the Pope to have extorted from him some secrets (as I am told) of great worth both as to medicine & profit, but hee escaped into Holland where they have granted him a guard. I think he usually goes clothed in green, pray enquire wt you can of him, & whither his ingenuity bee any profit to the Dutch. 5 You may inform your selfe whither ye Dutch have any tricks to keep their ships from being all worm eaten in their voyages to ye Indys. Whither Pendulum clocks doe any service in finding out ye longitude &c. I am very weary & shall not stay to part wth a long complement only I wish you a Good Journey & God bee wth you.

Is NEWTON.

Pray let us heare from you in your Travells. I have given your 2 books to Ds Arrowsmith.

*Newton's masterpiece, and the work that more than any
other created the new science, was* Philosophiae Naturalis
Principia Mathematica (The Mathematical Principles of
Natural Philosophy), *published in 1687. In the* Principia,
*Newton laid out his rules of reasoning, which presumably
had led him to his great discoveries.*

Rules of Reasoning in Philosophy BY ISAAC NEWTON

RULE I

*We are to admit no more causes of natural things than such as are both true
and sufficient to explain their appearances.*

To this purpose the philosophers say that Nature does nothing in vain,
and more is in vain when less will serve; for Nature is pleased with
simplicity, and affects not the pomp of superfluous causes.

RULE II

*Therefore to the same natural effects we must, as far as possible, assign the
same causes.*

As to respiration in a man and in a beast; the descent of stones in
Europe and in *America;* the light of our culinary fire and of the sun; the
reflection of light in the earth, and in the planets.

RULE III

*The qualities of bodies, which admit neither intensification nor remission of
degrees, and which are found to belong to all bodies within the reach of our
experiments, are to be esteemed the universal qualities of all bodies whatsoever.*

For since the qualities of bodies are only known to us by experiments,
we are to hold for universal all such as universally agree with experiments;
and such as are not liable to diminution can never be quite taken away. We are
certainly not to relinquish the evidence of experiments for the sake of dreams
and vain fictions of our own devising; nor are we to recede from the analogy
of Nature, which is wont to be simple, and always consonant to itself. We no
other way know the extension of bodies than by our senses, nor do these

Sir Isaac Newton's Mathematical Principles of Natural Philosophy and His System of the World
(1947), pp. 398–400, translated by Andrew Motte (1729); translation revised by Florian Cajori.
Reprinted by permission of University of California Press.

reach it in all bodies; but because we perceive extension in all that are
sensible, therefore we ascribe it universally to all others also. That abundance
of bodies are hard, we learn by experience; and because the hardness of the
whole arises from the hardness of the parts, we therefore justly infer the
hardness of the undivided particles not only of the bodies we feel but of all
others. That all bodies are impenetrable, we gather not from reason, but from
sensation. The bodies which we handle we find impenetrable, and thence
conclude impenetrability to be an universal property of all bodies whatsoever.
That all bodies are movable, and endowed with certain powers (which we
call the inertia) of persevering in their motion, or in their rest, we only infer
from the like properties observed in the bodies which we have seen. The
extension, hardness, impenetrability, mobility, and inertia of the whole, result
from the extension, hardness, impenetrability, mobility, and inertia of the
parts; and hence we conclude the least particles of all bodies to be also all
extended, and hard and impenetrable, and movable, and endowed with their
proper inertia. And this is the foundation of all philosophy. Moreover, that
the divided but contiguous particles of bodies may be separated from one
another, is matter of observation; and, in the particles that remain undivided,
our minds are able to distinguish yet lesser parts, as is mathematically
demonstrated. But whether the parts so distinguished, and not yet divided,
may, by the powers of Nature, be actually divided and separated from one
another, we cannot certainly determine. Yet, had we the proof of but one
experiment that any undivided particle, in breaking a hard and solid body,
suffered a division, we might by virtue of this rule conclude that the undivided as well as the divided particles may be divided and actually separated
to infinity.

Lastly, if it universally appears, by experiments and astronomical observations, that all bodies about the earth gravitate towards the earth, and that
in proportion to the quantity of matter which they severally contain; that the
moon likewise, according to the quantity of its matter, gravitates towards the
earth; that, on the other hand, our sea gravitates towards the moon; and all
the planets one towards another; and the comets in like manner towards the
sun; we must, in consequence of this rule, universally allow that all bodies
whatsoever are endowed with a principle of mutual gravitation. For the
argument from the appearances concludes with more force for the universal
gravitation of all bodies than for their impenetrability; of which, among
those in the celestial regions, we have no experiments, nor any manner of
observation. Not that I affirm gravity to be essential to bodies: by their *vis
insita* I mean nothing but their inertia. This is immutable. Their gravity is
diminished as they recede from the earth.

RULE IV

*In experimental philosophy we are to look upon propositions inferred by
general induction from phenomena as accurately or very nearly true, not-*

withstanding any contrary hypotheses that may be imagined, till such time as other phenomena occur, by which they may either be made more accurate, or liable to exceptions.

This rule we must follow, that the argument of induction may not be evaded by hypotheses.

4   The Origins of the Scientific Revolution

*The late Alexandre Koyré was one of the leading historians
of the Scientific Revolution. He is the strongest advocate of
the position that the Scientific Revolution was basically a
philosophical reorientation of Western thought and had
nothing to do with the needs of society or anything else.*

FROM *Galileo and Plato* BY ALEXANDRE KOYRÉ

THE NAME OF GALILEO GALILEI is indissolubly linked with the
scientific revolution of the sixteenth century, one of the profoundest, if not
the most profound, revolution of human thought since the invention of the
Cosmos by Greek thought: a revolution which implies a radical intellectual
"mutation," of which modern physical science is at once the expression and
the fruit.

This revolution is sometimes characterized, and at the same time
explained, as a kind of spiritual upheaval, an utter transformation of the
whole fundamental attitude of the human mind; the active life, the *vita
activa* taking the place of the θεωρία, the *vita contemplativa,* which until
then had been considered its highest form. Modern man seeks the domination of nature, whereas medieval or ancient man attempted above all its
contemplation. The mechanistic trend of classical physics—of the Galilean,
Cartesian, Hobbesian physics, *scientia activa, operativa,* which was to
render man "master and possessor of nature"—has, therefore to be explained by this desire to dominate, to act; it has to be considered purely
and simply an outflow of this attitude, an application to nature of the
categories of thinking of *homo faber.* The science of Descartes—and *a
fortiori* that of Galileo—is nothing else than (as has been said) the science
of the craftsman or of the engineer.

I must confess that I do not believe this explanation to be entirely
correct. It is true, of course, that modern philosophy, as well as modern ethics

Alexandre Koyré, "Galileo and Plato," *Journal of the History of Ideas,* IV (1943), 400–5, 406–8,
417–9, 421–4.

and modern religion, lays much more stress on action . . . than ancient and medieval thought. And it is just as true of modern science: I am thinking of the Cartesian physics and its analogies of pulleys, strings and levers. Still the attitude we have just described is much more that of Bacon—whose rôle in the history of science is not of the same order—than that of Galileo or Descartes. Their science is made not by engineers or craftsmen, but by men who seldom built or made anything more real than a theory. The new ballistics was made not by artificers and gunners, but against them. And Galileo did not learn *his* business from people who toiled in the arsenals and shipyards of Venice. Quite the contrary: he taught them *theirs*. Moreover, this theory explains too much and too little. It explains the tremendous scientific progress of the seventeenth century by that of technology. And yet the latter was infinitely less conspicuous than the former. Besides, it forgets the technological achievements of the Middle Ages. It neglects the lust for power and wealth which, throughout its history, inspired alchemy.

Other scholars have insisted on the Galilean fight against authority, against tradition, especially against that of Aristotle: against the scientific and philosophical tradition, upheld by the Church and taught in the universities. They have stressed the rôle of observation and experience in the new science of nature. It is perfectly true, of course, that observation and experimentation form one of the most characteristic features of modern science. It is certain that in the writings of Galileo we find innumerable appeals to observation and to experience, and bitter irony toward men who didn't believe their eyes because what they saw was contrary to the teaching of the authorities, or, even worse, who (like Cremonini) did not want to look through Galileo's telescope for fear of seeing something which would contradict their traditional theories and beliefs. It is obvious that it was just by building a telescope and by looking through it, by careful observation of the moon and the planets, by his discovery of the satellites of Jupiter, that Galileo dealt a crushing blow to the astronomy and the cosmology of his times.

Still one must not forget that observation and experience, in the sense of brute, common-sense experience, did not play a major rôle—or, if it did, it was a negative one, the rôle of obstacle—in the foundation of modern science. The physics of Aristotle . . . was . . . much nearer to common sense experience than those of Galileo and Descartes. It is not "experience," but "experiment," which played—but only later—a great positive rôle. Experimentation is the methodical interrogation of nature, an interrogation which presupposes and implies a *language* in which to formulate the questions, and a dictionary which enables us to read and to interpret the answers. For Galileo, as we know well, it was in curves and circles and triangles, in mathematical or even more precisely, in *geometrical language*—not in the language of common sense or in that of pure symbols—that we must speak to Nature and receive her answers. Yet obviously the choice of the language, the decision to employ it, could not be determined by the experience which its use was to make possible. It had to come from other sources.

I shall not try to explain here the reasons and causes that produced the spiritual revolution of the sixteenth century. It is for our purpose sufficient to describe it, to describe the mental or intellectual attitude of modern science by two (connected) characteristics. They are: 1) the destruction of the Cosmos, and therefore the disappearance in science of all considerations based on that notion; 2) the geometrization of space—that is, the substitution of the homogeneous and abstract space of Euclidian geometry for the qualitatively differentiated and concrete world-space conception of the pre-galilean physics. These two characteristics may be summed up and expressed as follows: the mathematization (geometrization) of nature and, therefore, the mathematization (geometrization) of science.

The dissolution of the Cosmos means the destruction of the idea of a hierarchically-ordered finite world-structure, of the idea of a qualitatively and ontologically differentiated world, and its replacement by that of an open, indefinite and even infinite universe, united and governed by the same universal laws; a universe in which, in contradiction to the traditional conception with its distinction and opposition of the two worlds of Heaven and of Earth, all things are on the same level of Being. The laws of Heaven and the laws of Earth are merged together. Astronomy and physics become interdependent, and even unified and united. And this implies the disappearance from the scientific outlook of all considerations based on value, on perfection, on harmony, on meaning and on purpose. They disappear in the infinite space of the new Universe. It is in this new Universe, in this new world of a geometry made real, that the laws of classical physics are valid and find their application.

The dissolution of the Cosmos—I repeat what I have already said: this seems to me to be the most profound revolution achieved or suffered by the human mind since the invention of the Cosmos by the Greeks. It is a revolution so profound and so far-reaching that mankind—with very few exceptions, of whom Pascal was one—for centuries did not grasp its bearing and its meaning; which, even now, is often misvalued and misunderstood.

Therefore what the founders of modern science, among them Galileo, had to do, was not to criticize and to combat certain faulty theories, and to correct or to replace them by better ones. They had to do something quite different. They had to destroy one world and to replace it by another. They had to reshape the framework of our intellect itself, to restate and to reform its concepts, to evolve a new approach to Being, a new concept of knowledge, a new concept of science—and even to replace a pretty natural approach, that of common sense, by another which is not natural at all.

This explains why the discovery of things, of laws, which today appear so simple and so easy as to be taught to children—the laws of motion, the law of falling bodies—required such a long, strenuous, and often unsuccessful effort of some of the greatest geniuses of mankind, a Galileo, a Descartes. This fact in turn seems to me to disprove the modern attempt to minimize, or even to deny, the originality, or at least the revolutionary character, of

Galileo's thinking; and to make clear that the apparent continuity in the development of medieval and modern physics (a continuity so emphatically stressed by Caverni and Duhem) is an illusion.

Aristotelian physics is false, of course; and utterly obsolete. Nevertheless, it is a "physics," that is, a highly though non-mathematically elaborated science. It is not a childish phantasy, nor a brute and verbal restatement of common sense, but a theory, that is, a doctrine which, starting of course with the data of common sense, subjects them to an extremely coherent and systematic treatment.

The facts or data which serve as a basis for this theoretical elaboration are very simple, and in practice we admit them just as did Aristotle. It still seems to all of us "natural" to see a heavy body fall "down." And just like Aristotle or St. Thomas, we should be deeply astonished to see a ponderous body—a stone or a bull—rise freely in the air. This would seem to us pretty "unnatural"; and we would look for an explanation in the action of some hidden mechanism.

In the same way we still find it "natural" that the flame of a match points "up," and that we place our pots and pans "on" the fire. We should be astonished and should seek for an explanation if, for instance, we saw the flame turn about and point "down." Shall we call this conception, or rather this attitude, childish and simple? Perhaps. We can even point out that according to Aristotle himself science begins precisely by looking for an explanation for things that appear natural. Still, when thermodynamics asserts as a principle that "heat" passes from a hot to a cold body, but not from the cold to a hot one, does it not simply translate an intuition of common sense that a "hot" body "naturally" becomes cold, but that a cold one does not "naturally" become hot? And even when we are stating that the center of gravity of a system tends to take the lowest position and does not rise by itself, are we not simply translating an intuition of common sense, the self-same intuition which Aristotelian physics expresses by its distinction of movement into "natural" and "violent"?

Moreover, Aristotelian physics no more rests content than thermodynamics with merely expressing in its language the "fact" of common sense just mentioned; it transposes it, and the distinction between "natural" and "violent" movements takes its place in a general conception of physical reality, a conception of which the principal features seem to be: (a) the belief in the existence of qualitatively determined "natures," and (b) the belief in the existence of a Cosmos—that is, the belief in the existence of principles of order in virtue of which the entirety of real beings form a hierarchically-ordered whole.

Whole, cosmic order, and harmony: these concepts imply that in the Universe things are (or should be) distributed and disposed in a certain determined order; that their location is not a matter of indifference (neither for them, nor for the Universe); that on the contrary each thing has, according to its nature, a determined "place" in the Universe, which is in some sense its own. A place for everything, and everything in its place: the concept of "natural place" expresses this theoretical demand of Aristotelian physics.

We are too well acquainted with, or rather too well accustomed to, the principles and concepts of modern mechanics; so well that it is almost impossible for us to see the difficulties which had to be overcome for their establishment. They seem to us so simple, so natural, that we do not notice the paradoxes they imply and contain. Yet the mere fact that the greatest and mightiest minds of mankind—Galileo, Descartes—had to struggle in order to make them theirs, is in itself sufficient to indicate that these clear and simple notions—the notion of movement or that of space—are not so clear and simple as they seem to be. Or they are clear and simple only from a certain point of view, only as part of a certain set of concepts and axioms, apart from which they are not simple at all. Or, perhaps, they are too clear and too simple: so clear and so simple that, like all prime notions, they are very difficult to grasp.

Movement, space—let us try to forget for a while all we have learnt at school; let us try to think out what they mean in mechanics. Let us try to place ourselves in the situation of a contemporary of Galileo, a man accustomed to the concepts of Aristotelian physics which *he* learnt at *his* school, and who encounters for the first time the modern concept of motion. What is it? In fact something pretty strange. It is something which in no way affects the body which is endowed with it: to be in motion or to be at rest does not make any difference for, nor any change in, the body in motion or at rest. The body, as such, is utterly and absolutely indifferent to both. Therefore, we are not able to ascribe motion to a determined body considered in itself. A body is in motion only in relation to some other body which we assume to be at rest. All motion is relative. And therefore we may ascribe it to the one or to the other of the two bodies, *ad libitum*.

Thus motion seems to be a relation. But at the same time it is a *state,* just as rest is another *state,* utterly and absolutely opposed to the former; besides which they are both *persistent states.* The famous first law of motion, the law of inertia, teaches us that a body left to itself persists eternally in its state of motion or of rest, and that we must apply a force in order to change a state of motion to a state of rest, and *vice versa.* Yet not every kind of motion is thus endowed with an eternal being, but only uniform movement in a straight line. Modern physics affirms, as well we know, that a body once set in motion conserves eternally its direction and speed, provided of course it is not subject to the action of any external force. Moreover, to the objection of the Aristotelian that though as a matter of fact he is acquainted with eternal motion, the eternal circular motion of the heavenly spheres, he has never yet encountered a persistent rectilinear one, modern physics replies: of course! rectilinear, uniform motion is utterly impossible, and can take place only in a vacuum.

Let us think it over, and perhaps we will not be too harsh on the Aristotelian who felt himself unable to grasp and to accept this unheard-of notion, the notion of a persistent, substantial relation-state, the concept of something which to him seemed just as abstruse, and just as impossible, as the ill-fated substantial forms of the scholastics appear to us. No wonder that the Aristotelian felt himself astonished and bewildered by this amazing attempt to explain the real by the impossible—or, which is the same thing, to explain real being by mathematical being, because, as I have mentioned already, these bodies moving in straight lines in infinite empty space are not *real* bodies moving in *real* space, but *mathematical* bodies moving in *mathematical* space.

Once more, we are so accustomed to mathematical science, to mathematical physics, that we no longer feel the strangeness of a mathematical approach to Being, the paradoxical daring of Galileo's utterance that the book of Nature is written in geometrical characters. For us it is a foregone conclusion. But not for the contemporaries of Galileo. Therefore it is the right of mathematical science, of the mathematical explanation of Nature, in opposition to the non-mathematical one of common sense and of Aristotelian physics, much more than the opposition between two astronomical systems, that forms the real subject of the *Dialogue on the Two Greatest Systems of the World*. As a matter of fact the *Dialogue,* as I believe I have shown . . . is not so much a book on *science* in our meaning of the term as a book on philosophy—or to be quite correct and to employ a disused but time-honored expression, a book on *natural philosophy*—for the simple reason that the solution of the astronomical problem depends on the constitution of a new Physics; which in turn implies the solution of the *philosophical* question of the rôle played by mathematics in the constitution of the science of Nature.

One sees that for the scientific and philosophical consciousness of the time—Buonamici and Mazzoni are only giving expression to the *communis opinio*—the opposition, or rather the dividing line, between the Aristotelian and the Platonist is perfectly clear. If you claim for mathematics a superior status, if more than that you attribute to it a real value and a commanding position in Physics, you are a Platonist. If on the contrary you see in mathematics an abstract science, which is therefore of a lesser value than those—physics and metaphysics—which deal with real being; if in particular you pretend that physics needs no other basis than experience and must be built directly on perception, that mathematics has to content itself with the secondary and subsidiary rôle of a mere auxiliary, you are an Aristotelian.

What is in question in this discussion is not certainty—no Aristotelian has ever doubted the certainty of geometrical propositions or demonstrations —but Being; not even the use of mathematics in physical science—no Aristotelian has ever denied our right to measure what is measurable and to count what is numerable—but the structure of science, and therefore the structure of Being.

These are the discussions to which Galileo alludes continuously in the course of his *Dialogue*. Thus at the very beginning Simplicio, the Aristotelian, points out that "concerning natural things we need not always seek the necessity of mathematical demonstrations." To which Sagredo, who allows himself the pleasure of misunderstanding Simplicio, replies: "Of course, when you cannot reach it. But, if you can, why not?" Of course. If it is possible in questions pertaining to natural things to achieve a demonstration possessing a mathematical necessity, why shouldn't we try to do it? But is it possible? That is precisely the problem, and Galileo, in the margin of the book, sums up the discussion and formulates the real meaning of the Aristotelian: "In natural demonstrations," says he, "one must not seek mathematical exactitude."

One must not. Why? Because it is impossible. Because the nature of physical being is qualitative and vague. It does not conform to the rigidity and the precision of mathematical concepts. It is always "more or less." Therefore, as the Aristotelian will explain to us later, philosophy, that is the science of the real, does not need to look at details, nor need it have recourse to numerical determinations in formulating its theories of motion; all that it has to do is to develop its chief categories (natural, violent, rectilinear, circular) and to describe its general qualitative and abstract features.

The modern reader is probably far from being convinced. He finds it difficult to admit that "philosophy" had to content itself with abstract and vague generalization and not try to establish precise and concrete universal laws. The modern reader does not know the real reason of this necessity, but Galileo's contemporaries knew it quite well. They knew that quality, as well as form, being non-mathematical by nature, cannot be treated in terms of mathematics. Physics is not applied geometry. Terrestrial matter can never exhibit exact mathematical figures; the "forms" never "inform" it completely and perfectly. There always remains a gap. In the skies, of course, it is different; and therefore mathematical astronomy is possible. But astronomy is not physics. To have missed that point is precisely the error of Plato and of those who follow Plato. It is useless to attempt to build up a mathematical philosophy of nature. The enterprise is doomed even before it starts. It does not lead us to truth but to error.

"All these mathematical subtleties," explains Simplicio, "are true *in abstracto*. But applied to sensible and physical matter, they do not work." In real nature there are no circles, no triangles, no straight lines. Therefore it is useless to learn the language of mathematical figures: the book of Nature, in spite of Galileo and Plato, is not written in them. In fact, it is not only useless, it is dangerous: the more a mind is accustomed to the precision and to the rigidity of geometrical thought, the less it will be able to grasp the mobile, changing, qualitatively determined variety of Being.

This attitude of the Aristotelian is very far from being ridiculous. To me, at least, it seems perfectly sensible. You cannot establish a mathematical theory of quality, objects Aristotle to Plato; not even one of motion. There is no motion in numbers. . . . And the Aristotelian of Galileo's time could add that the greatest of the Platonists, the *divus* Archimedes himself, was never able to establish more than a statics. Not a dynamics. A theory of rest. Not one of motion.

The Aristotelian was perfectly right. It is impossible to furnish a mathematical deduction of quality. And well we know that Galileo, like Descartes somewhat later, and for just the same reason, was forced to drop the notion of quality, to declare it subjective, to ban it from the realm of nature. This at the same time implies that he was obliged to drop sense-perception as the source of knowledge and to proclaim that intellectual, and even *a priori* knowledge, is our sole and only means of apprehending the essence of the real.

As for dynamics, and the laws of motion—the *posse* is only to be proved by the *esse;* in order to show that it is possible to establish mathematical laws of nature, you have to do it. There is no other way and Galileo is perfectly conscious of it. It is therefore by giving mathematical solutions to concrete physical problems—the problem of falling bodies, the problem of projectile motion—that he leads Simplicio to the confession "that to want to study natural problems without mathematics is to attempt something that cannot be done."

It is of this science, the true "philosophic" knowledge which is knowledge of the very essence of Being, that Galileo proclaims: "And I, I say to you that if one does not know the truth by himself, it is impossible for anyone else to give him that knowledge. It is indeed possible to teach those things that are neither true nor false; but the true, by which I mean necessary things, that is, those for which it is impossible to be otherwise, every average mind either knows by itself, or it is impossible for it ever to learn them." Assuredly. A Platonist cannot be of a different opinion because for him to know is nothing else than to understand.

Robert Merton is a sociologist at Columbia University who has turned the instruments of modern sociology on the Scientific Revolution. His analysis is based upon the use of sociological method to resolve a historical problem.

FROM *Science and Economy of 17th Century England*
BY ROBERT K. MERTON

THE INTERPLAY between socio-economic and scientific development is scarcely problematical. To speak of socio-economic influences upon science in general unanalyzed terms, however, barely poses the problem. The sociologist of science is specifically concerned with the *types* of influence involved (facilitative and obstructive); the *extent* to which these types prove effective in different social structures; and the *processes* through which they operate. But these questions cannot be answered even tentatively without a clarification of the conceptual tools employed. All too often, the sociologist who repudiates the mythopeic or heroic interpretation of the history of science lapses into a vulgar materialism which seeks to find simple parallels between social and scientific development. Such misguided efforts invariably result in a seriously biased and untenable discussion.

FORMULATION OF THE PROBLEM

At least three common but unsound postulates must be avoided. The first and most illusive is the identification of personal utilitarian motivation of scientists with the structural determinants of their research. Second is the belief that socio-economic factors serve to account exhaustively for the entire complex of scientific activity; and third is the imputation of "social needs" where these needs are, in any significant sense, absent.

*   *   *

Motives may range from the desire for personal aggrandisement to a wholly "disinterested desire to know" without necessarily impugning the demonstrable fact that the thematics of science in seventeenth century England were in large part determined by the social structure of the time. Newton's own motives do not alter the fact that astronomical observations, of which he made considerable use, were a product of Flamsteed's work in the Greenwich Observatory, which was constructed at the command of Charles II for the benefit of the Royal Navy. Nor do they vitiate the striking influence upon Newton's work of such practically-oriented scientists as Halley, Hooke, Wren, Huyghens and Boyle. . . . It is neither an idle nor unguarded generalization that *every English scientist of this time* who was of sufficient distinction to merit mention in general histories of science at one point or another explicitly related at least some of his scientific research to immediate practical problems. But in any case, analysis exclusively in terms of (imputed) motives is seriously misleading and tends to befog the question of the modes of socio-economic influence upon science.

Thus it is important to distinguish the personal attitudes of individual men of science from the social role played by their research. Clearly, some scientists were sufficiently enamored of their subject to pursue it "for its own sake," at times with little consideration of its practical bearings. Nor need we assume that *all* individual researches are directly linked to technical tasks. The relation between science and social needs is two-fold: direct, in the sense that some research is advisedly and deliberately pursued for utilitarian purposes; and indirect, insofar as certain problems and materials for their solution come to the attention of scientists although they need not be cognizant of the practical exigencies from which they derive.

*   *   *

There remains the third problem—of ascertaining social needs—which can best be handled in specific empirical terms. The widely accepted notion that need precipitates appropriate inventions and canalizes scientific interests demands careful restatement. Specific emergencies have often focused attention upon certain fields, but it is equally true that a multitude of "human needs" have gone unsatisfied throughout the ages. In the technical sphere, needs far from being exceptional, are so general that they explain little. Each invention *de facto* satisfies a need or is an attempt to achieve such satisfaction. It is necessary to realize that certain needs may not exist for the society under observation, precisely because of its particular social structure. It is only when the goal is actually part and parcel of the culture in question, only when it is actually perceived as such by some members of the society, that one may properly speak of a need directing scientific and technological interest in certain channels. Moreover, economic needs may be satisfied not only technologically but also by changes in social organization. But given the routine of fulfilling certain types of needs by technologic invention, a pattern which was becoming established in the seventeenth century; given the prerequisite accumulation of technical and scientific knowledge which provides the basic fund for innovation; given (in this case) an *expanding* capitalistic economy; and it may be said that necessity is the (foster) mother of invention and the grandparent of scientific advance.

TRANSPORT AND SCIENCE

The burgeoning of capitalistic enterprise in seventeenth century England intensified interest in more adequate means of transport and communication. St. Helena, Jamaica, North America were but the beginnings of England's great colonial expansion. This and the relatively low cost of water-transport led to the marked growth of the merchant marine. More than forty per cent of the English production of coal was carried by water. Similarly, internal trade enhanced the need for improved facilities for land and river transport. Proposals for turnpikes and canals were common throughout the century.

Foreign trade was assuming world-wide proportions. The best available, though defective, statistics testify to these developments. Imports and exports increased by almost 300 per cent between 1613 and 1700.

*   *   *

These developments were accompanied by increased emphasis upon a number of technical problems. Above all, the increase of commercial voyages to distant points—India, North America, Africa, Russia—stressed anew the need for accurate and expedient means of determining position at sea, of finding latitude and longitude. Scientists were profoundly concerned with possible solutions to these problems. Both mathematics and astronomy were signally advanced through research oriented in this direction.

Napier's invention of logarithms, expanded by Henry Briggs, Adrian Vlacq (in Holland), Edmund Gunter and Henry Gellibrand, was of incalculable aid to astronomer and mariner alike. Adam Anderson possibly reflects the general attitude toward this achievement when he remarks that "logarithms are of great special utility to mariners at sea in calculations relating to their course, distance, latitude, longitude, etc." Sprat, the genial historiographer of the Royal Society, asserted that the advancement of navigation was one of the chief aims of the group.

*   *   *

A ballad written shortly after the Society began to meet at Gresham College reflects the popular appreciation of this interest, as is manifest in the following excerpt:

> This College will the whole world measure
> Which most impossible conclude,
> And navigation make a pleasure,
> By finding out the longitude:
> Every Tarpaulian shall then with ease
> Saile any ship to the Antipodes.

Meeting officially as the Royal Society or foregathering at coffee-houses and private quarters, the scientific coterie discussed without end technical problems of immediate concern for the profit of the realm. Hooke's recently published diary discloses the varied pressure exerted upon him by the Society, the King and interested nobles to devote his studies to "things of use." He would frequently repair to Garaways or Jonathans, the coffee-houses in Change Alley, where, with Christopher Wren and others of their company, he would "discourse about Celestiall Motions" over a pot of tea while at nearby tables more mundane speculations engrossed the attention of stock-jobbers and lottery touts. Problems considered at Garaways were often made the object of special inquiry by the Society. In short, the prevailing picture is not that of a group of "economic men" jointly or severally seeking to improve their economic standing, but one of a band of curious students coöperatively delving into the arcana of nature. The demands of economically-derived needs posed new questions and emphasized old, opening up fresh avenues of research and coupling with this a persistent pressure for the solution of these problems.

A CASE: PROBLEM OF THE LONGITUDE

This engrossing problem of finding the longitude perhaps illustrates best the way in which practical considerations focused scientific interest upon certain fields. There can be no doubt that the contemporary astronomers were thoroughly impressed with the importance of discovering a satisfactory way of finding the longitude, particularly at sea. . . .

The various methods proposed for finding longitude led to the following investigations:

1. Computation of lunar distances from the sun or from a fixed star. First widely used in the first half of the sixteenth century and again in the latter seventeenth century.
2. Observations of the eclipses of the satellites of Jupiter. First proposed by Galileo in 1610; adopted by Hooke, Halley, G. D. Cassini, Flamsteed and others.
3. Observations of the moon's transit of the meridian. Generally current in the seventeenth century.
4. The use of pendulum clocks, and other chronometers, at sea, aided by Huyghens, Hooke, Halley, Messy, Sully, and others.

Newton clearly outlined these procedures, as well as the scientific problems which they involved, upon the occasion of Ditton's claim of the reward for an accurate method of determining longitude at sea. The profound interest of English scientists in this subject is marked by an article in the first volume of the *Philosophical Transactions,* describing the use of pendulum clocks at sea. As Sprat put it, the Society had taken the problem "into its peculiar care." Hooke attempted to improve the pendulum clock and, as he says, "the success of these [trials] made me further think of improving it for finding the Longitude, and . . . quickly led me to the use of Springs instead of Gravity for the making a Body vibrate in any posture. . . ." A notorious controversy then raged about Hooke and Huyghens concerning priority in the successful construction of a watch with spiral balance spring. Howsoever the question of priority be settled, the very fact that two such eminent men of science, among others, focused their attention upon this sphere of inquiry is itself significant. These simultaneous inventions are a resultant of two forces: the intrinsically scientific one which provided the theoretical materials employed in solving the problem in hand, and the non-scientific, largely economic, factor which served to direct interest toward the general problem. The limited range of practicable possibilities leads to independent duplicate inventions.

*   *   *

It is precisely these examples, with their acknowledged practical implications, which clearly illustrate the role of utilitarian elements in furthering scientific advance. For it may be said, upon ample documentary grounds, that Giovanni Domenico Cassini's astronomical discoveries were largely a result of utilitarian interests. In almost all of Cassini's papers in the *Transactions* he emphasizes the value of observing the moons of Jupiter for determining longitude, by means of the method first suggested by Galileo. It is perhaps not too much to say that from this interest derived his discovery of the rotation of Jupiter, the double ring of Saturn, and the third, fourth, fifth, sixth and eighth satellites of Saturn for, as he suggests, astronomical observations of this sort were "incited" because of their practical implications. . . .

Newton was likewise deeply interested in the same general problem. Early in his career, he wrote a now famous letter of advice to his friend, Francis Aston, who was planning a trip on the Continent, in which he suggested among other particulars that Aston "inform himself whether pendulum clocks be of any service in finding out the longitude." In a correspondence which we have reason to believe ultimately led Newton to the completion of the *Principia*, both Halley and Hooke urged Newton to continue certain phases of his research because of its utility for navigation.

*   *   *

Newton's lunar theory was the climactic outcome of scientific concentration on this subject. . . . Halley, who had decided that the various methods of determining longitude were all defective and had declared that "it would be scarce possible ever to find the Longitude at sea sufficient for sea uses, till such time as the Lunar Theory be fully perfected," constantly prompted Newton to continue his work. Flamsteed, and (from 1691 to 1739) Halley also endeavored to rectify the lunar tables sufficiently to attain "the great objects, of finding the Longitude with the requisite degree of exactness." Observations of the eclipses of the moon were recommended by the Royal Society for the same purpose.

*   *   *

Thus we are led to see that the scientific problems emphasized by the manifest value of a method for finding longitude were manifold. If the scientific study of various possible means of achieving this goal was not invariably dictated by the practical utility of the desired result, it is clear that at least part of the continued diligence exercised in these fields was due to it. In the last analysis it is impossible to determine with exactitude the extent to which practical concern focused scientific attention upon certain problems. What can be conscionably suggested is a certain correspondence between the subjects most intensively investigated by the contemporary men of science and the problems raised or emphasized by economic developments. It is an inference—usually supported by the explicit statements of the scientists themselves—that these economic requirements or, more properly, the technical needs deriving from these requirements, provoked research in particular channels. The finding of the longitude was one problem which, engrossing the attention of many scientists, furthered profound developments in astronomy, geography, mathematics, mechanics, and the invention of clocks and watches.

*   *   *

THE EXTENT OF ECONOMIC INFLUENCE

In a sense, the foregoing discussion provides materials illustrative only of the connections we have been tracing. We still have to determine the extent to which socio-economic influences were operative. The minutes of the Royal Society as transcribed in Birch's *History of the Royal Society* provide one basis for such a study. A feasible, though in several manifest respects inadequate, procedure consists of a classification and tabulation of the researches discussed at these meetings, together with an examination of the context in which the various problems came to light. This should afford some ground for deciding *approximately* the extent to which extrinsic factors operated.

Meetings during the four years 1661, 1662, 1686 and 1687 will be considered. There is no reason to suppose that these did not witness meetings "typical" of the general period. The classification employed is empirical rather than logically symmetrical. Items were classified as "directly related" to socio-economic demands when the individual conducting the research explicitly indicated some such connection or when the immediate discussion of the research evidenced a prior appreciation of some such relation. Items classified as "indirectly related" comprise researches which had a clear-cut connection with current practical needs, intimated in the context, but which were not definitely so related by the investigators. Researches which evidenced no relations of this sort were classified as "pure science." Many items have been classified in this category which have (for the present-day observer) a conceivable relation to practical exigencies but which were not so regarded explicitly in the seventeenth century. Thus, investigations in the field of meteorology could readily be related to the practical desirability of forecasting the weather but when these researches were not explicitly related to specific problems they were classified as pure science. Likewise, much of the work in anatomy and physiology was undoubtedly of value for medicine and surgery, but the same criteria were employed in the classification of these items. It is likely, therefore, that if any bias was involved in this classification, it was in the direction of over-estimating the scope of "pure science."

Each research discussed was "counted" as one "unit." It is obvious that this procedure provides only a gross approximation to the extent of extrinsic influences upon the selection of subjects for scientific study, but when greater precision is impossible one must perforce rest temporarily content with less. The results can merely suggest the relative extent of the influences which we have traced in a large number of concrete instances.

From this tabulation it appears that less than half (41.3%) of the investigations conducted during the four years in question are classifiable as "pure science." If we add to this the items which were but indirectly related to practical needs, then about seventy per cent of this research had no explicit practical affiliations. Since these figures are but grossly approximate, the results may be summarized by saying that from forty to seventy per cent occurred in the category of pure science; and conversely that from thirty to sixty per cent were influenced by practical requirements.

Again, considering only the research directly related to practical needs, it appears that problems of marine transport attracted the most attention. This is in accord with one's impression that the contemporary men of science were well aware of the problems raised by England's insular position—problems both military and commercial in nature—and were eager to rectify them. Of almost equal importance was the influence of military exigencies. Not only were there some fifty years of actual warfare during this century, but also the two greatest revolutions in English history. Problems of a military nature left their impress upon the culture of the period, including scientific development.

Likewise, mining which developed so markedly during this period, as we may see from the studies of Nef and other economic historians, had an appreciable influence. In this instance, the greater part of scientific, if one may divorce it from technologic, research was in the fields of mineralogy and metallurgy with the aim of discovering new utilizable ores and new methods of extracting metals from the ore.

It is relevant to note that, in the latter years considered in this summary, there was an increasing proportion of investigation in the field of pure science. A conjectural explanation is not far to seek. It is probable that at the outset the members of the Society were anxious to justify their activities (to the Crown and the lay public generally) by deriving practical results as soon as possible. Hence, the initially marked orientation toward practical problems. Furthermore, many of the problems which were at first advisedly investigated because of their utilitarian importance may later be studied with no awareness of their practical implications. On the basis of the (perhaps biased) criteria adopted in this compilation, some of the later researches would arbitrarily be classified as pure science.

On the grounds afforded by this study it seems justifiable to assert that the range of problems investigated by seventeenth century English scientists was appreciably influenced by the socio-economic structure of the period.

Rupert Hall, Professor of the History of Science at Imperial College, London, has published extensively on the nature of the Scientific Revolution. The selection that follows was delivered as a lecture at a symposium at the University of Wisconsin in 1957.

FROM *The Scholar and the Craftsman in the Scientific Revolution* BY RUPERT HALL

NEVER HAS THERE BEEN such a time as that during the later sixteenth and the seventeenth centuries for the great diversity of men in the forefront of scientific achievement. A proportion of those who contributed to the swelling literature of science were in a broad sense professionals: indeed, a sizable proportion, since many minor figures enlarge this group. Among these professionals were university teachers, professors of mathematics, anatomy, and medicine; teachers of these subjects, especially applied mathematics, outside the universities; and their various practitioners—physicians, surveyors, mariners, engineers and so on; and lastly the instrument-makers, opticians, apothecaries, surgeons, and other tradesmen, though their great period in science is to be found rather in the eighteenth century than in the seventeenth. These men, widely divergent as they were in social origins and intellectual attainments, at least occupied positions in a recognizable scientific hierarchy. Some had won them through academic study, others through private education and research, others again by apprenticeship and pursuit of an occupation closely related to scientific inquiry. All were trained men in some way, whether in mathematics, physic and dissection, or the exercise of a manual craft. Now it is surprising enough, whether we make comparison with the scientific world of recent times, or with that of the later Middle Ages, to find such disparity in the professional group, that is, to find that the definition of scientific professionalism must be so loosely drawn; yet it is still more astonishing that many minor figures in the history of seventeenth-century science, and not a few notable ones, constitute an even more heterogeneous collection. Among these true "amateurs" of science (the distinction has really little meaning), some, it is true, had been exposed to scientific influences of a kind in college or university; yet the creation of a permanent interest thus, in an ordinary passing student, must have been as rare then as

Reprinted with permission of the copyright owners, the Regents of the University of Wisconsin, from Rupert Hall, "The Scholar and the Craftsman in the Scientific Revolution," in Marshall Clagett, *Critical Problems in the History of Science,* 1959, pp. 3–23, The University of Wisconsin Press.

the acquisition of a taste for Latin verse is now. A few also, no doubt, were quietly encouraged by discerning fathers or by private patrons. The rest remain as "sports"; diffusionist and environmental principles hardly suffice to explain their appearance on the scene. One thinks of such men as William Petty, son of a clothier, Otto von Guericke, Mayor of Magdeburg, John Flamsteed, an independent gentleman of modest means, or, most extraordinary of all, Antony van Leeuwenhoek, an unschooled borough official.

Thus one can never predict the social circumstances or personal history of a seventeenth-century scientist. Given the taste, the ability, and freedom from the immediate necessities of the struggle for subsistence, any man who could read and write might become such. Latin was no longer essential, nor mathematics, nor wide knowledge of books, nor a professorial chair. Publication in journals, even membership in scientific societies, was open to all; no man's work needed the stamp of academic approval. This was the free age between the medieval M.A. and the modern Ph.D. In the virtual absence of systematic scientific training, when far more was learned from books than from lectures, the wholly self-educated man was hardly at a disadvantage as compared with his more fortunate colleague who had attended the seats of learning, except perhaps in such special fields as theoretical astronomy or human anatomy. There were no important barriers blocking entry into the newer areas of exploration, such as chemistry, microscopy, qualitative astronomy, where all types of ability, manual and intellectual, were almost equally required. Obviously it was statistically more probable that a scientist would spring from the gentry class (if I may use this disputed term) than any other, and that he would be a university man rather than not. But the considerations determining the probability were sociological rather than scientific; if the texture of science was almost infinitely receptive of first-rate ability of any kind, the texture of society was such that it was more likely to emerge from some quarters than from others.

It is needful to traverse this familiar ground in order to set in perspective the dichotomy to which I shall turn—that of craftsman and scholar. It is a quadruple dichotomy—social, intellectual, teleological, and educational. It marks off, broadly, men of one class in society from another—those who earn their bread from scientific trades of one kind or another from those who do not. It distinguishes likewise those achievements in science which are in the main practical or operational from those which are cerebral or conceptual. Thirdly, it draws attention to the different objects of those who seek mainly practical success through science, and those who seek mainly understanding. And finally, if we consider only the group whom I have previously called professional, we may discern on the one hand the "scholars" who have been introduced to science by university or similar studies, and on the other the "craftsmen" who have learnt something of practical science in a trade. But we must be cautious in detecting polar opposites where there is in reality a spectrum. The scientific movement of the seventeenth century was infinitely varied, its successes demanded an infinite range of different qualities, and it is against this background of wide inclusion that we must set any attempt at analysis in particular terms.

By far the most closely-knit, homogeneous, and intellectually influential of the groups I have described was that of the university men, including both those who remained as teachers and those who departed to other walks of life. Some of the harshest critics of the contemporary "schools," like Bacon, Descartes, or Webster, were nevertheless their products. The opponents of the Aristotelian "forms and qualities" had been firmly grounded in that doctrine; many future scientists found stimulus in the universally required mathematical studies. To exemplify this point, one may consider the earliest membership of the Royal Society in 1663. Of the 115 names listed, I find that 65 had definitely attended a university, while only 16 were certainly non-academic. The remaining 34 are doubtful, but at any rate the university men had the majority. It is still more telling to single out the names which have a definite association-value on inspection; I rate 38 on this test, of whom 32 are "U" and only 6 "non-U." Whether or not we term such men "scholars" is largely a rather unimportant question of definition: at any rate they had in common a knowledge of Latin, some training in mathematics, and an introduction at least to logic and natural philosophy; quite a proportion would also have had such experience of the biological and medical sciences as was available at the time.

It appears then that the medieval association of scientific activity with the universities was weakened, but not disrupted, in the seventeenth century, though the association certainly became less strong as the century advanced. It was weakened not only by the importance in science of men who were not academically trained at all, but by the shift in the locus of scientific activity from the universities, where it had remained securely fixed throughout the Middle Ages, to new institutions like Gresham College, to the scientific societies meeting in capital cities, and to the circles basking in the patronage of a Montmor or a Medici. If a majority of creative scientists had been at the university, they were so no longer in their mature age. Moreover, while in the medieval university there had been little disparity between the instruction given to the student, and the advanced researches of the master, this was no longer the case in the seventeenth century. In the schools of the fourteenth century the master who remained to teach pushed forward his knowledge, in the main, within the framework of ideas, and through study of authorities, with which he had become familiar at a more elementary level. The seventeenth-century university, on the other hand, almost ignored observational and experimental science. The unprecedented advances in scientific technique occurring in physics, astronomy, botany and zoology, and chemistry were not made widely available to students: there was a fairly good grounding only in mathematics and human medicine. The potential investigator had to learn the techniques he required from practice, by the aid of books, and through personal contact with an experienced scientist, often only obtainable elsewhere. Perhaps even more serious was the absence from university courses of the leading principles of the scientific revolution and of the ideas of the new natural philosophy. In the last quarter of the seventeenth century Cartesian science was indeed expounded in some of the colleges of France, and less widely elsewhere, but dissemination of the thought of Galileo, of Bacon, and of the exponents of the mechanical philosophy owed little to university courses. . . . If the universities could produce scholars, they were ill-adapted to turning out scientists; the scientist had to train himself. Many who accomplished this transition regarded it, indeed, as a revulsion from the ordinary conception of scholarship. The learning they genuinely prized, in their own scientific disciplines, they had hardly won for themselves. It would surely be absurd to argue that Newton was less a self-made scientist than Huyghens, or Malpighi than Leeuwenhoek, because the former had attended a university and the latter not.

It lies outside my brief to discuss the fossilization of the universities, which, from what I can learn, the Renaissance did little to diminish so far as science was concerned, nor the rise of the new science as a rejection of academic dogma. Recent investigations would, I believe, tend to make one hesitant in concluding that the innovations and criticisms in the academic sciences—astronomy, physics, anatomy—which we call the scientific revolution, were the product solely, or even chiefly, of forces and changes operating outside the universities. Rather it would seem that, in relation to these subjects, it was a case of internal strife, one party of academic innovators trying to wrest the field from a more numerous one of academic conservatives. Certainly this was the case with Vesalius and his fellow-anatomists, with Copernicus, with Galileo. It was the academic and professional world that was passionately divided on the question of the inviolability of the Galenic, Aristotelian, or Ptolemaic doctrines; these quarrels of learned men had as little to do with capitalism as with the protestant ethic. Only towards the middle of the seventeenth century were they extended through the wider range of the educated class.

In the long run—that is to say within a century or so in each instance—the innovators won. In the short run they were defeated; academic conservatism prevented the recognition and implementation of the victories of the revolution in each science until long after they were universally applauded by thoughtful men outside. Whereas in the thirteenth century the schools had swung over to the Greeks and Muslims, despite their paganism and their often unorthodox philosophy, whereas in the fourteenth century the development of mechanics, of astronomy theoretical and practical, of anatomical and other medical studies, had been centered upon them, in the later sixteenth and seventeenth centuries teaching failed to adapt itself to the pace with which philosophy and science were moving. In the mid-sixteenth century the universities could still have formed the spear-head of this astonishing intellectual advance; in Galileo's life-time the opportunity was lost, and despite the invaluable efforts of individual teachers, as institutions the universities figured only in the army of occupation, a fantastic position not reversed until the nineteenth century. The innovators really failed, at the critical period, to capture the universities and bring them over to their side as centers of teaching and research in the new scientific manner. There were, for instance, many schemes in the seventeenth century for organizing scientific research, and for the provision of observatories, museums, laboratories and so on: yet no one, I think, thought of basing such new institutions on a university.

* * *

The passage in the *Discourse on Method* may be recalled, in which Descartes reviews critically the content of education and learning as ordinarily understood:

> Of philosophy I will say nothing, except that when I saw it had been cultivated for many ages by the most distinguished men, and that yet there is not a single matter within its sphere which is not still in dispute, and nothing therefore which is above doubt, I did not presume to anticipate that my success would be greater in it than that of others; and further, when I considered the number of conflicting opinions touching a single matter that may be upheld by learned men, while there can be but one true, I reckoned as well-nigh false all that was only probable.

After observing that the other sciences derived their principles from philosophy, which was itself infirm, so that "neither the honour nor the gain held out by them was sufficient to determine one to their cultivation," Descartes abandoned the study of letters "and resolved no longer to seek any other science than the knowledge of myself, or of the great book of the world." With this one may compare Bacon's "surprise, that among so many illustrious colleges in Europe, all the foundations are engrossed by the professions, none being left for the free cultivation of the arts and sciences." This restriction, he declares, "has not only dwarfed the growth of the sciences, but been prejudicial to states and governments themselves." The candid appraisal of the first chapter of the *Advancement of Learning* could have been applied to many academic institutions more than two centuries after it was penned.

* * *

The object of the preceding remarks is to justify my conception of the scientific scholar of the sixteenth and seventeenth centuries, as a man learned not merely in recent scientific activities and methods, but in the thought of the past. It seems superfluous to argue that the majority of the scientists of the time were of this type, neither technicians nor ignorant empiricists.

Certainly the learning of Galileo, or Mersenne, or Huyghens, or Newton, was not quite like learning in the medieval or Renaissance conception; they may have been as deficient in the subtleties of Thomist philosophy as in the niceties of Greek syntax; but to deny that they were learned scholars in their field and in their outlook, would be to deny that any scientist is entitled to be called learned.

I have tried also to trace in outline the way in which, at this time, scientific learning diverged from other branches of scholarship, without wholly severing its affiliations with academic institutions. One might also ask the question: how far was the new scientific spirit of the seventeenth century brought into being by activities of a purely scholarly kind—for example, through the evolution of certain principles of logic during the Middle Ages, or through the activities of the persistent students of Greek science in the Renaissance?

The latter especially furnished the core of an interpretation of the scientific revolution which held favor until recent times. To put it crudely, the scientific revolution was seen, according to this view, as the terminal stage of a scientific renaissance beginning about the mid-fifteenth century, and characterized chiefly by its full exploration of classical scientific texts, which was aided particularly by the invention of printing; the scientific renaissance was itself regarded as a classical reaction against the gothic barbarity of the Middle Ages. This interpretation is in effect an extension of Bacon's, to which I referred earlier; an extension which Bacon himself was unable to make because he did not know that the revolution he sought was going on around him. Clearly, if such a view is accepted, it attaches a very great importance indeed to the activity of the scholar-scientists of the Renaissance, who besides polishing and extending the works of the most authoritative ancient authors, shed a full light on others, such as Lucretius, Celsus, and Archimedes, whose writings had not previously been widely studied.

The merits of this hypothesis of the origin of the scientific revolution are as obvious as its defects. It draws attention to the weight of the contribution of sheer scholarship, and of the amazing Hellenophile instinct of the Renaissance, to the change in science which occurred between 1550 and 1700. No one would deny the connection between the mechanical, corpuscular philosophy of the seventeenth century, and *De natura rerum;* nor the significance for anatomy of the intensive study of Galen; nor would he dispute that the virtual rediscovery of Archimedes transformed geometry, and ultimately algebra. Equally, however, it is clear that this is far from being the whole story: the instances I have quoted are not universally typical ones. The history of mechanics before Galileo, which has been so elaborately worked out in the present half-century, proves the point. Medieval science was not abruptly cut short by a classical revival called a renaissance: it had much—how much must be the subject of continuing research—to contribute to the formation of modern science. Very important threads in the scientific revolution are not really traceable to antiquity at all, at least not through the channels of scholarship; here the chemical sciences furnish examples. Above all, the renaissance-scholarship interpretation fails to account for the *change* in science. If anything is fairly certain, it is that the intention of the Renaissance was the imitation of antiquity, and there is evidence that this ideal extended to the scholar-scientists. Yet the pursuit of this ideal seems to have endured least long in science, of all the learned subjects; it had ceased to have force long before the end of the sixteenth century. There never was a true Palladian age in science, and the limitations that had bound the Greeks themselves were relatively soon transcended in Europe. Why this was so is really the whole point at issue, and the Renaissance-scholarship interpretation does not squarely face it.

*   *   *

There is a point here . . . that deserves fuller consideration, and allows the craftsman to enter on the scene. For while we recognize science as a scholarly activity, and the reform of science as an act of learned men, it may plausibly be asked whether the impulse to reform was spontaneously generated among the learned. Was it perhaps stimulated elsewhere? Some support for this suspicion might seem to spring from the emphasis that has been laid on empiricism, not merely in the scientific revolution itself, but among its philosophical precursors. Thus, to quote Dr. Crombie: "The outstanding scientific event of the twelfth and thirteenth centuries was the confrontation of the empiricism long present in the West in the practical arts, with the conception of rational explanation contained in scientific texts recently translated from Greek and Arabic." It is unnecessary to dwell on the well-known interest of at least a few learned men, during the Middle Ages, in such fruits of empirical invention as the magnetic compass, the grinding of lenses, and above all, the important advances in the chemical and metallurgical arts. Similarly, everyone is familiar with the arguments of the Baconian school: that true command—and therefore real if unwitting knowledge—of natural processes had been won by the arts rather than by sciences, and that the scholar would often become more learned if he would consent to apprentice himself to the craftsman. All this might suggest that the increasingly spectacular achievements of empirical technology arrested the attention of scholarly scientists, enforcing some doubt of the rectitude of their own procedures, and still more, leading them to accept as an ideal of science itself that subjection of the natural environment to human purposes which had formerly seemed to belong only to the arts and crafts.

There are two issues here. One is the fact of technological progress, which some philosophical critics contrasted with the stagnation of science. The other is the reaction of learned men to the state of technology, and this is more properly our concern. Technological progress was not simply a feature of the Middle Ages and Renaissance: it occurred in the ancient empires, in the Greek world, under the Roman dominion, and even in the so-called "Dark Ages." It would be difficult to think of a long period of complete technical stagnation in European history, though individual arts suffered temporary periods of decline. Some craftsmen at some places seem always to have been making their way forward by trial and error. In short, a philosoper of antiquity had as great an opportunity of appreciating the inventiveness of craftsmen as his successors of the sixteenth and seventeenth centuries, and of drawing the same lessons as were drawn then. Indeed, ancient writers were aware of the importance of the crafts in creating the means of civilized existence, and praised works of ingenuity and dexterity; where they differed from the moderns was in their preservation of the distinction between *understanding* and *doing*. They did not conclude that the progressive success of the crafts set up any model of empiricism for philosophy to emulate. They would not have written, as Francis Bacon did, in the opening lines of the *Novum Organum:* "Man, as the minister and interpreter of nature, does and understands as much as his observations on the order of nature, either with regard to things or the mind, permit him, and neither knows nor is capable of more. The unassisted hand and the understanding left to itself possess but little power. . . . Knowledge and human power are synonymous."

It is the philosopher who has modified his attitude, not the craftsman, and the change is essentially subjective. The success of craft empiricism was nothing new in late medieval and early modern times, and if the philosopher became conscious of its significance for science it was not because such success was more dramatic now than in the past. It was always there to be seen, by those who had eyes to see it, and the change was in the eye of the beholder. It is absurd, for instance, to suppose that the introduction of gunpowder and cannon into warfare was in any serious sense the cause of a revival of interest in dynamics, and especially in the theory of the motion of projectiles, during the sixteenth and early seventeenth century. The ancient torsion artillery provided equally dramatic machines in its day, not to mention the crossbow, mangonel and trebuchet of the Middle Ages. The simplest methods of hurling projectiles—the human arm, the sling, the bow —pose problems of motion no less emphatically than more complex or powerful devices, and as everyone knows, appeal to practical experience of this primitive kind was the basis for the development of the concept of impetus. The earliest "scientific" writers on explosive artillery . . . did no more than transfer this concept to the operation of a different device.

Such an example reminds us that it may be naive to assume that even major technological advances suggested, contemporaneously, such questions worthy of scientific enquiry as would, indeed, immediately spring to our own minds. The scientific examination of the three useful forms of iron— cast-iron, wrought iron, and steel—did not begin until the early eighteenth century; the geometrical theory of gear-wheels was initiated about fifty years earlier; the serious study of the chemistry of the ceramics industry was undertaken a little later. I choose deliberately examples of practical science each associated with notable developments in late-medieval craftsmanship: the introduction, respectively, of the effective blast-furnace; of the gear-train in the windmill, water-mill, mechanical clock, and other devices; and of fine, brightly pigmented, tin-glazed earthenware. The time-lag in each instance between the establishment of a new craft-skill, and the effective appearance of scientific interest in it, is of the order of 250 years, and in each of these examples it appears *after* the scientific revolution was well under way. If there is some truth in the view that interest in crafts promoted a change in scientific procedures, it is also true that, at a later date, the very success of the new scientific knowledge and methods opened up the possibility of examining craft procedures systematically, which had not existed before.

*   *   *

In any case, I hesitate to conclude that the behavior of an empirical scientist—that is, I take it, one who observes and experiments, both to discover new information and to confirm his statements and ideas—is derivable by virtually direct imitation from the trial-and-error, haphazard, and fortuitous progress of the crafts. This seems to me to be the defect of the view that sees the new scientist of the seventeenth century as a sort of hybrid between the older natural philosopher and the craftsman. It is easy enough to say that the philosopher thought much and did little, while the craftsman did much but had no ideas, and to see the scientist as one who both thinks and does. But is such a gross simplification really very helpful in describing or explaining a complex historical transition? Neither Copernicus, nor Vesalius, nor Descartes, to name only three, were more craftsmanlike than Ptolemy, Galen, or Aristotle. Surely scientific empiricism is itself a philosophical artefact, or at least the creation of learned men . . . and it stands in about the same relation to craftsmanship as the theory of evolution does to the practices of pigeon-fanciers. It is a highly sophisticated way of finding out about the world in which we live; on the other hand, the notion that direct immersion in the lore of tradesmen was the essential baptism preceding scientific discovery was one of the sterile by-paths from which the scientists of the seventeenth century fortunately emerged after a short time. Modern studies combine in revealing that the empirical element in the scientific revolution, taking the word in its crudest, least philosophical and most craftsmanlike sense, has been greatly exaggerated; correspondingly we are learning to attach more and more significance to its conceptual and intellectual aspects.

*   *   *

Perhaps I may illustrate this in the following way. The contributions of craftsmanship to the development of scientific knowledge in the sixteenth and seventeenth centuries seem to be analyzable under five heads:

1. the presentation of striking problems worthy of rational and systematic enquiry;
2. the accumulation of technological information susceptible to scientific study;
3. the exemplification of techniques and apparatus adaptable from the purposes of manufacture to those of scientific research;
4. the realization of the scientific need for instruments and apparatus;
5. the development of topics not embraced in the organization of science proper.

The incidence of these contributions is highly variable among the individual sciences. None are strongly relevant in anatomy, medicine, or indeed any biological science, except that 4 would apply to microscopy. All the sciences demonstrate an increasing dependence on the instrument-maker's craft. Again, 4 is relevant to astronomy, while mechanics draws very slightly upon 1 and 2. Chemistry, on the other hand, exemplifies all these possible contributions, and most forms of applied science—other than mathematical sciences—owe much to the fifth contribution. All we can conclude, therefore, is an obvious truism: that those sciences in whose development empiricism played the greatest part are those in which elements derived from craftsmanship have the most effect. It does not follow, however, that the empirical sciences are those that best exhibit the profundity or the nature of the change in scientific thought and work, nor that the theoretical function of scholars is insignificant even in these sciences. . . . The academic and above all the mathematical sciences were not only those that advanced fastest, but they were already regarded as the models for the structure of other sciences, when these should have reached a sufficiently mature stage. In an ascending scale of sophistication, it was regarded as desirable to render all physical science of the same pattern as mechanics and astronomy, and to interpret all other phenomena in terms of the basic physical laws. The first great step towards the attainment of such an ambition was Newton's *Principia,* a work soon regarded by many as the ultimate manifestation of man's capacity for scientific knowledge. I believe it would be wrong to suppose that the scientists of the late seventeenth century, with such rich examples before them, were content to remain indefinitely at the level of empiricism or sublimated craftsmanship, though indeed in many branches of enquiry it was not yet possible to soar far above it. They were aware that the more abstruse and theoretical sciences, where the contributions of learned men had been greatest, were of a higher type than this.

Perhaps I may now summarize the position I have sought to delineate and justify in the following six propositions, in which it is assumed as an axiom that a science is distinguished by its coherent structure of theory and explanation from a mass of information about the way the world is, however carefully arranged.

1. The scientific revolution appears primarily as a revolution in theory and explanation, whether we view it in the most general fashion, considering the methods and philosophy of the new scientists, or whether we consider the critical points of evolution in any single science.

2. There is a tradition of logical (or, more broadly, philosophical) preoccupation with the problem of understanding natural phenomena of which the later stages, from the thirteenth to the seventeenth century, have at the lowest estimate some bearing on the attitudes to this problem of seventeenth century scientists.

3. Some of the most splendid successes of the scientific revolution sprang from its novel treatment of questions much discussed by medieval scholars.

4. These may be distinguished from the "contrary instances" of success (or an approximation to it) in handling types of natural phenomena previously ignored by philosophers, though familiar in technological experience.

5. While "scholars" showed increasing readiness to make use of the information acquired by craftsmen, and their special techniques for criticizing established ideas and exploring phenomena afresh, it is far less clear that craftsmen were apt or equipped to criticize the theories and procedures of science.

6. Though the early exploitation of observation and experiment as methods of scientific enquiry drew heavily on straightforward workshop practice, the initiative for this borrowing seems to be with scholars rather than craftsmen.

I dislike dichotomies: of two propositions, so often neither *a* nor *b* by itself can be wholly true. The roles of the scholar and the craftsman in the scientific revolution are complementary ones, and if the former holds the prime place in its story, the plot would lack many rich overtones had the latter also not played his part. The scholar's function was active, to transform science; the craftsman's was passive, to provide some of the raw material with which the transformation was to be effected. If science is not constructed from pure empiricism, neither can it be created by pure thought. I do not believe that the scientific revolution was enforced by a necessity for technological progress, but equally in a more backward technological setting it could not have occurred at all. If the genesis of the scientific revolution is in the mind, with its need and capacity for explanation, as I believe, it is also true that the nascent movement would have proved nugatory, had it not occurred in a world which offered the means and incentive for its success.

The Origins of the French Revolution—Popular Misery, Social Ambitions, or Philosophical Ideas?

CONTENTS

QUESTIONS FOR STUDY

1   *In what ways do Montesquieu and Rousseau criticize the foundations of the French state in the eighteenth century?*

2   *How desperate was the plight of the peasantry in France in 1789?*

The great cataclysm of modern European history was the French Revolution. Neither Europe nor the rest of the world was ever to be the same again. It is not surprising, considering the scope and importance of the French Revolution, that interpretations of its origins have been so various. Furthermore, it is not a mere academic debate—the history of Europe and the world since 1789 has been one of almost constant revolution; therefore, any insight into the origins of the French Revolution can offer guidelines to the understanding of contemporary revolutions. Basically, the question comes down to the reasons for men taking revolutionary action against established governments. Is it because they are starving and without hope? Is it because they find their ambitions thwarted by an Establishment? Is it because new theories of man and the state reveal their governments to be hopelessly out of date? Or is it some combination of all these motives?

---

3 *How does the Declaration of the Rights of Man reflect the influence of ideas on the makers of the Revolution? In what ways does it deal with very practical concerns?*

4 *Who were the makers of the French Revolution? In what ways could their motives be affected by misery, social ambitions, and ideas?*

5 *What do you feel to be sufficient motives for revolutionary action?*

1 The Coming of the French Revolution

In brief compass, Robert Palmer of Princeton University reviews the issues involved in the origins of the French Revolution and introduces the various interpretations that will be examined in some detail later.

FROM *Preface to Lefebvre's The Coming of the French Revolution* BY R. R. PALMER

THAT THERE HAVE BEEN diverse schools on the French Revolution is a reflection of wide differences within modern France on all social and political questions, differences which in turn resulted from the fact that the Revolution, though it became very violent, never exterminated its enemies, and in fact never even attempted to do so. It made enemies of the Church, the aristocracy, the upper bourgeoisie and in many ways even the peasants; but the violence used against these groups was only enough to terrify and disgust them, so that they remained, after the troubles subsided, resentful of the great Revolution and fearful of all signs of its renewal. That the revolutionary movement was renewed, in 1830, 1848 and 1870, confirmed and gave new life to these old feelings. The Revolution remained a continuing movement, spasmodically reappearing; counterrevolution therefore remained a continuing movement also. People in France have always been either for or against the great events of '89 and '93. Historians, far from serving as the arbiters and ultimate judges that they are sometimes expected to be, have generally taken one side or another, and their work has in fact intensified the differences of opinion.

These differences on the French Revolution, as on any revolution,

Georges Lefebvre, *The Coming of the French Revolution*, pp. vi–xvi, translated by R. R. Palmer. Reprinted by permission of Princeton University Press. Copyright 1947 by Princeton University Press.

ultimately revolve about unanswerable questions. Was the Revolution "necessary"? Or how much of it was "necessary," and at what point in its progressive course did the "excesses" begin? At one extreme is the belief that no revolution was necessary at all in 1789, either because the Old Regime was a satisfactory society (which few maintain), or because wiser and more statesmanlike policies could have met and mastered the problems of the day without revolution. This latter view was expressed at the time by Edmund Burke, and has attracted followers ever since; but no one has ever been able to suggest positively by what means the crisis of 1789 could have been met within the limits of the prevailing regime, so that partisans of this view usually reveal themselves negatively, by dwelling on the errors and imbecilities of the original revolutionaries. At the other extreme is the view that the whole Revolution was necessary, from the Oath of the Tennis Court in June 1789 to the so-called Great Terror of the early summer of 1794; that the whole sequence of events was a *bloc* which stands or falls together; and that each successive wave of revolutionary action, each going farther than the last, was necessary to prevent relapse into the Old Regime and loss of all gains accomplished, so that, strictly speaking, there were no "excesses." This theory too is incapable of proof, and suffers from the fact that most of the revolutionary leaders themselves did not believe it, since one group after another, each in turn concluding that the movement was going "too far," dissociated itself from it and went over to the counterrevolution, or at least to what was called counterrevolution by the newly emerging revolutionary party. Thus there are various middle grounds, in which the early phases of the Revolution are called wise and constructive, the later phases ruinous or fanatical. In general, the argument that the Revolution was necessary, wholly or in part, reveals itself in the argument of self-defense: the revolutionaries *had* to do thus and so because of the threats and provocations of their opponents. Contrariwise, writers who sympathize with what may be called the relatively conservative forces in the Revolution, the king or the aristocracy in 1789, or the Girondists or Dantonists in 1793–1794, also resort to arguments of necessity and self-defense: these elements, they seem to say, *had* to rally against the uncalled-for, impolitic or unnecessary provocations of the Left.

Necessity in these contexts does not mean a necessity imposed by a superhuman determinism or indemonstrable dialectic. It is a necessity compatible with freedom of choice, a necessity flowing from judgment, purpose and policy, expressible in the formula that one must do so-and-so in order to achieve such-and-such ends. It is the familiar necessity of practical life, that one who wills an objective must will the means to attain it, or, if the means are unacceptable, change the objective. This is essentially what happened in the French Revolution: many Frenchmen in 1789 shared in similar objectives; but some, continuing to hold to the objective, "had" to adopt means which they disliked (Robespierre, for example, did not "like" the Terror), while others, unable sooner or later to accept the means, "had" to change their objective, i.e., turn against the Revolution. Differences of opinion over what was necessary turn into differences as to what objectives were legitimate. So long as one thinks it to have been wise, feasible or legitimate to try to introduce a kind of political democracy in France in the eighteenth century, one must regard as necessary, in the judgment of the present translator, virtually all the steps taken by the revolutionaries down to the dictatorship of 1793–1794. To consider these steps unnecessary, deploring them as "excesses," requires one to say that the objective of political democracy in France at the time was a false or impossible one, which should have been given up as the means necessary to attain it became apparent. At the far pole, in this direction, lies the doctrine of Burke, who held in effect that the wise, feasible and legitimate policy for the French in 1789 was to maintain the aristocratic class structure and established Church of the day, and that the whole Revolution from the beginning was therefore an unnecessary outburst of irresponsible extremism. On the relative merits of the two polar viewpoints represented by Robespierre and Burke there can never be general agreement, nor will the same person, if judicious, always and in all moods be of exactly the same opinion. This is because the issue is a question of policy, and questions of policy are not and should not be matters of dogma.

More concretely, the modern schools on the French Revolution may be symbolized by the names of Taine, Aulard and Mathiez. Taine, who wrote seventy years ago but has had many followers, was unnerved by the specter of proletarian upheaval in the Commune of 1871, and made it his business to expose and excoriate the revolutionary tradition which agitated France. He regarded the Revolution which began in 1789 as a very poor and unnecessary solution to the problems then confronting the nation; he emphasized the role of willful minorities, the atrocities committed by mobs and the impractical and visionary character of the revolutionary leaders. Aulard, whose principal work was done in the twenty years preceding 1914, was on the other hand a kind of official apologist for the Third Republic of his day, and saw in the Revolution a necessary stage by which the advantages of the Third Republic had been reached. He undertook to discredit Taine, to show that the Revolution of 1789 had been a substantially peaceable and sensible movement, a majestic unfolding of ideas so liberal and humane that no man of good will could decently oppose them. In Aulard's picture material motives and violence were infrequent, except on the side of the aristocracy; the revolutionists, if they resorted to force, did so for purely defensive reasons; mobs were always the "people," and generally aimed consciously at high-minded political ends. Though Aulard had no love for what he called the bourgeoisie, he was no partisan of the working class of his own day either; he made little of economic classes, but was vehemently anticlerical, believing that the inveterate enemy of the Revolution and all it stood for was the Church.

*   *   *

The small volume now presented in English is written for a more general audience than the others. Though it carries the story only to October 1789, tracing the last years of the Old Regime and the first stages of the Revolution, it incorporates and summarizes some of the best findings of the author's more specialized books. Despite its brevity, it probably gives the best-rounded picture of the Old Regime available in English since Tocqueville. On the Revolution, though it treats only its advent, it presents the issues of the whole Revolution clearly, and illustrates the dynamics by which the Revolution continued to be moved. It thus touches on most of the more general questions on which opinion has been divided, and offers answers on which all but the most stubborn dissidents can agree.

That the Revolution was necessary M. Lefebvre does not doubt: the old government simply failed to function, and its officials either would not or could not take the measures necessary to maintain political life. He grants that opinion may differ on whether it was necessary for the Revolution to go so far. He holds, however, that if the desideratum was to create a regime at all democratic, avoiding an aristocratic order either like the Old Regime in France or like the regime then prevailing in England, it was probably necessary for the movement to work itself out about as it did. On the debated question of who "started" the Revolution, whose provocation it was which justified the subsequent tumult, he answers that all classes were in one way or another responsible; that the aristocracy, the bourgeoisie, the urban masses and the peasants, each independently and for reasons of its own, initiated revolutionary action. On the charge that the Revolution was pushed forward by small, determined minorities, little anonymous societies of extremists or committees of correspondence, he declares that this is in fact so, that all political movements require leaders and that in any case such highhanded methods were first used by the aristocracy. He thus disarms those critics, mainly upper-class Frenchmen, who have given the impression that the Revolution was something unleashed on the nation by little bands of irresponsible middle-class radicals. On the matter of mob violence and atrocities, M. Lefebvre admits freely that they occurred. He points out, unlike Aulard, that popular fury impelled statesmen onward, and that mobs aiming at short-run material ends helped to force acceptance of far-reaching ideas which they did not understand. He concedes to Taine that disreputable and murderous characters filtered into the insurgent crowds, but he does not think that such characters affected the course of the Revolution. He somewhat resembles Taine in dwelling on violence, but he insists that it was by resorting to violence that the French people freed themselves of many ancient burdens. He somewhat resembles Aulard in insisting that the use of violence by the revolutionaries was fundamentally defensive, arising as early as July 1789 from fear of an "aristocratic conspiracy" against the Third Estate.

It is perhaps in his exact perception of social classes that M. Lefebvre is at his best. His exhaustive knowledge of the French peasantry of the eighteenth century makes him a sure guide into the society of the time, for four-fifths of the people were peasants, most wealth was in land and most income derived from it, and the social position of the aristocracy, the bourgeoisie and the town laboring classes was defined largely by their relation to the rural population. Antagonisms between nobles and bourgeois, and between bourgeoisie and proletariat, are for Lefebvre only part of a much larger and more complicated structure. He shows that among the peasants themselves there were all sorts of class divisions, and that peasant opinion would have prevented a systematic redistribution of property or full social revolution. He notes that when the Revolution began the bourgeoisie probably owned as much rural land in France as did the nobility, a fact singularly awkward to a purely materialist theory of class conflict. He observes that between bourgeoisie and wage-earning class there was no sharp dividing line, and adds that, if there had been, the French Revolution as we know it could not have occurred, since the bourgeoisie would have been afraid to accept the support of the lower classes, and would probably have come to terms with the titled aristocracy instead, as, he says, later happened in Germany. But he shows too that the bourgeoisie and the masses obtained very different benefits from the Revolution; that the masses of city workers and poorer peasants wished to perpetuate the old controlled and regulated economy, with collective rights for the peasant communities, rather than to accept the regime of economic individualism and commercial freedom with which the Revolution presented them, in this respect continuing the tendency of the monarchy.

The different interests of social classes in the Revolution are nowhere more clearly and succinctly set forth than in this book. Yet it is not the struggle of classes that occupies the author, so much as their potential fusion. M. Lefebvre shows how all classes combined, under the leadership of the aristocracy, to overthrow the absolutist Bourbon regime and demand a constitutional order guaranteeing individual rights. Division thereafter took place, for the aristocracy, being only human, hesitated to surrender all the privileges of its position. The bourgeoisie came to the fore, taking advantage of popular insurrection in town and country. But the regime introduced by the bourgeoisie was not an instrument of class domination; it had something to offer to everybody, and indeed postulated that no such things as fixed classes existed. Within the bourgeois order, because of the liberties which it gave, could arise eventually a new order aiming at a fuller realization of social justice. This was because of the great flexibility and high level of abstraction of the philosophy of natural rights as expressed in the Declaration of the Rights of Man and the Citizen, which M. Lefebvre analyzes at some length. It was in this way, he seems to feel, that the philosophy of the eighteenth century influenced the Revolution. The writings of Rousseau, Voltaire and others like them did not "cause" the Revolution, which arose from a perfectly definite series of concrete political events; but the Revolution, once started, expressed itself in the broad conceptions of eighteenth century thought, in which "man" was the fundamental reality, with all classes, nations and races of merely secondary importance. Thus the Revolution addressed itself to all men alike, as did the Christian religion; and, seeing the similarity, M. Lefebvre is both firmly republican and not at all anticlerical or antireligious. In general, it is obviously a source of great pride to him that the French Revolution of 1789 knew no pariah classes, races or nations, but presented a universal philosophy in which, were it only accepted, all human beings could at least in principle live at peace, equal in dignity and treating one another as equals.

2 Man and the State in the Age of Reason

Charles de Secondat, Baron de Montesquieu (1689–1755), was one of the keenest political analysts of the eighteenth century. His most influential work was The Spirit of the Laws.

FROM *The Spirit of the Laws*

BY BARON DE MONTESQUIEU

OF THE LAWS WHICH ESTABLISH POLITICAL LIBERTY, WITH REGARD TO THE CONSTITUTION

A GENERAL IDEA

I MAKE A DISTINCTION between the laws that establish political liberty, as it relates to the constitution, and those by which it is established, as it relates to the citizen. . . .

DIFFERENT SIGNIFICATIONS OF THE WORD, LIBERTY

There is no word that admits of more various significations, and has made more different impressions on the human mind, than that of *liberty*. Some have taken it for a facility of deposing a person on whom they had conferred a tyrannical authority: others, for the power of choosing a superior whom they are obliged to obey; others, for the right of bearing arms, and of being thereby enabled to use violence: others, in fine, for the privilege of being governed by a native of their own country, or by their own laws. A certain nation, for a long time, thought liberty consisted in the privilege of wearing a long beard. Some have annexed this name to one form of government exclusive of others: those who had a republican taste applied it to this species of polity: those who liked a monarchical state gave it to monarchy. Thus

The Complete Works of M. de Montesquieu, translated from the French in Four Volumes, I (1778), 195–212.

they have all applied the name of *liberty* to the government most suitable to their own customs and inclinations; and as, in republics, the people have not so constant and so present a view of the causes of their misery, and as the magistrates seem to act only in conformity to the laws, hence liberty is generally said to reside in republics, and to be banished from monarchies. In fine, as in democracies the people seem to act almost as they please, this sort of government has been deemed the most free, and the power of the people has been confounded with their liberty.

IN WHAT LIBERTY CONSISTS

It is true that, in democracies, the people seem to act as they please; but political liberty does not consist in an unlimited freedom. In governments, that is, in societies directed by laws, liberty can consist only in the power of doing what we ought to will, and in not being constrained to do what we ought not to will.

We must have continually present to our minds the difference between independence and liberty. Liberty is a right of doing whatever the laws permit; and, if a citizen could do what they forbid, he would be no longer possessed of liberty, because all his fellow-citizens would have the same power.

THE SAME SUBJECT CONTINUED

Democratic and aristocratic states are not in their own nature free. Political liberty is to be found only in moderate governments; and even in these it is not always found. It is there only when there is no abuse of power: but constant experience shews us that every man invested with power is apt to abuse it, and to carry his authority as far as it will go. Is it not strange, though true, to say, that virtue itself has need of limits?

To prevent this abuse, it is necessary, from the very nature of things, power should be a check to power. A government may be so constituted, as, no man shall be compelled to do things to which the law does not oblige him, nor forced to abstain from things which the law permits.

OF THE END OR VIEW OF DIFFERENT GOVERNMENTS

Though all governments have the same general end, which is that of preservation, yet each has another particular object. Increase of dominion was the object of Rome; war, that of Sparta; religion, that of the Jewish laws; commerce, that of Marseilles; public tranquillity, that of the laws of China; navigation, that of the laws of Rhodes; natural liberty, that of the policy of the savages; in general, the pleasure of the prince, that of despotic states; that of monarchies, the prince's and the kingdom's glory: the independence of individuals is the end aimed at by the laws of Poland; from thence results the oppression of the whole.

One nation there is also in the world, that has, for the direct end of its constitution, political liberty. We shall presently examine the principles on which this liberty is founded: if they are sound, liberty will appear in its highest perfection.

To discover political liberty in a constitution, no great labour is requisite. If we are capable of seeing it where it exists, it is soon found, and we need not go far in search of it.

OF THE CONSTITUTION OF ENGLAND

In every government there are three sorts of power; the legislative; the executive in respect to things dependent on the law of nations; and the executive in regard to matters that depend on the civil law.

By virtue of the first, the prince or magistrate enacts temporary or perpetual laws, and amends or abrogates those that have been already enacted. By the second, he makes peace or war, sends or receives embassies, establishes the public security, and provides against invasions. By the third, he punishes criminals, or determines the disputes that arise between individuals. The latter we shall call the judiciary power, and the other, simply, the executive power of the state.

The political liberty of the subject is a tranquility of mind arising from the opinion each person has of his safety. In order to have this liberty, it is requisite the government be so constituted as one man need not be afraid of another.

When the legislative and executive powers are united in the same person, or in the same body of magistrates, there can be no liberty; because apprehensions may arise, lest the same monarch or senate should enact tyrannical laws, to execute them in a tyrannical manner.

Again, there is no liberty if the judiciary power be not separated from the legislative and executive. Were it joined with the legislative, the life and liberty of the subject would be exposed to arbitrary controul; for the judge would be then the legislator. Were it joined to the executive power, the judge might behave with violence and oppression.

There would be an end of every thing, were the same man, or the same body, whether of the nobles or of the people, to exercise those three powers, that of enacting laws, that of executing the public resolutions, and of trying the causes of individuals.

Most kingdoms in Europe enjoy a moderate government, because the prince, who is invested with the two first powers, leaves the third to his subjects.

In Turkey, where these three powers are united in the sultan's person, the subjects groan under the most dreadful oppression.

In the republics of Italy, where these three powers are united, there is less liberty than in our monarchies. Hence their government is obliged to have recourse to as violent methods, for its support, as even that of the Turks; witness the state-inquisitors, and the lion's mouth into which every informer may at all hours throw his written accusation.

In what a situation must the poor subject be, under those republics! The same body of magistrates are possessed, as executors of the laws, of the whole power they have given themselves in quality of legislators. They may plunder the state by their general determinations; and, as they have likewise the judiciary power in their hands, every private citizen may be ruined by their particular decisions.

The whole power is here united in one body; and, though there is no external pomp that indicates a despotic sway, yet the people feel the effects of it every moment.

Hence it is that many of the princes of Europe, whose aim has been levelled at arbitrary power, have constantly set out with uniting, in their own persons, all the branches of magistracy, and all the great offices of state.

I allow, indeed, that the mere hereditary aristocracy of the Italian republics does not exactly answer to the despotic power of the Eastern princes. The number of magistrates sometimes moderates the power of the magistracy; the whole body of the nobles do not always concur in the same design; and different tribunals are erected, that temper each other. Thus, at Venice, the legislative power is in the *council,* the executive in the *pregadi,* and the judiciary in the *quarantia.* But the mischief is, that these different tribunals are composed of magistrates all belonging to the same body; which constitutes almost one and the same power.

The judiciary power ought not to be given to a standing senate; it should be exercised by persons taken from the body of the people, at certain times of the year, and consistently with a form and manner prescribed by law, in order to erect a tribunal that should last only so long as necessity requires.

By this method, the judicial power, so terrible to mankind, not being annexed to any particular state or profession, becomes, as it were, invisible. People have not then the judges continually present to their view; they fear the office, but not the magistrate.

In accusations of a deep and criminal nature, it is proper the person accused should have the privilege of choosing, in some measure, his judges, in concurrence with the law; or, at least, he should have a right to except against so great a number, that the remaining part may be deemed his own choice.

The other two powers may be given rather to magistrates or permanent bodies, because they are not exercised on any private subject; one being no more than the general will of the state, and the other the execution of that general will.

But, though the tribunals ought not to be fixt, the judgements ought; and to such a degree, as to be ever conformable to the letter of the law. Were they to be the private opinion of the judge, people would then live in society without exactly knowing the nature of their obligations.

The judges ought likewise to be of the same rank as the accused, or, in other words, his peers; to the end, that he may not imagine he is fallen into the hands of persons inclined to treat him with rigour.

If the legislature leaves the executive power in possession of a right to imprison those subjects who can give security for their good behaviour, there is an end of liberty; unless they are taken up in order to answer, without delay, to a capital crime; in which case they are really free, being subject only to the power of the law.

But, should the legislature think itself in danger, by some secret conspiracy against the state, or by a correspondence with a foreign enemy, it might authorize the executive power, for a short and limited time, to imprison suspected persons, who, in that case, would lose their liberty only for a while, to preserve it for ever.

And this is the only reasonable method that can be substituted to the tyrannical magistracy of the *Ephori,* and to the *state inquisitors* of Venice, who are also despotical.

As, in a country of liberty, every man who is supposed a free agent ought to be his own governor, the legislative power should reside in the whole body of the people. But, since this is impossible in large states, and in small ones is subject to many inconveniences, it is fit the people should transact by their representatives what they cannot transact by themselves.

The inhabitants of a particular town are much better acquainted with its wants and interests than with those of other places; and are better judges of the capacity of their neighbours than of that of the rest of their countrymen. The members, therefore, of the legislature should not be chosen from the general body of the nation; but it is proper, that, in every considerable place, a representative should be elected by the inhabitants.

The great advantage of representatives is their capacity of discussing public affairs. For this, the people collectively are extremely unfit, which is one of the chief inconveniences of a democracy.

*   *   *

When the deputies, as Mr. Sidney well observes, represent a body of people, as in Holland, they ought to be accountable to their constituents; but it is a different thing in England, where they are deputed by boroughs.

All the inhabitants of the several districts ought to have a right of voting at the election of a representative, except such as are in so mean a situation as to be deemed to have no will of their own.

*   *   *

Neither ought the representative body to be chosen for the executive part of government, for which it is not so fit; but for the enacting of laws, or to see whether the laws in being are duly executed; a thing suited to their abilities, and which none indeed but themselves can properly perform.

In such a state, there are always persons distinguished by their birth, riches, or honours: but, were they to be confounded with the common people, and to have only the weight of a single vote, like the rest, the common liberty would be their slavery, and they would have no interest in supporting it, as most of the popular resolutions would be against them. The share they have, therefore, in the legislature ought to be proportioned to their other advantages in the state; which happens only when they form a body that has a right to check the licentiousness of the people, as the people have a right to oppose any encroachment of theirs.

The legislative power is, therefore, committed to the body of the nobles, and to that which represents the people; each having their assemblies and deliberations apart, each their separate views and interests.

Of the three powers abovementioned, the judiciary is, in some measure, next to nothing: there remain, therefore, only two: and, as these have need of a regulating power to moderate them, the part of the legislative body composed of the nobility is extremely proper for this purpose.

The body of the nobility ought to be hereditary. In the first place, it is so in its own nature; and, in the next, there must be a considerable interest to preserve its privileges: privileges that, in themselves, are obnoxious to popular envy, and of course, in a free state, are always in danger.

But, as an hereditary power might be tempted to pursue its own particular interests, and forget those of the people, it is proper, that, where a singular advantage may be gained by corrupting the nobility, as in the laws relating to the supplies, they should have no other share in the legislation than the power of rejecting, and not that of resolving.

By the *power of resolving* I mean the right of ordaining by their own authority, or of amending what has been ordained by others. By the *power of rejecting,* I would be understood to mean the right of annulling a resolution taken by another, which was the power of the tribunes at Rome. And, though the person possessed of the privilege of rejecting may likewise have the right of approving, yet this approbation passes for no more than a declaration that he intends to make no use of his privilege of rejecting, and is derived from that very privilege.

The executive power ought to be in the hands of a monarch, because this branch of government, having need of dispatch, is better administered by one than by many: on the other hand, whatever depends on the legislative power, is oftentimes better regulated by many than by a single person.

But, if there were no monarch, and the executive power should be committed to a certain number of persons, selected from the legislative body, there would be an end of liberty, by reason the two powers would be united; as the same persons would sometimes possess, and would be always able to possess, a share in both.

Were the legislative body to be a considerable time without meeting, this would likewise put an end to liberty. For, of two things, one would naturally follow: either that there would be no longer any legislative resolutions, and then the state would fall into anarchy; or that these resolutions would be taken by the executive power, which would render it absolute.

*   *   *

The legislative body should not meet of itself. For a body is supposed to have no will but when it is met: and besides, were it not to meet unanimously, it would be impossible to determine which was really the legislative body, the part assembled, or the other. And if it had a right to prorogue itself, it might happen never to be prorogued; which would be extremely dangerous, in case it should ever attempt to encroach on the executive power. Besides, there are seasons (some more proper than others) for assembling the legislative body: it is fit, therefore, that the executive power should regulate the time of meeting, as well as the duration, of those assemblies, according to the circumstances and exigences of a state, known to itself.

Were the executive power not to have a right of restraining the encroachments of the legislative body, the latter would become despotic: for, as it might arrogate to itself what authority it pleased, it would soon destroy all the other powers.

But it is not proper, on the other hand, that the legislative power should have a right to stay the executive. For, as the execution has its natural limits, it is useless to confine it: besides, the executive power is generally employed in momentary operations.

*   *   *

Here, then, is the fundamental constitution of the government we are treating of. The legislative body being composed of two parts, they check one another by the mutual privilege of rejecting. They are both restrained by the executive power, as the executive is by the legislative.

These three powers should naturally form a state of repose or inaction: but, as there is a necessity for movement in the course of human affairs, they are forced to move, but still in concert.

As the executive power has no other part in the legislative than the privilege of rejecting, it can have no share in the public debates. It is not even necessary that it should propose; because, as it may always disapprove of the resolutions that shall be taken, it may likewise reject the decisions on those proposals which were made against its will.

*   *   *

Were the executive power to determine the raising of public money otherwise than by giving its consent, liberty would be at an end; because it would become legislative in the most important point of legislation.

If the legislative power were to settle the subsidies, not from year to year, but for ever, it would run the risk of losing its liberty, because the executive power would be no longer dependent; and, when once it was possessed of such a perpetual right, it would be a matter of indifference whether it held it of itself or of another. The same may be said if it should come to a resolution of intrusting, not an annual, but a perpetual, command of the fleets and armies to the executive power.

To prevent the executive power from being able to oppress, it is requisite that the armies with which it is intrusted should consist of the people, and have the same spirit as the people, as was the case at Rome till the time of *Marius*. To obtain this end, there are only two ways; either that the persons employed in the army should have sufficient property to answer for their conduct to their fellow-subjects, and be enlisted only for a year, as was customary at Rome; or, if there should be a standing-army composed chiefly of the most despicable part of the nation, the legislative power should have a right to disband them as soon as it pleased; the soldiers should live in common with the rest of the people; and no separate camp, barracks, or fortress should be suffered.

OF THE MONARCHIES WE ARE ACQUAINTED WITH

The monarchies we are acquainted with have not, like that we have been speaking of, liberty for their direct view: the only aim is the glory of the subject, of the state, and of the sovereign. But from hence there results a spirit of liberty, which, in those states, is capable of achieving as great things, and of contributing as much, perhaps, to happiness, as liberty itself.

Here the three powers are not distributed and founded on the model of the constitution above-mentioned: they have each a particular distribution, according to which they border more or less on political liberty; and, if they did not border upon it, monarchy would degenerate into despotic government.

As the French Revolution developed, increasing attention was given to the ideas of Jean Jacques Rousseau (1712–1778). It soon became possible to claim Rousseau as the most important philosophical instigator of the Revolution. Robespierre himself was proud to be known as a disciple. Some of Rousseau's most important ideas are to be found in his essay on the social contract.

FROM *An Inquiry into the Nature of the Social Contract* BY J. J. ROUSSEAU

OF THE SOCIAL COMPACT

WE WILL SUPPOSE that men in a state of nature are arrived at that crisis, when the strength of each individual is insufficient to defend him

An Inquiry into the Nature of the Social Contract; or Principles of Political Right, translated from the French of John James Rousseau (1791), pp. 33–49.

from the attacks he is subject to. This primitive state can therefore subsist no longer; and the human race must perish, unless they change their manner of life.

As men cannot create for themselves new forces, but merely unite and direct those which already exist, the only means they can employ for their preservation is to form by aggregation an assemblage of forces that may be able to resist all assaults, be put in motion as one body, and act in concert upon all occasions.

This assemblage of forces must be produced by the concurrence of many: and as the force and the liberty of a man are the chief instruments of his preservation, how can he engage them without danger, and without neglecting the care which is due to himself? This doubt, which leads directly to my subject, may be expressed in these words:

"Where shall we find a form of association which will defend and protect with the whole aggregate force the person and the property of each individual; and by which every person, while united with ALL, shall obey only HIMSELF, and remain as free as before the union?" Such is the fundamental problem, of which the Social Contract gives the solution.

The articles of this contract are so unalterably fixed by the nature of the act, that the least modification renders them vain and of no effect. They are the same everywhere, and are everywhere understood and admitted, even though they may never have been formally announced: so that, when once the social pact is violated in any instance, all the obligations it created cease; and each individual is restored to his original rights, and resumes his native liberty, as the consequence of losing that conventional liberty for which he exchanged them.

All the articles of the social contract will, when clearly understood, be found reducible to this single point—THE TOTAL ALIENATION OF EACH ASSOCIATE, AND ALL HIS RIGHTS, TO THE WHOLE COMMUNITY. For every individual gives himself up entirely—the condition of every person is alike; and being so, it would not be the interest of anyone to render himself offensive to others.

Nay, more than this—the alienation is made without any reserve; the union is as complete as it can be, and no associate has a claim to anything: for if any individual was to retain rights not enjoyed in general by all, as there would be no common superior to decide between him and the public, each person being in some points his own proper judge, would soon pretend to be so in everything; and thus would the state of nature be revived, and the association become tyrannical or be annihilated.

In fine, each person gives himself to ALL, but not to any INDIVIDUAL: and as there is no one associate over whom the same right is not acquired which is ceded to him by others, each gains an equivalent for what he loses, and finds his force increased for preserving that which he possesses.

If, therefore, we exclude from the social compact all that is not essentially necessary, we shall find it reduced to the following terms:

"We each of us place, in common, his person, and all his power, under the supreme direction of the general will; and we receive into the body each member as an indivisible part of the whole."

From that moment, instead of so many separate persons as there are contractors, this act of association produces a moral collective body, composed of as many members as there are voices in the assembly; which from this act receives its unity, its common self, its life, and its will. This public person, which is thus formed by the union of all the private persons, took formerly the name of *city,* and now takes that of *republic* or *body politic.* It is called by its members *state* when it is passive, and *sovereign* when in activity: and whenever it is spoken of with other bodies of a similar kind, it is denominated *power.* The associates take collectively the name of *people,* and separately that of *citizens,* as participating in the sovereign authority: they are also styled *subjects,* because they are subjected to the laws. But these terms are frequently confounded, and used one for the other; and a man must understand them well to distinguish when they are properly employed.

OF THE SOVEREIGN POWER

It appears from this form that the act of association contains a reciprocal engagement between the public and individuals; and that each individual contracting as it were with himself, is engaged under a double character; that is, as a part of the *sovereign power* engaging with individuals, and as a member of the *state* entering into a compact with the *sovereign power.* But we cannot apply here the maxim of civil right, that no person is bound by any engagement which he makes with himself; for there is a material difference between an obligation contracted towards *one's self* individually, and towards a collective body of which *one's self* constitutes a part.

It is necessary to observe here that the will of the public, expressed by a majority of votes—which can enforce obedience from the subjects to the sovereign power in consequence of the double character under which the members of that body appear—cannot bind the sovereign power to itself; and that it is against the nature of the body politic for the sovereign power to impose any one law which it cannot alter. Were they to consider themselves as acting under one character only, they would be in the situation of individuals forming each a contract with himself: but this is not the case; and therefore there can be no fundamental obligatory law established for the body of the people, not even the social contract. But this is of little moment, as that body could not very well engage itself to others in any manner which would not derogate from the contract. With respect to foreigners, it becomes a single being, an individual only.

But the body politic, or sovereign power, which derives its existence from the sacredness of the contract, can never bind itself, even towards others, in any thing that would derogate from the original act; such as alienating any portion of itself, or submitting to another sovereign: for by violating the contract its own existence would be at once annihilated; and by nothing nothing can be performed.

As soon as the multitude is thus united in one body, you cannot offend one of its members without attacking the whole; much less can you offend the whole without incurring the resentment of all the members. Thus duty and interest equally oblige the two contracting parties to lend their mutual aid to each other; and the same men must endeavour to unite under this double character all the advantages which attend it.

The sovereign power being formed only of the individuals which compose it, neither has, or can have, any interest contrary to theirs; consequently the sovereign power requires no guarantee towards its subjects, because it is impossible that the body should seek to injure all its members: and we shall see presently that it can do no injury to any individual. The sovereign power by its nature must, while it exists, be everything it ought to be: but it is not so with subjects towards the sovereign power; to which, notwithstanding the common interest subsisting between them, there is nothing to answer for the performance of their engagements, if some means is not found of ensuring their fidelity.

In fact, each individual may, as a man, have a private will, dissimilar or contrary to the general will which he has as a citizen. His own particular interest may dictate to him very differently from the common interest; his mind, naturally and absolutely independent, may regard what he owes to the common cause as a gratuitous contribution, the omission of which would be less injurious to others than the payment would be burthensome to himself; and considering the moral person which constitutes the state as a creature of the imagination, because it is not a man, he may wish to enjoy the rights of a citizen, without being disposed to fulfil the duties of a subject: an injustice which would in its progress cause the ruin of the body politic.

In order therefore to prevent the social compact from becoming a vain form, it tacitly comprehends this engagement, which alone can give effect to the others—That whoever refuses to obey the general will, shall be compelled to it by the whole body, which is in fact only forcing him to be free; for this is the condition which guarantees his absolute personal independence to every citizen of the country: a condition which gives motion and effect to the political machine; which alone renders all civil engagements legal; and without which they would be absurd, tyrannical, and subject to the most enormous abuses.

OF THE CIVIL STATE

The passing from a state of nature to a civil state, produces in man a very remarkable change, by substituting justice for instinct, and giving to his actions a moral character which they wanted before.

It is at the moment of that transition that the voice of duty succeeds to physical impulse; and a sense of what is right, to the incitements of appetite. The man who had till then regarded none but himself, perceives that he must act on other principles, and learns to consult his reason before he listens to his propensities.

3   Conditions of Life on the Eve of the Revolution

Arthur Young (1741–1820) was a wealthy English farmer whose passion was the study of agriculture. In 1787 he set out to see how England's neighbor, France, conducted farming operations. His descriptions of various parts of France provide a vivid picture of the peasant's standard of living in the years immediately preceding the Revolution.

FROM *Travels in France during the Years 1787, 1788, 1789* BY ARTHUR YOUNG

POVERTY AND POOR CROPS to Amiens; women are now ploughing with a pair of horses to sow barley. The difference of the customs of the two nations is in nothing more striking than in the labours of the sex; in England, it is very little that they will do in the fields except to glean and make hay; the first is a party of pilfering, and the second of pleasure: in France, they plough and fill the dung cart. . . .

*   *   *

To La Ferté Lowendahl, a dead flat of hungry sandy gravel, with much heath. The poor people, who cultivate the soil here, are *métayers,* that is, men who hire the land without ability to stock it; the proprietor is forced to provide cattle and seed, and he and his tenant divide the produce; a miserable system, that perpetuates poverty and excludes instruction. . . .

*   *   *

The same wretched country continues to La Loge; the fields are scenes of pitiable management, as the houses are of misery. Yet all this country is highly improveable, if they knew what to do with it: the property, perhaps,

Arthur Young, *Travels in France during the Years 1787, 1788, 1789* (1889), pp. 8–9, 19, 27, 61, 123, 125, 189, 198, 201.

of some of those glittering beings, who figured in the procession the other day at Versailles. Heaven grant me patience while I see a country thus neglected—and forgive me the oaths I swear at the absence and ignorance of the possessors. . . .

Pass Payrac, and meet many beggars, which we had not done before. All the country, girls and women, are without shoes or stockings; and the ploughmen at their work have neither sabots nor feet to their stockings. This is a poverty, that strikes at the root of national prosperity; a large consumption among the poor being of more consequence than among the rich; the wealth of a nation lies in its circulation and consumption; and the case of poor people abstaining from the use of manufactures of leather and wool ought to be considered as an evil of the first magnitude. It reminded me of the misery of Ireland.

*   *   *

Take the road to Moneng, and come presently to a scene which was so new to me in France, that I could hardly believe my own eyes. A succession of many well built, tight, and COMFORTABLE farming cottages, built of stone, and covered with tiles; each having its little garden, inclosed by clipt thorn hedges, with plenty of peach and other fruit-trees, some fine oaks scattered in the hedges, and young trees nursed up with so much care, that nothing but the fostering attention of the owner could effect any thing like it. To every house belongs a farm, perfectly well inclosed, with grass borders mown and neatly kept around the corn fields, with gates to pass from one inclosure to another. The men are all dressed with red caps, like the highlanders of Scotland. There are some parts of England (where small yeomen still remain) that resemble this country of Bearne; but we have very little that is equal to what I have seen in this ride of twelve miles from Pau to Moneng. It is all in the hands of little proprietors, without the farms being so small as to occasion a vicious and miserable population. An air of neatness, warmth, and comfort breathes over the whole. It is visible in their new built houses and stables; in their little gardens; in their hedges; in the courts before their doors; even in the coops for their poultry, and the sties for their hogs. A peasant does not think of rendering his pig comfortable, if his own happiness hangs by the thread of a nine years lease. We are now in Bearne, within a few miles of the cradle of Henry IV. Do they inherit these blessings from that good prince? The benignant genius of that good monarch, seems to reign still over the country; each peasant has *the fowl in the pot*.

*   *   *

September 1st. To Combourg, the country has a savage aspect; husbandry not much further advanced, at least in skill, than among the Hurons, which appears incredible amidst inclosures; the people almost as wild as their country, and their town of Combourg one of the most brutal filthy places that can be seen; mud houses, no windows, and a pavement so broken, as to impede all passengers, but ease none—yet here is a chateau, and inhabited; who is this Mons. de Chateaubriant, the owner that has nerves strung for a residence amidst such filth and poverty? Below this hideous heap of wretchedness is a fine lake, surrounded by well wooded inclosures. . . .

*   *   *

1788

To Montauban. The poor people seem poor indeed; the children terribly ragged, if possible worse clad than if with no cloaths at all; as to shoes and stockings they are luxuries. A beautiful girl of six or seven years playing with a stick, and smiling under such a bundle of rags as made my heart ache to see her: they did not beg and when I gave them any thing seemed more surprized than obliged. One third of what I have seen of this province seems uncultivated, and nearly all of it in misery. What have kings, and ministers, and parliaments, and states, to answer for their prejudices, seeing millions of hands that would be industrious, idle and starving, through the execrable maxims of despotism, or the equally detestable prejudices of a feudal nobility. . . .

*   *   *

1789

The 12th. Walking up a long hill, to ease my mare, I was joined by a poor woman, who complained of the times, and that it was a sad country; demanding her reasons, she said her husband had but a morsel of land, one cow, and a poor little horse, yet they had a *franchar* (42 lb.) of wheat, and three chickens, to pay as a quit-rent to one Seigneur; and four *franchar* of oats, one chicken and 1 £. to pay to another, besides very heavy tailles and other taxes. She had seven children, and the cow's milk helped to make the soup. But why, instead of a horse, do not you keep another cow? Oh, her husband could not carry his produce so well without a horse; and asses are little used in the country. It was said, at present, that *something was to be done by some great folks for such poor ones, but she did not know who nor how,* but God send us better, *car les tailles & les droits nous écrasent.*—This woman, at no great distance, might have been taken for sixty or seventy, her figure was so bent, and her face so furrowed and hardened by labour,—but she said she was only twenty-eight. An Englishman who has not travelled. cannot imagine the figure made by infinitely the greater part of the country-women in France; it speaks, at the first sight, hard and severe labour: I am inclined to think, that they work harder than the men, and this, united with the more miserable labour of bringing a new race of slaves into the world, destroys absolutely all symmetry of person and every feminine appearance. To what are we to attribute this difference in the manners of the lower people in the two kingdoms? To GOVERNMENT. . . .

*   *   *

Nangis is near enough to Paris for *the people* to be politicians; the perruquier that dressed me this morning tells me, that every body is determined to pay no taxes, should the National Assembly so ordain. But the soldiers will have something to say. No, Sir, never:—be assured as we are, that the French soldiers will never fire on the people: but, if they should, it is better to be shot than starved. He gave me a frightful account of the misery of the people; whole families in the utmost distress; those that work have a pay insufficient to feed them—and many that find it difficult to get work at all. I enquired of Mons. de Guerchy concerning this, and found it true. By order of the magistrates no person is allowed to buy more than two bushels of wheat at a market, to prevent monopolizing. It is clear to common sense, that all such regulations have a direct tendency to increase the evil, but it is in vain to reason with people whose ideas are immovably fixed. Being here on a market-day, I attended, and saw the wheat sold out under this regulation, with a party of dragoons drawn up before the market-cross to prevent violence. The people quarrel with the bakers, asserting the prices they demand for bread are beyond the proportion of wheat, and proceeding from words to scuffling, raise a riot, and then run away with bread and wheat for nothing: this has happened at Nangis, and many other markets; the consequence was, that neither farmers nor bakers would supply them till they were in danger of starving, and, when they did come, prices under such circumstances must necessarily rise enormously, which aggravated the mischief, till troops became really necessary to give security to those who supplied the markets. . . .

*   *   *

Letters from Paris! all confusion! the ministry removed: Mons. Necker ordered to quit the kingdom without noise. The effect on the people of Nancy was considerable.—I was with Mons. Willemet when his letters arrived, and for some time his house was full of enquires; all agreed, that it was fatal news, and that it would occasion great commotions. *What will be the result at Nancy?* The answer was in effect the same from all I put this question to: *We are a provincial town, we must wait to see what is done at Paris; but every thing is to be feared from the people, because bread is so dear, they are half starved, and are consequently ready for commotion.*—This is the general feeling; they are as nearly concerned as Paris; but they dare not stir; they dare not even have an opinion of their own till they know what Paris thinks; so that if a starving populace were not in question, no one would dream of moving. This confirms what I have often heard remarked, that the *deficit* would not have produced the revolution but in concurrence with the price of bread. Does not this shew the infinite consequence of great cities to the liberty of mankind? Without Paris, I question whether the present revolution, which is fast working in France, could possibly have had an origin.

The peasant was not always as miserable as he seemed.

FROM *The Confessions of Jean Jacques Rousseau*

ONE DAY, AMONGST OTHERS, having purposely turned out of my way to get a nearer view of a spot which appeared worthy of admiration, I was so delighted with it, and went round it so often that, at last, I completely lost myself. After several hours of useless walking, tired, and dying of hunger and thirst, I entered a peasant's hut, not much to look at, but the only dwelling I saw in the neighbourhood. I expected to find it the same as in Geneva, or Switzerland, where all the well-to-do inhabitants are in a position to show hospitality. I begged him to give me dinner, and offered to pay for it. He offered me some skimmed milk and coarse barley bread, saying that that was all he had. I drank the milk with delight, and ate the bread, husks and all; but it was not very invigorating fare for a man exhausted by fatigue. The peasant, who examined me closely, estimated the truth of my story by my appetite, and immediately afterwards declared that he could see that I was a good and honourable young man, who had not come there to betray him for money. He opened a little trapdoor near the kitchen, went down, and came up a minute afterwards with a nice brown wheaten loaf, a very tempting-looking ham, although considerably cut down, and a bottle of wine, the sight of which rejoiced my heart more than all the rest; to this he added a substantial omelette, and I made a dinner such as none but a pedestrian ever enjoyed. When it came to the question of payment, his uneasiness and alarm returned; he would take none of my money, and refused it with singular anxiety; and the amusing thing was that I could not imagine what he was afraid of. At last, with a shudder, he uttered the terrible words, "Revenue officers and excisemen." He gave me to understand that he hid his wine on account of the excise, that he hid his bread on account of the tax, and that he was a lost man, if anyone had a suspicion that

The Confessions of Jean Jacques Rousseau (Modern Library ed., n.d.), pp. 169–70.

he was not starving. All that he said to me on this subject, of which I had not the least idea, made an impression upon me which will never be forgotten. It was the germ of the inextinguishable hatred which subsequently grew up in my heart against the oppression to which these unhappy people are subject, and against their oppressors. This man, although in good circumstances, did not dare to eat the bread which he had obtained by the sweat of his brow, and could only escape utter ruin by displaying the same poverty as prevailed around him. I left his house, equally indignant and touched, lamenting the lot of these beautiful countries, upon which Nature has only lavished her gifts to make them the prey of barbarous farmers of taxes.

The French Revolution is unique among revolutions in that there was an extensive sampling of public opinion immediately preceding the Revolution itself. Once the decision was made to call the Estates-General, the king was prevailed upon to order the compilation of notebooks (cahiers) of grievances to be drawn up by the three estates (Clergy, Nobility, Third). It was the first attempt to sample "grass roots" opinion, for literally every French subject was forced to think of the ills that afflicted France and was given the opportunity to make his views known.

The number of cahiers *that have survived is immense. The one that follows is typical of those submitted by the Third Estate.*

FROM *The Notebook of Grievances of the Third Estate of the Parish of Saint-Vaast*

TODAY, SUNDAY, the twenty-ninth day of March 1789, following vespers, at the sound of the church bell, in the customary way, the inhabitants of the parish of Saint-Vaast, Bailiwick of Auge, citizens of the Third-Estate, assembled according to the terms of the letters of convocation given by His Majesty at Versailles, the 24th of January 1789, for the convocation and holding of the Estates-general of the realm, and according to the ordinance

M. J. Mavidal and M. E. Laurent, *Archives parlementaires de 1787 à 1860,* Première Série, V (1879), 609–12, translated by L. Pearce Williams.

of the Lieutenant General of the Bailiwick of Auge at Pont-l'Evêque, dated the 16th of this month and announced in the pulpit of this parish on Sunday the 22nd of this month, and affixed to the main door of the Church on the same day, to the effect that they should confer among themselves and proceed to the writing of their notebook of grievances, complaints and remonstrances, means and advice that they wish to propose to the general assembly of the nation:

Begin, by assuring the King that they are ready to sacrifice their fortunes and their very persons for him and for the State;

And vote unanimously that the representatives of this province, in the Assembly of the Estates-general, before consenting to any new taxes to pay the debts of the government, shall employ their efforts and their zeal to the end that there shall be drawn up a *Declaration of the Rights of the French Nation* as a charter between the King, head of the nation and sole executor of the laws, and the nation, which will include the following:

NATIONAL CONSTITUTION

1. That the King consents to a law of *habeas corpus* which will guarantee every citizen, no matter how low his condition, from ever being subjected to the abuse of *lettres de cachet* or letters of exile, as well as from the actions and the arbitrary power of ministers, of governors and of intendants of provinces exercised through sealed letters.
2. That only the nation has the right to tax itself, that is to say, to accede to or refuse taxes, to regulate their size, their use, their assesssment and their scope; the nation can also ask for an account and must be consulted before loans are made. Any other means of taxation or of borrowing are declared unconstitutional, illegal and of no force.
3. That the periodical and regular reconvening of the Estates-general be set for every four years, at a specific time of the year, so that the nation can there consider the state of the realm, the use of taxes granted in the previous session in order to decide whether to continue or suppress them, and to propose, besides, reforms and other helps for all branches of the political economy.
4. That in the case (unhappily too frequent) where, by the intrigues of an ambitious minister intent upon administering everything according to his caprice, the lines of communication between the nation and its king are broken so that the convocation of the Estates-general does not take place as provided for in the *national charter,* the particular Estates of this province (of which more later) shall be authorized to oppose the levy of all taxes, and the parlements shall be authorized to publish their opposition by an ordinance which shall be sent to all lesser tribunals in their circuit and which will permit the public authorities to prosecute those who continue to collect them for malfeasance of office.

5. That all taxes on real and personal property shall be levied equally on all the goods of ecclesiastics, nobles and commoners, on perpetual rents and those of recent creation, and that all privileges which are really subsidies shall be wiped out.

6. That the Third-Estate, greatly superior in number to the two other orders, in order that it may be judged at least in part by its peers, as it was in the old exchequer court, will have, in the parlement of this undivided and indivisible province, forty magistrates drawn from this Estate; reason and experience have shown that the laws which guarantee the property, the liberty and the rights of the Third-Estate from the attacks and pretensions of the clergy and the nobility are illusory, useless and poorly obeyed so long as the maintenance and execution of justice rest in the hands of the two first orders to the exclusion of the third.

These representatives of the Third-Estate, presented to the King by the province and armed by the King with their powers, will be chosen among those of his subjects who have shown proof of their capacity by their study of the law and in the exercise of their talents at the bar, during ten years, either before the parlement or before other, lesser, courts. But, they shall cease to be the representatives of the Third-Estate, and their mandate shall become null and void if and when they are ennobled, no matter by what means.

*   *   *

The small income of a commoner should be no reason for exclusion from the parlement. The magistrature should not be based on the brilliance coming from opulence but on the brilliance of knowledge; this is especially true of a sense of justice which nothing can tarnish. How worthy of respect is the man who is always just!

The undersigned also vote that the representatives of this province to the Estates-general will insist that His Majesty grant, before they consent to any new taxes:

PROVINCIAL ESTATES

1. The re-establishment of the particular Estates of this province, which shall meet at Caen, center of Normandy, or elsewhere, each year, composed of a number of members of the Third-Estate equal to those of the two orders of the clergy and of the nobility together. . . .

2. *The unlimited liberty of the press,* with the requirement that the printer or the author place his name at the bottom of the printed matter so that he may be held responsible for whatever is contrary to dominant religious sentiments, or to the respect of the sovereign, public decency and the honor of citizens.

3. The destruction of all particular commissions of attribution or evocation,

for whatever cause, so that no citizen can ever be transferred from out his own jurisdiction. . . .

4. Great modifications in the ordinance of 1669, called the *Hunting Code,* most of which turns free commoners into true serfs. It is contrary to human rights that a cultivator who owns his land cannot lift a finger to destroy the wild animals which devastate his harvest, which is even more destroyed by those who chase these animals with great noise and numbers. The too abundant nature of the wild game (hitherto given greater privileges than the cultivator) leads to the real destruction of property; it also is contrary to reason as well as to the principle of liberty that a peaceful inhabitant of the country, merely because he is a commoner, can be seized from the center of his family and sent to prison by order of the governor of the province, simply because he has a gun to assure his own safety and is, therefore, suspect of having killed a Lord's rabbit.

In order to reconcile the interests of the possessors of fiefs with those of the commoner vassal (who is, after all, a man), it is necessary that the representatives of the Third-Estate solicit and obtain from the sovereign a hunting law such that:

No game warden can be believed on his own word unless he produce two witnesses who will swear to the day and the hour of the crime and to the person of the criminal. . . .

*   *   *

That game wardens who have killed commoners who were armed or caught hunting, or without authorization in the woods, shall no longer be immune from punishment, as has been the case recently in this province, among others in four recent cases of killing by the wardens of Madame A. . . . , of Madame N. . . . , of a prelate and of a Marshal of France, and others, all residents of this province.

That the cultivator be authorized to shoot, but not to carry away, the pigeons which devastate his harvest, from July 15 to August 20, as well as during the sowing season. This is the only way to force the Lords to close their dovecotes during this short time, since the laws passed on this point are not enforced since their enforcement is in the hands of those who have an interest in perpetuating the abuse.

Madame Roland was the wife of a moderate revolutionary who served for a time as Minister of the Interior before his execution in the Terror. Madame Roland followed him to the scaffold. Her memoirs were written as she awaited

*execution; in them she recalls her own feelings as a young
girl confronted with the pretensions of the nobility.*

FROM *The Private Memoirs of Madame Roland*

MY GRANDMOTHER ONE DAY took it into her head to pay a visit to
Madame de Boismorel, either for the pleasure of seeing her, or of displaying
her little daughter. Great preparations in consequence; long toilet in the
morning: at length behold us setting off with Aunt Angélique for the *rue
Saint-Louis, au Marais,* where we arrived about noon. On entering the house
every one, beginning with the *portier,* salutes Madame Phlipon with an air
of respect and affection, emulous who shall treat her with the greatest
civility. She repays their attention with courtesy, tinged at the same time
with dignity. So far very well; but her grandaughter is perceived; and, not
satisfied with pointing her out to one another, they proceed to pay her a
number of compliments. . . . We go on; a tall lackey announces us, and we
enter the *salon,* and find the lady seated, with her lap-dog beside her, upon
what we called then, not an *ottomane,* but a *canapé,* gravely embroidering
tapestry. Madame de Boismorel was about the age, the height, and the figure
of my grandmother; but her dress betokened the pride of wealth, rather than
taste; and her countenance, far from expressing any plebeian desire to please,
plainly demanded that all attention should be bestowed upon herself, and
manifested her consciousness of deserving it. . . . The rouge, spread one
layer over another, lent to eyes naturally dull a much greater air of fierceness
than was sufficient to make me fix mine upon the ground.

"Ah, Mademoiselle Rotisset, good morning to you," cried, in a loud and
cold tone, Madame de Boismorel, as she rose to meet us. (*"Mademoiselle!"*
So my grandmother is mademoiselle in this house.) "Upon my honor I am
very glad to see you. And this pretty child is your granddaughter? She will
make a fine woman. Come here, my dear, sit down by my side. . . . Did you
never venture in the lottery?"

"Never, madame; I am not fond of gaming."

"So, so! very likely indeed! At your age children are apt to think their
game is sure. . . . She is so grave too: I suppose you have a devotional
turn?"

"I know my duty to God, and I endeavor to fulfil it."

"That is a good girl! You wish to take the veil: is it not so?"

"I do not know my future destination, and I do not seek to pry into
it." . . .

The Private Memoirs of Madame Roland, edited, with an Introduction, by Edward Gilpin
Johnson (1900), pp. 121-5, 136-7, 200-5.

The conversation next turned upon the family and friends of the mistress of the house. . . . for example of Madame Roudé, who, notwithstanding her great age, was still absurd enough to pretend to a fine bosom, and accordingly greatly exposed this part of her person, except when she got in and out of her carriage, for which occasion she had always an immense handkerchief ready in her pocket, because, as she observed, it is not decent to make such an exhibition to the footmen. . . . I did not at this age ask myself, why my grandmother did not sit upon the *canapé,* or for what reason in particular Madame de Boismorel always called her *"Mademoiselle"* Rotisset; but I had the feeling that led to this reflection, and I saw the end of the visit with joy, as if I were just liberated from some hard confinement.

*   *   *

Mademoiselle d'Hannache, at that time at law for the inheritance of her uncle, "the captain," was accommodated in the house of my mother, and resided with us nearly a year and a half. During this interval I was her secretary; I wrote her letters, copied her precious genealogy, drew up the petitions she presented to the president and the attorney-general of the Parliament of Paris, the administrators of some annuities bequeathed by a M. de Saint-Vallier to females of rank in reduced circumstances, and accompanied her sometimes in her solicitations to various persons, which her affairs made necessary. I observed upon these occasions that, notwithstanding her ignorance, her illiterate language, her starched manners, her old-fashioned dress, and her other absurdities, she was treated with respect on account of her pedigree. They listened with attention to the names of her ancestors, which she never failed to enumerate, and were ready to side with her in her claims to the disputed inheritance. I could not but contrast this honorable treatment with the reception I had met with at Madame de Boismorel's, which had left a deep impression on my mind. It was impossible to conceal from myself my superiority to Mademoiselle d'Hannache, who, with all her genealogy and her forty years to boot, could not write a letter that was either legible, or dignified with a word of common sense; and I thought mankind extremely unjust, and the institutions of society extravagantly absurd.

*   *   *

The old Haudry, creator of the vast fortune of the family, was deceased, and had left a large estate to his son, who, born and educated in opulence, was fashioned to dissipate it. This son, who had already lost a charming wife, lived extravagantly, and, according to the custom of the rich, spent a part of the year at his château of Soucy, whither he transplanted the manners and mode of life of the town, instead of adopting those of the country. He had several neighboring estates, of which that nearest to Soucy (Fontenay), had an old mansion belonging to it that he loved to have occupied; and he had prevailed on M. and Madame Besnard to accept apartments there, in which they passed a part of the summer. This at once contributed to keep up the place, and to give that air of magnificence to his establishments, of which he was ambitious. M. and Madame Besnard were well accommodated, and enjoyed the use of the park, the wildness of which made an agreeable contrast with that of Soucy, and delighted me more than the artificial luxury, which distinguished the abode of the *fermier-général*. Soon after our arrival, Madame Besnard requested us to make a visit with her to Soucy, where the sister-in-law and stepmother of Haudry resided with him and did the honors of his house. This visit was modestly paid before dinner; and I entered, without the least feeling of pleasure, into the *salon,* where Madame Pénault and her daughter received us, with great politeness, it is true, but a politeness that savored a little of superiority. The propriety of my mother's behavior, and something too that appeared in me, in spite of that air of timidity which is produced by a feeling of our value and a doubt whether it will be appreciated by others, scarcely allowed them to exercise it. . . .

The ladies did not fail, a few days after, to return our visit. Three or four persons accompanied them, who happened to be at the château, their paying their respects to us serving merely for the termination of their walk. Upon this occasion I was more agreeable, and succeeded in infusing into my part of the reception the proportion of modest and decent politeness which re-established the equilibrium. Madame Pénault invited us to dinner; but I was never more astonished than on learning that it was not to her own table, but to that of the servants. I was sensible, however, that, as M. Besnard had formerly been in that station, I ought not, out of respect to him, to appear averse to accompanying them; but I felt that Madame Péneault ought to have arranged things otherwise, or spared us this contemptuous civility. My aunt saw it in the same light; but, to avoid any little scene, we accepted the invitation. These inferior household deities were a new spectacle to me, for I had formed no conception of ladies'-maids personating grandeur. They were prepared to receive us; and, indeed, aped their superiors admirably well. Toilet, gesture, affectation, graces, nothing was forgotten. The cast-off dresses of their mistresses gave to the female part of the household a richness of appearance that honest tradespeople would think out of character to themselves. The caricature of *bon ton* added to their garb a sort of elegance, not less foreign to *bourgeois* simplicity than odious in the eye of an artist. In spite of all this, however, the fluency of their prate and the multiplicity of their grimaces would no doubt have inspired awe into rustics. It was still worse with the men. The sword of "M. *le maître,*" the attentions of "M. *le chef,*" the graces and fine clothes of the valets, could not cloak their *gaucheries* or the jargon they affected when they wished to seem distinguished, or their native vulgarity of speech when for a moment they forgot their assumed gentility. The conversation glittered with marquises, counts, financiers, whose titles, fortunes, and alliances shed a second-hand splendor on those who so glibly discoursed of them. The superfluities of the first table were transferred to the second with an order and despatch that made them appear as if then served for the first time, and with a profusion that sufficed to deck a third table, that of the servants—for it seems the domestics of the first grade called themselves *"officiers."* After dinner, cards were introduced: the stake was high; it was that for which these *"demoiselles"* were accustomed to play, and they played every day. I was introduced to a new world, in which were reflected the prejudices, the vices, and the follies of the great world, the value of which is not really superior, though the show be somewhat more dazzling. I had heard a thousand times of the beginnings of old Haudry, of his coming to Paris from his village, and rising by degrees to the accumulation of thousands at the expense of the public; of his marrying his daughter to Montule, his granddaughters to the Marquis du Chillau and Count Turpin, and leaving his son heir to immense treasures. I agreed with Montesquieu that financiers support the state, just as the cord supports the criminal. I judged that publicans who found means to enrich themselves to this degree, and to use their wealth as an engine by which to unite themselves with families of rank, which the policy of courts regards as essential to the glory and safety of a kingdom—I judged that characters like these could belong only to a detestable government and a depraved nation.

4　The Ideals of the Revolution

On August 27, 1789, the National Assembly decreed the Declaration of the Rights of Man as the preamble to the Constitution of France yet to be written. It was, like the American Bill of Rights, to serve as the basic definition of the goals of the Revolution.

Declaration of the Rights of Man and of the Citizen

THE REPRESENTATIVES OF THE FRENCH PEOPLE, organized as a national assembly, believing that the ignorance, neglect or contempt of the rights of man are the sole causes of public calamities and of the corruption of governments, have determined to set forth in a solemn declaration, the natural, inalienable and sacred rights of man, in order that this declaration, being constantly before all the members of the social body, shall remind them continually of their rights and duties; in order that the acts of the legislative power, as well as those of the executive power, may be compared at any moment with the ends of all political institutions and may thus be more respected; in order that the grievances of the citizens, based hereafter upon simple and incontestable principles, shall tend to the maintenance of the constitution and redound to the happiness of all. Hence the national assembly recognizes and proclaims in the presence and under the auspices of the Supreme Being the following rights of man and of the citizen:

ARTICLE I. Men are born and remain free and equal in rights. Social distinctions can only be founded upon the general good.

2. The aim of all political association is the preservation of the natural and imprescriptible rights of man. These rights are liberty, property, security, and resistance to oppression.

3. The principle (*principe*) of all sovereignty resides essentially in the

J. H. Robinson, ed., "The French Revolution, 1789–91," in *Translations and Reprints from the Original Sources of European History*, I, No. 5 (1897), 6–8.

nation. No body nor individual may exercise any authority which does not proceed directly from the nation.

4. Liberty consists in being able to do everything which injures no one else; hence the exercise of the natural rights of each man has no limits except those which assure to the other members of the society the enjoyment of the same rights. These limits can only be determined by law.

5. Law can only prohibit such actions as are hurtful to society. Nothing may be prevented which is not forbidden by law, and no one may be forced to do anything not provided for by law.

6. Law is the expression of the general will. Every citizen has a right to participate personally or through his representative in its formation. It must be the same for all, whether it protects or punishes. All citizens being equal in the eyes of the law are equally eligible to all dignities and to all public positions and occupations according to their abilities and without distinction except that of their virtues and talents.

7. No person shall be accused, arrested or imprisoned except in the cases and according to the forms prescribed by law. Any one soliciting, transmitting, executing or causing to be executed any arbitrary order shall be punished. But any citizen summoned or arrested in virtue of the law shall submit without delay as resistance constitutes an offence.

8. The law shall provide for such punishments only as are strictly and obviously necessary, and no one shall suffer punishment except it be legally inflicted in virtue of a law passed and promulgated before the commission of the offence.

9. As all persons are held innocent until they shall have been declared guilty, if arrest shall be deemed indispensable all severity not essential to the securing of the prisoner's person shall be severely repressed by law.

10. No one shall be disquieted on account of his opinions, including his religious views provided their manifestation does not disturb the public order established by law.

11. The free communication of ideas and opinions is one of the most precious of the rights of man. Every citizen may, accordingly, speak, write and print with freedom, being responsible, however, for such abuses of this freedom as shall be defined by law.

12. The security of the rights of man and of the citizen requires public military force. These forces are, therefore, established for the good of all and not for the personal advantage of those to whom they shall be entrusted.

13. A common contribution is essential for the maintenance of the public forces and for the cost of administration. This should be equitably distributed among all the citizens in proportion to their means.

14. All the citizens have a right to decide either personally or by their representatives as to the necessity of the public contribution, to grant this freely, to know to what uses it is put, and to fix the proportion, the mode of assessment, and of collection, and the duration of the taxes.

15. Society has the right to require of every public agent an account of his administration.
16. A society in which the observance of the law is not assured nor the separation of powers defined has no constitution at all.
17. Property being an inviolable and sacred right, no one shall be deprived thereof except where public necessity, legally determined shall clearly demand it, and then only on condition that the owner shall have been previously and equitably indemnified.

5 The Origins of the Revolution

FROM *On the Revolution of France*
BY ARTHUR YOUNG

THE GROSS INFAMY which attended *lettres de cachet* and the Bastille, during the whole reign of Louis XV made them esteemed in England, by people not well informed, as the most prominent features of the despotism of France. They were certainly carried to an access [*sic*] hardly credible; to the length of being sold, with blanks, to be filled up with names at the pleasure of the purchaser; who was thus able, in the gratification of private revenge, to tear a man from the bosom of his family, and bury him in a dungeon, where he would exist forgotten, and die unknown!—But such excesses could not be common in any country; and they were reduced almost to nothing, from the accession of the present King. The great mass of the people, by which I mean the lower and middle ranks, could suffer very little from such engines, and as few of them are objects of jealousy, had there been nothing else to complain of, it is not probable they would ever have been brought to take arms. The abuses attending the levy of taxes were heavy and universal. The kingdom was parcelled into generalities, with an intendant at the head of each, into whose hands the whole power of the crown was delegated for every thing except the military authority; but particularly for all affairs of finance. The generalities were subdivided into elections, at the head of which was a *sub-délégué,* appointed by the intendant. The rolls of the *taille, capitation, vingtièmes,* and other taxes, were distributed among districts, parishes, and individuals, at the pleasure of the intendant, who could exempt, change, add, or diminish, at pleasure. Such an enormous power, constantly acting, and from which no man was free, might in the nature of things, degenerate in many cases into absolute tyranny. It must be obvious, that the friends, acquaintances, and dependents of the intendant, and of all his *sub-délégués,* and the friends of these friends, to a long chain of dependence, might be favoured in taxation at the expence of their miserable neighbours; and that noblemen, in favour at court, to whose protection the intendant himself would naturally look up, could find little difficulty in

Arthur Young, *Travels in France during the Years 1787, 1788, 1789* (1889), pp. 313–5, 316–7, 322–3.

throwing much of the weight of their taxes on others, without a similar support. Instances, and even gross ones, have been reported to me in many parts of the kingdom, that made me shudder at the oppression to which numbers must have been condemned, by the undue favours granted to such crooked influence. But, without recurring to such cases, what must have been the state of the poor people paying heavy taxes, from which the nobility and clergy were exempted? A cruel aggravation of their misery, to see those who could best afford to pay, exempted because able!

—The inrolments for the militia, which the *cahiers* call *an injustice without example,* were another dreadful scourge on the peasantry; and, as married men were exempted from it, occasioned in some degree that mischievous population which brought beings into the world, in order for little else than to be starved. The *corvées,* or police of the roads, were annually the ruin of many hundreds of farmers; more than 300 were reduced to beggary in filling up one vale in Loraine: all these oppressions fell on the *tiers état* only; the nobility and clergy having been equally exempted from *tailles,* militia, and *corvées.*

The *Capitaineries* were a dreadful scourge on all the occupiers of land. By this term, is to be understood the paramountship of certain districts, granted by the king, to princes of the blood, by which they were put in possession of the property of all game, even on lands not belonging to them; and, what is very singular, on manors granted long before to individuals; so that the erecting of a district into a *capitainerie,* was an annihilation of all manorial rights to game within it. This was a trifling business, in comparison to other circumstances; for, in speaking of the preservation of the game in these *capitaineries,* it must be observed, that by game it must be understood whole droves of wild boars, and herds of deer not confined by any wall or pale, but wandering, at pleasure, over the whole country, to the destruction of crops; and to the peopling of the gallies by the wretched peasants, who presumed to kill them, in order to save that food which was to support their helpless children. The game in the *capitainerie* of Montceau, in four parishes only, did mischief to the amount of 184,263 liv. per annum. . . . Now, an English reader will scarcely understand it without being told, that there were numerous edicts for preserving the game which prohibited weeding and hoeing, lest the young partridges should be disturbed; steeping seed, lest it should injure the game; manuring with night soil, lest the flavour of the partridges should be injured by feeding on the corn so produced; mowing hay, &c. before a certain time, so late as to spoil many crops; and taking away the stubble, which would deprive the birds of shelter. The tyranny exercised in these *capitaineries,* which extended over 400 leagues of country, was so great, that many *cahiers* demanded the utter suppression of them.

*   *   *

It is impossible to justify the excesses of the people on their taking up arms; they were certainly guilty of cruelties; it is idle to deny the facts, for they have been proved too clearly to admit of a doubt. But is it really the people to whom we are to impute the whole?—Or to their oppressors who had kept them so long in a state of bondage? He who chooses to be served by slaves, and by ill-treated slaves, must know that he holds both his property and life by a tenure far different from those who prefer the service of well-treated freemen; and he who dines to the music of groaning sufferers, must not, in the moment of insurrection, complain that his daughters are ravished, and then destroyed; and that his sons' throats are cut. When such evils happen, they surely are more imputable to the tyranny of the master, than to the cruelty of the servant. The analogy holds with the French peasants—the murder of a seigneur, or a chateau in flames, is recorded in every newspaper; the rank of the person who suffers, attracts notice; but where do we find the register of that seigneur's oppressions of his peasantry, and his exactions of feudal services, from those whose children were dying around them for want of bread? Where do we find the minutes that assigned these starving wretches to some vile petty-fogger, to be fleeced by impositions, and a mockery of justice, in the seigneural courts? Who gives us the awards of the intendant and his *sub-délégués,* which took off the taxes of a man of fashion, and laid them with accumulated weight, on the poor, who were so unfortunate as to be his neighbours? Who has dwelt sufficiently upon explaining all the ramifications of despotism, regal, aristocratical, and ecclesiastical, pervading the whole mass of the people; reaching, like a circulating fluid, the most distant capillary tubes of poverty and wretchedness? In these cases, the sufferers are too ignoble to be known; and the mass too indiscriminate to be pitied. But should a philosopher feel and reason thus? should he mistake the cause for the effect? and giving all his pity to the few, feel no compassion for the many, because they suffer in his eyes not individually, but by millions? The excesses of the people cannot, I repeat, be justified; it would undoubtedly have done them credit, both as men and christians, if they had possessed their new acquired power with moderation. But let it be remembered, that the populace in no country ever use power with moderation; excess is inherent in their aggregate constitution: and as every government in the world knows, that violence infallibly attends power in such hands, it is doubly bound in common sense, and for common safety, so to conduct itself, that the people may not find an interest in public confusions. They will always suffer much and long, before they are effectually roused; nothing, therefore, can kindle the flame, but such oppressions of some classes or order in the society, as give able men the opportunity of seconding the general mass; discontent will soon diffuse itself around; and if the government take not warning in time, it is alone answerable for all the burnings, and plunderings, and devastation, and blood that follow. The true judgment to be formed of the French revolution, must surely be gained, from an attentive consideration of the evils of the old government: when these are well understood—and when the extent and universality of the oppression under which the people groaned—oppression which bore upon them from every quarter, it will scarcely be attempted to be urged, that a revolution was not absolutely necessary to the welfare of the kingdom.

> *The most eloquent opponent of the French Revolution in Europe was Edmund Burke (1729–1797). He is the classic spokesman for Conservatism, and he used the happenings of the French Revolution to illustrate his thesis that abstract reasoning is no substitute for a slow, careful, organic growth of the state.*

FROM *Reflections on the Revolution in France*

BY EDMUND BURKE

Dear Sir,

YOU ARE PLEASED TO CALL AGAIN, and with some earnestness, for my thoughts on the late proceedings in France.

I flatter myself that I love a manly, moral, regulated liberty as well as any gentleman of that society, be he who he will; and perhaps I have given as good proofs of my attachment to that cause, in the whole course of my public conduct. I think I envy liberty as little as they do, to any other nation. But I cannot stand forward, and give praise or blame to any thing which relates to human actions, and human concerns, on a simple view of the object, as it stands stripped of every relation, in all the nakedness and solitude of metaphysical abstraction. Circumstances (which with some gentlemen pass for nothing) give in reality to every political principle its distinguishing colour, and discriminating effect. The circumstances are what render every civil and political scheme beneficial or noxious to mankind. Abstractedly speaking, government, as well as liberty, is good; yet could I, in common sense, ten years ago, have felicitated France on her enjoyment of a government (for she then had a government) without enquiry what the nature of that government was, or how it was administered? Can I now congratulate the same nation upon its freedom? Is it because liberty in the abstract may be classed amongst the blessings of mankind, that I am seriously to felicitate a madman, who has escaped from the protecting restraint and wholesome darkness of his cell, on his restoration to the enjoyment of

Edmund Burke, *Reflections on the Revolution in France, and on the Proceedings in Certain Societies in London Relative to that Event,* 6th ed. (1790), pp. 1, 7–9, 11, 35–6, 50–1, 74–5, 86–9, 90–2, 115.

light and liberty? Am I to congratulate an highwayman and murderer, who has broke prison, upon the recovery of his natural rights? This would be to act over again the scene of the criminals condemned to the gallies, and their heroic deliverer, the metaphysic Knight of the Sorrowful Countenance.

The effect of liberty to individuals is, that they may do what they please: We ought to see what it will please them to do, before we risque congratulations, which may be soon turned into complaints. Prudence would dictate this in the case of separate insulated private men; but liberty, when men act in bodies, is *power*. Considerate people before they declare themselves will observe the use which is made of *power*; and particularly of so trying a thing as *new* power in *new* persons, of whose principles, tempers, and dispositions, they have little or no experience, and in situations where those who appear the most stirring in the scene may possibly not be the real movers.

It looks to me as if I were in a great crisis, not of the affairs of France alone, but of all Europe, perhaps of more than Europe. All circumstances taken together, the French revolution is the most astonishing that has hitherto happened in the world. The most wonderful things are brought about in many instances by means the most absurd and ridiculous; in the most ridiculous modes; and apparently, by the most contemptible instruments. Every thing seems out of nature in this strange chaos of levity and ferocity, and of all sorts of crimes jumbled together with all sorts of follies. In viewing this monstrous tragi-comic scene, the most opposite passions necessarily succeed, and sometimes mix with each other in the mind; alternate contempt and indignation; alternate laughter and tears; alternate scorn and horror.

A few years ago I should be ashamed to overload a matter, so capable of supporting itself, by the then unnecessary support of any argument; but this seditious, unconstitutional doctrine is now publicly taught, avowed, and printed. The dislike I feel to revolutions, the signals for which have so often been given from pulpits; the spirit of change that is gone abroad; the total contempt which prevails with you, and may come to prevail with us, of all ancient institutions, when set in opposition to a present sense of convenience, or to the bent of a present inclination: all these considerations make it not unadviseable, in my opinion, to call back our attention to the true principles of our own domestic laws; that you, my French friend, should begin to know, and that we should continue to cherish them. We ought not, on either side of the water, to suffer ourselves to be imposed upon by the counterfeit wares which some persons, by a double fraud, export to you in illicit bottoms, as raw commodities of British growth though wholly alien to our soil, in order afterwards to smuggle them back again into this country, manufactured after the newest Paris fashion of an improved liberty.

You might, if you pleased, have profited of our example, and have given to your recovered freedom a correspondent dignity. Your privileges, though discontinued, were not lost to memory. Your constitution, it is true, whilst you were out of possession, suffered waste and dilapidation; but you possessed in some parts the walls, and in all the foundations of a noble and venerable castle. You might have repaired those walls; you might have built on those old foundations. Your constitution was suspended before it was perfected; but you had the elements of a constitution very nearly as good as could be wished. In your old states you possessed that variety of parts corresponding with the various descriptions of which your community was happily composed; you had all that combination, and all that opposition of interests, you had that action and counteraction which, in the natural and in the political world, from the reciprocal struggle of discordant powers, draws out the harmony of the universe. These opposed and conflicting interests, which you considered as so great a blemish in your old and in our present constitution, interpose a salutary check to all precipitate resolutions. They render deliberation a matter not of choice, but of necessity; they make all change a subject of *compromise,* which naturally begets moderation; they produce *temperaments,* preventing the sore evil of harsh, crude, unqualified reformations; and rendering all the headlong exertions of arbitrary power, in the few or in the many, for ever impracticable. Through that diversity of members and interests, general liberty had as many securities as there were separate views in the several orders; whilst by pressing down the whole by the weight of a real monarchy, the separate parts would have been prevented from warping and starting from their allotted places.

You had all these advantages in your antient states; but you chose to act as if you had never been moulded into civil society, and had every thing to begin anew. You began ill, because you began by despising every thing that belonged to you. You set up your trade without a capital. If the last generations of your country appeared without much lustre in your eyes, you might have passed them by, and derived your claims from a more early race of ancestors. Under a pious predilection of those ancestors, your imaginations would have realized in them a standard of virtue and wisdom, beyond the vulgar practice of the hour; and you would have risen with the example to whose imitation you aspired. Respecting your forefathers, you would have been taught to respect yourselves. You would not have chosen to consider the French as a people of yesterday, as a nation of low-born servile wretches until the emancipating year of 1789.

*   *   *

Nothing is a due and adequate representation of a state, that does not represent its ability, as well as its property. But as ability is a vigorous and active principle, and as property is sluggish, inert, and timid, it never can be safe from the invasions of ability, unless it be, out of all proportion, predominant in the representation. It must be represented too in great masses of accumulation, or it is not rightly protected. The characteristic essence of property, formed out of the combined principles of its acquisition and conservation, is to be *unequal.* The great masses therefore which excite envy, and tempt rapacity, must be put out of the possibility of danger. Then they form a natural rampart about the lesser properties in all their gradations. The same quantity of property, which is by the natural course of things divided among many, has not the same operation. Its defensive power is weakened as it is diffused. In this diffusion each man's portion is less than what, in the eagerness of his desires, he may flatter himself to obtain by dissipating the accumulations of others. The plunder of the few would indeed give but a share inconceivably small in the distribution to the many. But the many are not capable of making this calculation; and those who lead them to rapine, never intend this distribution.

*   *   *

Far am I from denying in theory; full as far is my heart from withholding in practice (if I were of power to give or to withhold) the *real* rights of men. In denying their false claims of right, I do not mean to injure those which are real, and are such as their pretended rights would totally destroy. If civil society be made for the advantage of man, all the advantages for which it is made become his right. It is an institution of beneficence; and law itself is only beneficence acting by a rule. Men have a right to live by that rule; they have a right to justice; as between their fellows, whether their fellows are in politic function or in ordinary occupation. They have a right to the fruits of their industry; and to the means of making their industry fruitful. They have a right to the acquisitions of their parents; to the nourishment and improvement of their offspring; to instruction in life, and to consolation in death. Whatever each man can separately do, without trespassing upon others, he has a right to do for himself; and he has a right to a fair portion of all which society, with all its combinations of skill and force, can do in his favour. In this partnership all men have equal rights; but not to equal things. He that has but five shillings in the partnership, has as good a right to it, as he that has five hundred pound has to his larger proportion. But he has not a right to an equal dividend in the product of the joint stock; and as to the share of power, authority, and direction which each individual ought to have in the management of the state, that I must deny to be amongst the direct original rights of man in civil society; for I have in my contemplation the civil social man, and no other. It is a thing to be settled by convention.

If civil society be the offspring of convention, that convention must be its law. That convention must limit and modify all the descriptions of constitution which are formed under it. Every sort of legislative, judicial, or executory power are its creatures. They can have no being in any other state of things; and how can any man claim, under the conventions of civil society, rights which do not so much as suppose its existence? Rights which are absolutely repugnant to it? One of the first motives to civil society, and which becomes one of its fundamental rules, is, *that no man should be judge in his own cause*. By this each person has at once divested himself of the first fundamental right of uncovenanted man, that is, to judge for himself, and to assert his own cause. He abdicates all right to be his own governor. He inclusively, in a great measure, abandons the right of self-defence, the first law of nature. Men cannot enjoy the rights of an uncivil and of a civil state together. That he may obtain justice he gives up his right of determining what it is in points the most essential to him. That he may secure some liberty, he makes a surrender in trust of the whole of it.

Government is not made in virtue of natural rights, which may and do exist in total independence of it; and exist in much greater clearness, and in a much greater degree of abstract perfection: but their abstract perfection is their practical defect. By having a right to every thing they want every thing. Government is a contrivance of human wisdom to provide for human *wants*. Men have a right that these wants should be provided for by this wisdom. Among these wants is to be reckoned the want, out of civil society, of a sufficient restraint upon their passions. Society requires not only that the passions of individuals should be subjected, but that even in the mass and body as well as in the individuals, the inclinations of men should frequently be thwarted, their will controlled, and their passions brought into subjection. This can only be done *by a power out of themselves*; and not, in the exercise of its function, subject to that will and to those passions which it is its office to bridle and subdue. In this sense the restraints on men, as well as their liberties, are to be reckoned among their rights. But as the liberties and the restrictions vary with times and circumstances, and admit of infinite modifications, they cannot be settled upon any abstract rule; and nothing is so foolish as to discuss them upon that principle.

*   *   *

The science of constructing a commonwealth, or renovating it, or reforming it, is, like every other experimental science, not to be taught *a priori*. Nor is it a short experience that can instruct us in that practical science; because the real effects of moral causes are not always immediate; but that which in the first instance is prejudicial may be excellent in its remoter operation; and its excellence may arise even from the ill effects it produces in the beginning. The reverse also happens; and very plausible schemes, with very pleasing commencements, have often shameful and lamentable conclusions. In states there are often some obscure and almost latent causes, things which appear at first view of little moment, on which a very great part of its prosperity or adversity may most essentially depend. The science of government being therefore so practical in itself, and intended for such practical purposes, a matter which requires experience, and even more experience than any person can gain in his whole life, however sagacious and observing he may be, it is with infinite caution that any man ought to venture upon pulling down an edifice which has answered in any tolerable degree for ages the common purposes of society, or on building it up again, without having models and patterns of approved utility before his eyes.

These metaphysic rights entering into common life, like rays of light which pierce into a dense medium, are, by the laws of nature, refracted from their straight line. Indeed in the gross and complicated mass of human passions and concerns, the primitive rights of men undergo such a variety of refractions and reflections, that it becomes absurd to talk of them as if they continued in the simplicity of their original direction. The nature of man is intricate; the objects of society are of the greatest possible complexity; and therefore no simple disposition or direction of power can be suitable either to man's nature, or to the quality of his affairs. When I hear the simplicity of contrivance aimed at and boasted of in any new political constitutions, I am at no loss to decide that the artificers are grossly ignorant of their trade, or totally negligent of their duty. The simple governments are fundamentally defective, to say no worse of them. If you were to contemplate society in but one point of view, all these simple modes of polity are infinitely captivating. In effect each would answer its single end much more perfectly than the more complex is able to attain all its complex purposes. But it is better that the whole should be imperfectly and anomalously answered, than that, while some parts are provided for with great exactness, others might be totally neglected, or perhaps materially injured, by the over-care of a favourite member.

The pretended rights of these theorists are all extremes; and in proportion as they are metaphysically true, they are morally and politically false. The rights of men are in a sort of *middle,* incapable of definition, but not impossible to be discerned. The rights of men in governments are their advantages; and these are often in balances between differences of good; in compromise sometimes between good and evil, and sometimes, between evil and evil. Political reason is a computing principle; adding, subtracting, multiplying, and dividing, morally and not metaphysically or mathematically, true moral denominations.

*   *   *

On the scheme of this barbarous philosophy, which is the offspring of cold hearts and muddy understandings, and which is as void of solid wisdom, as it is destitute of all taste and elegance, laws are to be supported only by their own terrors, and by the concern, which each individual may find in them, from his own private speculations, or can spare to them from his own private interests. In the groves of *their* academy, at the end of every vista, you see nothing but the gallows. Nothing is left which engages the affections on the part of the commonwealth. On the principles of this mechanic philosophy, our institutions can never be embodied, if I may use the expression, in persons; so as to create in us love, veneration, admiration, or attachment. But that sort of reason which banishes the affections is incapable of filling their place. These public affections, combined with manners, are required sometimes as supplements, sometimes as correctives, always as aids to law. . . . There ought to be a system of manners in every nation which a well-formed mind would be disposed to relish. To make us love our country, our country ought to be lovely.

But power, of some kind or other, will survive the shock in which manners and opinions perish, and it will find other and worse means for its support. The usurpation which, in order to subvert antient institutions, has destroyed antient principles, will hold power by arts similar to those by which it has acquired it. When the old feudal and chivalrous spirit of *Fealty,* which, by freeing kings from fear, freed both kings and subjects from the precautions of tyranny, shall be extinct in the minds of men, plots and assassinations will be anticipated by preventive murder and preventive confiscation, and that long roll of grim and bloody maxims, which form the political code of all power, not standing on its own honour, and the honour of those who are to obey it. Kings will be tyrants from policy when subjects are rebels from principle.

When antient opinions and rules of life are taken away, the loss cannot possibly be estimated. From that moment we have no compass to govern us; nor can we know distinctly to what port we steer. Europe undoubtedly, taken in a mass, was in a flourishing condition the day on which your Revolution was compleated. How much of that prosperous state was owing to the spirit of our old manners and opinions is not easy to say; but as such causes cannot be indifferent in their operation, we must presume, that, on the whole, their operation was beneficial.

> *Hippolyte Taine (1828–1893) was a literary critic by training. After having lived through the upheaval of the Paris Commune of 1871, he turned to the study of the French Revolution in order to find the origins of the class struggle that racked the France of his day. He found it in the misery of the lower orders of society on the eve of the Revolution.*

FROM *The Ancient Regime* BY HIPPOLYTE TAINE

I

EXAMINE ADMINISTRATIVE CORRESPONDENCE for the last thirty years preceding the Revolution. Countless statements reveal excessive

Hippolyte Taine, *The Ancient Regime* (1876), pp. 335–48, translated by John Durand.

suffering, even when not terminating in fury. Life to a man of the lower class, to an artisan, or workman, subsisting on the labor of his own hands, is evidently precarious; he obtains simply enough to keep him from starvation and he does not always get that. Here, in four districts, "the inhabitants live only on buckwheat," and for five years, the apple crop having failed, they drink only water. There, in a country of vineyards, "the vine-dressers each year are reduced, for the most part, to begging their bread during the dull season." Elsewhere, several of the day-laborers and mechanics, obliged to sell their effects and household goods, die of the cold; insufficient and unhealthy food generates sickness, while in two districts, thirty-five thousand persons are stated to be living on alms. In a remote canton the peasants cut the grain still green and dry it in the oven, because they are too hungry to wait. The intendant of Poitiers writes that "as soon as the workhouses open, a prodigious number of the poor rush to them, in spite of the reduction of wages and of the restrictions imposed on them in behalf of the most needy." The intendant of Bourges notices that a great many *métayers* have sold off their furniture and that "entire families pass two days without eating," and that in many parishes the famished stay in bed most of the day because they suffer less. The intendant of Orléans reports that "in Sologne, poor widows have burned up their wooden bedsteads and others have consumed their fruit trees" to preserve themselves from the cold, and he adds, "nothing is exaggerated in this statement; the cries of want cannot be expressed; the misery of the rural districts must be seen with one's own eyes to obtain an idea of it." From Rioni, from La Rochelle, from Limoges, from Lyons, from Montauban, from Caen, from Alençon, from Flanders, from Moulins come similar statements by other intendants. One might call it the interruptions and repetitions of a funeral knell; even in years not disastrous it is heard on all sides. In Burgundy, near Chatillon-sur-Seine, "taxes, seignioral dues, the tithes, and the expenses of cultivation, divide up the productions of the soil into thirds, leaving nothing for the unfortunate cultivators, who would have abandoned their fields, had not two Swiss manufacturers of calicoes settled there and distributed about the country forty thousand francs a year in cash." In Auvergne, the country is depopulated daily; many of the villages have lost, since the beginning of the century, more than one-third of their inhabitants. "Had not steps been promptly taken to lighten the burden of a downtrodden people," says the provincial assembly in 1787, "Auvergne would have forever lost its population and its cultivation." In Comminges, at the outbreak of the Revolution, certain communities threaten to abandon their possessions, should they obtain no relief. "It is a well-known fact," says the assembly of Haute-Guyenne, in 1784, "that the lot of the most severely taxed communities is so rigorous as to have led their proprietors frequently to abandon their property. Who is not aware of the inhabitants of Saint-Servin having abandoned their possessions ten times and of their threats to resort again to this painful proceeding in their recourse to the administration? Only a few years ago an abandonment of the community of Boisse took place through the combined action of the inhabitants, the seignior and the *décimateur* of the community"; and the desertion would be still greater if the law did not forbid persons liable to the *taille* abandoning overtaxed property, except by renouncing whatever they possessed in the community. In the Soissonais, according to the report of the provincial assembly, "misery is excessive." In Gascony the spectacle is "heart-rending." In the environs of Toule, the cultivator, after paying his taxes, tithes and other dues, remains empty-handed. "Agriculture is an occupation of steady anxiety and privation, in which thousands of men are obliged to painfully vegetate." In a village in Normandy, "nearly all the inhabitants, not excepting the farmers and proprietors, eat barley bread and drink water, living like the most wretched of men, so as to provide for the payment of taxes with which they are overburdened." In the same province, at Forges, "many poor creatures eat oat bread, and others bread of soaked bran, this nourishment causing many deaths among infants." People evidently live from day to day; whenever the crop proves poor they lack bread. Let a frost come, a hailstorm, an inundation, and an entire province is incapable of supporting itself until the coming year; in many places even an ordinary winter suffices to bring on distress. On all sides hands are seen outstretched to the king, who is the universal almoner. The people may be said to resemble a man attempting to wade through a pool with the water up to his chin, and who, losing his footing at the slightest depression, sinks down and drowns. Existent charity and the fresh spirit of humanity vainly strive to rescue them; the water has risen too high. It must subside to a lower level and the pool be drawn off through some adequate outlet. Thus far the poor man catches breath only at intervals, running the risk of drowning at every moment.

II

Between 1750 and 1760, the idlers who eat suppers begin to regard with compassion and alarm the laborers who go without dinners. Why are the latter so impoverished, and by what mischance, on a soil as rich as that of France, do those lack bread who grow the grain? In the first place many farms remain uncultivated, and, what is worse, many are deserted. According to the best observers "one-quarter of the soil is absolutely lying waste; . . . Hundreds and hundreds of *arpents* of heath and moor form extensive deserts." "Let a person traverse Anjou, Maine, Brittany, Poitou, Limousin, la Marche, Berry, Nivernais, Bourbonnais and Auvergne, and he finds one-half of these provinces in heaths, forming immense plains all of which might be cultivated." In Touraine, in Poitou and in Berry they form solitary expanses of thirty thousand *arpents*. In one canton alone, near Preuilly, forty thousand *arpents* of good soil consist of heath. The agricultural society of Rennes declares that two-thirds of Brittany is lying waste. This is not sterility but decadence. The régime invented by Louis XIV has produced its effect; the soil for a century past is reverting back to a wild state. "We see only abandoned and ruinous chateaux; the principal towns of the fiefs, in which the nobility formerly lived at their ease, are all now occupied by poor *métayer* herdsmen whose scanty labor hardly suffices for their subsistence and a remnant of tax ready to disappear through the ruin of the proprietors and the desertion of the settlers." In the election-district of Confolens a piece of property rented for 2,956 *livres* in 1665, brings in only 900 *livres* in 1747. On the confines of la Marche and of Berry a domain which, in 1660, honorably supported two seignioral families is now simply a small unproductive *métayer*-farm; "the traces of the furrows once made by the ploughshare being still visible on the surrounding heaths." Sologne, once flourishing, becomes a marsh and a forest; a hundred years earlier it produced three times the quantity of grain; two-thirds of its mills are gone; not a vestige of its vineyards remains; "grapes have given way to the heath." Thus abandoned by the spade and the plough, a vast portion of the soil ceases to feed man, while the rest, poorly cultivated, scarcely provides the simplest necessities.

In the first place, on the failure of a crop, this portion remains untilled; its occupant is too poor to purchase seed; the intendant is often obliged to distribute seed, without which the disaster of the current year would be followed by sterility the following year. Every calamity, accordingly, in these days affects the future as well as the present; during the two years of 1784 and 1785, around Toulouse, the drought having caused the loss of all draft animals, many of the cultivators are obliged to let their fields lie fallow. In the second place, cultivation, when it does take place, is carried on according to mediaeval modes. Arthur Young, in 1789, considers that French agriculture has not progressed beyond that of the tenth century. Except in Flanders and on the plains of Alsace, the fields lie fallow one year out of three and oftentimes one year out of two. The implements are poor; there are no ploughs made of iron; in many places the plough of Virgil's time is still in use. Cart-axles and wheel-tires are made of wood, while a harrow often consists of the trestle of a cart. There are few animals and but little manure; the capital bestowed on cultivation is three times less than that of the present day. The yield is slight; "our ordinary farms," says a good observer, "taking one with another return about six times the seed sown." In 1778, on the rich soil around Toulouse, wheat returns about five for one, while at the present day it yields eight to one and more. Arthur Young estimates that, in his day, the English acre produces twenty-eight bushels of grain, and the French acre eighteen bushels, and that the value of the total product of the same area for a given length of time is thirty-six pounds sterling in England and only twenty-five in France. As the parish roads are frightful, and transportation often impracticable, it is clear that, in remote cantons, where poor soil yields scarcely three times the seed sown, food is not always obtainable. How do they manage to live until the next crop? This is the question always under consideration previous to, and during, the Revolution. I find, in manuscript correspondence, the syndics and mayors of villages estimating the quantities for local subsistence at so many bushels in the granaries, so many sheaves in the barns, so many mouths to be filled, so many days to wait until the August wheat comes in, and concluding on short supplies for two, three and four months. Such a state of inter-communication, and of agriculture condemns a country to periodical famines, and I venture to state that, alongside of the small-pox which, out of eight deaths, causes one, another endemic disease exists, as prevalent and as destructive, and this disease is starvation.

We can easily imagine the people as sufferers by it, and, especially, the peasant. An advance in the price of bread prevents him from getting any, and even without that advance, he obtains it with difficulty. Wheat bread costs, as at the present day, three *sous* per pound, but as the average day's work brought only nineteen *sous* instead of forty, the day-laborer, working the same time, could buy only the half of a loaf instead of a full loaf. Taking everything into account, and wages being estimated according to the price of grain, we find that the husbandman's manual labor then procured him 959 *litres* of wheat, while nowadays it gives him 1,851 *litres;* his well-being, accordingly, has advanced ninety-three per cent; which suffices to show to what extent his predecessors suffered privations. And these privations are peculiar to France. Through analogous observations and estimates Arthur Young shows that in France those who lived on field labor, and they constituted the great majority, are seventy-six per cent less comfortable than the same laborers in England, while they are seventy-six per cent less well in health. The result is that, in seven-eighths of the kingdom, there are no farmers but simply *métayers*. The peasant is too poor to undertake cultivation on his own account, possessing no agricultural capital. "The proprietor, desirous of improving his land, finds no one to cultivate it but miserable creatures possessing only a pair of hands; he is obliged to advance everything for its cultivation at his own expense, animals, implements and seed, and even to advance the wherewithal to this *métayer* to feed him until the first crop comes in." "At Vatan, for example, in Berry, the *métayers,* almost every year, borrow bread of the proprietor in order to await the harvesting." "Very rarely is one found who is not indebted to his master at least one hundred *livres* a year." Frequently the latter proposes to abandon the entire crop to them on condition that they demand nothing of him during the year; "these miserable creatures" have refused; left to themselves, they would not be sure of keeping themselves alive. In Limousin and in Angoumois their poverty is so great "that, deducting the taxes to which they are subject, they have no more than from twenty-five to thirty *livres* each person per annum to spend; and not in money, it must be stated, but counting whatever they consume in kind out of the crops they produce. Frequently they have less, and when they cannot possibly make a living the master is obliged to support them. . . . The *métayer* is always reduced to just what is absolutely necessary to keep him from starving." As to the small proprietor, the villager who ploughs his land himself, his condition is but little better. "Agriculture, as our peasants practise it, is a veritable drudgery; they die by thousands in childhood, and in maturity they seek places everywhere but where they should be." In 1783, throughout the plain of the Toulousain they eat only maize, a mixture of flour, common seeds and very little wheat; those on the mountains feed, a part of the year, on chestnuts; the potato is hardly known, and, according to Arthur Young, ninety-nine out of a hundred peasants would refuse to eat it. According to the reports of intendants, the basis of food, in Normandy, is oats; in the election-district of Troyes, buckwheat; in the Marche and in Limousin, buckwheat with chestnuts and radishes; in Auvergne, buckwheat, chestnuts, milk-curds and a little salted goat's meat; in Beauce, a mixture of barley and rye; in Berry, a mixture of barley and oats. There is no wheat bread; the peasant consumes inferior flour only because he is unable to pay two *sous* a pound for his bread. There is no butcher's meat; at best he kills one pig a year. His dwelling is built of clay (*pise*), roofed with thatch, without windows, and the floor is the beaten ground. Even when the soil furnishes good building materials, stone, slate and tile, the windows have no sashes. In a parish in Normandy, in 1789, "most of the dwellings consist of four posts." They are often mere stables or barns "to which a chimney has been added made of four poles and some mud." Their clothes are rags, and often, in winter these are muslin rags. In Quercy and elsewhere, they have no stockings, or shoes or *sabots* (wooden shoes). "It is not in the power of an English imagination," says Arthur Young, "to figure the animals that waited on us here at the *Chapeau Rouge*. Some things that called themselves by courtesy Souillac women, but in reality walking dung-hills. But a neatly dressed, clean waiting-girl at an inn, will be looked for in vain in France." On reading descriptions made on the spot we see in France a similar aspect of country and of peasantry as in Ireland, at least in its broad outlines.

III

In the most fertile regions, for instance, in Limagne, both cottages and faces denote "misery and privation." "The peasants are generally feeble, emaciated and of slight stature." Nearly all derive wheat and wine from their homesteads, but they are forced to sell this to pay their rents and imposts; they eat black bread, made of rye and barley, and their sole beverage is water poured on the lees and the husks. "An Englishman who has not travelled can not imagine the figure made by infinitely the greater part of the countrywomen in France." Arthur Young, who stops to talk with one of these in Champagne, says that "this woman, at no great distance, might have been taken for sixty or seventy, her figure was so bent and her face so hardened and furrowed by labor, but she said she was only twenty-eight." This woman, her husband and her household, afford a sufficiently accurate example of the condition of the small proprietary husbandmen. Their property consists simply of a patch of ground, with a cow and a poor little horse; their seven children consume the whole of the cow's milk. They owe to one seignior a *franchard* (forty-two pounds) of flour, and three chickens; to another three *franchards* of oats, one chicken and one *sou,* to which must be added the *taille* and other imposts. "God keep us!" she said, "for the *tailles* and the dues crush us." What must it be in districts where the soil is poor! "From Ormes (near Chatellerault), as far as Poitiers," writes a lady, "there is a good deal of ground which brings in nothing, and from Poitiers to my residence (in Limousin) twenty-five thousand *arpents* of ground consist wholly of heath and sea-grass. The peasantry live on rye, of which they do not remove the bran, and which is as black and heavy as lead. In Poitou, and here, they plough up only the skin of the ground with a miserable little plough without wheels. . . . From Poitiers to Montmorillon it is nine leagues, equal to sixteen of Paris, and I assure you that I have seen but four men on the road and, between Montmorillon and my own house, which is four leagues, but three; and then only at a distance, not having met one on the road. You need not be surprised at this in such a country. . . . Marriage takes place as early as with the grand seigniors," doubtless for fear of the militia. "But the population of the country is no greater because almost every infant dies. Mothers having scarcely any milk, their infants eat the bread of which I spoke, the stomach of a girl of four years being as big as that of a pregnant woman. . . . Their rye crop this year was ruined by the frost on Easter day; flour is scarce; of the twelve *métairies* owned by my mother, four of them may, perhaps, have some on hand. There has been no rain since Easter; no hay, no pasture, no vegetables, no fruit. You see the lot of the poor peasant. There is no manure, and there are no cattle. . . . My mother, whose granaries used to be always full, has not a grain of wheat in them, because, for two years past, she has fed all her *métayers* and the poor."

"The peasant is assisted," says a seignior of the same province," "protected, and rarely maltreated, but he is looked upon with disdain. If kindly and pliable he is made subservient, but if ill-disposed he becomes soured and irritable. . . . He is kept in misery, in a abject state, by men who are not at all inhuman but whose prejudices, especially among the nobles, lead them to regard him as of a different species of being. . . . The proprietor gets all he can out of him; in any event, looking upon him and his oxen as domestic animals, he puts them into harness and employs them in all weathers for every kind of journey, and for every species of carting and transport. On the other hand, this *métayer* thinks of living with as little labor as possible, converting as much ground as he can into pasturage, for the reason that the product arising from the increase of stock costs him no labor. The little ploughing he does is for the purpose of raising low-priced provisions suitable for his own nourishment, such as buckwheat, radishes, etc. His enjoyment consists only of his own idleness and sluggishness, hoping for a good chestnut year and doing nothing voluntarily but procreate"; unable to hire farming hands he begets children. The rest, ordinary laborers, have small supplies, "living on the spontaneous, and on a few goats which devour everything." Often again, these, by order of Parlement, are killed by the keepers. A woman, with two children in swaddling clothes, having no milk, "and without an inch of ground," whose two goats, her sole resource, had thus been slain, and another, with one goat slain in the same way, and who begs along with her boy, present themselves at the gate of the chateau; one receives twelve *livres,* while the other is admitted as a domestic, and henceforth, "this village is all bows and smiling faces." In short, they are not accustomed to benefactions; the lot of all these poor people is to endure. "As with rain and hail, they regard as inevitable the necessity of being oppressed by the strongest, the richest, the most skillful, the most in repute," and this stamps on them, "if one may be allowed to say so, an air of painful suffering."

In Auvergne, a feudal country, covered with extensive ecclesiastic and seignioral domains, the misery is the same. At Clermont-Ferrand, "there are many streets that can for blackness, dirt and scents only be represented by narrow channels cut in a night dunghill." In the inns of the largest bourgs, "closeness, misery, dirtiness and darkness." That of Pradelles is "one of the worst in France." That of Aubenas, says Young, "would be a purgatory for one of my pigs." The senses, in short, are paralyzed. The primitive man is content so long as he can sleep and get something to eat. He gets something to eat, but what kind of food? To put up with the indigestible mess a peasant here requires a still tougher stomach than in Limousin; in certain villages where, ten years later, every year twenty or twenty-five hogs are to be slaughtered, they now slaughter but three. On contemplating this temperament, rude and intact since Vercingetorix, and, moreover, rendered more savage by suffering, one cannot avoid being somewhat alarmed. The Marquis de Mirabeau describes "the votive festival of Mont-Doré, savages descending from the mountain in torrents, the curate with stole and surplice, the justice in his wig, the police corps with sabres drawn, all guarding the open square before letting the bagpipers play; the dance interrupted in a quarter of an hour by a fight; the hootings and cries of children, of the feeble and other spectators, urging them on as the rabble urge on so many fighting dogs; frightful-looking men, or rather wild beasts covered with coats of coarse wool, wearing wide leather belts pierced with copper nails, gigantic in stature, which is increased by high *sabots,* and making themselves still taller by standing on tiptoe to see the battle, stamping with their feet as it progresses and rubbing each other's flanks with their elbows, their faces haggard, and covered with long matted hair, the upper portion pallid, and the lower distended, indicative of cruel delight and a sort of ferocious impatience. And these folks pay the *taille!* And now they want to take away their salt! And they know nothing of those they despoil, of those whom they think they govern, believing that, by a few strokes of a cowardly and careless pen, they may starve them with impunity up to the final catastrophe! Poor Jean-Jacques, I said to myself, had any one despatched you, with your system, to copy music amongst these folks he would have had some sharp replies to make to your discourses!" Prophetic warning and admirable foresight in one whom an excess of evil does not blind to the evil of the remedy! Enlightened by his feudal and rural instincts, the old man at once judges both the government and the philosophers, the Ancient Régime and the Revolution.

IV

Misery begets bitterness in a man; but ownership coupled with misery renders him still more bitter. He may have submitted to indigence but not to spoilation—which is the situation of the peasant in 1789, for, during the eighteenth century, he had become the possessor of land. But how could he maintain himself in such destitution? The fact is almost incredible, but it is nevertheless true. We can only explain it by the character of the French peasant, by his sobriety, his tenacity, his rigor with himself, his dissimulation, his hereditary passion for property and especially for that of the soil. He had lived on privations, and economized *sou* after *sou*. Every year a few pieces of silver are added to his little store of crowns buried in the most secret recess of his cellar; Rousseau's peasant, concealing his wine and bread in a pit, assuredly had a yet more secret hiding-place; a little money in a woolen stocking or in a jug escapes, more readily than elsewhere, the search of the clerks. Dressed in rags, going barefoot, eating nothing but coarse black bread, but cherishing the little treasure in his breast on which he builds so many hopes, he watches for the opportunity which never fails to come. "In spite of privileges," writes a gentleman in 1775, "the nobles are daily being ruined and reduced, the Third-Estate making all the fortunes." A number of domains, through forced or voluntary sales, thus pass into the hands of financiers, of men of the quill, of merchants, and of the well-to-do bourgeois. Before undergoing this total dispossession, however, the seignior, involved in debt, is evidently resigned to partial alienations of his property. The peasant who has bribed the steward is on hand with his hoard. "It is poor property, my lord, and it costs you more than you get from it." This may refer to an isolated patch, one end of a field or meadow, sometimes a farm whose farmer pays nothing, and generally worked by a *métayer* whose wants and indolence make him an annual expense to his master. The latter may say to himself that the alienated parcel is not lost since, some day or other, through his right of repurchase, he may take it back, while in the meantime, he enjoys a *cens,* drawbacks, and the lord's dues. Moreover, there is on his domain and around him, extensive open spaces which the decline of cultivation and depopulation have left a desert. To restore the value of this he must surrender its proprietorship. There is no other way by which to attach man permanently to the soil. And the government helps him along in this matter. Obtaining no revenue from the abandoned soil, it assents to a provisional withdrawal of its too weighty hand. By the edict of 1766, a piece of cleared waste land remains free of the *taille* for fifteen years, and, thereupon, in twenty-eight provinces four hundred thousand *arpents* are cleared in three years.

This is the mode by which the siegnioral domain gradually crumbles away and decreases. Towards the last, in many places, with the exception of the chateau and the small adjoining farm, which brings in two or three thousand francs a year, nothing is left to the seignior but his feudal dues; the rest of the soil belongs to the peasantry. Forbonnais already remarks, towards 1750, that many of the nobles and of the ennobled "reduced to extreme poverty but with titles to immense possessions," have sold off portions to small cultivators at low prices, and often for the amount of the *taille*. Towards 1760, one-quarter of the soil is said to have already passed into the hands of agriculturists. In 1772, in relation to the *vingtième,* which is levied on the net revenue of real property, the intendant of Caen, having completed the statement of his quota, estimates that out of one hundred and fifty thousand "there are perhaps fifty thousand whose liabilities did not exceed five *sous* and perhaps still as many more not exceeding *twenty sous."* Contemporary observers authenticate this passion of the peasant for real property. "The savings of the lower classes, which elsewhere are invested with individuals and in the public funds, are wholly destined in France to the purchase of land." "Accordingly the number of small rural holdings is always on the increase. Necker says that there is an *immensity* of them." Arthur Young, in 1789, is astonished at their great number and "inclines to think that they form one-third of the kingdom." That would already be about the proportion, and the proportion would still be the same, were we to compare the number of proprietors with the number of inhabitants.

The small cultivator, however, in becoming a possessor of the soil assumes its charges. Simply as day-laborer, and with his arms alone, he was only partially affected by the taxes; "where there is nothing the king loses his dues." But now, vainly is he poor and declaring himself still poorer; the fisc has a hold on him and on every portion of his new possessions. The collectors, peasants like himself, and jealous, by virtue of being his neighbors, know how much his property, exposed to view, brings in; hence they take all they can lay their hands on. Vainly has he labored with renewed energy; his hands remain as empty, and, at the end of the year, he discovers that his field has produced him nothing. The more he acquires and produces the more burdensome do the taxes become. In 1715, the *taille* and the poll-tax, which he alone pays, or nearly alone, amounts to sixty-six millions of *livres;* the amount is ninety-three millions in 1759 and one hundred and ten millions in 1789. In 1757, the imposts amount to 283,156,000 *livres;* in 1789 to 476,294,000 *livres.*

Theoretically, through humanity and through good sense, there is, doubt- less, a desire to relieve the peasant and pity is felt for him. But, in practice, through necessity and routine, he is treated according to Cardinal Richelieu's precept, as a beast of burden to which oats are measured out for fear that he may become too strong and kick, "a mule which, accustomed to his load, is spoiled by more long repose than by work."

Alphonse Aulard was the leading historian of the French Revolution in the generation between Taine and Lefebvre.

He was also the foremost proponent of the primary role of the ideas of the eighteenth century in bringing about the French Revolution.

FROM *The French Revolution* BY A. AULARD

ON AUGUST 10, 1792, the Legislative Assembly, in establishing universal suffrage, constituted France a democratic State, and the Convention, in establishing the Republic on the following September 22nd, gave to this democracy the form of government which in the eyes of the Convention was logically expedient.

Can we say that by these two acts a preconceived system was brought into being? Many have thought so; many of our teachers and writers, with much eloquence, have advanced the theory that democracy and the Republic sprang, fully fledged, from the eighteenth-century philosophy, from the works of the Encyclopaedists, from the doctrine of the precursors of the Revolution. Let us see if the facts, and the written word, justify these assertions.

One prime and important fact is this: that in 1789, at the time of the convocation of the Estates-General, there was no Republican party in France.

Now the best testimony to be found as to contemporary French opinion is contained in the *cahiers* in which the people embodied their grievances and their desires. Of these we have many, different in origin and in kind, and in none is a republic demanded, nor even a change of dynasty; and I think my study of these justifies the assertion that in none is there found any criticism, even indirect, of the King's conduct. It would seem that none of the petitioners dream of attributing their stated grievances to the Monarchy, nor even to the King. In all these documents the French are seen imbued with an ardent royalism, a warm devotion to the person of Louis XVI. Above all, in documents of the more humble kind, petitions from parishes, and the like, there is a note of confidence, love, and gratitude. "Our good King! The King our father!"—so the peasants and the workers address him. The nobles and the clergy, less ingenuously enthusiastic, appear equally loyal.

*   *   *

If all Frenchmen were at one in wishing to maintain the Monarchy, they were not agreed as to the manner of regulating the royal authority, and we

Reprinted with the permission of Charles Scribner's Sons from *The French Revolution*, pp. 79–81, 89–99, 125–6, 127–32, by A. Aulard, translated by Bernard Miall (1910).

may go so far as to say that they did not all see the throne with the same eyes.

The masses of the people, in their unreasoned loyalty, did not, it would appear, discern the excesses of the royal prerogative. No doubt the commissaries were unpopular. But complaints of "ministerial despotism," as they preferred to call it, came from the nobles, the *bourgeoisie,* the rich and enlightened classes, rather than from the peasantry. The latter more especially lamented a "feudal despotism," because, in fact, they were the greatest sufferers from it.

Far from regarding the King as responsible for the conduct of his agents, the people would say that his agents deceived the King, that they annulled or hampered his power of doing good. The popular idea was to deliver the King from these unjust stewards in order that he might be enlightened, the better to direct his omnipotent power, to the profit of the nation, against the remnants of feudalism. The masses were beginning to have a certain idea of their rights, yet, so far were they from thinking to restrain his royal omnipotence, that it was precisely on that omnipotence that all their hopes were based. One petition said that, in order that all should go well, it was only necessary for the King to cry: *"To me, my people!"*

Enlightened Frenchmen, on the other hand, knowing well what manner of men Louis XIV and XV had been, feared the abuse of the royal power, and were not all reassured by the paternal character of Louis XVI's despotism. They wished to restrain, by means of political institutions, this fantastic and capricious power, so that it should no longer be dangerous to liberty, while leaving it sufficient force to destroy the aristocracy and what remained of the feudal system, thus making France a nation. To ensure that the King should govern according to the laws—this was what they called "organising the Monarchy."

The way to this organisation of the Monarchy was prepared by the writers of the eighteenth century.

They, with the logical spirit natural to the French, did not attempt merely to prevent abuses and to regulate the exercise of sovereign power; they discussed the very essence of this power, of the pretended right Divine; they sapped the Catholic faith by which the throne was propped, sought publicly for the origins of sovereignty and authority, in history, in the assent of subjects, and in the national will.

Thus, without desiring to establish a republic, and solely with a view to "organising" the Monarchy, they attacked the monarchical principle, and put in circulation republican ideals of such a nature that, although in 1789 no one wished for a republic, yet whoever thought at all was impregnated with these republican ideas; and this is why, in 1792, when circumstances made the Republic necessary, there was a sufficient number of thinking men prepared to accept, and to force on others, a form of government of which they had already adopted the principles.

A few examples will show the diffusion and elaboration of republican ideas before the Revolution.

*   *   *

Montesquieu, in 1748, in his *l'Esprit des Lois,* defined a republic: "The republican form of government," he says, "is that in which the people as a whole, or one party only of the people, exercises the sovereign power." This definition became classic. In 1765 it was reproduced in the article on "Republics" in the *Encyclopédie* (vol. xiv.), which consists entirely of quotations from Montesquieu.

Could not such a republic exist under a king? Montesquieu does not think so; but Mably does—when, for instance, he dreams of a "republican monarchy"; and the same idea is held by those whom we shall find, in 1789, speaking of a "monarchical democracy."

Montesquieu undoubtedly pronounces against a republic, and is of opinion that in a republic "the laws are evaded with greater danger than they can be violated by a prince, who, being always the chief citizen of the State, has the greatest interest in its conservation. None the less, we see how he elsewhere commends the republican form of government, as when he says that virtue is its very mainspring, while a monarchy is founded upon respect and honour; or when, in approval of the popular elections, he writes: "It is an admirable thing that the people should select those to whom they are bound to confide some part of their authority."

It was after reading Montesquieu that Frenchmen became accustomed to regard the republican form of government—which they did not desire to see in France—as a theoretically noble and interesting form.

This theorist of the Monarchy thus found that he had deprived monarchical government of some of its prestige; and, by his views upon the separation of the three forms of authority, he touched royalty itself to the quick—that royalty which pretended, by Divine right, to concentrate all authority in itself.

In this manner did Montesquieu, so admired, so widely read, contribute towards the development of republican ideas and the formation of the republican spirit.

*   *   *

Jean-Jacques Rousseau, in his *Contrat social,* had written "that, in general, government by democracy was suited to small States, government by aristocracy to those of medium size, and government by Monarchy to large States." He further stated "that there is no form of government so liable to civil wars and internecine tumult as the democratic or popular," and that "if there existed a nation of gods, they would govern themselves by a democracy: so perfect a government is unsuited to mankind." But he was preparing for the ruin of the monarchical system when he said that "the two principle objects of every system of legislation should be liberty and equality." Prudent and reserved though he was in theory, he preached revolt by his conduct, in his speeches, and in his romantic writings—revolt, in the name of Nature, against the vicious and artificial social system of his time; and, although fundamentally a Christian, he replaced the mystical ideals of charity and humility by the republican ideal of fraternity.

*　　*　　*

From the writings of these philosophers one idea stands out, an idea that quickly became almost general: that the nation is above the King; and is not this a republican idea? Although these writers wish to maintain the Monarchy, they habitually speak of the republican system in honourable terms. A posthumous work of d'Argenson's, *Considérations sur le Gouvernement,* published in 1765, recommends the fortification of the Monarchy by an "infusion" of republican institutions; and d'Argenson praises the government which he does not desire for his own country in terms so sympathetic as to invite misconception, so greatly does this work of royalist tendencies, which was much read at the time, do honour to the republican idea.

*　　*　　*

The idea that the King should be only a citizen subject to the law, causing the law to be executed, had gradually become popularised; of its popularity there is endless proof. When Voltaire wrote, in his tragedy of *Don Pèdre* (1775):

> A king is but a man with name august,
> First subject of the laws: and, by law, just,

he knew well that he would win applause. And if it be objected that this tragedy was not presented, that these lines were not actually heard by the theatre-going public, I will cite the line borrowed by Favart from a poem by Louis Racine, published in 1744, which drew applause in the *Trois Sultanes,* at the *Théâtre des Italiens,* on April 9, 1761:

> Each citizen a king, under a citizen king.

That such maxims were applauded in the theatre, nearly thirty years before the Revolution, that the Government was obliged to tolerate them: does not this prove that public opinion had already, so to say, despoiled the King and his kingship of the mystical principle of sovereignty? And is not this idea of the "citizen king," so unanimously applauded, one of the most startling signs of the republicanisation of the general mind?

*　　*　　*

To sum up: no one on the eve of the Revolution had ever dreamed of the establishment of a republic in France: it was a form of government that seemed impossible in a great State in course of unification. It was through the King that men sought to establish a free government. Men wished to organise the monarchy, not to destroy it. No one dreamed of calling the ignorant mass of the people to political life; the necessary revolution was to be brought about by the better class of the nation, the educated, property-owning class. It was believed that the people, blind and inconstant as they were thought, could only prove an instrument of reaction in the hands of the privileged. However, the future date of democracy was announced in the proclamation of the principle of the sovereignty of the people: and the republic, the logical form of democracy, was prepared by the diffusion of republican ideas—for example, from America; by the sight of an impotent monarchy, and by the continual proclamation of the necessity of a violent revolution, which, undertaken in order to reform the monarchy, was to expose its very existence to the dangers of a general upheaval. The ruling classes of society were steeped in republicanism. Such a state of mind was so prevalent that if the King, in whom men saw the historically indispensable guide to a new France, were to fail in his mission, or discard, for example, his authority as hereditary defender of French independence, a republic would be accepted without dislike and without enthusiasm, first by the better class, and then by the mass of the nation.

*   *   *

We have seen that in 1789 there appeared to be two Frances; the enlightened France and the ignorant France, a rich France and a poor France. As for the political rights which the publicists of the day were demanding, it was only for the well-to-do and the educated that these rights were claimed. Owners of property were to be "active citizens"; they alone having the right to vote. Those without property were to be "passive citizens." In short, "the nation is the *bourgeoisie.*"

Between the *bourgeoisie* and the people there is a gulf. The richer classes exaggerate the stupidity and obliviousness of the people—above all, of the rural masses. There is ill-feeling and misunderstanding between the two classes. To clear up this misunderstanding will require a conference, a general meeting and mingling of the middle classes with the people as a whole.

Such a result will follow the convocation of the Estates-General.

At the Parish Assemblies the Third Estate is admitted almost without exception, under a slight property restriction, to fulfil the condition of being "included in the roll of taxpayers." This is very nearly universal suffrage.

Had royalty established this suffrage, so contrary to the ideas of the century, for the very reasons that induced the philosophers and the writers in favour of reform to reject it? Did the King hope, in the poor and ignorant masses, to find an element of resistance against the new and revolutionary ideas of the middle class? I have not found any documentary evidence which will allow me to answer this question precisely, but to me it does not seem impossible that the King did have some confused idea of appealing to universal suffrage against the opposition of the middle class, to darkness against light.

If such a calculation did really exist, it was disproved by the event.

To be sure, the *cahiers* are more timid than the books and pamphlets of the time; but as a general thing they demand a Constitution, and a Constitution is the end of absolutism—it is, to some extent, the Revolution.

Moreover, there are *cahiers* which are bold in the extreme.

However, neither the hopes of royalty nor the fears of the *bourgeoisie* were realised—supposing that such hopes and fears existed.

In any case, we must note how the misunderstanding between the *bourgeoisie* and the people was dissipated or diminished on the occasion of convocation and the drawing up of the *cahiers*.

Collaboration took place between the *bourgeoisie* and the people in the drafting of the *cahiers* of the first degree, or the parish *cahiers;* and in general we must not, in the case of rural communities, regard these *cahiers* as the personal work of peasants. It was usually a man of the middle classes who held the pen, and in most localities, even in the most rustic, there were a few educated men. The majority of the parish *cahiers* that we possess testify to a considerable amount of culture—a culture higher than that of the provincial middle classes of today.

If the *cahier* is not dictated by peasants, it is at least read to and approved by them. There is an assembly at which peasants and middle classes mingle together, chat with one another, and publicly discuss and debate. It is the first time such a colloquy has taken place; the occasion is a fraternal one, and the classes are quickly in agreement. The middle-class man sees that the peasant is more intelligent or less imbecile than he had supposed; that—by what obscure channels who knows?—the spirit of the times has touched him. The peasants, once they have met together, soon rise to the idea of a common interest; they have the sense that they are many and powerful, and they obtain, from the middle classes, a perception of their rights. For them this Parish Assembly is a civic apprenticeship.

We must not picture the whole peasantry rising at once to the revolutionary idea of the mother-country. But they take the Convocation seriously; they feel that it will bring about an event which will be beneficial to themselves, and they conceive an image of the King, an image which is a reflection of the idea of country. To them, it appears in deadly earnest that the King is going to concern himself with the cure of the ills which afflict them; it is in earnest that they recount these ills, or, rather, accept the account of them that the gentlemen of the village write for them; and when they sign with a cross at the bottom of the document, they have no fear that this cross will subject them to surcharges of taxation and the nuisance of collectors. By no means; their signature is an act of confidence and hope.

We have here no longer the vile populace, slighted and feared by Mably, Rousseau, and Condorcet. But it is not as yet the sovereign people. They are men who at last are counting on being treated as men; almost candidates for the dignity of citizen; and who, tomorrow, by an electric impulse issuing, at the fall of the Bastille, from Paris, will feel themselves animated by an impetus of union and agglomeration from which will issue the new nation, the new France.

Let us repeat that the middle classes also have found somewhat to learn at these assemblies—namely, to be less scornful of the poor and the ignorant. It is true that men will still declaim against the populace, and the middle class will even establish itself as a caste politically privileged. But enlightened Frenchmen will no longer, after this royal experiment in universal suffrage, be unaminous in declaring the unlettered to be incapable of exercising political rights. A democratic party is about to declare itself, and will soon be fully formed. The method of convening the Third Estate at the Estates-General allows us almost to foretell the advent of universal suffrage, and, as a consequence, the establishment of the Republic, the national form of Democracy.

Georges Lefebvre devoted his whole scholarly life to the study of the French Revolution. In 1939, his unmatched knowledge of the origins of the Revolution was distilled into the little book from which the following selections are drawn.

FROM *The Coming of the French Revolution*

BY GEORGES LEFEBVRE

THE PEASANTRY

THERE WAS SCARCELY ANY QUESTION of the peasants before July 14. Yet they formed at least three quarters of the population of the kingdom, and we realize today that without their adherence the Revolution could with difficulty have succeeded. Their grievances had been disregarded

Georges Lefebvre, *The Coming of the French Revolution*, pp. 131–7, 140–7, 209–12, 214–20, translated by R. R. Palmer. Reprinted by permission of Princeton University Press. Copyright 1947 by Princeton University Press.

in the drafting of the bailiwick petitions, or had at best received little emphasis. Their complaints were by no means uppermost among the interests of the National Assembly, in which there were no peasant members. Then suddenly they too revolted, taking their cause into their own hands and delivering a death blow to what was left of the feudal and manorial system. The peasant uprising is one of the most distinctive features of the Revolution in France.

THE PEASANT AND THE LAND

In 1789 the great majority of the French peasants had been free for many generations, i.e., they could move about and work as they wished, possess property and bring suit in the law courts. Some "serfs" could still be found, principally in Franche-Comté and the Nivernais, but they were no longer really attached to the soil, and in 1779 the king had even abolished the right of pursuit, which had allowed the lord to make good his claims over the serf wherever the latter might go. The main characteristic of serfdom in France was lack of freedom in disposing of goods. The serf was a *mainmortable* or man under a mortmain; if, at his death, he did not have at least one living child residing with him, all his possessions reverted to the lord. In France the serf was far better off than in central and eastern Europe, where the peasantry was left under the nobleman's arbitrary jurisdiction. In France the king's justice protected the rights and person of both serf and free man.

Not only were most French peasants not serfs. Many were landowners, differing in this respect from the peasants of England, who in general had been reduced by the landed aristocracy to the status of wage laborers. The size and number of peasant properties varied greatly from one region to another. They were most extensive in Alsace, Flanders, Limousin, parts of Normandy, the Loire valley, the plains of the Saône and the Garonne and generally throughout southern France more than in the North. In these regions peasants owned from half to three-quarters of the soil. Elsewhere the proportion fell much lower, notably in barren, marshy or forested regions and in the neighborhood of cities. Of the land around Versailles peasant ownership accounted for no more than one or two per cent. Thirty per cent is a probable average for the kingdom as a whole. The remaining land was owned by the clergy (probably a tenth of the kingdom), the nobles (over twice as much) and the bourgeoisie (perhaps a fifth). The clergy was especially wealthy in the North, less so as one went west and south. The nobles seem to have been wealthiest in the North, East and West. Bourgeois ownership of rural land was characteristic of the South.

Yet everywhere there were propertyless peasants. Rarely was the number of these rural proletarians negligible: it has been estimated at about a fifth of family heads in Limousin, 30 to 40 per cent in the Norman woodlands, 70 per cent around Versailles and as high as 75 per cent in maritime Flanders. Some of these unpropertied peasants found land to rent. Ecclesiastics, noblemen and bourgeois seldom exploited their own lands, except in the wine country and in some parts of the South. Instead, they put them in the hands of farmers, or more often of sharecroppers with whom they divided the produce. Moreover, their estates consisted in many small unconnected parcels, which they were glad to lease out separately bit by bit. Hence the laborer could manage to procure a patch for himself, and the peasant owner, for his part, could supplement his own holdings with additional parcels taken on lease. In this way the rural proletariat in the strict sense, or peasants who had no land either by ownership or by leasehold, was substantially reduced while never disappearing entirely. Hence also rural society had as many gradations as society in the cities. The most well to do were the large farmers, who often owned no land themselves. Next came the substantial class, called *laboureurs*, who worked considerable tracts which they owned wholly or in part. They were followed, in downward order, by the small farmer, the sharecropper, the peasant having the use of some land but not enough to live on, the laborer possessing a house and garden plus some small parcel on lease and finally the laborer who had nothing but his hands.

Unfortunately the holdings of the overwhelming majority of the peasants were not large enough to support them and their families. Backward methods of cultivation were in part the cause. In the North and East the village lands were subdivided into countless long and narrow strips, which were grouped in three "fields." One field was sown with winter wheat, one with a spring crop, while the third lay fallow, i.e., uncultivated, each field changing its role from year to year. South of a line running from eastern Normandy to Burgundy and passing by Beauce there were only two fields, of which one always lay fallow. In the West, in Limousin and in the mountains, the cultivated areas, enclosed by hedges, comprised an even smaller fraction of the soil, the remaining land being worked only from time to time, sometimes only one year in ten, sometimes even less often. In any case, triennial or biennial rotation left a third or half the arable soil unproductive. Hence the peasant needed more land than today. In the region later comprised in the department of Nord nine families out of ten had too little to live on. The situation had grown worse since the middle of the eighteenth century, for the population had increased perceptibly, probably by three million. The number of proletarians had risen, while through division of inheritances the shares of property owners had become smaller. There was, therefore, at the end of the Old Regime, an agrarian crisis.

Hence many peasants invaded the commons when the king, in 1764 and 1766, granted exemption from tithes and taxes to persons who cleared new land. Borders of the forests, and open places within them, swarmed with barefoot pioneers who built themselves cabins, cleared what they could and felled timber either for sale or for conversion into charcoal. The marshes likewise hid a wretched population which lived by fishing or cutting peat. Peasant landowners, in the grievance-lists, roundly criticized the nobles and clergy who exploited their own estates directly, and demanded also that the big properties be leased out, not to a few large farmers, but to many small ones. In Picardy and Hainaut, when the owners tried to change farmers, the latter fought back against eviction, even to the point of arson and murder. It is therefore not surprising to find some parishes asking for alienation of the crown lands and even of part of the property of the clergy. But it is characteristic of the time that the property of individuals was never questioned. At the height of the Terror, when the property of *émigrés* and of persons condemned for political offenses was sold, and when it was decided also to confiscate the property of mere suspects, the principle was always that of penalizing enemies of the country. Nobles who stayed in France, and remained peaceable, never at any time during the Revolution saw their property threatened. This was because the land, when it was not the property of the peasants, was already in their hands on leasehold terms. Farm rentals, it is true, had almost doubled during the eighteenth century, while prices had gone up on the average not more than sixty-five per cent. Sharecropping too had become less favorable to the peasant; in general, the owner still took only half the crop or half the increment of livestock, but he increasingly imposed obligations of many kinds and even a supplemental payment in cash, especially in cases where sharing arrangements were managed through a "farmer-general," who found it to his advantage to bring pressure on the croppers. There was much bitter complaint on this score in Bourbonnais, Nivernais and Beaujolais. Nevertheless, despite all these grievances, the farmer or sharecropper would have nothing to gain by exchanging his leased holdings for the tiny parcel which a general redistribution of property would procure for him. And it is obvious that those peasants who already owned property would not have favored any such redistribution.

TAXES, TITHES, FEES, DUES

Keeping in mind that the agrarian crisis was real and pressing, we must recognize that there was only one matter on which the whole rural population could unanimously agree—namely, the obligations imposed by the king and the aristocracy.

The peasant was almost alone in paying the *taille* and drawing lots for militia service. He alone was held for road work and for aid in military transportation. From him came most of the proceeds of the poll-tax and the twentieth-taxes. Yet it was the indirect taxes that he detested the most, especially the government salt monopoly, which held the price of salt as high as thirteen sous a pound in a large part of the kingdom. The royal demands had steadily risen during the eighteenth century, and the parish grievance-lists of 1789 invariably complained of them, but we cannot say, in view of the general rise in the price level, whether they actually took a greater part of the national income in 1789 than a half century before. Probably they did. In Walloon Flanders, a region having Provincial Estates and hence getting off fairly lightly, the increase in direct taxes in the reign of Louis XVI alone has been estimated at twenty-eight per cent. The peasants, while critical of the bourgeois, observing that commercial wealth paid less than its proper share, were most especially aroused to a state of fury by the privileges of the aristocracy.

The royal taxation, a relatively new burden superimposed on the payments made from time immemorial to the aristocracy, undoubtedly had the indirect consequence of making these payments far more hateful. To the clergy was due the tithe, variable in amount but almost always less than a tenth, levied on the "great" grains, wheat, rye, oats and barley (the "great tithe"), and on other grains and vegetables and fruits (the "small tithe"), and on a few animal products. From the peasant grievance-lists it is evident that the tithe would have been more willingly paid if the proceeds, instead of going in most cases to bishops, abbeys or chapters, or even to lay lords to whom the tithe might be "subinfeudated" (the parish priest receiving the small tithe at most), had been used, as they should have been, to support public worship, the parish church and parsonage and above all the poor. But the peasant, after paying the tithe, saw most of the expense for such purposes still falling upon himself. In addition the tithe had all the disadvantages of a levy collected in kind. The tithe owner had to come and take it away himself; if he delayed, the whole crop might suffer from bad weather; the peasant was deprived of straw, a material necessary to manure, and the only one known to him. The tithe also blocked the progress of land clearance and of new methods of cultivation. Since it was collected in kind, a rise in prices made it more profitable to the collector; in 1789 the gross product was thought to be worth 120,000,000 livres. The profit was greatest in times of scarcity, at the cost of the peasant's very subsistence; and in any case, at all times, the tithe collector seemed a food hoarder by his very nature.

What there was left of feudalism was even more disliked. The strictly feudal should be distinguished from the manorial. From the feudal point of view land consisted of fiefs, depending one upon another and all finally upon the king. Fiefs were subject to a law of their own, of which the law of primogeniture is the best known; and with each change of owner the suzerain required the vassal to make due acknowledgment, submit a survey of the estate and pay a fee. Unless the peasant had bought a fief, which was rare at least in the North, this system did not concern him. If he had bought a fief he paid the king, as did the bourgeois in the same circumstances, a special fee called the *franc-fief*.

During the eighteenth century the demands of manorial lords, like those of the king, had become more burdensome for the peasants. Since the system had been criticized by the philosophers and economists, manorial lords thought it necessary to reaffirm their rights by frequently renewing the manor rolls in which they were written down and by requiring exact payment. Increasingly they farmed out their rights to professional collectors, who were inexorable in their work, reviving and enforcing almost obsolete obligations, if indeed not broadening them in a way that was positively an abuse. Where claims were contested, the manorial courts and the Parliaments always decided against the peasants. But what exasperated the rural people, since they had in any case too little land for a livelihood, was the encroachment on their collective rights, on which their existence depended.

*   *   *

Numerous are the peasant grievance-lists which complain, and complain bitterly, of these constant encroachments, as of the generally growing exactions of the feudal class. They insist on the damage done to agriculture by the hunting rights, the dovecotes and the rabbit warrens in the absence of proper regulation and of any recourse. Payments in kind were subjected to the same criticism as was the tithe. The petitions call attention to the crushing weight of all these dues taken together, finding it heavier than the parallel burden of the royal taxes. More rare are the petitions which propose remedies, such as suppression of certain rights considered particularly repugnant, or authorization to buy up the manorial dues. The principle of the system is never questioned, but we must note that the peasants did not express all that was on their minds, and that on the matter of manorial rights the bourgeois who assumed leadership over them were often reticent in their opinions, since manorial rights were a form of property, which some bourgeois had themselves purchased, and in which others had an interest as judges or agents for the manorial lords. Still, the deeper workings of the peasant mind can be seen in one way, when their petitions demand that the original document specifying payments in return for holdings be produced, and that in its absence such payments be brought to an end. The peasant proprietor, it is clear, thought himself the only legitimate owner of his land, and considered the payments due the lord, unless there was proof to the contrary, to have originated in nothing but violence. In some cases peasant rancor against lordly "bloodsuckers" did in fact express itself plainly. . . .

Against the aristocracy the peasants had far more substantial grievances than did the people of the cities, and it is natural therefore that they took it upon themselves to deal the blow by which the aristocracy was laid low.

THE AGRARIAN REVOLTS AND
THE GREAT FEAR

The hatred of the peasants for the lords was not a thing of yesterday. The history of France abounds in *jacqueries*. In the eighteenth century the collection of manorial dues more than once led to troubles, and in particular engendered innumerable lawsuits which the peasants sustained with incredible tenacity. Yet if they were brought to a state of general rebellion in 1789 one reason is to be found in the convocation of the Estates-General. . . . The bailiwick lieutenant of Saumur observed, as the most unsettling feature of convocation of the Estates, that the electoral assemblies of the parishes thought themselves invested with sovereign authority, and that the rustics believed themselves already rid of the manorial dues. Cries of alarm rose everywhere in the kingdom in the course of the spring: the peasants were declaring their intention to make no payments at the coming harvest. Class solidarity asserted itself strongly. During the disturbances at Chatou the peasants took aside one of their number who seemed suspect, demanded of him, "Are you for the Third Estate?" and when he gave a negative answer told him, "Then we'll give you the idea!" The agrarian insurrections, more even than those of the cities, were genuine mass movements.

At the same time the idea of an "aristocratic conspiracy" grew up and rooted itself even more strongly than in the bourgeois, for the peasants knew by centuries of experience that in the eyes of the lord the manorial dues were untouchable—his social superiority depending on them as well as his income. That the lord would make every effort to deceive the "good king"; that if he failed in this he would take up arms to crush the Third Estate—all this seemed obvious and inevitable to the peasants. The inaction of the Estates-General and their silence on matters of concern to the peasants were attributed to an aristocratic conspiracy. When news came of the resort to force, what doubt could there be? And when it was learned that the king, visiting his insurgent capital, had given his approval to the resistance which had blocked the aristocrats, what reservations could any longer be felt? During the ensuing revolts the peasants insisted that they were executing the king's will. Smuggled orders circulated among them, ostensibly emanating from the king.

*   *   *

Yet the same observation must be made of the country as of the towns. The peasant rising would be inconceivable without the excitement produced by the calling of the Estates-General. But it is undeniable also that the economic crisis contributed powerfully to it, and reinforced also the idea of an aristocratic plot. The rural masses suffered cruelly from food shortages, contrary to what might be supposed, for most peasants raised too little to subsist on, and when the harvest was bad the number of those in want increased perceptibly as the year went on. They would go to make purchases at the neighboring market, become involved in the disturbances there and on returning spread trouble and a sense of insecurity through their home parishes. In the open country they would stop shipments of food without hesitation, so that during the summer of 1789 disorder became universal. As for the causes and possible remedies for the problem, they held the same views as the small people of the towns. Regulation was their panacea, the hoarder their enemy.

*   *   *

Hence the economic crisis had revolutionary consequences in two ways. On the one hand it enflamed the peasants by turning them against the tithe owners and lords who took away part of their livelihood through the manorial dues. On the other hand, by multiplying the number of those in want, it generalized a sense of insecurity which in the end was blamed on a conspiracy of the aristocrats.

THE AGRARIAN REVOLTS

Just as fear in no sense dated from July 14, so it would be wrong to imagine that the peasant waited for the example of the capital to revolt. The example of the nearest town was sufficient, and even this was by no means indispensable. At the end of March the high price of bread led to popular uprisings at Toulon and Marseilles, from which agitation spread immediately to all upper Provence. The villages of the Avance Valley, in the region of Gap, rose in insurrection against their lord on April 20. On May 6 a riot broke out at Cambrai; the whole Cambrésis was instantly aflame; the contagion spread to Picardy. Near Paris and Versailles the peasants organized a systematic extermination of game, pillaged the forests and fired on the wardens.

*   *   *

These disturbances were all aimed against the aristocracy.

CONCLUSION

The Revolution of 1789 consisted first of all in the fall of absolute monarchy and advent of a liberty henceforth guaranteed by constitutional government; nor on this score can it be doubted that it was a national revolution, since the privileged orders as well as the Third Estate demanded a constitution and a regime in which individual rights would be respected.

But it was also the advent of equality before the law, without which liberty would be but another privilege of the powerful. For the French of 1789 liberty and equality were inseparable, almost two words for the same thing; but had they been obliged to choose, it is equality that they would have chosen; and when the peasants, who formed the overwhelming majority, cheered the conquest of liberty they were in fact thinking of the disappearance of the authority of the manorial lord, and his reduction to the status of a mere citizen. They were thinking, that is, of equality.

Thus made free and equal in rights, the French founded the nation anew, one and indivisible, by voluntary consent, in the movements called federations and especially in the Federation of July 14, 1790. This third characteristic of the Revolution of 1789 was one of its most original features, and the assertion that a people has the right to dispose of itself, and cannot be annexed to another without its own adherence freely expressed, has exerted an influence by no means yet exhausted in the world.

Moreover, the men of 1789 never entertained the idea that the rights of man and citizen were reserved for Frenchmen only. Christianity drew no distinction among men; it called on them all to meet as brothers in the divine city. In the same way the revolutionaries thought of liberty and equality as the common birthright of mankind. Imagining that all peoples would emulate their example, they even dreamed for an instant that the nations, in becoming free, would be reconciled forever in universal peace.

In the view of the lawyers, who represented and guided the bourgeoisie, the Revolution was to be a peaceful readjustment, imposed by opinion and translated rather simply into new juridical formulations. And in fact the essential work of the Revolution of 1789 may be found registered in the resolutions of August 4 and in the Declaration of Rights of Man and the Citizen. But it would be childish to emphasize only these legislative enactments, throwing into the background the events which gave them birth; childish likewise, and indeed more so, to select from among these events certain ones to compose a legend. The Estates-General skillfully and boldly defended the cause of the Third Estate which was the cause of the nation, but as even Buchez admitted, a peace-loving and Catholic democrat of 1848, "The Assembly would have achieved nothing without the insurrections." The Old Regime did not bend before the juridical revolution. Having taken to force, it was destroyed by force, which the people, descending into the street, put at the service of what they regarded as right, though even their own representatives had not dared to ask such assistance from them.

Whether the resort to violence was *in principle* necessary or unnecessary the historian cannot know. He observes simply that in the spring of 1789 the French people still had no thought of it, and that two years earlier they did not even suspect the regime to be nearing its end. It was the aristocracy that precipitated the Revolution by forcing the king to call the Estates-General. Once the Third Estate obtained the right to express itself, the possibility of concessions which would have satisfied it for a time depended on the nobles and on the king. The issue was not so much political in character as social; for the transformation of the monarchy into a constitutional government was a reform on which nobles and bourgeois agreed, and by which Louis XVI would have lost little authority; but the great majority of the nobles, while prepared to make concessions in the direction of fiscal equality, were determined, more from pride than from material interest, to preserve their other privileges and remain a nation within the nation. One wonders whether the year 1789 might not have become the first phase of an evolutionary movement, during which the nobles would have gradually come to accept the status of mere citizens. It is possible, and, if one likes, even probable; but, since we cannot run history over like an experiment in a laboratory, opinions on this question will always be divided. In any case, what actually happened is that the necessary decisions were not made in time, that the Court turned to force to protect the aristocracy and that the problem was therefore presented in all its fullness. The Third Estate, driven to the wall, had to choose between resistance and surrender, so that in fact insurrection became inevitable, considering that fundamentally the Third was resolved to stand its ground.

*   *   *

Still it need hardly be said that many motives combined to bring the French people to their supreme dilemma. We have attempted to single them out. Class interests and personal interests, humbled pride, mass suffering, philosophical propaganda all made their contribution, in proportions different for each individual, but with the net effect of producing in the Third Estate a collective mentality that was strangely complex, but which in summary expressed itself as a belief in an aristocratic conspiracy, a belief which in turn aroused passionate feelings, the fear, the frenzy for fighting, the thirst for revenge that characterized the days of July.

Dismayed by popular excesses, the bourgeoisie tried to blame them on provocative agents, foreigners, "brigands" and criminals such as inevitably mingled with the insurgents. It is true that men who are the dregs of society are not the last to take part in mobs. But the allegations of the Assembly and the bourgeois authorities have a note of apology. The ordinary people neither condemned nor repudiated the murders of July, nor did Barnave or Mme. Roland. The elements in the revolutionary complex cannot be taken apart. In this sense Clemenceau was right: the Revolution is a *bloc,* a single thing. The moralist must praise heroism and condemn cruelty; but the moralist does not explain events.

*   *   *

Much labor has been spent in contesting the originality of the Declaration, in deducing its substance, for example, from the bills of rights adopted by the American colonists in the struggle that won their independence. The men of the Constituent Assembly were undoubtedly familiar with these documents, especially the one issued by Virginia on May 10, 1776. The inspiration and content of the American and French declarations were the same. It was in fact with Jefferson, as early as January 1789, that La Fayette discussed his project; the text that he presented to the Assembly on July 11, with the accompanying letter, has been found in the papers of the ambassador of the United States, annotated by his own hand. The influence of America is beyond question. But this is not to say that without America the French declaration would not have seen the light. The whole philosophic movement in France in the eighteenth century pointed to such an act; Montesquieu, Voltaire and Rousseau had collaborated in its making. In reality, America and France, like England before them, were alike tributaries to a great stream of ideas, which, while expressing the ascendancy of the bourgeoisie, constituted a common ideal that summarized the evolution of western civilization.

*   *   *

Many objections have been made to the Declaration. Some have already been mentioned because they apply to the circumstances in which it was debated in the Assembly. Others of more general bearing merit a moment's further attention.

The Declaration, it has been said, is a mere abstraction from real life. Some men may be worthy of the rights it proclaims; some are less so; some, indeed, are hardly human. For cannibals, for example, the rights of man can have no real application; and if it be argued that even cannibals are human beings, still they are scarcely human in our sense. Nor, it is alleged, does the Declaration allow for circumstances. If war or economic crisis endanger a nation's existence, are the rights of its citizens to have the same free scope as in times of prosperity? And if individual rights are not inherently limited, will not the government be granted the power to limit them?

There is no force in this criticism except when the Declaration is confused with a legal code, whereas its nature is that of moral principle, not of positive legislation. We are bound by moral principle, for example—as well as by the Declaration—not to do to another what we should not wish him to do to us. Moral principle does not specify what our conduct should be in each particular case; it leaves this task to the moralist or the casuist. Similarly the Declaration proclaims the rights of man, but leaves to the law, which may vary with circumstances, the task of determining the extent, which may also vary with circumstances, to which these rights may be exercised, always providing that the law is the true expression of the general will, i.e., of the majority of the community. That the members of the National Assembly considered this to be the character of the Declaration is clear from the debates in which, a month before its adoption, they discussed the operations of counter-revolutionaries and considered setting up a special court: governing in wartime is not like governing in peacetime, observed Gouy d'Arsy, anticipating Robespierre. Again, when the question of slavery arose, the relativism in the Declaration became apparent; it was judged impossible to transfer the Negroes abruptly, without apprenticeship in freedom, from slavery to the full status of citizenship. And the Assembly reached by implication the same conclusion for France, when it made the right to vote depend on degree of economic well-being, and the right to be elected depend on the owning of real estate, because, rightly or wrongly, it regarded such economic well-being, and especially the ownership of land, as the only means of assuring the enlightenment and self-restraint thought necessary to the exercise of the rights of man and of citizenship. These rights then are relative to circumstances. The Declaration is an ideal to be realized. It is a *direction of intention.*

Another criticism, vehemently raised in our day, is that it favored one class at the expense of others, namely the bourgeoisie that drew it up, and that it thus provoked a disorder that threatens the community with disruption. The Declaration did indeed list property among the rights of man, and its authors meant property as it then existed and still does; moreover, economic liberty, though not mentioned, is very much in its spirit. This amounts to saying that the man who holds the land and the other instrumentalities of labor, i.e., capital, is in fact master of those who possess nothing but their muscles and their intelligence, because they depend on him for the opportunity to earn their living. The evil is made worse, it is added, by the inheritance of property, which endows certain children, irrespective of merit or capacity, with the *means* over and above the *rights* which are all that others receive. The Declaration, in short, is blamed for having allowed capitalism to develop without control and for having thus caused the proletariat to rise against it—to have had as a consequence a new class struggle of an always accelerating violence, all for want of some power of arbitration that can be granted only to the state. Contrariwise, those who deny such a power to the state have not failed to invoke the Declaration, elaborating upon it with ideas drawn from its own authors, who undoubtedly held to *laissez-faire* and unlimited competition as universal panaceas, and conceived of property as an absolute right to use or to abuse.

Here again, for a reply, we must appeal to the Constituents themselves. They had before their eyes a society in which modern capitalism was barely beginning, and in which the increase of productive capacity seemed the essential corrective to poverty and want. Even to those who gave thought to the poor it seemed not impossible that every man might own a few acres or a shop that would make him self-sufficient; and this ideal, which was that of the *sans-culottes,* remained alive well into the nineteenth century. Experience has not justified these hopes. Rousseau had already observed, long before 1789, that democracy is not compatible with an excessive inequality of wealth. It is for the community to examine whether the changes since 1789 in the economic and social structure of society do not justify intervention by the law, so that the excess of *means* in the hands of some may not reduce the *rights* of others to an empty show. By what procedure? That too is for the community to decide, in the spirit of the Declaration, which in proclaiming liberty did not mean an aristocratic liberty reserved for a few, such as Montalambert demanded in 1850, but which rather, confiding to the law the task of delimiting the rights of citizens, left it to take the measures that may be suitable to prevent social disruption.

Finally, according to other critics, the Declaration regards law as simply the will of the citizens; but what would become of the nation if the majority oppressed the minority, or if it refused to make the necessary sacrifices which in time of war may reach to life itself? The community, this school concludes, cannot be identified with the citizens who make it up at a given moment; extending beyond them in time, it is hierarchically above them, for without it they would not exist; it is really embodied in the state, which in consequence cannot depend on the will of ephemeral citizens, and for that reason has the right to coerce them. With this idea, it need hardly be said, we return to the personal absolutism of the Old Regime, for the state, whatever may be said, has itself no effective existence except in individual persons, who by and large would confer their mandates upon themselves. Still less need it be remarked that this system is in radical contradiction with the Declaration in reducing the individual to be a mere instrument in the hands of the state, depriving him of all liberty and all self-determination.

But these answers do not remove the difficulty, as too often we delude ourselves into believing. It is perfectly true that the Declaration carries with it a risk, as do absolutism and dictatorship, though the risk is of another kind. The citizens must be made to face their responsibilities. Invested with the rights of governing themselves, if they abuse their powers with respect to one another, above all if they refuse from personal selfishness to assure the welfare of the community, the community will perish, and with it their liberty, if not indeed their existence.

We come here to the deeper meaning of the Declaration. It is a direction of intention; it therefore requires of the citizens an integrity of purpose, which is to say a critical spirit, patriotism in the proper sense of the word, respect for the rights of others, reasoned devotion to the national community, "virtue" in the language of Montesquieu, Rousseau and Robespierre. "The soul of the Republic," wrote Robespierre in 1792, "is virtue, love of country, the generous devotion that fuses all interests into the general interest." The Declaration in proclaiming the rights of man appeals at the same time to discipline freely consented to, to sacrifice if need be, to cultivation of character *and to the mind*. Liberty is by no means an invitation to indifference or to irresponsible power; nor is it the promise of unlimited well-being without a counterpart of toil and effort. It supposes application, perpetual effort, strict government of self, sacrifice in contingencies, civic and private virtues. It is therefore more difficult to live as a free man than to live as a slave, and that is why men so often renounce their freedom; for freedom is in its way an invitation to a life of courage, and sometimes of heroism, as the freedom of the Christian is an invitation to a life of sainthood.

The Industrial Revolution in England—Blessing or Curse to the Working Man?

CONTENTS

QUESTIONS FOR STUDY

1   *What was the condition of the rural workers in the eighteenth century?*

2   *What were the essential changes required of a person when a shift was made
from the country to a manufacturing city?*

3   *What working conditions were detrimental to the children employed in
factories? What conditions might be beneficial?*

4   *What are the main points at issue between the Hammonds and Ashton?
Between Mantoux and Ashton?*

5   *By what criteria can a judgment be made on whether the Industrial Revolution
was a blessing or a curse to the working man?*

The very term "Industrial Revolution" brings to mind a violent upheaval and implies the drastic dislocation of a whole segment of society. The dice would thus seem to be loaded in favor of the view that, at least in the short run, it brought nothing but ill to those whose sweat made it possible. Yet it should not be forgotten that it took almost a century for the Industrial Revolution to occur—the standard dates are 1760–1830—and one wonders if "Revolution" is the proper term. Furthermore, there were other economic changes in this period that were both independent of, and supplementary to, the Industrial Revolution. British agriculture was changing rapidly and at some human cost. Would there have been less misery had the Industrial Revolution not been contemporary with the acceleration of the Enclosure movement? Or would there have been more? Is there, in fact, a "price" that must always be paid for industrialization, as so many people believe today when a nation must industrialize or die?

1   The Industrial Revolution Defined

The term "Industrial Revolution" was first given common currency in the lectures of Arnold Toynbee (1852–1883). It is in one of these lectures that he gave the classic definition of the fundamental economic changes that England had undergone in the years following 1750.

FROM *Lectures on the Industrial Revolution of the 18th Century in England* BY ARNOLD TOYNBEE

THE ESSENCE OF THE INDUSTRIAL REVOLUTION is the substitution of competition for the mediaeval regulations which had previously controlled the production and distribution of wealth. . . .

Coming to the facts of the Industrial Revolution, the first thing that strikes us is the far greater rapidity which marks the growth of population. Before 1751 the largest decennial increase, so far as we can calculate from our imperfect materials, was 3 per cent. For each of the next three decennial periods the increase was 6 per cent.; then between 1781 and 1791 it was 9 per cent.; between 1791 and 1801, 11 per cent.; between 1801 and 1811, 14 per cent.; between 1811 and 1821, 18 per cent. This is the highest figure ever reached in England, for since 1815 a vast emigration has been always tending to moderate it; between 1815 and 1880 over eight millions (including Irish) have left our shores. But for this our normal rate of increase would be 16 or 18 instead of 12 per cent. in every decade.

Next we notice the relative and positive decline in the agricultural population. In 1811 it constituted 35 per cent. of the whole population of Great Britain; in 1821, 33 per cent.; in 1831, 28 per cent. And at the same time its actual numbers have decreased. In 1831 there were 1,243,057 adult males employed in agriculture in Great Britain; in 1841 there were 1,207,989. In

Arnold Toynbee, *Lectures on the Industrial Revolution of the 18th Century in England* (1887), pp. 85, 87–93.

1851 the whole number of persons engaged in agriculture in England was 2,084,153; in 1861 it was 2,010,454, and in 1871 it was 1,657,138. Contemporaneously with this change, the centre of density of population has shifted from the Midlands to the North; there are at the present day 458 persons to the square mile in the countries north of the Trent, as against 312 south of the Trent. And we have lastly to remark the change in the relative population of England and Ireland. Of the total population of the three kingdoms, Ireland had in 1821 32 per cent., in 1881 only 14.6 per cent.

An agrarian revolution plays as large part in the great industrial change of the end of the eighteenth century as does the revolution in manufacturing industries, to which attention is more usually directed. Our next inquiry must therefore be: What were the agricultural changes which led to this noticeable decrease in the rural population? The three most effective causes were: the destruction of the common-field system of cultivation; the enclosure, on a large scale, of common and waste lands; and the consolidation of small farms into large. We have already seen that while between 1710 and 1760 some 300,000 acres were enclosed, between 1760 and 1843 nearly 7,000,000 underwent the same process. Closely connected with the enclosure system was the substitution of large for small farms. In the first half of the century Laurence, though approving of consolidation from an economic point of view, had thought that the odium attaching to an evicting landlord would operate as a strong check upon it. But these scruples had now disappeared. Eden in 1795 notices how constantly the change was effected, often accompanied by the conversion of arable to pasture; and relates how in a certain Dorsetshire village he found two farms where twenty years ago there had been thirty. The process went on uninterruptedly into the present century. Cobbett, writing in 1826, says: "In the parish of Burghclere one single farmer holds, under Lord Carnarvon, as one farm, the lands that those now living remember to have formed fourteen farms, bringing up in a respectable way fourteen families." The consolidation of farms reduced the number of farmers, while the enclosures drove the labourers off the land, as it became impossible for them to exist without their rights of pasturage for sheep and geese on common lands.

Severely, however, as these changes bore upon the rural population, they wrought, without doubt, distinct improvement from an agricultural point of view. They meant the substitution of scientific for unscientific culture. "It has been found," says Laurence, "by long experience, that common or open fields are great hindrances to the public good, and to the honest improvement which every one might make of his own." Enclosures brought an extension of arable cultivation and the tillage of inferior soils; and in small farms of 40 to 100 acres, where the land was exhausted by repeated corn crops, the farm buildings of clay and mud walls and three-fourths of the estate often saturated with water, consolidation into farms of 100 to 500 acres meant rotation of crops, leases of nineteen years, and good farm buildings. The period was one of great agricultural advance; the breed of cattle was improved, rotation of crops was generally introduced, the steam-plough was invented, agricultural societies were instituted. In one respect alone the change was injurious. In consequence of the high prices of corn which prevailed during the French war, some of the finest permanent pastures were broken up. Still, in spite of this, it was said in 1813 that during the previous ten years agricultural produce had increased by one-fourth, and this was an increase upon a great increase in the preceding generation.

Passing to manufactures, we find here the all-prominent fact to be the substitution of the factory for the domestic system, the consequence of the mechanical discoveries of the time. Four great inventions altered the character of the cotton manufacture; the spinning-jenny, patented by Hargreaves in 1770; the water-frame, invented by Arkwright the year before; Crompton's mule introduced in 1779, and the self-acting mule, first invented by Kelly in 1792, but not brought into use till Roberts improved it in 1825. None of these by themselves would have revolutionised the industry. But in 1769—the year in which Napoleon and Wellington were born—James Watt took out his patent for the steam-engine. Sixteen years later it was applied to the cotton manufacture. In 1785 Boulton and Watt made an engine for a cotton-mill at Papplewick in Notts, and in the same year Arkwright's patent expired. These two facts taken together mark the introduction of the factory system. But the most famous invention of all, and the most fatal to domestic industry, the power-loom, though also patented by Cartwright in 1785, did not come into use for several years, and till the power-loom was introduced the workman was hardly injured. At first, in fact, machinery raised the wages of spinners and weavers owing to the great prosperity it brought to the trade. In fifteen years the cotton trade trebled itself; from 1788 to 1803 has been called "its golden age;" for, before the power-loom but after the introduction of the mule and other mechanical improvements by which for the first time yarn sufficiently fine for muslin and a variety of other fabrics was spun, the demands became such that "old barns, cart-houses, out-buildings of all descriptions were repaired, windows broke through the old blank walls, and all fitted up for loom-shops; new weavers' cottages with loom-shops arose in every direction, every family bringing home weekly from 40 to 120 shillings per week." At a later date, the condition of the workman was very different. Meanwhile, the iron industry had been equally revolutionised by the invention of smelting by pit-coal brought into use between 1740 and 1750, and by the application in 1788 of the steam-engine to blast furnaces. In the eight years which followed this latter date, the amount of iron manufactured nearly doubled itself.

A further growth of the factory system took place independent of machinery, and owed its origin to the expansion of trade, an expansion which was itself due to the great advance made at this time in the means of communication. The canal system was being rapidly developed throughout the country. In 1777 the Grand Trunk canal, 96 miles in length, connecting the Trent and Mersey, was finished; Hull and Liverpool were connected by one canal while another connected them both with Bristol; and in 1792, the Grand Junction canal, 90 miles in length, made a waterway from London through Oxford to the chief midland towns. Some years afterwards, the roads were greatly improved under Telford and Macadam; between 1818 and 1829 more than a thousand additional miles of turnpike road were constructed; and the next year, 1830, saw the opening of the first railroad. These improved means of communication caused an extraordinary increase in commerce, and to secure a sufficient supply of goods it became the interest of the merchants to collect weavers around them in great numbers, to get looms together in a workshop, and to give out the warp themselves to the workpeople. To these latter this system meant a change from independence to dependence; at the beginning of the century the report of a committee asserts that the essential difference between the domestic and the factory system is, that in the latter the work is done "by persons who have no property in the goods they manufacture." Another direct consequence of this expansion of trade was the regular recurrence of periods of over-production and of depression, a phenomenon quite unknown under the old system, and due to this new form of production on a large scale for a distant market.

These altered conditions in the production of wealth necessarily involved an equal revolution in its distribution. In agriculture the prominent fact is an enormous rise in rents. Up to 1795, though they had risen in some places, in others they had been stationary since the Revolution. But between 1790 and 1833, according to Porter, they at least doubled. In Scotland, the rental of land, which in 1795 had amounted to £2,000,000, had risen in 1815 to £5,278,685. A farm in Essex, which before 1793 had been rented at 10s. an acre, was let in 1812 at 50s., though, six years after, this had fallen again to 35s. In Berks and Wilts, farms which in 1790 were let at 14s., were let in 1810 at 70s., and in 1820 at 50s. Much of this rise, doubtless, was due to money invested in improvements—the first Lord Leicester is said to have expended £400,000 on his property—but it was far more largely the effect of the enclosure system, of the consolidation of farms, and of the high price of corn during the French war. Whatever may have been its causes, however, it represented a great social revolution, a change in the balance of political power and in the relative position of classes. The farmers shared in the prosperity of the landlords; for many of them held their farms under beneficial leases, and made large profits by them. In consequence, their character completely changed; they ceased to work and live with their labourers, and became a distinct class. The high prices of the war time thoroughly demoralised them, for their wealth then increased so fast, that they were at a loss what to do with it. Cobbett has described the change in their habits, the new food and furniture, the luxury and drinking, which were the consequences of more money coming into their hands than they knew how to spend. Meanwhile, the effect of all these agrarian changes upon the condition of the labourer was an exactly opposite and most disastrous one. He felt all the burden of high prices, while his wages were steadily falling, and he had lost his common-rights. It is from this period, viz., the beginning of the present century, that the alienation between farmer and labourer may be dated.

Exactly analogous phenomena appeared in the manufacturing world. The new class of great capitalist employers made enormous fortunes, they took little or no part personally in the work of their factories, their hundreds of workmen were individually unknown to them; and as a consequence, the old relations between masters and men disappeared, and a "cash nexus" was substituted for the human tie. The workmen on their side resorted to combination, and Trades-Unions began a fight which looked as if it were between mortal enemies rather than joint producers. The misery which came upon large sections of the working people at this epoch was often, though not always, due to a fall in wages, for, as I said above, in some industries they rose. But they suffered likewise from the conditions of labour under the factory system, from the rise of prices, especially from the high price of bread before the repeal of the corn-laws, and from those sudden fluctuations of trade, which, ever since production has been on a large scale, have exposed them to recurrent periods of bitter distress. The effects of the Industrial Revolution prove that free competition may produce wealth without producing wellbeing. We all know the horrors that ensued in England before it was restrained by legislation and combination.

2   The World That Was Lost

Arthur Young (1741–1820) was a prosperous farmer who devoted his life to the improvement of agriculture. He traveled widely, keeping a journal in which he noted the condition of the countryside and reporting what he saw in the journal, Annals of Agriculture, *or in separate publications. These reports give an excellent insight into the conditions of Great Britain just as she plunged into the Industrial Revolution.*

In the first document, Young provides figures for the amount of capital required to set up as a farmer, leasing enough land to bring in an annual income of 100 pounds a year. Then he gives indications of the standard of living of cottagers (the poorest farmers).

FROM *Tours in England and Wales*

BY ARTHUR YOUNG

To Hire a Farm of 100l. a Year.

5 Horses at 15l.	£.75	0	0
12 Cows at 7l.	84	0	0
8 Young cattle 3l.	24	0	0
60 Sheep at 10s.	30	0	0
2 Sows at 50s.	5	0	0
1 Waggon,	25	0	0
2 Tunbrils 10l.	20	0	0
1 Harvest cart,	7	0	0
2 Ploughs,	3	0	0

Arthur Young, *Tours in England and Wales selected from the Annals of Agriculture* (1932), pp. 1, 2–3, 5, 9, 45, 47–9, 87–90, 145, 157–8, 205, 217, 223–4, 274–5. Reprinted by permission of The London School of Economics and Political Science, London.

2 Harrows,	*3*	*0*	*0*
1 Roller,	*1*	*0*	*0*
Harness,	*5*	*0*	*0*
Sundries,	*15*	*0*	*0*
Furniture,	*50*	*0*	*0*
Tythe,	*12*	*0*	*0*
Rates, &c.	*5*	*0*	*0*
Housekeeping,	*25*	*0*	*0*
2 Men and 1 boy,	*19*	*0*	*0*
2 Maids,	*6*	*0*	*0*
1 Labourer,	*18*	*0*	*0*
60 Acres seed 12s.	*36*	*0*	*0*
	468	*0*	*0*

Land sells at 30 years purchase, in 10 years risen much, now at a stand. Land-tax at 4s. not more than 1s. the county through. Tythes not much gathered; computed 2s. to 3s. in the pound. Poor rates, 1s. to 1s. 6d. doubled in 10 years. Tea general, leases 7s. to 14s. or 21s. many, but going out.

Labour

In harvest 1s. 4d. 1s. 6d. and board
—Hay 1s. 2d. 1s. 4d. and beer.
—Winter 1s.
Man's wages 8l.
Lad 3l.
Maid 3l. to 3l. 10s.
Woman at hay 6d. and beer.
  Rise of labour, none for 6 years, but in 15 years ⅓d

Provision

Cheese 3d.
Butter 6d. 9d.
Beef 4d.
Bacon 6d. 7d.
Potatoes 1s. 6d. 2s. strike,
Labourer's house rent 40s.

Mutton 4d.
Veal 4d.
Pork 4d.
Firing, seldom buy more
  than 12s. for 1 stack coal.
Tools 5s.

Building

Bricks 15s. formerly 9s.

Tiles 20s.

Oak 40s. a ton, very little advanced.

Ash do.

Poplar 30s.

Carpenter 1s. 6d. 1s. 8d.

Mason do.

Building a cottage 25l.

A Farm

300	Acres	8	Horses
124	Grass	16	Cows
176	Arable	4	Fatting
33	Wheat	30	Young
50	Barley	100	Sheep
8	Oats	3	Men
17	Pease	2	Maids
60	Clover	2	Labourers
8	Fallow		

*　　*　　*

The state of the poor, in general, in this country is advantageous, owing very much to lace making. The following account will shew this, in the receipt and expenditure of a poor family, viz. a man, his wife, and five children, the eldest sixteen years of age.

Earnings

	£.	s.	d.
Twenty-six weeks winter, at 7s. raised to that rate by taking work by the great	9	2	0
Five harvest, at 9s.	2	5	0
Four week's hay, going upwards (towards London)	3	3	0
Seventeen weeks summer, at 8s.	6	16	0
The son 3s. a week, and 16s. extra in hay and harvest	8	12	0
The rest of the family, 2s. a week	5	4	0
	35	2	0

Expenses

	£.	s.	d.
Bread, half the year (winter), barley, and half wheaten, at 6s. 6d. a week, on an average including baking, 4d. barm, 2d. and salt, 1d.	0	6	6
Salt for other uses,	0	0	0½
Bacon, 2 lb. a week	0	1	4
Tea, sugar, and butter	0	1	0
Cheese, half a pound	0	0	2½
Beer (four bushel of malt, at 5s. 6d. and 3 lb. hops, 3s.) per week	0	0	6
Soap (half a pound in three weeks), and starch, and blue	0	0	2
Candles	0	0	3
Thread, half an ounce a week, 1½d. worsted, 2d.	0	0	3½
	0	10	3¼
Per annum	26	15	2
Rent	1	15	0
Wood	0	12	0
Lying in and sickness	1	0	0

				£.	s.	d.
Cloaths. The man's shoes	0	15	0			
shirts	0	8	0			
stockings	0	4	0			
hat, &c.	0	1	6			
jacket	0	6	0			
	1	14	6			
Family	2	0	0			
				3	14	6
				33	16	8
Earnings				35	2	0
Expenses				33	16	8
To lay up, or expend in additional cloaths				1	5	4

In the selections that follow, Young describes the conditions of rural life in a number of places throughout England and Wales.

OCTOBER 23, 1776, landed at Milford haven from Ireland. The whole country is inclosed, without such a thing as a common field. The food of the poor, bread and cheese, with broth made of salt meat, paid in at the cheapest season; much fish also eaten by them. Many keep cows; no goats on the mountains. The cottages many of them not a wh't better than Irish cabbins, without an equal show of pigs, poultry and cows. Labour 8d. in the winter, and 10d. in summer, the year round. The whole country is in gentle inequalities; and, if wooded would be beautiful.

To Narbarth. Several cottages building in the Irish way, of mud with straw. The poor people seem well cloathed and fed. They use through all this country small heavy carts with two oxen and two or three horses, the driver sits on the front of the cart, and drives with reins.

October 24th to St. Clear. From Narbarth to Hubberston the course is, Rents 7s. 6d. to 10s. the whole farm through; to 14s. on some farms. Farms rise to very large ones, but in general small. The Irish cottar system is found here—3 or 4 cottages to a farm of 40 or 50l. a year. They are always at the call of the farmers, they are allowed two or three grass fields at a moderate rent, a cow or two, but no pigs, unless one in a year, to kill at Christmas. Strangers get in winter 4d. a day, and food; without food 8d. in harvest 1s. 1s. 6d. and food. They live on bread and cheese, and milk, or water; no beer, nor meat, except on a Sunday. The culture of potatoes increases much, more planted last year than ever known before. The poor eat them; and every cabbin has a garden with some in it. Many iron furnaces, the ore dug in the country. The poor people spin a good deal of wool, and weave it into flannel for their own wear, no linen is worn by them, flannel supplying the place. Query, to the physicians of the country—Is the rheumatism known here as much as in other countries where linen is worn? They make cloth also for their own wear. Weavers earn 1s. a day, and sometimes more. The poor live on barley-bread, cheese, and butter; not one in ten have either cows or pigs, fare very poorly and rarely touch meat. Their little gardens they plant with cabbages, carrots, leeks, and potatoes. Rent of a cottage and garden, 10s. to 20s. Building a mud cabbin costs 10l.

*   *   *

The Earl of Shelburne, though his attention has not been particularly applied to husbandry, yet having kept large tracts of land in his own hands and with very liberal views, his Lordship has planned a system of conduct which cannot fail of having excellent effects upon the husbandry of his extensive estate, and the neighbourhood in general. . . . It is his idea, that a man of large fortune keeping land in his hands with a view only of uniting the profits of the landlord and the farmer, is acting from very poor motives: That he ought to apply to farming either as a mere amusement, or which is better, as a means in which he can be of very great service to the country.

That in the first place he should have his grounds to exhibit to his tenants and others, cultivated in the most masterly manner which the climate and soil will admit of; that they may at all times see the culture of all those new plants which are recommended to farmers from the fields of gentlemen, that seeing the produce, the application, and the effect, they may, by degrees, be induced to make experiments themselves, and choose between objects, once equally unknown to them. That they may see the plants, to which they have always been accustomed, carried to the highest degree of perfection, by new successions of arrangement, new modes of culture and new exertions in manuring. From fields thus managed a farmer must always return wiser than he came.

In another line, who, says his Lordship, should introduce improvements in the breed of cattle and sheep; in the implements of husbandry; and in various other circumstances? the farmer, who, probably, sees little beyond what he has used and to whom a failure in success would be a heavy loss, or the landlord, who must necessarily have opportunities of seeing such variation and their effects, and to whom losses are an insignificant object?

Before I quit this country, I may remark, that I was much struck all through it, to find the Lombardy poplar so generally introduced; there is scarcely a house without some, and many of them very finely grown. But the cause to which this and other circumstances may be referred, is an article that escaped me when I was here before. It is, there being a great number of landlords the occupiers of their own lands. Alderton especially, is full of them; gentlemen farmers from 200 to 500l. a-year, who cultivating their own property, do it with a spirit that very few leases will permit. Within a very few years there are a great number of well-built brick houses, with inclosed and well-managed gardens; many new cottages; much planting; which, added to the excellent husbandry in the fields, give a beautiful appearance to the country, and prove, beyond a million of arguments, the admirable effects which flow from a wealthy yeomanry; a race of men so greatly decreased in this kingdom; and is a strong confirmation of what I have more than once remarked, that it is not the union of little farms we should complain of, but the accumulation of little estates, which, when they happen to be cultivated by their owners, promote, beyond any thing else, the prosperity of the national agriculture.

All this country abounds greatly in game, especially pheasants, which are so plentiful, that every little copse is full of them. At Boyton Mr. Woolnough, when I was here before, had them in his garden, and in severe weather they come to the corn stacks: besides a general plenty of game the country abounds greatly with the best sorts of fresh water fish; there is not a pond, or scarcely a large dyke at Alderton, Hollesley, Shottisham, or Bawdsey, that has not good carp and tench; carp rise to eight pound each, tench four pound, perch two pounds; and there are several fresh water creeks that communicate with the sea, in which they abound of the largest size; when to this we add wild fowl in plenty, a dry sandy but fertile soil, and the sea contiguous almost to every parish, it will not be doubted that few parts of the kingdom possess so many circumstances to make a residence in every respect plentiful, and in most agreeable. I know but one drawback; in the spots near the marshes they are plagued with agues, but the high sandy situations are free from them. Those marshes are narrow tracts on the river.

Next we went to Capel St. Andrews. Mr. Gross's great farm of 2700 acres, of whom, repeating our enquiries, we found, that he had been accustomed to cultivate carrots, even to last year, but his crops were so eaten up by the innumerable number of hares which his landlord, Lord Archibald Hamilton, preserved, that he has determined to sow no more. In these cases the tenant doubtless has his recompense in the rent, but the public has none. The profusion of game in this and another of his lordship's farms, Butley Abbey, Mr. Chandler's, which are together above 5000 acres, puts a barrier to good husbandry, and prevents one of the best articles of culture in the kingdom from spreading. It is not only the hares that do the mischief, but their preservation nurses up a breed of rabbits which add to the evil. The reflection I have added is my own, and not the farmer's, who seemed very well inclined to second his landlord's wishes.

* * *

Crossed the Severn at the ferry at Lincoln Hill, in the midst of a most noble scenery of exceeding bold mountainous tracts, with that river rolling at the bottom. The opposite shore is one immense steep of hanging wood, which has the finest effect imaginable. Mounted through that wood, thickly scattered with cottages, the inhabitants busily employed in the vast works of various kinds carried on in the neighbourhood. One circumstance I remarked which gave me much pleasure. There was not a single cottage in which a fine hog did not seem to make a part of every family; not a door without a stone trough with the pig eating his supper, in company with the children at the same business playful about the threshold. It was a sight which shewed that chearfulness and plenty crowned the board of the humble but happy inhabitants of this romantic spot.

About St. Neot's a vast improvement by an inclosure, which took place 16 years ago, which makes the country much more beautiful, and has been a great benefit to the community. A gentleman of the town however complained, as I rode thither with him, that, notwithstanding the productiveness of the soil was certainly greater, yet that the poor were ill-treated by having about half a rood given them in lieu of a *cow keep,* the inclosure of which land costing more than they could afford, they sold the lots at 5l. the money was drank out at the ale-house, and the men, spoiled by the habit, came, with their families, to the parish; by which means poor rates had risen from 2s. 6d. to 3s. and 3s. 6d. But pray, sir, have not rates arisen equally in other parishes, where no inclosure has taken place? Admitted. And what can be the good of commons, which would not prevent poor rates coming to such a height? Better modes of giving the poor a share might easily, and have been, as in other cases, adopted.

*   *   *

In the open fields the farms are generally small, usually about 70l. a-year: these little occupations with which the Duke of Grafton, and other good landlords have patience in order to nurse up industrious families, are yet a heavy loss in repairs: and sometimes in other circumstances: inclosed farms rise to 300l. which is the greatest; there are but few of 200l. to 250l. In farms of a tolerable size, the tenantry are substantial, and it gave me great pleasure to find them with such confidence in their landlord, as to raise considerable erections on the Duke's farms at their own expence, in articles beyond the common demands of the country; as a hay barn, &c. &c. and this while tenants at will; a sure proof that they regard their landlord as their father and their friend.

The 7th. To Measham, where Mr. Wilkes shewed us his many and great improvements; the manor and estate he purchased some years ago of Mr. Wollaston, of Finborough, in Suffolk, for 50,000l. The buildings erected and erecting will speedily change the face of it. Here are two cotton and a corn mill, two steam engines; many weaving-shops, and a number of cottages built; a large and handsome inn; . . . a few of the old thatched hovels remain to shew what this place was; what it will be may easily be conceived. But what is done here in ten or a dozen years by one man, who has been at the same time engaged in many other great undertakings, who, in union with Mr. Peele, is giving a new face to Faseley and Tamworth, cannot but make any one from the Continent admire at the wonderful exertions active in this kingdom—and in this kingdom only, for there is nothing out of it in the manufacturing world that is not, comparatively speaking, fast asleep.

A manufacturing town—Birmingham in the 1790s.

These immense works, which wear so animated a face of business, correspond well with the prodigious increase of the town, which I viewed to good advantage from the top of the new church of St. Paul: it is now a very great city indeed; and it was abundantly curious to have it pointed out to me the parts added since I was here. They form the greatest part of the town, and carry in their countenance undoubted marks of their modern date. In

1768 the population was under 30,000; now the common calculation is 70,000, but more accurate calculation extend it to 80,000, which I am told is the number assigned by Dr. Priestley. In the last 10 years above 4000 new houses have been built: and the increase is at present going on much more rapidly, for I was told that the number this year is not less than 700.

The earnings of the workmen in the manufacture are various, but in general very high: a boy of 10 or 12 years, 2s. 6d. to 3s. a week; a woman from 4s. to 20s. a week, average about 6s.; men from 10s. to 25s. a week, and some much higher; colliers earn yet more. These are immense wages, when it is considered that the whole family is sure of constant steady employment; indeed they are so great, that I am inclined to think labour higher at Birmingham than in any place in Europe: a most curious circumstance for the politician to reflect on, and which shews of how little effect to manufactures is cheap labour, for here is the most flourishing fabric that was perhaps ever known, paying the highest rates of labour. Such an instance ought to correct those common notions that have been retailed from hand to hand a thousand times, that cheap provisions are necessary for the good of manufactures, because cheap provisions suppose cheap labour, which is a combination founded in ignorance and error. Provisions at Birmingham are at the same rate as every where else in England, for it is remarkable that the level of price at present is very general, except the division of the east and west of the kingdom for corn; but while Birmingham and Norwich eat their provisions at nearly the same price (with allowance that the former is much the more quick, ready, and active market), the price of labour is at least 150 per cent. higher in one of those places than the other. Why then I enquire, what has provisions to do with the rate of labour? If one was to form our ideas from a very enlarged view of all the great fabrics in Europe, we should be apt to think that a great and flourishing fabric could not subsist, either with cheap provisions, or with cheap labour.

I tried hard to pick up some data, on which to calculate the amount of the fabric, but difficulties of various kinds prevented any accuracy in the estimation. In conversation with a very ingenious gentleman, who has written an able work on the town, and who was rewarded for it by having his house burnt down in the late riots, I mean Mr. Hutton, he informed me that ten years ago there were many estimates made with a good deal of care; and that on multiplied experiments it was found, that the returns per week, was equal to the rent per annum; including all the houses of the town on an average; all shops; all trades: the houses were then about 9000, and the rent 9l. each, on a medium; now the houses are about 13,000, and as I find, on enquiry, that the little houses, which have been built in such numbers for manufacturers, are let at 6l. 10s. the lowest; 7l. and 8l. each; 9l. on a general average of rents must now be much too low; however let us call it no more than 10l. this would make the rental of the town 130,000l. a year, and the returns of all its trade 6,760,000l. per annum: out of which a very great deduction is to be made for all the trades and professions of common life, supported by the manufacture, but not composing it. If I should form any idea corrective of this, it would be that the estimate is carried too high: let us suppose the population 80,000, then there are about 40,000 males, of these deduct 5000 not employed in the manufacture, remain 35,000; three-fourths of that number are of an age to be employed, or 26,250. Suppose these to earn, including manufacturers and merchants profit, 15s. a week, it amounts to 1,023,724l. a year. Of the 40,000 women 20,000 may be supposed to be employed, and to earn 6s. including, as above; the year's earnings will be 312,000l. in all 1,335,000l. double this, to include all raw materials, and you have 2,670,000l. for the amount of the manufacture. Now I am ready to grant, that here is a great deal of supposition in this estimate, but at the same time it is not altogether without data; and though the total may exceed this, possibly half a million, yet I think as much might be said to shew the calculation high, as to prove it low. It is true the ratio of the earnings is taken rather low, including, as it ought to do, the profit both of the manufacturer and of the merchant, which cannot well be less than 20 per cent.; but then the number of the workmen can scarcely exceed the supposition, probably not equal to it, 20,000 females, in particular are a high allowance.

> *Robert Southey (1774–1843) was Poet Laureate of England and intimately connected with the Romantic school of William Wordsworth and Samuel Taylor Coleridge. The Romantics tended to idealize the rural life and see in it a purity and simplicity that often was invisible to their contemporaries.*
>
> > *The selection that follows takes the form of a dialogue between Sir Thomas More's ghost and a man who speaks for Southey's time.*

FROM *Sir Thomas More* BY ROBERT SOUTHEY

SIR THOMAS MORE. . . . The spirit which built and endowed monasteries is gone. Are you one of those persons who think it has been superseded for the better by that which erects steam-engines and cotton mills?

MONTESINOS. They are indeed miserable politicians who mistake wealth for welfare in their estimate of national prosperity; and none have committed this great error more egregiously than some of those who have been called statesmen by the courtesy of England. Yet the manufacturing system

---

Robert Southey, *Sir Thomas More; or, Colloquies on the Progress and Prospects of Society,* I (1829), 158–9, 166–7, 170–1, 173–4.

is a necessary stage in the progress of society. Without it this nation could not have supported the long and tremendous conflict which has delivered Europe from the yoke of military despotism, . . . the worst of all evils. If England had not been enabled by the use of steam-engines to send out every year myriads of brave men, and millions of specie, . . . what had Europe, and what had England itself been now? This inestimable benefit we have seen and felt. And from the consequences of that skill in machinery which the manufacturing system alone could have produced, we may expect ultimately to obtain the greatest advantages of science and civilization at the least expense of human labour.

*   *   *

SIR THOMAS MORE. There is an example before our eyes. Yonder children are on the way to a manufactory, where they pass six days out of the seven, from morning till night. Is it likely that the little they learn at school on the seventh (which ought to be their day of recreation as well as rest); should counteract the effects of such an education, when the moral atmosphere wherein they live and move and have their being, is as noxious to the soul, as the foul and tainted air which they inhale is to their bodily constitution?

MONTESINOS. Yet the most celebrated minister of the age, the only minister who for many generations has deserved to be called a Premier, the minister whom our best and wisest statesmen at this day profess entirely to admire and implicitly to follow, . . . he made his boast of this very evil, and congratulated Parliament that the nation had a new source of wealth and revenue in the labour of children: so completely had the political system in which he was trained up seared his heart and obscured his understanding.

SIR THOMAS MORE. Confess that this is an evil which had no existence in former times! There are new things under the sun, . . . new miseries, . . . new enormities, . . . this portentous age produces them.

*   *   *

SIR THOMAS MORE. What then shall we say of a system which in its direct consequences debases all who are engaged in it? a system that employs men unremittingly in pursuits unwholesome for the body, and unprofitable for the mind, . . . a system in which the means are so bad, that any result would be dearly purchased at such an expense of human misery and degradation, and the end so fearful, that the worst calamities which society has hitherto endured may be deemed light in comparison with it?

MONTESINOS. Like the whole fabric of our society it has been the growth of circumstances, not a system foreplanned, foreseen and deliberately chosen. Such as it is we have inherited it, . . . or rather have fallen into it, and must get out of it as well as we can. We must do our best to remove its evils, and to mitigate them while they last, and to modify and reduce it till only so much remains as is indispensable for the general good.

SIR THOMAS MORE. The facts will not warrant you in saying that it has come upon the country unsought and unforeseen. You have prided your-selves upon this system, you have used every means for extending it; you have made it the measure of your national prosperity. It is a wen, a fungous excrescence from the body politic: the growth might have been checked if the consequences had been apprehended in time; but now it has acquired so great a bulk, its nerves have branched so widely, and the vessels of the tumour are so inosculated into some of the principal veins and arteries of the natural system, that to remove it by absorption is impossible, and excision would be fatal.

MONTESINOS. Happily, this is but a metaphor; and the body politic, like its crowned head, never dies.

By this time we had reached the bank above Applethwaite. The last question of my companion was one to which I could make no reply, and as he neither talked for triumph, nor I endeavoured to elude the force of his argument, we remained awhile in silence, looking upon the assemblage of dwellings below. Here, and in the adjoining hamlet of Millbeck, the effects of manufactures and of agriculture may be seen and compared. The old cottages are such as the poet and the painter equally delight in beholding. Substantially built of the native stone without mortar, dirtied with no white-lime, and their long low roofs covered with slate, if they had been raised by the magic of some indigenous Amphion's music, the materials could not have adjusted them-selves more beautifully in accord with the surrounding scene; and time has still farther harmonized them with weather stains, lichens and moss, short grasses and short fern, and stone plants of various kinds. The ornamented chimnies, round or square, less adorned than those which, like little turrets, crest the houses of the Portugueze peasantry, and yet not less happily suited to their place; the hedge of clipt box beneath the windows, the rose bushes beside the door, the little patch of flower ground with its tall holyocks in front, the garden beside, the bee-hives, and the orchard with its bank of daffodils and snowdrops, (the earliest and the profusest in these parts,) indicate in the owners some portion of ease and leisure, some regard to neatness and comfort, some sense of natural and innocent and healthful enjoyment. The new cottages of the manufacturers, are . . . upon the manu-facturing pattern . . . naked, and in a row.

How is it, said I, that every thing which is connected with manufactures, presents such features of unqualified deformity? From the largest of Mam-mon's temples down to the poorest hovel in which his helotry are stalled, the edifices have all one character. Time cannot mellow them; Nature will neither clothe nor conceal them; and they remain always as offensive to the eye as to the mind!

3 Working Conditions in the Industrial Revolution

The rapid industrialization of Great Britain, added to the hardships of the wars of the French Revolution and Napoleon, created serious conditions among the poor. Many members of the upper classes were troubled by the burgeoning of manufactures and by the use of small children in producing them. The children were a necessary part of the new cotton textile industry for, because of their small size, they could move freely under the machinery to repair broken threads and keep the looms and spindles working. The moral question raised by such employment could not long be ignored, and in 1816 a parliamentary committee was appointed to find out if the employment of children was detrimental to their health and morals.

FROM *Report . . . on the State of the Children Employed . . .*

The first witness is Matthew Baillie, M.D. The Chairman of the Committee is Sir Robert Peel, himself an industrialist and the father of the future Prime Minister.

IN SPEAKING OF THE INJURY to young persons arising from labour, do you mean to speak of labour which requires great bodily exertion?—I did not suppose that children at so early an age were employed in great

Report of the Minutes of Evidence taken before the Select Committee on the State of the Children employed in the Manufactories of the United Kingdom, 25 April—18 June, 1816, pp. 30–1, 46–8, 50–2, 178–81, 222–3.

bodily exertion, but I meant any bodily exertion in which they were confined in a given space, and their minds not allowed to wander into the various channels of thought, and their limbs allowed the sort of irregular exercise which takes place in children who are living in the usual manner.

Is not the state of maturity of children very different in those brought up in the country, to those brought up in town?—With regard to children who are brought up in the country, they are more vigorous; and I have no doubt, in many instances, their progress towards maturity may be more rapid than in children who are reared in a large town.

And your experience has principally been in town?—Entirely, I may say.

Have you been called to give any opinion, or to know the state of health in different manufactories?—I have not.

What is the state of heat, as ascertained by a thermometer, in which children might work without injury?—I should say, that the temperature which is upon the whole most favourable, is about sixty degrees of heat.

In giving your opinion upon this subject, do you take into your consideration the situation in which children would be placed, if, at an early period, they were not employed in such factories?—I do not know that the whole of this pressed on my mind, but certainly it was not absent from it; I drew the comparison between those children as employed in manufactories, and the ordinary employment of children in the country.

Would children of the age of ten be employed in the ordinary business of the country?—No; but they would be doing a good deal of work of various kinds, as going of errands, or weeding, and a thousand employments, which I cannot at present call up to my mind.

That answer seems to refer more particularly to children in the country, as the manufactories are generally in towns, it does not apply to them; therefore the Committee wish to know whether you conceive, if children at an early period of life were prevented by Act of Parliament from working in factories, their situation would be better than it is?—I conceive it would be more favourable to health to be at large, although they might sometimes be not well nourished; and although sometimes they would be in hot rooms, they would have a great deal more time in which they could be playing about, and using their faculties of observation.

Then if those children were left on the parish for support, and many sent to the workhouse, their situation would be better than at present?—I think that children would be better situated in a workhouse, were they not so employed, than in manufactories.

Do you give this as an opinion that you derive from an accurate observation of facts, with respect to the condition of children in factories, or do you give it upon general reasoning?—Upon general reasoning.

Then you are not really acquainted with the condition of children employed in such manufactories?—I am not really acquainted with the condition of children employed in such manufactories; but I mention what I suppose must be more or less the influence of confinement which children are subject to in those manufactories upon their health, from the general principles that guide us in ascertaining the causes that maintain health or lead to sickness, with respect to the human body generally.

In a factory consisting of 875 persons, the annual deaths in which were not more than from two to five, should you conceive that the employment was inconsistent with the health of the people employed?—I should say it does not appear from that statement to have been inconsistent; I conceive, a great many of those children might not be in vigorous health, not in the same health in which they would otherwise be, and yet not be attacked with diseases which would occasion death.

Your answer refers to the number of deaths in a particular year; but if the average for seven years should be about the same, would not you consider that fact as tolerable evidence of the health of the employment?— Indeed I should think so.

Then if in another factory consisting of 289 persons, two only died in the year 1815; and on the 13th of April, one only was sick; would not that afford a tolerable inference of the healthiness of the persons employed in that factory?—It certainly would; but as I stated before, I can easily believe that those children may not be attacked by diseases which should lead to death; but at the same time, be many of them less vigorous than they otherwise would be if employed in the usual manner.

Then in factories, where on the average persons are employed seven years, and where a great portion remain from fourteen to twenty; if the general state of health has been good, would not that be tolerably good evidence of the healthiness of the employment?—I think so.

Have you ever had reason to conceive that there exists in the lower classes of people, a want of affection and tenderness for their children?—I believe you will find very often less affection, both of fathers and mothers for their children in the lower classes, than in the middle ranks: But at the same time there are many strong instances of the purest maternal and paternal affection in the lowest classes of society, where there may be very great difficulty to rear children: they will often submit to every kind of privation respecting themselves, in order to rear the children with some degree of comfort.

Then the lowest class are not the persons where the greatest degree of affection is found for their children?—I think not.

Does not a family press much harder on a poor man, than on any other class?—No doubt.

And is it not of greater importance to him to superintend the care of those children, than to any other class of persons in life?—It must be of more importance to him to superintend, if he can, the education and the bringing up of his children, because in other ranks of life, there are persons who can be procured to do that office for them.

Does not any sickness or want of health in the children of the poor, press upon the parents more than upon any other class of persons?—Certainly.

In the communications you have received from other practitioners, have you ever heard of any great detriment that has occurred to children from too intense employment in manufactories?—I do not recollect that I have ever received a communication upon the subject.

Have you had opportunities of observation upon the condition of the children of the poor not employed in manufactories in large towns?—I have been engaged almost from the beginning of my medical life, in the middle and higher ranks of society.

*   *   *

Sir Gilbert Blane, M.D., was also examined.

May it not happen, by those children being kept employed not in hard labour but in that kind of gentle occupation that gives exercise without superinducing too great fatigue, for twelve hours in a day, in factories, where the air was pure and salutary?—That is a question that, from my want of knowing in detail what is the nature of the employment, I cannot answer; if it was not sedentary but loco-motive, ten hours would not be too much.

Must not a great deal of the power of performance on the part of children, depend on the nourishment and cloathing which they receive?—Not the least doubt much must depend upon the quantity and quality of food.

May not, both in men and animals, an increased degree of maturity be attained in consequence of the food that they receive?—No doubt of it; but there is a greater latitude in the human species than in any other; a man, so speaking, is more an animal of mixed food than any other.

May not children of ten years of age, by being better fed and better care taken of them, be capable of doing more work, without injury to his health, than a child of the same age could have done twenty years ago?—I am clearly of that opinion, from the habits of life, which I have watched with great accuracy.

In referring to the powers of children, are we not to refer, not to what they were, but to what they actually are, from the improvements that have been made?—No doubt of it.

Has it ever occurred to you, to contemplate what has been the increased consumption of animal food within the last fifty years?—I have frequently attended to it, and I think with advantage to mankind, particularly to the young.

Is not the increase of animal food, to young and old, ten times what it was fifty years ago?—It has certainly increased, but I should think that was too high a ratio; it has been increased, to the benefit of all ages, and particularly to the young.

In your observations, has not the consumption of animal food greatly increased within the last fifty years?—It has greatly increased.

Has it not greatly increased within the last twenty years?—Certainly it has, according to my observation.

And that has had a material influence on the strength and health of the people?—I suppose that that has had some share in the decreased mortality which appears.

Is the Committee to understand, that you consider the employment of children, under the age of ten years, to be wholly improper and inconvenient?—By no means wholly improper; I should think if it was limited to five or six hours, that would not only not be pernicious, but salutary.

And you think the employment of children from ten to sixteen, ought not to exceed ten hours a day?—Yes, that might be without prejudice.

You were understood to say, you conceived the state of the atmosphere in which the children worked, was of more importance than the labour itself?—Certainly; they would suffer more from foul air than from the actual labour: the manual labour is the least evil I think.

You say, that the employment of children under ten, might, under certain restrictions, not only be not detrimental, but even beneficial?—I should have no objection to five or six hours.

Are there any restrictions, in point of time or kind of work, that would make it proper to employ children under six years old?—I am so little acquainted with the nature of the occupations in manufactories, I cannot answer that.

Suppose a great number are kept together in the same room, and not exposed to the open air, and in a sedentary posture, or at any rate not taking exercise, do you conceive that at the age of five or six, such occupation, however limited in point of time, is wholesome?—I should apprehend it is wholesome if very limited.

At the age of five or six?—Even as low as that, very limited in time, and in apartments well ventilated and not crowded.

Do you mean, if during the other parts of the day the children should be allowed to play or amuse themselves in the open air?—Most assuredly I understood it so.

Is the proportion between the cubic feet of air in a room, and the number of persons employed in it, of great importance to their health?—Very great; that is a subject I have particularly studied.

In rooms properly ventilated, and where the quantity of respirable air allowed to each person is 1,440 cubic feet, do you think that employment is likely to be prejudicial to such persons?—There is ample space for pure air there; in a hospital there is 700 feet to a patient, and we consider that a safe and proper space, still more so where they are in health and walk about. In a hospital well ventilated, we find 700 cubic feet is a safe and proper space for each patient.

Are you of opinion, that the air in such rooms as have been alluded to, and the employment in them, are likely to be more or less healthy than such rooms as children are employed in by inferior tradesmen, such as tailors and shoemakers?—I apprehend that is a superior degree of ventilation to what they have in the apartments of the labouring poor.

Is it important to the health of children and others, that the temperature of the rooms in which they are employed in winter should be comfortable, and as nearly uniform as is consistent with proper ventilation?—There is no doubt of it; I think comfortable and salutary to be one and the same thing; nature points out what is salutary.

Your attention seems to have been particularly called to the proportion of deaths in different places in this country; do you conceive, that in a factory where in 1811 the number being 873, the deaths in that year being only three; in 1812 the number being 891, the deaths only two; and in 1813 the number being 879, and the deaths only two, such facts to be an indication of the healthiness of the employment in such factory?—It is an indication of the greatest possible health; but it so far exceeds the common course of nature, that if I had it not from such respectable authority I should greatly doubt it.

Would you be surprized at the statement, if you were informed that when children are ill, and likely to die, they are removed from the manufactories?—That alters the case totally.

Are you of opinion, that in another factory, wherein the numbers were 289 employed in 1815, the deaths being two, and where, on the 13th of April only one person out of all that number was sick, such facts are evidence that such factory is healthy?—The same answer; it is evidence of extreme healthiness.

Are you aware, in the most healthy communities, what the proportion of deaths to the persons in life, usually is?—The average in England is one in forty-nine, including Wales one in fifty; and according to the Parliamentary Returns of the beginning of this century, it was one in forty-four; by the Parliamentary Return of 1801.

Healthiness has been somewhat increasing?—Yes.

Did the surprize expressed in a former question, refer to this turning out to be six times less than the average mortality in healthy situations in this country?—To be sure, that made me say it was against the common course of nature; there are no tables that I ever saw, that quoted so high a proportion in the most healthy period of life.

Are you of opinion, that in no situation peculiarly favourable to health in this country, the proportion of deaths is less than that which you have just now stated?—I should have said, had I not been assured of this fact, that that was a rate of mortality that was not to be found any where in the world.

You stated one in forty-four as the average health in healthy districts; the question is, whether, in any particular districts, you have heard of the proportion being smaller than one in forty-four?—Yes; according to the last enumeration the mortality in Cardiganshire is only one in seventy-three, in Monmouthshire one in sixty-four, in Cornwall one in sixty-two, in Gloucestershire one in sixty-one; all the others are under one in sixty. The highest mortality is in the Metropolis and the aguish districts.

Would your surprize of the small mortality cease, if you were informed that no persons are employed under nine years of age, only fifty-nine of the number under ten at the larger factory, and perhaps not forty out of the number above forty years of age, and the factory situated in the healthful county of Ayr, with which you are acquainted?—That renders it somewhat less marvellous.

Have you the means of informing the Committee, what the general mortality is in healthy districts in this country, upon healthy persons between the age of ten and eighteen?—I had lately occasion to make enquiry about that. From some calculations I have made, I found that the mortality in England, between twenty and forty, was about one in eighty.

*   *   *

A deposition was later offered on the part of Charles Pennington, M.D., as a report on the health of the people employed in the mill at Papplewick.

Nottingham, 6th May 1816.

Gentlemen,

Having been desired to communicate to you, as delegates in London from the proprietors of cotton mills and factories in Nottingham and its neighbourhood, my opinion respecting the general state of health of the persons employed in the cotton mills in and near Papplewick, belonging to Mr. James Robinson and Son, I hereby certify to you and to the Honourable the Committee of the House of Commons, that for more than thirty years I have been very frequently called upon in my professional character to attend the family of Mr. Robinson, and the persons employed in his extensive manufactory; and that I have uniformly remarked the most humane attention and careful regard to the health, the morals and the comforts of all engaged in this concern; and that when under medical care, every thing, without any regard to its cost, has been always freely and largely afforded. Further, I may add, that during the greater part of this period, I have had a considerable practice in the town of Nottingham, in a very populous district, for many miles around it, and also in the Infirmary and Lunatic Asylum, amongst all classes and descriptions of people; and after a careful review of the more important circumstances connected with the health of the parties, my conviction is, that the persons employed in the cotton-spinning manufactories are as healthy and strong as any engaged in sedentary pursuits in general; more healthy and strong than the frame-work-knitter; and much more so than the shoemaker and the tailor.

I am, very respectfully, Gentlemen,
Your obedient Servant,
Charles Pennington, M.D.
Honorary Physician to the General Hospital,

Messrs. Stanton and Heygate.   and Physician to the Lunatic Asylum

Mr. Archibald Buchanan, a mill owner, also took the stand.

Do you know of any person whose health was beginning to fail, leaving the manufactory?—I have known many instances of that kind; and I have known many instances of persons of delicate health coming into the manufactory, as being an easy employment.

Did you ever know of a sickly or delicate child coming into the manufactory?—A great many.

And did they, from a more regular life and a more constant supply of food and regular habits, get better?—Their parents had difficulty in getting employment for them otherwise, and they were glad to get them into the works as being easy; there are some parts of it where they may either sit or stand; and there are many parts of the work where lame people can be employed; and gentlemen in the neighbourhood, and frequently parishes, make application to me to have these people taken in to obtain a subsistence.

And from these circumstances, particularly the material one of having a regular supply of good food, did you observe that those children improved in their health?—I have observed very great improvement from their getting good food.

*   *   *

Did you ever, in the course of your visits at the different manufactories, see any establishments . . . under better regulations than those of Messrs. Finlay & Company, and those of Messrs. Phillips & Company?—I suppose there are none better regulated, in general, than that of Messrs. Phillips & Company.

Or than that of Messrs. Finlay & Company?—I have great delicacy in saying that, I believe many others are equally well regulated. I would beg to state to the Committee, that when the girls grow up, we do not object to their going to service; we rather recommend it; they go away for six months, and twelve months; and if they let us know when they wish to return to the works again, we endeavour to employ them. Many of these young women get married, and of course we take no further account of them; after that, we do not enter the deaths of those people.

In the changes that took place in the year 1811, had you reason to think that a considerable proportion of those changes took place in consequence of your dismissing sick persons?—I know no instance of sick persons being dismissed; it must be understood, however, that when these persons become sickly, they go away; and they are received back into the works when they recover, if they are people of good character, and well behaved.

If those persons had quitted the works from sickness, and not quitted the village, would your attention have been directed to them, and would you have considered them as persons employed in the manufactory in your returns?—I certainly should.

Then have you any reason to believe, that on the change, to the extent of twenty persons, supposed to have taken place in 1811, more of those persons were sick, and that a greater proportion of deaths took place among them, than among the persons remaining in the factory?—I do not suppose there was a greater proportion.

Your supposition of course must depend upon the number out of the twenty who remained under your eye in the village?—I understand the twenty all to have gone away.

Do you mean, all to have gone away out of the village?—No; only to have left the works.

Is the account from which you have spoken, prepared by yourself, or by one of the principal persons under your direction?—It was prepared by myself, so far as I could obtain information; it is entered in the hand-writing of one of our clerks.

And has reference to every person employed, during the period you have spoken of, at your works?—At the time that these enquiries were made, and the number of deaths taken, we could have no contemplation of any investigation of this kind; they were taken for the satisfaction of those concerned, and they were taken accurately to the best of my knowledge; at the same time it is possible that a death or two might not be entered.

Have you a conviction of their general accuracy?—I believe it.

Have you any doubt of their accuracy?—I have no reason to doubt it.

Have you reason to suppose, that the years that have been selected were peculiarly healthy, or do you conceive them to be a fair specimen of the state of mortality in the village of Catrine?—The years are not selected, they are the last five years.

Do you suppose that the last four years to which your account refers, were peculiarly healthy, or that they are a fair specimen of the state of mortality in the village of Catrine?—I have no means of knowing the state of mortality in the village; it is a healthy situation, and I can only state that of late years; indeed it has been progressive: the people that we employ are becoming more healthy; that I attribute to a greater degree of cleanliness in the works, but especially to their getting liberal wages, and being well fed and clothed.

*   *   *

Do you know what proportion the persons employed in the manufactory bear to the whole population of the village?—The village contains something above 2,000.

Including those employed in the manufactory?—Yes.

Do you know any thing of the total number of deaths in the village?—I do not.

Do you mean to give to the Committee the impression, that the average number of deaths of the persons employed in the manufactory, at all resembles the total average number of deaths in the village?—I should think that the deaths belonging to the manufactory were less; I have been frequently told by the medical gentleman who attends our people, that in the course of his practice, he finds less disease existing with the people employed in the works, than in the general population of the surrounding country.

Do you mean to lead the Committee to apprehend, that the deaths, upon the remaining eleven hundred who live in the village, are in any thing resembling an equal proportion to that of the deaths in the manufactory?—I am of opinion that they are considerably more; I beg leave to state, that parents with a large family often come to the village and get their children employed; the parents frequently do little or nothing at home, and of course there are a smaller proportion of grown up people in our works than are to be found among the inhabitants of the village.

Those in your works are at the more healthy periods of life?—Yes.

*　　　*　　　*

In the population of the village, are the greater proportion of those not now in your works out of employment?—I have stated in my former evidence, that a great number of those who have formerly been employed in the mills have grown up and gone to other trades; a great number of them are masons, joiners, shoemakers, tailors, and in fact, engaged in every kind of trade almost.

And you have not observed, that those people who have been formerly employed in the works, have been affected in their health?—They are very similar to those who have been brought up in the country; and I mentioned also, that tradesmen generally prefer those brought up in the works to people from the country, on account of their having been brought up in industry, and having acquired a great degree of ingenuity.

*　　　*　　　*

MR. JOHN MOSS, CALLED IN, AND EXAMINED

Where do you live?—At Preston workhouse.

In Lancashire?—Yes.

What is your occupation?—My present occupation is that of governor of the workhouse.

Were you ever employed as the master of the apprentices at a cotton mill?—I was engaged to attend the apprentice-house at Backbarrow. I was over the children.

*   *   *

Up to what period were they apprenticed?—One-and-twenty.

What were the hours of work?—From five o'clock in the morning till eight at night.

Were fifteen hours in the day the regular hours of work?—Those were their regular hours of work.

Was that the regular time all the year through?—Yes.

What time was allowed for meals?—Half an hour for breakfast and half an hour for dinner.

*   *   *

Had they any refreshment in the afternoon?—Yes, they had their drinking taken to the mill; their bagging, they call it.

You mean luncheon?—Yes.

Did they work while they ate their afternoon refreshment?—Yes.

They had no cessation after dinner till eight o'clock at night?—No.

At what hour was the breakfast?—At seven in the morning; they came to their breakfast at seven o'clock, and then the bell rang for them at half past seven.

Did they leave the mill at breakfast time?—Yes, they always left the mill and came to the house.

What was the dinner hour?—Twelve o'clock.

And at what time did they return to the mill?—Half past twelve.

Did they, beyond working those fifteen hours, make up for any loss of time?—Yes, always.

Did the children actually work fourteen hours in the day?—Yes.

And one hour was allowed for the two meals, making fifteen hours in the whole?—Yes.

When the works were stopped for the repair of the mill, or for any want of cotton, did the children afterwards make up for the loss of that time?—Yes.

When making up lost time, how long did they continue working at night?— Till nine o'clock, and sometimes later; sometimes ten.

Was this before the Apprentice Bill or after?—It was last year, and it is in practice now.

How long were they making up lost time?—I have known them to be three weeks or more making up lost time.

Have you known them for three weeks together working from five in the morning till nine or ten at night, with the exception of the hour for meals?—Yes, I have.

What time did they rise from bed?—I always got up at half past four to get them ready to be at the mill by five.

How far was their sleeping room from the mill?—It might be not above a hundred yards; hardly so much.

Did they rise at half past four in the winter season?—They were always to be at the mill by five o'clock winter and summer, and never later.

Were there two mills?—Yes.

When you had only water for one mill, did the children work night and day?—When there was only water for one mill, one worked in the day and the other at night.

Have you ever known the children work all night on Saturday, until six o'clock on Sunday morning?—Yes, I have once; they have gone to work at eight o'clock on Saturday night, and stayed till six on Sunday morning.

At what hour on Sunday night did those children begin to work again? —They have begun at twelve o'clock on Sunday night again, and worked till five in the morning; then the other children for the day began at the other mill, and worked till eight at night.

Did they work as late on Saturday night as on other nights?—Always the same; I never knew any abatement.

Did any children work on the Sundays as cleaners of the machinery?— Yes.

Did they do this regularly?—Regularly every Sunday; I do not know that ever they missed one Sunday while I was there.

Through the year?—Yes.

How many hours did they work on a Sunday?—Their orders were from six till twelve.

Did you remonstrate against this?—Yes, I did.

Frequently?—Yes.

What was the consequence of your remonstrance?—It was never much better; there were not so many went to the mill; I believe that they went from their own accord sometimes, and I wished the book-keeper to give in a paper of the names of those who were to attend.

Did the children take it in rotation?—It was just according to what wanted cleaning.

Who gave orders what children were to work on a Sunday?—The book-keeper sent me a written note of the names of those who were to attend.

Did he give you a written order in consequence of your remonstrance? —Yes.

Do you remember any Sunday when they did not work while you were at the mills?—I do not remember one Sunday when they did not go to work.

If they had left off work a little earlier on Saturday, could not they have avoided the necessity of going to the mills on a Sunday?—Yes.

Were the children paid for the Sunday-work?—Yes.

Did the children ever attend church?—Yes.

Would the children rather get money by working on a Sunday than attend church?—I thought there was a motive, which made me put a stop to it, by having a written order who was to attend.

Did they absent themselves sometimes from church, under the pretence of going to the mill to clean the machinery?—Yes.

Did the overlookers ever give you any orders for the children to work till twelve o'clock on Saturday night?—Yes.

Did you remonstrate against this also?—Yes.

For what reason?—Because we had the children to wash and clean after they had done work on Saturday night, therefore it was late before we got to bed; but they have sometimes worked till ten, the whole of the children; and when they have been short of water, that set that went on to work at eight at night was worked till twelve.

Did the masters ever express any concern for such excessive labour?—No.

Was it at the desire of the proprietors of the mill, or of the overlookers, that the children worked till twelve o'clock on Saturday night?—It was the master of the mill that wished them to work till twelve o'clock at night, when they were short of water; but it was the overlookers that wished the whole of them to work till twelve o'clock at night, in order to make up lost time, that they might get done the sooner; the whole of them never did work together later than ten.

Were they very strict in keeping them to their time?—Yes.

Did the children sit or stand to work?—Stand.

The whole of their time?—Yes.

Were there any seats in the mill?—None.

Were they usually much fatigued at night?—Yes, some of them were very much fatigued.

Where did they sleep?—They slept in the apprentice-house.

Did you inspect their beds?—Yes, every night.

For what purpose?—Because there were always some of them missing, some sometimes might be run away, others sometimes I have found have been asleep in the mill.

Upon the mill-floor?—Yes.

Did the children frequently lie down upon the mill-floor at night when their work was over, and fall asleep before their supper?—I have found them frequently upon the mill-floors, after the time they should have been in bed.

At what time did they go to bed?—Nine o'clock was their hour, when they worked their usual time.

In summer time did you allow them to sit up a little later?—Yes, sometimes till half past nine.

Were any children injured by the machinery?—Very frequently.

Were their fingers often crushed?—Very often their fingers were caught; and one had his arm broken.

Were any of the children deformed?—Yes, several of them were deformed; there were two or three that were very crooked.

Do you know whether those children were straight when they first came to the mill?—They told me they were.

Who told you they were?—The children themselves.

Were any of the children in-kneed, or what is called knock-kneed?—Yes, there were ten or a dozen of them, I dare say, that were in-kneed.

Did you understand from them whether they were so when they came to the mill?—I do not know that they were.

Do you think they were not?—I am pretty sure some of them were not, but some of them were lame when they came.

Did the parish officers of the parishes to which they belonged, ever come to the mills to visit and inspect the children?—No; there was one from Liverpool; the overseer of Liverpool.

Do you remember his name?—Hardman, I believe.

Was there any other inspection by magistrates, or any other persons?—No, there was no magistrates ever came into the childrens house.

Is the mill in a healthy situation?—Very.

Remarkably so?—Yes.

As the children grew up, did they in general appear to be healthy, or otherwise?—There were some who were very healthy children, and there were others that were sickly looking.

What was their general appearance?—Their general appearance was as well as most of the farmers children, some of them; some of them looked sickly, but then they were not sick.

They appeared to be sick, but were not so?—Yes; we scarcely ever had any sickness in the house.

How many died during the year you were at the mill?—There was only one.

How were the children lodged?—They had very good lodgings when we left them.

Had they good lodgings when you first went there?—No.

Did you make any complaints of their bedding when you first went?—Yes.

Will you state to the Committee what was the condition of their bedding when you first went?—When I first went there; their bedding was very bad, they had only a blanket to lie on, and a thin blanket to lie at top, and a horse cover, and some of them were very bad.

Could they be preserved cleanly with sleeping only on blankets?—They were not altogether clean.

Did you make complaint of that?—Yes.

Did the parish officer from Liverpool complain of it?—Yes.

Was it in consequence of his complaints and yours, that the bedding was improved?—Yes, it was; we got after that sheets and covers for every bed, and there never were sheets for any bed in the house I believe, before.

Did they spin fine or coarse yarn at those mills?—Very coarse.

Were the rooms as warm as where they spin fine?—No, I believe not.

Do you understand that they require greater heat for fine threads?—I have heard them say so; they have no heat in their rooms in the summer, in the winter they have heat from steam.

Were the children fed well?—Very well.

Before your time at Backbarrow mill, were the children turned out on the high road to beg their way to their former parishes, when the former proprietor stopped payment?—I was informed they were.

Did you converse with any of the children that were so turned out?—Yes.

Were they taken from the mill in a cart, and then turned adrift near the sands on the Lancaster road?—Yes, I was informed they were.

Do you know what became of them afterwards?—There was one of them I heard was taken in at Caton factory, and employed there for some time; and I heard there were some of them taken into Lancaster workhouse.

Did you hear that the gentlemen of Lancaster complained of this inhumanity?—Yes.

Were any fetched back in consequence of these complaints?—Yes, I believe there were.

Were they then turned over to Messrs. Ainsworth the present proprietors?—Yes.

After they had served out their apprenticeship to Messrs. Ainsworth, were they not compelled to serve extra time, under the pretence that so much time was lost by being turned out on the road and obliged to go to Lancaster?—Yes, there was one boy out of his time while I was there, and when the day came his master said that he had to serve six weeks, I think, longer, in consequence of his having run away; he said he never had ran away, he was turned out, and he had worked at Caton factory, and they made him serve that time out; his name is Henry Carter.

Do you know of Messrs. Watson's apprentices being turned out in the same manner?—I have heard it said so, but I never knew anything of it.

Were the children bad in their morals?—Yes, they were.

How did they behave one to another?—They did not behave well one to another.

Who looked over them in the mill?—Generally the older apprentices were overlookers over the younger ones.

Did the bigger boys beat the others?—Yes.

Frequently?—Yes.

What was the general character of the children?—Very bad characters.

What was the reason you left the mill?—It was in consequence of their bad behaviour.

4   Evaluation of the Industrial Revolution

Thomas Babington Macaulay (1800–1859) is most generally remembered for his history of England in the seventeenth century. He was also an essayist of devastating wit and power. Nothing was more calculated to arouse his ire than an attack on the idea of progress; and Southey's romanticism seemed to him such an attack. This review reveals Macaulay at his polemical best.

FROM *Southey's Colloquies* BY T. B. MACAULAY

IT WOULD BE SCARCELY POSSIBLE for a man of Mr. Southey's talents and acquirements to write two volumes so large as those before us, which should be wholly destitute of information and amusement. Yet we do not remember to have read with so little satisfaction any equal quantity of matter, written by any man of real abilities. We have, for some time past, observed with great regret the strange infatuation which leads the Poet Laureate to abandon those departments of literature in which he might excel, and to lecture the public on sciences of which he has still the very alphabet to learn. He has now, we think, done his worst. The subject which he has at last undertaken to treat is one which demands all the highest intellectual and moral qualities of a philosophical statesman, an understanding at once comprehensive and acute, a heart at once upright and charitable. Mr. Southey brings to the task two faculties which were never, we believe, vouchsafed in measure so copious to any human being, the faculty of believing without a reason, and the faculty of hating without a provocation.

It is, indeed, most extraordinary, that a mind like Mr. Southey's, a mind richly endowed in many respects by nature, and highly cultivated by study, a mind which has exercised considerable influence on the most enlightened generation of the most enlightened people that ever existed, should be utterly destitute of the power of discerning truth from falsehood. Yet such is the

Critical and Historical Essays contributed to the Edinburgh Review by Lord Macaulay, I (1903), 205, 207, 215–8.

fact. Government is to Mr. Southey one of the fine arts. He judges of a theory, of a public measure, of a religion or a political party, of a peace or a war, as men judge of a picture or a statue, by the effect produced on his imagination. A chain of associations is to him what a chain of reasoning is to other men; and what he calls his opinions are in fact merely his tastes.

*   *   *

Now in the mind of Mr. Southey reason has no place at all, as either leader or follower, as either sovereign or slave. He does not seem to know what an argument is. He never uses arguments himself. He never troubles himself to answer the arguments of his opponents. It has never occurred to him, that a man ought to be able to give some better account of the way in which he has arrived at his opinions than merely that it is his will and pleasure to hold them. It has never occurred to him that there is a difference between assertion and demonstration, that a rumour does not always prove a fact, that a single fact, when proved, is hardly foundation enough for a theory, that two contradictory propositions cannot be undeniable truths, that to beg the question is not the way to settle it, or that when an objection is raised, it ought to be met with something more convincing than "scoundrel" and "blockhead."

*   *   *

We now come to the conversations which pass between Mr. Southey and Sir Thomas More, or rather between two Southeys, equally eloquent, equally angry, equally unreasonable, and equally given to talking about what they do not understand. Perhaps we could not select a better instance of the spirit which pervades the whole book than the passages in which Mr. Southey gives his opinion of the manufacturing system. There is nothing which he hates so bitterly. It is, according to him, a system more tyrannical than that of the feudal ages, a system of actual servitude, a system which destroys the bodies and degrades the minds of those who are engaged in it. He expresses a hope that the competition of other nations may drive us out of the field; that our foreign trade may decline; and that we may thus enjoy a restoration of national sanity and strength. But he seems to think that the extermination of the whole manufacturing population would be a blessing, if the evil could be removed in no other way.

Mr. Southey does not bring forward a single fact in support of these views; and, as it seems to us, there are facts which lead to a very different conclusion. In the first place, the poor-rate is very decidedly lower in the manufacturing than in the agricultural districts. If Mr. Southey will look over the Parliamentary returns on this subject, he will find that the amount of parochial relief required by the labourers in the different counties of England is almost exactly in inverse proportion to the degree in which the manufacturing system has been introduced into those counties. The returns for the years ending in March 1825, and in March 1828, are now before us. In the former year we find the poor-rate highest in Sussex, about twenty shillings to every inhabitant. Then come Buckinghamshire, Essex, Suffolk, Bedfordshire, Huntingdonshire, Kent, and Norfolk. In all these the rate is above fifteen shillings a head. We will not go through the whole. Even in Westmoreland and the North Riding of Yorkshire, the rate is at more than eight shillings. In Cumberland and Monmouthshire, the most fortunate of all the agricultural districts, it is at six shillings. But in the West Riding of Yorkshire, it is as low as five shillings; and when we come to Lancashire, we find it at four shillings, one fifth of what it is in Sussex. The returns of the year ending in March 1828 are a little, and but a little, more unfavourable to the manufacturing districts. Lancashire, even in that season of distress, required a smaller poor-rate than any other district, and little more than one fourth of the poor-rate raised in Sussex. Cumberland alone, of the agricultural districts, was as well off as the West Riding of Yorkshire. These facts seem to indicate that the manufacturer is both in a more comfortable and in a less dependent situation than the agricultural labourer.

As to the effect of the manufacturing system on the bodily health, we must beg leave to estimate it by a standard far too low and vulgar for a mind so imaginative as that of Mr. Southey, the proportion of births and deaths. We know that, during the growth of this atrocious system, this new misery, to use the phrases of Mr. Southey, this new enormity, this birth of a portentous age, this pest which no man can approve whose heart is not seared or whose understanding has not been darkened, there has been a great diminution of mortality, and that this diminution has been greater in the manufacturing towns than any where else. The mortality still is, as it always was, greater in towns than in the country. But the difference has diminished in an extraordinary degree. There is the best reason to believe that the annual mortality of Manchester, about the middle of the last century, was one in twenty-eight. It is now reckoned at one in forty-five. In Glasgow and Leeds a similar improvement has taken place. Nay, the rate of mortality in those three great capitals of the manufacturing districts is now considerably less than it was, fifty years ago, over England and Wales, taken together, open country and all. We might with some plausibility maintain that the people live longer because they are better fed, better lodged, better clothed, and better attended in sickness, and that these improvements are owing to that increase of national wealth which the manufacturing system has produced.

Much more might be said on this subject. But to what end? It is not from bills of mortality and statistical tables that Mr. Southey has learned his political creed. He cannot stoop to study the history of the system which he abuses, to strike the balance between the good and evil which it has produced, to compare district with district, or generation with generation. We will give his own reason for his opinion, the only reason which he gives for it, in his own words:—

"We remained awhile in silence looking upon the assemblage of dwellings below. Here, and in the adjoining hamlet of Millbeck, the effects of manufactures and of agriculture may be seen and compared. The old cottages are such as the poet and the painter equally delight in beholding. Substantially built of the native stone without mortar, dirtied with no white lime, and their long low roofs covered with slate, if they had been raised by the magic of some indigenous Amphion's music, the materials could not have adjusted themselves more beautifully in accord with the surrounding scene; and time has still further harmonized them with weather stains, lichens, and moss, short grasses, and short fern, and stone-plants of various kinds. The ornamented chimneys, round or square, less adorned than those which, like little turrets, crest the houses of the Portuguese peasantry; and yet not less happily suited to their place, the hedge of clipt box beneath the windows, the rose-bushes beside the door, the little patch of flower ground, with its tall hollyhocks in front; the garden beside, the beehives, and the orchard with its bank of daffodils and snow-drops, the earliest and the profusest in these parts, indicate in the owners some portion of ease and leisure, some regard to neatness and comfort, some sense of natural, and innocent, and healthful enjoyment. The new cottages of the manufacturers are upon the manufacturing pattern—naked, and in a row.

"How is it," said I, "that every thing which is connected with manufactures presents such features of unqualified deformity? From the largest of Mammon's temples down to the poorest hovel in which his helotry are stalled, these edifices have all one character. Time will not mellow them; nature will neither clothe nor conceal them; and they will remain always as offensive to the eye as to the mind."

Here is wisdom. Here are the principles on which nations are to be governed. Rose-bushes and poor-rates, rather than steam-engines and independence. Mortality and cottages with weather-stains, rather than health and long life with edifices which time cannot mellow. We are told, that our age has invented atrocities beyond the imagination of our fathers; that society has been brought into a state compared with which extermination would be a blessing; and all because the dwellings of cotton-spinners are naked and rectangular. Mr. Southey has found out a way, he tells us, in which the effects of manufactures and agriculture may be compared. And what is this way? To stand on a hill, to look at a cottage and a factory, and to see which is the prettier. Does Mr. Southey think that the body of the English peasantry live, or ever lived, in substantial or ornamented cottages, with box-hedges, flower-gardens, beehives, and orchards? If not, what is his parallel worth? We despise those mock philosophers, who think that they serve the cause of science by depreciating literature and the fine arts. But if any thing could excuse their narrowness of mind, it would be such a book as this. It is not strange that, when one enthusiast makes the picturesque the test of political good, another should feel inclined to proscribe altogether the pleasures of taste and imagination.

> *The work from which this selection is taken has long been regarded as the standard work in its field. First published in 1906, it utilized the full panoply of the historian's art and resources to reach an essentially negative judgment on the immediate effect of the Industrial Revolution on the working men who were caught up in it.*

FROM *The Industrial Revolution in the Eighteenth Century* BY PAUL MANTOUX

INTERMIXED WITH THE MEN'S GRIEVANCES against machinery was their hatred of the factory. The feeling of repulsion which it aroused is easily understood, as, to a man used to working at home, or in a small workshop, factory discipline was intolerable. Even though at home he had to work long hours to make up for the lowness of his wage, yet he could begin and stop at will, and without regular hours. He could divide up the work as he chose, come and go, rest for a moment, and even, if he chose, be idle for days together. Even if he worked in the master-manufacturer's house, his freedom, though less complete, was still fairly great. He did not feel that there was an impassable gulf between himself and his employer, and their relations still retained something of a personal character. He was not bound by hard and fast regulations, as relentless and as devoid of sympathy as the machinery itself. He saw little difference between going to a factory and entering a barracks or a prison. This is why the first generation of manufacturers often found real difficulty in obtaining labour. They would have found it still more difficult, had there not been a floating population available, which the changes in rural conditions were driving from agriculture into industry and from the country to the towns. Other workers were attracted from the poorer parts of the Kingdom, from the bogs of Ireland and from the mountains of Scotland or Wales. Thus the origin of factory labour is to be found partly in a class of men forcibly uprooted from their employment, and partly among populations to whom industry offered better opportunities than did their former employment.

From *The Industrial Revolution in the Eighteenth Century,* rev. ed. (1928), pp. 419–28, 486–9, by Paul Mantoux, translated by Marjorie Vernon. Reprinted by permission of Harcourt, Brace & World, Inc., Mrs. Mathilde Mantoux, and Jonathan Cape Ltd., London.

In the textile trades the manufacturers found another way out of the difficulty, by resorting largely to women and child labour. Spinning was quickly learned and needed little strength, while for certain processes the small size of the children and their delicacy of touch made them the best aids to the machines. They were preferred, too, for other and more conclusive reasons. Their weakness made them docile, and they were more easily reduced to a state of passive obedience than grown men. They were also very cheap. Sometimes they were given a trifling wage, which varied between a third and a sixth of an adult wage; and sometimes their only payment was food and lodging. Lastly they were bound to the factory by indentures of apprenticeship, for at least seven years, and usually until they were twenty-one. It was obviously to the spinners' interest to employ as many as possible and thus to reduce the number of workmen. The first Lancashire factories were full of children. Sir Robert Peel had over a thousand in his workshops at once.

The majority of these wretched children were paupers, supplied (one might almost say sold) by the parishes where they belonged. Especially during the first period of machine industry, when factories were built outside, and often far from, the towns, manufacturers would have found it impossible to recruit the labour they needed from the immediate neighbourhood. And the parishes on their side were only too anxious to get rid of their paupers. Regular bargains, beneficial to both parties, if not to the children, who were dealt with as mere merchandise, were entered into between the spinners on the one hand and the Poor Law authorities on the other. Lots of fifty, eighty or a hundred children were supplied and sent like cattle to the factory, where they remained imprisoned for many years. Certain parishes drove even better bargains and stipulated that the buyer should take idiots in the proportion of one to every twenty children sent. At the beginning, these "parish apprentices" were the only children employed in the factories. The workmen, very justifiably, refused to send their own. But unfortunately this resistance did not last long, as they were soon driven by want to a step which at first had so much horrified them.

The only extenuating circumstance in the painful events which we have now to recount as shortly as we can, was that forced child labour was no new evil. In the domestic system of manufacture, children were exploited as a matter of course. Among the Birmingham ironmongers, apprenticeship began at seven years of age. Among the weavers of the North and the South-west, children worked at five or even four years old, as soon in fact as they were considered capable of attention and obedience. Far from regarding this with indignation, men at that time thought it an admirable system. Yarranton recommended the establishment of "industrial schools" such as he had seen in Germany. There, two hundred little girls, under a matron's rod, sat spinning without a moment's relaxation and in complete silence, and were beaten if they did not spin quickly or well enough: "In these parts I speak of, a man that has most children lives best; whereas here he that has most is poorest. There the children enrich the father, but here beggar him." When Defoe visited Halifax, he was lost in admiration at the sight of four-year-old children earning their living like grown-up people. William Pitt's statement on child labour, which Michelet, with his usual exaggeration of sentiment and language, quoted against him as though it were a crime, was only a common-place reference to an accepted opinion.

It might be said that in the earlier forms of industry the child was at any rate an apprentice in the true sense, for he learned a trade, instead of merely being a part of the plant, as he was in the factory. But real apprenticeship could only begin when the child was old enough to benefit by it, and therefore for several years the child could only be a workman's drudge, paid either nothing or next to nothing. It might also be said that the conditions under which the child lived were less unfavourable to its physical development; but, with regard to hygiene, we know only too well the condition of the domestic workshop. Was it kindly treated and not overworked? Under the sting of necessity, parents were often the most exacting, if not the harshest of taskmasters.

But, even with these reservations, we must acknowledge that the fate of these parish apprentices, in the early spinning mills, was particularly miserable. Completely at the mercy of their employers, kept in isolated buildings, far from anyone who might take pity on their sufferings, they endured a cruel servitude. Their working day was limited only by their complete exhaustion, and lasted fourteen, sixteen and even eighteen hours. The foreman, whose wages were dependent on the amount of work done in each workshop, did not permit them to relax their efforts for a minute. In most factories forty minutes were allowed for the chief or the only meal of the day, and of these about twenty were taken up in cleaning the machines. In some factories work went on ceaselessly day and night, so that the machines might never stop. In such cases, the children were divided up into shifts, and "the beds never got cold." Accidents were very common, especially towards the end of the over-long day, when the exhausted children almost fell asleep at their work. The tale never ended of fingers cut off and limbs crushed in the wheels.

Discipline was savage, if the word discipline can be applied to such indescribable brutality, and sometimes such refined cruelty, as was exercised at will on defenceless creatures. The well-known catalogue of the sufferings of the factory apprentice, Robert Blincoe, makes one sick with horror. At Lowdham (near Nottingham), whither he was sent in 1799 with a batch of about eighty other boys and girls, they were only whipped. It is true that the whip was in use from morning till night, not only as a punishment for the slightest fault, but also to stimulate industry and to keep them awake when they were dropping with weariness. But at the factory at Litton matters were very different. There, the employer, one Ellice Needham, hit the children with his fists and with a riding whip, he kicked them, and one of his little attentions was to pinch their ears until his nails met through the flesh. The foremen were even worse, and one of them, Robert Woodward, used to devise the most ingenious tortures. It was he who was responsible for such inventions as hanging Blincoe up by his wrists over a machine at work, so that he was obliged to keep his knees bent up, making him work almost naked in winter, with heavy weights on his shoulders, and filing down his teeth. The wretched child had been so knocked about that his scalp was one sore all over. By way of curing him, his hair was torn out by means of a cap of pitch. If the victims of these horrors tried to escape, their feet were put in irons. Many tried to commit suicide, and one girl, who took advantage of a moment when the supervision relaxed and threw herself into the river, thus regained her freedom: she was sent away, as her employer "was afraid the example might be contagious."

Of course, not all factories witnessed such scenes, but they were less rare than their incredible horror would lead one to suppose, and were repeated until a system of strict control was set up. Even if they had not been ill-treated, excessive labour, lack of sleep and the nature of the work forced on children during the critical period of their growth, would have been quite enough to ruin their health and deform their bodies. The food, too, was often bad and insufficient. They had black bread, oatmeal porridge and rancid bacon. At Litton Mill the apprentices used to struggle with the pigs fattening in the yard, in order to get some of the food in their troughs. The factories were usually unhealthy, as their builders cared as little for health as they did for beauty. The ceilings were low in order to economize as much space as possible, the windows were narrow and almost always closed. In the cotton mills, fluff filled the air and gave rise to serious lung diseases. In flax-spinning mills, where wet spinning was usual, the air was saturated with moisture and the workers' clothes were dripping wet. Overcrowding in unventilated rooms, where the atmosphere was further vitiated by candle smoke at night, favoured the spreading of a contagious disorder resembling prison fever. The first cases of this "factory fever" broke out near Manchester in 1784. It very soon spread to nearly all the industrial districts and there were many deaths. Lastly, the promiscuity of both workshops and dormitories gave scope for immorality, and this was, unfortunately, encouraged by the bad behaviour of some of the employers and foremen, who took advantage of it to satisfy their low instincts. Thus to a puritan conscience, the factory, with its mixture of depravity and suffering, of barbarity and vice, offered a perfect picture of hell.

Among those who lived through the cruel period of apprenticeship, many bore its brand for life in the shape of crooked backs, and limbs deformed by rickets or mutilated by accidents with machinery. With "flaccid features, a stunted growth, very often tumid bellies they were already marked down as the victims of all the infections to which, during their later life, they were but too frequently exposed. Their moral and intellectual condition was no better. They left the factory ignorant and corrupt. During their miserable period of servitude not only did they receive no teaching of any kind, but in spite of the formal clauses of their indenture of apprenticeship, they did not even acquire enough technical knowledge to enable them to earn their living. They had learned nothing beyond the mechanical routine to which they had been bound during so many long hard years, and they were thus condemned to remain mere slaves, tied to the factory as of old the serf to the soil.

It must not be assumed that the status of all workers under the factory system was like that of the apprentices in the spinning mills. But, even though adults were not treated with quite the same revolting cruelty, their life in the factory was hard enough. They, too, suffered from too many working hours, from overcrowded and unhealthy workshops, and from tyrannical foremen and overseers. With them, the despotic employer, instead of physical violence, resorted to fraud; one of the most frequent abuses of which the workmen had to complain was that, in order to lengthen the working day, of which every minute meant money to the employer, they were literally robbed of their rest hours. During the dinner hour, the speed of the factory clock appeared miraculously to accelerate, so that work was resumed five or ten minutes before the hour had actually struck. Sometimes the means used to the same end were even simpler and less hypocritical: the meal times and closing times were at the discretion of the employer, and the workers were forbidden to carry watches.

Here we come to the real cause of the evils attributed to machine industry, namely the absolute and uncontrolled power of the capitalist. In this, the heroic age of great undertakings, it was acknowledged, admitted and even proclaimed with brutal candour. It was the employer's own business, he did as he chose, and did not consider that any other justification of his conduct was necessary. He owed his employees wages, and, once those were paid, the men had no further claim on him: put shortly, this was the attitude of the employer as to his rights and his duties. A cotton spinner, on being asked whether he did anything to help sick apprentices, answered: "When we engage a child, it is with the approbation of the parents, and it is an engagement to give a certain quantity of money for a certain quantity of labour. If the labour is not performed, the child is supported by the parents. —Then there is no security afforded to the child, that in sickness the master will support it?—It is an act of bounty in the master." Pure bounty, indeed, on which it was wiser not to count. The same man, when questioned as to why he had decided to stop his machinery at night, explained that he did it in order to allow water to accumulate in a tank, as the stream of the neighbouring river was insufficient: "Then if the stream had been more ample, you would have continued your night work?—As long as the trade had been sufficiently lucrative.—Then there is nothing now to restrain you from working day and night, but want of water or want of trade?—I know of no law to restrain me for so doing: I never heard of any." This was unanswerable, so long as the law remained unchanged.

*   *   *

In the first decade of the nineteenth century, which closes the period we set out to study, the industrial revolution was far from being completed. The use of machinery was still limited to certain industries, and in these industries to certain specialities or certain districts. Side by side with great metal works such as Soho and Coalbrookdale the small workshops of the Birmingham toyman and of the Sheffield cutlers continued to exist, and survived for many decades. Side by side with the Lancashire cotton mills and the West Riding woollen mills, thousands of weavers went on working at home on their old hand looms. Steam, which was to multiply and generalize the results of all other mechanical inventions, had hardly begun its triumphant progress. Nevertheless the modern industrial system did already exist, with all its essential features, and it is possible to detect, in the developments which had taken place at that time, the main characteristics of the great change.

From the technical point of view the industrial revolution consists in the invention and use of processes which make it possible to speed up and constantly to increase production: some are mechanical processes, as in the textile industries, others chemical, as in the metal-working industries; they help either to prepare the raw material, or to determine the form of the finished product, and the phrase machine industry is inadequate to the variety and to the possibilities offered by such developments. The invention of such processes (at least in the beginning) owed little to conclusions drawn from purely scientific discoveries. It is established fact that most of the first inventors were anything but scientists. They were technical men who, being faced with a practical problem, used their natural faculties and their expert knowledge of the habits and needs of the industry to solve it. Highs, Crompton, Hargreaves, Dudley, Darby and Cort were men of this type. A few others, such as Wyat and Cartwright, undertook their researches instinctively and out of pure curiosity, without either scientific or professional training. Under the pressure of necessity, and on purely concrete data, they set to work without a definite plan, and only reached their goal after much groping in the dark. They represent economic necessity, silently and powerfully moulding men to its will, overcoming obstacles and forging its own instruments. Science came later, and brought its immense reserves of power to bear on the development which had already begun, thus giving at once to partial developments in different industries a common direction and a common speed. This is specially noticeable in the case of Watt and the steam engine. Thus two streams from different sources met, and though it was to their combined power that the industrial revolution owed its actual size and strength, yet the change had already begun and its first results were conspicuous.

From the economic point of view, the industrial revolution is characterized by the concentration of capital and the growth of large undertakings, the existence and working of which, from being only exceptional, came to be the normal conditions of industry. Though, not without reason, this concentration is often considered as the result of technical inventions, yet to a certain extent it preceded such inventions. It was essentially a commercial phenomenon, and was connected with the gradual hold obtained by merchants over industry. Not only was it accompanied, but it was also prepared, by the expansion of trade and credit. Its necessary conditions were internal security, the development of communications and of maritime trade. The historical transition between the master craftsman of the middle ages and the modern industrialist was provided by the merchant manufacturer. We find him at first, so to speak, on the margin of industry, with the sole function of linking up producers with markets which were becoming too large and too distant for them. Later on, as his capital grew and the manufacturer came to rely on him more and more, he became the master of production, and finally the owner of all raw material, buildings and equipment, while independent workmen were degraded to the rank of mere wage-earners. This concentration of the means of production in the hands of capitalists who were more concerned with trade than with industry is a fact of paramount importance. No doubt "manufacture," with the great number of men it employed, the highly specialized division of its labour, and its many likenesses to the factory system, was a more striking fact, but it played a much smaller part in the evolution of industry. It marked a stage on the road, but a stage no sooner reached than passed. Economists, studying this evolution, have conceived and described it as a simple development, one phase following another like the different parts of a geometrical curve. But to the eyes of the historian a movement of such complexity is more like a river, which does not always flow at the same pace, but sometimes slackens its course, sometimes rushes on, now running through narrow gorges and now spreading out over the plain, now breaking up into many divergent branches, and now winding about, so that it seems to curve back on itself. Merely to enumerate the different points it passes by, is not to describe it. To do this, we must follow, step by step, its varied winding course, which in spite of its changes of direction, remains continuous like the slope which bears it to its end.

From the social point of view, the industrial revolution had such extensive and profound results that it would be presumptuous for us to attempt to summarize them in a short formula. Even though, unlike political revolutions, it did not actually alter the legal form of society, yet it modified its very substance. It gave birth to social classes whose progress and mutual opposition fill the history of our times. It would be easy, by quoting some of the facts mentioned in this very book, to try and show that, in this respect, there has been no revolution, that the same social classes were already in existence, that their opposition had begun long before, its nature and cause always remaining the same. One of the objects we have always kept in mind was precisely to show the continuity of the historical process underlying even the most rapid changes. None of these changes took place suddenly, as by a miracle, but each of them had been expected, prepared and outlined before it actually took place. It would be an equal error either to undervalue those preliminaries, or to take them for what they only foreshadowed. We know that there were machines before the era of machinery, "manufacture" before factories, combinations and strikes before the formation of industrial capitalism and of the "factory proletariat." But, in the slow-moving mass of society, a new element does not make itself felt immediately. And we have not only to note its presence, but its relation to its environment and, as it were, the space it occupies, in history. The industrial revolution is precisely the expansion of undeveloped forces, the sudden growth and blossoming of seeds which had for many years lain hidden or asleep.

After the beginning of the nineteenth century the growth of the factory system was visible to all. It was already influencing the distribution, as well as the material condition, of the population. To the factory system were due the importance and sudden prosperity of districts such as Lancashire, South Wales and part of the Lowlands of Scotland, which, until then, had been considered as being among the least prosperous parts of the country. It was the factory system which, following on the redistribution of landed property, quickened the migration of the rural population towards the factories. When the census of 1811 was taken, sixty or seventy per cent. of the inhabitants in the counties of Middlesex, Warwickshire, Yorkshire and Lancashire were employed in trade or industry, and at least fifty per cent. of those of Cheshire, Leicestershire, Nottinghamshire and Staffordshire. In these new centres, full of such intense activity, with their contrasting extremes of wealth and poverty, the data of the social problem, much as we know them to-day, could already be descried. The moment was not far off when that problem was to be defined for the first time by Robert Owen, in his *Letter to the Manufacturers of England* and his *Observations on the Consequences of the Factory System*. And he spoke not for England alone, but for all the nations of the West, for while the factory system continued to develop in the country of its birth, it had already begun to spread to other countries. It had made its appearance on the Continent, and from that time onward its history was no longer English but European—until it extended to the whole world.

The Hammonds, both educated at Oxford, could find little good in the Industrial Revolution. To them, it was comparable to slavery, and they make their case with skill and verve.

FROM *The Rise of Modern Industry*

BY JOHN L. AND BARBARA HAMMOND

ROME IMPORTED SLAVES to work in Italy: Englishmen counted it one of the advantages of the slave trade that it discouraged the competition of British colonists with British manufacturers. For the slaves were chiefly needed for industries like sugar planting, in which Englishmen at home were not engaged. Thus it might be argued that England had escaped the fate of Rome and that she so used the slave trade as to make it a stimulus rather than a discouragement to native energy and skill.

Yet England did not escape the penalty. For it was under this shadow that the new industrial system took form and grew, and the immense power with which invention had armed mankind was exercised at first under conditions that reproduced the degradation of the slave trade. The factory system was not like war or revolution a deliberate attack on society: it was the effort of men to use will, energy, organization and intelligence for the service of man's needs. But in adapting this new power to the satisfaction of its wants England could not escape from the moral atmosphere of the slave trade: the atmosphere in which it was the fashion to think of men as things.

In the days of the guilds the workman was regarded as a person with some kind of property or status; the stages by which this character is restricted to a smaller and smaller part of the working classes, and more and more of the journeymen and apprentices fall into a permanently inferior class have been described by historians. In the early nineteenth century the workers, as a class, were looked upon as so much labour power to be used at the discretion of, and under conditions imposed by, their masters; not as men and women who are entitled to some voice in the arrangements of their life and work. The use of child labour on a vast scale had an important bearing on the growth of this temper.

The children of the poor were regarded as workers long before the Industrial Revolution. Locke suggested that they should begin work at three; Defoe rejoiced to see that in the busy homes of the Yorkshire clothiers "scarce anything above four years old, but its hands were sufficient for its own support." The new industrial system provided a great field for the

John L. and Barbara Hammond, *The Rise of Modern Industry* (1925), pp. 194–5, 196–9, 200–1, 210, 211–3, 217–20, 222–4, 226–32. Reprinted by permission of Methuen & Co. Ltd., London.

employment of children, and Pitt himself, speaking in 1796, dwelt on this prospect with a satisfaction strange to modern minds, and disturbing even to some who heard him. One of the most elaborate of all Bentham's fantasies was his scheme for a great series of Industry Houses, 250 in number, each to hold 2,000 persons, for whose work, recreation, education, and marriage most minute regulations were laid down. An advantage he claimed for his system was that it would enable the apprentices to marry at "the earliest period compatible with health," and this was made possible by the employment of children. "And to what would they be indebted for this gentlest of all revolutions? To what, but to economy? Which dreads no longer the multiplication of man, now that she has shown by what secure and unperishable means infant man, a drug at present so much worse than worthless, may be endowed with an indubitable and universal value." Infant man soon became in the new industrial system what he never was in the old, the basis of a complicated economy.

Most children under the old domestic system worked at home under their parents' eyes, but in addition to such children there were workhouse children, who were hired out by overseers to every kind of master or mistress. Little care was taken to see that they were taught a trade or treated with humanity by their employers, and though London magistrates like Fielding did what they could to protect this unhappy class, their state was often a kind of slavery. The number of children on the hands of the London parishes was largely increased in the latter part of the eighteenth century, because an Act of Parliament, passed in 1767 in consequence of the exertions of Jonas Hanway, compelled the London parishes to board out their young children, and to give a bonus to every nurse whose charge survived. Until this time very few parish pauper children grew up to trouble their betters.

The needs of the London workhouses on the one hand, and those of the factory on the other, created a situation painfully like the situation in the West Indies. The Spanish employers in America wanted outside labour, because the supply of native labour was deficient in quantity and quality. The new cotton mills placed on streams in solitary districts were in the same case. The inventions had found immense scope for child labour, and in these districts there were only scattered populations. In the workhouses of large towns there was a quantity of child labour available for employment, that was even more powerless and passive in the hands of a master than the stolen negro, brought from his burning home to the hold of a British slave ship. Of these children it could be said, as it was said of the negroes, that their life at best was a hard one, and that their choice was often the choice between one kind of slavery and another. So the new industry which was to give the English people such immense power in the world borrowed at its origin from the methods of the American settlements.

How closely the apologies for this child serf system followed the apologies for the slave trade can be seen from Romilly's description of a speech made in the House of Commons in 1811. "Mr. Wortley, who spoke on the same side, insisted that, although in the higher ranks of society it was true that to cultivate the affections of children for their family was the source of every virtue, yet that it was not so among the lower orders, and that it was a benefit to take them away from their miserable and depraved parents. He said too that it would be highly injurious to the public to put a stop to the binding of so many apprentices to the cotton manufacturers, as it must necessarily raise the price of labour and enhance the price of cotton manufactured goods."

It was not until 1816 that Parliament would consent to reform this system of transportation. In that year a Bill that had been repeatedly introduced by Mr. Wilbraham Bootle passed both Houses, and it was made illegal for London children to be apprenticed more than forty miles away from their parish. But by this time the problem had changed, for steam-power had superseded water-power and mills could be built in towns; in these towns there were parents who were driven by poverty to send their children to the mills. In the early days of the factory system there had been a prejudice against sending children to the mill, but the hand-loom weaver had been sinking steadily from the beginning of the century into deeper and deeper poverty, and he was no longer able to maintain himself and his family. Sometimes too an adult worker was only given work on condition that he send his child to the mill. Thus the apprentice system was no longer needed. It had carried the factories over the first stage and at the second they could draw on the population of the neighbourhood.

These children, who were commonly called "free-labour children," were employed from a very early age. Most of them were piecers: that is they had to join together or piece the threads broken in the several roving or spinning machines. But there were tasks less skilled than these, and Robert Owen said that many children who were four or five years old were set to pick up waste cotton on the floor. Their hours were those of the apprentice children. They entered the mill gates at five or six in the morning and left them again at seven or eight at night. They had half an hour for breakfast and an hour for dinner, but even during meal hours they were often at work cleaning a standing machine; Fielden calculated that a child following the spinning machine could walk twenty miles in the twelve hours. Oastler was once in the company of a West Indian slave-master and three Bradford Spinners. When the slave-master heard what were the children's hours he declared: "I have always thought myself disgraced by being the owner of slaves, but we never in the West Indies thought it possible for any human being to be so cruel as to require a child of nine years old to work twelve and a half hours a day."

This terrible evil fastened itself on English life as the other fastened itself on the life of the Colonies. Reformers had an uphill struggle to get rid of its worst abuses. Throughout this long struggle the apologies for child labour were precisely the same as the apologies for the slave trade. Cobbett put it in 1833 that the opponents of the Ten Hours Bill had discovered that

England's manufacturing supremacy depended on 30,000 little girls. This was no travesty of their argument. The champions of the slave trade pointed to the £70,000,000 invested in the sugar plantations, to the dependence of our navy on our commerce, and to the dependence of our commerce on the slave trade. This was the argument of Chatham in one generation and Rodney in another. When Fox destroyed the trade in 1806 even Sir Robert Peel complained that we were philosophizing when our looms were idle, and George Rose, that the Americans would take up the trade, and that Manchester, Stockport and Paisley would starve. . . .

The argument for child labour followed the same line. In the one case the interests of Liverpool, in the other those of Lancashire, demanded of the nation that it should accept one evil in order to escape from another. Cardwell, afterwards the famous army reformer, talked of the great capital sunk in the cotton industry and the danger of the blind impulse of humanity. Sir James Graham thought that the Ten Hours Bill would ruin the cotton industry and with it the trade of the country. The cotton industry had taken the place in this argument that had been held by the navy in the earlier controversy. Our population, which had grown so rapidly in the Industrial Revolution, was no longer able to feed itself: the food it bought was paid for by its manufactures: those manufactures depended on capital: capital depended on profits: profits depended on the labour of the boys and girls who enabled the manufacturer to work his mills long enough at a time to repay the cost of the plant and to compete with his foreign rivals. This was the circle in which the nation found its conscience entangled.

The life of man had been regulated before by the needs of a particular order or the pattern of a particular society: the government of king or church or lord had defined narrow limits within which a man was to run his course. The new master was a world force, for this economy could make its profits, so it was believed, where it chose, and when Englishmen rebelled against its rule it would seek its gains and bestow its blessings elsewhere. This way of looking at the new industrial system put man at the mercy of his machines, for if the new power was not made man's servant, it was bound to become his master. If at every point the governing claim was not man's good but the needs of the machine, it was inevitable that man's life and the quality of his civilization should be subordinated to this great system of production.

Nobody could argue that the ordinary worker before the Industrial Revolution was a free man, whether he was a peasant in the country or a journeyman in the town, but the age which watched the change from domestic to factory industry in Lancashire and Yorkshire could see that a great many men and women lost what they had possessed of initiative and choice.

* * *

What happened at the Industrial Revolution was that all the restraints that the law imposed on workmen in particular industries, were standardized into a general law for the whole of the expanding world of industry, and all the regulations and laws that recognized him as a person with rights were withdrawn or became inoperative. The workman, as we have seen, lost one by one the several Acts of Parliament that gave him protection from his master in this or that industry. His personal liberty was circumscribed by a series of Acts, beginning with the Act of 1719, which made it a crime for him to take his wits and his skills into another country: a law that applied to the artisan but not to the inventor. At the end of the century the masters were given complete control of their workmen, by a Combination Act which went far beyond the Acts against combinations already on the Statute book. By the Combination Act of 1799 any workman who combined with any other workman to seek an improvement in his working conditions was liable to be brought before a single magistrate—it might be his own employer—and sent to prison for three months. This Act, the chief authors of which were Pitt and Wilberforce, was modified next year, when Parliament decided that two magistrates were necessary to form a court, and that a magistrate who was a master in the trade affected should not try offences, but these modifications did not affect in practice the power that the law gave to employers. Under cover of this Act it often happened that a master would threaten his workman with imprisonment or service in the fleet in order to compel him to accept the wages he chose to offer. In 1824 Place and Hume, taking advantage of the reaction from the worst of the panics produced by the French Revolution, managed to carry the repeal of the Combination Laws. Next year, after their repeal had been celebrated by an outburst of strikes, a less stringent law was put in their place. But the view of the new system as a beneficent mechanism which the mass of men must serve with a blind and unquestioning obedience was firmly rooted in the temper of the time, and thus anyone who tried to think of Englishmen in the spirit of Burke's description of a man, found himself strangely out of tune in a world where the workman was refused education, political rights and any voice in the conditions of his employment.

"At Tyldesley," it was said in a pamphlet published during a strike, "they work fourteen hours per day, including the nominal hour for dinner; the door is locked in working hours, except half an hour at tea time; the workpeople are not allowed to send for water to drink, in the hot factory: and even the rain water is locked up, by the master's order, otherwise they would be happy to drink even that." In this mill a shilling fine was inflicted on a spinner found dirty, or found washing, heard whistling or found with his window open in a temperature of 84 degrees. The men who were thrust into this discipline, however hard and bare their lives, had been accustomed to work in their own homes at their own time. The sense of servitude that was impressed on the age by this discipline, by the methods of government, the look of the towns and the absence of choice or initiative in the lives of the mass of the work-people, was strengthened by the spectacle of the new power. "While the engine runs," wrote an observer, "the people must work—

men, women and children yoked together with iron and steam. The animal machine—breakable in the best case, subject to a thousand sources of suffering—is chained fast to the iron machine which knows no suffering and no weariness."

"Two centuries ago not one person in a thousand wore stockings; one century ago not one person in five hundred wore them; now not one person in a thousand is without them." This sentence from *The Results of Machinery* (1831), one of the publications of the Society for the Diffusion of Useful Knowledge, illustrates a feature of the Industrial Revolution that made a profound impression on the imagination of the time. When capital was applied to production on a large scale, it gained its profits by producing in bulk; producing, that is, for mass consumption. Energy and brains were now devoted to satisfying, not the luxurious taste of the classes that were served by the commerce of medieval Europe, but the needs of the poor consumer.

It was natural for the age that witnessed the first triumphs of the new system to worship production for profit. This great addition to the wealth of the world seemed to follow automatically when men were left to acquire at their pleasure. Swift success is a dazzling spectacle, and the new industrial system provided a new miracle every day. . . .

The English people, from the whole tone and cast of its thought and politics, was specially liable to be swept off its balance by this revolution. The positive enthusiasms of the time were for science and progress: for material development and individual liberty. The restraints of custom, tradition and religion had never been so frail over the classes that held power. In the Middle Ages the Church had laid a controlling or checking hand on manners: the Guilds had hampered individual enterprise by a corporate discipline. But the Church of the eighteenth century was merely part of the civil order, without standards, authority or conscience of its own; the Guilds were dead, and their successors stood not for corporate spirit, but for property and nothing else. Thus neither Church nor Guild survived to offer any obstacle to the view that headlong wealth was the sovereign good for society and for the individual, for cities and for men.

This view was powerfully encouraged by the philosophy of confidence which the eighteenth century had substituted for a religion of awe. Medieval religion had watched man's instincts with anxious eyes, as instincts needing to be disciplined, coerced, held fast by Pope and priest; the Puritans, though they gave him different masters, were not less suspicious of the natural man. The new philosophy, on the other hand, regarded man's instincts as the best guide to conduct, and taught that left to himself man so acted as to serve rather than injure the society to which he belonged. Capital was a magical power; man was a benevolent creature. Thus so far as an age lives by a system of belief, this age drew its wisdom from a philosophy that found nothing but good in the new force to which it had submitted.

The state of politics was also congenial to this impulse. Neither Conservative nor Radical offered any distracting or competing motive, for while they disagreed about political and administrative reform, they did not disagree about the advantages of a system under which acquisition and profit-making were unimpeded. If it was the manufacturers who promoted the new system in industry, the landowners were equally active in promoting it on their estates. The most important force in making the English an industrial people was the destruction of the village. Nations that kept the peasant could never be completely absorbed in the new industrial system, and it was the land-owner, often of course the new landowner, who had come from the world of finance and industry, who pushed the English peasant out.

England was on the eve of a great expansion of resources, numbers, wealth and power. What were the new towns to be like? What their schools, their pleasures, their houses, their standards of a good life, their plans for co-operation and fellowship? What the fate of the mass of people who did not feel or force their way through the doors thrown open to enterprise? To all these questions the Industrial Revolution gave the same answer: "Ask Capital." And neither Conservative nor Radical, the man defending or the man attacking bad laws and bad customs, thought that answer wrong. But that answer meant that the age had turned aside from making a society in order to make a system of production.

The effect of this concentration is seen in the towns of the age. They were left, like everything else, to the mercy and direction of the spirit of profit. . . .

Yet the Industrial Revolution which had given these men their fortunes had made it much easier to supply the needs of the towns that sprang up beside their great establishments. One of the products of that revolution was gas lighting; the Soho Works were lighted with gas in 1802 to celebrate the Peace of Amiens. Great factories at Manchester and Leeds soon followed the example of Boulton and Watt. Another product was the cheap water-pipe. At the end of the American War English ironmasters were exporting water-pipes to Paris and New York. The Romans had no cheap water-pipes made by the help of mechanical power, but they could supply their towns with clean water, whereas the people of Merthyr Tydfil, their streets echoing by day and night with the clamour of forge and furnace, had to drink whatever the river brought them.

The rage for production had swept England, as the rage for piety had swept the age of the monarchists. And production had taken a form that was intensely isolating; the successful man kept his secrets, tried to find his neighbours' secrets, strove for personal gain, took personal risks, made his way by personal initiative and personal enterprise.

This concentration led to the complete neglect of the most urgent tasks of the age. In the first twenty years of the nineteenth century the population of Manchester increased from 94,000 to 160,000; of Bolton from 29,000 to 50,000; Leeds more than doubled its population between 1801 and 1831; Bradford, which had 23,000 inhabitants in 1831, grew grass in its streets at the end of the eighteenth century. Oldham, which had 38,000 inhabitants in

1821, had three or four hundred in 1760. In the twenty years from 1801 to 1821 the population of Lancashire grew from 672,000 to 1,052,000; in the next twenty years it grew to 1,701,000. The population of Merthyr increased from 7,700 to 35,000 between 1801 and 1841, and that of the two counties of Glamorgan and Monmouth from 126,000 to 305,000. Industry was accumulating dense masses of people into particular districts, where the workman was shut up in melancholy streets, without gardens or orchards. England was passing from a country to a town life, as she passed from a peasant to an industrial civilization. What this meant is clear if we compare the state of the towns as revealed in the health statistics, with that of the country districts. In 1757 Dr. Percival put the death-rate for Manchester at 1 in 25, for Liverpool at 1 in 27. In Monton, a few miles from Manchester, the ratio was at that time 1 in 68, at Horwich, between Bolton and Chorley, 1 in 66, at Darwen, three miles from Blackburn, 1 in 56. The Industrial Revolution was to spread the conditions of town life over places like Monton, Horwich and Darwen.

The problem of arranging and controlling the expansion of the towns was thus the most urgent of the problems created by the Industrial Revolution. Its importance was illustrated by a picture of some cottages near Preston published by the Health of Towns Commission in 1844. These cottages stood in two rows, separated by little back yards, with an open sewer running the whole length. The picture was given as an example of dangerous and disgusting drainage. But this is not its chief significance. One would suppose that these huddled cottages, without gardens of any kind, were built in a crowded town, where not an inch of space was available for amenities. They were in fact in the open country. Clearly then there was more here than a problem of drainage, for if it was left to private enterprise to develop this district, under the guidance of an uncontrolled sense for profit, these rows would spring up all round, and Preston would have another slum on her hands. This is what happened in the new industrial districts. When the Health of Towns Commission investigated towns like Manchester, they were told that the worst evils were not the evils of the past, for new Manchester was reproducing the slums and alleys of the old, and spreading them, of course, over a far wider surface. Of no other problem was it so true that neglect by one generation tied the hands and the mind of the next. . . .

The importance of preserving amenities, footpaths, and something of the look of the country was impressed on Parliament. The most significant comment of the neglect of these proposals is to be found in the recurring complaint that runs through all the Reports on Health and Housing that were issued in the nineteenth century. Town planning never found its way into an Act of Parliament until the twentieth century, and back-to-back houses (made illegal in 1909) were built in great numbers two generations after Normanby's Bill had proposed to forbid them. The Commission which sat in 1867 found in existence the main evils that were revealed by the Committee of 1840; the Commission of 1884 found in existence the main evils that had been revealed by the Commission of 1867. In many towns the death-rate was higher in 1867 than in 1842, and Cross, speaking as Home Secretary in 1871, could match the terrible revelations by which Chadwick had tried to rouse the indignation and fear of the Parliaments of Melbourne and Peel.

Before each Commission the large towns disclosed the same difficulties. The law did not enable them to control expansion, or to prevent the creation on their circumference of the evils they were trying to suppress at the centre. The Committee of 1840 had pointed out that back-to-back houses were being introduced into towns that had been free from them. Town Clerks told the Commission of 1867 that whole streets were still being built on "a foundation composed of old sweepings, refuse from factories, old buildings and other objectionable matter." Parliament passed Public Health Acts and set up authorities with sharply limited powers, but the fatal blindness to the character of the problem, as a problem in the organization and planning of town life, which marked the early phases of the Industrial Revolution, persisted. England learnt sooner than other countries how to cleanse her towns, but towns still continued to grow at the pleasure of the profit seeker. Each generation looked wistfully back to its predecessor as living in a time when the evil was still manageable, and over the reforms of the century could be inscribed the motto "the Clock that always loses." For the creed of the first age of the Industrial Revolution, that the needs of production must regulate the conditions of life, and that the incidence of profits must decide in what kind of town, in what kind of streets, and in what kind of houses a nation shall find its home, had cast its melancholy fatalism over the mind of the generations that followed. The trouble was not merely that the evil was greater when a town had a quarter of a million of inhabitants instead of a hundred thousand. It was that men still saw with the eyes of their grandfathers, and that they were busy polishing the life of the slum, when a race that was free and vigorous in its mind could have put an end to it. With the consequences and the traditions of this neglect industrial civilization is still fighting an up-hill battle.

The other task that became immensely more important with the Industrial Revolution was the task of education. Adam Smith had pointed out that the division of labour, though good for production, was bad for the mind of the labourer. Men, women and children lost range, diversity and incentive in their work, when that work was simplified to a single process, or a monotonous routine. Life was more versatile and interesting when craftsmanship was combined with agriculture. Under the new system a boy or youth learnt one process and one process only; a great part of his mind was never exercised; many of his faculties remained idle and undeveloped. Moreover, apprenticeship was declining, and thus an important method of education was passing out of fashion.

Nor were these the only reasons why popular education was needed more urgently in this than in previous ages. Men learn from their leisure as well as from their work. Now the common life of the time was singularly wanting in inspiration, comparing in this respect unfavourably with the life of the ancient or that of the medieval world. The Greeks and the Romans put a great deal of beauty into their public buildings; they made provision, in some cases barbarous provision, for public amusement; they did not isolate art and pleasure for the delight of a small class. Life in Manchester or Merthyr was very different. Mr. and Mrs. Webb, who have described the work of the several bodies of Improvement Commissioners at this time, remark that even the most energetic among them made no provision for parks, open spaces, libraries, picture galleries, museums, baths, or any kind of education. The workmen put it that their sports had been converted into crimes, and their holidays into fast days. Rich men in the Roman Empire spent their money on things that were for common enjoyment as rich men in the Middle Ages spent their money on things that were for common salvation. Pliny gave to his native Como, a library, a school endowment, a foundation for the nurture of poor children and a Temple of Ceres with spacious colonnades to shelter the traders who visited the great fair. The wealthy Herodes Atticus, tutor of Marcus Aurelius, gave a theatre to Athens with a roof of cedar to hold 6,000 persons, another theatre to Corinth, and a race-course to Delphi. Such gifts were common in the days of the Antonines. But in the England of the early Industrial Revolution all diversions were regarded as wrong, because it was believed that successful production demanded long hours, a bare life, a mind without temptation to think or to remember, to look before or behind. Some Lancashire magistrates used to refuse on this ground to license public-houses where concerts were held. Long hours did not begin with the Industrial Revolution, but in the Middle Ages the monotony of industrial work was broken for the journeyman by frequent holidays, saints' days and festivals; for medieval Europe, like Rome, gave some place in common life to the satisfaction of the imagination and the senses.

Perhaps nothing served so directly to embitter the relations of class in the Industrial Revolution as this fashionable view, that the less amusement the worker had, the better. The love of amusement has a place of special significance in the English character. If the English workman stints himself for his holiday week at Blackpool, as the Scottish peasant stints himself to send his son into the Ministry, or the Irish or French peasant stints himself to own a little property, it is not merely because he sets his holiday high among the enjoyments of life. The satisfaction of this desire is connected with his self-respect. The football field and the holiday resort represent a world in which the poor man feels himself the equal of the rich: a corner of life in which he has not bargained away any rights or liberties. It might be said of the early Radicals, that they sought to extend to his view of politics, and of the early Socialists, that they sought to extend to his views of property, the spirit that ruled the workman's outlook on his pleasures: that they sought to make him resent in those spheres the inequalities he was so quick to resent, when employer or magistrate tried to keep from him amusements that other classes enjoyed.

The need for popular education became in these circumstances specially urgent. The reading of print is one way of using and exercising the mind, and its value at any moment depends on circumstances. In the days of pageants and spectacles, when story-tellers went from village to village, when pedlars and pilgrims brought tales of adventure or war or the habits of foreign countries, a man might be unable to read or write, and yet take a share in the culture of the time. Buildings, plays, music, these may be greater influences on the mind than book or pamphlet or newspaper. But the youth of the early nineteenth century who found no scope for initiative or experiment or design in his work, found no stimulus or education for his fancy from the spectacles and amusements provided for his recreation. Science was improving the mechanical contrivances of life, but the arts of life were in decline. To take advantage of these improvements, the power to read and write was essential. In a world depending on newspapers, the man who cannot read lives in the darkest exile; when the factory was taking the place of the craft, the newspaper the place of the pageant, illiteracy was the worst disfranchisement a man could suffer.

Horner, reporting in 1839 that a population of over a hundred thousand persons in a district of Lancashire comprising Oldham and Ashton was without a single public day-school for poor scholars, the Commissioner who said of South Wales in 1842 that not one grown male in fifty could read, both spoke of an age in which the story-teller had left the village, and the apprenticeship system was leaving the town. Adam Smith had argued that as the division of labour deprived the worker of opportunities of training his mind, the State ought to provide opportunities by public education. The ruling class argued, on the contrary, that with the new methods of specialization, industry could not spare a single hour for the needs of the men who served it. In such a system education had no place. The great majority of the ruling class believed, as one of them put it, that the question to ask was not whether education would develop a child's faculties for happiness and citizenship, but whether it "would make him a good servant in agriculture and other laborious employments to which his rank in society had destined him."

Thus England asked for profits and received profits. Everything turned to profit. The towns had their profitable dirt, their profitable smoke, their profitable slums, their profitable disorder, their profitable ignorance, their profitable despair. The curse of Midas was on this society: on its corporate life, on its common mind, on the decisive and impatient step it had taken from the peasant to the industrial age. For the new town was not a home where man could find beauty, happiness, leisure, learning, religion—the influences that civilize outlook and habit; but a bare and desolate place, without colour, air or laughter, where man, woman and child worked, ate and slept. This was to be the lot of the mass of mankind: this the sullen rhythm of their lives. The new factories and the new furnaces were like the Pyramids, telling of man's enslavement, rather than of his power, casting their long shadow over the society that took such pride in them.

The foremost proponent of the necessity for revising the traditional accounts of the Industrial Revolution is T. S. Ashton, Professor Emeritus of Economic History at the University of London.

FROM *The Treatment of Capitalism by Historians*
BY T. S. ASHTON

THE STUDENT OF ENGLISH ECONOMIC HISTORY is fortunate in having at his disposal the reports of a long series of Royal Commissions and Committees of Inquiry beginning in the eighteenth century but reaching full stream in the 1830's, 1840's, and 1850's. These reports are one of the glories of the early Victorian age. They signalized a quickening of social conscience, a sensitiveness to distress, that had not been evident in any other period or in any other country. Scores of massive folios provided statistical and verbal evidence that all was not well with large numbers of the people of England and called the attention of legislators and the reading public to the need for reform. The economic historians of the succeeding generations could do no other than draw on their findings; and scholarship, no less than society, benefited. There was, however, loss as well as gain. A picture of the economic system constructed from Blue Books dealing with social grievances, and not with the normal processes of economic development, was bound to be one-sided. It is such a picture of early Victorian society that has become fixed in the minds of popular writers. . . . A careful reading of the reports would, indeed, lead to the conclusion that much that was wrong was the result of laws, customs, habits, and forms of organization that belonged to earlier periods and were rapidly becoming obsolete. It would have brought home to the mind that it was not among the factory employees but among the domestic workers, whose traditions and methods were those of the eighteenth century, that earnings were at their lowest. It would have provided evidence that it was not in the large establishments making use of steam power but in the garret or cellar workshops that conditions of employment were at their worst. It would have led to the conclusion that it was not in the growing manufacturing towns or the developing coal fields but in remote villages and the countryside that restrictions on personal freedom and the evils of truck were most marked. But few had the patience to go carefully through these massive volumes. It was so much easier to pick out the more sensational evidences of distress and work them into a dramatic story of exploitation. The result has been that a generation that had the enterprise and industry to assemble the facts, the honesty to reveal them, and the energy to set about the task of reform has been held up to obloquy as the author, not of the Blue Books, but of the evils themselves. Conditions in the mills and the factory town were so bad, it seemed, that there must have been deterioration; . . . and, since the supposed deterioration had taken place at a time when machinery had increased, the machines, and those who owned them, must have been responsible.

At the same time the romantic revival in literature led to an idyllic view of the life of the peasant. The idea that agriculture is the only natural and healthy activity for human beings has persisted, and indeed spread, as more of us have escaped from the curse of Adam—or, as the tedious phrase goes, "become divorced from the soil." A year ago an examinee remarked profoundly that "in earlier centuries agriculture was widespread in England" but added sorrowfully, "Today it is confined to the rural areas." There was a similar idealization of the condition of the domestic worker, who had taken only the first step in the proceedings for divorce. Bear with me while I read some passages with which Friedrich Engels (who is usually acclaimed a realist) opens his account of *The Condition of the Working Classes in England in 1844*. It is, of course, based on the writings of the Reverend Philip Gaskell, whose earnestness and honesty are not in doubt, but whose mind had not been confused by any study of history. Engels' book opens with the declaration that "the history of the proletariat in England begins with the invention of the steam-engine and of machinery for working cotton." Before their time, he continues,

> the workers vegetated throughout a passably comfortable existence, leading a righteous and peaceful life in all piety and probity; and their material condition was far better than that of their successors. They did not need to overwork; they did no more than they chose to do, and yet earned what they needed. They had leisure for healthful work in garden or field, work which, in itself, was recreation for them, and they could take part beside in the recreation and games of their neighbours, and all these games—bowling, cricket, football, etc. contributed to their physical health and vigour. They were, for the most part, strong, well-built people, in whose physique little or no difference from that of their peasant neighbours was discoverable. Their children grew up in fresh country air, and, if they could help their parents at work, it was only

occasionally; while of eight or twelve hours work for them there was no question.

It is difficult to say whether this or the lurid picture of the lives of the grandchildren of these people presented in later pages of the book is more completely at variance with the facts. Engels had no doubt whatsoever as to the cause of the deterioration in the condition of labor. "The proletariat," he repeats, "was called into existence by the introduction of machinery." "The consequences of improvement in machinery under our present social conditions," he asserts, "are, for the working-man, solely injurious, and often in the highest degree oppressive. Every new advance brings with it loss of employment, want and suffering."

Engels has had many disciples, even among those who do not accept the historical materialism of Marx, with which such views are generally connected. Hostility to the machine is associated with hostility to its products and, indeed, to all innovation in consumption. One of the outstanding accomplishments of the new industrial age is to be seen in the greatly increased supply and variety of fabrics offered on the market. Yet the changes in dress are taken as evidence of growing poverty: "The clothing of the working-people in a majority of cases," Engels declares, "is in a very bad condition. The material used for it is not of the best adapted. Wool and linen have almost vanished from the wardrobes of both sexes, and cotton has taken their place. Skirts are made of bleached or coloured cotton goods, and woollen petticoats are rarely to be seen on the wash-line." The truth is that they never had been greatly displayed on the wash line, for woolen goods are liable to shrink. The workers of earlier periods had to make their garments last (second or third hand as many of these were), and soap and water were inimical to the life of clothing. The new, cheap textiles may not have been as hard-wearing as broadcloth, but they were more abundant; and the fact that they could be washed without suffering harm had a bearing, if not on their own life, at least on the lives of those who wore them.

The same hostility is shown to innovation in food and drink. Generations of writers have followed William Cobbett in his hatred of tea. One would have thought that the enormous increase in consumption between the beginning of the eighteenth and the middle of the nineteenth century was one element in a rising standard of comfort; but only a few years ago Professor Parkinson asserted that it was "growing poverty" that made tea increasingly essential to the lower classes as ale was put beyond their means. (This, I may add, unfortunately meant that they were forced to consume sugar, and one must suppose that this practice also led to a fall in the standard of living.) Similarly, Dr. Salaman has recently assured us that the introduction of the potato into the diet of the workers at this time was a factor detrimental to health and that it enabled the employers to force down the level of wages—which, it is well known, is always determined by the minimum of food required for subsistence.

Very gradually those who held to these pessimistic views of the effects of industrial change have been forced to yield ground. The painstaking researches of Bowley and Wood have shown that over most of this period, and later, the course of real wages was upward. The proof is not at all easy, for it is clear that there were sections of the working classes of whom it was emphatically not true. In the first half of the nineteenth century the population of England was growing, partly because of natural increase, partly as the result of the influx of Irish. For those endowed with little or no skill, marginal productivity, and hence earnings, remained low. A large part of their incomes was spent on commodities (mainly food, drink, and housing), the cost of which had hardly been affected by technical development. That is why so many of the economists, like McCulloch and Mill, were themselves dubious about the beneficial nature of the industrial system. There were, however, large and growing sections of skilled and better-paid workers whose money incomes were rising and who had a substantial margin to spend on the products of the machine, the costs of which were falling progressively. The controversy really rests on which of the groups was increasing most. Generally it is now agreed that for the majority the gain in real wages was substantial.

But this does not dispose of the controversy. Real earnings might have risen, it was said, but it was the quality of life and not the quantity of goods consumed that mattered. In particular, it was the evil conditions of housing and the insanitary conditions of the towns that were called as evidence that the circumstances of labor had worsened. "Everything which here arouses horror and indignation," wrote Engels of Manchester in 1844, "is of recent origin, belongs to the industrial epoch"—and the reader is left to infer that the equally repulsive features of cities like Dublin and Edinburgh, which were scarcely touched by the new industry, were, somehow or other, also the product of the machine.

This is the legend that has spread round the world and has determined the attitude of millions of men and women to labor-saving devices and to those who own them. Indians and Chinese, Egyptians and Negroes, to whose fellow-countrymen today the dwellings of the English of the mid-nineteenth century would be wealth indeed, solemnly declare, in the scripts I have to read, that the English workers were living in conditions unworthy of beasts. They write with indignation about the inefficiency of the sanitation and the absence of civic amenities—the very nature of which is still unknown to the urban workers of a large part of the earth.

Now, no one who has read the reports of the Committee on the Sanitary Condition of the Working Classes of 1842 or that of the Commission on the Health of Towns of 1844 can doubt that the state of affairs was, from the point of view of modern Western civilization, deplorable. But, equally, no one who has read Dorothy George's account of living conditions in London in the eighteenth century can be sure that they had deteriorated. Dr. George herself believes that they had improved, and Clapham declared that the

English towns of the mid-century were "less crowded than the great towns of other countries and not, universally, more insanitary." The question I wish to raise, however, is that of responsibility. Engels, as we have seen, attributed the evils to the machine; others are no less emphatic in attributing them to the Industrial Revolution, which comes to much the same thing. No historian, as far as I know, has looked at the problem through the eyes of those who had the task of building and maintaining the towns.

There were two main aspects: the supply of houses in relation to the demand and the technical matters of drainage, sanitation, and ventilation. In the early nineteenth century, according to one of these scripts, "the workers were pressed into back-to-back houses, like sardines in a rabbit warren." Many of the houses were certainly unsubstantial and insanitary, and for this it is usual to blame the industrialist who put them up, a man commonly spoken of as the jerry-builder. I had often wondered who this man was. When I was young, the parson of the church I attended once preached a sermon on Jerry, who, he asserted with complete conviction, was at that very moment burning in hell for his crimes. I have searched for records of him, but in vain. It appears from Weekley's *Etymological Dictionary of Modern English* that "jerry" is a corruption of "jury"—a word of nautical origin applied to any part of a ship contrived for temporary use, as in "jury mast" and "jury rig," and extended to other things, such as "jury leg" for "wooden leg." "Jerry," then, means temporary, or inferior, or makeshift; and no doubt other uses of the word as a makeshift in an emergency will come to the mind. According to Partridge's *Dictionary of Slang and Unconventional English,* it was first used in Liverpool about 1830. The place and time are significant. Liverpool was the port for the rapidly developing industrial area of southeastern Lancashire; it was the chief gate of entry for the swarms of Irish immigrants. It was probably here that the pressure of population on the supplies of accommodation was most acute. Houses were run up rapidly, and many of them were flimsy structures, the outer walls of which were only 4½ inches in thickness. On December 5, 1822, some of them, along with many buildings elsewhere, were blown down in a great storm that swept over the British Isles; and in February, 1823, the grand jury at Liverpool called the attention of the magistrates "to the dreadful effects of the late storm . . . in consequence of the modern insecure mode of building." A year later the same body referred again to "the slight and dangerous mode of erecting dwelling houses now practised in this town and neighbourhood" and asked for steps to be taken "to procure a Legislative enactment, which might empower a proper Officer carefully to survey every building hereafter to be erected, and in case of insecurity to cause the danger to be removed."

The sudden collapse of buildings was no new experience. In 1738 Samuel Johnson had written of London as a place where "falling houses thunder on your head"; and, to give a specific instance, in 1796 two houses fell, burying sixteen people, in Houghton Street, where the concrete buildings of the School of Economics now stand. The chief trouble seems to have been the use of inferior material, such as ashes and street sweepings, in the making of bricks and the unsubstantial walls erected whenever the building lease was for only a short run of years. It would appear from the Liverpool evidence, however, that matters had taken a turn for the worse in the early 1820's; and complaints of inferior building in other quarters reinforce the belief. The explanation is not far to seek. It lies in the fact that the early twenties saw a revival of housebuilding after a long period of suspension (or, at best, feeble activity) during nearly a quarter of a century of war and that this revival took place in circumstances when building costs had been raised to an inordinate height.

It is necessary to take account of the organization of the industry. The typical builder was a man of small means, a bricklayer or a carpenter who bought a small plot of land, carried out himself only a single operation, such as that of laying the bricks, and employed craftsmen on contract for the other processes of construction. By the middle of the nineteenth century, it is true, large-scale firms were growing up, controlled by men like Thomas Cubitt, but these were concerned with the erection of public buildings or mansions and not with the dwellings of the poor. The jerry-builders were not, in the usual sense of the word, capitalists, but workingmen. Says Chadwick's *Report* of 1842:

> In the rural districts, the worst of the new cottages are those erected on the borders of commons by the labourers themselves. In manufacturing districts, the tenements erected by building clubs and by speculating builders of the class of workmen, are frequently the subject of complaint, as being the least substantial and the most destitute of proper accommodation. The only conspicuous instances of improved residences found in the rural districts are those which have been erected by opulent and benevolent landlords for the accommodation of the labourers on their own estates: and in the manufacturing districts, those erected by wealthy manufacturers for the accommodation of their own workpeople.

In Liverpool the builders of so-called "slop houses," or scamped houses, were usually Welshmen, drawn largely from the quarrymen of Caernarvonshire. They were backed by attorneys who had land to dispose of on lease but were not themselves willing to become builders. They bought their materials, which were of a cheap and shoddy type, on three months' credit. They tended to employ a high proportion of apprentices, and so, it was said, workmanship was of low quality. They needed credit at every stage: to obtain the building lease, to purchase the materials, and to meet the claims of the joiners, plasterers, slaters, plumbers, painters, etc., who performed their special tasks as contractors or subcontractors. The price of money was an important element in building costs. Under the operation of the usury laws it was illegal to offer, or demand, more than 5 per cent, and this meant that, at times when the state itself was offering 4½ or more per cent, it was impossible for the builders to obtain loans at all. By allowing the rate of interest to rise to 4½ or 5 per cent on the public debt, and prohibiting the industrialist from offering more, the state had been successful in damping down the activities of the builders for more than twenty years and so had deflected to itself the resources of men and materials required for the prosecution of the war against Napoleon. After 1815 the rate of interest fell tardily; it was not until the early twenties that the builders could resume operations. They were faced with a demand that had swollen enormously as the result of a vast increase of population, which now included an abnormally large number of young adults seeking homes of their own.

They were faced also by an enormous increase in costs. In 1821, according to Silberling's index number, wholesale prices in general stood about 20 per cent above the level of the year 1788. In the same period the price of building materials had risen far more: bricks and wainscot had doubled; deals had risen by 60 per cent and lead by 58 per cent. The wages of craftsmen and laborers had gone up by anything from 80 to 100 per cent. The costs of a large number of specific operations are given annually in the *Builders' Price Books* published in London. They show an increase in the cost of plain brickwork of 120 per cent. Oak for building purposes had gone up by 150 per cent, and fir by no less than 237 per cent. The cost of common painting had doubled, and that of glazing with crown glass had increased by 140 per cent.

It was not, in the main, the producer of materials who was responsible. During the war the duties levied by the state on bricks and tiles, stone, slate, and wallpaper had increased enormously. At this time the cost of timber was the chief element in the total cost of building materials, amounting, according to one estimate, to fully a half of the whole. Almost prohibitive duties had been laid on the supplies of timber and deals from the Baltic, and the builders of working-class houses had to make use of what were generally said to be inferior woods, brought at great cost across the Atlantic from Canada. Joseph Hume declared, in 1850, that, if the duties on bricks and timber were removed, a cottage which cost £60 to build, as things were, could be put up for £40.

*   *   *

In the years that followed the long war, then, the builders had the task of making up arrears of housing and of meeting the needs of a rapidly growing population. They were handicapped by costs, a large part of which arose from fiscal exactions. The expenses of occupying a house were loaded with heavy local burdens, and so the net rent that most workingmen could afford to pay was reduced. In these circumstances, if the relatively poor were to be housed at all, the buildings were bound to be smaller, less substantial, and less well provided with amenities than could be desired. It was emphatically not the machine, not the Industrial Revolution, not even the speculative bricklayer or carpenter that was at fault. Few builders seem to have made fortunes, and the incidence of bankruptcy was high. The fundamental problem was the shortage of houses. Those who blame the jerry-builder remind one of the parson, referred to by Edwin Cannan, who used to upbraid the assembled worshipers for the poor attendance at church.

Stress has rightly been laid by many writers on the inadequacy of the provisions for safeguarding the public against overcrowding of houses on limited sites. But London, Manchester, and other large towns had had their Building Acts for generations, and no one who has looked at the *Builders' Price Books* can possibly believe that Londoners suffered from a deficiency of regulations. Mr. John Summerson, indeed, has suggested that the depressing monotony of the newer streets of the capital were the direct result, not, as is often assumed, of free enterprise, but of the provisions of what the builders called the Black Act of 1774—a measure that runs to about thirty-five thousand words. It is true that what was uppermost in the minds of those who framed this act was the avoidance of fire. But some writers like the Webbs (as Redford has shown) have done less than justice to the work of the early organs of local government in such matters as the paving, lighting, and cleaning of streets. If more was not done, the fault did not rest on the builders. Thomas Cubitt told the House of Commons that he would not allow a house to be built anywhere unless it could be shown that there was a good drainage and a good way to get rid of water. "I think there should be a public officer paid at the public expense, who should be responsible for that." If the towns were ridden with disease, some at least of the responsibility lay with legislators who, by taxing windows, put a price on light and air and, by taxing bricks and tiles, discouraged the construction of drains and sewers. Those who dwell on the horrors that arose from the fact that the products of the sewers often got mixed up with the drinking water, and attribute this, as all other horrors, to the Industrial Revolution, should be reminded of the obvious fact that without the iron pipe, which was one of the products of that revolution, the problem of enabling people to live a healthy life together in towns could never have been solved.

If my first complaint against commonly accepted views of the economic developments of the nineteenth century is concerned with their pessimism, my second is that they are not informed by any glimmering of economic sense. In the generation of Adam Smith and his immediate successors many treatises appeared dealing with the history of commerce, industry, coinage, public revenue, population, and pauperism. Those who wrote them—men like Anderson, Macpherson, Chalmers, Colquhoun, Lord Liverpool, Sinclair, Eden, Malthus, and Tooke—were either themselves economists or at least were interested in the things that were the concern of Adam Smith, Ricardo, and Mill. There were, it is true, many rebels, on both the right and the left, against the doctrines propounded by the economists; but few of these, it so happened, were historically minded. There was, therefore, no sharply defined cleavage between history and theory. In the second half of the nineteenth century, however, a wide breach appeared. How far it was due to the direct influence of the writings of Marx and Engels, how far to the rise of the Historical School of economists in Germany, and how far to the fact that the English economic historians, following Toynbee, were primarily social re-formers, I must not stay to discuss. There can be no doubt, however, that the tendency was to write the story in other than economic terms. A whole series of labels was introduced to indicate what were believed to be the dominant characteristics of successive periods of time, and most of these were political rather than economic in connotation. The arresting phrase, the "Industrial Revolution," was coined (as Miss Bezanson has shown) not by English industrialists or economists but by French writers of the late eighteenth century, under the spell of their own great political ferment. It was seized upon by Engels and Marx and was used by Arnold Toynbee as the title of his pioneer work. It may be questioned whether it has not now outlived its usefulness, for it has tended to support the view that the introduction of large-scale production was catastrophic, rather than beneficial, in its effects. Even more unfortunate, I would urge, has been the intrusion into economic history of another phrase of political intent, struck at the same mint but at an even earlier period. Professor Macgregor has traced back the term "laissez faire" to 1755, when it was first used by the Marquis d'Argenson as both a political and an economic principle. He has charted its curious evolution from the time when it meant noninterference with industry to its use, in 1907, by Alfred Marshall to mean "let the State be up and doing." In view of the dubiety of its intention, it is perhaps not to be wondered at that it should have been fastened by some onto a period of English history that is known to others as the Age of Reform—again a phrase drawn from the vocabulary of politics and not of economics. One could not feel too harshly, therefore, about the candidate who declared that "about the year 1900 men turned their backs on laissez-faire and began to do things for themselves." The title of a work written by Mr. Fisher Unwin in 1904 has fastened on the decade that saw the railway boom and the repeal of the Corn Laws the stigma of "the hungry forties," and only the other day a magazine called *Womanfare* referred to the decade before the recent war as "the hungry thirties." A legend is growing up that the years 1930–39 were marked throughout by misery. In the next generation "the hungry thirties" may be common form.

For two generations economic historians have shirked economic ques-tions or have dealt with them superficially. They have never made up their minds on such elementary matters as to whether it is abundance or scarcity that is to be sought, but generally it is restrictionism they favor. The efforts of Lancashire to provide cheap cottons for people who had previously gone seminaked is acknowledged only in a sentence to the effect that "the bones of the cotton weavers whitened the plains of India." In the same elementary textbook I am told that the tax on imports of wheat led to poverty and distress in the first half of the nineteenth century and that the absence of such a tax to act as a dam against the flood of cheap wheat that poured across the Atlantic was the prime cause of the poverty and distress of the later decades of the century—the period so unhappily known as the Great Depression. Some economic historians have written chapters designed to answer such questions as to whether trade arises from industry or industry from trade, whether transport develops markets or markets give occasion for transport. They have concerned themselves with inquiries as to where the demand comes from that makes production possible. Whenever a real problem is encountered, it is passed over with some such comment as that "a crisis arose" or that "speculation became rife," though why or what nature is rarely disclosed. And, when details are given, logic is often thrown to the winds. In explaining the French depression of 1846, Professor Clough declares that "reduced agricultural production lowered the purchasing power of the farmers, and the high cost of living prevented the industrial population from buying much else than food." This surely is a case of making the worst of both worlds. It has often been said that, at least before Keynes, the economic theorist moved in a world of abstractions and had nothing worth while to offer the historian. But, if only historians had pondered a little on marginal analysis, they would have been saved from such foolish assertions as that trade can arise only when there is a surplus or that investment abroad takes place only when the capital market at home is sated. Ignorance of the elements of economic theory led historians to give political interpretations to every favorable trend. In scores of books the improvement in conditions of labor in the nineteenth century has been attributed to factory legislation; in hardly any is it pointed out that rising productivity of male labor had something to do with the decline of the number of children exploited in the factories or the number of women degraded in the mines. Until Professor Rostow wrote his work on the *British Economy of the Nineteenth Century* in 1948, there had been scarcely any discussion by historians of the relation between investment and earnings.

No one has laid more stress on the need for theory in the writing of history than Sombart. "Facts are like beads," he declares; "they require a string to hold them together. . . . No theory—no history." It is to be deplored that he found his own theory, not in the writings of the economists of his day, but in those of Karl Marx; for, although later he reacted strongly against the interpretations of Marx, his writings have led large numbers of historians in Germany, Britain, and the United States to thread their facts on a Marxist string. In particular, everything that has happened, since the early Middle Ages, is explained in terms of capitalism—a term if not coined at least given wide currency by Marx. Marx, of course, associated it with exploitation. Sombart used it to mean a system of production differing from the handicraft system by reason of the fact that the means of production are owned by a class distinct from the workers—a class whose motive is profit and whose methods are rational, as opposed to the traditional methods, of the handicraftsmen. Above all, he stressed the capitalist spirit. Other elements, such as that innovations in the system are carried out by borrowed money, or credit, have been added by later writers like Schumpeter. But nearly all agree that capitalism implies the existence of a rational technique, a proletariat that sells its labor (and not the product of its labor), and a class of capitalists whose aim is unlimited profit. The assumption is that at some stage of human history—perhaps in the eleventh century A.D.—men became, for the first time, rational and acquisitive. The main business of the economic historians who followed Sombart was to trace the origins of rationality and acquisitiveness. It was what they called the "genetic approach" to the problem of capitalism.

A thousand years is an unmanageably long period, and so capitalism had to be presented as a series of stages—the epochs, respectively, of early, full, and late capitalism, or of mercantile capitalism, industrial capitalism, finance capitalism, and state capitalism. It is admitted, of course, by those who make use of these categories that there is overlapping: that the late stage of one epoch is the early (or, as they say, the emergent) stage of the next. But to teach economic history in this way—to suggest that commerce, industry, finance, and state control are *successive* dominant forces—is to hide from the student, I suggest, the interaction and interdependence of all these at every period of time. It is bad economics.

Those who write so tend to torture the facts. It is part of the legend that the dominant form of organization under industrial capitalism, the factory, arose out of the demands, not of ordinary people, but of the rich and the rulers. Let me quote Professor Nussbaum here. "In personal terms," he says, "it was the interests of the princes [the state] and of the industrialists; in impersonal terms, war and luxury favoured—one might almost say, caused—the development of the factory system." To support this monstrous thesis, he gives a list of the capitalized industries about the year 1800. It includes "sugar, chocolate, lace, embroidery, novelties, tapestries, mirrors, porcelains, jewellery, watches and book printing." All I can say is that, apart from that of sugar, I cannot find a single instance of the production of any one of these things in a factory in England at this time. Nussbaum admits that cotton clothes "offered a field for almost exclusively capitalistic organisation" but says that this was because they were "at first and for a long time luxury goods." Apparently he thinks Arkwright and his fellows were making fine muslins and cambrics for royal courts and not calicoes for English workers and the peasants of India. But this legend about war and luxury is too absurd to need refutation by anyone who has taken the trouble to glance at the records of the first generation of factory masters in England.

FROM *The Industrial Revolution* BY T. S. ASHTON

MUCH HAS BEEN WRITTEN about the effects of the industrial revolution on the workers. Some, impressed by the lot of those who went down in

T. S. Ashton, *The Industrial Revolution 1760–1830* (1948), pp. 157–61. Reprinted by permission of Oxford University Press, London.

the struggle against the machine, have declared that technological change brought little but misery and poverty, and a statistician of repute has set on record his opinion that by the early years of the nineteenth century the standard of life of the British worker had been forced down to Asiatic levels. Mr. Colin Clark can hardly have looked at the statistics which more than a generation of research has produced. The careful studies of Mrs. Gilboy indicate that, over the eighteenth century, the material well-being of the labourer in the woollen area of the South-West had, indeed, fallen, but that the lot of his fellow in the textile region of the North had steadily improved, and that the labourer of London more than held his own. It is true that the rise of prices after 1793 made many humble people poorer. But before the end of the war (as Professor Silberling has shown) industrial wages in England caught up with retail prices, and in the 'twenties the gain was pronounced. In 1831 the cost of living was 11 per cent higher than in 1790, but over this span of time urban wages had increased, it appears, by no less than 43 per cent.

It would have been strange, indeed, if the industrial revolution had simply made the rich richer and the poor poorer. For the commodities to which it gave rise were not, in general, luxuries, but necessaries and capital goods. The tardiness with which the last of these yielded their fruit to the consumer has already been explained. But by the 'twenties the effects of the war were passing away and the cottons and woollens, and food and drink, which now became available, were consumed not by the few, but by the masses. Some of the products of the factories and ironworks were sent abroad, but the return cargoes did not consist, in the main, of wines and silks, but of sugar, grain, coffee, and tea for the people at large. Much has been made of the suggestion that the prices of the things Britain exported fell more rapidly than those of the things she brought back: there was no revolution to reduce costs in overseas agriculture; and British lending abroad may also have helped to give the terms of trade an unfavourable turn. But, though such influences may explain why, in the 'thirties and 'forties, real wages were lower than might have been expected, they had little effect, it would seem, between 1815 and 1830. The diet of the worker almost certainly improved: there was a substitution of "flower of wheat" for rye and oatmeal; and meat, which had been a rarity, became, with potatoes, the staple dish on the artisan's table. Not all the coal raised from the pits went to feed the furnaces and steam-engines: a warm hearth and a hot meal were of no small consequence to the man who came home wet from the fields.

In 1802 George Chalmers remarked that the laborious classes were "too wealthy to covet the pittance of the soldier, or too independent to court the dangers of the sailor." There were, true enough, many vagrants and paupers, but, even before the new Poor Law came in, the hordes of the "indigent and distressed" had probably shrunk. Hours of labour were long, and holidays few; there is a mass of evidence that employment in factories was harmful to the health and morals of the young. A leading politician has recently spoken of the "mechanized horrors of the industrial revolution," and there can be little doubt that the deeper mines and more complicated machines brought new risks of mutilation and death. But against all this must be set the lessening of strain on those who worked in the heavy trades, and the decline in the number of crippled and deformed people that followed the introduction of power in places like Sheffield. There must be set, also, the reduction of sweating of women and young children, the rise in family earnings, the greater regularity of pay, and the gain in welfare that came as industrial work was taken out of the home.

Whether the houses themselves were becoming better or worse is diffi-cult to determine: much depends on the periods compared. Many of the dwellings provided for the workers by the country factory masters have survived—at Cromford, Mellor, and Styal. They have design and proportion, and, even by modern standards, are not wanting in amenity and comfort. But these were put up when building materials were plentiful, wages relatively low, and money relatively cheap. After 1793 the import of timber from the Baltic was restricted, and the price of labour of bricklayers and carpenters went up. At least two-thirds of the rent of a dwelling consists of interest charges: rates of interest were rising, and for more than a generation they remained high. This meant that if dwellings were to be let at rents which the workers could afford to pay they had to be smaller and less durable than those of the 'eighties. The rows of ill-built, back-to-back houses, into which the rapidly growing population of the towns was pressed, were largely the product of wartime conditions.

After 1815 matters were made worse by the influx of Irish, who, gregar-ious by instinct, crowded into the seaports and the towns of the North. Careful estimates made by members of the Manchester Statistical Society in the middle 'thirties led to the conclusion that about one-sixth of the families in Manchester were Irish, and that the percentage of the people living in cellars was 11.75. In Liverpool, where again there were many Irish, no less than 15 per cent of the inhabitants were in cellars. But in the newer towns, which were the special creation of the industrial revolution, conditions were far less grim. In Bury, where there were few Irish (and few hand-loom weavers) only 3.75 per cent, and in Ashton-under-Lyne only 1.25 per cent, of the people were housed in this way. In these places, the investigators re-ported, the houses of the workers were not only less crowded, but also better furnished and cleaner than those of the cities.

An historian has written of "the disasters of the industrial revolution." If by this he means that the years 1760–1830 were darkened by wars and made cheerless by dearth, no objection can be made to the phrase. But if he means that the technical and economic changes were themselves the source of calamity the opinion is surely perverse. The central problem of the age was how to feed and clothe and employ generations of children outnumbering by far those of any earlier time. Ireland was faced by the same problem. Failing to solve it, she lost in the 'forties about a fifth of her people by emigration or starvation and disease. If England had remained a nation of cultivators and craftsmen, she could hardly have escaped the same fate, and, at best, the weight of a growing population must have pressed down the spring of her spirit. She was delivered, not by her rulers, but by those who, seeking no doubt their own narrow ends, had the wit and resource to devise new instruments of production and new methods of administering industry. There are to-day on the plains of India and China men and women, plague-ridden and hungry, living lives little better, to outward appearance, than those of the cattle that toil with them by day and share their places of sleep by night. Such Asiatic standards, and such unmechanized horrors, are the lot of those who increase their numbers without passing through an industrial revolution.

Nationalism—Friend or Foe of Liberalism?

CONTENTS

QUESTIONS FOR STUDY

1   What does Snyder feel are the essential elements of nationalism? To what extent would Fichte agree with him?

2   What did Fichte think were the essential elements of German nationalism? Who would he consider a German?

3   In what ways do Schurz and Baumgarten differ as examples of German liberals?

4   Was it inevitable that liberalism and nationalism come into conflict in Germany?

It could be argued that nationalism has always been with us. Pro patria mori *(to die for one's country) was considered the highest good in ancient Rome, and the cry, "God acts through France," echoed through the Middle Ages. But these manifestations of nationalism were sporadic and submerged beneath strong feelings of local custom and tradition. It was the French Revolution that created the upsurge of national feeling that was to swell and grow throughout the nineteenth century until the principle of national self-determination was recognized as a natural right in the twentieth. The French Revolution also gave great impetus to liberalism, to the idea that men have natural rights and that the purpose of the state is to guarantee them. One of the great questions of the nineteenth century was what to do when there was, as yet, no national state that could effectively guarantee the rights of man. Was it not obvious that the state must first be created if rights were to have any meaning? Or was it enough to struggle for rights in the hopes that the small principality would be too weak to suppress them? But what then of one's stronger neighbors? Who would protect the citizen's rights if, as during the Napoleonic wars, the state fell to an invader? These questions were basic to the evolution of the German state in the nineteenth century, and it is the conflict among some of them that forms the basis of this problem.*

1 The Nature of Nationalism

Nationalism is not a simple idea to define. It is a whole constellation of philosophical and emotional factors that combine to create a feeling of being a part of a national group. The dimensions of this feeling, as it applies to Germany, are described by Professor Snyder of the City College of New York.

FROM *German Nationalism* BY LOUIS L. SNYDER

THERE IS GENERAL AGREEMENT among historians on the existence of nationalism as an idea of enormous significance that has penetrated into every phase of modern life. The attitude which ascribes to national individuality a high place in the hierarchy of values is not only an idea in the Platonic sense, but a reality which is of great importance in the study of history. On the corollary of "national character," however, there is a strong, often bitter, difference of opinion. Three points of view may be noted: (1) there is no such thing as "national character"; (2) "national character" is a demonstrable historical idea produced by variable social influences, and it remains constant among a people from first to last; and (3) the persuasion that certain types of character belong to certain people in certain areas has a limited validity if it intends to convey the idea that certain values have been inculcated within cultures by responses to different calls from without—by traditions, by ethical institutions, and by education. The first two points of view represent extremist thinking on the problem, while the third recognizes the existence of national character without minimizing the difficulties faced in determining its meaning and nature.

Until recently the idea of national character was regarded by respectable social scientists as only a metaphysical dream shot through with fallacious generalizations and unreflecting prejudice. With a little ingenuity and sophistry, it was said, it is possible to deduce two entirely different sets of characteristics for any nation. The contention that each nation has a char-

Louis L. Snyder, *German Nationalism: The Tragedy of a People* (1952), pp. 1–5, 7–12, 16–20. Reprinted by permission of The Stackpole Company.

acter of its own, it was further claimed, is mere superstition, and so-called national differences can be fully accounted for by the undeniable characteristics of individual psychology.

The second point of view, which goes to the opposite extreme, was expressed by Henry Morley in the statement that "in the literature of any people we perceive under all contrasts of form produced by variable social influences the one national character from first to last." The idea of a fundamental national character, a concept borrowed from Montesquieu by some German writers, notably Herder, in the late eighteenth century, developed in the nineteenth century into a persuasion that national characters existed which helped to mould the destiny of nations. This school had so much faith in fixed national character that it gave the concept an important place as a prime moulder of political, social, and economic institutions. The procedure was to prove that the *Volksgeist* (people's spirit), the *Volksstimme* (people's voice), and the *Volksseele* (people's soul), were compounded of certain desirable characteristics which showed the superiority of one people over another. By the same token, other peoples were regarded as inferior national groups. Emphasis was placed upon such externals as language, dress, and social habits. From this school believing in a permanent, stable national character arose such stereotypes as the realistic and volatile Frenchman, the emotional and cynical Italian, the phlegmatic and self-assured Englishman, the frugal Scotsman, and the aggressive and naïve American. These sweeping generalizations have little scientific validity without careful frequency analysis, but they have persisted as popular beliefs.

The third position, and the one we shall accept here, recognizes the limited validity of the idea of national character, but does not reject it for that reason. It is aware of the difficulties encountered both in defining national character and in measuring its quality. The term has validity only if it is intended to convey the idea that within certain cultures distinct values have been inculcated by environmental conditions, historical institutions, and formal education. It is intended to show that different aspects of the complex character of man respond to different environmental conditions, and that separate groups, as well as individuals, react socially in diverse ways. From this point of view it is unwise to reject altogether the psychological differences among nations in favor of the more impersonal factors of economics and military power.

It will be noted that nothing has been said in this position about national character as if it were something biologically inherited. Much of the confusion that has existed in treating this problem in the past has been due to the common practice of confusing the term with the obscure designation "racial character." Since racialism has been exposed as a meaningless fraud, few historians now speak of national character as if it were inheritable. It is obvious that national character could not possibly consist of such inherited characteristics as are organic and inborn. Because of this confusion of meaning, many historians tend to shy away completely from the term "national character," on the assumption that, no matter how carefully they distinguish between nationalism and racialism, they will be accused of subjective thinking and propaganda.

It is useless to insist upon a rigid constancy of national character. Throughout history there have been frequent characterizations of common attitudes and traits of peoples, some of which persist for a long time and others of which apparently change under the influence of historical developments. It is possible that an important transformation can take place in the character traits of a people. The French of the early eighteenth century were generally considered to be a stolid, peace-loving people, yet, within a century, they had undergone a violent revolution and were attempting to impress their ideas upon the rest of Europe by means of Napoleon's sword. Similarly, the once impractical, comfortable Germans of the Holy Roman Empire and the Confederation, petty and bourgeois in their ideas, emerged into a leading position in industry and business in the late nineteenth century, and, proud, hard, and arrogant, found themselves involved in two world wars. The English, once regarded as a people inclined to revolution, are today considered to be one of the most stolid and stable people on earth. Clearly, then, the notion of a *permanent* national character cannot be sustained.

That there is at least a *relative* uniformity of national character is an entirely different matter. Indeed, some national traits show an extraordinary persistence and power of survival. Each individual is exposed to those forces which make up the idea of nationalism—common history, common institutions, common historical traditions, common historical heroes, and, perhaps, common language, literature, and religion. The individual tends to identify himself with the predominant group of the age in which he lives; in other words, he treats the events that happen to the group as though they happened to him, as if the body of society were his own body. This process of identification, partly sensible and objective, and partly imaginative and false, accounts for the obvious intensity of group life. The individual may or may not absorb all the qualities of the national character, especially since in modern, complex, industrialized societies the factors conditioning character may be involved or contradictory. Nor does it necessarily follow that the national character will be the sum total of the individuals' characters, as there may be extraneous factors existing over which the individual has little or no control. The majority of people in a given country may abhor the idea of war; nevertheless, they find themselves part of an aggressive people bent upon seeking for themselves "a place in the sun." The national character may be at variance with the personality of the individual member of the nation, as there are always large numbers in any society who fail to conform to type. It is possible that even a conforming individual may act atypically on occasion.

*   *   *

The role of the historian in the new study of national character stems from the fact that institutions often reflect mainly the influence of dominant groups, hence "analysis of a nation's current institutions must be supplemented by historical and causal studies." The course of German history has shown that there is a conspicuous lack of balance in the national character. The duality of German conduct is a striking phenomenon. German greatness of purpose and achievement have often been combined with a vague, romantic foolhardiness. The Germans may be sentimental and good-hearted and at the same time unpredictable and dangerous. The tradition of internal quarreling made the Germans either frivolous or ruthless, or else they took refuge in philosophy and mysticism because the world seemed to be too harsh for them. The number of eccentric types in Germany is inordinately large. Harmony in the Germans is rare.

The outstanding fact of German history is a polarity of development and a dichotomy of ideas and procedures that has never been resolved. The history of the Germans has been the history of the unending struggle between the continental Teutons for a working compromise between uniformity and disruption. Uniformity was, and is, contrary to the ethnic, political, and cultural divergences of the Germans. At no time in German history has there been one central power strong enough to crush the centrifugal tendencies of the component parts. At no time were the individual parts weak enough to allow themselves to be merged into one highly centralized body, with the exception of the short-lived Hitler Reich.

*　　　*　　　*

. . . The idea of the independent unit was an early theme in German history. Both Caesar and Tacitus testified to the fierce sense of independence of the early Germanic barbarians. German feudalism in the Middle Ages was torn by disintegration.

Superimposed on this dualism of centralism versus particularism was an even greater dichotomy—the conflict between national unity and theocratical world monarchy. While England and France emerged in early modern times as national states, in the Germanies there was a fruitless pursuit of idealistic dreams of a theocratical world monarchy.

*　　　*　　　*

The persistent dichotomy appeared again in the struggle between Austria and Prussia for domination of Germany. The Austrian monarchy controlled a consolidated territory that extended from the Swiss-Tyrolean border to the Polish frontier. Starting as a product of German particularism, Prussia expanded on eastern colonial ground, and, by the time of the reign of Frederick the Great, had arisen to a place of importance in Europe. The dualism between Austria and Prussia continued through the first half of the nineteenth century. After the Congress of Vienna in 1815, the Metternichian policy or domination was imposed on Prussia until Metternich's collapse in 1848. The professors of the Frankfort Assembly had a golden opportunity to create once and for all time the hotly desired German unity, but these well-meaning men found themselves on the horns of a dilemma. Was there to be a "Big German" (*grossdeutsch*) solution, which would include the Germans of Austria, or a "Little German" (*kleindeutsch*) settlement, which would leave out the Austrian Germans? German liberalism was to be submerged in the frustrations of this dualism.

Once German unity had been fashioned in the crucible of Bismarck's wars, and once the German Empire of William II felt itself ready for expansion, it might have been expected that the tragic dichotomy would be resolved. But not so. This time Germany was caught between East (*Drang nach Osten*) and West. The Empire created by Bismarck in 1871 sought a solution in a kind of half-hearted combination between Western constitutionalism and Eastern authoritarianism. Prussia, the state of soldiers and officials, was the determining force in the government, and the voice of the people was heard but faintly in the *Reichstag,* an ineffectual debating society. The German Emperor, who was at the same time King of Prussia, exercised semi-autocratic powers through his Prussian office.

*   *   *

There is a strong historical reason for the curious German predilection for philosophic systems, abstract ideas, and cosmopolitan dreams. With little opportunity to take part in practical political affairs, the Germans sought to exercise their minds in intellectual contemplation, as indicated by the enormous popularity of philosophy in nineteenth-century Germany. Following the lead of Kant, German philosophers, such as Hegel, Schelling, Fichte, and others, and the historical school of law and politics, such as Savigny, Adam Müller, Friedrich Stahl, and others, sought to give ideas and ideals a predominant position in the scale of human values and to convert them into an exclusive pillar of the universe. Hegel, especially, made liberty the pivot of political philosophy, but withdrew this liberty from the individual and transferred it to the State, thus bringing about a union between idealism and absolutism. Unlike the earlier philosophers, the Germans took, not man, but *German man* as their primary concern, thus making the objective of the mind, which in Europe generally had been considered the universal good, the particular good of German nationalism. Treitschke expressed this trend in a revealing passage: "Depth of thought, idealism, cosmopolitan views; a transcendental philosophy which boldly oversteps (or freely looks over) the separate barriers of finite existence; familiarity with every thought and feeling, the desire to traverse the worldwide realm of ideas in common with the foremost intellects of all nations and all times—all that has at all times been held to be characteristic of the Germans and has always been praised as the privilege of German character and breeding." This preference for philosophic systems, accompanied by a self-righteous rejection of the actual forces at work in the world, resulted in a dangerous political immaturity.

The end result of this predisposition toward philosophical abstractions was a gradual shifting to a mythological attitude which was, in effect, a battle against the temper of Western civilization. Aurel Kolnai described this defiance of reason and morals in a significant passage:

> This self-conscious subjectivism, this deliberate sacrifice of the intellect, this methodological training to barbarian *naïveté* has an almost touching air of heroic perversity about it. What is its meaning? Apart from the general "weariness of civilization" and the historical antagonism to the nations and forces that represent it, roused to fever-pitch by the War and its sequel, the Call for Mythology is also in line with the political conception of the Totalitarian Tribe and the anthropological and religious conception of the Master Man, the Superior Race, the Sacred We. Objective Truth, enduring and detached (be it of the religious or the scientific order), portends deadly injury to the triple identity of Tribal Egotism: the identification of the racial Self, the Master Set, and Deity. . . . In brief, the call for mythology indicates the will to break the spiritual backbone of man, to supersede personality, with its consciousness of eternal relations, by a flabby vital stock of ethnic purity, to pull down the last strongholds of the mind in which human freedom and dignity could entrench themselves against the totalitarian encroachment of an insane and godless tyranny.

The point of view expressed by L. B. Namier, Professor of Modern History in the University of Manchester, England, is one for which the remainder of this book will attempt to present historical evidence in various fields:

> Most types of social groups can be found, in one form or another, in all nations, but attaining various degrees of development and importance; and some nations develop into one or two forms into dominant patterns which express national character and their communal life. Thus the pattern forms of England are Parliament and the team, of Germany the State and the army, or perhaps rather the army and the State. Characteristic of the English social groups is the degree of freedom which they leave to the individual and the basic equality of their members, the voluntary submission to the rules of "the game" and the curious mixture of elasticity and rigidity in these rules; most of all, the moral standards which these groups enforce or to which they aspire.
>
> Characteristic of the German social groups is the utter, conscious, subordination of the individual, the iron discipline which they enforce, the high degree of organization and efficiency which they attain, and their resultant inhumanity. The State is an aim in itself, while that of

the army is essentially a-moral—to smash the enemy. Whatever characteristics in the individual members of the two nations have gone to form these patterns, and whatever share circumstances had in their development, once crystallized these patterns powerfully react on the individual and mould him in turn. Removed from this setting the individual may develop, or at least seem to develop, in a different manner: still, it is the pattern which expresses the national character.

The contention that national extremism was a bolt out of the heavens, a "catastrophe" that suddenly appeared to plague the German people, is inaccurate and untenable. German extremism did not occur in a vacuum; its roots lay deep in German history for the last century and a half. Behind it was a pattern of thinking tempered by nationalism, romanticism, and historicism. The Germans who were shocked and amazed by the excesses of Hitlerism never understood that the political régime which almost led them to national destruction was the logical outcome of a long and dangerous intellectual tradition.

*　　　*　　　*

It would be incorrect to assume that the line leading to German integral nationalism was absolutely clear and unchallenged as it ran through the course of the nineteenth century. The golden age of German universalism, epitomized in the thinking and works of Lessing, Humboldt, Goethe, Schiller, Beethoven, and Mozart, ended in the frustrations of the nineteenth century as the Germans apparently became exhausted by their sudden and dizzy ascent to politico-economic power. But even in that century, in which the German character was moulded in the Prussian tradition, there were some thinkers who were appalled and disgusted with the rapidly accelerating extremism. Heine and even Nietzsche ("nationalism is disease and madness") heaped ridicule on German provincialism and urged their fellow-countrymen to mature into citizens of the world. As other countries, Prusso-Germany had a supply of liberals, rationalists, socialists, internationalists, cosmopolitans, and pacifists, but they were always a relatively small and isolated group with voices crying in the wilderness. Their ineffectiveness testifies to the strength of the culture-power advocates who moulded the German mind in their own image. The masses were so politically inarticulate and immature that even socialism, which was supposed to stem from the yearnings of the lower classes, received its stamp from above and became "Prussian socialism" and "national socialism."

Our procedure will be to select representatives of various fields and show what they contributed to the rise of extremist thinking in Germany. Several advocates of German liberalism are included to demonstrate the weakness of the liberal position contra extremism.

2 Liberalism and Nationalism in Post-Napoleonic Germany

In 1806 Napoleon's army crushed the Prussians at Jena, and Prussia found herself, for the first time, a subject nation. It was in answer to the despair that gripped the Fatherland that Johann Gottlieb Fichte (1762–1814) gave a series of addresses intended to reveal the uniqueness of the German nation and its historical destiny.

FROM *Address to the German Nation* BY J. G. FICHTE

I SPEAK FOR GERMANS SIMPLY, of Germans simply, not recognizing, but setting aside completely and rejecting, all the dissociating distinctions which for centuries unhappy events have caused in this single nation. You, gentlemen, are indeed to my outward eye the first and immediate representatives who bring before my mind the beloved national characteristics, and are the visible spark at which the flame of my address is kindled. But my spirit gathers round it the educated part of the whole German nation, from all the lands in which they are scattered. It thinks of and considers our common position and relations; it longs that part of the living force, with which these addresses may chance to grip you, may also remain in and breathe from the dumb printed page which alone will come to the eyes of the absent, and may in all places kindle German hearts to decision and action. Only of Germans and simply for Germans, I said. In due course we shall show that any other mark of unity or any other national bond either never had truth and meaning or, if it had, that owing to our present position these bonds of union have been destroyed and torn from us and can never recur; it is only by means of the common characteristic of being German that we can avert the downfall of our nation which is threatened by its fusion with

Johann Gottlieb Fichte, *Addresses to the German Nation* (1922), pp. 3–4, 206–9, 227–33, 235–6, translated by R. F. Jones and G. H. Turnbull. Reprinted by permission of The Open Court Publishing Company, La Salle, Illinois.

foreign peoples, and win back again an individuality that is self-supporting and quite incapable of any dependence upon others. With our perception of the truth of this statement its apparent conflict (feared now, perhaps, by many) with other duties and with matters that are considered sacred will completely vanish.

Therefore, as I speak only of Germans in general, I shall proclaim that many things concern us which do not apply in the first instance to those assembled here, just as I shall pronounce as the concern of all Germans other things which apply in the first place only to us. In the spirit of which these addresses are the expression, I perceive that organic unity in which no member regards the fate of another as the fate of a stranger. I behold that unity (which shall and must arise if we are not to perish altogether) already achieved, completed, and existing.

*   *   *

. . . He who lets himself go without paying heed to himself, and allows himself to be moulded by circumstances just as they please, soon accustoms himself to any possible order of things. However much his eye may have been offended by something when he first saw it, let it only present itself anew every day in the same way and he accustoms himself to it. Later, he finds it natural, and in the end he even gets to like it as something inevitable; he would not thank you for the restoration of the original and better state of things, because this would tear him out of the mode of life to which he has become accustomed. In this way men become accustomed even to slavery, if only their material existence is not thereby affected, and in time they get to like it. It is just this that is the most dangerous thing about a state of subjection; it makes men insensitive to all true honour, and, moreover, for the indolent man it has its very pleasant side, because it relieves him of many a care and of the need of thinking for himself.

Let us be on our guard against being taken unawares by this sweetness of servitude, for it robs even our posterity of the hope of future emancipation. If our external activity is restricted and fettered, let us elevate our spirit all the more boldly to the thought of freedom; let us rise to live in this thought and make it the sole object of our wish and longing. What if freedom disappear for a time from the visible world? Let us give it a place of refuge in our innermost thoughts, until there shall grow up round about us the new world which has the power of manifesting our thoughts outwardly. In the sphere where no one can deprive us of the freedom to do as we think best—in our own minds let us make ourselves a pattern, a prophecy, and a guarantee of that which will become a reality when we are gone. Let us not allow our spirit, as well as our body, to be bent and subjected and brought into captivity.

If you ask me how this is to be brought about, the only entirely comprehensive answer is this: We must at once become what we ought to be in any case, namely, Germans. We are not to subject our spirit; therefore we must before all things provide a spirit for ourselves, and a firm and certain spirit; we must become earnest in all things and not go on existing frivolously, as if life were a jest; we must form for ourselves enduring and unshakable principles which will serve as a sure guide for all the rest of our thoughts and actions. Life and thought with us must be of one piece and a solid and interpenetrating whole; in both we must live according to nature and truth, and throw away foreign contrivances; in a word, we must provide character for ourselves; for to have character and to be German [*Charakter haben und deutsch sein*] undoubtedly mean the same; and the thing has no special name in our language, because it is intended to proceed immediately from our very existence without any knowledge or reflection on our part.

We must first of all set our own thoughts to work and think about the great events of our days, their relation to us, and what we have to expect from them; and we must provide ourselves with a firm and clear view of all these matters, and a definite and unchangeable Yes or No in answer to the questions that arise out of them. Everyone who makes the slightest claim to culture is bound to do that. The animal life of man proceeds in all ages according to the same laws, and in this every age is alike. Only to the understanding are there such things as different ages; and only the man whose conception penetrates them lives in them, and only he exists in his own age; any other kind of life is nothing but the life of plants and animals. To let everything that happens pass by one unperceived, perhaps to close eye and ear diligently to its urgent message, and even to boast of such thoughtlessness as if it were great wisdom—this may be the proper thing for a rock on which the waves of the sea beat without its feeling them, or for a tree-trunk dashed to and fro by storms without its perceiving them; but in no wise does it beseem a thinking being. Even the thinker who dwells in the higher spheres is not absolved from this general obligation of understanding his own age. Everything that is on the higher plane must want to influence the immediate present in its own fashion; and he who truly lives in the former lives at the same time in the latter also; if he did not live in the latter also, it would be a proof that he did not live in the former either, but only dreamed in it. That lack of heed to what is going on before our eyes, and the artful distraction to other objects of the attention that is everywhere aroused, would be the best thing that an enemy of our independence could wish to find. If he is sure that nothing will set us thinking, he can do anything he wishes with us, as if we were lifeless tools. It is precisely this thoughtlessness that accustoms itself to anything; but where clear and comprehensive thought, and in that thought the image of what ought to be, always remains watchful, there is no question of becoming accustomed to such things.

These addresses have in the first place invited you, and they will invite the whole German nation, in so far as it is possible at the present time to assemble the nation around a speaker by means of the printed book, to come to a definite decision and to be at one with themselves in their own minds on the following questions:

1. Whether it is true or untrue that there is a German nation, and that its continued existence in its peculiar and independent nature is at the present time in danger;
2. Whether it is worth the trouble, or not worth the trouble, to maintain this nation;
3. Whether there is any sure and thorough means of maintaining it, and what this means is.

*   *   *

If only the German nation had remained united, with a common will and a common strength! Then, though the other Europeans might have wanted to murder each other on every sea and shore, and on every island too, in the middle of Europe the firm wall of the Germans would have prevented them from reaching each other. Here peace would have remained, and the Germans would have maintained themselves, and with themselves also a part of the other European peoples, in quiet and prosperity.

That things should remain thus did not suit the selfishness of foreign countries, whose calculations did not look more than one moment ahead. They found German bravery useful in waging their wars and German hands useful to snatch the booty from their rivals. A means had to be found to attain this end, and foreign cunning won an easy victory over German ingenuousness and lack of suspicion. It was foreign countries which first made use of the division of mind produced by religious disputes in Germany —Germany, which presented on a small scale the features of Christian Europe as a whole—foreign countries, I say, made use of these disputes to break up the close inner unity of Germany into separate and disconnected parts. Foreign countries had already destroyed their own unity naturally, by splitting into parts over a common prey; and now they artificially destroyed German unity. They knew how to present each of these separate States that had thus arisen in the lap of the one nation—which had no enemy except those foreign countries themselves, and no concern except the common one of setting itself with united strength against their seductive craft and cunning—foreign countries, I say, knew how to present each of these States to the others as a natural enemy, against which each State must be perpetually on its guard. On the other hand, they knew how to make themselves appear to the German States as natural allies against the danger threatening them from their own countrymen—as allies with whom alone they would themselves stand or fall, and whose enterprises they must in turn support with all their might. It was only because of this artificial bond that all the disputes which might arise about any matter whatever in the Old World or the New became disputes of the German races in their relation to each other. Every war, no matter what its cause, had to be fought out on German soil and with German blood; every disturbance of the balance had to be adjusted in that nation to which the whole fountainhead of such relationship was unknown; and the German States, whose separate existence was in itself contrary to all nature and reason, were compelled, in order that they might count for something, to act as make-weights to the chief forces in the scale of the European equilibrium, whose movement they followed blindly and without any will of their own. Just as in many States abroad the citizens are designated as belonging to this or that foreign party, or voting for this or that foreign alliance, but no name is found for those who belong to the party of their own country, so it was with the Germans; for long enough they belonged only to some foreign party or other, and one seldom came across a man who supported the party of the Germans and was of the opinion that this country ought to make an alliance with itself.

This, then, is the true origin and meaning, this the result for Germany and for the world, of that notorious doctrine of a balance of power to be artificially maintained between the European States. If Christian Europe had remained one, as it ought to be and as it originally was, there would never have been any occasion to think of such a thing. That which is one rests upon itself and supports itself, and does not split up into conflicting forces which must be brought to an equilibrium. Only when Europe became divided and without a law did the thought of a balance acquire a meaning from necessity. To this Europe, divided and without a law, Germany did not belong. If only Germany at any rate had remained one, it would have rested on itself in the centre of the civilized world like the sun in the centre of the universe; it would have kept itself at peace, and with itself the adjacent countries; and without any artificial measures it would have kept everything in equilibrium by the mere fact of its natural existence. It was only the deceit of foreign countries that dragged Germany into their own lawlessness and their own disputes; it was they who taught Germany the treacherous notion of the balance of power, for they knew it to be one of the most effective means of deluding Germany as to its own true advantage and of keeping it in that state of delusion. This aim is now sufficiently attained, and the result that was intended is now complete before our eyes. Even if we cannot do away with this result, why should we not at any rate extirpate the source of it in our own understanding, which is now almost the only thing over which we still have sovereign power? Why should the old dream still be placed before our eyes, now that disaster has awakened us from sleep? Why should we not now at any rate see the truth and perceive the only means that could have saved us? Perhaps our descendants may do what we see ought to be done, just as we now suffer because our fathers dreamed. Let us understand that the conception of an equilibrium to be artificially maintained might have been a consoling dream for foreign countries amid the guilt and evil that oppressed them; but that this conception, being an entirely foreign product, ought never to have taken root in the mind of a German, and that the Germans ought never to have been so situated that it could take root among them. Let us understand that now at any rate we must perceive the utter worthlessness of such a conception, and must see that the salvation of all is to be found, not in it, but solely in the unity of the Germans among themselves.

*   *   *

Now, at last, let us be bold enough to look at the deceptive vision of a universal monarchy, which people are beginning to hold up for public veneration in place of that equilibrium which for some time has been growing more and more preposterous, and let us perceive how hateful and contrary to reason that vision is. Spiritual nature was able to present the essence of humanity in extremely diverse gradations in individuals and in individuality as a whole, in peoples. Only when each people, left to itself, develops and forms itself in accordance with its own peculiar quality, and only when in every people each individual develops himself in accordance with that common quality, as well as in accordance with his own peculiar quality—then, and then only, does the manifestation of divinity appear in its true mirror as it ought to be; and only a man who either entirely lacks the notion of the rule of law and divine order, or else is an obdurate enemy thereto, could take upon himself to want to interfere with that law, which is the highest law in the spiritual world. Only in the invisible qualities of nations, which are hidden from their own eyes—qualities as the means whereby these nations remain in touch with the source of original life—only therein is to be found the guarantee of their present and future worth, virtue, and merit. If these qualities are dulled by admixture and worn away by friction, the flatness that results will bring about a separation from spiritual nature, and this in its turn will cause all men to be fused together to their uniform and conjoint destruction. As for the writers who console us for all our ills with the prospect that we, too, shall be subjects of the new universal monarchy that is beginning—are we to believe them when they say that someone or other has decided upon such a grinding together of all the germs of what is human in humanity, in order to press the unresisting dough into some new form, and that so monstrous an act of brutality or enmity against the human race is possible in this age of ours? Even if, in the first place, we were willing to make up our minds to believe such an utterly incredible thing, the further question arises: By what instrument is such a plan to be carried out? What sort of people is it to be which, in the present state of European culture, shall conquer the world for some new universal monarch?

*   *   *

The ideas we have mentioned, and all ideas of this kind, are products of a form of thinking which merely plays a game with itself and sometimes, too, gets caught in its own cobwebs—a form of thinking which is unworthy of German thoroughness and earnestness. At best, some of these ideas, as, for example, that of a political equilibrium, are serviceable guiding-lines to enable one to find one's way about in the extensive and confused multiplicity of phenomena and to set it in order; but to believe that these things exist in nature, or to strive to realize them, is the same as to expect to find the poles, the meridians, and the tropics, by which our survey of the earth is guided, actually marked and indicated on the surface of the globe. May it become the custom in our nation, not merely to think idly and as it were experimentally, just to see what will come of it, but to think in such a way that what we think shall be true and have a real effect in life! Then it will be superfluous to warn people against such phantoms of a political wisdom whose origin is foreign and which only deludes the Germans.

This thoroughness, earnestness, and weightiness in our way of thinking, once we have made it our own, will show itself in our life as well. We are defeated; whether we are now to be despised as well, and rightly despised, whether in addition to all other losses we are to lose our honour also—that will still depend on ourselves. The fight with weapons has ended; there arises now, if we so will it, the new fight of principles, of morals, of character.

Let us give our guests a picture of faithful devotion to friends and fatherland, of incorruptible uprightness and love of duty, of all civic and domestic virtues, to take home with them as a friendly gift from their hosts; for they will return home at last some time or other. Let us be careful not to invite them to despise us; there would, however, be no surer way for us to do this than if we either feared them beyond measure or gave up our own way of life and strove to resemble them in theirs. Be it far from us as individuals to be so unmannerly as to provoke or irritate individuals; but, as to the rest, our safest measure will be to go our own way in all things, as if we were alone with ourselves, and not to establish any relation that is not laid upon us by absolute necessity; and the surest means to this will be for each one to content himself with what the old national conditions are able to afford him, to take up his share of the common burden according to his powers, but to look upon any favour from foreigners as a disgrace and a dishonour.

In 1813, the Germans, led by the Prussians, rose up against their French conquerors and contributed significantly to the downfall of Napoleon. Some of the veterans of this war returned to their studies at the universities, inspired with the ideal they had served. They banded together into a fraternal organization, the Allgemeine Deutsche Burschenschaft, *which was intended to keep their ideal alive. It is expressed in the two selections that follow.*

This speech by theology student Riemann, Knight of the Iron Cross, was delivered in the Hall of the Minnesingers at the Wartburg, October 18, 1817.

Theology Student Riemann's Speech

MY ASSEMBLED BROTHERS, today for the fourth time the bonfire will flame up to heaven, to remind us of the past and to urge us on to the future. Since that battle, four long years have passed; the German people held fine hopes then, but these have all been dissipated. The event has betrayed our expectation; many a great and glorious task, which could have been accomplished and which must be accomplished, has been left undone; many a holy and noble passion has been contaminated by contempt and scorn. Of all the princes of Germany, only one has made good the pledge he gave—he, in whose free land we celebrate the battle festival. Many a stouthearted man has grown discouraged with such an outcome; many a man thinks that the much-praised nobility of the German people has no meaning, withdraws from the public life which showed such glorious promise, and seeks compensation in the silent pursuit of science.

Others prefer to seek a new fatherland, in the far regions of the earth where new life stirs.

But now I ask you who are gathered here, in the bloom of youth, with all the enthusiasm supplied by the fresh young force of life—you who one day will be the teachers, the representatives and the magistrates of the people, upon whom the fatherland bases its hopes—you who have fought, some with weapons in hand, but all in spirit and will, for the weal of the fatherland—I ask you whether you are at one with such sentiments. No! Now and always, no! In times of need we saw God's will and followed it. And that which we recognized then we will hold to now, as long as a drop of blood runs in our veins. The spirit which has brought us together here, the spirit of truth and justice, shall lead us through all our life, that we, all brothers and sons of one and the same fatherland, may build a brazen wall against the internal and external enemies of that fatherland; that raging death may not affright us in the open fight or make us fear to endure the fiercest onslaught when the aggressor threatens; that when truth and justice are at stake, the glory of

P. Joachimsen, ed., *Die Nationalbewegung von 1815–49* (1928), translated in T. C. Mendenhall, B. D. Henning, and A. S. Foord, *The Quest for a Principle of Authority in Europe 1715–Present* (1948), pp. 208–9. Reprinted by permission of Holt, Rinehart and Winston, Inc.

thrones of kings may not blind us [to our duty] of speaking the strong free word—and that in our hearts the desire for truth, the desire for every human and patriotic virtue, may never be extinguished!

This charter was announced on the 18th day of the Month of Victory, 1818.

Constitutional Charter of the Universal German Burschenschaft

I.

THE UNIVERSAL GERMAN *Burschenschaft* is the free association of all young German scholars, who are now being educated in the *Hochschule,* in one union, founded upon the relationship of German youth to the growing unity of the German people.

II.

As a free community, the Universal German *Burschenschaft* sets forth the following principles as the focus of its activity: (*a*) unity, freedom, and the mutual equality of all *Burschen;* equality of all rights and duties: (*b*) the development of all our spiritual and physical powers for the service of the fatherland, according to German-Christian principles.

III.

The companionship of all German *Burschen* in the spirit of these propositions represents the highest ideal of the Universal German *Burschenschaft:* the spiritual and physical union of all German *Burschen.*

IV.

The Universal German *Burschenschaft* comes into existence in this way, so that it may present, increasingly as time goes on, a model of a people prospering in freedom and unity, that it may maintain, in the development

P. Joachimsen, ed., *Die Nationalbewegung von 1815–49* (1928), translated in T. C. Mendenhall, B. D. Henning, and A. S. Foord, *The Quest for a Principle of Authority in Europe 1715–Present* (1948), pp. 208–9. Reprinted by permission of Holt, Rinehart and Winston, Inc.

of all spiritual and physical forces, a national brotherly way of life, and may prepare its members for public life in this free, equal, and orderly community, with the end that each of them will be exalted to such a grade of self-assurance that his pure individuality will reflect the noble glory of German folk life.

3 The Confrontation of Liberalism and Nationalism

> *Carl Schurz, born in 1829, represented a generation once removed from the stirring events of 1813. In 1848 he was a student, a liberal, and a nationalist. The three seemed perfectly compatible then; Schurz was soon to find that, as conditions changed, certain strains were introduced. Ultimately, Schurz fled Germany and came to the United States.*
>
> *In the selection that follows, Schurz gives his analysis of German history to 1848 and an account of what happened then.*

FROM *The Reminiscences of Carl Schurz*

THEN CAME, IN 1813, after long suffering and debasement, the great popular uprising against Napoleonic despotism, and with it a period of a new German national consciousness. To this feeling appealed the famous manifesto, issued from the town of Kalisch, in which the king of Prussia, allied with the Russian Czar, after Napoleon's defeat in Russia, called the German people to arms, promising at the same time a new national union and participation of the people in the business of government under constitutional forms. The new birth of a united German national empire, the abolition of arbitrary government by the introduction of free political institutions—that was the solemn promise of the Prussian king as the people understood it—that was the hope which inspired the people in the struggle against Napoleonic rule with enthusiastic heroism and a self-sacrifice without limit, and ended in a final victory. It was one of the periods in history when a people proved itself ready to sacrifice all for the attainment of an ideal. But after the victories of Leipzig and Waterloo followed another time

The Reminiscences of Carl Schurz, I (1907), 103–6, 109–10, 112–4, 118–21, 124–6, 134–8, 141–5, 154–6, 161–3.

of bitter disappointment. Against the formation of a united Germany arose not only the jealous opposition of non-German Europe, but also the selfish ambitions of the smaller German princes, especially of those who, as members of the "Rheinbund," such as Bavaria, Würtemberg, Baden, etc., had been raised in their rank. And this opposition was strengthened by the intriguing policy of Austria, which, with her possessions outside of Germany, had also un-German interests and designs. And this Austrian policy was conducted by Prince Metternich, the prime minister of Austria, to whom every emotion of German patriotism was foreign, as he hated and feared every free aspiration among the people. Thus the peace was far from bringing to the German people the reward for their sacrifices which they had deserved and expected. From the Congress of Vienna, in 1814 and 1815, which disposed of peoples as of herds of cattle in order to establish a permanent balance of power in Europe, nothing issued for the German nation but a treaty of alliance between German states, the famous "Deutsche Bund," the organ of which was to be the "Bundestag"; and this organ was to be composed of the representatives of the various German kings and princes, without any vestige of a representation of the people. There was no mention of any guarantee of civic rights, of a popular vote, of a free press, of the freedom of assembly, of a trial by jury. On the contrary, the "Bundestag," impotent as an organ of the German nation in its relations to the outside world, developed itself only as a mutual insurance society of despotic rulers— as a central police board for the suppression of all national and liberal movements. The king of Prussia, Frederick William III, the same who had made the promises to the people contained in the proclamation of Kalisch, had probably in the days of distress and of national uprising honestly meant to do what he promised. But his mind was narrow and easily disposed to consider autocratic authority on his part as necessary for the well-being of the world. . . .

Hope revived when Frederick William III's son and successor, Frederick William IV, ascended the Prussian throne in 1840. He was regarded as a man of high intelligence and had, as crown-prince, excited fair expectations. Many considered him incapable of continuing the stupid and sterile policy of his father. Indeed, the first utterances of the new king and the employment of able men in high positions encouraged the hope that he harbored a national heart, in sympathy with the patriotic aspirations of the German people, and that the liberal currents of the time would find in him appreciative understanding. But fresh disappointment followed. As soon as the demand was publicly made, that now at last the old promises of a representative government should be fulfilled, the king's attitude changed. These demands were bluntly repelled, and the censorship of the press was enforced with renewed severity.

*   *   *

There had indeed long been some revolutionary agitators who, in their isolation, had passed for dreamers and could win but a slim following. But now the feeling began to spread in large circles that the real thunder-storm was coming, although hardly anybody anticipated how soon it would come. In former days people had excited themselves about what Thiers and Guizot had said in the French chambers, or Palmerston and Derby in the English parliament, or even what Hecker, Rotteck and Welker had said in the little Diet of the grand duchy of Baden. But now everybody listened with nervous eagerness to every word that in the United Diet of the most important of German states had fallen from the lips of Camphausen, Vincke, Beckerath, Hansemann and other liberal leaders. There was a feeling in the air as if this United Diet, in its position and the task to be performed by it, was not at all unlike the French assembly of the year 1789.

We university students watched these events with perhaps a less clear understanding, but with no less ardent interest, than our elders. As I have already mentioned, the "Burschenschaft" had its political traditions. Immediately after the wars of liberation—1813 to 1815—it had been among the first in line to raise the cry for the fulfillment of the pledges given by the princes. It had cultivated the national spirit with zeal, although sometimes with exaggerated demonstrations. It had furnished many victims in the persecutions of so-called demagogues. The political activity of the old Burschenschaft had indeed not been continued by the younger associations; but "God, Liberty, Fatherland," had still remained the common watchword; we still wore the prohibited black-red-golden ribbon under our coats, and very many members of the new Burschenschaft societies still recognized it as their duty to keep themselves well informed of what happened in the political world and to devote to it as active an interest as possible. Thus the liberal currents of our time found among us enthusiastic partisans, although we young people could not give a very definite account of the practical steps to be taken.

In the prosecution of my studies I had taken up with ardor the history of Europe at the period of the great Reformation. I expected to make this my specialty as a professor of history. The great characters of that period strongly attracted me and I could not resist the temptation to clothe some of them in dramatic form. So I planned a tragedy, the main figure of which was to be Ulrich von Hutten, and I began to elaborate some scenes in detail.

*   *   *

One morning, toward the end of February, 1848, I sat quietly in my attic-chamber, working hard at my tragedy of "Ulrich von Hutten," when suddenly a friend rushed breathlessly into the room, exclaiming: "What, you sitting here! Do you not know what has happened?"

"No; what?"

"The French have driven away Louis Philippe and proclaimed the republic."

I threw down my pen—and that was the end of "Ulrich von Hutten." I never touched the manuscript again. We tore down the stairs, into the street, to the market-square, the accustomed meeting-place for all the student societies after their midday dinner. Although it was still forenoon, the market was already crowded with young men talking excitedly. There was no shouting, no noise, only agitated conversation. What did we want there? This probably no one knew. But since the French had driven away Louis Philippe and proclaimed the republic, something of course must happen here, too. Some of the students had brought their rapiers along, as if it were necessary at once to make an attack or to defend ourselves. We were dominated by a vague feeling as if a great outbreak of elemental forces had begun, as if an earthquake was impending of which we had felt the first shock, and we instinctively crowded together. Thus we wandered about in numerous bands—to the "Kneipe," where our restlessness, however, would not suffer us long to stay; then to other pleasure resorts, where we fell into conversation with all manner of strangers, to find in them the same confused, astonished and expectant state of mind; then back to the market-square, to see what might be going on there; then again somewhere else, and so on, without aim and end, until finally late in the night fatigue compelled us to find the way home.

The next morning there were the usual lectures to be attended. But how profitless! The voice of the professor sounded like a monotonous drone coming from far away. What he had to say did not seem to concern us. The pen that should have taken notes remained idle. At last we closed with a sigh the notebook and went away, impelled by a feeling that now we had something more important to do—to devote ourselves to the affairs of the fatherland. And this we did by seeking as quickly as possible again the company of our friends, in order to discuss what had happened and what was to come. In these conversations, excited as they were, certain ideas and catchwords worked themselves to the surface, which expressed more or less the feelings of the people. Now had arrived in Germany the day for the establishment of "German Unity," and the founding of a great, powerful national German Empire. In the first line the convocation of a national parliament. Then the demands for civil rights and liberties, free speech, free press, the right of free assembly, equality before the law, a freely elected representation of the people with legislative power, responsibility of ministers, self-government of the communes, the right of the people to carry arms, the formation of a civic guard with elective officers, and so on—in short, that which was called a "constitutional form of government on a broad democratic basis." Republican ideas were at first only sparingly expressed. But the word democracy was soon on all tongues, and many, too, thought it a matter of course that if the princes should try to withhold from the people the rights and liberties demanded, force would take the place of mere petition. Of course the regeneration of the fatherland must, if possible, be accomplished by peaceable means. A few days after the outbreak of this commotion I reached my nineteenth birthday. I remember to have been so entirely absorbed by what was happening that I could hardly turn my thoughts to anything else. Like many of my friends, I was dominated by the feeling that at last the great opportunity had arrived for giving to the German people the liberty which was their birthright and to the German fatherland its unity and greatness, and that it was now the first duty of every German to do and to sacrifice everything for this sacred object. We were profoundly, solemnly in earnest.

*   *   *

The enthusiastic elation was followed by a short time of anxious expectancy. At last came the report of the awful events that had taken place in the capital.

The king of Prussia, Frederick William IV, at first received the petitions rushing in upon him with sullen silence. He had so recently, and then so emphatically, even so defiantly, proclaimed his inflexible determination never to consent to any constitutional limitation of his kingly power, that the thought of yielding to popular pressure anything that he fancied should be only a free emanation of the royal will was well-nigh inconceivable to him. But the situation became more threatening from day to day. Not only the language of the deputations arriving from various parts of the kingdom constantly grew more and more impetuous and peremptory, but the people of Berlin began to hold mass meetings counting by thousands and to greet with thundering acclamations the political watchwords uttered by popular orators. The municipal authorities, too, were swept into the current and entreated the king to make concessions. At last he saw the necessity of yielding something. On the 14th of March he gave a "gracious" answer to an address presented by the city council, but that answer was still too evasive and indefinite to satisfy public opinion. Meanwhile bloody collisions occurred between the police supported by military detachments and the multitude thronging the public squares and streets, in which a merchant and a university student were killed. The bitterness of feeling caused by these events was somewhat assuaged by a rumor that the king had resolved upon further and more important concessions, which would be publicly announced on the 18th. He had indeed concluded to issue an edict opening a prospect of steps to be taken in favor of national unity and abolishing the censorship of the press.

On the afternoon of the fateful 18th of March an immense concourse of people assembled on the open square in front of the royal palace, hoping to hear the authoritative announcement that the popular demands had been granted. The king appeared on the balcony and was received with enthusiastic cheers. He attempted to speak, but could not be heard. In the belief, however, that he had granted all that was asked for, the people were ready for a jubilee. Then a cry arose for the removal of the bodies of troops surrounding the palace and appearing to separate the king from his people. It seemed to be expected that this would be granted, too, for an effort was made to open a passage for the soldiers through the dense crowd, when a roll of drums was heard. This was regarded as a signal for the departure of the soldiery; but, instead of the troops withdrawing, heavy bodies of infantry and cavalry pressed upon the multitude for the evident purpose of clearing the square. Then two shots rang from the infantry line and the whole scene suddenly and frightfully changed. Frantic cries arose: "We are betrayed! We are betrayed!" In an instant the mass of people who but a moment before had joyously acclaimed the king, dispersed in the adjoining streets with the angry shout, "To arms, to arms!" In all directions the thoroughfares were soon blocked with barricades. The pavingstones seemed to leap from the ground and to form themselves into bulwarks surmounted by black-red-gold flags, and manned by citizens, university students, tradesmen, artists, laborers, professional men—hastily armed with all sorts of weapons, from rifles and shotguns down to pikes, axes and hammers. There was no preparation, no plan, no system, in the uprising; everybody seemed to follow a common instinct. Then the troops were ordered to the assault. When, after a fierce fight they had taken one barricade, they were at short distances confronted by another and another. Behind the barricades women were busy bringing food and drink for the fighters and caring for the wounded. During the whole night the city resounded with the roar of cannon and the rattle of musketry.

The king seemed at first sternly determined to put down the insurrection at any cost; but as the street battle proceeded he became painfully conscious of its terrible character. Reports arrived in rapid succession. He would now give an order to stop the fight and then an order to go on. Shortly after midnight he wrote with his own hand an address to "My dear Berliners." He began by saying that the firing of the two shots which had caused the excitement had been a mere accident, that a band of miscreants, mostly foreigners, had taken advantage of this misunderstanding to goad many of his good subjects into the fratricidal fight. Then he promised to withdraw the troops as soon as the insurgents would remove the barricades, and he implored them "to listen to the fatherly voice of their king, to which the grievously suffering queen joined her affectionate and tearful prayers." But the address failed to produce the desired effect. It was accompanied with the roar of cannon and the rattle of musketry, and the fighting citizens rather resented being called "a band of miscreants."

At last, on the afternoon of Sunday, the 19th of March, when one of the high commanders of the troops, General Möllendorf, had been captured by the citizens, the withdrawal of the troops was resolved upon. Peace was concluded on the understanding that the army should leave Berlin, that there should be freedom of the press, and that Prussia should have a constitution on a broad democratic basis. When the soldiery had marched off something happened that in dramatic force and significance has never been surpassed in the history of revolutions. From all parts of the city solemn and silent processions moved toward the royal palace. They escorted the bodies of those of the people who had been killed in the battle; the corpses of the slain were carried aloft on litters, their gaping wounds uncovered, their heads wreathed with laurel branches and immortelles. So the processions marched into the inner palace court, where the litters were placed in rows in ghastly parade, and around them the multitude of men with pallid faces, begrimed with blood and powder smoke, many of them still carrying the weapons with which they had fought during the night; and among them women and children bewailing their dead. Then the king was loudly called for. He appeared in an open gallery, pale and dejected, by his side the weeping queen. "Hat off!" the multitude shouted, and the king took off his hat to the dead below. Then a deep voice among the crowd intoned the old hymn, "Jesus, meine Zuversicht"—"Jesus, my Refuge," in which all present joined. The chorus finished, the king silently withdrew and the procession moved away in grim solemnity.

* * *

Suddenly after a prolonged fermentation, and following an impulse from abroad, the German people rose up in strength. The kings and princes now conceded everything that they had refused before, and the people found themselves all at once in full possession of an unaccustomed power. Is it to be wondered at that these surprising changes brought forth some confused desires and misdirected endeavors? Would it not have been more astonishing if the people had at once clearly defined and wisely limited their desires, and promptly found the right means for the attainment of the right objects? Do we expect that the beggar who suddenly becomes a millionaire will instantly know how to make the best use of his unwonted wealth? And yet, it cannot be said of the large majority of the German people that, however vague their political notions may have been, they asked in the revolutionary movements of the year 1848 in the main for anything that was unreasonable or unattainable. Much of what they at that period sought to accomplish has since been realized. The errors committed by them in 1848 were more in the means employed than in the ends aimed at. And the greatest of these errors sprang from the childlike confidence with which they expected the complete fulfillment of all the promises which the kings and princes, especially the King of Prussia, had made under stress of circumstances. It is idle to indulge in speculations about that which might have been if that which was had been different. But one thing is certain: If the princes had not permitted themselves to be seduced by the machinations of the reactionary parties on the one side, nor to be frightened by occasional popular excesses on the other, but had with unflinching fidelity and with the exertion of all their power done that which in March, 1848, they had given the people reason to expect of them, the essential objects fought for at that period would have proved themselves entirely practicable. It was indeed not prudent on the part of the people in their enthusiastic enjoyment of what they called the "Volkerfrühling"—the People's Springtime—an enjoyment to which they gave themselves with such ingenuous elation, to cherish that credulous confidence, instead of assuring themselves of the necessary guarantees against a reaction bound to come; but this imprudence sprang from no ignoble source. He surely wrongs the German people who lays solely at their and their leaders' doors the responsibility for the failures of the years 1848–49, overlooking the tergiversations of the princes.

*   *   *

The national parliament at Frankfurt elected in the spring, which represented the sovereignty of the German people in the large sense and was to give to the united German nation a national government, counted among its members a great many men illustrious in the fields, not of politics, but of science and literature. It soon showed a dangerous tendency of squandering in brilliant, but more or less fruitless, debates much of the time which was sorely needed for prompt and decisive action to secure the legitimate results of the revolution against hostile forces.

But our eyes were turned still more anxiously upon Berlin. Prussia was by far the strongest of the purely German states. The Austrian empire was a conglomeration of different nationalities—German, Magyar, Slavic and Italian. The German element, to which the dynasty and the political capital belonged, had so far been the predominant one. It was most advanced in civilization and wealth, although inferior in numbers. But the Slavs, the Magyars and the Italians, stimulated by the revolutionary movements of 1848, were striving for national autonomy, and although Austria had held the foremost place in the later periods of the ancient German empire and then after the Napoleonic wars in the German Confederacy, it seemed problematic whether her large non-German interests would permit her to play a leading part now in the political unification of Germany under a constitutional government. In fact, it turned out subsequently that the mutual jealousies of the different races enabled the Austrian central government to subjugate to despotic rule one by the other, in spite of the hopeful beginnings of the revolution, and that the non-German interests of Austria and those of the dynasty were predominant in her policy. But Prussia, excepting a comparatively small Polish district, was a purely German country, and by far the strongest among the German states in point of numbers, of general education, of economic activity and especially of military power. It was, therefore, generally felt that the attitude of Prussia would be decisive in determining the fate of the revolution.

For a while the Prussian king, Frederick William IV, seemed to be pleased with the rôle of a leader in the national movement which the revolution had made him assume. His volatile nature seemed to be warmed by a new enthusiasm. He took walks on the streets and talked freely with the people. He spoke of constitutional principles of government to be introduced as a matter of course. He loudly praised the noble generosity which the people of Berlin had manifested toward him in the hours of stress. He ordered the army to wear the black-red-gold cockade together with the Prussian. On the parade ground at Potsdam he declared to the sulking officers of the guards "that he felt himself perfectly safe, free and happy among the citizens of Berlin; that all the concessions made by him had been made of his own free will and according to his own convictions, and that nobody should dare to question this." But when the Prussian constituent assembly had met in Berlin and began to pass laws, and to design constitutional provisions, and to interfere with the conduct of the government in the spirit of the revolution, the king's mind gradually opened itself to other influences, and those influences gained access to him and surrounded him all the more readily since he removed his residence from Berlin to his palace at Potsdam, a little town preponderantly inhabited by courtiers and soldiers and other dependents of the government. Thus the king's immediate contact with the people ceased, his conferences with the newly appointed liberal ministers were confined to short formal "audiences," and voices appealing to old sympathies, prepossessions and partialities were constantly nearest to his ear.

There was the army, traditionally the pet of the Hohenzollerns, smarting under the "disgrace" of its withdrawal from Berlin after the street battle, and pining for revenge and restoration of its prestige. There was the court nobility, whose business it always had been to exalt and flatter the royal person. There was the landed aristocracy, the "Junker" element, whose feudal privileges were theoretically denied by the revolutionary spirit and practically invaded by the legislative action of the representatives of the people, and who artfully goaded the king's pride. There was the old bureaucracy, the power of which had been broken by the revolution, although its personnel had but little been changed, and which sought to recover its former sway. There was the "old Prussian" spirit which resented any national aspirations that might encroach upon the importance and self-appreciation of specific Prussiandom, and which still had strength in the country immediately surrounding Berlin and in some of the eastern provinces. All these forces, which in a general term were popularly called "the reaction," worked together to divert the king from the course he had ostensibly taken immediately after the revolution of March, with the hope of using him for the largest possible restoration of the old order of things—well knowing that if they controlled him, they would, through him, control the army, and then with it a tremendous, perhaps decisive, force in the conflicts to come. And this "reaction" was greatly strengthened by the cunning exploitation of some street excesses that happened in Berlin—excesses which in a free country like England might, indeed, have brought forth some vigorous measures of repression by the police, but would certainly not have induced anybody to call the practicability of civil freedom or of the constitutional principles of government in question. But these occurrences were used in Prussia with considerable effect to frighten the timid men of the bourgeoisie with the specter of general anarchy, and to persuade the king that after all the restoration of unrestrained royal power was necessary for the maintenance of law and order.

On the other hand, the visible development of the reaction had the effect of producing among many of those who stood earnestly for national unity and constitutional government, a state of mind more open to radical tendencies. The rapid progress of these developments was clearly perceptible in my own surroundings. Our democratic club was composed in almost equal parts of students and citizens, among whom there were many of excellent character, of some fortune and good standing, and of moderate views, while a few others had worked themselves into a state of mind resembling that of the terrorists in the French Revolution. Kinkel was the recognized leader of the club, and I soon became a member of the executive committee. At first the establishment of a constitutional monarchy with universal suffrage and well-secured civil rights would have been quite satisfactory to us. But the reaction, the threatened rise of which we were observing, gradually made many of us believe that there was no safety for popular liberty except in a republic. From this belief there was only one step to the further conclusion, that in a republic, and only in a republic, all evils of the social body could be cured, and the solution of all the political problems would be possible. The idealism which saw in the republican citizen the highest embodiment of human dignity we had imbibed from the study of classic antiquity; and the history of the French Revolution satisfied us that a republic could be created in Germany and could maintain its existence in the European system of states. In that history we found striking examples of the possibility of accomplishing the seemingly impossible, if only the whole energy resting in a great nation were awakened and directed with unflinching boldness. Most of us indeed recoiled from the wild excesses which had stained with streams of innocent blood the national uprising in France during the Reign of Terror. But we hoped to stir up the national energies without such terrorism. At any rate the history of the French Revolution furnished to us models in plenty that mightily excited our imagination. How dangerously seductive such a play of the imagination is, we were of course then unaware.

*   *   *

On a bright September morning I sailed up the Rhine from Bonn to Mainz. I should have enjoyed it with the fullness of youthful spirits had I been able to drive away the disquieting thoughts which were stirred up by confused rumors of a riot and street-battle in Frankfurt. In fact, upon my arrival in that city I found those rumors distressingly verified.

The revolt in Frankfurt was the outcome of the following events. I have already mentioned that the popular uprising in the duchies of Holstein and Schleswig against the Danish rule had been sanctioned as a national cause by the old Diet of the German Confederation, and then by the national parliament and by all the several German governments. Prussian and other German troops had marched into the duchies and won considerable advantages over the Danish army on the field of battle. Everything promised a speedy and happy termination of the war. It was therefore a painful surprise when the Prussian government, whose head, Frederick William IV, had as usual permitted himself to be intimidated by the other European powers, concluded in the name of the German Confederation a truce with Denmark —the so-called "truce of Malmö"—in which it was agreed that the victorious German troops were to retire from the duchies, that the duchies were to lose their own provisional government, and that a commission composed of two Prussians, two Danes and a fifth member to be elected by them was to govern the disputed country. At the same time all the laws and ordinances that had been issued by the Schleswig-Holstein authorities since the days of March, 1848, were declared invalid. This truce called forth the greatest indignation all over Germany. The representative assembly of Schleswig-Holstein protested. The national parliament in Frankfurt, which saw not only the honor of Germany grievous compromised, but its own authority overruled by these proceedings of the Prussian government, resolved on September 5 to refuse the recognition of the truce of Malmö and to demand the suspension of all the measures stipulated therein. But after several failures to form a new ministry on the basis of this resolution, and not daring to bring the question of authority between itself and the Prussian government to a direct issue, the parliament revoked the resolution of September 5, ten days later, and declared at the same time that the execution of the truce of Malmö could apparently no longer be hindered. This declaration, which seemed to strike the sympathies of the German people full in the face, caused immense excitement, of which the revolutionary leaders in Frankfurt and the surrounding country at once took advantage. On the next day a large mass meeting was held on a meadow near Frankfurt. Inflammatory speeches goaded the passions of the multitude to fury, and the meeting adopted resolutions by which the members of the majority of the national parliament in Frankfurt were branded as traitors to the German nation. Troops of armed democrats poured in from all sides, and an attempt was made to force the parliament to revoke the hateful declaration, or to drive out the traitorous majority. Two prominent conservative members of the parliament, Count Auerswald and Prince Lichnowsky, fell into the hands of the revolutionists and were killed; and then followed a bloody struggle in the streets of Frankfurt, in which the insurgents soon succumbed to the quickly concentrated troops.

When on my way to Eisenach I arrived in Frankfurt, the victorious soldiery still bivouacked on the streets around their burning campfires; the barricades had not yet been removed; the pavement was still stained with blood, and everywhere the heavy tramp of military patrols was heard. With difficulty I made my way to the hotel "Zum Schwan," where I was to meet, according to agreement, some Heidelberg students, in order to continue in their company the journey to Eisenach. With hearts full of gloom we sat together deep into the night, for we all felt that the cause of liberty and of popular sovereignty had received a terrible blow. The royal Prussian government had successfully defied the national parliament, which represented the sovereignty of the German nation. Those who called themselves "the people" had made a hostile attempt upon the embodiment of popular sovereignty which had issued from the revolution, and this embodiment of popular sovereignty had been obliged to call upon the armed forces of the princes for protection against the hatred of "the people." Thus the backbone of the revolution begun in March, 1848, was substantially broken. We young students indeed did not see so far. But we felt that terrible mischief had been done. Our youthful spirits, however, consoled themselves with the hope that what was lost might still be recovered by well-directed and energetic action under more favorable circumstances.

The next day I visited with some of my friends the gallery of St. Paul's Church, in which the national parliament held its sessions. With that profound reverence, the organ of which (to express myself in the language of phrenology) has always been with me very strongly developed, I looked at that historic spot, in which the fate of the revolution of 1848 was already foretold. On "the right" there sat, with a smile of triumph on their lips, men whose principal aim it was to restore the old order of things; in "the center" the advocates of a liberal constitutional monarchy, tormented by anxious doubt as to whether they could control the revolutionary tendencies without making the absolutist reaction all-powerful; on "the left" the democrats and republicans with the oppressive consciousness that the masses of the people, in whom they were to find the source of their power, had grievously compromised them by this wild eruption of passion at Frankfurt and had thus put the most dangerous weapon into the hands of the reactionists.

I remember well the men whom my eyes most eagerly sought. On "the right" Radowitz, whose finely chiseled face, somewhat oriental in its character, looked like a sealed book containing the secret of reactionary politics; in "the center" Heinrich von Gagern, with his imposing stature and heavy eyebrows; on "the left" the Silenus-head of Robert Blum, whom many regarded as the ideal man of the people; and the little shriveled figure of the old poet, Ludwig Uhland, whose songs we had so often sung, and who with such touching fidelity stood by that which he believed to be the good right of his people!

*   *   *

Since March the Prussian government had moved in constitutional forms, and the ministry, at the head of which stood the liberal General von

Pfuel, showed itself willing to fulfill the promises that had been given. But the king and his immediate surroundings had on various occasions manifested a disposition which hardly harmonized with those pledges and called forth grave apprehensions. On October 31 the Prussian Constituent Assembly gave voice to the general sympathy with the struggling people of Vienna and resolved to request his Majesty's government "to take speedy and energetic steps to induce the German central power in Frankfurt to effectually protect the imperiled liberties of the people in the German districts of Austria, and to restore peace." The president of the ministry, General von Pfuel, supported this resolution. The next day he found himself compelled to resign, and the king then appointed a ministry of decidedly reactionary character, at the head of which he put Count Brandenburg, and the leading spirit of which was Herr von Manteuffel. The Constituent Assembly solemnly protested, but in vain. On November 9 the Brandenburg ministry presented itself to the Assembly with a royal message which transferred the meetings of that body to another place and prorogued its sessions until November 27. By a large majority the Assembly denied the right of the royal government to do these things, but the next day the house was surrounded by large bodies of troops under General Wrangel, who gave the order that nobody should be permitted to enter, but anybody might leave the building. On November 11 the civil guard of Berlin was dissolved and in a few days disarmed. The Assembly moved from one place to another, constantly followed by the soldiery, until finally on November 15, at its last meeting, it refused to vote the supplies, and declared "that this ministry had no right to dispose of the moneys of the state or to levy taxes, so long as the Constituent Assembly could not undisturbed continue its deliberations in Berlin." These events called forth immense excitement all over the country. They seemed to prove that the reactionary court-parties were determined to sweep away by force all the fruits of the revolution.

That the Constituent Assembly in opposing the "coup d'état" was altogether within its right, admitted of no doubt in the minds of the democrats. They blamed it only for not having made the fullest use of its right by calling the people directly to arms, and for having at this moment of great decision limited itself to the weak-kneed policy of "passive resistance." But they thought that this passive resistance by means of a general refusal to pay taxes might finally force the government to yield, assuming that the refusal to pay taxes would become general and be maintained with inflexible steadiness.

*   *   *

Now it appeared to us unnecessary to seize upon the general machinery of the tax-department. The next day a committee, of which I was a member, appeared at the city hall to take possession of it. The Burgomaster received us with great politeness and listened quietly to what we had to say to him about the authority of the Constituent Assembly and its power to stop the payment of taxes; but he tried to amuse us with all sorts of evasive talk. At last we became impatient and demanded an immediate and definite answer according to which we would resolve upon further measures. Suddenly we noticed a change in the expression of the Burgomaster's face. He seemed to hearken to something going on outside and then, still politely but with a sort of triumphant smile on his lips, he said: "Gentlemen, your answer you will have to receive from somebody else. Do you hear that?" Now we hearkened too, and heard a still distant, but approaching, sound of a military band playing the Prussian national air. The music sounded nearer and nearer in the street leading up, from the Rhine. In a few minutes it reached the market-place and behind it came the heavy tramp of an infantry column which presently filled a large part of the square in front of the city hall. Our conversation with the Burgomaster of course came to a sudden end and we thought it very decent on his part that he permitted us to leave the building undisturbed.

*   *   *

Of the large parliamentary bodies that had issued from the revolution of March, only the national parliament in Frankfurt was still in existence. That existence it had owed to the longing of the German people, or rather the German peoples, for national unity, and it was its natural and universally understood mission to weld the German peoples under a common constitution of national government into one great nation. Immediately after the revolution of March, 1848, the different German governments, and with them also Austria, because of her German possessions, had recognized this object as a legitimate one, and it was with their co-operation that in May the elections for the national parliament had taken place. The large majority of that body, in fact, the German people in general, regarded the Frankfurt parliament as the specific representative of the sovereignty of the German nation. It was to be expected that the princes and those of their adherents, who may be designated as court-parties, would submit to this conception of the powers of the parliament only so long, and only so far, as they found themselves forced to do so. But few of the princes, if any, were sufficiently liberal to accept a limitation of their princely prerogatives with equanimity. Every gain of the people in the matter of political power they felt to be their own loss. Of course they were also opposed to the institution of a strong national government for the reason that this would be conditioned upon the surrender to the national authority of many of the sovereignty-rights of the different states. It was not only a national republic that the individual German sovereigns feared, but they also dreaded a national Kaiser who would be apt to reduce them to the condition of mere vassals. The German princes, with the exception of the one who could hope himself to occupy the imperial throne, were therefore the natural adversaries of German unity, embodied in a strong national government. There may have been some men of national sentiment among them capable of overcoming this reluctance, but certainly there were very few. Austria desired a united Germany in some form, only if it could hope to occupy in it the position of the leading power.

Face to face with the princes and their parties stood the national parliament in Frankfurt, that child of the revolution, which might then have almost been called the orphan of the revolution. It had at its immediate disposal no administrative machinery, no army, no treasury, only its moral authority; all the other things were in the hands of the different German state governments. The only power of the national parliament consisted in the will of the people. And this power was sufficient for the fulfillment of its mission so long as the will of the people proved itself strong enough, even through revolutionary action in case of necessity, to counteract the adverse interests of the princes. The parliament would have been sure of success in creating a constitutional German empire, if it had performed that task quickly and elected and put into office its Kaiser while the revolutionary prestige of the people was still unbroken—that is to say, in the first two or three months after the revolution of March. No German prince would then have declined the imperial crown with a constitution ever so democratic, and not one of them would have dared to refuse the sacrifice of any of his sovereignty-rights to the national power.

But that parliament was laboring under an overabundance of learning and virtue and under a want of that political experience and sagacity which recognizes that the better is often the enemy of the good, and that the true statesman will be careful not to imperil that which is essential by excessive insistence upon things which are of comparatively little consequence. The world has probably never seen a political assembly that contained a larger number of noble, learned, conscientious and patriotic men, and it will be difficult to find a book of the same character richer in profound knowledge and in models of lofty eloquence than its stenographic reports. But it did not possess the genius that promptly discerns opportunity and with quick resolution takes fortune by the forelock; it was not mindful of the fact that in times of great commotion the history of the world does not wait for the theoretical thinker. And thus it failed.

The failure of the Frankfurt Assembly was greeted with joy by the German conservatives who saw liberalism as the enemy. German unity, on the other hand, was something else again, and Otto von Bismarck, who was ultimately to lead Prussia to the dominant position in a united Germany, put the matter quite bluntly in his famous speech of 1862. It

*should be noted that rarely has a leader of a powerful
nation expended less blood and utilized less iron in the
successful pursuit of his policies than the "Iron Chancellor."*

FROM *Otto von Bismarck's Speech to the Budget
Commission*

OUR BLOOD IS TOO HOT; we prefer to wear armor which is too heavy
for our slender body; but we should use it nonetheless. The eyes of Germany
are fixed not upon Prussia's liberalism, but upon her armed might. Bavaria,
Württemberg, and Baden may indulge in liberal experiments; therefore no
one will assign to them Prussia's role. Prussia must harbor and maintain her
strength for the favorable moment—a moment which has already, on one
occasion, slipped by; Prussia's boundaries, as drawn by the Vienna treaties,
are not suitable for a healthy state life. The great questions of the day will
not be decided by speeches or by majority decisions—that was the mistake of
1848 and 1849—but by blood and iron!

> *In 1866, the Prussians, under the shrewd leadership of Otto
> von Bismarck, were able to provoke Austria into a war. In a
> few weeks it was all over, and Prussia emerged as un-
> doubted leader of North Germany. The first striking vic-
> tory on the road to German unity had been won.*
>
> *Baumgarten was a German liberal who felt it necessary
> to re-examine the tenets of German liberalism in the light
> of the national triumph just achieved.*

FROM *German Liberalism* BY H. BAUMGARTEN

IT WOULD BE OF CONSIDERABLE VALUE for us to be acquainted
in detail with the historical development of liberalism in the years from 1815

P. Joachimsen, ed., *Die Nationalbewegung von 1815–49* (1928), translated in T. C. Mendenhall,
B. D. Henning, and A. S. Foord, *The Quest for a Principle of Authority in Europe 1715–
Present* (1948), p. 220. Reprinted by permission of Holt, Rinehart and Winston, Inc.

H. Baumgarten, "Der Deutsche Liberalismus, Eine Selbstkritik," *Preussische Jahrbücher*, 18
(1866), 468–79, 499–501, 507–12, translated by Eleanore L. Miller.

to 1848. . . . If we want to be honest, we must admit that during the period mentioned liberalism did indeed achieve much in the petty states. In individual states it considerably improved conditions in many respects and often prevented a turn for the worse. Above all, it kept alive the spirit of the nation and gave it its first political schooling. However, on the whole the liberal movement remained small, uninstructive, and unproductive. It could not grant the nation what it so desperately needed. Liberalism was not to blame for this; rather it was the circumstances. *In order to be effective within the state, the man must above all have a state; all those individual German territories, however, to which liberalism found itself confined because of the resignation of Prussia, were not states. . . .*

Justice demands the recognition of the fact that these petty states on the average accomplished more under the given circumstances than one in all probability could have predicted. Actually, only the modesty and conscientiousness of the Germans made it possible for this pitiful particularism on the whole to be efficient in administration. We owe it to the administration that a large part of the German people, in spite of the most unfavorable nature of the political situation, made gratifying progress economically and spiritually after 1815. The unselfishness and peaceful domesticity of our nature were required to produce untiring and honest officials for all these petty states. Men whose ambitions are directed towards great things, towards splendor and power, men different from us, would not have borne this misery—which only later appeared to be misery in our eyes and which even today is regarded by many as our greatest pride. Even though in these petty states the quiet detailed work of the official flourished most of all, even though burghers and peasants felt comfortable in the narrowest and most indigent circle, and even though idealism was not prevented from constructing the most magnificent castles in the air, it was nonetheless altogether impossible for these phantom states to aid in the development of real political life.

But it should not be forgotten that our primary concern was to acquire the first elements of a political education. After an absolutely unpolitical past of centuries, our primary concern was to take the first step from an existence entirely fulfilled by private interests and by domestic, scientific, poetic, and religious endeavours to the stage of political life. This step could be taken successfully only if the most distinguished minds of the nation participated most enthusiastically and only if great objectives beckoned them from their books and out of their homes to the market place. However, where in God's name did the German petty states present such goals and such circumstances during those years? Everything conspired to discourage even the political enthusiasts. And even if we had had men, endowed by nature with the greatest talents for successful political activity, they would have been deterred from pursuing a political career because of the utter impossibility of achieving satisfactory results or of even practicing these talents.

And so it happened that among the great numbers of distinguished scholars, artists, industrialists, judges, and officials whom Germany had produced in the thirty-three years following the establishment of the Confederation, few individuals can be mentioned to whom we can ascribe political importance. Many of the most important leaders of liberalism at that time stood intellectually far below the level to which men like Niebuhr and Savigny had raised our conception of the state. And even though on the whole their less sophisticated practice met the demands of the times more adequately than the wisdom of those conservatives, a more penetrating investigation clearly reveals that their opposition to the *Bundestag* arose from strongly particularistic motives. It also reveals that their liberalism did not hesitate, circumstances permitting, to disregard patriotic duty and national interest. One needs only to read Paul Pfizer's excellent correspondence between two Germans (1832) to realize how willing they were to promote constitutional interests with French help. One needs only to recall the strong opposition with which the *Zollverein* met in these liberal circles of the southwest to recognize the insecure and dubious basis which supported the beginnings of a free life. To be sure, each German chamber had its great representatives; to be sure, great men appeared here and there whose words echoed beyond the narrow borders of the land. There were even individuals whom the enthusiastic youth of the nation looked to with admiration. However, with a few exceptions, all these great men sank into the sweet sleep of oblivion after twenty or thirty years. Go into the various territories and inquire about the leaders of the opposition in 1820 or 1830. You will find only a few grateful people who have preserved a living memory of the patriotic deeds of those men who undertook to liberate their people from disgraceful conditions and who sacrificed a life filled with toil and self-denial for a cause which could not be achieved.

The abnormal attitude of our nobility was particularly responsible for the extreme difficulties with which this task met in every respect. In every monarchistic state the nobility is the truly political class. Not only has it been the case for centuries in England that the various classes of the nobility have almost exclusively borne the burden of political tasks, but also, on the continent, the nobility has without exception played a significant role in the affairs of state. The rather unsuccessful role of the nobility in the modern constitutional history of France and Spain is basically responsible for the small amount of progress which these countries have made to date in organized political freedom. On the other hand, Italy owes its unexpected success primarily to the intelligent and patriotic participation of its nobility in the great struggle for national rebirth.

The unalterable nature of circumstances is the reason for the following phenomenon which appears everywhere in the same manner: monarchic states have the choice either of achieving a modified constitution and parliamentary forms with the help of the nobility or of remaining under the rule of a bureaucratic and more or less absolute government. In all modern states the bourgeoisie became an important economic power and a proud authority of scientific and industrial intelligence. All modern states rest primarily on the work of the bourgeoisie; therefore, all modern states will have to grant the bourgeoisie an important role in political life. However, the middle class lacks the proper prerequisites for real political action. The middle class will always be a major factor in political life; its insight, its activity, and its wealth are above all demanded by the state. Its interests and inclinations will have to be considered foremost by every intelligent statesman. But the nature of its social position, the effect of its professional activity on lifelong habits, forms of character, and trends of thought will only in rare instances enable the middle-class man to work successfully in major political affairs. He will provide the chambers with the most prudent and knowledgeable members, but only seldom with leaders who are capable of mastering the entire situation with the grasp of a statesman, and of taking decisive action at the critical moment. He will provide the ministries with excellent advisers, but only seldom with ministers who are capable of associating as skillfully with the ruling masters as with the delegates. The burgher is cut out for work but not for command; and the essential task of the statesman is to rule.

The most able members of the bourgeoisie have worked themselves up from the bottom. Their cradles stood in narrow little rooms. In a limited and poor environment their youth was a struggle against all kinds of misery. Only later did they attain a position which allowed them a freer view of the world; work and toil for their family as a rule remains their lot until their creative energy is consumed. Such a life is most conducive to human competence. It builds character and freedom and purity of the soul. But he who worked his way up in this manner, is, so to speak, too good for politics. He has learned to trust his own strength in all things and to follow his own convictions; he does not yield or cringe; he bears within both a strong sense of masculine pride and humble modesty; he is strong, but awkward; he is conscientious, but stubborn. Place such a man into a circle of diplomats or place him beside a throne. In his heart he will look down upon them, and still he will be duped by them. The splendor of the castle will at times impress him too much and at times repulse him. He will always feel he is in a strange world, and he will yearn for the peace and independence of his bourgeois labor. Actually, at the core of its being the bourgeoise is democratic. This basic democratic feature will always place him in certain opposition to the aristocrats, who surround and support every monarch. This antagonism will have as its result that he either will act contrary to his nature and plunge into servile submission or will unprofitably expend a great deal of his best energy in constant friction.

But all these weaknesses are minor when compared to the fact that the bourgeois man entered politics rather late and from a totally different profession. He was not trained or educated to be a statesman, and he therefore lacked the knowledge, practice, and skills which are absolutely essential to the statesman. It is one of the most fatal errors, for which our totally unpolitical way of thinking and the lack of any important political experience are responsible, to believe that every conscientious scholar, lawyer, merchant, and official who is interested in public affairs and who diligently reads the newspaper is capable of actively engaging in politics. It is also one of our most fatal errors to believe that absolutely no specific preparation or education is required and that politics can be pursued successfully together with other professional duties. To be sure, if this kind of politics does not have greater objectives than to putter around with bills in some little chamber or to discharge a clerk here and a policeman there or to provide the constituency with a road or a railroad station, then intelligent burgomasters, officials, and judges under the direction of a somewhat more sagacious professor or lawyer would certainly comprise a very good council. However, no one will maintain that anything of significance will be accomplished with this kind of parliamentary activity. And as happens in even the smallest German chamber, decisions have to be made which require more than the mediocre knowledge of a constituency or the insight of a provincial philistine; more than the integrity of a dependent official. What would happen then? I know of no more curious sight than the one presented by our German chambers when they have to solve real political problems. The serious, conscientious, and thorough German people appear in those persons —whom they have entrusted with the power to decide their most important problems—in a manner which contrasts most unfavorably with their true nature. The men who sit on the green or red benches in those important moments are certainly recognized for their professional ability. How would they have otherwise won the confidence of the voters? But now they are supposed to decide issues which lie outside their range of vision—about which they can form no independent judgment and of which they have no thorough knowledge. They will either become the prey of ministerial superiority—which often forces them by the most obvious tricks to pass resolutions of whose consequences they are unaware; or they will be courageous enough to vote in opposition. This, however, has no practical results because the opposition only rarely has men at its disposal who would be in a position to take over the government. These men, however, are wanting because the assembly—with disappearing exceptions—is composed of persons who engage in politics only by the way. A chamber whose parties are not led by true statesmen is a monstrosity; statesmen, however—just as competent physicians, lawyers, and philologists—are not created overnight. Statesmen do not emerge from a dilettantish occupation in the state, but from earnest life-long service to the state. Politics is a profession, just as jurisprudence and medicine. It is the most noble and difficult profession to which a man can dedicate himself. It is a real offence against the German nation and the German name that we, who pursue the smallest things with the thorough concentration of all our energy, believe we can dispose of the greatest and noblest human matters, the affairs of state, with a playful dilettantism—we, who of all nations have to solve the most difficult political task with the most modest political talents.

If, however, important political achievements can be expected only from men who pursue politics as a life's profession, and if the middle class is not suited for a truly political career, it follows that the assistance of the nobility is essential to every people if it wants to solve great political tasks. We ourselves, among whom bourgeois character, views, and aspirations have attained undue predominance, have learned in our provincial life that the few truly outstanding political minds as a rule are members of the nobility! . . .

* * *

Only under the condition that the bourgeoisie send its best representatives into the real political class can the bourgeoisie leave the supreme command of the state to the nobility. And only upon the prudent partnership of interests among the various elements of the political community can a powerful state rest. The exact opposite of this normal relationship was true of Germany. Consequently our political development followed the most unpleasant path.

Nowhere in Europe except in Germany has the nobility long been the ally of absolutism; nowhere except in Germany has the nobility systematically advocated bureaucratic forms of government as opposed to the demand for self-government in which an important role falls to the nobility —whereas it is powerless next to the bureaucracy with all its courtly and military connections. This absurd attitude of our nobility completely poisoned the political struggles of liberalism in the small states, for it deprived liberalism of its natural leaders. In addition to the absolutist pressures of the two great powers, the attitude of the nobility was a further factor in sentencing liberalism to the role of unfruitful opposition. This attitude of the nobility finally gave liberalism a radical tendency, which became dangerous perhaps for the monarchy, but certainly for liberalism. . . .

* * *

In all military questions liberal opinion had submitted to rather radical views. There was a series of factors which made it possible to anticipate the opposition of public opinion to any increase of the military burden: a peace of almost fifty years, the dissatisfaction with the high and, as it appeared, superfluous expenditure for standing armies, the tempting example of Switzerland and the United States, the deceiving memory of the great achievements of the *Landwehr* from 1813 to 1815, hostility towards the absolutist tendencies of the military aristocracy, and an abhorrence in general of all the disturbances caused by war—which was only too natural at a time when industrialism continued to rise to ascendancy. It was quite obvious that for precisely these reasons only a liberal administration had a chance of obtaining the consent of the territorial representatives for such a reorganization. However, it was equally certain that liberal ministers could hope to solve this problem successfully only if they simultaneously removed all suspicion from liberalism in the eyes of the people and persuaded or assured them that additional expenditures in the military budget would be offset by the abolition of other burdens and obstacles, under whose pressure the country had suffered for many years. Precisely this reciprocal relationship presented the most valuable chance for the liberal system.

Those individuals and classes to whom the military reform was a matter of the greatest consequence for their particular proclivities and interests, at the same time caused the liberalism of the ministry the greatest difficulties. Thus the ministers found themselves in the unique position of having to relate the military question to the entire political problem, of having to court the one through the favor of the other and of having to join their assistance to the one with the desired concessions for the other. In January of 1860 Mr. von Manteuffel made the absolutely correct observation: If the Liberals were clever, they would oust us from office forever by means of the military problem.

At this first great opportunity to secure a firm and lasting liberal policy for the Prussian state, the Liberals evidenced a fatal lack of skill. Even before the public had received any details of the intended reorganization, the sudden resignation of the popular minister of war, von Bonin, became a bad omen for the further development of the matter. In general, von Bonin was considered to be a liberal military man. Of course, it was assumed that he had resigned because the reorganization of the army was to take place along reactionary lines, but in fact, completely different motives led to the minister's resignation. In reality, he would hardly have been equal to the problem which had to be solved. But the manner in which his resignation came about—without appropriate interest on the part of the other ministers —indicated that they had not known how to adopt the correct attitude with regard to a question which involved the existence of the entire government. Neither did they appear to have this attitude during the futher formulation of the proposal. Obviously it was not sufficient that they had obtained approval from the regent for a series of beneficial bills. They had to demand the guarantee that these bills would actually become law and would not be killed by the powerful influences in the ministries of the previous regime; in the highest posts of the provincial administration; in the *Herrenhaus;* and in the entourage of the prince himself.

Although the mood of the country in the last months had regrettably soured because of several events—for example the Schiller festival—nothing major was actually required to restore public confidence. It was not a question of translating bold experiments into legislation or of mercilessly purifying all the personnel. If the ministry had actually abolished some of the most oppressive abnormalities of the previous situation, if it had given evidence of its seriousness by discharging some of the officials who were hated with good reason, and if it had, above all, created in the *Herrenhaus* the necessary support for its policies, it cannot be doubted that the country would have agreed to accept a considerable increase in the financial burden. Above all, it was not of utmost importance to come to grips with the somewhat dull judgment of public opinion, but rather to come to an agreement with the leaders of the Chamber of Deputies and with the party members of long standing, one which excluded any unfounded suspicion from either side.

The party to which the majority of the ministers belonged now formed the overwhelming majority in the Chamber of Deputies. It would not now be difficult to convince the most respected members of the majority of the necessity of the military reform. They needed only to be informed of the entire situation. Nor would it be difficult to win their support—even if it were not immediately possible to offer the Chamber of Deputies the entire sum of constitutional guarantees in return. Such an open and frank exchange between the ministers and their very influential friends in the Chamber of Deputies could also make up for the serious difficulties in the ministerial position.

I do not believe it can be said that exaggerated demands of an ideal policy have been developed in the above paragraphs. They contained only what was absolutely obvious and essential. On the other hand, if one points out the great difficulties which the ministers encountered in pursuing this policy, one would have to reply that great problems are always bound up with great difficulties. Indeed, we were dealing with something great. It was a question of leading Prussia from the wrong path of revolutionary and counterrevolutionary excesses back to the secure path of sound and constantly progressive politics. It was a question of giving the German problem a beneficial turn through a strong Prussia and of reviving through a Prussia backed up by Germany the old order of Europe, which was visibly out of joint, in a way demanded by the interests of Prussia and Germany and of civilization in general. No instance could be thought of which had offered true statecraft more propitious circumstances. In Prussia, in Germany, and in Europe the most dynamic elements lay scattered. A policy with a goal in mind could set these elements in motion for its own purposes. In Prussia and Germany everyone longed for a power which knew how to sever itself only somewhat favorably well from the gloomy past. To be certain, the European situation held dangers; but it also presented the unique opportunity for raising Prussia from forty years of insignificance to a position of appropriate influence.

*   *   *

In the January (1860) issue of the Prussian annuals I drew special attention to the following point: "In review of the sad events of the previous year it was stated that their experiences should really stimulate us to think seriously about ourselves! For, whatever we might say, each of us was partly to blame. For almost a decade we all, with a few exceptions, had postponed the essential political work, which, to be sure, was a difficult and thankless task. Everybody was more concerned with his private affairs and more or less forgot the issues common to all. Eleven years ago we set about like dilettantes pursuing the rich pleasures of an interesting public life; we quickly outdid ourselves. When the fruits of politics became bitter, most of the people became disgusted, and they returned to their comfortable private libraries and their offices. When the storm which had suddenly gathered called us back to public life, we had on the whole learned little and forgotten much. Public duties cannot be undertaken in such a sporadic fashion. Like any other kind of learning or art, politics requires loyal devotion and serious energy. And if it appeals little to our customs and inclinations to devote our best energy to restless and thankless activity in the market place of public life, nonetheless reason should aid us in recognizing that it is impossible for us to overcome the particularly great difficulties of satisfactorily organizing the German state. If a respectable number of gifted men does not dedicate itself to the Fatherland, reason should help us to recognize that all our erudition, education, and prosperity are built upon sand, as long as the foundation of everything—a sound state—is lacking."

*   *   *

Hitherto we Germans have squandered so much valuable energy largely because this political way of thinking is extremely alien to our nature. We are students of theory, who make a judgment about things completely independent of all circumstances. We are children of a religious past, and religion does not question the circumstances. We have grown up in a quiet home where firm virtue is justifiably more important than cautious shrewdness. Even where our activity approaches political practice, we prefer to follow the letter of the law or instruction rather than an independent conception of the circumstances. Whoever is guided by the latter is quickly reproached for arbitrary action. In politics, however, this purely pertinent settlement of business leads to the worst blunders. This manner of settling affairs is customary in our chambers. It was followed by the liberals in the Prussian Chamber of Deputies in the fatal session of 1860.

*   *   *

By a bold offensive Prussia rose, grew, and was delivered from the misery of 1807. Because of the circumstances this offensive became Prussia's natural law. It could not remain what it was. It had to become very great or small again. The destiny of Prussia and of Germany could be fulfilled only if the borders of Prussian power were extended to those of Germany. Only in Germany could the strength be found which would secure Prussia's existence, if it had no European alliance. Only Germany could give Prussia the supplement, which it could not dispense with, if it were to transfer the overwrought state of its financial and military resources—which in the long run would have been intolerable—to a normal effort. The national uprising of Italy aroused of necessity similar efforts in Germany. . . . And what was the result? The states of secondary importance gathered in Würzburg and drafted a great conspiracy against Prussia. They rejected the proposals for the reform of the Confederate military organization, which by far did not meet the demands established by Prussia. They attempted to draw maritime affairs into the sphere of the Confederacy. In the question of Electoral Hesse they adhered to the old oppression. Mr. von Borries disclosed the intrinsic meaning of this coalition with the notorious words of May 1st: that the German princes would prefer to call for the help of foreign states rather than recognize the leading position of Prussia. And as people in various parts of Germany expressed their indignation at this manifestation of patriotism in those states, the King of Hanover confirmed the dictum of his minister by elevating him to earldom.

Lay not a serious danger for Prussia in those circumstances? Could even at that time an unbiased observer doubt that this German chaos could only be ordered, if either the Prussian sword were unsheathed or if it were at least to threaten the petty kings with considerable heat. Or if one had perchance the proper patience to let the German question completely rest for some time, it would have been impossible for one to have the patience not to requisition a certain part of German strength for the European position of Prussia. However, one could depend upon this only if Prussian military power stood alert and prepared for a strong offensive attack, only if Prussia cast off the bonds of a military organization directed totally towards defense, and only if it were in a position to calmly confront alone a bellicose threat by a major European power. Prussia did not have to fear the intrigues of its royal neighbors only if they trembled before its power.

*   *   *

A political way of thinking had to come to the conclusion that the acceptance of the military bill was unavoidable. In spite of everything a political manner of dealing with the question had to have considerable support, which would allow the acceptance of the military bill to appear not merely as a difficult sacrifice. The Chamber of Deputies had the power to place the European and German questions in the foreground in such a way that even superficial liberalism would automatically learn to view military affairs in a different manner. Of course, precisely in this point of foreign politics the Liberal Party suffered from a serious lack of fundamental knowledge and rich experience. Hardly any members of the liberal party had ever exercised practical activity in this field; least of all from books can one obtain useful information in the practical aspects of politics. However, even that which literature offered in this respect was unknown to many. Foreign politics had lain almost totally outside the range of even the Prussian liberals. This was a natural result of the fact that since 1815 Prussia had no foreign policy worth mentioning. In general, the Chamber of Deputies had to discard the fetters which bound it to small details and to the limitations of bureaucratic diligence in the commissions. It had to pursue politics. It had to impress opponents and support friends in the ministry, and it had to guide public opinion instead of being guided by it. Had the ministers in the palace not taken the proper stand, then there were individual delegates who could have corrected this error. Perhaps these were nothing but demands which exceeded the usual range of accomplishments. But was not something crucial at stake? Was it worthy of serious men to allow an extremely important attempt to fail before the last bit of energy had been expended?

However, we unfortunately take a different attitude toward political tasks than we do to all others. We look down upon the man who in scientific or industrial affairs shrinks from being completely serious. For us it is understood that business of a private nature, where great decisions are involved, must be pursued with complete dedication. On the other hand, a defeat in public affairs is nothing disgraceful to us. In public affairs acquiescence is understood among us. These affairs lay almost beyond our feeling of duty. They hardly touch our innermost sentiments. For us they do not form an existential problem.

With this resignation the Chamber of Deputies also set about the problem of the army. The circumstances were simply accepted as given. The ministers, the crown, the *Herrenhaus,* the press, and public opinion had fashioned the situation in such a way that the approval of the new military budget appeared to be impossible. It would have been a question of improving this situation with creative energy. People accepted the situation as a misfortune which had to be tolerated. People suffered instead of acting. And finally a compromise was reached which became the source of the most vexing quarrels. To agree to the military reform as provisional readiness for war was certainly a thought which attested to the active wish for settlement, as well as to the hopeless confusion of the situation.

The Liberal Party had failed just as had the liberal ministry. The fact that the liberal system was able to stay in power for another two years seems to indicate that this system would have had a great opportunity if it had taken a different attitude toward the affairs of government. I believe that not only the country but also the ruler vigorously maintained the position he had chosen when he assumed power, and that it was difficult for him to personally alter the system. But after the session of 1860 it was almost impossible to entertain any hope for the policies of the new era. The necessary understanding between the government and public opinion, between public opinion and the Chamber of Deputies, had been too thoroughly shattered.

4 The Historians' Views

Guido de Ruggiero's study of liberalism is a classic. In the selection that follows he examines the factors in Germany that led to the conflict between liberalism and nationalism.

FROM The History of European Liberalism in the Nineteenth Century BY GUIDO DE RUGGIERO

HEGEL'S DOCTRINE is a theoretical synthesis of two opposed German tendencies struggling for predominance in the first half of the nineteenth century. In the field of militant politics their effective reconciliation, so far at least as concerns the fundamentals of public law, had to wait till a much later date.

Prussian Liberalism, which flourished after Jena, made its last appearance in the customs law of 1818, conceived according to the principle of free trade and containing only in a minor degree measures of retaliation against the protectionism of other nations; implicitly against that of England, which in 1815 had limited the importation of grain. In a country which was essentially an exporter of agricultural produce and devoid of industry, as Prussia was in 1815, this free trade was natural enough without appeal to the feeling for liberty, which at this time had almost vanished from the governing classes. But the Liberal consequences of the law were important, because it formed the centre round which all the other German States grouped themselves into the Zollverein of 1833. Thus the consequences of liberty survived the eclipse of the Liberal spirit in Prussia, and offer to political history a striking proof of the importance of liberty as a means towards national unification. Liberal opinion, widely diffused among the German States of the west and south, extracted from the Zollverein a powerful motive

Guido de Ruggiero, *The History of European Liberalism*, pp. 241–51, translated by R. G. Collingwood. Reprinted by permission of Beacon Press and The Clarendon Press, Oxford. First published by the Oxford University Press in 1927. First published as a Beacon Paperback in 1959.

for a close union between the idea of freedom and that of the Fatherland, and for bringing pressure on Prussia to induce her to promote a general political movement towards liberty and to take the lead towards national unification.

But Prussia was now governed according to the ideals of the Holy Alliance, and disappointed all Liberal hopes. And the complications which Liberalism introduced into the national problem aggravated the Austrian government's inherent anti-Liberalism. Metternich realized that a Liberal Prussia would mean the end of the Austrian hegemony and of the Austro-Prussian equilibrium in the German federation; he therefore made every effort not only to arouse all Austrophil Germans against the Liberals, but also to encourage Frederick William III of Prussia in his policy of reaction. He regarded a monarchy tempered by representation of the feudal classes as the best government for Prussia; a view shared by the Prussian government, which in 1823 reorganized the provincial diets, redistributing them into three orders according to their territorial possessions, so as to give a safe majority to the landed aristocracy, the owners of the so-called *Rittergüter,* while the *bourgeois* not possessed of land, professional men, capitalists, and tradesmen, were entirely unrepresented.

The States of Southern Germany enjoyed a far more Liberal régime than that of Prussia. In most of them the constitutions of the period from 1814 to 1848 were modelled on the charter of Louis XVIII. The Liberal theories of these countries, too, much resembled the constitutionalism of Constant, Royer-Collard, and Daunou. They were represented in great part by university professors, the two Rottecks, Welcker, Friedrich Gagern, Jacob Grimm, Stockmar, Rümelin, Robert Mohl, Gervinus, and others. The programme of Carl Rotteck, the earliest of them, and therefore interesting as the original document of the school, is a defence of rational rights as against historic rights. By this Rotteck means a legal and political system directed to attaining the rational ends of man, and recognizing, in a Kantian spirit, the claim of every individual to a freedom compatible to that of the rest. In all these writers Liberal feeling is combined with national feeling, thus originating the movement of thought which was to have its epilogue in the parliament of Frankfurt.

But the first struggles of university Liberalism were conducted within the schools and by academic weapons. Only the extreme autonomy of the German universities could permit professors living in the centre of Europe, between a reactionary Prussia and a reactionary Austria, to expound Liberal ideas to their students. Thus when, owing to government pressure, the freedom of teaching was here and there violated, the universities became centres and hotbeds of revolt. The most famous example is the protest of the historian Dahlmann of Göttingen, which bore the signatures of the brothers Grimm, Gervinus, Eduard Albrecht, and others, against the Hanoverian government in 1837 on its violating the constitution it had sworn to respect. The protest was the more significant in that not only the liberty of the university but that of the country at large was at stake, and the professors felt the incompatibility of their function with the act of a government that failed to abide by its solemn pledges. "Must I," said Dahlmann and the court-counsellor Albrecht, "teach henceforward that the supreme principle of the State is that whatever pleases those in power is law? As a man of honour, I would cease to teach rather than sell to my audience for truth that which is a lie and a deceit."

The seven professors who signed the protest were expelled from their chairs; but the people of Göttingen, mindful of the Liberalism which they had learnt to value under English government, opened a public subscription on their behalf. And the defences of their conduct written after their reappointment by Dahlmann and Jacob Grimm are rightly regarded by Germans as the loftiest examples of their own Liberal literature. In them the peculiar *forma mentis* of German Liberalism stands out, in contrast not only with an arbitrary absolutism, but also with the anti-historical rationalism dear to the Liberal extremists most influenced by France. Thus Dahlmann denies the right of the people to take the law into its own hands; and Grimm, answering those Liberals who despised the barbarism of the Middle Ages, does not conceal his deep sympathy for the ancient medieval liberties of the people, and his delight in slaking his thirst at the far-off springs of German life.

The greatest obstacle to the success of the national Liberal programme was the attitude of Prussia. Frederick William IV, coming to the throne in 1840, carried yet farther the reactionary tendencies of his predecessor. He was a belated Romantic, moved by the contradictory desires for a revived medievalism and a legitimatistic assertion of the divine right of kings. The great development of the *bourgeoisie* during the twenty years of his reign took place unobserved beneath his very eyes. Surrounded by a little clique of catholicizing Romantics, he devoted his political energies to a revival of the old feudal classes, and on the very eve of the Revolution of 1848 set about altering his predecessor's constitution by erecting a House of Lords above the representatives of the three classes, as if to accentuate a class distinction in order to impress the *bourgeoisie*. In convoking the new diet, he insisted on the special position of his State between the three Great Powers, by ordaining which "it pleases God to make Prussia great by means of the sword, the sword of war without, the sword of the spirit within; not the negative spirit of our age, but the spirit of discipline and order." He added:

> No power on earth shall ever persuade me to exchange the natural relation between prince and people for a contractual and constitutional relation; or to countenance the insertion, between our Lord in Heaven and this country, of a piece of written paper, like a second providence, to rule by its paragraphs and to take the place of ancient sacred loyalty.

The increasing rigidity of Prussia in her traditional attitude formed a serious obstacle to the execution of the Liberal programme of a national unification by means of liberty, and split the party into two camps. The more moderate Liberals continued to hope for a change of heart on the part of Prussia, in the sense that if the king saw an opportunity to make a bid for the crown of all Germany, a feeling for his own dynastic interests might induce him to form a *mariage de convenance* with freedom; the more radical Liberals began to look for a unification in spite of Prussia, at the price of the absorption of the Prussian kingdom in a Liberal Germany.

But in Prussia the same politicians who were farthest from the romantic spirit of the king, and shared with the Liberals a hope of national unification, recoiled from this extreme of radicalism. In their opinion the hegemony of an armed Prussia was the only guarantee for true unity, the only force capable of permanently uniting the numerous petty States of Germany, overcoming their anarchical particularism and arousing their dormant political feeling. Thus to the Liberal idea of a federation of autonomous sovereign States (*Staatenbund*) they opposed the idea of a federal State (*Bundesstaat*) with Prussia as its centre. The reactionary policy of Frederick William IV they regarded as an antiquated and out-of-date, but none the less providential, method of resisting the disintegrating forces of Liberalism, and saving the Prussian State in its existing form for its future task.

Thus the medievalism of the king became the vehicle of a highly modern imperialistic conception of the nation, in contrast with the Liberal conception. The realization of this change is the clearest proof of the profound historical sense of Ranke, Droysen, and Sybel, and of the political astuteness shown by Bismarck in his role of reactionary during the Revolution of 1848.

For these politicians the national idea was an inference from historical premisses resembling those of Romanticism; but far from exhausting itself in a sterile reminiscence and passive admiration of the past, it brought its forces, drawn from the tradition of centuries, to bear upon the present and point towards the future, towards the expansion and domination of the German people. Not the nation as a vague sentimental entity, but the nation as an instrument of power, was the object of their love and, still more, of their political activity. They did not reject the nation of the Romantics; they wished to use its conservative energies, its archaic but solid structure, its narrow but powerful monarchy, as a platform on which to construct the new Germany. They took up the cause of Prussia not out of love of the old feudal Prussia, but because a strong Prussia could give to all Germany the form of a State, and enable it to take a place in the great international competition. Unlike their allies or tools, the pure reactionaries, they did not ignore the importance of the rapidly rising *bourgeoisie,* but wished to wean it from the philistinic ideals of a barren individualism, indoctrinate it with their own conceptions, and convert it into a progressive force to operate upon the sluggish landed aristocracy. While English and French Liberalism tended to shape the nation upon the mould of middle-class economic life, they proposed to mould this economic life to the needs of the nation, combining it with pre-existent and even outworn forces in such a way that each class should make its contribution to the common cause.

This was the motive of their protectionism, formulated for the first time, and with full consciousness of its national end, by Friedrich List in his *National System of Political Economy* in 1841. In this system the author's opposition to competition and *laissez-faire* is based not upon the social and humanitarian motives of the French and English Conservatives, nor upon the purely technical motives of Utopian Socialism, but on a totally different order of ideas. The aim of free competition, according to the classical school, was to increase the present wealth available for national consumption; the predominant consideration was that of value in exchange. List, on the other hand, introduced into the discussion two new ideas: the idea of nationality, as opposed to that of international free trade, and the idea of productive power, as opposed to that of exchange value. As against cosmopolitanism, he showed that individual prosperity closely depends upon the political power of the nation. As against the idea that productive activity ought to tend towards the creation of the maximum quantity of exchangeable values, he asserted the necessity of safeguarding the sources of labour and economic life, and ensuring the future development of these energies, on the ground that the power to create riches is infinitely more important than riches themselves.

Now according to the theory of free trade, it cannot pay a nation to create an industry when, as was the case with Germany about the year 1840, it can purchase the industrial products which it needs cheaper in foreign countries, in exchange for agricultural products which it can produce more cheaply. But this narrowly utilitarian calculation would, according to List, deprive the nation of its best energies. Industry best develops the moral energies of a people. The desire for a constant increase of intellectual and moral goods, the love of emulation and liberty, is characteristic of an industrial and commercial state; under the régime of a uniform agriculture, dullness of mind, sloth of body, and attachment to old ideas and habits are the rule. Even agriculture is powerfully stimulated by the presence of manufactures. The State, therefore, by suitable legislation must encourage the birth and growth of industries.

Here economics are clearly subordinated to national organization. But not economics only; all the other energies of the people are to be treated in the same way. Freedom also, with its autonomous institutions, is a source of national energy; and the arguments which we have reproduced led List to distinguish clearly between the cause of protection and that of anti-Liberalism. Indeed, in the rise of industry, even under protection, he saw a means of a liberal education for the people. But freedom, like industry, like agriculture, like intellectual culture, has the value of a mere means to a higher national end. In a spirit not unlike that of List, Bismarck, the reactionary of 1848, later granted the nation universal suffrage when he came to see in this a useful means of consolidating the Empire; he was willing either to form an alliance with the Liberal Party or to set on foot the *Kulturkampf,* whose anti-Liberal character is obvious.

The danger of this tendency to subordinate and sacrifice every value to the idol of nationality is that the spirit of the people may lose its sense of direction, and that stability and firmness may disappear from the current of public opinion through the prevalence of the idea that these values are contingent and accidental; and in minds of a lower order, less strongly sustained by the consciousness of the higher end, this means degeneration into a cynical opportunism. The nationalism of Bismarck, Droysen, and Treitschke failed to create a true governing class, because it was too much of an original work of art, requiring for its perfection a lofty intellect capable of mastering a recalcitrant and uninspiring matter. Now a political tradition cannot base its continuity upon a succession of great men. Bismarck could only create lieutenants; and when he vanished from the political stage, the technical and administrative subordinates who had worked under him in a complex and highly organized machine showed themselves unable to perform a task of synthesis for which they had not been trained.

Another danger of this form of nationalism is that by turning the nation into a weapon of aggression and conquest it threatens to destroy the basis on which the idea of the nation, and therefore the possibility of the coexistence of different nations, is built. The imperialism which inevitably proceeds from such a tendency not only claims the right of enslaving weaker nations, but runs the risk of corrupting the spirit of the conquering nation, by disintegrating its forces into a super-State composed of heterogeneous elements whose artificial cohesion demands a diversion of these forces from their normal function in the historical life of the nation. While the reactionary nationalism of the Romantics sacrificed the future of the national life to the love of the past, the new imperialism, which was not unconnected with its predecessor, sacrificed to ambitious hopes for the future the traditional historic character of the German people.

At this point the fundamental contrast between this conception and the political idea of the nation becomes clear. The one considers the nation only as an element in the power of the State; the other erects it into an independent value superior to the State, enclosing and entrenching the latter within the inviolable limits of the nation. Thus for Liberalism the peaceful coexistence of a number of nations, each organized as a State and conducting its relations with its neighbours on the same principles that govern the relations of free and self-conscious individuals, is a necessary condition of political stability and progress. From this point of view it is possible to appreciate the great difference between the national claims of most European peoples during the nineteenth century, directed to the achievement, through revolution and war, of a work of emancipation, and the projects of expansion and hegemony inspired by the spirit of an imperialistic nationalism.

The great campaign of German Liberalism for national unity was fought in 1848. The Liberals put forward three closely connected proposals:

to liberate the German States from the paternalism of Austria; to obtain, especially in Prussia, genuinely modern constitutions in place of the old feudal diets; and to make these constitutions a bond of political union for the whole German people.

The first of these proposals could be carried out easily and almost instantaneously. Austria, weakened by a revolutionary crisis at home, a war against Italy, and a rebellion in Hungary, could offer little resistance to the German federation in its struggle for freedom. The weakness of Austria resulted in the paralysis of the pro-Austrian party, which called itself the Great German Party, and proposed to include the Austrian nation in a Greater Germany. This party, in a small minority at the parliament of Frankfurt, disappeared from the scene together with its patroness Austria, and the partisans of a smaller Germany remained masters of the field.

The second point in the Liberal programme was won at the first attack by the *bourgeois* revolution, which wrested from the terrified rulers the constitutional concessions that had long been demanded. This revolution was particularly violent in Prussia, where the monarchical reaction had been most energetic. Unlike the contemporary revolution in France, it had no marked social character, because industry had not yet developed in Prussia, and the agricultural masses were still in a backward state of feudal civilization which prevented their infection by the revolutionary feeling of the lesser *bourgeoisie*. The soul of the revolution was the city *bourgeoisie,* led by professors and students, the educated classes among which the claims of Liberalism had been longer felt and more vividly realized. But absolutism, defeated in the towns, was uninjured and ready for the counter-attack in the country, the stronghold of feudalism. Bismarck gives in his *Memoirs* an interesting picture of this state of mind, which he expounded to the king in order to engage him on the side of reaction. But Frederick William no longer needed such aids. In the army, a force of feudal origin so far as officers and men were concerned, but educated in the school of monarchy, he possessed the quintessence of the forces of ancient and modern Prussia; and once the first period of dismay was over he employed this powerful weapon to put down the revolution.

The third task of the German Liberals was more complicated. It was taken in hand under the happy auspices of the revolutionary victory in Prussia, which favoured the hope of a unification of Germany with a Liberal Prussia at its head. It expressed an ideal towards which no party, even the most reactionary, could display a *fin de non-reçevoir*. Yet this ideal was opposed by the best representatives of culture and politics, who, as we have seen, were partisans of a new nationalism. These agreed in desiring unification, but not by an act of popular sovereignty, which would create a weak State, at the mercy of parties, and condemn Prussia to a secondary position where she could make no use of her actual military superiority. Hence we find an alliance in common opposition to the Liberal programme taking shape, between the old conservative classes, anxious for internal reaction, and the most modern representatives of imperialism, ready to use the former's power of resistance in order to oppose the revolutionary project of a federation of German States. The ancient alliance between the monarchy and the feudal nobility was reasserted and confirmed.

And while the conservative classes seconded the efforts of "King Grapeshot" (as the King of Prussia was nicknamed) to suppress the Liberal revolution, the nationalists criticized and ridiculed the debates in the parliament of Frankfurt, which, intended to settle the question of national unity, were gradually degenerating into empty verbal disputes as the people's representatives lost their prestige beneath the rising tide of reaction, and found themselves impotent to obtain any practical sanction for their resolutions. Nationalist historians have described the Frankfurt sessions as shining examples of doctrinaire abstraction and practical ineffectiveness. Partisan passions have prevented them from coolly realizing the exceptional conditions under which the representatives of the people were compelled to work, fettered by the heavy diplomatic yoke of two Great Powers, and, even more serious, hampered in carrying out their mandate by a permanent conflict between the sovereignty of parliament and that of the confederated States in whose hands any final decision must lie. But for the nationalists, the manifest impotence of the parliament was enough to discredit popular assemblies as such, and to create in the public mind a sense of distrust towards the futile and abstract sham-politics of professors and lawyers. The example of Frankfurt, aggravated by the historians' misrepresentations, was fatal to German political Liberalism. The people lost all interest in representative institutions, and made up its mind, to its own loss, that its political future depended wholly upon the Crown.

The closing scenes of the Frankfurt parliament, by a fiasco striking enough to impress itself permanently on the memory of the people, crowned the work of the doctrinaire impotence displayed by the representatives during the whole session. In the sitting of the 28th of March 1849, the assembly, after settling the internal crisis between the Prussian and Austrian parties in favour of the former, in spite of the Prussian reaction then in full swing, elected Frederick William IV Emperor of the Germans by 290 votes, 248 abstaining. But the King of Prussia refused the crown offered him by the representatives of the people, and explained in private why he had done so: the crown which a Hohenzollern could accept, he said, was not a crown created, even with the consent of princes, by a revolutionary assembly. If the ancient crown of the German nation, he added, which for forty-two years had lain idle, was to be conferred upon any one, it ought to have been conferred by himself and his equals, the other princes.

The king's haughty legitimism was a generation behind the times; but in its effects, if not in its motives, it harmonized admirably with the views of the most advanced politicians, who regarded unification as a problem of sheer force, to be solved by the sword. History has shown that both the king and politicians were right; for the Empire was created by the military strength of the Hohenzollerns, combined with the *Realpolitik* of the nationalists, to the complete exclusion of any expression of popular consent, or any aid from the spirit of an "antiquated" Liberalism. Yet the Liberal sense of nationality, outwardly ignored, never ceased to live and work silently in the depths of the popular mind; and in the darkest hour of the Empire, when the force which was to be its only effectual bond had failed, the nation was able to maintain its unity as a State in virtue of a right based on purely Liberal principles, and thus to feel itself still firmly united in spite of threats of internal disruption. The representatives united at Weimar at last did justice to the Utopian generosity of Frankfurt.

Hans Kohn of the City College of New York is one of the foremost modern students of nationalism and its consequences in the modern world.

FROM *The Mind of Germany* BY HANS KOHN

HEINRICH HEINE DIED IN 1856—in the midst of a profound change in the political and moral climate of Germany. As late as 1840 liberals were influencing major decisions, but by 1870 most of the liberals had turned into nationalists. To the historian Friedrich Sell this was a tragedy. Tragic indeed were the consequences, but the word *tragedy* is misleading, for it implies that the German liberals were unwittingly tangled in events outside their control. The truth is that most liberals were convinced that they had to choose between a free society and a unified power state. Wittingly and willingly they preferred national power to individual liberty.

The turning point meant a break not only with the West but also with most of Germany's past. For Goethe the small town and principality of Weimar set the stage for a wide-open world of cultural intercourse and for the intensity of fruitful daily work. For the generation of 1870 the Prussian power-state alone seemed to guarantee a worthwhile national and personal life. Goethe as we have seen had no use for the Middle Ages. Now the Prussian dynasty of the Hohenzollern was greeted as the legitimate successor of the Hohenstaufen.

The interest in their empire was revived in the 1820's by a number of historical and poetical works. Friedrich von Raumer, Professor at the University of Berlin, began publication in 1823 of a six-volume "History of the Hohenstaufen and their Times." It presented the Hohenstaufen Reich not only as the first European power of its times, but also as a much more centralized national state than was actually the case. Under the influence of Raumer's widely read work, Karl Leberecht Immermann wrote a tragedy, "Kaiser Friedrich II," in 1828, and Ernst Benjamin Raupach wrote a cycle of not less than sixteen plays called "Die Hohenstaufen," which in spite of the fact that today his name has long been forgotten, were very popular in their day, so popular that in 1832 young Richard Wagner wrote an overture on this subject. More talented than Raupach was Christian Dietrich Grabbe; his two plays on the same subject may be read even today. In 1849 Raumer was a member of the delegation which on behalf of the German National Assembly offered the imperial crown to the Hohenzollern King. He lived long enough to witness, as a nonagenarian in 1871, the assumption by the Hohenzollern of the imperial title which popular imagination confounded with that of the Hohenstaufen. But the two had nothing in common. The Hohenstaufen Reich was rooted in southern Germany; in its religion it was Catholic; in its concept it was universal; and many of the Hohenstaufen felt more Mediterranean than German.

In the mid-nineteenth century the Prussian historian, Heinrich von Sybel, proposed a new interpretation of German history, which, under the impact of the Prussian victories was soon generally accepted. The new interpretation shifted the center of German history to the northeast, made Protestantism its dominant and creative religion, and based this religion upon a strictly nation-centered concept. Its outlook was not only anti-Roman and anti-Mediterranean, but antiwestern. It saw German history after the fall of the Hohenstaufen reaching its first climax in the War of Liberation fought under Prussia's leadership against France, and finding its fulfillment in Prussia's victory over France in 1871.

Such were the forces that brought about the close co-operation of most German liberal intellectuals with the Prussian authoritarian monarchy. The co-operation was originally not sought by either of the two sides. They neither loved nor trusted each other. But Prussia, which had little liking for modern liberalism, seemed the only country to offer what so many liberals desired, power to achieve national greatness and to restore Germany, as in the time of the Hohenstaufen, to the imperial leadership in Europe. In the end, after some resistance, but not too unwillingly or ungraciously, most liberals capitulated to Prussia. In return, the latter made minor concessions to the liberals, concessions without which a modern power-state could not have existed but which did not go far enough to transform Prussia into a durable and viable modern society.

There was nothing traditional or hallowed about the Prussian monarchy. The kingdom came into existence on January 18, 1701, when the Elector of Brandenburg assumed the title of king in Prussia. This took place in Königsberg, a city in the extreme northeast of Germany, then politically and spiritually outside Germany proper. It was a German outpost surrounded on all sides by Slav and Lithuanian populations which had been subjugated in the late Middle Ages by the Teutonic Knights. From its original domain, the March of Brandenburg, itself a frontier territory occupying former Slav lands east of the Elbe River, the power of the House of Hohenzollern had spread over many territorially disconnected possessions, which were united only by two factors: the dynasty and the need of defending long frontiers in a shapeless plain, a landscape much more characteristic of eastern than of western Europe. From the end of the seventeenth century Brandenburg, until then a minor German state, was bent upon glory and expansion. It lacked natural resources and its soil was poor; thus, it could achieve military strength only by the most efficient and economical administration and by giving full precedence to the military.

Life in eighteenth century Prussia was dominated by a stern sense of duty and service, by frugality and cultural insensibility. The emphasis was on efficiency, self-reliance, and thrift, not, as in the middle-class world of puritanism, for the sake of the individual and of religion but for the sake of the authoritarian state and of military power. Its own historians praised the Prussian state as the personification of political power. The state became the fountainhead of ethical life and the center of devotion.

In the eighteenth century Prussia was alien to the German mind and suspect to the German intellectuals who hated its garrison-spirit. The princes who founded Prussian greatness in that century, the dedicated soldier-king Frederick William I and his more complex and famous son Frederick II, had no regard or understanding for German cultural life. Prussia owed little to Germany and gave little. Its astonishing growth was dominated by only one goal—power—and only one norm—Prussia.

During the Napoleonic period a generation of great reformers, almost all of them born outside Prussia, tried to infuse Prussian power with a German spirit and to liberalize the monarchy. Their efforts saved Prussia and made victory in the war of 1813 possible. After that, reforms were halted. The University of Berlin, founded in 1810 as a part of the reform movement, became in many ways a model of scholarship and efficiency, but its professors accepted the authority of the state so willingly that one of the leading scholars there could call himself and his colleagues "the intellectual bodyguard of the Hohenzollern." This description was intended by the author and received by his colleagues as high praise. It was to this unreformed Prussia, the openly acknowledged bulwark of authoritarianism and conservative militarism, that most German liberals turned for guidance and inspiration.

This change in the attitude of the German liberals can best be followed in the writing of the German historians, from Johann Gustav Droysen, born in 1808, to Heinrich von Treitschke who died in 1896. Leopold von Ranke, whom they acknowledged as their master, belonged to an older generation.

He never was a liberal. Nevertheless, his political thought influenced many of those who called themselves liberal. "Ranke asserted the right of any state to follow its own logic of politics, its right to be different from the strict standard of liberalism," writes Professor Theodore H. von Laue in his study of Ranke's formative years. "The consequences of this assertion were momentous. It implied a break with the political development in France, England, and the United States. Under its guidance Prussia preserved the absolutist state of the eighteenth century instead of following the western trend toward democracy, and the more pacifist evaluation of international relations. The philosophy which Ranke so clearly stated was one of the landmarks in the revolt against the West, upholding against the advocates of western liberalism a new Prussophilism, which in time grew into a Germanophilism."

What separated Ranke from his successors was not merely his conservatism. Like Hegel, Ranke was no nationalist. He accepted the Europe of his time and believed in the concert of nations, whereas an historian like Droysen demanded the pre-eminence of the one nation clearly marked out for leadership. Ranke believed in the authoritarian monarchical state; Droysen believed in the German nation-state. Ranke still participated in the open world of Goethe, and in the balanced Europe of Metternich. Droysen finally embraced nothing except Germany and its national self-interest.

German historians and the German people ultimately accepted the idealization of state and power which Ranke held in common with Hegel, and as time went on oversimplified and vulgarized it. Perhaps the most generous judgment on Ranke's influence on nineteenth century German thought was expressed in 1886, on the occasion of Ranke's ninetieth birthday, by a Dutch historian, Robert Fruin, a master of the critical method himself and a liberal in the western sense of the word. "To us, who find more in the history of mankind than just the impact of power, and who care for other interests besides those of the State, Ranke's writings, however beautiful, will always appear lacking in something and unsatisfying. . . . Is it an injustice to our German neighbors to suggest that it is this characteristic attitude which has earned for Ranke the position of the historian *par excellence* of present-day Germany? Or is it not true that to the rulers and leaders of opinion in that country the power of the State is the overriding consideration? That to it everything else must give way and is, if need be, sacrificed? Prosperity, trade, and industry, are not promoted in accordance with their own needs and the laws of political economy, but are managed with an eye to the demands of State power, in the interests of the unity and efficiency of the Reich. Everything is regarded as lawful in these, and alas in other, respects, whenever German unity and German ascendancy in Europe might otherwise be thought to suffer."

*   *   *

Looking back to the War of Liberation, the liberals of this generation rejoiced in the recollection of the high moral standard maintained by the German people in their struggle against the French. Droysen's colleague Friedrich Christoph Dahlmann could not conceal his disgust for French frivolity when, in 1815, he came to deliver an academic address celebrating the victory over Napoleon. "Any one of us in the future who considers the French and the Germans merely as two hostile nations fighting with equal right on each side, any one of us who goes on believing that he would act in the same way if he were born a Frenchman, any one of us who compares this people who have so ignominiously degenerated, this rapacious people who commit perjury and deny God, with the noble and self-sacrificing Germans, he, wherever he be born, is really French and deserves so to be regarded in Germany." On behalf of the University Dahlmann stressed that all scholarship was meaningless if it did not enrich society and that scholars more than anyone else were called to preserve the sacred flame of the love of the Fatherland.

Before 1848 this dedication to an exclusive patriotism and this emphasis on the power-state were in no way characteristic of German liberals. In southwestern Germany and in the Rhineland the desire to follow western ways prevailed. The year 1819 saw the introduction of parliamentary institutions in Bavaria, Baden, and Württemberg. The leader of the liberal opposition in Baden was Karl von Rotteck who taught history and political science at the University of his native town, Freiburg. In his time his influence on the educated middle class in southern Germany was very great. His multivoluminous *Universal History* reached its 25th printing twenty-six years after his death. His *Encyclopedia of Political Science (Staatslexikon)* which he edited with his young colleague, Karl Theodor Welcker, was, in the 1830's, a powerful vehicle for spreading western liberal ideas. The Chamber of Deputies in Baden, originally modeled after that of the French Charte of 1814 became after 1831, with the growing influence of French liberalism, the first school of parliamentary life in Germany.

Rotteck's spiritual home was not the War of Liberation but the Enlightenment. The state to him was primarily the embodiment not of might, but of right. Like so many other eighteenth century Germans, he lavished no praise on great conquerors and least of all on Frederick II of Prussia. Like most German liberals of 1830 he demanded the restoration of Poland's independence. In his *History* he called the partition of Poland "the most horrible violation of international law and of the sacred right of mankind in modern times, infinitely more terrible than the horrors of the Huns and the Vandals." Rotteck believed in natural law, which the Germans called *Vernunftrecht*, rational law. He also admired the United States. "There no secret police, no censorship, no suspension of personal liberty, no closing of the borders, no terrorist measures were needed to maintain public tranquility and the respect for authority." Rotteck was neither a revolutionary nor a republican. He sought to transform Baden and southwestern Germany into a bulwark of western liberty rivaling England, France, and Belgium. "For Rotteck," writes Professor Sell, "liberty unquestionably took precedence over nationalism. In the Napoleonic period he proved himself a patriot; Napoleon as he saw it had suppressed liberty." But he was reluctant to sacrifice the liberty acquired in a small German state for the nation at large if that were less liberal. He preferred being the citizen of a constitutional free state to being the subject of a great power. After the German Festival of Hambach in 1832 he delivered a speech in Badenweiler in which he exclaimed: "I do not desire [national] unity without [political] liberty, and I prefer liberty without unity to unity without liberty. I reject unity under the wings of the Prussian or Austrian eagle." When war between liberal France and reactionary Prussia threatened to break out Rotteck was of the opinion that in such a case liberal Germany should side with France.

*　　　　*　　　　*

When the Prussian army under Prince William, the future William I, moved southward to suppress democracy in Germany, it found the stiffest resistance in Baden. There Lorenz Brentano, a lawyer from Mannheim, proclaimed a republic with the support of the majority of the population. The people fought well. The Swiss poet Gottfried Keller, who was then in Heidelberg and could observe the war at close range, wrote: "The Prussians paid dearly for their victory though they had superior forces. Especially the Baden artillerymen showed great heroism. As it was very hot, they worked at their guns in shirtsleeves as bakers do in front of the oven, and yet they were in high spirits. They shot their own wounded comrades to death to prevent them from falling into Prussian hands." The superior equipment and numbers of the Prussian army rendered resistance hopeless.

What the Russian troops did at about the same time in Hungary, Prussian soldiers accomplished in south-western Germany. German liberty was extinguished in a reign of terror. Nearly a thousand men were sentenced to long terms of hard labor, and over forty were executed. Out of a population of nearly one and one half million, eighty thousand citizens left Baden for Switzerland, England, and the United States. Almost equally great was the number who fled the Palatinate and the Rhineland. The revolutions of 1849 in Baden and the Palatinate were the last attempt to introduce democracy into Germany. An authoritarian exclusive nationalism triumphed in 1848 and carried Germany along a road far removed from that traced by Rotteck and Gervinus.

Before 1848 German liberals hoped to achieve both national unity and political liberty. In the nineteenth century in western Europe nationalism and democratic liberalism supported and strengthened each other. The same process took place during the century in most Germanic lands—in Switzerland, in the Netherlands, and in Scandinavia. The Germans, however, did not succeed in uniting the two forces. The great majority of them desired national power even above liberty.

There were those who hoped that liberty would come after the creation of a strong nation-state. Recalling Periclean Athens and Elizabethan England, they insisted that great civilizations flourish under a strong government. But history exhibits many examples of artistic activity under weak governments, to mention only the Italian Renaissance and the ferment of Germany in Goethe's generation. But whatever might have been the hopes and illusions of the German national liberals, they preferred nationalism, and their liberalism was short-lived. Two critical years in the surrender of liberalism were 1848 and 1866. In both cases few Germans could resist the lure of power, a power embodied in the Prussian military monarchy.

After the Revolution of 1848 in Paris fanned the hopes of democracy in central Europe, the German liberals had to choose one of two alternatives. One was to reform the governments in the various German states, to call democratic assemblies in each, and thus to replace the absolutist authorities by popular institutions. Later on, the new democratic German states could have formed, by democratic means, a closer and more perfect union. In their haste to establish national unity, the German liberals proceeded otherwise. Instead of reforming and democratizing the various individual states—as the Swiss did in their cantons after 1831—and thus laying the foundations for German democracy, they ignored local institutions, traditional seats of loyalty and power, and called a democratically elected National Assembly to Frankfurt-am-Main, an assembly which rested on no real foundations and was not supported by any existing political structure. It was an overly ambitious project. For that very reason it achieved neither liberty nor unity. During the many months that it took to work out a democratic constitution for the whole of Germany the authoritarian governments of the various German lands, which in the spring of 1848 had briefly lost control of the situation, reasserted themselves, and the democratic constitution was doomed. Unity was achieved twenty years later by a determined adversary of liberal democracy, by Bismarck.

The National Assembly went further in predetermining the course of German history. No German prince of the time stood in as sharp an opposition to all western concepts of liberty and parliamentarism as did King Frederick William IV of Prussia. When he opened, on April 11, 1847, the first session of the United Estates (*Vereinigte Landtag*) representing the various provinces of his kingdom, he warned the assembly against the un-Germanic and impractical illusion that it might be possible to realize in Germany parliamentary institutions. No power on earth, he solemnly professed, would ever succeed in making him change the natural relation between prince and people into a constitutional one. He swore that he would never allow a constitution, a piece of paper, to come between our Lord in Heaven and his (the king's) country, "to govern us with its articles and to replace old and sacred loyalties." He was convinced that his people would resist the wiles of seduction, that they did not wish to share in the government through their representatives and to break the plenitude of power entrusted by God to their kings. "I and my House, we wish to serve the Lord."

At the time this medieval approach aroused general consternation. Only Ranke was so naive as to believe that since King David no king had uttered more beautiful words. "I say definitely," he wrote, "that I know nothing since the psalms where the idea of a religious monarchy has been expressed more powerfully and more nobly. It has great passages of historical truth." Though the national liberals in Frankfurt did not share Ranke's profound devotion and put their hope instead in a liberal Prussia, they were so fascinated by Prussian power that in April, 1849, they offered the imperial crown of Germany to King Frederick William IV. The king, more faithful to his principles than the majority of liberals in the National Assembly were to theirs, rejected the crown offered to him by the democratically elected representatives of the nation. The Prussian ruling class had no faith in nation or people, in democracy or parliament. They expected the regeneration of Prussia from Prussia's traditional pillar of strength, the army. *"Gegen Demokraten helfen nur Soldaten"*—Only soldiers are of help against democrats—expressed the then prevailing mood in Berlin. After the failure of the Frankfurt Assembly to achieve German unity, many of the national liberals came to share their faith in Prussia's mission and in Prussia's army.

Before 1848 the national liberals expected Prussia to be absorbed in Germany. In an article published in the *Deutsche Zeitung* on January 1, 1848, Dahlmann pleaded for an hereditary imperial monarchy under the Hohenzollern. But he rejected the idea of Prussian domination over Germany and insisted that the German parliament must not meet in Berlin. On the contrary, he demanded, "the German Reichstag should have its seat anywhere but on Prussian soil. . . . In a short time there must be no Prussian region which has not felt the rejuvenating breath of free German life." Prussia was to be Germanized, not Germany Prussianized. There was widespread hope among the liberals that Prussia could be dissolved into its various provinces which would become in their own right part of the united Germany. Thus the threat presented to German liberty and cultural life by Prussia's overwhelming power and tradition might be averted. This seemed not impossible in 1847. Most Prussian provinces were still corporate personalities with their own traditions, their own Estates, and their own administrations. In March, 1848, a strong separatist movement made itself felt in the Prussian Rhineland.

The experience of the year 1848–49 changed the outlook of the national liberals. In a recent book, *Liberal Thought at the Time of the Frankfurt Assembly,* the young German historian Wolfgang Hock has carefully followed the progress of many German intellectuals from an initial clear distinction between national might and self-interest on the one hand and right and morality on the other, to their harmonization and identification.

Gustav Rümelin took this to be the mission which "our German people received from history," to make morality ever more political and politics ever more moral. Such an attempt at the harmonization of might and morality was facilitated by several factors: the educated German middle class lacked political experience. It had not shared in the political life of the country or in the administration of the state, which was reserved for the closed caste of professional bureaucrats. German thought had been predominantly philosophical and poetical and had neglected the realities of state and power as well as the task of responsible self-government and political education of the citizen.

Now the intellectuals seized upon the revelation of power—from the exercise of which they remained excluded—with typical German thoroughness, and with the enthusiasm of converts to a new faith. They overestimated and idealized power and the state as much as they had formerly underestimated them. They overlooked the necessary limits and inherent dangers of power. They were convinced that these dangers did not exist when power was in the right hands, in the hands of a morally superior and better educated governing class or nation. The new vision of power and national greatness was intoxicating. The danger was all the greater the more sincerely these educated Germans were convinced of their own morality and rationality. They lacked even a slight—and often healthy—dash of humor, of cynicism, or of self-criticism. They were deeply in earnest. Thus they easily succumbed to temptation without even being aware of it. Jacob Burckhardt saw this clearly. On August 23, 1848, he wrote to his German friend, Hermann Schaumburg: "Do what you wish or must do, only don't imagine that you are free while in reality the darkest elemental spirits dwell in you and drive you on (*die dunkelsten Elementargeister ihr Wesen mit Euch treiben*)."

An understandable desire for action, for a new fulness of life, animated the educated German middle class. They no longer wished to be a people of thinkers, poets, and dreamers. Impatiently they longed for great deeds on the world stage. The pettier the present appeared to them the mightier was their vision of the future. They knew that German classical literature was great. In their eyes it represented a unique re-embodiment of the heritage of Greece. But now its task was fulfilled. The time had come to assert German political leadership as Luther had three centuries before established German religious leadership. A man like Luther was needed, not in the field of religion but in the realm of politics. How could such a great destiny be realized without the help of those in power?

Dahlmann, in the speech of January 22, 1849, in which he proposed the imperial crown for Prussia, voiced the growing conviction that power was more important than liberty. "The path of power," he declared, "is the only one which can satisfy and satiate our urge for liberty. For this urge does not primarily aspire to liberty; to a greater degree it lusts for power which has so far been denied to it. This can be accomplished only through Prussia. Prussia

can not thrive (genesen) without Germany nor Germany without Prussia."
The same shift to a preference for state-power over liberty can be traced, as
Professor Felix Gilbert has shown, in the thought of another great liberal
historian, Droysen. In 1847 he had written that history teaches us everywhere
that the longing for power and glory deludes nations and states, for it
overstimulates and finally brutalizes and debilitates them. But at the end of
1848, in the midst of the popular uprisings, he confessed that he saw in the
[Prussian] army a great moral force, and that power alone could save
Germany. "The State is Power," he proclaimed as did Treitschke later.
Droysen now abandoned the hope that Prussia would become Germanized
and a part of Germany; on the contrary, Prussia in its full power and armed
with the Prussian tradition appeared as the political savior of Germany. In a
revolutionary year men and movements travel rapidly a long road, some
forward to liberty, others backward to the apparent security of great power.

*   *   *

The Germans of the Age of Nationalism had no liberal statesman, no
Gladstone, not even a Cavour, Clemenceau, or Masaryk, to direct their
national energies into democratic channels. Instead, they had Bismarck.
What the revolution of 1848 failed to do, his revolution of 1866 accomplished.
It laid the foundations of a unified German nation-state. Bismarck put the
Hohenzollern into the position which the Hohenstaufen once occupied. But
the foundations laid by Bismarck seemed stronger at that time than they
were shown to be a few decades later. Solitary voices crying in the wilderness
of national self-satisfaction warned Bismarck's admirers in vain against
overestimating power and underestimating liberty. For 1866 failed even
more disastrously than 1848 in securing liberty and infusing nationalism
with the spirit of democracy.

> *Dr. Neill views the alliance and conflict of liberalism and*
> *nationalism in terms of social classes.*

FROM *The Rise and Decline of Liberalism*

BY THOMAS P. NEILL

IN THE FIRST HALF of the nineteenth century Liberalism was inextricably bound in with the all-pervading romanticism of the age, and outside of

Thomas P. Neill, *The Rise and Decline of Liberalism* (1953), pp. 123–30, 132. Reprinted by
permission of The Bruce Publishing Company.

England and France with nationalism. Liberalism and nationalism are frequently called twin offspring of the French Revolution, twins who supported and helped each other grow in the first half of the century, but who turned against each other about 1850 with the ever stronger nationalism eventually smothering the ever weakening Liberalism. Italy is perhaps the best example of the close association, almost identification, of Liberalism and nationalism in the first part of the century. Germany and Poland are other good examples. At this time there was no geographic Italy or Germany or Poland. Italy was cut up into a number of states, some under foreign and others under native control. Nationalists who wanted to create a united Italy therefore instinctively embraced Liberal doctrines as excellent weapons to turn against the existing authorities. So it was with Germans who were divided among thirty-nine states, or Poles who lived under the rule of Prussia, Austria, and Russia.

In each of these areas the nationalists imported Liberal theory from abroad, and though it served their revolutionary purpose, it was an abstract kind of thought not associated with their national traditions or their various histories. When a national state was finally created in Italy in 1861 and in Germany a decade later, it was therefore easy for the new governments to suppress Liberalism as annoying and as dangerous to the established government. Thus Liberalism tended to lose out to nationalism in the latter part of the century, but it did not disappear without leaving its mark on each country, and in many countries it continued as the program of a minority group. As an opposition party in Germany, for example, the Liberals kept their theory alive and pushed upon Bismarck a number of measures he might otherwise never have adopted. So it was in Italy, in Spain, in Portugal, and in other countries where Liberalism tended to disappear as a doctrine or as a party label.

Liberalism failed to take root in the countries outside France, we have suggested, principally because there was no large middle class anywhere else in Europe in the early nineteenth century. And the middle class is the good ground in which the seed of Liberal doctrine takes root and grows. It is worth noting in this connection that Liberalism spread chiefly in the Rhineland, in Belgium and Holland, in northern Italy, and in other local areas where there was a numerous middle class. But nowhere outside England, France, Holland, and Belgium were the bourgeoisie numerous or influential enough to control the nation as a whole. The Rhinelanders, for example, were in a Prussia dominated by the *Junkertum* of the East, and the bourgeoisie of northern Italy had to contend with the central and southern provinces as well as opponents in their own area. It is this lack of a large middle class, more than any other single factor, which explains the failure of Liberalism in such countries as Hungary and Poland, where the political and social situation seemed otherwise ideally cast for the triumph of Liberalism.

The near success and the ultimate failure of Liberalism in Germany is more important for the subsequent history of the movement than its fate anywhere else in central or southern Europe. It should be remembered that the western and southern parts of the German-speaking world had been within the orbit of French influence throughout the eighteenth century, that the Liberal ideas of such writers as Montesquieu and Voltaire and Rousseau and of such groups as the Encyclopedists and Physiocrats were well known in these parts of Germany. This thought developed into a German brand of the Enlightenment, known as the *Aufklärung,* which prepared the way intellectually for the advance of Liberalism in the early nineteenth century.

The first Liberal victories, paradoxically, were not won by Liberals but were imposed on Prussians by their government. These were the Liberal reforms of Hardenberg and vom Stein, a part of that larger movement in Prussian history early in the nineteenth century when the country of Frederick the Great came to life again after its humiliations at Napoleon's hands. The Prussian government had watched Napoleon's conscript army, fired by a burning nationalism and an intense love of liberty, tear their professional army to pieces time and time again. After Prussia's worst humiliations of all, the defeats of Jena and Auerstadt and the partitioning of the country at Tilsit in 1807, the ministry set about reviving the country and readying it for a "war of liberation" against Napoleon.

Military reform under men like Gneisenau and Scharnhorst was of a liberal character. Social and political and economic reforms were likewise liberal, enough so at any rate to satisfy the modest requests of Rhineland Liberals and to serve as the springboard for future Liberal demands for constitutional government and a bill of rights. Vom Stein and Hardenberg, leaders in the Prussian revival after 1807, wanted to destroy the relics of feudalism so as to set up a society of free men, partly because the French experience proved free men better soldiers and partly because men like vom Stein and Hardenberg were influenced by the *Aufklärung.* A series of land reforms under vom Stein ended serfdom and threw the ownership of land open to all classes in Prussia. At the same time freedom of occupation was asserted for all citizens.

The most important Liberal change in politics was the setting up of a system of local self-government which, it should be noted, was widely interpreted as the first step toward constitutional government on the English model. Thus Ruggiero has written:

> The projects of Hardenberg [and vom Stein] were permeated by this spirit of freedom. He demanded so much liberty and equality as was compatible with monarchy and a free civil society: the abolition of the privileges of the nobility with regard to public office, possession of baronial lands, and exemption from taxes: the abolition of the hereditary dependence of the peasants and the restrictions on the acquisition and use of land: and the institution of national representation so far as this did not prejudice the principle of monarchy.

Thus it seemed a good beginning was made toward the triumph of Liberalism in Prussia by the time Napoleon was sent off to St. Helena in 1815. Moreover, the great German thinkers of this age seemed favorably disposed toward the development of a full Liberalism; the professional classes were inclined toward Liberal doctrine; and the universities, the freest and most advanced in Europe, promised to be seedbeds of future Liberal thought. However, the destinies of Germany did not lie in such persons' hands, but rather in the ruling classes', especially in Austria and Prussia. The governments of these two states proved abnormally fearful of all Liberal thought. Metternich believed that Liberalism would dissolve his world. His mission was to preserve that world as long as he was in power, and until 1848 he controlled German destinies through the Confederation set up at Vienna after Napoleon's defeat.

Liberalism was realized in a modified way, however, in some of the smaller states, especially those in the southwest, where new constitutions were adopted on the model of the French *Charte* of 1814. Baden and Bavaria received such constitutions in 1818, Württemberg adopted one in 1819, and after the disturbances of 1830 Saxony and Hanover adopted moderately Liberal constitutions. Until the Revolution of 1848 Liberalism achieved no other notable victories in the German Confederation. Prussia unintentionally promoted the growth of the middle class, and indirectly therefore of Liberalism, by following a vigorous free trade policy throughout these years. Such a policy derived from political necessity rather than Liberal theory, for the Prussian government found that it could not enforce tariff duties in a state with such long, broken, and irregular borders as it had after 1815. It therefore followed a policy of free trade with neighboring states, and eventually by 1834 created the famous *Zollverein* or Customs Union of German states clustering in a free trade area around Prussia. This measure, together with a few minor enactments, such as a law of 1838 encouraging the construction of railroads, or the Prussian Code of Labor of 1845 based on freedom of contract for workers, promoted the growth of the middle class in Prussia and to some extent in neighboring German states.

The growth of a commercial and industrial class in Germany after 1815 was of course helpful for the development of Liberalism. Until about 1830 German Liberals were generally writers, students, and professors; after that date more and more commercial and industrial leaders appear in the Liberal camp, men such as David Hansemann, a merchant of Aachen, and Ludwig Camphausen, Liberal Prussian statesman of 1848. Industrialism had not developed sufficiently by 1848, however, to produce a class in Germany such as existed in England two decades earlier, a class capable of taking over the revolution of that year and directing it along practical Liberal lines. Control was exercised instead by the professors, who at mid-century were still the dominant Liberal class in Germany.

It is customary to divide German Liberalism of this period into radical and moderate camps, with the radicals found mostly in the southern states and the moderates found chiefly in the Rhineland. For our purposes it is sufficient to note that all Liberals came to agree on this program: they must liberate the German states from the paternalism of Austria and the influence of Metternich; they must obtain genuinely Liberal constitutions for all these states, especially for Prussia, which must lead the Liberal struggle against Austria; finally, they must join these states together into a united German state. Thus the Liberals found themselves tied in with the national movement to create a united German state.

These Liberals differed from other nationalists chiefly in their insistence on the rights and liberties of German citizens, which for them were as important as the goal of German unity. Carl Rotteck, called "a typical representative of unhistorical, doctrinaire Liberalism," modeled his thought closely on that of Royer-Collard. Rotteck based human rights on abstract reason rather than on historical precedent. In a fashion strongly similar to the French Doctrinaires he drew up plans for ideal constitutional government and formulated a set of guarantees to preserve such government from royal tyranny or mob despotism. Liberals such as Rotteck conspired in romantic fashion to seize the reins of government and to unify the German states whenever the opportunity should present itself. Several times in the thirty years after 1815 they thought the time for such revolutionary Liberalism had come, but it was not until 1848 that they had a real chance to direct their nation's destiny.

In that year of universal revolution the Liberals had an opportunity to take over every government on the Continent—and for a few months it seemed that they would succeed everywhere. German revolutionary activity began toward the end of February in Baden, where Liberal agitators demonstrated and Liberal politicians came to power without violence or bloodshed. Similar spontaneous upheavals occurred at once in Bavaria and other southwestern German states. Within a few weeks the governments of other such states as Hanover and Saxony had fallen and the Liberals were in control. Early in March demonstrations began in the streets of Vienna. Metternich was forced to resign and flee to England. A new ministry made the typical Liberal promises to satisfy the urban-manned insurrection: the Imperial Estates would be summoned to draw up a constitution; censorship would be abolished; a bourgeois national guard would be organized. In Berlin the Prussian king capitulated to a demonstrating crowd, appointed a more liberal ministry, and called for elections to a constituent assembly.

Thus by the end of March, 1848, Liberalism seemed triumphant throughout the thirty-nine German states. Constitutions were being made according to Liberal theory. The old regime had collapsed everywhere, and it only remained for the new Liberal governments to consolidate their position and to create a Liberal national German state. To accomplish this latter important task Liberal leaders had summoned a parliament to meet at

Frankfurt in May. For a time all went well in this "professors' parliament." There was much heated debate on a bill of rights and on the form of government best suited for Liberal society. Eventually the new constitution was finished, and the smaller states were generally in favor of adopting it. But meanwhile the anti-Liberal leaders of Prussia and Austria had recovered their positions and had come back to rule in Berlin and Vienna. Their refusal to accept the Liberal national constitution of Frankfurt, together with the inability of the "professors" parliament to force its solution on the two major states, spelled the ruin of Liberalism throughout the Germanies.

Liberalism had failed to stay in power for a number of reasons. It had taken hold only in the cities, which in Germany did not contain a sizable proportion of the population. When the revolution spread out into the countryside, therefore, urban Liberalism was swamped under rural conservatism. Liberalism, moreover, had taken root only in the middle class, and in Germany this was not a sufficiently strong or large class to govern by itself. The movement did not receive active support from peasant, artisan, or aristocratic elements in the nation. Finally, Liberal leadership was incredibly inefficient. It achieved its initial successes only because the existing governments had been caught off guard by spontaneous demonstrations in the various capitals. When Liberals found themselves in power, however, they were unprepared to rule. The "professors' parliament" characteristically talked long about fundamental rights when they should have been solving the more pressing problem of what to do with Austria and Prussia in the proposed national state.

*　　　*　　　*

Perhaps the Frankfurt Assembly was too much interested in getting a constitution on paper and formulating a full declaration of rights, and not enough concerned with practical problems of government. Whatever the causes—and the story of 1848 is a very confused and complex one—the Liberals failed to stem the tide of reaction under the old professional ruling classes. Their failure meant the failure of Liberalism as a political philosophy and a system of government. "The example of Frankfurt, aggravated by the historians' misrepresentations, was fatal to German political Liberalism. The people lost all interest in representative institutions, and made up its mind, to its own loss, that its political future depended wholly upon the Crown. The tradition of a paternal state was too strong, especially in Prussia, for a single assembly of Liberals to destroy it with a declaration of fundamental rights and liberties of the German citizen. Nationalism remained the more pressing issue after 1848. The Liberals had failed to create a national state when they had their chance. The next opportunity was to fall to Bismarck, who, disgusted by the professorial verbiage at Frankfurt, decided that unification was to be accomplished not by words but by blood and iron.

Professor Hayes of Columbia University was a life-long stu-
dent of nationalism. In the following essay he sums up what
he considers to be the inevitable result of the clash of liberal-
ism and nationalism, particularly in cases similar to that of
Germany.

FROM *Essays on Nationalism*
BY CARLTON J. H. HAYES

LET US SUPPOSE that a nationality has waged several wars of self-determination and finally established a sovereign national state. Let us suppose, further, that this state has been successful in irredentist struggles and has acquired every bit of territory inhabited by any considerable number of fellow nationals. Let us concede that the wars of national self-determination were of the nature of enthusiastic popular rebellions against intolerable abuses of alien tyranny and that they evoked from the rebels the noblest idealism and the most heroic deeds. Let us concede, too, even in respect of the subsequent irredentist conflicts, that they were precipitated by muddling attempts of a corrupt empire to restrict the liberties of its dissident national-ities and that they represent an honest and just effort to "redeem" a popula-tion, the large majority of whom truly yearned to become citizens of the emancipating national state. It is reasonable to infer from the circumstances that "liberals" and "radicals" and "humanitarians" and "progressives" in all countries acclaimed with one voice the spiritual grandeur of that nationality, that the wealthier among them contributed to relief funds in aid of its wounded and destitute and subscribed to the war-bonds of its government, and that the more romantic volunteered their lives in its military service and their pens in its journalistic propaganda.

We might imagine, if we knew no history and were incorrigible opti-mists, that such a nationality, that such a national state, would thenceforth be an exemplar of justice and charity to all other nationalities and national states and a pillar of world-peace. Unfortunately, however, the history of the nineteenth and twentieth centuries, whilst it gives ample support to our suppositions concerning the altruism and lofty purpose of wars of national self-determination and even of irredentist wars, affords little or no evidence that the attainment of national independence and unity is a sure preliminary

Carlton J. H. Hayes, *Essays on Nationalism* (1926), pp. 156–9. Reprinted by permission of Evelyn Carroll Hayes.

to international peace and brotherhood. On the contrary, it bears witness to the disquieting fact that nationalism does not exhaust its functions and resources when it unites a dismembered nationality and erects a national state; it shows that almost invariably nationalism is heightened rather than lessened by the attainment of national sovereignty and that a national state, so soon as it is solidly established, proceeds to evolve a "national policy," which is as bellicose as it is nationalist.

What this "national policy" is, has been nicely indicated in an illuminating essay by Mr. J. L. Stocks: ". . . the 'national' policy of an established State . . . means, of course, a policy of national selfishness and aggrandisement, a 'sacred egoism,' made sacred, presumably, by the sentiment of nationality. Internally its effort is to strengthen and tighten the national bond by every means in its power; externally to make the nation feared or 'respected' by a bold and firm foreign policy, backed by a sufficiency of military force, and to obtain for it a share in the riches of the undeveloped portions of the earth's surface. It appeals to the cruder forms of patriotism. Its love of country turns readily into hatred of the foreigner, its desire for prosperity into competition for territory; and the duty of service is interpreted as a duty to maintain national unity by unquestioning assent to every decision of government. The appropriate political ideas are instilled into the citizen by the machinery of public education and by compulsory military service; and direct inducement not to surrender these ideas in later life is easily supplied if the state keeps control over appointments in some of the main professions, especially the teaching profession, and is liberal in its rewards to right-thinking leaders of opinion. Such a policy is necessarily the antithesis of nineteenth-century liberalism. In the interest of national unity it will ruthlessly suppress dissentient groups within the nation, and will be prepared for whatever sacrifice may be necessary of the principle of free speech and thought. It will develop a national economy with all its machinery of tariffs, subsidies, and concessions. In every sphere it will tend to penalise the foreigner, in its colonies by frank preference for the trade and capital of the home country, at home by interposing obstacles to immigration and naturalisation. The rulers of Germany perceived further that a certain measure of what is called State Socialism is of assistance to the objects of this policy, which are to make nationality overwhelmingly important to the citizen and so strengthen the hands of government."

In other words, an established national state evolves, under nationalism, "national interests" at home and abroad; its citizens similarly develop "national rights," more national rights perhaps when they are abroad than when they are at home; and, above all, the aggregate of national state and its citizens come to possess a peculiarly precious "national honour." Now, to assure national interests and national rights and to preserve national honour, an established state, even more than a would-be nation, must be prepared to use force and to wage war. Militarism thus becomes an abiding characteristic of nationalism and the chief means to nationalist ends. Militarism is not merely a temporary instrument thrust by a fortuitous Providence into the hands of oppressed nationalities and idyllic irredentists and enabling them to recast political geography on reasonable national lines. Militarism, with its displays of might and threats of force, is a permanent feature of triumphant nationalism in a world in which non-national empires have largely been replaced by national states.

The Marxists—Revolutionaries or Reformers?

CONTENTS

QUESTIONS FOR STUDY

1 How do Marx and Engels define social classes in the Communist Manifesto? Why does this definition make class conflict inevitable?

2 What is the goal of revolution in the Communist Manifesto?

3 How has Engels' position changed from the time of the Manifesto to that of the letter to Van Patten?

4 Why did Engels feel, in 1894, that revolution could be avoided?

5 What is the basis for the disagreement between Carr and Ulam?

6 What function does revolution play in Lenin's system?

"*A* *spectre is haunting Europe"* *are the opening words of the Communist Manifesto, in which Karl Marx and Friedrich Engels threw down their challenge to the bourgeois world of 1848. The specter today haunts the whole world. One of the many reasons that the noncommunist world reacts so violently to the threat of communist take-over is the Marxist doctrine of revolution. The prospect of the violent overthrow of institutions and traditions is not one that appeals to any but those who feel that their society is fundamentally unjust, unreasonable, or unbearable.*

One of the great debates in the last 100 years centers around the question of the inevitability of revolution. Marx's system was based on a profound study of history, and Marxism claims to be the one true science of history. Does this science predict the inevitable fall of capitalism as physics predicts the inevitable fall of rain? And must this fall be accomplished only *by revolutionary means? They are questions of some moment in the modern world.*

1 The Road to Revolution

In 1848, Karl Marx (1818–1883) and Friedrich Engels (1820–1895) brought out the Manifesto of the Communist Party. It could not have appeared at a more opportune time; the manuscript was delivered to the printer in London a few weeks before the French revolution of February, 1848. A French translation was published shortly before the insurrection of the workers in Paris in June, 1848. Thought and deed thus seemed to go together, and the Manifesto became the rallying point for those who saw in revolution the only course for the oppressed workers of the world.

FROM *Manifesto of the Communist Party*
BY KARL MARX AND FRIEDRICH ENGELS

A SPECTRE IS HAUNTING EUROPE—the spectre of Communism. All the Powers of old Europe have entered into a holy alliance to exorcise this spectre; Pope and Czar, Metternich and Guizot, French Radicals and German police-spies.

Where is the party in opposition that has not been decried as communistic by its opponents in power? Where the Opposition that has not hurled back the branding reproach of Communism, against the more advanced opposition parties, as well as against its re-actionary adversaries?

Two things result from this fact.

1. Communism is already acknowledged by all European Powers to be itself a Power.
2. It is high time that Communists should openly, in the face of the whole world, publish their views, their aims, their tendencies, and meet this nursery tale of the Spectre of Communism with a Manifesto of the party itself.

Karl Marx and Friedrich Engels, *Manifesto of the Communist Party* (1911), pp. 11–30, 32–6, 42–7.

To this end, Communists of various nationalities have assembled in London, and sketched the following manifesto, to be published in the English, French, German, Italian, Flemish and Danish languages.

I. BOURGEOIS AND PROLETARIANS

The history of all hitherto existing society is the history of class struggles.

Freeman and slave, patrician and plebeian, lord and serf, guild-master and journeyman, in a word, oppressor and oppressed, stood in constant opposition to one another, carried on an uninterrupted, now hidden, now open fight, a fight that each time ended either in a revolutionary re-constitution of society at large, or in the common ruin of the contending classes.

In the earlier epochs of history, we find almost everywhere a complicated arrangement of society into various orders, a manifold gradation of social rank. In ancient Rome we have patricians, knights, plebeians, slaves; in the middle ages, feudal lords, vassals, guild-masters, journeymen, apprentices, serfs; in almost all of these classes, again, subordinate gradations.

The modern bourgeois society that has sprouted from the ruins of feudal society, has not done away with class antagonisms. It has but established new classes, new conditions of oppression, new forms of struggle in place of the old ones.

Our epoch, the epoch of the bourgeoisie, possesses, however, this distinctive feature; it has simplified the class antagonisms. Society as a whole is more and more splitting up into two great hostile camps, into two great classes directly facing each other: Bourgeoisie and Proletariat.

From the serfs of the Middle Ages sprang the chartered burghers of the earliest towns. From these burgesses the first elements of the bourgeoisie were developed.

The discovery of America, the rounding of the Cape, opened up fresh ground for the rising bourgeoisie. The East-Indian and Chinese markets, the colonisation of America, trade with the colonies, the increase in the means of exchange and in commodities generally, gave to commerce, to navigation, to industry, an impulse never before known, and thereby, to the revolutionary element in the tottering feudal society, a rapid development.

The feudal system of industry, under which industrial production was monopolised by close guilds, now no longer sufficed for the growing wants of the new markets. The manufacturing system took its place. The guild-masters were pushed on one side by the manufacturing middle-class; division of labour between the different corporate guilds vanished in the face of division of labour in each single workshop.

Meantime the markets kept ever growing, the demand, ever rising. Even manufacture no longer sufficed. Thereupon, steam and machinery revolutionised industrial production. The place of manufacture was taken by the giant, Modern Industry, the place of the industrial middle-class, by industrial millionaires, the leaders of whole industrial armies, the modern bourgeois.

Modern industry has established the world-market, for which the discovery of America paved the way. This market has given an immense development to commerce, to navigation, to communication by land. This development has, in its turn, reacted on the extension of industry; and in proportion as industry, commerce, navigation, railways extended, in the same proportion the bourgeoisie developed, increased its capital, and pushed into the background every class handed down from the Middle Ages.

We see, therefore, how the modern bourgeoisie is itself the product of a long course of development, of a series of revolutions in the modes of production and of exchange.

Each step in the development of the bourgeoisie was accompanied by a corresponding political advance of that class. An oppressed class under the sway of the feudal nobility, an armed and self-governing association in the mediaeval commune, here independent urban republic (as in Italy and Germany), there taxable "third estate" of the monarchy (as in France), afterwards, in the period of manufacture proper, serving either the semi-feudal or the absolute monarchy as a counterpoise against the nobility, and, in fact, corner stone of the great monarchies in general, the bourgeoisie has at last, since the establishment of Modern Industry and of the world-market, conquered for itself, in the modern representative State, exclusive political sway. The executive of the modern State is but a committee for managing the common affairs of the whole bourgeoisie.

The bourgeoisie, historically, has played a most revolutionary part.

The bourgeoisie, wherever it has got the upper hand, has put an end to all feudal, patriarchal, idyllic relations. It has pitilessly torn asunder the motley feudal ties that bound man to his "natural superiors," and has left remaining no other nexus between man and man than naked self-interest, than callous "cash payment." It has drowned the most heavenly ecstasies of religious fervour, of chivalrous enthusiasm, of philistine sentimentalism, in the icy water of egotistical calculation. It has resolved personal worth into exchange value, and in place of the numberless indefeasible chartered freedoms, has set up that single, unconscionable freedom—Free Trade. In one word, for exploitation, veiled by religious and political illusions, it has substituted naked, shameless, direct, brutal exploitation.

The bourgeoisie has stripped of its halo every occupation hitherto honoured and looked up to with reverent awe. It has converted the physician, the lawyer, the priest, the poet, the man of science, into its paid wage-labourers.

The bourgeoisie has torn away from the family its sentimental veil, and has reduced the family relation to a mere money relation.

The bourgeoisie has disclosed how it came to pass that the brutal display of vigour in the Middle Ages, which Reactionists so much admire, found its fitting complement in the most slothful indolence. It has been the first to shew what man's activity can bring about. It has accomplished wonders far surpassing Egyptian pyramids, Roman aqueducts, and Gothic cathedrals; it has conducted expeditions that put in the shade all former Exoduses of nations and crusades.

The bourgeoisie cannot exist without constantly revolutionising the instruments of production, and thereby the relations of production, and with them the whole relations of society. Conservation of the old modes of production in unaltered form, was, on the contrary, the first condition of existence for all earlier industrial classes. Constant revolutionising of production, uninterrupted disturbance of all social conditions, everlasting uncertainty and agitation distinguish the bourgeois epoch from all earlier ones. All fixed, fast-frozen relations, with their train of ancient and venerable prejudices and opinions, are swept away, all new-formed ones become antiquated before they can ossify. All that is solid melts into air, all that is holy is profaned, and man is at last compelled to face with sober senses, his real conditions of life, and his relations with his kind.

The need of a constantly expanding market for its products chases the bourgeoisie over the whole surface of the globe. It must nestle everywhere, settle everywhere, establish connexions everywhere.

The bourgeoisie has through its exploitation of the world-market given a cosmopolitan character to production and consumption in every country. To the great chagrin of Re-actionists, it has drawn from under the feet of industry the national ground on which it stood. All old-established national industries have been destroyed or are daily being destroyed. They are dislodged by new industries, whose introduction becomes a life and death question for all civilised nations, by industries that no longer work up indigenous raw material, but raw material drawn from the remotest zones; industries whose products are consumed, not only at home, but in every quarter of the globe. In place of the old wants, satisfied by the productions of the country, we find new wants, requiring for their satisfaction the products of distant lands and climes. In place of the old local and national seclusion and self-sufficiency, we have intercourse in every direction, universal interdependence of nations. And as in material, so also in intellectual production. The intellectual creations of individual nations become common property. National one-sidedness and narrow-mindedness become more and more impossible, and from the numerous national and local literatures there arises a world-literature.

The bourgeoisie, by the rapid improvement of all instruments of production, by the immensely facilitated means of communication, draws all, even the most barbarian, nations into civilisation. The cheap prices of its commodities are the heavy artillery with which it batters down all Chinese walls, with which it forces the barbarian's intensely obstinate hatred of foreigners to capitulate. It compels all nations, on pain of extinction, to adopt the bourgeois mode of production; it compels them to introduce what it calls civilisation into their midst, i.e., to become bourgeois themselves. In a word, it creates a world after its own image.

The bourgeoisie has subjected the country to the rule of the towns. It has

created enormous cities, has greatly increased the urban population as compared with the rural, and has thus rescued a considerable part of the
population from the idiocy of rural life. Just as it has made the country
dependent on the towns, so it has made barbarian and semi-barbarian
countries dependent on the civilised ones, nations of peasants on nations of
bourgeois, the East on the West.

The bourgeoisie keeps more and more doing away with the scattered
state of the population, of the means of production, and of property. It has
agglomerated population, centralised means of production, and has concentrated property in a few hands. The necessary consequence of this was
political centralisation. Independent, or but loosely connected provinces, with
separate interests, laws, governments and systems of taxation, became
lumped together in one nation, with one government, one code of laws, one
national class-interest, one frontier and one customs-tariff.

The bourgeoisie, during its rule of scarce one hundred years, has created
more massive and more colossal productive forces than have all preceding
generations together. Subjection of Nature's forces to man, machinery, application of chemistry to industry and agriculture, steam-navigation, railways,
electric telegraphs, clearing of whole continents for cultivation, canalization
of rivers, whole populations conjured out of the ground—what earlier century had even a presentiment that such productive forces slumbered in the
lap of social labour?

We see then: the means of production and of exchange on whose
foundation the bourgeoisie built itself up, were generated in feudal society.
At a certain stage in the development of these means of production and of
exchange, the conditions under which feudal society produced and exchanged, the feudal organisation of agriculture and manufacturing industry,
in one word, the feudal relations of property became no longer compatible
with the already developed productive forces; they became so many fetters.
They had to burst asunder; they were burst asunder.

Into their places stepped free competition, accompanied by a social and
political constitution adapted to it, and by the economical and political sway
of the bourgeois class.

A similar movement is going on before our own eyes. Modern bourgeois
society with its relations of production, of exchange and of property, a society
that has conjured up such gigantic means of production and of exchange, is
like the sorcerer, who is no longer able to control the powers of the nether
world whom he has called up by his spells. For many a decade past the
history of industry and commerce is but the history of the revolt of modern
productive forces against modern conditions of production, against the
property relations that are the conditions for the existence of the bourgeoisie
and of its rule. It is enough to mention the commercial crises that by their
periodical return put on its trial, each time more threateningly, the existence
of the entire bourgeois society. In these crises a great part not only of the
existing products, but also of the previously created productive forces, are

periodically destroyed. In these crises there breaks out an epidemic that, in all earlier epochs, would have seemed an absurdity—the epidemic of over-production. Society suddenly finds itself put back into a state of momentary barbarism; it appears as if a famine, a universal war of devastation had cut off the supply of every means of subsistence; industry and commerce seem to be destroyed; and why? Because there is too much civilisation, too much means of subsistence, too much industry, too much commerce. The produc-tive forces at the disposal of society no longer tend to further the develop-ment of the conditions of bourgeois property; on the contrary, they have become too powerful for these conditions, by which they are fettered, and so soon as they overcome these fetters, they bring disorder into the whole of bourgeois society, endanger the existence of bourgeois property. The con-ditions of bourgeois society are too narrow to comprise the wealth created by them. And how does the bourgeoisie get over these crises? On the one hand by enforced destruction of a mass of productive forces; on the other, by the conquest of new markets, and by the more thorough exploitation of the old ones. That is to say, by paving the way for more extensive and more destructive crises, and by diminishing the means whereby crises are pre-vented.

The weapons with which the bourgeoisie felled feudalism to the ground are now turned against the bourgeoisie itself.

But not only has the bourgeoisie forged the weapons that bring death to itself; it has also called into existence the men who are to wield those weapons—the modern working-class—the proletarians.

In proportion as the bourgeoisie, i. e., capital, is developed, in the same proportion is the proletariat, the modern working-class, developed, a class of labourers, who live only so long as they find work, and who find work only so long as their labour increases capital. These labourers, who must sell themselves piecemeal, are a commodity, like every other article of commerce, and are consequently exposed to all the vicissitudes of competition, to all the fluctuations of the market.

Owing to the extensive use of machinery and to division of labour, the work of the proletarians has lost all individual character, and, consequently, all charm for the workman. He becomes an appendage of the machine, and it is only the most simple, most monotonous, and most easily acquired knack that is required of him. Hence, the cost of production of a workman is restricted, almost entirely, to the means of subsistence that he requires for his maintenance, and for the propagation of his race. But the price of a com-modity, and also of labour, is equal to its cost of production. In proportion, therefore, as the repulsiveness of the work increases, the wage decreases. Nay more, in proportion as the use of machinery and division of labour increases, in the same proportion the burden of toil also increases, whether by pro-longation of the working hours, by increase of the work enacted in a given time, or by increased speed of the machinery, etc.

Modern industry has converted the little workshop of the patriarchal master into the great factory of the industrial capitalist. Masses of labourers, crowded into the factory, are organised like soldiers. As privates of the industrial army they are placed under the command of a perfect hierarchy of officers and sergeants. Not only are they the slaves of the bourgeois class, and of the bourgeois State, they are daily and hourly enslaved by the machine, by the over-looker, and, above all, by the individual bourgeois manufacturer himself. The more openly this despotism proclaims gain to be its end and aim, the more petty, the more hateful and the more embittering it is.

The less the skill and exertion or strength implied in manual labour, in other words, the more modern industry becomes developed, the more is the labour of men superseded by that of women. Differences of age and sex have no longer any distinctive social validity for the working class. All are instruments of labour, more or less expensive to use, according to their age and sex.

No sooner is the exploitation of the labourer by the manufacturer, so far, at an end, that he receives his wages in cash, than he is set upon by the other portions of the bourgeoisie, the landlord, the shopkeeper, the pawnbroker, etc.

The lower strata of the middle class—the small tradespeople, shopkeepers, and retired tradesmen generally, the handicraftsmen and peasants—all these sink gradually into the proletariat, partly because their diminutive capital does not suffice for the scale on which Modern Industry is carried on, and is swamped in the competition with the large capitalists, partly because their specialised skill is rendered worthless by new methods of production. Thus the proletariat is recruited from all classes of the population.

The proletariat goes through various stages of development. With its birth begins its struggle with the bourgeoisie. At first the contest is carried on by individual labourers, then by the workpeople of a factory, then by the operatives of one trade, in one locality, against the individual bourgeois who directly exploits them. They direct their attacks not against the bourgeois conditions of production, but against the instruments of production themselves; they destroy imported wares that compete with their labour, they smash to pieces machinery, they set factories ablaze, they seek to restore by force the vanished status of the workman of the Middle Ages.

At this stage the labourers still form an incoherent mass scattered over the whole country, and broken up by their mutual competition. If anywhere they unite to form more compact bodies, this is not yet the consequence of their own active union, but of the union of the bourgeoisie, which class, in order to attain its own political ends, is compelled to set the whole proletariat in motion, and is moreover yet, for a time, able to do so. At this stage, therefore, the proletarians do not fight their enemies, but the enemies of their enemies, the remnants of absolute monarchy, the landowners, the nonindustrial bourgeois, the petty bourgeoisie. Thus the whole historical movement is concentrated in the hands of the bourgeoisie, every victory so obtained is a victory for the bourgeoisie.

But with the development of industry the proletariat not only increases in number; it becomes concentrated in greater masses, its strength grows, and it feels that strength more. The various interests and conditions of life within the ranks of the proletariat are more and more equalised, in proportion as machinery obliterates all distinctions of labour, and nearly everywhere reduces wages to the same low level. The growing competition among the bourgeois, and the resulting commercial crises, make the wages of the workers ever more fluctuating. The unceasing improvement of machinery, ever more rapidly developing, makes their livelihood more and more precarious; the collisions between individual workmen and individual bourgeois take more and more the character of collisions between two classes. Thereupon the workers begin to form combinations (Trades' Unions) against the bourgeois; they club together in order to keep up the rate of wages; they found permanent associations in order to make provision beforehand for these occasional revolts. Here and there the contest breaks out into riots.

Now and then the workers are victorious, but only for a time. The real fruit of their battles lies, not in the immediate result, but in the ever expanding union of the workers. This union is helped on by the improved means of communication that are created by modern industry, and that place the workers of different localities in contact with one another. It was just this contact that was needed to centralise the numerous local struggles, all of the same character, into one national struggle between classes. But every class struggle is a political struggle. And that union, to attain which the burghers of the Middle Ages, with their miserable highways, required centuries, the modern proletarians, thanks to railways, achieve in a few years.

This organisation of the proletarians into a class, and consequently into a political party, is continually being upset again by the competition between the workers themselves. But it ever rises up again, stronger, firmer, mightier. It compels legislative recognition of particular interests of the workers, by taking advantage of the divisions among the bourgeoisie itself. Thus the ten-hours'-bill in England was carried.

Altogether collisions between the classes of the old society further, in many ways, the course of development of the proletariat. The bourgeoisie finds itself involved in a constant battle. At first with the aristocracy; later on, with those portions of the bourgeoisie itself, whose interests have become antagonistic to the progress of industry; at all times, with the bourgeoisie of foreign countries. In all these battles it sees itself compelled to appeal to the proletariat, to ask for its help, and thus, to drag it into the political arena. The bourgeoisie itself, therefore, supplies the proletariat with its own elements of political and general education, in other words, it furnishes the proletariat with weapons for fighting the bourgeoisie.

Further, as we have already seen, entire sections of the ruling classes are, by the advance of industry, precipitated into the proletariat, or are at least threatened in their conditions of existence. These also supply the proletariat with fresh elements of enlightenment and progress.

Finally, in times when the class-struggle nears the decisive hour, the process of dissolution going on within the ruling class, in fact within the whole range of old society, assumes such a violent, glaring character, that a small section of the ruling class cuts itself adrift, and joins the revolutionary class, the class that holds the future in its hands. Just as, therefore, at an earlier period, a section of the nobility went over to the bourgeoisie, so now a portion of the bourgeoisie goes over to the proletariat, and in particular, a portion of the bourgeois ideologists, who have raised themselves to the level of comprehending theoretically the historical movements as a whole.

Of all the classes that stand face to face with the bourgeoisie to-day, the proletariat alone is a really revolutionary class. The other classes decay and finally disappear in the face of modern industry; the proletariat is its special and essential product.

*   *   *

Though not in substance, yet in form, the struggle of the proletariat with the bourgeoisie is at first a national struggle. The proletariat of each country must, of course, first of all settle matters with its own bourgeoisie.

In depicting the most general phases of the development of the proletariat, we traced the more or less veiled civil war, raging within existing society, up to the point where that war breaks out into open revolution, and where the violent overthrow of the bourgeoisie lays the foundation for the sway of the proletariat.

Hitherto, every form of society has been based, as we have already seen, on the antagonism of oppressing and oppressed classes. But in order to oppress a class, certain conditions must be assured to it under which it can, at least, continue its slavish existence. The serf, in the period of serfdom, raised himself to membership in the commune, just as the petty bourgeois, under the yoke of feudal absolutism, managed to develop into a bourgeois. The modern labourer, on the contrary, instead of rising with the progress of industry, sinks deeper and deeper below the conditions of existence of his own class. He becomes a pauper, and pauperism develops more rapidly than population and wealth. And here it becomes evident, that the bourgeoisie is unfit any longer to be the ruling class in society, and to impose its conditions of existence upon society as an over-riding law. It is unfit to rule, because it is incompetent to assure an existence to its slave within his slavery, because it cannot help letting him sink into such a state that it has to feed him, instead of being fed by him. Society can no longer live under this bourgeoisie, in other words, its existence is no longer compatible with society.

The essential condition for the existence, and for the sway of the bourgeois class, is the formation and augmentation of capital; the condition for capital is wage-labour. Wage-labour rests exclusively on competition between the labourers. The advance of industry, whose involuntary promoter is the bourgeoisie, replaces the isolation of the labourers, due to competition, by their involuntary combination, due to association. The development of Modern Industry, therefore, cuts from under its feet the very foundation on which the bourgeoisie produces and appropriates products. What the bourgeoisie therefore produces, above all, are its own grave-diggers. Its fall and the victory of the proletariat are equally inevitable.

II. PROLETARIANS AND COMMUNISTS

In what relation do the Communists stand to the proletarians as a whole?

The Communists do not form a separate party opposed to other working-class parties.

They have no interests separate and apart from those of the proletariat as a whole.

They do not set up any sectarian principles of their own, by which to shape and mould the proletarian movement.

The Communists are distinguished from the other working-class parties by this only: 1. In the national struggles of the proletarians of the different countries, they point out and bring to the front the common interests of the entire proletariat, independently of all nationality. 2. In the various stages of development which the struggle of the working class against the bourgeoisie has to pass through, they always and everywhere represent the interests of the movement as a whole.

The Communists, therefore, are on the one hand, practically, the most advanced and resolute section of the working class parties of every country, that section which pushes forward all others; on the other hand, theoretically, they have over the great mass of the proletariat the advantage of clearly understanding the line of march, the conditions, and the ultimate general results of the proletarian movement.

The immediate aim of the Communists is the same as that of all the other proletarian parties: formation of the proletariat into a class, overthrow of the bourgeois supremacy, conquest of political power by the proletariat.

The theoretical conclusions of the Communists are in no way based on ideas or principles that have been invented, or discovered, by this or that would-be universal reformer.

They merely express, in general terms, actual relations springing from an existing class struggle, from a historical movement going on under our very eyes. The abolition of existing property-relations is not at all a distinctive feature of Communism.

All property relations in the past have continually been subject to historical change consequent upon the change in historical conditions.

The French Revolution, for example, abolished feudal property in favour of bourgeois property.

The distinguishing feature of Communism is not the abolition of property generally, but the abolition of bourgeois property. But modern bourgeois private property is the final and most complete expression of the system of producing and appropriating products, that is based on class antagonism, on the exploitation of the many by the few.

In this sense, the theory of the Communists may be summed up in the single sentence: Abolition of private property.

We Communists have been reproached with the desire of abolishing the right of personally acquiring property as the fruit of a man's own labour, which property is alleged to be the ground work of all personal freedom, activity and independence.

Hard-won, self-acquired, self-earned property! Do you mean the property of the petty artisan and of the small peasant, a form of property that preceded the bourgeois form? There is no need to abolish that; the development of industry has to a great extent already destroyed it, and is still destroying it daily.

Or do you mean modern bourgeois private property?

But does wage-labour create any property for the labourer? Not a bit. It creates capital, i.e., that kind of property which exploits wage-labour, and which cannot increase except upon condition of getting a new supply of wage-labour for fresh exploitation. Property, in its present form, is based on the antagonism of capital and wage-labour. Let us examine both sides of this antagonism.

To be a capitalist, is to have not only a purely personal, but a social status in production. Capital is a collective product, and only by the united action of many members, nay, in the last resort, only by the united action of all members of society, can it be set in motion.

Capital is therefore not a personal, it is a social power.

When, therefore, capital is converted into common property, into the property of all members of society, personal property is not thereby transformed into social property. It is only the social character of the property that is changed. It loses its class-character.

Let us now take wage-labour.

The average price of wage-labour is the minimum wage, i. e., that quantum of the means of subsistence, which is absolutely requisite to keep the labourer in bare existence as a labourer. What, therefore, the wage-labourer appropriates by means of his labour, merely suffices to prolong and reproduce a bare existence. We by no means intend to abolish this personal appropriation of the products of labour, an appropriation that is made for the maintenance and reproduction of human life, and that leaves no surplus wherewith to command the labour of others. All that we want to do away with is the miserable character of this appropriation, under which the labourer lives merely to increase capital, and is allowed to live only in so far as the interest of the ruling class requires it.

In bourgeois society, living labour is but a means to increase accumulated labour. In Communist society, accumulated labour is but a means to widen, to enrich, to promote the existence of the labourer.

In bourgeois society, therefore, the past dominates the present; in Communist society, the present dominates the past. In bourgeois society capital is independent and has individuality, while the living person is dependent and has no individuality.

And the abolition of this state of things is called by the bourgeois, abolition of individuality and freedom! And rightly so. The abolition of bourgeois individuality, bourgeois independence, and bourgeois freedom is undoubtedly aimed at.

By freedom is meant, under the present bourgeois conditions of production, free trade, free selling and buying.

* * *

The charges against Communism made from a religious, a philosophical, and generally, from an ideological standpoint, are not deserving of serious examination.

Does it require deep intuition to comprehend that man's ideas, views, and conceptions, in one word, man's consciousness, changes with every change in the conditions of his material existence, in his social relations and in his social life?

What else does the history of ideas prove, than that intellectual production changes in character in proportion as material production is changed? The ruling ideas of each age have ever been the ideas of its ruling class.

When people speak of ideas that revolutionize society, they do but express the fact, that within the old society, the elements of a new one have been created, and that the dissolution of the old ideas keeps even pace with the dissolution of the old conditions of existence.

When the ancient world was in its last throes, the ancient religions were overcome by Christianity. When Christian ideas succumbed in the 18th century to rationalist ideas, feudal society fought its death-battle with the then revolutionary bourgeoisie. The ideas of religious liberty and freedom of conscience, merely gave expression to the sway of free competition within the domain of knowledge.

"Undoubtedly," it will be said, "religious, moral, philosophical and juridical ideas have been modified in the course of historical development. But religion, morality, philosophy, political science, and law, constantly survived this change.

"There are, besides, eternal truths, such as Freedom, Justice, etc., that are common to all states of society. But Communism abolishes eternal truths, it abolishes all religion, and all morality, instead of constituting them on a new basis; it therefore acts in contradiction to all past historical experience."

What does this accusation reduce itself to? The history of all past society has consisted in the development of class antagonisms, antagonisms that assumed different forms at different epochs.

But whatever form they may have taken, one fact is common to all past ages, viz., the exploitation of one part of society by the other. No wonder, then, that the social consciousness of past ages, despite all the multiplicity and variety it displays, moves within certain common forms, or general ideas, which cannot completely vanish except with the total disappearance of class antagonisms.

The Communist revolution is the most radical rupture with traditional property-relations; no wonder that its development involves the most radical rupture with traditional ideas.

But let us have done with the bourgeois objections to Communism.

We have seen above, that the first step in the revolution by the working class is to raise the proletariat to the position of ruling class, to win the battle of democracy.

The proletariat will use its political supremacy to wrest, by degrees, all capital from the bourgeoisie, to centralise all instruments of production in the hands of the State, i.e., of the proletariat organised by the ruling class; and to increase the total of productive forces as rapidly as possible.

Of course, in the beginning, this cannot be effected except by means of despotic inroads on the rights of property, and on the conditions of bourgeois production; by means of measures, therefore, which appear economically insufficient and untenable, but which, in the course of the movement, outstrip themselves, necessitate further inroads upon the old social order, and are unavoidable as a means of entirely revolutionising the mode of production.

These measures will of course be different in different countries.

Nevertheless in the most advanced countries the following will be pretty generally applicable:

1. Abolition of property in land and application of all rents of land to public purposes.
2. A heavy progressive or graduated income tax.
3. Abolition of all right of inheritance.
4. Confiscation of the property of all emigrants and rebels.
5. Centralisation of credit in the hands of the State, by means of a national bank with State capital and an exclusive monopoly.
6. Centralisation of the means of communication and transport in the hands of the State.
7. Extension of factories and instruments of production owned by the State; the bringing into cultivation of waste lands, and the improvement of the soil generally in accordance with a common plan.
8. Equal liability of all to labour. Establishment of industrial armies, especially for agriculture.
9. Combination of agriculture with manufacturing industries; gradual abolition of the distinction between town and country, by a more equable distribution of the population over the country.
10. Free education for all children in public schools. Abolition of children's factory labour in its present form. Combination of education with industrial production, etc., etc.

When, in the course of development, class distinctions have disappeared, and all production has been concentrated in the hands of a vast association of the whole nation, the public power will lose its political character. Political power, properly so called, is merely the organised power of one class for oppressing another. If the proletariat during its contest with the bourgeoisie is compelled, by the force of circumstances, to organise itself as a class, if, by means of a revolution, it makes itself the ruling class, and, as such, sweeps away by force the old conditions of production, then it will, along with these conditions, have swept away the conditions for the existence of class antagonisms, and of classes generally, and will thereby have abolished its own supremacy as a class.

In place of the old bourgeois society, with its classes and class antagonisms, we shall have an association in which the free development of each is the condition for the free development of all.

> *The Marxist condemnation of bourgeois society had unexpected results. Marx and Engels had used all their rhetoric to prove that capitalist society was evil. Moreover, they had proven that the State, as such, was the instrument of oppression. It should not have surprised them to find that their conclusions were eagerly grasped by a group—the Anarchists—who saw the whole purpose of the coming struggle between proletariat and bourgeoisie as the destruction of the State. It was this view that Engels countered in the selection that follows. What must be gained is the control of the State, not its destruction. This principle, in turn, left the door open to those who argued that control could come by other means than revolution.*

Friedrich Engels' Letter to Philip van Patten

London, April 18, 1883

Dear Comrade:

MY REPLY to your inquiry of April 2 regarding Karl Marx's attitude toward the anarchists in general and toward Johann Most in particular will be brief and to the point.

Frederick Engels, *Letters to Americans, 1848–1895: A Selection*, pp. 137–8. Reprinted by permission of International Publishers Co., Inc. Copyright 1953 International Publishers Co., Inc.

Since 1845 Marx and I have held the view that one of the ultimate results of the future proletarian revolution will be the gradual dissolution of the political organizations known by the name of *state*. The main object of this organization has always been to secure, by armed force, the economic oppression of the laboring majority by the minority which alone possesses wealth. With the disappearance of an exclusive wealth-possessing minority there also disappears the need for an armed force of suppression, or state power. At the same time, however, it was always our opinion that in order to attain this and the other far more important aims of the future social revolution, the working class must first take possession of the organized political power of the state and by its aid crush the resistance of the capitalist class and organize society anew. This is to be found as early as the *Communist Manifesto* of 1847, Chapter II, conclusion.

The anarchists stand the thing on its head. They declare that the proletarian revolution must *begin* by abolishing the political organization of the state. But the only organization that the proletariat finds ready to hand after its victory is precisely the state. This state may require very considerable alterations before it can fulfill its new functions. But to destroy it at such a moment would mean to destroy the only organism by means of which the victorious proletariat can assert its newly conquered power, hold down its capitalist adversaries, and carry out that economic revolution of society without which the whole victory must end in a new defeat and in a mass slaughter of the workers similar to that after the Paris Commune.

Does it require my express assurance that Marx opposed this anarchist nonsense from the first day it was put forward in its present form by Bakunin? The whole internal history of the International Workingmen's Association proves it. Ever since 1867 the anarchists tried, by the most infamous methods, to seize the leadership of the International; the main hindrance in their way was Marx. The five-year struggle ended, at the Hague Congress in September 1872, with the expulsion of the anarchists from the International; and the man who did most to effect this expulsion was Marx. Our old friend, Friedrich Anton Sorge, in Hoboken, who was present as a delegate, can give you further details if you wish.

By 1895, when Engels wrote this introduction, the position of the Left had changed considerably. Many of the revolutionary demands of the Communist Manifesto had been written into law, as the result not of violent revolution but of peaceful politicking. Was it possible that the "inevitability" of revolution, to which all Marx's and Engels' writing

*in the 1840s logically led, was a mistake? Engels took a
long look at the question in the selection that follows.*

FROM *Introduction to Marx's The Class Struggles in France* BY FRIEDRICH ENGELS

IN JUDGING THE EVENTS and series of events of day-to-day history, it
will never be possible for anyone to go right back to the final economic
causes. Even today, when the specialised technical press provides such rich
materials, in England itself it still remains impossible to follow day by day
the movement of industry and trade in the world market and the changes
which take place in the methods of production, in such a way as to be able to
draw the general conclusion, at any point of time, from these very complicated and ever changing factors: of these factors, the most important, into
the bargain, generally operate a long time in secret before they suddenly and
violently make themselves felt on the surface. A clear survey of the economic
history of a given period is never contemporaneous; it can only be gained
subsequently, after collecting and sifting of the material has taken place.
Statistics are a necessary help here, and they always lag behind. For this
reason, it is only too often necessary, in the current history of the time, to
treat the most decisive factor as constant, to treat the economic situation
existing at the beginning of the period concerned as given and unalterable
for the whole period, or else to take notice only of such changes in this
situation as themselves arise out of events clearly before us, and as, therefore,
can likewise be clearly seen. Hence, the materialist method has here often to
limit itself to tracing political conflicts back to the struggles between the
interests of the social classes and fractions of classes encountered as the result
of economic development, and to show the particular political parties as the
more or less adequate political expression of these same classes and fractions
of classes.

It is self-evident that this unavoidable neglect of contemporaneous
changes in the economic situation, of the very basis of all the proceedings
subject to examination, must be a source of error. But all the conditions of a
comprehensive presentation of the history of the day unavoidably imply
sources of error—which, however, keeps nobody from writing contemporary
history.

When Marx undertook this work, the sources of error mentioned were,

Karl Marx, *The Class Struggles in France* (1848–50) (1895), pp. 9–10, 13–4, 15, 19–28.

to a still greater degree, impossible to avoid. It was quite impossible during the period of the Revolution of 1848–49 to follow the economic transformations which were being consummated at the same time, or even to keep a general view of them. It was just the same during the first months of exile in London, in the autumn and winter of 1849–50. But that was just the time when Marx began this work. And in spite of these unfavourable circumstances, his exact knowledge both of the economic situation in France and of the political history of that country since the February Revolution, made it possible for him to give a picture of events which laid bare their inner connections in a way never attained since, and which later brilliantly withstood the double test instituted by Marx himself.

*   *   *

When the Paris upheaval found its echo in the victorious insurrections in Vienna, Milan and Berlin; when the whole of Europe right up to the Russian frontier was swept into the movement; when in Paris the first great battle for power between the proletariat and the bourgeoisie was joined; when the very victory of their class so shook the bourgeoisie of all countries that they fled back into the arms of the monarchist-feudal reaction which had just been overthrown—for us under the circumstances of the time, there could be no doubt that the great decisive struggle had broken out, that it would have to be fought out in a single, long and changeful period of revolution, but that it could only end with the final victory of the proletariat.

*   *   *

But we, too, have been shown to have been wrong by history, which has revealed our point of view of that time to have been an illusion. It has done even more: it has not merely destroyed our error of that time; it has also completely transformed the conditions under which the proletariat has to fight. The mode of struggle of 1848 is today obsolete from every point of view, and this is a point which deserves closer examination on the present occasion.

*   *   *

History has proved us, and all who thought like us, wrong. It has made it clear that the state of economic development on the Continent at that time was not, by a long way, ripe for the removal of capitalist production; it has proved this by the economic revolution which, since 1848, has seized the whole of the Continent, has really caused big industry for the first time to take root in France, Austria, Hungary, Poland and, recently, in Russia, while it has made Germany positively an industrial country of the first rank—all on a capitalist basis, which in the year 1848, therefore, still had great capacity for expansion. But it is just this industrial revolution which has everywhere for the first time produced clarity in the class relationships, which has removed a number of transition forms handed down from the manufacturing period and in Eastern Europe even from guild handicraft, and has created a genuine bourgeoisie and a genuine large-scale industrial proletariat and pushed them into the foreground of social development. But owing to this, the struggle of these two great classes, which, apart from England, existed in 1848 only in Paris and, at the most, a few big industrial centres, has been spread over the whole of Europe and has reached an intensity such as was unthinkable in 1848. At that time the many obscure evangels of the sects, with their panaceas; today the one generally recognised, transparently clear theory of Marx, sharply formulating the final aims of the struggle. At that time the masses, sundered and differing according to locality and nationality, linked only by the feeling of common suffering, undeveloped, tossed to and fro in their perplexity from enthusiasm to despair; today a great international army of Socialists, marching irresistibly on and growing daily in number, organisation, discipline, insight and assurance of victory. If even this mighty army of the proletariat has still not reached its goal, if, a long way from winning victory with one mighty stroke, it has slowly to press forward from position to position in a hard, tenacious struggle, this only proves, once and for all, how impossible it was in 1848 to win social reconstruction by a simple surprise attack.

*   *   *

The war of 1870–71 and the defeat of the Commune had transferred the centre of gravity of the European workers' movement for the time being from France to Germany, as Marx foretold. In France it naturally took years to recover from the bloodletting of May 1871. In Germany, on the other hand, where industry was, in addition, furthered (in positively hot-house fashion) by the blessing of the French milliards and developed more and more quickly, Social-Democracy experienced a much more rapid and enduring growth. Thanks to the understanding with which the German workers made use of the universal suffrage introduced in 1866, the astonishing growth of the Party is made plain to all the world by incontestable figures. 1871, 102,000; 1874, 352,000; 1877, 493,000 Social-Democratic votes. Then came recognition of this advance by high authority in the shape of the Anti-Socialist Law: the Party was temporarily disrupted; the number of votes sank to 312,000 in 1881. But that was quickly overcome, and then, though oppressed by the Exceptional Law, without press, without external organisation and without the right of combination or meeting, the rapid expansion really began: 1884, 550,000; 1887, 763,000; 1890, 1,427,000 votes. Then the hand of the state was paralysed. The Anti-Socialist Law disappeared; socialist votes rose to 1,787,000—over a quarter of all the votes cast. The government and the ruling classes had exhausted all their expedients—uselessly, to no purpose, and without success. The tangible proofs of their impotence, which the authorities, from night watchman to the imperial chancellor, had had to accept—and that from the despised workers—these proofs were counted in millions. The state was at the end of its Latin [*sic— L.P.W.*], the workers only at the beginning of theirs.

But the German workers did a second great service to their cause in addition to the first, which they rendered by their mere existence as the strongest, best disciplined, and most rapidly growing Socialist Party. They supplied their comrades of all countries with a new weapon, and one of the sharpest, when they showed them how to use universal suffrage.

There had long been universal suffrage in France, but it had fallen into disrepute through the misuse to which the Bonapartist government had put it. After the Commune there was no workers' party to make use of it. Also in Spain it had existed since the republic, but in Spain boycott of the elections was ever the rule of all serious opposition parties. The Swiss experiences of universal suffrage, also, were anything but encouraging for a workers' party. The revolutionary workers of the Latin countries had been wont to regard the suffrage as a snare, as an instrument of government trickery. It was otherwise in Germany. *The Communist Manifesto* had already proclaimed the winning of universal suffrage, of democracy, as one of the first and most important tasks of the militant proletariat, and Lassalle had again taken up this point. When Bismarck found himself compelled to introduce the franchise as the only means of interesting the mass of the people in his plans; our workers immediately took it in earnest and sent August Bebel to the first constituent Reichstag. And from that day on, they have used the franchise in a way which has paid them a thousandfold and has served as a model to the workers of all countries. The franchise has been, in the words of the French Marxist programme, . . . transformed from a means of deception, which it was heretofore, into an instrument of emancipation. And if universal suffrage had offered no other advantage than that it allowed us to count our numbers every three years; that by the regularly established, unexpectedly rapid rise in the number of votes it increased in equal measure the workers' certainty of victory and the dismay of their opponents, and so became our best means of propaganda; that it accurately informed us concerning our own strength and that of all hostile parties, and thereby provided us with a measure of proportion for our actions second to none, safeguarding us from untimely timidity as much as from untimely foolhardiness—if this had been the only advantage we gained from the suffrage, then it would still have been more than enough. But it has done much more than this. In election agitation it provided us with a means, second to none, of getting in touch with the mass of the people, where they still stand aloof from us; of forcing all parties to defend their views and actions against our attacks before all the people; and, further, it opened to our representatives in the Reichstag a platform from which they could speak to their opponents in Parliament and to the masses without, with quite other authority and freedom than in the press or at meetings. Of what avail to the government and the bourgeoisie was their Anti-Socialist Law when election agitation and socialist speeches in the Reichstag continually broke through it?

With this successful utilisation of universal suffrage, an entirely new mode of proletarian struggle came into force, and this quickly developed further. It was found that the state institutions, in which the rule of the bourgeoisie is organised, offer still further opportunities for the working class to fight these very state institutions. They took part in elections to individual diets, to municipal councils and to industrial courts; they contested every post against the bourgeoisie in the occupation of which a sufficient part of the proletariat had its say. And so it happened that the bourgeoisie and the government came to be much more afraid of the legal than of the illegal action of the workers' party, of the results of elections than of those of rebellion.

For here, too, the conditions of the struggle had essentially changed. Rebellion in the old style, the street fight with barricades, which up to 1848 gave everywhere the final decision, was to a considerable extent obsolete.

Let us have no illusions about it: a real victory of an insurrection over the military in street fighting, a victory as between two armies, is one of the rarest exceptions. But the insurgents, also, counted on it just as rarely. For them it was solely a question of making the troops yield to moral influences, which, in a fight between the armies of two warring countries do not come into play at all, or do so to a much less degree. If they succeed in this, then the troops fail to act, or the commanding officers lose their heads, and the insurrection wins. If they do not succeed in this, then, even where the military are in the minority, the superiority of better equipment and training, of unified leadership, of the planned employment of the military forces and of discipline makes itself felt. The most that the insurrection can achieve in actual tactical practice is the correct construction and defence of a single barricade. Mutual support; the disposition and employment of reserves; in short, the cooperation and harmonious working of the individual detachments, indispensable even for the defence of one quarter of the town, not to speak of the whole of a large town, are at best defective, and mostly not attainable at all; concentration of the military forces at a decisive point is, of course, impossible. Hence the passive defence is the prevailing form of fight: the attack will rise here and there, but only by way of exception, to occasional advances and flank assaults; as a rule, however, it will be limited to occupation of the positions abandoned by the retreating troops. In addition, the military have, on their side, the disposal of artillery and fully equipped corps of skilled engineers, resources of war which, in nearly every case, the insurgents entirely lack. No wonder, then, that even the barricade struggles conducted with the greatest heroism—Paris, June 1848; Vienna, October 1848; Dresden, May 1849—ended with the defeat of the insurrection, so soon as the leaders of the attack, unhampered by political considerations, acted from the purely military standpoint, and their soldiers remained reliable.

The numerous successes of the insurgents up to 1848 were due to a great variety of causes. In Paris in July 1830 and February 1848, as in most of the Spanish street fights, there stood between the insurgents and the military a civic militia, which either directly took the side of the insurrection, or else by its lukewarm, indecisive attitude caused the troops likewise to vacillate, and supplied the insurrection with arms into the bargain. Where this citizens' guard opposed the insurrection from the outset, as in June 1848 in Paris, the insurrection was vanquished. In Berlin in 1848, the people were victorious partly through a considerable accession of new fighting forces during the night and the morning of the 19th, partly as a result of the exhaustion and bad victualling of the troops, and, finally, partly as a result of the paralysed command. But in all cases the fight was won because the troops failed to obey, because the officers lost their power of decision or because their hands were tied.

Even in the classic time of street fighting, therefore, the barricade produced more of a moral than a material effect. It was a means of shaking the steadfastness of the military. If it held out until this was attained, then victory was won; if not, there was defeat. This is the main point, which must be kept in view, likewise when the chances of contingent future street fights are examined.

$$*\qquad*\qquad*$$

But since then there have been very many more changes, and all in favour of the military. If the big towns have become considerably bigger, the armies have become bigger still. Paris and Berlin have, since 1848, grown less than fourfold, but their garrisons have grown more than that. By means of the railways, the garrisons can, in twenty-four hours, be more than doubled, and in forty-eight hours they can be increased to huge armies. The arming of this enormously increased number of troops has become incomparably more effective. In 1848 the smooth-bore percussion muzzle-loader, today the small-calibre magazine breech-loading rifle, which shoots four times as far, ten times as accurately and ten times as fast as the former. At that time the relatively ineffective round-shot and grape-shot of the artillery; today the percussion shells, of which one is sufficient to demolish the best barricade. At that time the pick-axe of the sapper for breaking through walls; today the dynamite cartridge.

On the other hand, all the conditions on the insurgents' side have grown worse. An insurrection with which all sections of the people sympathise, will hardly recur; in the class struggle all the middle sections will never group themselves round the proletariat so exclusively that the reactionary parties gathered round the bourgeoisie well-nigh disappear. The "people," therefore, will always appear divided, and with this a powerful lever, so extraordinarily effective in 1848, is lacking. Even if more soldiers who have seen service were to come over to the insurrectionists, the arming of them becomes so much the more difficult. The hunting and luxury guns of the gunshops—even if

not previously made unusable by removal of part of the lock by the police—
are far from being a match for the magazine rifle of the soldier, even in close
fighting. Up to 1848 it was possible to make the necessary ammunition
oneself out of powder and lead; today the cartridges differ for each rifle, and
are everywhere alike only in one point, that they are a special product of big
industry, and therefore not to be prepared *ex tempore,* with the result that
most rifles are useless as long as one does not possess the ammunition
specially suited to them. And, finally, since 1848 the newly built quarters of
the big towns have been laid out in long, straight, broad streets, as though
made to give full effect to the new cannons and rifles. The revolutionary
would have to be mad, who himself chose the working class districts in the
North and East of Berlin for a barricade fight.

*   *   *

Does the reader now understand why the ruling classes decidedly want
to bring us to where the guns shoot and the sabres slash? Why they accuse us
today of cowardice, because we do not betake ourselves without more ado
into the street, where we are certain of defeat in advance? Why they so
earnestly implore us to play for once the part of cannon fodder?

*   *   *

Of course, our foreign comrades do not renounce their right to revolution. The right to revolution is, after all, the only real "historical right" the
only right on which all modern states without exception rest. . . .

But whatever may happen in other countries, German Social-Democracy
has a special situation and therewith, at least in the first instance, a special
task. The two million voters, whom it sends to the ballot box, together with
the young men and women who stand behind them as non-voters, form the
most numerous, most compact mass, the decisive *"shock force"* of the international proletarian army. This mass already supplies over a fourth of the
recorded votes; and as the by-elections to the Reichstag, the diet elections in
individual states, the municipal council and industrial court elections demonstrate, it increases uninterruptedly. Its growth proceeds as spontaneously, as
steadily, as irresistibly, and at the same time as tranquilly as a natural
process. All government interventions have proved powerless against it. We
can count even today on two and a half million voters. If it continues in this
fashion, by the end of the century we shall conquer the greater part of the
middle section of society, petty bourgeois and small peasants, and grow into
the decisive power in the land, before which all other powers will have to
bow, whether they like it or not. To keep this growth going without
interruption until of itself it gets beyond the control of the ruling governmental system *not to fritter away this daily increasing shock force in advance
guard fighting, but to keep it intact until the day of the decision,* that is our

main task. And there is only one means by which the steady rise of the socialist fighting forces in Germany could be momentarily halted, and even thrown back for some time: a clash on a big scale with the military, a bloodbath like that of 1871 in Paris. In the long run that would also be overcome. To shoot out of the world a party which numbers millions—all the magazine rifles of Europe and America are not enough for this. . . .

The irony of world history turns everything upside down. We, the "revolutionaries," the "rebels"—we are thriving far better on legal methods than on illegal methods and revolt. The parties of order, as they call themselves, are perishing under the legal conditions created by themselves. They cry despairingly with Odilon Barrot: . . . legality is the death of us; whereas we, under this legality, get firm muscles and rosy cheeks and look like eternal life. And if we are not so crazy as to let ourselves be driven into street fighting in order to please them, then nothing else is finally left for them but themselves to break through this legality so fatal to them.

2 The Scholars' Views

Marxism is both a program of political action and a theoretical analysis of society. The two are inextricably intertwined. This has created the problem of determining what is merely politically expedient and what follows necessarily from the theoretical premises of the Marxist argument. One of the central problems is that of the place of revolution in the coming of the Marxist society. Scholars have argued for a generation over this point: Must revolutionary action necessarily be taken, or can the Marxist society evolve from that of the bourgeoisie?

E. H. Carr is one of the foremost historians of Soviet Russia; from this vantage point he assesses the message of the Communist Manifesto.

FROM *Studies in Revolution* BY E. H. CARR

THE COMMUNIST MANIFESTO

THE WINTER OF 1847–48 (it is difficult to fix a more precise date for the celebration of the centenary) saw the birth of one of the capital documents of the nineteenth century—the *Communist Manifesto*. In the summer of 1847 a group consisting mainly of German craftsmen in London held the first congress of a new "Communist League." They had been in touch with Marx, then living in Brussels, for some time; and Engels attended the congress, which adjourned to a future congress the drafting of a programme for the League. Inspired by this prospect, Engels tried his hand and produced a catechism in twenty-five questions, which Marx and he took with them to the second League congress in London at the end of November. The congress thereupon charged Marx and Engels to draft their programme for them: it was to take the form of a manifesto. Marx worked away in Brussels

E. H. Carr, *Studies in Revolution* (1962), pp. 15–37. Reprinted by permission of Macmillan & Company Ltd., London, and The Macmillan Company of Canada Ltd., Toronto.

through December and January. The "Manifesto of the Communist Party" was published in London in German in February 1848, a few days before the revolution broke out in Paris.

The *Communist Manifesto* is divided into four parts. The first reviews the rise of the bourgeoisie on the ruins of the feudal system of property relations, government and morality which it destroyed; shows how "the powerful and colossal productive forces" which the bourgeoisie itself created have now grown to a point where they are no longer compatible with bourgeois property relations and bourgeois supremacy; and finally demonstrates that the proletariat is the new revolutionary class which can alone master the forces of modern industry and end the exploitation of man by man. The second part proclaims the policy of the Communist Party, as "the most progressive and resolute section of the working class of all countries," to promote the proletarian revolution which will destroy bourgeois power and "raise the proletariat to the position of the ruling class." The third part surveys and condemns other recent and existing schools of socialism; and the fourth is a brief tactical postscript on the relations of Communists to other left-wing parties.

A historic document like the *Communist Manifesto* invites examination from the point of view both of its antecedents and of its consequences. On the former count the *Manifesto* owes as much to predecessors and contemporaries as most great pronouncements; and the worst that can be said is that Marx's sweeping denunciations of predecessors and contemporaries sometimes mask the nature of the debt. Babeuf, who also called his proclamation a "manifesto," had announced the final struggle between rich and poor, between "a tiny minority" and "the huge majority." Blanqui had anticipated the class interpretation of history and the idea of the dictatorship of the proletariat (the phrase was not used by Marx himself till 1850). Lorenz von Stein had written that the history of freedom, society and political order was essentially dependent on the distribution of economic goods among the classes of the population. Proudhon also knew that "the laws of political economy are the laws of history" and measured the progress of society "by the development of industry and the perfection of its instruments"; and Pecqueur had predicted that, with the spread of commerce, "the barriers between nation and nation will be broken down" until the day when "every man becomes a citizen of the world." Such ideas were current coin in advanced circles when Marx wrote. But neither such borrowings, nor Marx's overriding debt to Hegel's immense synthesis, detract from the power of the conception presented to the world in the *Communist Manifesto*.

To-day it is more appropriate to study the famous manifesto in the light of its hundred-year influence on posterity. Though written when Marx was in his thirtieth year and Engels two years younger, it already contains the quintessence of Marxism. Beginning with a broad historical generalization ("the history of all hitherto existing society is the history of class struggles") and ending with an inflammatory appeal to the workers of all countries to unite for "the forcible overthrow of all existing social conditions," it presents Marxist methodology in its fully developed form—an interpretation of history which is at the same time a call to action. Some passages in Marx's writings, especially at the revolutionary crises of 1848 and 1871, appear to commend revolutionary action as a good thing in itself. Some passages, both earlier and later, appear to dwell on the iron laws of historical development in such a way as to leave little place for the initiative of the human will. But these momentary shifts of emphasis cannot be taken to impair the dual orthodoxy established by the *Communist Manifesto,* where interpretation and action, predestination and free will, revolutionary theory and revolutionary practice march triumphantly hand in hand. It propounds a philosophy of history, a dogma of revolution, belief in which will take the spontaneous form of appropriate action in the believer.

The *Communist Manifesto* is thus no broadsheet for the hoardings or the hustings. Marx—and many others who are not Marxists—would deny the possibility of any rigid separation of emotion and intellect; but using the terms in a popular sense, it is to the intellect rather than to the emotions that the *Manifesto* makes its primary appeal. The overwhelming impression which it leaves on the reader's mind is not so much that the revolution is desirable (that, like the injustice of capitalism in *Das Kapital,* is taken for granted as something not requiring argument) but that the revolution is inevitable. For successive generations of Marxists the *Manifesto* was not a plea for revolution—that they did not need—but a prediction about the way in which the revolution would inevitably happen combined with a prescription for the action required of revolutionaries to make it happen. The controversies of a hundred years ranged round the questions as to what Marx actually said or meant and how what he said should be applied to conditions diverging widely from those of his own time and place. Only the bold offered openly to "revise" Marx; the sagacious interpreted him. The *Communist Manifesto* has thus remained a living document. The centenary of the *Communist Manifesto* cannot be celebrated otherwise than in the light, and in the shadow, of the Russian revolution which was its culminating embodiment in history.

The *Communist Manifesto* sets out a coherent scheme of revolution. "The history of all hitherto existing society is the history of class struggles." In modern times Marx detects two such struggles—the struggle between feudalism and the bourgeoisie, ending in the victorious bourgeois revolution, and the struggle between the bourgeoisie and the proletariat, destined to end in the victorious proletarian revolution. In the first struggle a nascent proletariat is mobilized by the bourgeoisie in support of bourgeois aims, but is incapable of pursuing independent aims of its own: "every victory so obtained is a victory for the bourgeoisie." In the second struggle Marx recognizes the presence of the lower middle class—"the small manufacturer, the shopkeeper, the artisan, the peasant"—which plays a fluctuating role between bourgeoisie and proletariat, and a "slum proletariat" which is liable to "sell itself to reactionary forces." But these complications do not seriously affect the ordered simplicity of the main pattern of revolution.

The pattern had been framed in the light of Marx's reading in modern English and French history and in the works of French and British economists, and of Engels's study of factory conditions in England. The English bourgeois revolution, winning its victory in the seventeenth century, had fully consolidated itself by 1832. The French bourgeois revolution, more suddenly and dramatically triumphant after 1789, had succumbed to reaction only to re-emerge once more in 1830. In both countries the first revolutionary struggle of the modern age—the struggle between feudalism and bourgeoisie —was virtually over; the stage was set for the second struggle—between bourgeoisie and proletariat.

The events of 1848, coming hard on the heels of the *Manifesto,* did much to confirm its diagnosis and nothing to refute it. In England the collapse of Chartism was a set-back which none the less marked a stage in the consolidation of a class-conscious workers' movement. In France the proletariat marched shoulder to shoulder with the bourgeoisie in February 1848, as the *Manifesto* had said it would, so long as the aim was to consolidate and extend the bourgeois revolution. But once the proletariat raised its own banner of social revolution the line was crossed. Bourgeoisie and proletariat, allies until the bourgeois revolution had been completed and made secure, were now divided on opposite sides of the barricades by the call for proletarian revolution. The first revolutionary struggle was thus over: the second was impending. In Paris, in the June days of 1848, Cavaignac saved the bourgeoisie and staved off the proletarian revolution by massacring, executing and transporting the class-conscious workers. The pattern of the *Communist Manifesto* had been precisely followed. As Professor Namier, who is no Marxist, puts it: "The working classes touched off, and the middle classes cashed in on it."

> The June revolution [as Marx wrote at the time] for the first time split the whole of society into two hostile camps—east and west Paris. The unity of the February revolution no longer exists. The February fighters are now warring against each other—something that has never happened before; the former indifference has vanished and every man capable of bearing arms is fighting on one side or other of the barricades.

The events of February and June 1848 had provided a classic illustration of the great gulf fixed between bourgeois and proletarian revolutions.

Farther east the pattern of England and France did not fully apply, as the concluding section of the *Manifesto* admitted—almost by way of an afterthought.

In Germany the bourgeois revolution had not yet begun. The German bourgeoisie had not yet won the fundamental political rights which the English bourgeoisie had achieved in 1689 and the French a hundred years later. The task of the German proletariat was still therefore to support the bourgeoisie in the first revolutionary struggle against feudalism; in Germany, in the words of the *Manifesto,* "the Communist Party fights with the bourgeoisie whenever it acts in a revolutionary manner against the absolute monarchy, the feudal landlords and the petty bourgeoisie." But it could not be argued that Germany would simply follow the same path as England and France at a greater or less distance of time. The German revolution would occur "under the most advanced conditions of European civilization" which would give it a special character. Where the proletariat was already so advanced, thought Marx, the bourgeois revolution "can only be the immediate prelude to the proletarian revolution."

When Marx, in the brief concluding section of the *Manifesto,* devoted to Communist Party tactics, thus announced the prospect in Germany of an immediate transition from bourgeois to proletarian revolution without the intervening period of bourgeois rule, he showed a keen historical perception, even at the expense of undermining the validity of his own theoretical analysis. The events of 1848 in the German-speaking lands confirmed Marx's intuition of the impossibility in Germany of a period of established bourgeois supremacy comparable with that which has set so strong a mark on English and French history. This impossibility was due not so much to the strength of the German proletariat, which Marx perhaps exaggerated, as to the weakness of the German bourgeoisie. Whatever the prospects of an eventual proletarian revolution in mid-nineteenth-century Germany, the material for a bourgeois revolution such as England and France had long ago achieved was still conspicuously absent. Indeed, the bourgeoisie, far from bidding for power for itself, was plainly ready to ally itself with the surviving elements of feudalism for defence against the proletarian menace. It need hardly be added that the same symptoms, in a still more pronounced form, repeated themselves in Russia more than half a century afterwards.

The problem, therefore, which Germany presented in 1848 to the authors of the *Communist Manifesto* was the same which Russia would one day present to the theorists of her revolution. According to the revolutionary pattern of the *Communist Manifesto,* the function of the bourgeoisie was to destroy feudal society root and branch preparatory to its own destruction in the final phase of the revolutionary struggle by the proletariat. But what was to happen if the bourgeoisie through weakness or cowardice—or perhaps through some untimely premonition of its own eventual fate—was unable or unwilling to perform its essential function? Marx never provided a categorical answer to this question. But his answer was implicit in the doctrine of "permanent revolution," which he propounded in an address to the Communist League in 1850:

> While the democratic petty bourgeoisie wants to end the revolution as rapidly as possible . . . our interests and our task consist in making the revolution permanent until all the more or less possessing classes are removed from authority, until the proletariat wins State power.

The responsibility was thus placed on the proletariat to complete the task, which the bourgeoisie had failed to perform, of liquidating feudalism.

What form the liquidation was to take when the proletariat found itself directly confronted by a feudal society without any effective and independent bourgeoisie was not altogether clear. But if one insisted—as Marx apparently did, and Engels continued to do down to the end of his life—that "our party can come to power only under some such form as a democratic republic," then the conclusion followed that the immediate aim of the proletariat must be limited to the establishment of a political democracy in which it was interested only as a necessary stepping-stone to the proletarian social revolution. This was, however, a theoretical construction unlikely to be realized in practice—as the experience of both the German and the Russian revolutions was one day to show. Marx never really fitted his analysis of revolution to countries where the bourgeoisie was incapable of making its own revolution; and acrimonious controversy about the relation between bourgeois and proletarian revolutions continued to divide the Russian revolutionaries for several decades.

The economic corollary of this conclusion was still more startling. If the establishment of a democratic republic was a prerequisite of the proletarian revolution, so also was the full development of capitalism; for capitalism was the essential expression of bourgeois society and inseparable from it. Marx certainly held this view as late as 1859 when he wrote in the preface to the *Critique of Political Economy:* "No social form perishes until all the productive forces for which it provides scope have been developed." It appeared to follow, paradoxically enough, that in backward countries the interest of the nascent proletariat was to promote the most rapid development of capitalism and capitalist exploitation at its own expense.

Such was the view seriously propounded by Russian Marxists, Bolshevik and Menshevik alike, down to 1905—perhaps even down to 1917. Meanwhile, however, in the spring of 1905, Lenin's practical mind worked out a new scheme under which the proletariat was to seize power in conjunction with the peasantry, creating a "democratic dictatorship" of workers and peasants; and this became the official doctrine of the October revolution. The Mensheviks stuck to their guns, and their survivors and successors to-day attribute the shortcomings of the Russian revolution to its failure to pass through the bourgeois-democratic, bourgeois-capitalist phase on its way to the achievement of socialism. The issue is not to be settled by reference to Marx, who can hardly be acquitted of inconsistency on this point. Either he made a mistake in suggesting, in the last section of the *Communist Manifesto,* that Germany might pass immediately from the bourgeois to the proletarian revolution; or he failed to fit this new conception into the revolutionary framework of the earlier part of the *Manifesto.*

Marx was to encounter similar difficulties in applying the generalizations of the *Communist Manifesto* about nationalism, which were also based on British and French experience, to central and eastern Europe. The charge often brought against Marx of ignoring or depreciating national sentiment rests indeed on a misunderstanding. The famous remark that "the workers have no country," read in its context, is neither a boast nor a programme; it is a complaint which had long been a commonplace among socialist writers. Babeuf had declared that the multitude "sees in society only an enemy, and loses even the possibility of having a country"; and Weitling had connected the notion of country with the notion of property:

> He alone has a country who is a property owner or at any rate has the liberty and the means of becoming one. He who had not that, has no country.

In order to remedy this state of affairs (to quote once more from the *Manifesto*) "the proletariat must first conquer political power, must rise to be the dominant class of the nation, must constitute itself the nation, so that the proletariat is so far national itself, though not in the bourgeois sense."

The passage of the *Manifesto* in which these sentences occur is not free from ambiguities. But the thought behind it is clear. In Marx's view, which corresponded to the facts of English and French history, nationalism grew up as an attribute of bourgeois society at a time when the bourgeoisie was a revolutionary and progressive force. Both in England and in France the bourgeoisie, invoking the national spirit to destroy a feudalism which was at once particularist and cosmopolitan, had through a period of centuries built up a centralized State on a national basis. But the advance of capitalism was already making nations obsolete.

> National differences and antagonisms are to-day vanishing ever more and more with the development of the bourgeoisie, free trade in the world market, the uniformity of industrial production and the conditions of life corresponding thereto.
>
> With the victory of the proletariat they will vanish still faster. . . . With the disappearance of classes within the nation the state of enmity between nations will come to an end.

Hence the first step was for the proletariat of every country to "settle accounts with its own bourgeoisie." The way would then be open for a true international communist order. Like Mazzini and other nineteenth-century thinkers, Marx thought of nationalism as a natural stepping-stone to internationalism.

Unfortunately the national pattern of the *Manifesto,* far from being universal, proved difficult to extend beyond the narrow limits of the place (western Europe) or the time (the age of Cobden) in which it was designed. Beyond western Europe the same conditions which prevented the rise of a powerful bourgeoisie also prevented the development of an orderly bourgeois nationalism. In central Europe (the Hapsburg Empire, Prussia) as well as in Russia the centralized State had been brought into being under pressure of military necessity by feudal overlords indifferent to national feeling; and when in the nineteenth century, under the impetus of the French revolution, nationalism became for the first time a force to be reckoned with in central and eastern Europe, it appeared not—as in England and France—as an attribute and complement of the State but as a sentiment independent of any existing State organization.

Moreover, the relation of nation to State worked itself out in different ways and sometimes involved even the same national group in inconsistent attitudes. This was particularly true of the Hapsburg Empire. The growing national consciousness of the German-Austrian bourgeoisie did not diminish its support of imperial unity; the bourgeoisie of the other constituent national groups sought to destroy that unity or at least to dissolve it into a federation. The Hungarians asserted the rights of the Magyar nation against the German-Austrians, but denied the national rights of Croats and Slovaks.

In these circumstances it is not surprising that Marx and Engels never succeeded in working out, even for their own day and generation, a consistent theory of nationalism which would hold good throughout Europe. They supported the Polish claim to national independence; no revolutionary, no liberal, of the nineteenth century could have done otherwise. But Engels, at any rate, seemed mainly concerned that this claim should be satisfied at the expense of Russia rather than of Prussia, proposing on one occasion to offer the Poles Riga and Mitau in exchange for Danzig and Elbing; and in the candid outburst of a private letter to Marx he referred to the Poles as *"une nation foutue,* a serviceable instrument only until Russia herself is swept into the agrarian revolution." In the same spirit he rejected outright the national aspirations of the Slavs of the Hapsburg Empire, whose triumph would be, in his eyes, a subjugation "of the civilized west by the barbaric east."

In these judgments, from which Marx is not known to have dissented, Engels was indubitably swayed by national prejudice and in particular by hostility to Russia as the most reactionary Power of the day. But he was also moved by the recognition that these nationalisms of central and eastern Europe, whose economic basis was agrarian, had little or nothing to do with the bourgeois nationalism of which Marx and he had taken cognizance in the *Communist Manifesto.* It was not only a question of "the civilized west" and "the barbaric east": it was a question of the subjugation "of town by the country, of trade, manufacture and intelligence by the primitive agriculture of Slavonic serfs." On the presuppositions of the *Manifesto,* this seemed necessarily a retrograde step. The failure of Marx and Engels to take account of agrarian nationalism was one aspect of the other great lacuna of the *Manifesto*—the question of the peasant.

If, however, the theory of nationalism propounded in the *Communist Manifesto* could not be transplanted from western to central and eastern Europe, it equally failed to stand the test of time. The *Manifesto* contains indeed one reference to "the exploitation of one nation by another" and declares, by what seems a tautology in one sense and a *non sequitur* in another, that it will end when the exploitation of one individual by another ends. But Marx has little to say (nothing at all in the *Manifesto* itself) about the colonial question, touching on it in detail only in the case of Ireland; and here it is perhaps significant that, while in 1848 he was prepared to sacrifice the Irish in the same way as the Austrian Slavs, he had become convinced by 1869 that "the direct absolute interest of the English working class demands a rupture of the present connexion with Ireland." Marx did not, however, live to see the full development of the process by which the great nations, already victims of the contradictions of capitalism, vied with one another in bringing the whole world under their yoke in a desperate attempt to save themselves and the capitalist system—the process which Lenin was afterwards to analyse in his famous work on *Imperialism as the Highest Stage of Capitalism;* nor could he foresee that rise to national consciousness of innumerable "unhistorical" nations of which the Austrian Slavs had been the harbingers. The Soviet theory of nationality, in which the colonial question and the question of small nations divide the honours between them, can derive only a pale and faltering light from the simple and far-away formulation of the *Communist Manifesto*. But critics of the national theories, whether of Marx or of the Bolsheviks, may do well to reflect that bourgeois thinkers and statesmen have also not been able to formulate, and still less to apply, a consistent doctrine of national rights.

Marx's attitude to the tiller of the soil is more seriously open to criticism. Here too there is a foretaste of subsequent controversy—both the Mensheviks and Trotsky were accused, rightly from Lenin's point of view, of "underestimating" the peasant; and here too Marx ran into trouble because his initial theories had been primarily framed to fit western conditions. The *Communist Manifesto* praised the bourgeoisie for having, through its development of factories and towns, "delivered a great part of the population from the idiocy of country life"; and it classed peasant or peasant proprietor with handicraftsmen, small traders and shopkeepers as members of the "petty bourgeoisie"—an unstable and reactionary class, since it struggled against the greater bourgeoisie, not for revolutionary ends, but only in order to maintain its own bourgeois status. In England, in France (which in revolutionary circles was generally thought of as Paris writ large) and in Germany, the *Communist Manifesto* upheld the strict pattern of successive revolutions of which the bourgeoisie and the proletariat would be the respective driving forces, and reserved no independent place for the peasant.

Events were soon to show up the lacuna left by this scheme of things even in western Europe. The French peasants were unmoved when the revolutionary workers of Paris were shot down in June 1848 by the agents of the bourgeoisie, and voted solidly for the bourgeois dictatorship of Louis Napoleon. In fact they behaved exactly as the *Communist Manifesto* expected them to behave (which did not save them from incurring some of Marx's fiercest invective in *The Eighteenth Brumaire of Louis Napoleon*); but in so doing they showed how far things would have to travel before the French proletariat would be able to make another French revolution.

In Prussia and throughout Germany the revolution of 1848 was in the hands of intellectuals who thought as little of the peasants as Marx himself; and the peasants failed to move. In Austria the peasants did move. They rose in Galicia against the landlords and would have risen elsewhere with the right leadership. They formed a large and vocal group in the new democratic Reichstag. But the claims of the peasant encountered the hostility of the bourgeoisie and the indifference of the urban workers. Peasantry and proletariat were crushed separately in the absence of a leader and a programme to unite them; and in central Europe the surest moral of 1848 was that no revolution could succeed which did not win the peasant and give a high priority to his concerns.

In eastern Europe this was still more abundantly clear. As regards Poland, even the *Communist Manifesto* declared that "the Communists support the party that sees in agrarian revolution the means to national freedom, the party which caused the Cracow insurrection of 1846." But this passage, which occurs in the tactical postscript, is the only incursion of the *Manifesto* into eastern Europe and the only reference to agrarian revolution; and even here agrarian revolution is regarded as the ally of a bourgeois revolution leading to "national freedom," not of a proletarian revolution.

Spending the rest of his years in England, where there was no peasantry and no agrarian question, Marx never felt any strong impulse to fill this lacuna in the *Communist Manifesto*. In 1856, drawing a moral from the failure of 1848 in Germany, he spoke casually of the importance of backing up the future proletarian German revolution "with some second edition of the Peasants' War." But even here only a subsidiary role was assigned to the peasantry. It was towards the end of his life that Marx was called on to pass judgment on a controversy just opening in far-away Russia. The leading Russian revolutionaries, the Narodniks, regarded the Russian peasant commune with its system of common tenure of land as the seed-bed of the future Russian Socialist order. On the other hand, the first Russian Marxists were already beginning to argue that the way to socialism could only lie, in Russia as elsewhere, through a development of capitalism and the proletariat.

Four times did the Marx-Engels partnership attack this ticklish issue. In 1874, before the Russian Marxists had raised their head, Engels had recognized the possibility in favourable conditions of the direct transformation of the communal system into a higher form, "avoiding the intermediate stage of individualized bourgeois property." In 1877, in reply to an attack in a Russian journal, Marx confined himself to a doubtful admission that Russia had "the finest chance which history ever presented to a nation of avoiding the up-and-downs of the capitalist order." In 1881 Marx gave a more positive response to a direct personal inquiry from Vera Zasulich; and in the follow-ing year the last and most authoritative pronouncement appeared in the preface to a Russian translation of the *Communist Manifesto,* signed jointly by both its authors:

> If the Russian revolution is the signal for a workers' revolution in the west so that these complement each other, then the contemporary Russian system of communal ownership can serve as the starting-point for a Communist development.

Russian Social-Democrats of a later generation, both Bolshevik and Men-shevik, looked askance at this quasi-Narodnik deviation, and returned to the purer theoretical pattern of the *Manifesto* with its clear-cut dialectic of bourgeois and proletarian revolutions; and Lenin himself, not less than the Mensheviks, sternly maintained the paradox that the further development of capitalism in Russia was a necessary prelude to social revolution. Neverthe-less, Lenin, like Marx in his later years, recognized that no revolution, and no revolutionary, in eastern Europe could afford to ignore the peasant and his demands. After 1905—and before and after 1917—the Bolsheviks were obliged to devote an immense amount of energy and controversy to the task of fitting the Russian peasant into the western formulae of the *Communist Manifesto.*

Franz Mehring, Marx's best and most sympathetic biographer, remarks of the *Communist Manifesto* that "in many respects historical development has proceeded otherwise, and above all has proceeded more slowly, than its authors expected." This is true of the expectations of the two young men who composed the *Manifesto.* But how far were these expectations modi-fied? As regards pace, Marx in later life certainly no longer believed in the imminence of the proletarian revolution with all the eager confidence of 1848. But even the *Manifesto* in one of its more cautious passages had predicted temporary successes followed by set-backs and a slow process of "growing unity" among the workers before the goal was achieved. Marx came, with advancing years, to accept the necessity of a long course of education for the proletariat in revolutionary principles; and there is the famous *obiter dictum* in a speech of the 1870s, which admits that in certain advanced countries the victory of the proletariat may be achieved without revolutionary violence.

As regards the scheme of historical development, it would be difficult to prove that Marx, speaking theoretically and *ex cathedra,* ever abandoned the strict analysis of revolution which he had worked out in the *Communist Manifesto.* But he was not a pure theorist. He was willy-nilly the leader of a political party; and it was when he found himself compelled to make pronouncements in this capacity that he sometimes appeared to derogate from his principles. Thus in the last section of the *Manifesto* itself he had already foreseen that in Germany the bourgeois revolution would be the "immediate prelude" of the proletarian revolution, thus skipping over the period of bourgeois supremacy; in the next few years he was drawn into some uncomfortable compromises and inconsistencies on the national question; and towards the end of his life he was constrained to admit that a predominantly peasant country like Russia had the chance of achieving the social revolution without passing through the bourgeois capitalist phase at all, thus not merely modifying but side-tracking altogether the revolutionary analysis of the *Manifesto*.

It is curious and significant of the vitality of Marx's thought to watch how accurately this evolution was repeated in the Russian Social-Democratic Party. Its first leaders—Plekhanov and Axelrod, Lenin and Martov—accepted without question the scheme of the *Communist Manifesto*. After 1903 the Mensheviks, remaining consistent with themselves and with the Marxist scheme, ended in bankruptcy because they could find no way of applying it to Russian conditions. The more flexible Lenin took the scheme and brilliantly adapted it to those conditions; and the adaptations which he made followed—in broad outline, though not in every detail—those which Marx himself had admitted in his later years. The process can be justified. Marxism was never offered to the world as a static body of doctrine; Marx himself once confessed that he was no Marxist; and the constant evolution of doctrine in response to changing conditions is itself a canon of Marxism.

It is on such grounds that the Russian revolution can claim to be a legitimate child of the *Communist Manifesto*. The *Manifesto* challenged bourgeois society and offered a revaluation of bourgeois values. The Bolshevik revolution, with all its deviations, all its adaptations to specifically Russian conditions and all the impurities which always disfigure practice as opposed to theory, has driven home the challenge and sought to apply the revaluation. That bourgeois society has been put progressively on the defensive in the past hundred years, that its fate still hangs in the balance, few today will deny; and until that fate is settled, until some new synthesis has been achieved, the *Communist Manifesto* will not have said its last word.

Eduard Bernstein (1850–1932) was a German journalist and an important member of the German Social Democratic Party. Like Engels, he was an ardent Marxist, but, unlike Engels, he was not an apologist for Marx. Bernstein's views of the essential truths of Marxism were based upon an intimate study of the important texts, as well as a close acquaintance with German political reality in the

1890s. The work from which the following selection is drawn was first published in 1899.

FROM *Evolutionary Socialism* BY EDUARD BERNSTEIN

THE MARXIST DOCTRINE OF CLASS WAR AND OF THE EVOLUTION OF CAPITAL

THE DOCTRINE OF THE CLASS WARS rests on the foundation of the materialist conception of history. "It was found," writes Engels in *Anti-Dühring,* "that all history hitherto was the history of class wars, that the classes fighting each other are, each time, the outcome of the conditions of production and commerce—in one word, of the economic conditions of their epoch." . . . In modern society it is the class war between the capitalist owners of the means of production and the producers without capital, the wage workers, which imprints its mark on history in this respect. For the former class Marx took from France the term "Bourgeoisie," and for the latter the term "Proletariat." This class struggle between bourgeoisie and proletariat is accordingly the antagonism, transferred to men, which is in the conditions of production to-day, that is, in the private character of the method of appropriation and the social character of the method of production. The means of production are the property of individual capitalists who appropriate to themselves the results of the production, but the production itself has become a social process; that means, a production of commodities for use made by many workers on a basis of systematic division and organisation of labour. And this antagonism conceals in itself, or has, a second conflict, as a supplement: the systematic division and organisation of work within the establishments for production (workshop, factory, combination of factories, etc.) is opposed by the unsystematic disposal of the produce on the market.

The starting point of the class struggle between capitalists and workers is the antagonism of interests which follows from the nature of the utilisation of the labour of the latter by the former for profit.

*   *   *

The capitalist sells the products (manufactured with the help of the worker—that is, by the whole of the workers employed by him) in the goods market at a price which, as a rule and as a condition of the continuance of

Eduard Bernstein, *Evolutionary Socialism: A Criticism and Affirmation* (1909), pp. 18–20, 24–5, 146–50, 153–7, 159–65, translated by Edith C. Harvey. Reprinted by permission of the Independent Labour Party, London.

his undertaking, yields a surplus above the amount which the manufacture costs. What is, then, this surplus?

According to Marx it is the surplus value of the labour accomplished by the worker. The goods are exchanged on the market at a value which is fixed by the labour embodied in them, measured according to time. What the capitalist has put in in past—we would even say dead—labour in the form of raw material, auxiliary material, wear and tear of machinery, rent, and other costs of production, appears again unchanged in the value of the product. It is otherwise with the living work expended on it. This costs the capitalist wages; it brings him an amount beyond these, the equivalent of the value of labour. The labour value is the value of the quantity of labour worked into the product; the worker's wages is the selling price of the labour power used up in production. Prices, or the value of labour power, are determined by the cost of maintenance of the worker as it corresponds with his historically developed habits of life. The difference between the equivalent . . . of the labour-value and the labour-wage is the surplus value which it is the natural endeavour of the capitalist to raise as high as possible and in any case not to allow to sink.

*   *   *

So far, in the most concise compression possible, I have endeavoured to set forth the most important propositions of that part of the Marxist theory which we have to consider as essential to his socialism. Just as little as—or, rather, still less than—the materialist theory of history has this part of the theory sprung from the beginning in a perfected form from the head of its authors. Even more than in the former case can a development of the theory be shown which, whilst firmly maintaining the chief points of view, consists of limiting the propositions at first represented as absolute. In the preface to *Capital* (1867), in the preface to the new edition of the *Communist Manifesto* (1872), in the preface and a note to the new edition of the *Poverty of Philosophy* (1884), and in the preface to the *Class Struggles in the French Revolution* (1895), some of the changes are shown which in the course of time have been brought to pass with regard to various corresponding matters in the views of Marx and Engels. But not all the changes to be cited here and elsewhere with reference to single portions or hypoteses of the theory have found full consideration in its final elaboration. Marx and Engels confined themselves sometimes merely to hinting at, sometimes only to stating in regard to single points, the changes recognised by them in facts, and in the better analyses of these facts, which influenced the form and application of their theory. And even in the last respect contradictions are not wanting in their writings. They have left to their successors the duty of bringing unity again into their theory and of co-ordinating theory and practice.

But this duty can only be accomplished if one gives an account unreservedly of the gaps and contradictions in the theory. In other words, the further development and elaboration of the Marxist doctrine must begin with criticism of it.

*   *   *

The whole practical activity of social democracy is directed towards creating circumstances and conditions which shall render possible and secure a transition (free from convulsive outbursts) of the modern social order into a higher one. From the consciousness of being the pioneers of a higher civilisation, its adherents are ever creating fresh inspiration and zeal. In this rests also, finally, the moral justification of the socialist expropriation towards which they aspire. But the "dictatorship of the classes" belongs to a lower civilisation, and apart from the question of the expediency and practicability of the thing, it is only to be looked upon as a reversion, as political atavism. If the thought is aroused that the transition from a capitalist to a socialist society must necessarily be accomplished by means of the development of forms of an age which did not know at all, or only in quite an imperfect form, the present methods of the initiating and carrying of laws, and which was without the organs fit for the purpose, reaction will set in.

I say expressly transition from a capitalist to a socialist society, and not from a "civic society," as is so frequently the expression used to-day. This application of the word "civic" is also much more an atavism, or in any case an ambiguous way of speaking, which must be considered an inconvenience in the phraseology of German social democracy, and which forms an excellent bridge for mistakes with friend and foe. The fault lies partly in the German language, which has no special word for the idea of the citizen with equal civic rights separate from the idea of privileged citizens.

What is the struggle against, or the abolition of, a civic society? What does it mean specially in Germany, in whose greatest and leading state, Prussia, we are still constantly concerned with first getting rid of a great part of feudalism which stands in the path of civic development? No man thinks of destroying civic society as a civilised ordered system of society. On the contrary, social democracy does not wish to break up this society and make all its members proletarians together; it labours rather incessantly at raising the worker from the social position of a proletarian to that of a citizen, and thus to make citizenship universal. It does not want to set up a proletarian society instead of a civic society, but a socialist order of society instead of a capitalist one. It would be well if one, instead of availing himself of the former ambiguous expression, kept to the latter quite clear declaration. Then one would be quite free of a good portion of other contradictions which opponents, not quite without reason, assert do exist between the phraseology and the practice of social democracy. . . .

Finally, it is to be recommended that some moderation should be kept in the declaration of war against "liberalism." It is true that the great liberal movement of modern times arose for the advantage of the capitalist bourgeoisie first of all, and the parties which assumed the names of liberals were, or became in due course, simple guardians of capitalism. Naturally, only opposition can reign between these parties and social democracy. But with respect to liberalism as a great historical movement, socialism is its legitimate heir, not only in chronological sequence, but also in its spiritual qualities, as is shown moreover in every question of principle in which social democracy has had to take up an attitude.

Wherever an economic advance of the socialist programme had to be carried out in a manner, or under circumstances, that appeared seriously to imperil the development of freedom, social democracy has never shunned taking up a position against it. The security of civil freedom has always seemed to it to stand higher than the fulfilment of some economic progress.

The aim of all socialist measures, even of those which appear outwardly as coercive measures, is the development and the securing of a free personality. Their more exact examination always shows that the coercion included will raise the sum total of liberty in society, and will give more freedom over a more extended area than it takes away. The legal day of a maximum number of hours' work, for example, is actually a fixing of a minimum of freedom, a prohibition to sell freedom longer than for a certain number of hours daily, and, in principle, therefore, stands on the same ground as the prohibition agreed to by all liberals against selling oneself into personal slavery.

*   *   *

Liberalism had historically the task of breaking the chains which the fettered economy and the corresponding organisations of law of the middle ages had imposed on the further development of society. That it at first strictly maintained the form of bourgeois liberalism did not stop it from actually expressing a very much wider-reaching general principle of society whose completion will be socialism.

Socialism will create no new bondage of any kind whatever. The individual is to be free, not in the metaphysical sense, as the anarchists dreamed—*i.e.,* free from all duties towards the community—but free from every economic compulsion in his action and choice of a calling. Such freedom is only possible for all means of organisation. In this sense one might call socialism "organising liberalism," for when one examines more closely the organisations that socialism wants and how it wants them, he will find that what distinguishes them above all from the feudalistic organisations, outwardly like them, is just their liberalism, their democratic constitution, their accessibility. Therefore the trade union, striving after an arrangement similar to a guild, is, in the eyes of the socialist, the product of self-defence against the tendency of capitalism to overstock the labour market; but, at the same time, just on account of its tendency towards a guild, and to the degree in which that obtains, is it an unsocialistic corporate body.

*   *   *

To create the organisations described—or, so far as they are already begun, to develop them further—is the indispensable preliminary to what we call socialism of production. Without them the so-called social appropriation of the means of production would only result presumably in reckless devastation of productive forces, insane experimentalising and aimless violence, and the political sovereignty of the working class would, in fact, only be carried out in the form of a dictatorial, revolutionary, central power, supported by the terrorist dictatorship of revolutionary clubs. As such it hovered before the Blanquists, and as such it is still represented in the *Communist Manifesto* and in the publications for which its authors were responsible at that time. But "in presence of the practical experiences of the February revolution and much more of those of the Paris Commune when the proletariat retained political power for two months," the revolutionary programme given in the *Manifesto* has "here and there become out of date." "The Commune notably offers a proof that the working class cannot simply take possession of the state machinery and set it in motion for their own ends."

So wrote Marx and Engels in 1872 in the preface to the new edition of the *Manifesto*. And they refer to the work, *The Civil War in France*, where this is developed more fully. But if we open the work in question and read the part referred to (it is the third), we find a programme developed which, according to its political contents, shows in all material features the greatest similarity to the federalism of Proudhon.

"The unity of the nation was not to be broken, but on the contrary it was to be organised by the destruction of that power of the state which pretended to be the personification of that unity but wanted to be independent of, and superior to, the nation on whose body it was after all only a parasitic growth. Whilst they were occupied in cutting off the merely oppressive organs of the old governing power its rightful functions as a power which claimed to stand above the community were to be taken away and given over to the responsible servants of the community. Instead of deciding once in three or six years what member of the ruling class should trample on and crush the people in Parliament, universal suffrage should serve the people constituted in communities, as individual suffrage serves every other employer to select for his business workers, inspectors, and clerks."

"The antagonism between the commune and the power of the state has been looked on as an exaggerated form of the old fight against over-centralisation. . . . The constitution of the commune, on the contrary, would have restored to the community all the powers which until now the parasitic growth, the state, which lives on the community and hinders its free action, has absorbed."

Thus Marx wrote in the *Civil War in France*.

*   *   *

There is not the least doubt (and it has since then been proved many times practically) that the general development of modern society is along the line of a constant increase of the duties of municipalities and the extension of municipal freedom, that the municipality will be an ever more important lever of social emancipation. It appears to me doubtful if it was necessary for the first work of democracy to be such a dissolution of the modern state system and complete transformation of its organisation as Marx . . . pictured (the formation of the national assembly out of delegates from provincial or district assemblies, which in their turn were composed of delegates from municipalities) so that the form the national assemblies had hitherto taken had to be abolished. Evolution has given life to too many institutions and bodies corporate, whose sphere has outgrown the control of municipalities and even of provinces and districts for it to be able to do without the control of the central governments unless or before their organisation is transformed. . . .

But we are less concerned here with a criticism of separate items in the quoted programme than with bringing into prominence the energy with which it emphasises autonomy as the preliminary condition of social emancipation, and with showing how the democratic organisation from the bottom upwards is depicted as the way to the realisation of socialism, and how the antagonists Proudhon and Marx meet again in—liberalism.

The future itself will reveal how far the municipalities and other self-governing bodies will discharge their duties under a complete democracy, and how far they will make use of these duties. But so much is clear: the more suddenly they come in possession of their freedom, the more experiments they will make in number and in violence and therefore be liable to greater mistakes, and the more experience the working class democracy has had in the school of self-government, the more cautiously and practically will it proceed.

Simple as democracy appears to be at the first glance, its problems in such a complicated society as ours are in no way easy to solve. Read only in the volumes of *Industrial Democracy* by Mr. and Mrs. Webb how many experiments the English trade unions had to make and are still making in order to find out the most serviceable forms of government and administration, and of what importance this question of constitution is to trade unions. The English trade unions have been able to develop in this respect for over seventy years in perfect freedom. They began with the most elementary form of self-government and have been forced to convince themselves that this form is only suited to the most elementary organisms, for quite small, local unions. As they grew they gradually learned to renounce as injurious to their successful development certain cherished ideas of doctrinaire democracy (the imperative mandate, the unpaid official, the powerless central representation), and to form instead of it a democracy capable of governing with representative assemblies, paid officials, and central government with full powers.

* * *

Meantime we are not yet so far on, and it is not my intention to unfold pictures of the future. I am not concerned with what will happen in the more distant future, but with what can and ought to happen in the present, for the present and the nearest future. And so the conclusion of this exposition is the very banal statement that the conquest of the democracy, the formation of political and social organs of the democracy, is the indispensable preliminary condition to the realisation of socialism.

Feudalism, with its unbending organisations and corporations, had to be destroyed nearly everywhere by violence. The liberal organisations of modern society are distinguished from those exactly because they are flexible, and capable of change and development. They do not need to be destroyed, but only to be further developed. For that we need organisation and energetic action, but not necessarily a revolutionary dictatorship. . . .

> *The present is a revolutionary age, and the place of revolutions on the Marxist plan raises questions of global concern. Dr. Ulam, Professor of Government at Harvard University, views the Marxist analysis of the ills of contemporary society through modern (and somewhat jaundiced) eyes.*

FROM *The Unfinished Revolution* BY ADAM B. ULAM

THE ETERNAL BATTLE ARRAY of history always ranges the oppressor against the oppressed, most commonly the owner of the means of production against the man who works with them. Only in the very beginning of human society was there no class struggle, just as there will be none in its culmination. Between the most primitive tribal community and the socialist-communist era, "the history of all hitherto existing society is the history of

From *The Unfinished Revolution*, pp. 32–44, by Adam B. Ulam. © Copyright 1960 by Adam B. Ulam. Reprinted by permission of Random House, Inc.

class struggles." Capitalism witnesses this struggle in the most simplified form: the proletariat against the capitalists. The victory of the proletariat will bring with it the abolition of the class struggle. The discovery of private property disrupted the social innocence of mankind. The full utilization of mankind's productive powers under socialism will restore it. With the disappearance of private property and of the class struggle, most of the social evils will disappear and with them the rationale for oppressive institutions, including the state.

This is the most clear-cut and internally consistent of all Marxist arguments. From its ringing formulation in the *Communist Manifesto* to the end of their lives, Marx and Engels never doubted that they had found the operating pattern of history, that the reality of social and political life is expressed, not in the struggle of ideas, dynasties, or nations, but in the class struggle grounded in economic motivation. To their followers, the principle was a satisfactory explanation and a reliable guide to action, with none of the puzzling qualities of Marxist economics or overall philosophy. Class struggle became, in effect, the major portion of the revolutionary appeal of Marxism. Workers do not strike or storm the barricades in order to abolish surplus value. They strike and revolt against oppressive conditions, against the capitalists. From the point of view of political action, the slogan of class struggle is the simplest guide. It is also the simplest, most convincing revolutionary explanation of politics and history.

A deceptive simplicity! It has misled both the critics and the followers of Marxism. It has led Marxist movements too often to identify Marxist politics with a simple posture of opposition to the exploiting classes. The dominant faction of the German Social Democrats before World War I defined their Marxism as hostility to the imperial institutions and middle-class parties of their country. It led the Bolsheviks, in the first flush of their victory in 1917, to believe that by destroying the capitalists they were destroying capitalism. It has led people versed in Marxism to express surprise that many secondary features of capitalism "suddenly" made their appearance in Soviet Russia in the 1930's. Marxism became identified with insurrectionary action or with hostility, open and uncompromising, to capitalism and to everything and everyone connected with it.

It is necessary to repeat (as it will be again) what is perhaps the most pregnant sentence in Marx's view of social revolution, describing the role of the capitalist: "He thus forces the development of the productive powers of society, and creates *those material conditions, which alone can form the real basis of a higher form of society,* a society in which the full and free development of every individual forms the ruling principle." Nothing in the *main body* of Marx and Engels' writing suggests that any political development, even a seizure of power by the proletariat, can abrogate the laws governing the material development of mankind. From the earliest days of their association, the days filled with the most immediate revolutionary hope, Marx and Engels believed in the primacy of material factors over political action. It is always possible to find an incident or a statement by one or the other that would range them in the camp of believers in revolution pure and simple and hang the stage of economic development. (Thus the brief "Blanquist" period of Marx's early revolutionary activity, and, late in his life, his opinion that Russia might skip the full capitalist phase and pass into socialism from pre-capitalism.) But it is impossible to claim that such incidents or utterances represent the main tendency of Marxism or, as M. Rubel claims in his excellent biography, that Marx ultimately abandoned economic determinism in favor of unconditional faith in the ideal of human liberation.[1]

What bridges the gap between economic determinism on the one hand and class struggle and the call to the proletariat to seize power on the other is Marx's revolutionary optimism. In the 1840's and early '50's, he believed that capitalism was on its last legs, that the economic as well as the political conditions for its downfall were at hand. It is true, as M. Rubel reminds us, that Marx was a socialist long before he discovered his economic system. It is true that the fascination of political economy engrossed and captured him, pushing his thought in directions he had perhaps not envisaged as a young man. But his socialism and his "discovery" of the class struggle did not precede his distaste for the existing moralistic brands of socialism and the determination to place *his* socialism on a firm, materialistic, scientific basis.

Again, what is difficult for us to understand from the perspective of a hundred years becomes easier if we immerse ourselves in the feeling of the period. How could a man believe both that capitalism was a necessary phase of the development of mankind and that Western European capitalism circa 1850 had played its role and was ready to leave the stage? The simple answer is that Marx and Engels shared not only the expectations of many radicals and socialists of the day, but also the apprehensions of many capitalists and liberal economists. Social and economic unrest had risen in ascending proportion from the introduction of what are *to us* the rudimentary institutions of capitalism to the middle of the nineteenth century. Was it entirely unreasonable to expect a fairly early economic collapse as well as a political revolution? Or to see a democratic revolution as a far-reaching step toward socialism? Many revolutionaries live expecting their revolution to take place any day. In Marx the faith of a revolutionary was complemented by the analysis of a social scientist. It is easy for us to say that Marx was wrong: capitalism did not collapse in Europe in 1850 or in 1860. But he was also right, though on wrong premises: what he assumed were relatively late stages of capitalism in France and England were in effect the early stages of industrialization and modernization in those countries, and in those stages capitalism is most vulnerable to class struggle.

Without revolutionary optimism, the doctrine of the class struggle, when joined with economic determinism, is a somber and tragic lesson. Except at the turning points in history, there is nothing the oppressed can do against

[1] Maximilien Rubel, *Karl Marx: Essai de biographie intellectuelle,* Paris, 1957.

the oppressor. The slave cannot prevail against his master, the serf against the landowner; and one type of oppression disappears only to be reborn in a different form of exploitation of man by man. Class struggle is compounded in the character of law and civilization imposed by each dominant class. Systems of religion and ethics serve to reinforce and to conceal at the same time the interest of the dominant class. Ever since he had seen, as a young man, the diet of his province discuss draconic laws against the removal of timber from state and private forests by the poor, all of Marx's instincts rebelled at the myth of the impartial state, impartial law. The system of private property under capitalism embodies best the double deception by which each exploiting class masks its exploiting role. It protects the capitalist against any tampering with his property, and it seeks to create the illusion of equality and impartiality for all. The plea for democratic franchise that the bourgeoisie makes is likewise a weapon of its class struggle. It seeks to strip the landlords of the remnants of their power and to delude the proletariat into believing that the essential issues are political in nature. The principle of class struggle illuminates world history by stripping it of its theatrical aspects of national struggles or contests about principles, and by demonstrating its material nature. Marx's is the "inside story" of world history, with economic interest its moving principle.

The "exposure" of history and politics was not unique to Marx. The dominant role of "interest" in politics and recent history was a cardinal tenet of the liberalism of his time. The sense of politics consisted in the struggle of classes seeking the advancement of their material interests. Thus the political struggle in the England of the thirties and forties between the Whigs and the Tories was interpreted as centering around the contest between the agricultural and the manufacturing interests. Liberal economists saw in their doctrine a guide to public policies that would secure a "harmony of interests," but they were far from assuming that the correctness of their theories would of itself secure their adoption, or that a collusion of vested interests could not—as well as ignorance—hamper public welfare. The liberal version was already a "suspicious" theory of history, with the material interests of classes lurking behind the struggle for politics and principles.

Marx elevates this suspicion into certainty. Thus, for example, the Glorious Revolution of 1688 is not primarily a victory of parliamentarianism over royal despotism, but a harbinger of bourgeois domination, with the Stock Exchange and other rudimentary institutions of capitalism soon to be established. In a sense, the Marxist class-struggle interpretation of history is more "historical" than the liberal one. In the liberal outlook, history had been a period of darkness and superstition until the sixteenth and seventeenth centuries, and only then had scientific principle begun to assert itself in thinking about human affairs. To Marx, on the other hand, the class struggle provided the rationale of social systems and philosophies from earliest times; the pattern of history is always meaningful if we follow the class-struggle principle and its economic underpinning. The Middle Ages are thus not merely a period of darkness and obscurantism: their social and religious ideas are perfectly understandable in terms of the then dominant mode of production and system of property. Marxist historical analysis and methods of investigation have had an influence on many historians, some of whom would repudiate indignantly the charge of having anything to do with Marxism.

*   *   *

Marx cannot be reproached with having overlooked the differentiation and proliferation of social classes in his society. Indeed, ostensible political activity consists in various classes and subclasses playing for, or being played for, power in the state. But the essence of the class struggle and its eventual determination is much simpler. Only two classes really count—the capitalists and the proletariat. Other classes and subclasses play increasingly minor roles in the drama of capitalism. Sooner or later they retire into the wings, leaving the stage to the two great antagonists. Insofar as it is the logic of history, i.e., the development of productive forces, and not the temporary whims or affiliations of groups of population that ordain social stratifications, only two classes will remain, and they are "really" the only classes in the true sense of the word. Capitalism is already destroying the landowning nobility, and it will destroy the peasants.

*   *   *

The two classes that are to square off in the last phase of the class struggle are quite dissimilar in many characteristics. The capitalist class is forever growing smaller in numbers; the proletariat, the exploited, ever larger. The rationale of the capitalist process, while it makes the capitalists aware of certain interests they have in common, still obliges them to engage in suicidal competition. The capitalist-industrial process makes the workers more and more unified in the realization of their common interest and in their class solidarity. The peasants, for instance, because of their dispersion, because of the peculiarity of their way of living, can never achieve real solidarity and a real community of interest and feeling; and thus, apart from their marginal economic significance, they can never constitute a true class. The workers, on the contrary, are disciplined by the circumstances of their work, brought together in great aggregations where they can feel the community of their privations and realize the logic of capitalism as leading to socialism. The *spontaneous growth* of class consciousness accompanies the growth of the capitalist-industrial system. . . .

Here we may observe certain interesting connotations of the concept. It is *rationalistic* in the extreme. The working class will not be distracted from the obligation and the realization of the inevitability of the class struggle by nationalistic or religious slogans and considerations. Only a degenerate, rootless portion of it, the *Lumpenproletariat,* may capitulate to the schemes of reactionaries and adventurers. The vast majority of the workers will understand their historical position and historical mission. The vision of the working class is Hegelian in its underpinnings. The proletariat is the universal class, carrying in its future the destiny of mankind, thus parallel in its function to Rousseau's General Will and Hegel's State. The loss of individuality caused and made inevitable by factory labor, the worker's *alienation,* carries in it the seeds of the fullest assertion of individuality under socialism, which comes as a Hegelian "negation of a negation." In more prosaic terms, the factory system is inevitably oppressive and inevitably felt by the worker as such. This oppression *inherent* in the system produces the class feeling. Capitalism = factory system = class consciousness is the line of argument, and a closer examination of each term of the triad will illuminate the nature and conditions of the appeal of Marxism.

The doctrines of the classes and the class struggle have, within the context of the Marxist system, some further rather unexpected connotations. Take the class struggle between the bourgeoisie and the proletariat. The latter, through strikes and political action, resists the inevitable tendency of the capitalists to increase the exploitation of the workers. Yet nothing is clearer according to the logic of the doctrine than that the class struggle cannot paralyze capitalism until the system is fully developed and ready to pass on, or until the proletariat is fully capable of wresting power from the bourgeoisie. What might be called guerrilla class warfare, endemic industrial strife, which would paralyze the system, is clearly against the logic of Marxist thought, even if paradoxically within its spirit: the worker has to get used to the hated factory system, has to undergo exploitation, before the material conditions of the society will allow the transition to socialism. From the perspective of a hundred years, we may appreciate how the Russian and Chinese Communists have taken to heart the logic of the last proposition.

There is no *mystique* of the working class in early Marxism, no extolling of humble material circumstances as being conducive to virtue. Workers are not asserted or called upon to be heroic. They are asserted and called upon to be rational, to develop class consciousness. To Marx, nothing would have been more distasteful than the emotional undertones of later syndicalism. The ideal (in Weber's sense of the term) Marxist worker is a curiously unemotional creature. He has no country, no real family life; and his main objective in life is not an amelioration of his condition, but the overthrow of the whole capitalist system. His sense of suffering injustice, of being exploited, does not deceive him into immediate action against the immediate agents of oppression—the factory and the employer—but into a *planned* struggle against capitalism and the capitalist state. In his political writings and speeches, Marx makes eloquent and emotion-tinged appeals, but the fact is that the main tenet of his theory about the worker and the class struggle is coldly rational in its logic. Human passion and generosity cannot in the last analysis prevail against the facts of history. The drama of the class struggle and the heroic exploits of the working-class revolutionaries are secondary to the working out of material forces. One cannot divorce economic evolution from the human drama that underlies it, but one must not ignore the laws of economics in revolutionary action. It is only a superficial reader of Marxism who would read into it the assumption that the proletariat may by political or insurrectionary action void the laws of history and avoid, say, by seizing power before capitalism is fully established, the hardships and privation of the factory system.

The idea of the class struggle serves to disprove the facile optimism of the liberals for whom, in all the clashes of interests, an "invisible hand" assured in a rationally organized society the harmony of individual and class self-interest with the general welfare. Marx's "invisible hand" is the very visible forces of production, which by their evolution confront each succeeding civilization with a different type of class warfare until, finally developed, they bring about classless society.

The centering of the social problem around the individual is, according to Marx, another pious hypocrisy of liberalism. Individual liberty and due process of law are, within a capitalist society, simply contradictions in terms. They are at most scraps of concessions thrown by the bourgeois state to deceive the proletariat, and in the circumstances of the workers' life under capitalism, they are of no value to them. This contemptuous attitude toward civil liberties, of such great historical significance to Marxism, is attuned to the circumstances of the worst period of the Industrial Revolution: with the proletarian working twelve and fourteen hours a day, and his wife and underage children also in unregulated industrial labor, the Bill of Rights did not, in fact, appear of overwhelming importance to the working class. The class struggle becomes the doctrine of total distrust of the capitalist state, with its laws, bureaucracy, and ideology. The violence of this distrust and opposition, the difficulty Marx and Engels experienced in acknowledging even the slightest social-welfare aspect of the bourgeois state, have often led to the optical illusion that Marxism was opposed to the state as such. It has enabled the revolutionary Marxists to denounce *the state,* with all the accents and conviction of anarchists, forgetting, for the moment, that the centralized state, like the capitalism of which it is a necessary ingredient, is an inevitable part of the historical process.

*   *   *

Here, then, is a theory attuned even more closely than other parts of Marxism to the facts and feelings of an early period of industrialization. The class struggle is the salt of Marxism, its most operative revolutionary part. As a historical and psychological concept, it expresses a gross oversimplification, but it is the oversimplification of a genius. The formula of the class struggle seizes the essence of the mood of a great historical moment—a revolution in basic economy—and generalizes it into a historical law. It extracts the grievances of groups of politically conscious workers in Western Europe, then a very small part of the whole proletariat, and sees in it the portent and meaning of the awakening of the whole working class everywhere. The first reaction of the worker to industrialization, his feelings of grievance and impotence before the machine, his employer, and the state which stands behind the employer, are assumed by Marx to be typical of the general reactions of the worker to industrialization. What does change in the process of the development of industry is that the worker's feeling of impotence gives way to class consciousness, which in turn leads him to class struggle and socialism. Marx's worker is the historical worker, but he is the historical worker of a specific period of industrial and political development.

Even in interpreting the psychology of the worker of the transitional period, Marx exhibited a rationalistic bias. The worker's opposition to the capitalist order is a total opposition to its laws, its factories, and its government. But this revolutionary consciousness of the worker is to take him next to Marxist socialism, where he will accept the factory system and the state, the *only* difference being the abolition of capitalism. Why shouldn't the revolutionary protest of the worker flow into other channels: into rejection of industrialism as well as capitalism, into rejection of the socialist as well as the capitalist state? It is here that Marx is most definitely the child of his age, the child of rationalistic optimism: the workers will undoubtedly translate their anarchistic protests and grievances into a sophisticated philosophy of history. They will undoubtedly realize that the forces of industrialism and modern life, which strip them of property, status, and economic security, are in themselves benevolent in their ultimate effects and that it is only capitalism and the capitalists which make them into instruments of oppression. The chains felt by the proletariat are the chains of the industrial system. The chains Marx urges them to throw off are those of capitalism. Will the workers understand the difference? And if they do, will they still feel that in destroying capitalism they have a "world to win"?

3 The Participants' Views

> The real teachings of Marxism on revolution were of more
> than academic importance. The Marxist in many countries
> was betting his life on the truth of the system; a misinter-
> pretation could lead not only to the failure of the Socialist
> movement but also to imprisonment or death. It was a high
> price to pay for misreading the Marxist texts, and the
> leaders of the Socialist movement in the various countries
> of Europe were concerned to establish an official reading.
>
> The selections that follow illustrate two approaches:
> the "hard" one of Nikolai Lenin (1870–1924), to whom rev-
> olution was fundamental, and the "soft" one of Karl
> Kautsky (1854–1938), to whom revolution was no longer
> necessary.

FROM *State and Revolution* BY NIKOLAI LENIN

WE MUST . . . NOTE that Engels quite definitely regards universal suffrage as a means of bourgeois domination. Universal suffrage, he says, obviously summing up the long experience of German Social-Democracy, is
"an index of the maturity of the working class; it cannot, and never will, be
anything else but that in the modern state."

The petty-bourgeois democrats, such as our Socialist-Revolutionaries and
Mensheviks, and also their twin brothers, the social-chauvinists and opportunists of Western Europe, all expect "more" from universal suffrage. They
themselves share, and instil into the minds of the people, the wrong idea that
universal suffrage "in the *modern* state" is really capable of expressing the
will of the majority of the toilers and of assuring its realisation.

We can here only note this wrong idea, only point out that this perfectly
clear, exact and concrete statement by Engels is distorted at every step in the

V. I. Lenin, *State and Revolution*, pp. 14–20. Reprinted by permission of International Publishers
Co., Inc. Copyright 1932 by International Publishers Co., Inc.

propaganda and agitation of the "official" (*i.e.,* opportunist) Socialist parties.
A detailed analysis of all the falseness of this idea, which Engels brushes
aside, is given in our further account of the views of Marx and Engels on the
"modern" state.

A general summary of his views is given by Engels in the most popular
of his works in the following words:

> The state, therefore, has not existed from all eternity. There have
> been societies which managed without it, which had no conception of
> the state and state power. At a certain stage of economic development,
> which was necessarily bound up with the cleavage of society into classes,
> the state became a necessity owing to this cleavage. We are now rapidly
> approaching a stage in the development of production at which the
> existence of these classes has not only ceased to be a necessity, but is
> becoming a positive hindrance to production. They will disappear as
> inevitably as they arose at an earlier stage. Along with them, the state
> will inevitably disappear. The society that organises production anew on
> the basis of a free and equal association of the producers will put the
> whole state machine where it will then belong: in the museum of
> antiquities, side by side with the spinning wheel and the bronze axe.

It is not often that we find this passage quoted in the propaganda and
agitation literature of contemporary Social-Democracy. But even when we
do come across it, it is generally quoted in the same manner as one bows
before an icon, *i.e.,* it is done merely to show official respect for Engels,
without any attempt to gauge the breadth and depth of revolutionary action
presupposed by this relegating of "the whole state machine . . . to the
museum of antiquities." In most cases we do not even find an understanding
of what Engels calls the state machine.

*   *   *

Without fear of committing an error, it may be said that of this
argument by Engels so singularly rich in ideas, only one point has become an
integral part of Socialist thought among modern Socialist parties, namely,
that, unlike the Anarchist doctrine of the "abolition" of the state, according
to Marx the state "withers away." To emasculate Marxism in such a manner
is to reduce it to opportunism for such an "interpretation" only leaves the
hazy conception of a slow, even, gradual change, free from leaps and storms,
free from revolution. The current popular conception, if one may say so, of
the "withering away" of the state undoubtedly means a slurring over, if not a
negation, of revolution.

Yet, such an "interpretation" is the crudest distortion of Marxism, which
is advantageous only to the bourgeoisie; in point of theory, it is based on a
disregard for the most important circumstances and considerations pointed

out in the very passage summarising Engels' ideas, which we have just quoted in full.

In the first place, Engels at the very outset of his argument says that, in assuming state power, the proletariat by that very act "puts an end to the state as the state." One is "not accustomed" to reflect on what this really means. Generally, it is either ignored altogether, or it is considered as a piece of "Hegelian weakness" on Engels' part. As a matter of fact, however, these words express succinctly the experience of one of the greatest proletarian revolutions—the Paris Commune of 1871, of which we shall speak in greater detail in its proper place. As a matter of fact, Engels speaks here of the destruction of the bourgeois state by the proletarian revolution, while the words about its withering away refer to the remains of *proletarian* statehood *after* the Socialist revolution. The bourgeois state does not "wither away," according to Engels, but is "put an end to" by the proletariat in the course of the revolution. What withers away after the revolution is the proletarian state or semi-state.

Secondly, the state is a "special repressive force." This splendid and extremely profound definition of Engels' is given by him here with complete lucidity. It follows from this that the "special repressive force" of the bourgeoisie for the suppression of the proletariat, of the millions of workers by a handful of the rich, must be replaced by a "special repressive force" of the proletariat for the suppression of the bourgeoisie (the dictatorship of the proletariat). It is just this that constitutes the destruction of "the state as the state." It is just this that constitutes the "act" of "the seizure of the means of production in the name of society." And it is obvious that such a substitution of one (proletarian) "special repressive force" for another (bourgeois) "special repressive force" can in no way take place in the form of a "withering away."

Thirdly, as to the "withering away" or, more expressively and colourfully, as to the state "becoming dormant," Engels refers quite clearly and definitely to the period *after* "the seizure of the means of production [by the state] in the name of society," that is, *after* the Socialist revolution. We all know that the political form of the "state" at that time is complete democracy. But it never enters the head of any of the opportunists who shamelessly distort Marx that when Engels speaks here of the state "withering away," or "becoming dormant," he speaks of *democracy*. At first sight this seems very strange. But it is "unintelligible" only to one who has not reflected on the fact that democracy is *also* a state and that, consequently, democracy will *also* disappear when the state disappears. The bourgeois state can only be "put an end to" by a revolution. The state in general, *i.e.,* most complete democracy, can only "wither away."

Fourthly, having formulated his famous proposition that "the state withers away," Engels at once explains concretely that this proposition is directed equally against the opportunists and the Anarchists. In doing this, however, Engels puts in the first place that conclusion from his proposition about the "withering away" of the state which is directed against the opportunists.

One can wager that out of every 10,000 persons who have read or heard about the "withering away" of the state, 9,990 do not know at all, or do not remember, that Engels did not direct his conclusions from this proposition against the Anarchists *alone*. And out of the remaining ten, probably nine do not know the meaning of a "people's free state" nor the reason why an attack on this watchword contains an attack on the opportunists. This is how history is written! This is how a great revolutionary doctrine is imperceptibly adulterated and adapted to current philistinism! The conclusion drawn against the Anarchists has been repeated thousands of times, vulgarised, harangued about in the crudest fashion possible until it has acquired the strength of a prejudice, whereas the conclusion drawn against the opportunists has been hushed up and "forgotten"!

The "people's free state" was a demand in the programme of the German Social-Democrats and their current slogan in the 'seventies. There is no political substance in this slogan other than a pompous middle-class circumlocution of the idea of democracy. In so far as it referred in a lawful manner to a democratic republic, Engels was prepared to "justify" its use "at times" from a propaganda point of view. But this slogan was opportunist, for it not only expressed an exaggerated view of the attractiveness of bourgeois democracy, but also a lack of understanding of the Socialist criticism of every state in general. We are in favour of a democratic republic as the best form of the state for the proletariat under capitalism, but we have no right to forget that wage slavery is the lot of the people even in the most democratic bourgeois republic. Furthermore, every state is a "special repressive force" for the suppression of the oppressed class. Consequently, *no* state is either "free" or a "people's state." Marx and Engels explained this repeatedly to their party comrades in the 'seventies.

Fifthly, in the same work of Engels, from which every one remembers his argument on the "withering away" of the state, there is also a disquisition on the significance of a violent revolution. The historical analysis of its rôle becomes, with Engels, a veritable panegyric on violent revolution. This, of course, "no one remembers"; to talk or even to think of the importance of this idea is not considered good form by contemporary Socialist parties, and in the daily propaganda and agitation among the masses it plays no part whatever. Yet it is indissolubly bound up with the "withering away" of the state in one harmonious whole.

Here is Engels' argument:

> . . . That force, however, plays another rôle (other than that of a diabolical power) in history, a revolutionary rôle; that, in the words of Marx, it is the midwife of every old society which is pregnant with the new; that it is the instrument with whose aid social movement forces its way through and shatters the dead, fossilised political forms—of this

there is not a word in Herr Dühring. It is only with sighs and groans that he admits the possibility that force will perhaps be necessary for the overthrow of the economic system of exploitation—unfortunately! because all use of force, forsooth, demoralises the person who uses it. And this in spite of the immense moral and spiritual impetus which has resulted from every victorious revolution! And this in Germany, where a violent collision—which indeed may be forced on the people—would at least have the advantage of wiping out the servility which has permeated the national consciousness as a result of the humiliation of the Thirty Years' War. And this parson's mode of thought—lifeless, insipid and impotent—claims to impose itself on the most revolutionary party which history has known?

How can this panegyric on violent revolution, which Engels insistently brought to the attention of the German Social-Democrats between 1878 and 1894, *i.e.,* right to the time of his death, be combined with the theory of the "withering away" of the state to form one doctrine?

Usually the two views are combined by means of eclecticism, by an unprincipled, sophistic, arbitrary selection (to oblige the powers that be) of either one or the other argument, and in ninety-nine cases out of a hundred (if not more often), it is the idea of the "withering away" that is specially emphasised. Eclecticism is substituted for dialectics—this is the most usual, the most widespread phenomenon to be met with in the official Social-Democratic literature of our day in relation to Marxism. Such a substitution is, of course, nothing new; it may be observed even in the history of classic Greek philosophy. When Marxism is adulterated to become opportunism, the substitution of eclecticism for dialectics is the best method of deceiving the masses; it gives an illusory satisfaction; it seems to take into account all sides of the process, all the tendencies of development, all the contradictory factors and so forth, whereas in reality it offers no consistent and revolutionary view of the process of social development at all.

We have already said above and shall show more fully later that the teaching of Marx and Engels regarding the inevitability of a violent revolution refers to the bourgeois state. It *cannot* be replaced by the proletarian state (the dictatorship of the proletariat) through "withering away," but, as a general rule, only through a violent revolution. The panegyric sung in its honour by Engels and fully corresponding to the repeated declarations of Marx (remember the concluding passages of the *Poverty of Philosophy* and the *Communist Manifesto,* with its proud and open declaration of the inevitability of a violent revolution; remember Marx's *Critique of the Gotha Programme* of 1875 in which, almost thirty years later, he mercilessly castigates the opportunist character of that programme)—this praise is by no means a mere "impulse," a mere declamation, or a polemical sally. The necessity of systematically fostering among the masses *this* and just this point of view about violent revolution lies at the root of the *whole* of Marx's and

Engels' teaching. The neglect of such propaganda and agitation by both the present predominant social-chauvinist and the Kautskyist currents brings their betrayal of Marx's and Engels' teaching into prominent relief.

The replacement of the bourgeois by the proletarian state is impossible without a violent revolution. The abolition of the proletarian state, *i.e.,* of all states, is only possible through "withering away."

Marx and Engels gave a full and concrete exposition of these views in studying each revolutionary situation separately, in analysing the lessons of the experience of each individual revolution. We now pass to this, undoubtedly the most important part of their work.

Karl Kautsky (1854–1938) was one of the leading theoreticians of the German Social Democratic Party. The selection that follows—Kautsky's attempt to come to grips with the problem of the necessity of revolution in a state with democratic institutions—is from a book review written by him in 1893.

FROM *A Social Democratic Catechism*
BY KARL KAUTSKY

WE ARE REVOLUTIONARIES, and not merely in the sense that the steam engine is revolutionary. The social overturn at which we aim can only be achieved through a political revolution, through the conquest of political power by the fighting proletariat. And the specific form of government in which alone socialism can be realized is the republic, that is—as the phrase is commonly understood—in the democratic republic.

*   *   *

Social Democracy is a revolutionary—but not a revolution-making—party. We know that our aims can only be achieved through a revolution, but we also know that it is as little in our power to make that revolution as it is in the power of our enemies to prevent it. It does not occur to us, therefore, to want to either plot or instigate a revolution. And since the revolution cannot arbitrarily be made by us, we cannot even attempt to

Karl Kautsky, "Ein Sozialdemokratischer Katechismus," *Neue Zeit* (December, 1893), pp. 368–9, 402–5, 409–10, translated by Walter R. Weitzmann.

describe when, under what circumstances, and in which form it will break out. We do know that the class struggle between bourgeoisie and proletariat will not end before the latter has come into full possession of political power, which it will use to establish the socialist society. We do know that this class struggle must become more intensive and extensive, that the proletariat will grow in numbers and in moral and economic power and that, therefore, its victory and capitalism's defeat are inevitable. But we can venture only the vaguest guesses about how the last decisive battles in this social war will be fought.

*   *   *

Since we know nothing about the decisive battles of the social war we can, of course, say little about their character—whether they will be bloody, whether physical violence will play a dominant rôle, or whether they will be fought exclusively by means of economic, legislative, and moral pressures.

But we can say that it is very probable that in the revolutionary struggles of the proletariat the latter [non-violent] means will have greater predominance over the use of physical, i.e., military, force, than was the case in the revolutionary struggles of the bourgeoisie.

One reason why the coming revolutionary struggles will be fought less and less with military means is, as has often been said, that the equipment of government troops is today vastly superior to the weapons available to the "civilians." As a rule, this disparity makes all the latters' resistance hopeless from the start. On the other hand, today's revolutionary strata have available to them better weapons of economic, political and moral resistance than had those of the previous century. The only exception to this is Russia.

Freedom of association, of press, and universal suffrage (under some circumstances, universal military service, as well), are, however, not merely weapons that give the proletariat of modern nations an advantage not possessed by the classes that fought the revolutionary battles of the bourgeoisie. These institutions also spread over the power relations of individual classes and parties, and the spirit which animates them is a light which was missing during the absolutist era.

Then, the ruling classes as well as the revolutionary classes groped about in the dark. Because the expression of opposition was made impossible, neither the governments nor the revolutionaries had any way to measure their strengths. Each of the two groups was therefore in danger of overestimating its strength before it had tested it in battle with its opponent, and equally, of underestimating it when it suffered a single defeat—quickly throwing in the towel. This is probably the main reason why we find, in the era of the revolutionary bourgeoisie, so many *coups* so easily put down, and so many governments so easily toppled—a succession, therefore, of revolution and counterrevolution.

It is entirely different today, at least in countries with somewhat democratic institutions. These institutions have been called the safety valve of society. If one means by this that the proletariat in a democracy ceases to be revolutionary, that it remains satisfied with merely expressing its resentment and its suffering publicly, and that it renounces political and social revolution, then this designation is wrong. Democracy cannot do away with the class contradictions of capitalist society, and it cannot prevent their necessary final result, the overthrow of this social system. But it can do one thing: though it cannot prevent the revolution, it can prevent some foredoomed revolutionary attempts and forestall some revolutionary uprisings. Democracy produces clarity about the relative strength of different parties and classes; though it cannot resolve their opposition nor transform their final aims, it does tend to prevent the rising classes from attempting to solve problems which they are not yet strong enough to tackle, and it tends, in turn, to keep the ruling classes from denying concessions which they are no longer strong enough to do. The direction of development is not thereby changed, but its pace becomes steadier and calmer. In states with democratic institutions the advance of the proletariat will be accompanied by less striking successes than was the rise of the bourgeoisie during its revolutionary epoch. But neither will it be marked by as severe defeats. Since the awakening of the modern social democratic workers' movement in the sixties the European proletariat has suffered only one great defeat—in the Paris Commune of 1871. At that time France was still suffering from the imprint of the Empire which had deprived the people of truly democratic institutions; the French proletariat had reached only a low level of self-consciousness, and the uprising had been forced upon them.

The democratic parliamentary method of struggle may appear more tedious than the method used in the revolutionary epoch of the bourgeoisie. It is true that it is less dramatic and showy, but it also produces fewer casualties. This may be a matter of indifference to that aestheticised group of literati which dabbles in socialism solely to find interesting sport and copy, but it is not unimportant to those who have to wage the struggle.

The more effective the democratic institutions and the greater the political and economic awareness and self-control of the populace, the better are the chances that so-called peaceful means of class struggle, those that limit themselves to non-violent means such as parliamentarism, strikes, demonstrations, use of the press and other means of pressure, will be used.

Given any two opponents and everything else being equal, the one who feels superior to the other will most likely maintain his *sang-froid*. Someone who does not believe in himself and his cause is only too likely to lose his equanimity and control.

Now the class which in every modern country has the greatest faith in itself and its cause is the proletariat. To attain it it needs no false illusions. It needs only to examine the history of the last generation to see itself everywhere in uninterrupted advance. It needs only to study contemporary developments to gain the assurance that its victory is unavoidable. Hence, we should not expect the highly developed proletariat of a given country to easily lose its equanimity and self-control, or to inaugurate a policy of adventurism. The more educated and aware the working class and the more democratic the state, the less likely a policy of adventurism becomes.

But one cannot place equal confidence in the ruling class. Seeing and feeling themselves grow weaker every day, they become ever more anxious, and therefore unpredictable. Increasingly they sink into a mood where one must be prepared to see them seized by attacks of madness during which they fall upon their enemy in blind rage, intent upon finishing him off, mindless of the wounds they will thereby inflict upon all of society including themselves, and of the devastation they will wreak.

The political position of the proletariat is such that it will attempt as long as possible to advance by the aforementioned "legal" means. The danger that this aim will be frustrated lies in the jittery mood of the ruling classes.

The political leaders of the ruling classes hope for such madness to lay hold not just of the ruling classes but the indifferent masses as well, before Social Democracy is strong enough to resist. This is their only hope to delay the victory of socialism for at least another few years. But this is a desperate gamble. For if the bourgeoisie should fail in their mad attempt to suppress the proletariat, they will have exhausted their strength and will collapse even sooner while the proletariat triumphs even more quickly. But the predominant mood among many politicians of the ruling classes has already reached the point where they believe that nothing else can be done but to gamble everything on one card. They want to provoke civil war because they fear the revolution.

Social Democracy, on the other hand, has no reason to adopt such a policy of despair. It has every reason to avoid—and failing this to postpone—such madness in its rulers as long as possible. Ultimately, it must be delayed until the proletariat is strong enough to subdue and tame the maniacs, so that the havoc and its victims will be reduced and their attack be the last.

Social Democrats must, therefore, avoid and even combat anything that might be a purposeless provocation of the ruling classes; anything that might give their leaders an excuse to drive the bourgeoisie and its followers into a socialist-hating frenzy. Thus, when we declare that revolutions cannot be "made," when we condemn as nonsensical and dangerous the instigation of a revolution and act accordingly, we do this not to please the German state attorneys, but in the interest of the fighting proletariat. And in this position German Social Democrats stand united with their sister parties. Because of this stand it has so far been impossible for the leaders of the ruling classes to proceed against the fighting proletariat as they would have wished.

Though the political power of Social Democracy is still relatively small, socialists in modern nations are powerful enough to prevent bourgeois politicians from arbitrary actions. Minor regulations and ordinances cannot help them; they only embitter their subjects without discouraging them or reducing their fighting ability. Any attempt, however, to enact legislation that would seriously affect the proletariat's fighting capacity conjures up the danger of civil war which, whatever its outcome, would bring frightful devastation. This is fairly common knowledge. And though the bourgeois politicians may wish for a trial of strength with socialists before the latter are prepared, the bourgeois businessmen will have nothing to do with experiments which would ruin every one of them; at least in a rational state unaffected by the aforementioned madness. In a state of frenzy, the bourgeois can be gotten to support any measure, and the greater his fear, the wilder his cry for blood.

The interests of the proletariat demand even more authoritatively today than ever before that anything that might provoke the ruling classes into a policy of violence be avoided. Social Democrats act accordingly.

[*He then speaks of a tendency calling itself proletarian which advocates such a policy of provocation. This he calls "anarchism" and he spends the next five pages in showing that socialists must reject this anarchist direction which has been responsible for all the setbacks of socialism since the Paris Commune —L. P. W.*]

The main lever of our success is our revolutionary enthusiasm. We shall need it even more in the future for the most difficult days lie not behind, but ahead of us. Thus anything that might immobilize this lever would be most detrimental to our cause.

Our present position, by making us appear more "moderate" than we really are, carries with it a certain danger. The stronger we are, the more the practical tasks take precedence: the more we must extend our agitation beyond the circle of the industrial wage workers, and the more we must guard against useless provocations or hollow threats. This makes it extremely difficult to maintain the proper balance, to give full attention to the needs of the present without losing sight of the future; to engage in a dialogue with the peasantry and lower middle class and yet not surrender the proletarian standpoint; to avoid all provocation and yet to convince everyone that we are a party of struggle in irreconcilable opposition to the existing social system.

The Origins of Modern

Imperialism—Ideological

or Economic?

CONTENTS

QUESTIONS FOR STUDY

1 What are the arguments in favor of imperialism offered by Joseph Chamberlain?
2 Do they lend support to Lenin's analysis?
3 What is the nature of Langer's criticism of the Marxist analysis?
4 What is the relation of Kipling's poem to the attitude of Josiah Strong?
5 In what ways does Schumpeter disagree with Lenin?
6 Is there a legitimate argument in favor of imperialism?

For millennia tribes, peoples, and nations have engaged in aggressive expansion at the expense of their neighbors. In the period from about 1870 to the First World War the nations of Europe, the United States of America, and Japan were all particularly active in extending their influence and control over many areas of the world. These nations had many things in common: They were all industrial powers for whom commerce was very important; they extended their power over countries that were generally less industrial or not industrial at all; their control was sometimes not territorial but merely commercial. This "new imperialism," a consequence of the industrial era, quickly brought about the partition of the underdeveloped regions of the world among the great industrial powers and soon produced theories of imperialism. What were its causes, its purposes, its results?

1 Imperialism and Capitalism

The first full-scale economic explanation of imperialism was offered by John A. Hobson in 1902. It strongly influenced Lenin, who adapted it to suit Marxist principles and presented it in a form that has been very influential ever since.

FROM *Imperialism, the Highest Stage of Capitalism*

BY NIKOLAI LENIN

WE MUST NOW TRY to sum up and put together what has been said above on the subject of imperialism. Imperialism emerged as the development and direct continuation of the fundamental attributes of capitalism in general. But capitalism only became capitalist imperialism at a definite and very high stage of its development, when certain of its fundamental attributes began to be transformed into their opposites, when the features of a period of transition from capitalism to a higher social and economic system began to take shape and reveal themselves all along the line. Economically, the main thing in this process is the substitution of capitalist monopolies for capitalist free competition. Free competition is the fundamental attribute of capitalism, and of commodity production generally. Monopoly is exactly the opposite of free competition; but we have seen the latter being transformed into monopoly before our very eyes, creating large-scale industry and eliminating small industry, replacing large-scale industry by still larger-scale industry, finally leading to such a concentration of production and capital that monopoly has been and is the result: cartels, syndicates and trusts, and merging with them, the capital of a dozen or so banks manipulating thousands of millions. At the same time monopoly, which has grown out of free competition, does not abolish the latter, but exists over it and alongside of it, and thereby gives rise to a number of very acute, intense antagonisms, friction and conflicts. Monopoly is the transition from capitalism to a higher system.

V. I. Lenin, *Imperialism, the Highest Stage of Capitalism* (1939), pp. 88–98. Reprinted by permission of International Publishers Co., Inc.

If it were necessary to give the briefest possible definition of imperialism we should have to say that imperialism is the monopoly stage of capitalism. Such a definition would include what is most important, for, on the one hand, finance capital is the bank capital of a few big monopolist banks, merged with the capital of the monopolist combines of manufacturers; and, on the other hand, the division of the world is the transition from a colonial policy which has extended without hindrance to territories unoccupied by any capitalist power, to a colonial policy of monopolistic possession of the territory of the world which has been completely divided up.

But very brief definitions, although convenient, for they sum up the main points, are nevertheless inadequate, because very important features of the phenomenon that has to be defined have to be especially deduced. And so, without forgetting the conditional and relative value of all definitions, which can never include all the concatenations of a phenomenon in its complete development, we must give a definition of imperialism that will embrace the following five essential features:

1. The concentration of production and capital developed to such a high stage that it created monopolies which play a decisive role in economic life.
2. The merging of bank capital with industrial capital, and the creation, on the basis of this "finance capital," of a "financial oligarchy."
3. The export of capital, which has become extremely important, as distinguished from the export of commodities.
4. The formation of international capitalist monopolies which share the world among themselves.
5. The territorial division of the whole world among the greatest capitalist powers is completed.

Imperialism is capitalism in that stage of development in which the dominance of monopolies and finance capital has established itself; in which the export of capital has acquired pronounced importance; in which the division of the world among the international trusts has begun; in which the division of all territories of the globe among the great capitalist powers has been completed.

We shall see later that imperialism can and must be defined differently if consideration is to be given, not only to the basic, purely economic factors —to which the above definition is limited—but also to the historical place of this stage of capitalism in relation to capitalism in general, or to the relations between imperialism and the two main trends in the working class movement. The point to be noted just now is that imperialism, as interpreted above, undoubtedly represents a special stage in the development of capitalism. In order to enable the reader to obtain as well grounded an idea of imperialism as possible, we deliberately quoted largely from *bourgeois* economists who are obliged to admit the particularly incontrovertible facts regarding modern capitalist economy. With the same object in view, we have produced detailed statistics which reveal the extent to which bank capital, etc., has developed, showing how the transformation of quantity into quality, of developed capitalism into imperialism, has expressed itself. Needless to say, all boundaries in nature and in society are conditional and changeable, and, consequently, it would be absurd to discuss the exact year or the decade in which imperialism "definitely" became established.

In this matter of defining imperialism, however, we have to enter into controversy, primarily, with K. Kautsky, the principal Marxian theoretician of the epoch of the so-called Second International—that is, of the twenty-five years between 1889 and 1914.

Kautsky, in 1915 and even in November 1914, very emphatically attacked the fundamental ideas expressed in our definition of imperialism. Kautsky said that imperialism must not be regarded as a "phase" or stage of economy, but as a policy; a definite policy "preferred" by finance capital; that imperialism cannot be "identified" with "contemporary capitalism"; that if imperialism is to be understood to mean "all the phenomena of contemporary capitalism"—cartels, protection, the domination of the financiers and colonial policy—then the question as to whether imperialism is necessary to capitalism becomes reduced to the "flattest tautology"; because, in that case, "imperialism is naturally a vital necessity for capitalism," and so on. The best way to present Kautsky's ideas is to quote his own definition of imperialism, which is diametrically opposed to the substance of the ideas which we have set forth (for the objections coming from the camp of the German Marxists, who have been advocating such ideas for many years already, have been long known to Kautsky as the objections of a definite trend in Marxism).

Kautsky's definition is as follows:

> Imperialism is a product of highly developed industrial capitalism. It consists in the striving of every industrial capitalist nation to bring under its control and to annex increasingly big *agrarian* [Kautsky's italics] regions irrespective of what nations inhabit those regions.

This definition is utterly worthless because it one-sidedly, *i.e.,* arbitrarily, brings out the national question alone (although this is extremely important in itself as well as in its relation to imperialism), it arbitrarily and *inaccurately* relates this question *only* to industrial capital in the countries which annex other nations, and in an equally arbitrary and inaccurate manner brings out the annexation of agrarian regions.

Imperialism is a striving for annexations—this is what the *political* part of Kautsky's definition amounts to. It is correct, but very incomplete, for politically, imperialism is, in general, a striving towards violence and reaction. For the moment, however, we are interested in the *economic* aspect of the question, which Kautsky *himself* introduced into *his* definition. The inaccuracy of Kautsky's definition is strikingly obvious. The characteristic feature of imperialism is *not* industrial capital, *but* finance capital. It is not an accident that in France it was precisely the extraordinarily rapid development of *finance* capital, and the weakening of industrial capital, that, from 1880 onwards, gave rise to the extreme extension of annexationist (colonial) policy. The characteristic feature of imperialism is precisely that it strives to annex *not only* agricultural regions, but even highly industrialised regions (German appetite for Belgium; French appetite for Lorraine), because 1) the fact that the world is already divided up obliges those contemplating a *new* division to reach out for *any kind* of territory, and 2) because an essential feature of imperialism is the rivalry between a number of great powers in the striving for hegemony, *i.e.,* for the conquest of territory, not so much directly for themselves as to weaken the adversary and undermine *his* hegemony. (Belgium is chiefly necessary to Germany as a base for operations against England; England needs Bagdad as a base for operations against Germany, etc.)

Kautsky refers especially—and repeatedly—to English writers who, he alleges, have given a purely political meaning to the word "imperialism" in the sense that Kautsky understands it. We take up the work by the Englishman Hobson, *Imperialism,* which appeared in 1902, and therein we read:

> The new imperialism differs from the older, first, in substituting for the ambition of a single growing empire the theory and the practice of competing empires, each motivated by similar lusts of political aggrandisement and commercial gain; secondly, in the dominance of financial or investing over mercantile interests.

We see, therefore, that Kautsky is absolutely wrong in referring to English writers generally (unless he meant the vulgar English imperialist writers, or the avowed apologists for imperialism). We see that Kautsky, while claiming that he continues to defend Marxism, as a matter of fact takes a step backward compared with the *social-liberal* Hobson, who *more correctly* takes into account two "historically concrete" (Kautsky's definition is a mockery of historical concreteness) features of modern imperialism: 1) the competition between *several* imperialisms, and 2) the predominance of the financier over the merchant. If it were chiefly a question of the annexation of agrarian countries by industrial countries, the role of the merchant would be predominant.

Kautsky's definition is not only wrong and un-Marxian. It serves as a basis for a whole system of views which run counter to Marxian theory and Marxian practice all along the line. We shall refer to this again later. The argument about words which Kautsky raises as to whether the modern stage of capitalism should be called "imperialism" or "the stage of finance capital" is of no importance. Call it what you will, it matters little. The fact of the matter is that Kautsky detaches the politics of imperialism from its economics, speaks of annexations as being a policy "preferred" by finance capital, and opposes to it another bourgeois policy which, he alleges, is possible on this very basis of finance capital. According to his argument, monopolies in economics are compatible with non-monopolistic, non-violent, non-annexationist methods in politics. According to his argument, the territorial division of the world, which was completed precisely during the period of finance capital, and which constitutes the basis of the present peculiar forms of rivalry between the biggest capitalist states, is compatible with a non-imperialist policy. The result is a slurring-over and a blunting of the most profound contradictions of the latest stage of capitalism, instead of an exposure of their depth; the result is bourgeois reformism instead of Marxism.

Kautsky enters into controversy with the German apologist of imperialism and annexations, Cunow, who clumsily and cynically argues that: imperialism is modern capitalism, the development of capitalism is inevitable and progressive; therefore imperialism is progressive; therefore, we should cringe before and eulogise it. This is something like the caricature of Russian Marxism which the Narodniki drew in 1894–95. They used to argue as follows: if the Marxists believe that capitalism is inevitable in Russia, that it is progressive, then they ought to open a public-house and begin to implant capitalism! Kautsky's reply to Cunow is as follows: imperialism is not modern capitalism. It is only one of the forms of the policy of modern capitalism. This policy we can and should fight; we can and should fight against imperialism, annexations, etc.

The reply seems quite plausible, but in effect it is a more subtle and more disguised (and therefore more dangerous) propaganda of conciliation with imperialism; for unless it strikes at the economic basis of the trusts and banks, the "struggle" against the policy of the trusts and banks reduces itself to bourgeois reformism and pacifism, to an innocent and benevolent expression of pious hopes. Kautsky's theory means refraining from mentioning existing contradictions, forgetting the most important of them, instead of revealing them in their full depth; it is a theory that has nothing in common with Marxism. Naturally, such a "theory" can only serve the purpose of advocating unity with the Cunows.

Kautsky writes: "from the purely economic point of view it is not impossible that capitalism will yet go through a new phase, that of the extension of the policy of the cartels to foreign policy, the phase of ultra-imperialism," *i.e.,* of a super-imperialism, a union of world imperialisms and not struggles among imperialisms; a phase when wars shall cease under capitalism, a phase of "the joint exploitation of the world by internationally combined finance capital."

We shall have to deal with this "theory of ultra-imperialism" later on in order to show in detail how definitely and utterly it departs from Marxism. In keeping with the plan of the present work, we shall examine the exact economic data on this question. Is "ultra-imperialism" possible "from the purely economic point of view" or is it ultra-nonsense?

If, by purely economic point of view a "pure" abstraction is meant, then all that can be said reduces itself to the following proposition: evolution is proceeding towards monopoly; therefore the trend is towards a single world monopoly, to a universal trust. This is indisputable, but it is also as completely meaningless as is the statement that "evolution is proceeding" towards the manufacture of foodstuffs in laboratories. In this sense the "theory" of ultra-imperialism is no less absurd than a "theory of ultra-agriculture" would be.

If, on the other hand, we are discussing the "purely economic" conditions of the epoch of finance capital as an historically concrete epoch which opened at the beginning of the twentieth century, then the best reply that one can make to the lifeless abstractions of "ultra-imperialism" (which serve an exclusively reactionary aim: that of diverting attention from the depth of *existing* antagonisms) is to contrast them with the concrete economic realities of present-day world economy. Kautsky's utterly meaningless talk about ultra-imperialism encourages, among other things, that profoundly mistaken idea which only brings grist to the mill of the apologists of imperialism, *viz.*, that the rule of finance capital *lessens* the unevenness and contradictions inherent in world economy, whereas in reality it *increases* them.

R. Calwer, in his little book, *An Introduction to World Economics,* attempted to compile the main, purely economic, data required to understand in a concrete way the internal relations of world economy at the end of the nineteenth and beginning of the twentieth centuries. He divides the world into five "main economic areas," as follows: 1) Central Europe (the whole of Europe with the exception of Russia and Great Britain); 2) Great Britain; 3) Russia; 4) Eastern Asia; 5) America; he includes the colonies in the "areas" of the state to which they belong and "leaves out" a few countries not distributed according to areas, such as Persia, Afghanistan and Arabia in Asia; Morocco and Abyssinia in Africa, etc.

Here is a brief summary of the economic data he quotes on these regions:

Principal Economic Areas	*1 Central European*	*2 British*	*3 Russian*	*4 East Asian*	*5 American*
AREA *Million Sq. Km.*	27.6 (23.6) *	28.9 (28.6) †	22	12	30
POPULATION *Millions*	388 (146)	398 (355)	131	389	148
TRANSPORT *Railways* *Thous. Km.*	204	140	63	8	379
Mercantile Fleet *Million Tons*	8	11	1	1	6

* R. Calwer, *Einführung in die Weltwirtschaft*, Berlin, 1906.
† The figures in parentheses show the area and population of the colonies.

Principal Economic Areas	1 Central European	2 British	3 Russian	4 East Asian	5 American
TRADE					
Imports & Exports Billion Marks	41	25	3	2	14
INDUSTRY					
Output of Coal Million Tons	251	249	16	8	245
Output of Pig Iron Million Tons	15	9	3	0.02	14
No. of Cotton Spindles Millions	26	51	7	2	19

We notice three areas of highly developed capitalism with a high development of means of transport, of trade and of industry, the Central European, the British and the American areas. Among these are three states which dominate the world: Germany, Great Britain, the United States. Imperialist rivalry and the struggle between these countries have become very keen because Germany has only a restricted area and few colonies (the creation of "Central Europe" is still a matter for the future; it is being born in the midst of desperate struggles). For the moment the distinctive feature of Europe is political disintegration. In the British and American areas, on the other hand, political concentration is very highly developed, but there is a tremendous disparity between the immense colonies of the one and the insignificant colonies of the other. In the colonies, capitalism is only beginning to develop. The struggle for South America is becoming more and more acute.

There are two areas where capitalism is not strongly developed: Russia and Eastern Asia. In the former, the density of population is very low, in the latter it is very high; in the former political concentration is very high, in the latter it does not exist. The partition of China is only beginning, and the struggle between Japan, U.S.A., etc., in connection therewith is continually gaining in intensity.

Compare this reality, the vast diversity of economic and political conditions, the extreme disparity in the rate of development of the various countries, etc., and the violent struggles of the imperialist states, with Kautsky's silly little fable about "peaceful" ultra-imperialism. Is this not the reactionary attempt of a frightened philistine to hide from stern reality? Are not the international cartels which Kautsky imagines are the embryos of "ultra-imperialism" (with as much reason as one would have for describing the manufacture of tabloids in a laboratory as ultra-agriculture in embryo) an example of the division and the *redivision* of the world, the transition from peaceful division to non-peaceful division and *vice versa?* Is not American and other finance capital, which divided the whole world peacefully, with Germany's participation, for example, in the international rail syndicate, or in the international mercantile shipping trust, now engaged in *redividing* the world on the basis of a new relation of forces, which has been changed by methods *by no means* peaceful?

Finance capital and the trusts are increasing instead of diminishing the differences in the rate of development of the various parts of world economy. When the relation of forces is changed, how else, *under capitalism,* can the solution of contradictions be found, except by resorting to *violence?* Railway statistics provide remarkably exact data on the different rates of development of capitalism and finance capital in world economy. In the last decades of imperialist development, the total length of railways has changed as follows:

R A I L W A Y S (*Thousand Kilometres*)

	1890	1913	INCREASE
Europe	224	346	122
U.S.A.	268	411	143
Colonies (*total*)	82 ⎱	210 ⎱	128 ⎱
Independent and semi-dependent states of Asia and America	43 ⎰ 125	137 ⎰ 347	94 ⎰ 222
Total	617	1,104	

Thus, the development of railways has been more rapid in the colonies and in the independent (and semi-dependent) states of Asia and America. Here, as we know, the finance capital of the four or five biggest capitalist states reigns undisputed. Two hundred thousand kilometres of new railways in the colonies and in the other countries of Asia and America represent more than 40,000,000,000 marks in capital, newly invested on particularly advantageous terms, with special guarantees of a good return and with profitable orders for steel works, etc., etc.

Capitalism is growing with the greatest rapidity in the colonies and in overseas countries. Among the latter, *new* imperialist powers are emerging (*e.g.,* Japan). The struggle of world imperialism is becoming more acute. The tribute levied by finance capital on the most profitable colonial and overseas enterprises is increasing. In sharing out this "booty," an exceptionally large part goes to countries which, as far as the development of productive forces is concerned, do not always stand at the top of the list. In the case of the biggest countries, considered with their colonies, the total length of railways was as follows (in thousands of kilometres):

	1890	1913	INCREASE
U.S.A.	268	413	145
British Empire	107	208	101
Russia	32	78	46
Germany	43	68	25
France	41	63	22
Total	491	830	339

Thus, about 80 per cent of the total existing railways are concentrated in the hands of the five Great Powers. But the concentration of the *ownership* of these railways, of finance capital, is much greater still: French and English millionaires, for example, own an enormous amount of stocks and bonds in American, Russian and other railways.

Thanks to her colonies, Great Britain has increased the length of "her" railways by 100,000 kilometres, four times as much as Germany. And yet, it is well known that the development of productive forces in Germany, and especially the development of the coal and iron industries, has been much more rapid during this period than in England—not to mention France and Russia. In 1892, Germany produced 4,900,000 tons of pig iron and Great Britain produced 6,800,000 tons; in 1912, Germany produced 17,600,000 tons and Great Britain 9,000,000 tons. Germany, therefore, had an overwhelming superiority over England in this respect. We ask, is there *under capitalism* any means of removing the disparity between the development of productive forces and the accumulation of capital on the one side, and the division of colonies and "spheres of influence" for finance capital on the other side—other than by resorting to war?

2 The Economic Element

The most obvious motive for imperialism, economic gain, has not been neglected by theorists. Such contemporary proponents of empire as the English businessman and Liberal politician Joseph Chamberlain were not ashamed to admit to such a purpose. In the following selection he offers other practical advantages of empire as well. The speech was delivered to a sympathetic audience at Glasgow on October 6, 1903.

FROM *Imperial Union and Tariff Reform*

BY JOSEPH CHAMBERLAIN

MY FIRST DUTY is to thank this great and representative audience for having offered to me an opportunity of explaining for the first time in some detail the views which I hold upon the subject of our fiscal policy (cheers). I would desire no better platform than this ("Hear, hear," and cheers). I am in a great city, the second of the Empire; the city which by the enterprise and intelligence which it has always shown is entitled to claim something of a representative character in respect of British industry (cheers). I am in that city in which Free Trade took its birth ("hear, hear"), in that city in which Adam Smith taught so long, and where he was one of my most distinguished predecessors in the great office of Lord Rector of your University (cheers) which it will always be to me a great honour to have filled. Adam Smith was a great man. It was not given to him, it never has been given to mortals to foresee all the changes that may occur in something like a century and a half, but with a broad and far-seeing intelligence which is not common among men, Adam Smith did at any rate anticipate many of our modern conditions, and when I read his books I see how even then he was aware of the importance of home markets as compared with foreign ("hear, hear"); how he advocated retaliation under certain conditions; how he supported the

Joseph Chamberlain, *Imperial Union and Tariff Reform* (1903), pp. 19–34.

Navigation Laws; how he was the author of a sentence which we ought never to forget, that "Defence is greater than opulence" (cheers). When I remember, also, how he, entirely before his time, pressed for reciprocal trade between our Colonies and the Mother Country, I say he had a broader mind, a more Imperial conception of the duties of the citizens of a great Empire, than some of those who have taught also as professors (laughter and cheers), and who claim to be his successors (renewed laughter and cheering). Ladies and gentlemen, I am not afraid to come here (cheers, and a voice "Bravo!") to the home of Adam Smith, and to combat free imports (cheers), and still less am I afraid to preach to you preference with our Colonies ("hear, hear" and cheers)—to you in this great city whose whole prosperity has been founded upon its colonial relations (cheers). But I must not think only of the city, I must think of the country. It is known to every man that Scotland has contributed out of all proportion to its population to build up the great Empire of which we are all so proud—an Empire which took genius and capacity and courage to create ("hear, hear")—and which requires now genius and capacity and courage to maintain (loud cheers).

I do not regard this as a party meeting. I am no longer a party leader (laughter). I am an outsider (renewed laughter), and it is not my intention —I do not think it would be right—to raise any exclusively party issues. But after what has occurred in the last few days, after the meeting at Sheffield (cheers), a word or two may be forgiven to me, who, although no longer a leader, am still a loyal servant of the party to which I belong (cheers).

I say to you, ladies and gentlemen, that that party whose continued existence, whose union, whose strength I still believe to be essential to the welfare of the country and to the welfare of the Empire (cheers), has found a leader whom every member may be proud to follow (loud cheers). Mr. Balfour (cheers), in his position has responsibilities which he cannot share with us, but no one will contest his right—a right to which his high office, his ability, and his character alike entitle him—to declare the official policy of the party which he leads ("hear, hear"), to fix its limits, to settle the time at which application shall be given to the principles which he has put forward (loud cheers). For myself, I agree with the principles that he has stated. I approve of the policy to which he proposes to give effect, and I admire the courage and the resource with which he faces difficulties which even in our varied political history have hardly ever been surpassed ("hear, hear"). It ought not to be necessary to say any more. But it seems as though in this country there have always been men who do not know what loyalty and friendship mean ("hear, hear"), and to them I say that nothing that they can do will have the slightest influence or will affect in the slightest degree the friendship and confidence which exist and have existed for so many years between the Prime Minister and myself (loud cheers). Let them do their worst. Their insinuations pass us by like the idle wind, and I would say to my friends, to those who support me in the great struggle on which I have entered, I would say to them also, I beg of you to give no encouragement to these mean and libellous insinuations. Understand that in no conceivable circumstances will I allow myself to be put in any sort of competition, direct or indirect, with my friend and leader, whom I mean to follow (cheers). What is my position? I have invited a discussion upon a question which comes peculiarly within my province, owing to the office which I have so recently held. I have invited discussion upon it. I have not pretended that a matter of this importance is to be settled offhand. I have been well aware that the country has to be educated, as I myself have had to be educated before I saw, or could see, all the bearings of this great matter; and therefore I take up the position of a pioneer. I go in front of the army, and if the army is attacked, I go back to it (loud and prolonged cheers).

Meanwhile, putting aside all these personal and party questions, I ask my countrymen, without regard to any political opinions which they may have hitherto held, to consider the greatest of all great questions that can be put before the country, to consider it impartially if possible, and to come to a decision—and it is possible—I am always an optimist (laughter)—it is possible that the nation may be prepared to go a little further than the official programme ("hear, hear," and cheers). I have known them to do it before (laughter), and no harm has come to the party; no harm that I know has come to those who as scouts, or pioneers, or investigators, or discoverers have gone a little before it. Well, one of my objects in coming here is to find an answer to this question. Is the country prepared to go a little further? (Cries of "Yes," and cheers.)

I suppose that there are differences in Scotland, differences in Glasgow, as there are certainly in the southern country, but those differences, I hope, are mainly differences as to methods ("hear, hear"). For I cannot conceive that, so far as regards the majority of the country at any rate, there can be any differences as to our objects. What are our objects? They are two. In the first place, we all desire the maintenance and increase of the national strength and the prosperity of the United Kingdom (cheers). That may be a selfish desire; but in my mind it carries with it something more than mere selfishness. You cannot expect foreigners to take the same views as we of our position and duty. To my mind Britain has played a great part in the past in the history of the world, and for that reason I wish Britain to continue (cheers). Then, in the second place, our object is, or should be, the realisation of the greatest ideal which has ever inspired statesmen in any country or in any age—the creation of an Empire such as the world has never seen (loud cheers). We have to cement the union of the States beyond the seas; we have to consolidate the British race; we have to meet the clash of competition, commercial now—sometimes in the past it has been otherwise—it may be again in the future. Whatever it be, whatever danger threatens, we have to meet it no longer as an isolated country; we have to meet it fortified and strengthened, and buttressed by all those of our kinsmen, all those powerful and continually rising States which speak our common tongue and glory in our common flag (cheers).

Those are two great objects, and, as I have said, we all should have them in view. How are we to attain them? In the first place, let me say one word as to the method in which this discussion is to be carried on. Surely it should be treated in a manner worthy of its magnitude, worthy of the dignity of the theme ("hear, hear"). For my part I disclaim any imputation of evil motive and unworthy motive on the part of those who may happen to disagree with me; and I claim equal consideration from them ("hear, hear"). I claim that this matter should be treated on its merits—without personal feeling, personal bitterness, and, if possible, without entering upon questions of purely party controversy (cheers), and I do that for the reason I have given; but also because, if you are to make a change in a system which has existed for nearly sixty years, which affects more or less every man, woman, and child in the kingdom, you can only make that change successfully if you have behind you not merely a party support—if you do not attempt to force it by a small majority on a large and unwilling minority, but if it becomes, as I believe it will become (cheers), a national policy in consonance with the feelings, the aspirations, and the interests of the overwhelming proportion of the country (cheers).

I was speaking just now of the characteristics of Glasgow as a great city; I am not certain whether I mentioned that I believe it is one of the most prosperous of cities, that it has had a great and continuous prosperity; and if that be so, here, more than anywhere else, I have to answer the question, Why cannot you let well alone? ("Hear, hear.") Well, I have been in Venice —the beautiful city of the Adriatic—which had at one time a commercial supremacy quite as great in proportion as anything we have ever enjoyed. Its glories have departed; but what I was going to say was that when I was there last I saw the great tower of the Campanile rising above the city which it had overshadowed for centuries, and looking as though it was as permanent as the city itself. And yet the other day, in a few minutes, the whole structure fell to the ground. Nothing was left of it but a mass of ruin and rubbish. I do not say to you, gentlemen, that I anticipate any catastrophe so great or so sudden for British trade; but I do say to you that I see signs of decay; that I see cracks and crevices in the walls of the great structure; that I know that the foundations upon which it has been raised are not broad enough or deep enough to sustain it (cheers). Now, do I do wrong, if I know this—if I even think I know it—do I do wrong to warn you? Is it not a most strange and inconsistent thing that while certain people are indicting the Government in language which, to say the least of it, is extravagant, for not having been prepared for the great war from which we have recently emerged with success (cheers)—is it not strange that these same people should be denouncing me in language equally extravagant because I want to prepare you now, while there is time, for a struggle greater in its consequences than that to which I have referred (hear, hear)—a struggle from which, if we emerge defeated, this country will lose its place, will no longer count among the great nations of the world—a struggle which we are asked to meet with antiquated weapons and with old-fashioned tactics? (Cheers.)

I tell you that it is not well to-day with British industry ("hear, hear"). We have been going through a period of great expansion. The whole world has been prosperous. I see signs of a change, but let that pass. When the change comes I think even the Free Fooders will be converted (laughter). But meanwhile, what are the facts? The year 1900 was the record year of British trade. The exports were the largest we had ever known. The year 1902—last year—was nearly as good, and yet, if you will compare your trade in 1872, thirty years ago, with the trade of 1902—the export trade—you will find that there has been a moderate increase of twenty-two millions. That, I think, is something like 7½ per cent. Meanwhile, the population has increased 30 per cent. Can you go on supporting your population at that rate of increase, when even in the best of years you can only show so much smaller an increase in your foreign trade? The actual increase was twenty-two millions under our Free Trade. In the same time the increase in the United States of America was 110 millions, and the increase in Germany was fifty-six millions. In the United Kingdom our export trade has been practically stagnant for thirty years. It went down in the interval. It has now gone up in the most prosperous times. In the most prosperous times it is hardly better than it was thirty years ago.

Meanwhile the protected countries which you have been told, and which I myself at one time believed, were going rapidly to wreck and ruin, have progressed in a much greater proportion than ours. That is not all; not merely the amount of your trade remained stagnant, but the character of your trade has changed. When Mr. Cobden preached his doctrine, he believed, as he had at that time considerable reason to suppose, that while foreign countries would supply us with our food-stuffs and raw materials, we should remain the mart of the world, and should send them in exchange our manufactures. But that is exactly what we have not done. On the contrary, in the period to which I have referred, we are sending less and less of our manufactures to them, and they are sending more and more of their manufactures to us (cheers).

I know how difficult it is for a great meeting like this to follow figures. I shall give you as few as I can, but I must give you some to lay the basis of my argument. I have had a table constructed, and upon that table I would be willing to base the whole of my contention. I will take some figures from it. You have to analyse your trade. It is not merely a question of amount; you have to consider of what it is composed. Now what has been the case with regard to our manufactures? Our existence as a nation depends upon our manufacturing capacity and production. We are not essentially or mainly an agricultural country. That can never be the main source of our prosperity. We are a great manufacturing country. In 1872, we sent to the protected countries of Europe and to the United States of America, £116,000,000 of exported manufactures. In 1882, ten years later, it fell to £88,000,000. In 1892, ten years later, it fell to £75,000,000. In 1902, last year, although the general exports had increased, the exports of manufactures to these countries had decreased again to £73,500,000, and the total result of this is that, after thirty years, you are sending £42,500,000 of manufactures less to the great protected countries than you did thirty years ago (cheers). Then there are the neutral countries, that is, the countries which, although they may have tariffs, have no manufactures, and therefore the tariffs are not protective— such countries as Egypt and China, and South America, and similar places. Our exports of manufactures have not fallen in these markets to any considerable extent. They have practically remained the same, but on the whole they have fallen £3,500,000. Adding that to the loss in the protected countries, and you have lost altogether in your exports of manufactures £46,000,-000.

How is it that that has not impressed the people before now? Because the change has been concealed by our statistics. I do not say they have not shown it, because you could have picked it out, but they are not put in a form which is understanded of the people. You have failed to observe that the maintenance of your trade is dependent entirely on British possessions. While to these foreign countries your export of manufactures has declined by £46,000,000, to your British possessions it has increased £40,000,000 (cheers), and at the present time your trade with the Colonies and British possessions is larger in amount, very much larger in amount, and very much more valuable in the categories I have named, than our trade with the whole of Europe and the United States of America. It is much larger than our trade to those neutral countries of which I have spoken, and it remains at the present day the most rapidly increasing, the most important, the most valuable of the whole of our trade (cheers). One more comparison. During this period of thirty years in which our exports of manufactures have fallen £46,000,000 to foreign countries, what has happened as regards their exports of manufactures to us? They have risen from £63,000,000 in 1872 to £149,000,000 in 1902. They have increased £86,000,000. That may be all right. I am not for the moment saying whether that is right or wrong, but when people say that we ought to hold exactly the same opinion about things that our ancestors did, my reply is that I daresay we should do so if circumstances had remained the same (cheers).

But now, if I have been able to make these figures clear, there is one thing which follows—that is, that our Imperial trade is absolutely essential to our prosperity at the present time ("hear, hear"). If that trade declines, or if it does not increase in proportion to our population and to the loss of trade with foreign countries, then we sink at once into a fifth-rate nation (cheers). Our fate will be the fate of the empires and kingdoms of the past. We shall have reached our highest point, and indeed I am not certain that there are some of my opponents who do not regard that with absolute complacency (laughter). I do not (loud cheers). As I have said, I have the misfortune to be an optimist. I do not believe in the setting of the British star (cheers), but then, I do not believe in the folly of the British people (laughter). I trust them. I trust the working classes of this country (cheers), and I have confidence that they who are our masters, electorally speaking, will have the intelligence to see that they must wake up. They must modify their policy to suit new conditions. They must meet those conditions with altogether a new policy (cheers).

I have said that if our Imperial trade declines we decline. My second point is this. It will decline inevitably unless while there is still time we take the necessary steps to preserve it ("hear, hear"). Have you ever considered why it is that Canada takes so much more of the products of British manufacturers than the United States of America does per head? When you answer that, I have another conundrum (laughter). Why does Australia take about three times as much per head as Canada? And to wind up, why does South Africa—the white population of South Africa—take more per head than Australasia? When you have got to the bottom of that—and it is not difficult—you will see the whole argument. These countries are all protective countries. I see that the Labour leaders, or some of them, in this country are saying that the interest of the working class is to maintain our present system of free imports. The moment those men go to the Colonies they change. I will undertake to say that no one of them has ever been there for six months without singing a different tune (laughter). The vast majority of the working men in all the Colonies are Protectionists, and I am not inclined to accept the easy explanation that they are all fools (laughter). I do not understand why an intelligent man—a man who is intelligent in this country—becomes an idiot when he goes to Australasia (laughter). But I will tell you what he does do. He gets rid of a good number of old-world prejudices and superstitions (laughter). I say they are Protectionist, all these countries. Now, what is the history of Protection? In the first place a tariff is imposed. There are no industries, or practically none, but only a tariff; then gradually industries grow up behind the tariff wall. In the first place they are primary industries, the industries for which the country has natural aptitude or for which it has some special advantage—mineral or other resources. Then when those are established the secondary industries spring up, first the necessaries, then the luxuries, until at last all the ground is covered. These countries of which I have been speaking to you are in different stages of the protective process. In America the process has been completed. She produces everything; she excludes everything (laughter). There is no trade to be done with her beyond a paltry 6s. per head. Canada has been protective for a long time. The protective policy has produced its natural result. The principal industries are there, and you can never get rid of them. They will be there for ever, but up to the present time the secondary industries have not been created, and there is an immense deal of trade that is still open to you, that you may still retain, that you may increase. In Australasia the industrial position is still less advanced. The agricultural products of the country have been first of all developed. Accordingly, Australasia takes more from you per head than Canada. In South Africa there are, practically speaking, no industries at all.

Now, I ask you to suppose that we intervene in any stage of the process. We can do it now. We might have done it with greater effect ten years ago ("hear, hear"). Whether we can do it with any effect or at all twenty years hence I am very doubtful. We can intervene now. We can say to our great Colonies: "We understand your views and conditions. We do not attempt to dictate to you. We do not think ourselves superior to you. We have taken the trouble to learn your objections, to appreciate and sympathise with your policy. We know that you are right in saying you will not always be content to be what the Americans call a one-horse country, with a single industry and no diversity of employment. We can see that you are right not to neglect what Providence has given you in the shape of mineral or other resources. We understand and we appreciate the wisdom of your statesmen when they say they will not allow their country to be solely dependent on foreign supplies for the necessities of life. We understand all that, and therefore we will not propose to you anything that is unreasonable or contrary to this policy, which we know is deep in your hearts; but we will say to you, 'After all, there are many things which you do not now make, many things for which we have a great capacity of production—leave them to us as you have left them hitherto. Do not increase your tariff walls against us. Pull them down where they are unnecessary to the success of this policy to which you are committed. Do that because we are kinsmen—without injury to any important interest—because it is good for the Empire as a whole, and because we have taken the first step and have set you the example ("hear, hear"). We offer you a preference; we rely on your patriotism, your affection, that we shall not be losers thereby' " (cheers).

Now, suppose that we had made an offer of that kind—I won't say to the Colonies, but to Germany, to the United States of America—ten or twenty years ago. Do you suppose that we should not have been able to retain a great deal of what we have now lost and cannot recover? (Cheers.)

I will give you an illustration. America is the strictest of protective nations. It has a tariff which to me is an abomination. It is so immoderate, so unreasonable, so unnecessary, that, though America has profited enormously under it, yet I think it has been carried to excessive lengths, and I believe now that a great number of intelligent Americans would gladly negotiate with us for its reduction. But until very recent times even this immoderate tariff left to us a great trade. It left to us the tin-plate trade, and the American tin-plate trade amounted to millions per annum, and gave employment to thousands of British workpeople. If we had gone to America ten or twenty years ago and had said, "If you will leave the tin-plate trade as it is, put no duty on tin-plate—you have never had to complain either of our quality or our price—we in return will give you some advantage on some articles which you produce," we might have kept the tin-plate trade ("hear, hear"). It would not have been worth America's while to put a duty on an article for which it had no particular or special aptitude or capacity. If we had gone to Germany in the same sense there are hundreds of articles which are now made in Germany which are sent to this country, which are taking the place of goods employing British labour, which they might have left to us in return for our concessions to them.

We did not take that course. We were not prepared for it as a people. We allowed matters to drift. Are we going to let them drift now? ("No.") Are we going to lose the colonial trade? (Cries of "No.") This is the parting of the ways. You have to remember that if you do not take this opportunity it will not recur (cheers). If you do not take it I predict, and I predict with certainty, that Canada will fall to the level of the United States, that Australia will fall to the level of Canada, that South Africa will fall to the level of Australia, and that will only be the beginning of the general decline which will deprive you of your most important customers, of your most rapidly increasing trade (cheers). I think that I have some reason to speak with authority on this subject. The Colonies are prepared to meet us (cheers). In return for a very moderate preference they will give us a substantial advantage. They will give us in the first place, I believe they will reserve to us, much at any rate of the trade which we already enjoy. They will not—and I would not urge them for a moment to do so—they will not injure those of their industries which have already been created. They will maintain them, they will not allow them to be destroyed or injured even by our competition, but outside that there is still a great margin, a margin which has given us this enormous increase of trade to which I have referred. That margin I believe we can permanently retain ("hear, hear")—and I ask you to think, if that is of so much importance to us now, when we have only eleven millions of white fellow-citizens in these distant Colonies, what will it be when in the course of a period which is a mere moment of time in the history of States, what will it be when that population is forty millions or more? ("Hear, hear.") Is it not worth while to consider whether the actual trade which you may retain, whether the enormous potential trade which you and your descendants may enjoy, be not worth a sacrifice, if sacrifice be required? ("Hear, hear.") But they will do a great deal more for you. This is certain. Not only will they enable you to retain the trade which you have, but they are ready to give you preference on all the trade which is now done with them by foreign competitors (cheers). I never see any appreciation by the free importers of the magnitude of this trade. It will increase. It has increased greatly in thirty years, and if it goes on with equally rapid strides we shall be ousted by foreign competition, if not by protective tariffs, from our Colonies. It amounts at the present time to £47,000,000. But it is said that a great part of that £47,000,000 is in goods which we cannot supply. That is true, and with regard to that portion of the trade we have no interest in any preferential tariff, but it has been calculated, and I believe it to be accurate, that £26,000,000 a year of that trade might come to this country which now goes to Germany and France and other foreign countries, if reasonable preference were given to British manufactures (cheers). What does that mean? The Board of Trade assumes that of manufactured goods one-half the value is expended in labour—I think it is a great deal more, but take the Board of Trade figures—£13,000,000 a year of new employment. What does that mean to the United Kingdom? It means the employment of 166,000 men at 30s. a week (cheers). It means the subsistence, if you include their families, of 830,000 persons; and now, if you will only add to that our present export to the British possessions of £96,000,000, you will find that that gives, on the same calculation, £48,000,000 for wages, or employment at 30s. a week to 615,000 workpeople, and it finds subsistence for 3,075,000 persons ("hear, hear"). In other words, your Colonial trade as it stands at present with the prospective advantage of a preference against the foreigner means employment and fair wages for three-quarters of a million of workmen, and subsistence for nearly four millions of our population (cheers).

Ladies and gentlemen, I feel deeply sensible that the argument I have addressed to you is one of those which will be described by the Leader of the Opposition as a squalid argument (laughter). A squalid argument! I have appealed to your interests, I have come here as a man of business (loud cheers), I have appealed to the employers and the employed alike in this great city. I have endeavoured to point out to them that their trade, their wages, all depend on the maintenance of this Colonial trade, of which some of my opponents speak with such contempt, and, above all, with such egregious ignorance (loud laughter and cheers). But now I abandon that line of argument for the moment, and appeal to something higher, which I believe is in your hearts as it is in mine. I appeal to you as fellow-citizens of the greatest Empire that the world has ever known; I appeal to you to recognise that the privileges of Empire bring with them great responsibilities (cheers). I want to ask you to think what this Empire means, what it is to you and your descendants. I will not speak, or, at least, I will not dwell, on its area, greater than that which has been under one dominion in the history of the world. I will not speak of its population, of the hundreds of millions of men for whom we have made ourselves responsible. But I will speak of its variety, and of the fact that here we have an Empire which with decent organisation and consolidation might be absolutely self-sustaining (loud cheers). Nothing of the kind has ever been known before. There is no article of your food, there is no raw material of your trade, there is no necessity of your lives, no luxury of your existence which cannot be produced somewhere or other in the British Empire, if the British Empire holds together, and if we who have inherited it are worthy of our opportunities.

There is another product of the British Empire, that is, men (cheers). You have not forgotten the advantage, the encouragement, which can be given by the existence of loyal men (cheers), inhabitants, indeed, of distant States, but still loyal to the common flag (cheers). It is not so long since these men, when the old country was in straits, rushed to her assistance (cheers). No persuasion was necessary; it was a voluntary movement. That was not a squalid assistance (loud cheers). They had no special interest. They were interested indeed, as sons of the Empire. If they had been separate States they would have had no interest at all. They came to our assistance and proved themselves indeed men of the old stock (cheers); they proved themselves worthy of the best traditions of the British army (cheers), and gave us an assistance, a material assistance, which was invaluable. They gave us moral support which was even more grateful (loud cheers). That is the result of Empire (cheers). I should be wrong if, in referring to our white fellow-subjects, I did not also say, that in addition to them, if any straits befell us, there are millions and hundreds of millions of men born in tropical climes, and of races very different from ours, who, although they were prevented by political considerations from taking part in our recent struggle, would be in any death-throe of the Empire (loud cheers) equally eager to show their loyalty and their devotion (cheers). Now, is such a dominion, are such traditions, is such a glorious inheritance, is such a splendid sentiment—are they worth preserving? (Cheers.) They have cost us much. They have cost much in blood and treasure; and in past times, as in recent, many of our best and noblest have given their lives, or risked their lives, for this great ideal. But it has also done much for us. It has ennobled our national life, it has discouraged that petty parochialism which is the defect of all small communities. I say to you that all that is best in our present life, best in this Britain of ours, all of which we have the right to be most proud, is due to the fact that we are not only sons of Britain, but we are sons of Empire. I do not think, I am not likely to do you the injustice to believe, that you would make this sacrifice fruitless, that you would make all this endeavour vain. But if you want to complete it, remember that each generation in turn has to do its part, and you are called to take your share in this great work. Others have founded the Empire; it is yours to build firmly and permanently the great edifice of which others have laid the foundation (cheers). And I believe we have got to change somewhat our rather insular habits. When I have been in the Colonies I have told them that they are too provincial, but I think we are too provincial also. We think too much of ourselves ("hear, hear"), and we forget—and it is necessary we should remember—that we are only part of a larger whole ("hear, hear"). And when I speak of our Colonies, it is an expression; they are not ours—they are not ours in a possessory sense. They are sister States, able to treat with us from an equal position, able to hold to us, willing to hold to us, but also able to break with us. I have had eight years' experience (cheers). I have been in communication with many of the men, statesmen, orators, writers, distinguished in our Colonies. I have had intimate conversation with them. I have tried to understand them and I think I do understand them (cheers), and I say that none of them desire separation. There are none of them who are not loyal to this idea of Empire which they say they wish us to accept more fully in the future, but I have found none who do not believe that our present colonial relations cannot be permanent. We must either draw closer together or we shall drift apart.

3 The Mission of Empire

At least some imperialists were moved by motives that were not economic. Honor, decency, responsibility, and uplift were all offered as reasons for empire.

The White Man's Burden BY RUDYARD KIPLING

1899

(The United States and the Philippine Islands)

Take up the White Man's burden—
  Send forth the best ye breed—
Go bind your sons to exile
  To serve your captives' need;
To wait in heavy harness
  On fluttered folk and wild—
Your new-caught, sullen peoples,
  Half devil and half child.

Take up the White Man's Burden—
  In patience to abide,
To veil the threat of terror
  And check the show of pride;
By open speech and simple,
  An hundred times made plain,
To seek another's profit,
  And work another's gain.

Take up the White Man's burden—
  The savage wars of peace—
Fill full the mouth of Famine
  And bid the sickness cease;

And when your goal is nearest
   The end for others sought,
Watch Sloth and heathen Folly
   Bring all your hope to nought.

Take up the White Man's burden—
   No tawdry rule of kings,
But toil of serf and sweeper—
   The tale of common things.
The ports ye shall not enter,
   The roads ye shall not tread,
Go make them with your living,
   And mark them with your dead!

Take up the White Man's burden—
   And reap his old reward:
The blame of those ye better,
   The hate of those ye guard—
The cry of hosts ye humour
   (Ah, slowly!) toward the light:—
"Why brought ye us from bondage,
   "Our loved Egyptian night?"

Take up the White Man's burden—
   Ye dare not stoop to less—
Nor call too loud on Freedom
   To cloak your weariness;
By all ye cry or whisper,
   By all ye leave or do,
The silent, sullen peoples
   Shall weigh your Gods and you.

Take up the White Man's burden—
   Have done with childish days—
The lightly proffered laurel,
   The easy, ungrudged praise.
Comes now, to search your manhood
   Through all the thankless years,
Cold-edged with dear-bought wisdom,
   The judgment of your peers!

4　Race and Christianity

The advocates of imperialism included men convinced that the domination of backward areas by the more developed nations was a duty imposed upon the advanced countries by their racial superiority. According to the American clergyman Josiah Strong the Anglo-Saxon race, and especially the American branch of it, was morally bound to bring the message of Christianity and individual liberty to less favored peoples.

FROM *Our Country* BY JOSIAH STRONG

EVERY RACE WHICH HAS DEEPLY IMPRESSED ITSELF on the human family has been the representative of some great idea—one or more—which has given direction to the nation's life and form to its civilization. Among the Egyptians this seminal idea was life, among the Persians it was light, among the Hebrews it was purity, among the Greeks it was beauty, among the Romans it was law. The Anglo-Saxon is the representative of two great ideas, which are closely related. One of them is that of civil liberty. Nearly all of the civil liberty in the world is enjoyed by Anglo-Saxons: the English, the British colonists, and the people of the United States. To some, like the Swiss, it is permitted by the sufferance of their neighbors; others, like the French, have experimented with it; but, in modern times, the peoples whose love of liberty has won it, and whose genius for self-government has preserved it, have been Anglo-Saxons. The noblest races have always been lovers of liberty. That love ran strong in early German blood, and has profoundly influenced the institutions of all the branches of the great German family; but it was left for the Anglo-Saxon branch fully to recognize the right of the individual to himself, and formally to declare it the foundation stone of government.

The other great idea of which the Anglo-Saxon is the exponent is that of a pure *spiritual* Christianity. It was no accident that the great reformation of the sixteenth century originated among a Teutonic, rather than a Latin

Josiah Strong, *Our Country* (1885), pp. 159–62, 165, 172–80.

people. It was the fire of liberty burning in the Saxon heart that flamed up against the absolutism of the Pope. Speaking roughly, the peoples of Europe which are Celtic are Catholic, and those which are Teutonic are Protestant; and where the Teutonic race was purest, there Protestantism spread with the greatest rapidity. But, with rare and beautiful exceptions, Protestantism on the continent has degenerated into mere formalism. By confirmation at a certain age, the state churches are filled with members who generally know nothing of a personal spiritual experience. In obedience to a military order, a regiment of German soldiers files into church and partakes of the sacrament, just as it would shoulder arms or obey any other word of command. It is said that, in Berlin and Leipsic, only a little over one per cent. of the Protestant population are found in church. Protestantism on the continent seems to be about as poor in spiritual life and power as Catholicism. That means that most of the spiritual Christianity in the world is found among Anglo-Saxons and their converts; for this is the great missionary race. If we take all of the German missionary societies together, we find that, in the number of workers and amount of contributions, they do not equal the smallest of the three great English missionary societies. The year that Congregationalists in the United States gave one dollar and thirty-seven cents per caput to foreign missions, the members of the great German State Church gave only three-quarters of a cent per caput to the same cause. Evidently it is chiefly to the English and American peoples that we must look for the evangelization of the world.

It is not necessary to argue to those for whom I write that the two great needs of mankind, that all men may be lifted up into the light of the highest Christian civilization, are, first, a pure, spiritual Christianity, and, second, civil liberty. Without controversy, these are the forces which, in the past, have contributed most to the elevation of the human race, and they must continue to be, in the future, the most efficient ministers to its progress. It follows, then, that the Anglo-Saxon, as the great representative of these two ideas, the depository of these two greatest blessings, sustains peculiar relations to the world's future, is divinely commissioned to be, in a peculiar sense, his brother's keeper. Add to this the fact of his rapidly increasing strength in modern times, and we have well nigh a demonstration of his destiny. In 1700 this race numbered less than 6,000,000 souls. In 1800, Anglo-Saxons (I use the term somewhat broadly to include all English-speaking peoples) had increased to about 20,500,000, and in 1880 they numbered nearly 100,000,000, having multiplied almost five-fold in eighty years. At the end of the reign of Charles II. the English colonists in America numbered 200,000. During these two hundred years, our population has increased two hundred and fifty-fold. And the expansion of this race has been no less remarkable than its multiplication. In one century the United States has increased its territory ten-fold, while the enormous acquisition of foreign territory by Great Britain—and chiefly within the last hundred years—is wholly unparalleled in history. This mighty Anglo-Saxon race, though comprising only one-fifteenth part of mankind, now rules more than one-third of the earth's surface, and more than one-fourth of its people. And if this race, while growing from 6,000,000 to 100,000,000, thus gained possession of a third portion of the earth, is it to be supposed that when it numbers 1,000,000,000, it will lose the disposition, or lack the power to extend its sway? . . . It is not unlikely that, before the close of the next century, this race will outnumber all the other civilized races of the world. Does it not look as if God were not only preparing in our Anglo-Saxon civilization the die with which to stamp the peoples of the earth, but as if he were also massing behind that die the mighty power with which to press it? My confidence that this race is eventually to give its civilization to mankind is not based on mere numbers —China forbid! I look forward to what the world has never yet seen united in the same race; viz., the greatest numbers, *and* the highest civilization.

*   *   *

It may be easily shown, and is of no small significance, that the two great ideas of which the Anglo-Saxon is the exponent are having a fuller development in the United States than in Great Britain. There the union of Church and State tends strongly to paralyze some of the members of the body of Christ. Here there is no such influence to destroy spiritual life and power. Here, also, has been evolved the form of government consistent with the largest possible civil liberty. Furthermore, it is significant that the marked characteristics of this race are being here emphasized most. Among the most striking features of the Anglo-Saxon is his money-making power—a power of increasing importance in the widening commerce of the world's future. . . . although England is by far the richest nation of Europe, we have already outstripped her in the race after wealth, and we have only begun the development of our vast resources.

Again, another marked characteristic of the Anglo-Saxon is what may be called an instinct or genius for colonizing. His unequaled energy, his indomitable perseverance, and his personal independence, made him a pioneer. He excels all others in pushing his way into new countries. It was those in whom this tendency was strongest that came to America, and this inherited tendency has been further developed by the westward sweep of successive generations across the continent. So noticeable has this characteristic become that English visitors remark it. Charles Dickens once said that the typical American would hesitate to enter heaven unless assured that he could go further west.

Again, nothing more manifestly distinguishes the Anglo-Saxon than his intense and persistent energy; and he is developing in the United States an energy which, in eager activity and effectiveness, is peculiarly American. This is due partly to the fact that Americans are much better fed than Europeans, and partly to the undeveloped resources of a new country, but more largely to our climate, which acts as a constant stimulus. Ten years after the landing of the Pilgrims, the Rev. Francis Higginson, a good observer, wrote: "A sup of New England air is better than a whole flagon of English ale." Thus early had the stimulating effect of our climate been noted. Moreover, our social institutions are stimulating. In Europe the various ranks of society are, like the strata of the earth, fixed and fossilized. There can be no great change without a terrible upheaval, a social earthquake. Here society is like the waters of the sea, mobile; as General Garfield said, and so signally illustrated in his own experience, that which is at the bottom to-day may one day flash on the crest of the highest wave. Every one is free to become whatever he can make of himself; free to transform himself from a rail-splitter or a tanner or a canal-boy, into the nation's President. Our aristocracy, unlike that of Europe, is open to all comers. Wealth, position, influence, are prizes offered for energy; and every farmer's boy, every apprentice and clerk, every friendless and penniless immigrant, is free to enter the lists. Thus many causes co-operate to produce here the most forceful and tremendous energy in the world.

What is the significance of such facts? These tendencies infold the future; they are the mighty alphabet with which God writes his prophecies. May we not, by a careful laying together of the letters, spell out something of his meaning? It seems to me that God, with infinite wisdom and skill, is training the Anglo-Saxon race for an hour sure to come in the world's future. Heretofore there has always been in the history of the world a comparatively unoccupied land westward, into which the crowded countries of the East have poured their surplus populations. But the widening waves of migration, which millenniums ago rolled east and west from the valley of the Euphrates, meet to-day on our Pacific coast. There are no more new worlds. The unoccupied arable lands of the earth are limited, and will soon be taken. The time is coming when the pressure of population on the means of subsistence will be felt here as it is now felt in Europe and Asia. Then will the world enter upon a new stage of its history—*the final competition of races, for which the Anglo-Saxon is being schooled*. Long before the thousand millions are here, the mighty *centrifugal* tendency, inherent in this stock and strengthened in the United States, will assert itself. Then this race of unequaled energy, with all the majesty of numbers and the might of wealth behind it—the representative, let us hope, of the largest liberty, the purest Christianity, the highest civilization—having developed peculiarly aggressive traits calculated to impress its institutions upon mankind, will spread itself over the earth. If I read not amiss, this powerful race will move down upon Mexico, down upon Central and South America, out upon the islands of the sea, over upon Africa and beyond. And can any one doubt that the result of this competition of races will be the "survival of the fittest"? "Any people," says Dr. Bushnell, "that is physiologically advanced in culture, though it be only in a degree beyond another which is mingled with it on strictly equal terms, is sure to live down and finally live out its inferior. Nothing can save the inferior race but a ready and pliant assimilation. Whether the feebler and more abject races are going to be regenerated and raised up, is already very much of a question. What if it should be God's plan to people the world with better and finer material? Certain it is, whatever expectations we may indulge, that there is a tremendous overbearing surge of power in the Christian nations, which, if the others are not speedily raised to some vastly higher capacity, will inevitably submerge and bury them forever. These great populations of Christendom—what are they doing, but throwing out their colonies on every side, and populating themselves, if I may so speak, into the possession of all countries and climes?" To this result no war of extermination is needful; the contest is not one of arms, but of vitality and of civilization. "At the present day," says Mr. Darwin, "civilized nations are everywhere supplanting barbarous nations, excepting where the climate opposes a deadly barrier; and they succeed mainly, though not exclusively, through their arts, which are the products of the intellect?" Thus the Finns were supplanted by the Aryan races in Europe and Asia, the Tartars by the Russians, and thus the aborigines of North America, Australia and New Zealand are now disappearing before the all-conquering Anglo-Saxons. It would seem as if these inferior tribes were only precursors of a superior race, voices in the wilderness crying: "Prepare ye the way of the Lord!" The savage is a hunter; by the incoming of civilization the game is driven away and disappears before the hunter becomes a herder or an agriculturist. The savage is ignorant of many diseases of civilization which, when he is exposed to them, attack him before he learns how to treat them. Civilization also has its vices, of which the uninitiated savage is innocent. He proves an apt learner of vice, but dull enough in the school of morals. Every civilization has its destructive and preservative elements. The Anglo-Saxon race would speedily decay but for the salt of Christianity. Bring savages into contact with our civilization, and its destructive forces become operative at once, while years are necessary to render effective the saving influences of Christian instruction. Moreover, the pioneer wave of our civilization carries with it more scum than salt. Where there is one missionary, there are hundreds of miners or traders or adventurers ready to debauch the native. Whether the extinction of inferior races before the advancing Anglo-Saxon seems to the reader sad or otherwise, it certainly appears probable. I know of nothing except climatic conditions to prevent this race from populating Africa as it has peopled North America. And those portions of Africa which are unfavorable to Anglo-Saxon life are less extensive than was once supposed. The Dutch Boers, after two centuries of life there, are as hardy as any race on earth. The Anglo-Saxon has established himself in climates totally diverse—Canada, South Africa, and India—and, through several generations, has preserved his essential race characteristics. He is not, of course, superior to climatic influences; but, even in warm climates, he is likely to retain his aggressive vigor long enough to supplant races already enfeebled. Thus, in what Dr. Bushnell calls "the out-populating power of the Christian stock," may be found God's final and complete solution of the dark problem of heathenism among many inferior peoples.

Some of the stronger races, doubtless, may be able to preserve their integrity; but, in order to compete with the Anglo-Saxon, they will probably be forced to adopt his methods and instruments, his civilization and his religion. Significant movements are now in progress among them. While the Christian religion was never more vital, or its hold upon the Anglo-Saxon mind stronger, there is taking place among the nations a wide-spread intellectual revolt against traditional beliefs. "In every corner of the world," says Mr. Froude, "there is the same phenomenon of the decay of established religions. . . . Among Mohammedans, Jews, Buddhists, Brahmins, traditionary creeds are losing their hold. An intellectual revolution is sweeping over the world, breaking down established opinions, dissolving foundations on which historical faiths have been built up." The contact of Christian with heathen nations is awaking the latter to new life. Old superstitions are loosening their grasp. The dead crust of fossil faiths is being shattered by the movements of life underneath. In Catholic countries, Catholicism is losing its influence over educated minds, and in some cases the masses have already lost all faith in it. Thus, while on this continent God is training the Anglo-Saxon race for its mission, a complemental work has been in progress in the great world beyond. God has two hands. Not only is he preparing in our civilization the die with which to stamp the nations, but, by what Southey called the "timing of Providence," he is preparing mankind to receive our impress.

Is there room for reasonable doubt that this race, unless devitalized by alcohol and tobacco, is destined to dispossess many weaker races, assimilate others, and mold the remainder, until, in a very true and important sense, it has Anglo-Saxonized mankind? Already "the English language, saturated with Christian ideas, gathering up into itself the best thought of all the ages, is the great agent of Christian civilization throughout the world; at this moment affecting the destinies and molding the character of half the human race." Jacob Grimm, the German philologist, said of this language: "It seems chosen, like its people, to rule in future times in a still greater degree in all the corners of the earth." He predicted, indeed, that the language of Shakespeare would eventually become the language of mankind. Is not Tennyson's noble prophecy to find its fulfillment in Anglo-Saxondom's extending its dominion and influence—

> Till the war-drum throbs no longer, and the battle-flags are furl'd
> In the Parliament of man, the Federation of the world.

In my own mind, there is no doubt that the Anglo-Saxon is to exercise the commanding influence in the world's future; but the exact nature of that influence is, as yet, undetermined. How far his civilization will be materialistic and atheistic, and how long it will take thoroughly to Christianize and sweeten it, how rapidly he will hasten the coming of the kingdom wherein dwelleth righteousness, or how many ages he may retard it, is still uncertain; but *it is now being swiftly determined.* Let us weld together in a chain the various links of our logic which we have endeavored to forge. Is it manifest that the Anglo-Saxon holds in his hands the destinies of mankind for ages to come? Is it evident that the United States is to be the home of this race, the principal seat of his power, the great center of his influence? Is it true . . . that the great West is to dominate the nation's future? Has it been shown . . . that this generation is to determine the character, and hence the destiny, of the West? Then may God open the eyes of this generation! When Napoleon drew up his troops before the Mamelukes, under the shadow of the Pyramids, pointing to the latter, he said to his soldiers: "Remember that from yonder heights forty centuries look down on you." Men of this generation, from the pyramid top of opportunity on which God has set us, *we look down on forty centuries!* We stretch our hand into the future with power to mold the destinies of unborn millions.

> We are living, we are dwelling,
> In a grand and awful time,
> In an age on ages telling—
> To be living is sublime!

Nothwithstanding the great perils which threaten it, I cannot think our civilization will perish; but I believe it is fully in the hands of the Christians of the United States, during the next fifteen or twenty years, to hasten or retard the coming of Christ's kingdom in the world by hundreds, and perhaps thousands, of years. We of this generation and nation occupy the Gibraltar of the ages which commands the world's future.

5 Imperialism as a Social Atavism

As evidence for noneconomic and even nonrational motives for empire accumulated, the limits of the economic interpretation became obvious. Joseph Schumpeter offered a broader interpretation based on his understanding of world history since antiquity.

FROM *Imperialism and Social Classes*

BY JOSEPH SCHUMPETER

OUR ANALYSIS OF THE HISTORICAL EVIDENCE has shown, first, the unquestionable fact that "objectless" tendencies toward forcible expansion, without definite, utilitarian limits—that is, non-rational and irrational, purely instinctual inclinations toward war and conquest—play a very large role in the history of mankind. It may sound paradoxical, but numberless wars—perhaps the majority of all wars—have been waged without adequate "reason" —not so much from the moral viewpoint as from that of reasoned and reasonable interest. The most herculean efforts of the nations, in other words, have faded into the empty air. Our analysis, in the second place, provides an explanation for this drive to action, this will to war—a theory by no means exhausted by mere references to an "urge" or an "instinct." The explanation lies, instead, in the vital needs of situations that molded peoples and classes into warriors—if they wanted to avoid extinction—and in the fact that psychological dispositions and social structures acquired in the dim past in such situations, once firmly established, tend to maintain themselves and to continue in effect long after they have lost their meaning and their life-preserving function. Our analysis, in the third place, has shown the existence of subsidiary factors that facilitate the survival of such dispositions and structures—factors that may be divided into two groups. The orientation toward war is mainly fostered by the domestic interests of ruling classes,

Reprinted by permission of the President and Fellows of Harvard College from Joseph Schumpeter, *Imperialism and Social Classes* (New York: Augustus M. Kelley, Copyright 1951 by Elizabeth Schumpeter), pp. 64–73, translated by Heinz Norden.

but also by the influence of all those who stand to gain individually from a war policy, whether economically or socially. Both groups of factors are generally overgrown by elements of an altogether different character, not only in terms of political phraseology, but also of psychological motivation. Imperialisms differ greatly in detail, but they all have at least these traits in common, turning them into a single phenomenon in the field of sociology, as we noted in the introduction.

Imperialism thus is atavistic in character. It falls into that large group of surviving features from earlier ages that play such an important part in every concrete social situation. In other words, it is an element that stems from the living conditions, not of the present, but of the past—or, put in terms of the economic interpretation of history, from past rather than present relations of production. It is an atavism in the social structure, in individual, psychological habits of emotional reaction. Since the vital needs that created it have passed away for good, it too must gradually disappear, even though every warlike involvement, no matter how non-imperialist in character, tends to revive it. It tends to disappear as a structural element because the structure that brought it to the fore goes into a decline, giving way, in the course of social development, to other structures that have no room for it and eliminate the power factors that supported it. It tends to disappear as an element of habitual emotional reaction, because of the progressive rationalization of life and mind, a process in which old functional needs are absorbed by new tasks, in which heretofore military energies are functionally modified. If our theory is correct, cases of imperialism should decline in intensity the later they occur in the history of a people and of a culture. Our most recent examples of unmistakable, clear-cut imperialism are the absolute monarchies of the eighteenth century. They are unmistakably "more civilized" than their predecessors.

It is from absolute autocracy that the present age has taken over what imperialist tendencies it displays. And the imperialism of absolute autocracy flourished before the Industrial Revolution that created the modern world, or rather, before the consequences of that revolution began to be felt in all their aspects. These two statements are primarily meant in a historical sense, and as such they are no more than self-evident. We shall nevertheless try, within the framework of our theory, to define the significance of capitalism for our phenomenon and to examine the relationship between present-day imperialist tendencies and the autocratic imperialism of the eighteenth century.

The floodtide that burst the dams in the Industrial Revolution had its sources, of course, back in the Middle Ages. But capitalism began to shape society and impress its stamp on every page of social history only with the second half of the eighteenth century. Before that time there had been only islands of capitalist economy imbedded in an ocean of village and urban economy. True, certain political influences emanated from these islands, but they were able to assert themselves only indirectly. Not until the process we term the Industrial Revolution did the working masses, led by the entrepreneur, overcome the bonds of older life-forms—the environment of peasantry, guild, and aristocracy. The causal connection was this: A transformation in the basic economic factors (which need not detain us here) created the objective opportunity for the production of commodities, for large-scale industry, working for a market of customers whose individual identities were unknown, operating solely with a view to maximum financial profit. It was this opportunity that created an economically oriented leadership—personalities whose field of achievement was the organization of such commodity production in the form of capitalist enterprise. Successful enterprises in large numbers represented something new in the economic and social sense. They fought for and won freedom of action. They compelled state policy to adapt itself to their needs. More and more they attracted the most vigorous leaders from other spheres, as well as the manpower of those spheres, causing them and the social strata they represented to languish. Capitalist entrepreneurs fought the former ruling circles for a share in state control, for leadership in the state. The very fact of their success, their position, their resources, their power, raised them in the political and social scale. Their mode of life, their cast of mind became increasingly important elements on the social scene. Their actions, desires, needs, and beliefs emerged more and more sharply within the total picture of the social community. In a historical sense, this applied primarily to the industrial and financial leaders of the movement —the bourgeoisie. But soon it applied also to the working masses which this movement created and placed in an altogether new class situation. This situation was governed by new forms of the working day, of family life, of interests—and these, in turn, corresponded to new orientations toward the social structure as a whole. More and more, in the course of the nineteenth century, the typical modern worker came to determine the overall aspect of society; for competitive capitalism, by its inherent logic, kept on raising the demand for labor and thus the economic level and social power of the workers, until this class too was able to assert itself in a political sense. The working class and its mode of life provided the type from which the intellectual developed. Capitalism did not create the intellectuals—the "new middle class." But in earlier times only the legal scholar, the cleric, and the physician had formed a special intellectual class, and even they had enjoyed but little scope for playing an independent role. Such opportunities were provided only by capitalist society, which created the industrial and financial bureaucrat, the journalist, and so on, and which opened up new vistas to the jurist and physician. The "professional" of capitalist society arose as a class type. Finally, as a class type, the rentier, the beneficiary of industrial loan capital, is also a creature of capitalism. All these types are shaped by the capitalist mode of production, and they tend for this reason to bring other types—even the peasant—into conformity with themselves.

These new types were now cast adrift from the fixed order of earlier times, from the environment that had shackled and protected people for centuries, from the old associations of village, manor house, clan fellowship, often even from families in the broader sense. They were severed from the things that had been constant year after year, from cradle to grave—tools, homes, the countryside, especially the soil. They were on their own, enmeshed in the pitiless logic of gainful employment, mere drops in the vast ocean of industrial life, exposed to the inexorable pressures of competition. They were freed from the control of ancient patterns of thought, of the grip of institutions and organs that taught and represented these outlooks in village, manor, and guild. They were removed from the old world, engaged in building a new one for themselves—a specialized, mechanized world. Thus they were all inevitably democratized, individualized, and rationalized. They were democratized, because the picture of time-honored power and privilege gave way to one of continual change, set in motion by industrial life. They were individualized, because subjective opportunities to shape their lives took the place of immutable objective factors. They were rationalized, because the instability of economic position made their survival hinge on continual, deliberately rationalistic decisions—a dependence that emerged with great sharpness. Trained to economic rationalism, these people left no sphere of life unrationalized, questioning everything about themselves, the social structure, the state, the ruling class. The marks of this process are engraved on every aspect of modern culture. It is this process that explains the basic features of that culture.

These are things that are well known today, recognized in their full significance—indeed, often exaggerated. Their application to our subject is plain. Everything that is purely instinctual, everything insofar as it is purely instinctual, is driven into the background by this development. It creates a social and psychological atmosphere in keeping with modern economic forms, where traditional habits, merely because they were traditional, could no more survive than obsolete economic forms. Just as the latter can survive only if they are continually "adapted," so instinctual tendencies can survive only when the conditions that gave rise to them continue to apply, or when the "instinct" in question derives a new purpose from new conditions. The "instinct" that is *only* "instinct," that has lost its purpose, languishes relatively quickly in the capitalist world, just as does an inefficient economic practice. We see this process of rationalization at work even in the case of the strongest impulses. We observe it, for example, in the facts of procreation. We must therefore anticipate finding it in the case of the imperialist impulse as well; we must expect to see this impulse, which rests on the primitive contingencies of physical combat, gradually disappear, washed away by new exigencies of daily life. There is another factor too. The competitive system absorbs the full energies of most of the people at all economic levels. Constant application, attention, and concentration of energy are the conditions of survival within it, primarily in the specifically economic professions, but also in other activities organized on their model. There is much less excess energy to be vented in war and conquest than in any precapitalist society. What excess energy there is flows largely into industry itself, accounts for its shining figures—the type of the captain of industry—and for the rest is applied to art, science, and the social struggle. In a purely capitalist world, what was once energy for war becomes simply energy for labor of every kind. Wars of conquest and adventurism in foreign policy in general are bound to be regarded as troublesome distractions, destructive of life's meaning, a diversion from the accustomed and therefore "true" task.

A purely capitalist world therefore can offer no fertile soil to imperialist impulses. That does not mean that it cannot still maintain an interest in imperialist expansion. We shall discuss this immediately. The point is that its people are likely to be essentially of an unwarlike disposition. Hence we must expect that anti-imperialist tendencies will show themselves wherever capitalism penetrates the economy and, through the economy, the mind of modern nations—most strongly, of course, where capitalism itself is strongest, where it has advanced furthest, encountered the least resistance, and preeminently where its types and hence democracy—in the "bourgeois" sense —come closest to political dominion. We must further expect that the types formed by capitalism will actually be the carriers of these tendencies. Is such the case? The facts that follow are cited to show that this expectation, which flows from our theory, is in fact justified.

Throughout the world of capitalism, and specifically among the elements formed by capitalism in modern social life, there has arisen a fundamental opposition to war, expansion, cabinet diplomacy, armaments, and socially-entrenched professional armies. This opposition had its origin in the country that first turned capitalist—England—and arose coincidentally with that country's capitalist development. "Philosophical radicalism" was the first politically influential intellectual movement to represent this trend successfully, linking it up, as was to be expected, with economic freedom in general and free trade in particular. Molesworth became a cabinet member, even though he had publicly declared—on the occasion of the Canadian revolution—that he prayed for the defeat of his country's arms. In step with the advance of capitalism, the movement also gained adherents elsewhere— though at first only adherents without influence. It found support in Paris— indeed, in a circle oriented toward capitalist enterprise (for example, Frédéric Passy). True, pacifism as a matter of principle had existed before, though only among a few small religious sects. But modern pacifism, in its political foundations if not its derivation, is unquestionably a phenomenon of the capitalist world.

Wherever capitalism penetrated, peace parties of such strength arose that virtually every war meant a political struggle on the domestic scene. The exceptions are rare—Germany in the Franco-Prussian war of 1870–1871, both belligerents in the Russo-Turkish war of 1877–1878. That is why every war is carefully justified as a defensive war by the governments involved, and by all the political parties, in their official utterances—indicating a realization that a war of a different nature would scarcely be tenable in a political sense. (Here too the Russo-Turkish war is an exception, but a significant one.) In former times this would not have been necessary. Reference to an interest or pretense at moral justification was customary as early as the eighteenth century, but only in the nineteenth century did the assertion of attack, or the threat of attack, become the only avowed occasion for war. In the distant past, imperialism had needed no disguise whatever, and in the absolute autocracies only a very transparent one; but today imperialism is carefully hidden from public view—even though there may still be an unofficial appeal to warlike instincts. No people and no ruling class today can openly afford to regard war as a normal state of affairs or a normal element in the life of nations. No one doubts that today it must be characterized as an abnormality and a disaster. True, war is still glorified. But glorification in the style of King Tuglâi-palisharra is rare and unleashes such a storm of indignation that every practical politician carefully dissociates himself from such things. Everywhere there is official acknowledgment that peace is an end in itself— though not necessarily an end overshadowing all purposes that can be realized by means of war. Every expansionist urge must be carefully related to a concrete goal. All this is primarily a matter of political phraseology, to be sure. But the necessity for this phraseology is a symptom of the popular attitude. And that attitude makes a policy of imperialism more and more difficult—indeed, the very word imperialism is applied only to the enemy, in a reproachful sense, being carefully avoided with reference to the speaker's own policies.

The type of industrial worker created by capitalism is always vigorously anti-imperialist. In the individual case, skillful agitation may persuade the working masses to approve or remain neutral—a concrete goal or interest in self-defense always playing the main part—but no initiative for a forcible policy of expansion ever emanates from this quarter. On this point official socialism unquestionably formulates not merely the interests but also the conscious will of the workers. Even less than peasant imperialism is there any such thing as socialist or other working-class imperialism.

Despite manifest resistance on the part of powerful elements, the capital- ist age has seen the development of methods for preventing war, for the peaceful settlement of disputes among states. The very fact of resistance means that the trend can be explained only from the mentality of capitalism as a mode of life. It definitely limits the opportunities imperialism needs if it is to be a powerful force. True, the methods in question often fail, but even more often they are successful. I am thinking not merely of the Hague Court of Arbitration but of the practice of submitting controversial issues to conferences of the major powers or at least those powers directly concerned— a course of action that has become less and less avoidable. True, here too the individual case may become a farce. But the serious setbacks of today must not blind us to the real importance or sociological significance of these things.

Among all capitalist economies, that of the United States is least bur- dened with precapitalist elements, survivals, reminiscences, and power factors.

Certainly we cannot expect to find imperialist tendencies altogether lacking even in the United States, for the immigrants came from Europe with their convictions fully formed, and the environment certainly favored the revival of instincts of pugnacity. But we can conjecture that among all countries the United States is likely to exhibit the weakest imperialist trend. This turns out to be the truth. The case is particularly instructive, because the United States has seen a particularly strong emergence of capitalist interests in an imperialist direction—those very interests to which the phenomenon of imperialism has so often been reduced, a subject we shall yet touch on. Nevertheless the United States was the first advocate of disarmament and arbitration. It was the first to conclude treaties concerning arms limitations (1817) and arbitral courts (first attempt in 1797)—doing so most zealously, by the way, when economic interest in expansion was at its greatest. Since 1908 such treaties have been concluded with twenty-two states. In the course of the nineteenth century, the United States had numerous occasions for war, including instances that were well calculated to test its patience. It made almost no use of such occasions. Leading industrial and financial circles in the United States had and still have an evident interest in incorporating Mexico into the Union. There was more than enough opportunity for such annexation—but Mexico remained unconquered. Racial catch phrases and working-class interests pointed to Japan as a possible danger. Hence possession of the Philippines was not a matter of indifference—yet surrender of this possession is being discussed. Canada was an almost defenseless prize—but Canada remained independent. Even in the United States, of course, politicians need slogans—especially slogans calculated to divert attention from domestic issues. Theodore Roosevelt and certain magnates of the press actually resorted to imperialism—and the result, in that world of high capitalism, was utter defeat, a defeat that would have been even more abject, if other slogans, notably those appealing to anti-trust sentiment, had not met with better success.

These facts are scarcely in dispute. And since they fit into the picture of the mode of life which we have recognized to be the necessary product of capitalism, since we can grasp them adequately from the necessities of that mode of life and industry, it follows that capitalism is by nature anti-imperialist.

6 A Critique of the Marxist Analysis

> By 1935 the course of the "New Imperialism" had largely
> been run, and a proper historical evaluation was possible.
> The theories could be tested by facts, and the two did not
> necessarily agree.

A Critique of Imperialism BY W. L. LANGER

IT IS NOW ROUGHLY FIFTY YEARS since the beginning of that
great outburst of expansive activity on the part of the Great Powers of
Europe which we have come to call "imperialism." And it is about a
generation since J. A. Hobson published his "Imperialism: a Study," a book
which has served as the starting point for most later discussions and which
has proved a perennial inspiration for writers of the most diverse schools. A
reappraisal of it is therefore decidedly in order. The wonder is that it has not
been undertaken sooner.

Since before the outbreak of the World War the theoretical writing on
imperialism has been very largely monopolized by the so-called Neo-Marxians, that is, by those who, following in the footsteps of the master, have
carried on his historical analysis from the critique of capitalism to the study
of this further phase, imperialism, the significance of which Marx himself
did not appreciate and the very existence of which he barely adumbrated.
The Neo-Marxians, beginning with Rudolf Hilferding and Rosa Luxem-
burg, have by this time elaborated a complete theory, which has recently
been expounded in several ponderous German works. The theory hinges
upon the idea of the accumulation of capital, its adherents holding that
imperialism is nothing more nor less than the last stage in the development
of capitalism—the stage in which the surplus capital resulting from the
system of production is obliged by ever diminishing returns at home to seek

William L. Langer, "A Critique of Imperialism," *Foreign Affairs*, 14(1935–1936), 102–19.
Copyright by The Council on Foreign Relations, Inc., New York. Some footnotes omitted by
permission.

new fields for investment abroad. When this surplus capital has transformed the whole world and remade even the most backward areas in the image of capitalism, the whole economic–social system will inevitably die of congestion.

That the classical writers of the socialistic school derived this basic idea from Hobson's book there can be no doubt.[1] Lenin himself admitted, in his "Imperialism, the Latest Stage of Capitalism," that Hobson gave "a very good and accurate description of the fundamental economic and political traits of imperialism," and that Hobson and Hilferding had said the essentials on the subject. This, then, has been the most fruitful contribution of Hobson's essay. When we examine his ideas on this subject we refer indirectly to the larger part of the writing on imperialism since his day.

As a matter of pure economic theory it is most difficult to break down the logic of the accumulation theory. It is a fact that since the middle of the last century certain countries—first England, then France, Germany and the United States—have exported large amounts of capital, and that the financial returns from these investments in many instances came to overshadow completely the income derived by the lending countries from foreign trade. It is also indisputable that industry embarked upon the road to concentration and monopoly, that increased efficiency in production led to larger profits and to the amassing of ever greater surpluses of capital. We must recognize further that, as a general rule, the return from investments abroad was distinctly above the return on reinvestment in home industry. In other words, the postulates of the socialist theory undoubtedly existed. There is no mentionable reason why the development of the capitalist system should not have had the results attributed to it.

But, as it happens, the actual course of history refutes the thesis. The course of British investment abroad shows that there was a very considerable export of capital before 1875, that is, during the climax of anti-imperialism in England. Between 1875 and 1895, while the tide of imperialism was coming to the full, there was a marked falling off of foreign investment. Capital export was then resumed on a large scale in the years before the war, though England was, in this period, already somewhat disillusioned by the outcome of the South African adventure and rather inclined to be skeptical about imperialism. Similar observations hold true of the United States. If the promulgation of the Monroe Doctrine was an act of imperialism, where was the export of capital which ought to have been its condition? Let us concede that the war with Spain was an imperialist episode. At that time the United States was still a debtor nation, importing rather than exporting capital. In Russia, too, the heyday of imperialism coincided with a period of heavy borrowing rather than of lending.

---

[1] I strongly suspect that Hobson, in turn, took over the idea from the very bourgeois American financial expert, Charles A. Conant, whose remarkable article, "The Economic Basis of Imperialism," in the *North American Review*, September 1898, p. 326–340, is now forgotten, but deserves recognition.

There is this further objection to be raised against the view of Hobson and his Neo-Marxian followers, that the export of capital seems to have little direct connection with territorial expansion. France, before the war, had plenty of capital to export, and some of her earliest and most vigorous imperialists, like Jules Ferry, declared that she required colonies in order to have adequate fields for the placement of this capital. But when France had secured colonies, she did not send her capital to them. By far the larger part of her exported funds went to Russia, Rumania, Spain and Portugal, Egypt and the Ottoman Empire. In 1902 only two or two and a half billion francs out of a total foreign investment of some 30 or 35 billion francs was placed in the colonies. In 1913 Britain had more money invested in the United States than in any colony or other foreign country. Less than half of her total export of capital had been to other parts of the Empire. The United States put more capital into the development of Canada than did England; and when, after the war, the United States became a great creditor nation, 43 percent of her investment was in Latin America, 27 percent in Canada and Newfoundland, and 22 percent in European countries. What she sent to her colonies was insignificant. Or let us take Germany, which in 1914 had about 25 billion marks placed abroad. Of this total only three percent was invested in Asia and Africa, and of that three percent only a small part in her colonies. Pre-war Russia was a great imperialist power, but Russia had to borrow from France the money invested in her Far Eastern projects. In our own day two of the most outspokenly imperialist powers, Japan and Italy, are both nations poor in capital. Whatever the urge that drives them to expansion, it cannot be the need for the export of capital.

At the height of the imperialist tide, let us say from 1885 to 1914, there was much less talk among the advocates of expansion about the need for foreign investment fields than about the need for new markets and for the safeguarding of markets from the tariff restrictions of competitors. It is certain that in the opinion of contemporaries that was the mainspring of the whole movement. But this economic explanation, like the other, has not been borne out by the actual developments. Very few colonies have done even half of their trading with the mother country and many have done less. Taken in the large it can be proved statistically that the colonial trade has always played a relatively unimportant part in the total foreign commerce of the great industrial nations. These nations have always been each other's best customers and no amount of rivalry and competition has prevented their trade from following, not the flag, but the price-list. The position of Canada within the British Empire did not prevent her from levying tariffs against British goods, nor from developing exceedingly close economic relations with the United States. In the pre-war period German commerce with the British possessions was expanding at a relatively higher rate than was Britain's.

If one must have an economic interpretation of imperialism, one will probably find its historical evolution to have been something like this: In the days of England's industrial preëminence she was, by the very nature of the case, interested in free trade. In the palmiest days of Cobdenism she exported manufactured goods to the four corners of the earth, but she exported also machinery and other producers' goods, thereby preparing the way for the industrialization of the continental nations and latterly of other regions of the world. In order to protect their infant industries from British competition, these new industrial Powers threw over the teachings of the Manchester school and began to set up tariffs. The result was that the national markets were set aside, to a large extent, for home industry. British trade was driven to seek new markets, where the process was repeated. But the introduction of protective tariffs had this further effect, that it made possible the organization of cartels and trusts, that is, the concentration of industry, the increase of production and the lowering of costs. Surplus goods and low prices caused the other industrial Powers likewise to look abroad for additional markets, and, while this development was taking place, technological improvements were making transportation and communication safer and more expeditious. The exploration of Africa at that time was probably a pure coincidence, but it contributed to the movement toward trade and expansion and the growth of a world market. Fear that the newly opened areas of the world might be taken over by others and then enclosed in tariff walls led directly to the scramble for territory in Asia and Africa.

The socialist writers would have us believe that concentration in industry made for monopoly and that the banks, undergoing the same process of evolution, were, through their connection with industry, enabled to take over control of the whole capitalist system. They were the repositories of the surplus capital accumulated by a monopolistic system and they were therefore the prime movers in the drive for imperial expansion, their problem being to find fields for the investment of capital. This is an argument which does violence to the facts as they appear historically. The socialist writers almost to a man argue chiefly from the example of Germany, where cartellization came early and where the concentration of banking and the control of industry by the banks went further than in most countries. But even in Germany the movement towards overseas expansion came before the growth of monopoly and the amalgamation of the banks. In England, the imperialist country *par excellence,* there was no obvious connection between the two phenomena. The trust movement came late and never went as far as in Germany. The same was true of the consolidation of the banking system. One of the perennial complaints in England was the lack of proper coördination between the banks and industry. To a certain extent the English exported capital because the machinery for foreign investment was better than the organization for home investment. In the United States, to be sure, there was already a pronounced concentration of industry when the great outburst of imperialism came in the last years of the past century, but in general the trust movement ran parallel to the movement for territorial expansion. In any event, it would be hard to disprove the contention that the growth of world trade and the world market brought on the tendency toward better organization and concentration in industry, rather than the reverse. It is obvious not only that one large unit can manufacture more cheaply than many small ones, but that it can act more efficiently in competition with others in the world market.

But this much is clear—that territorial control of extra-European territory solved neither the trade problem nor the question of surplus capital. The white colonies, which were the best customers, followed their own economic interests and not even tariff restrictions could prevent them from doing so. In the backward, colored, tropical colonies, which could be more easily controlled and exploited, it proved difficult to develop a market, because of the low purchasing power of the natives. The question of raw materials, of which so much has always been made, also remained open. The great industrial countries got but a fraction of their raw materials from the colonies, and the colonies themselves continued to show a tendency to sell their products in the best market. As for the export of capital, that continued to flow in an ever broader stream, not because the opportunities for investment at home were exhausted, but because the return from foreign investment was apt to be better and because, in many cases, foreign investment was the easier course. Capital flowed from the great industrial countries of Europe, but it did not flow to their colonies. The United States and Canada, Latin America (especially the Argentine) and even old countries like Austria-Hungary and Russia, got the bulk of it. The export of capital necessarily took the form of the extension of credit, which in turn implied the transfer of goods. Not infrequently the granting of loans was made conditional on trade concessions by the borrowing country. So we come back to the question of trade and tariffs. In a sense the export of capital was nothing but a device to stimulate trade and to circumvent tariff barriers, which brings us back to the coincidence of the movement for protection and the movement toward imperialism.

This may seem like an oversimplified explanation and it probably is. Some may argue that imperialism is more than a movement toward territorial expansion and that financial imperialism in particular lays the iron hand of control on many countries supposedly independent. But if you try to divorce imperialism from territorial control you will get nowhere. Practically all writers on the subject have been driven to the conclusion that the problem cannot be handled at all unless you restrict it in this way. When Hobson wrote on imperialism, he had reference to the great spectacle of a few Powers taking over tremendous areas in Africa and Asia. Imperialism is, in a sense, synonymous with the appropriation by the western nations of the largest part of the rest of the world. If you take it to be anything else, you will soon be lost in nebulous concepts and bloodless abstractions. If imperialism is to mean any vague interference of traders and bankers in the affairs of other countries, you may as well extend it to cover any form of influence. You will have to admit cultural imperialism, religious imperialism, and what not. Personally I prefer to stick by a measurable, manageable concept.

But even though Hobson's idea, that imperialism "is the endeavor of the great controllers of industry to broaden the channel for the flow of their surplus wealth by seeking foreign markets and foreign investments to take off the goods and capital they cannot sell or use at home," proved to be the most stimulating and fertile of his arguments, he had the very correct idea that imperialism was also a "medley of aims and feelings." He had many other contributory explanations of the phenomenon. For example, he was keenly aware of the relationship between democracy and imperialism. The enfranchisement of the working classes and the introduction of free education had brought the rank and file of the population into the political arena. One result of this epoch-making change was the rise of the so-called yellow press, which catered to the common man's love of excitement and sensationalism. Northcliffe was one of the first to sense the value of imperialism as a "talking point." Colonial adventure and far-away conflict satisfied the craving for excitement of the industrial and white-collar classes which had to find some outlet for their "spectatorial lust." The upper crust of the working class, as Lenin admitted, was easily converted to the teaching of imperialism and took pride in the extension of empire.

No doubt this aspect of the problem is important. The mechanization of humanity in an industrial society is a phenomenon with which we have become all too familiar, and every thoughtful person now recognizes the tremendous dangers inherent in the powers which the demagogue can exercise through the press, the motion picture and the radio. In Hobson's day propaganda was still carried on primarily through the press, but later developments were already foreshadowed in the activities of a Northcliffe or a Hearst. Hobson himself was able to show how, during the war in South Africa, the English press took its information from the South African press, which had been brought very largely under the control of Rhodes and his associates. Even at that time Hobson and others were pointing out how imperialistic capital was influencing not only the press, but the pulpit and the universities. Indeed, Hobson went so far as to claim that the great inert mass of the population, who saw the tangled maze of world movements through dim and bewildered eyes, were the inevitable dupes of able, organized interests who could lure or scare or drive them into any convenient course.

Recognizing as we do that control of the public mind involves the most urgent political problems of the day, it is nevertheless important to point out that there is nothing inexorable about the connection of propaganda and imperialism. Even if you admit that a generation ago moneyed interests believed that imperialism was to their advantage, that these interests exercised a far-reaching control over public opinion, and that they used this control to dupe the comman man into support of imperial ventures, it is obvious that at some other time these same interests might have different ideas with regard to their own welfare, just as it is evident that public opinion may be controlled by some other agency—the modern dictator, for example.

But the same thing is not true of another influence upon which Hobson laid great stress, namely the biological conception of politics and international relations. During the last years of the nineteenth century the ideas of "social Darwinism," as it was called, carried everything before them. Darwin's catchwords—the struggle for existence and the survival of the fittest—which he himself always refused to apply to the social organism, were snapped up by others who were less scrupulous, and soon became an integral part of popular and even official thought on foreign affairs. It not only served to justify the ruthless treatment of the "backward" races and the carving up *in spe* of the Portuguese, Spanish, Ottoman and Chinese Empires and of other "dying nations," as Lord Salisbury called them, but it put the necessary imprimatur on the ideas of conflict between the great imperialistic Powers themselves, and supplied a divine sanction for expansion. It was currently believed, in the days of exuberant imperialism, that the world would soon be the preserve of the great states—the British, the American and the Russian—and it was deduced from this belief that survival in the struggle for existence was in itself adequate evidence of superiority and supernatural appointment. The British therefore looked upon their empire as a work of the divine will, while the Americans and Russians were filled with the idea of a manifest destiny. It will be at once apparent that glorification of war and joy in the conflict was intimately connected with the evolutionary mentality. Hobson, the most determined of anti-imperialists, was finally driven to define the whole movement as "a depraved choice of national life, imposed by self-seeking interests which appeal to the lusts of quantitative acquisitiveness and of forceful domination surviving in a nation from early centuries of animal struggle for existence."

The last phrases of this quotation will serve to lead us to the consideration of what has proved to be another fruitful thought of Hobson. He speaks, in one place, of imperialism as a sociological atavism, a remnant of the roving instinct, just as hunting and sport are left-overs of the physical struggle for existence. This idea of the roving instinct has made but little appeal to later writers, but the basic interpretation of imperialism as an atavism underlies the ingenious and highly intelligent essay of Joseph Schumpteter, "Zur Soziologie der Imperialismus," the only work from the bourgeois side which has had anything like the influence exerted by the writers of the socialist school. Schumpeter, who is an eminent economist, worked out a most convincing argument to prove that imperialism has nothing to do with capitalism, and that it is certainly not a development of capitalism. Capitalism, he holds, is by nature opposed to expansion, war, armaments and professional militarism, and imperialism is nothing but an atavism, one of those elements of the social structure which cannot be explained from existing conditions, but only from the conditions of the past. It is, in other words, a hang-over from a preceding economic order. Imperialism antedates capitalism, going back at least to the time of the Assyrians and Egyptians. It is, according to Schumpeter, the disposition of a state to forceful expansion without any special object and without a definable limit. Conquests are desired not so much because of their advantages, which are often questionable, but merely for the sake of conquest, success and activity.

Schumpeter's theory is in some ways extravagant, but it has served as the starting point for some very interesting speculation, especially among German scholars of the liberal persuasion. It is now fairly clear, I think, that the Neo-Marxian critics have paid far too little attention to the imponderable, psychological ingredients of imperialism. The movement may, without much exaggeration, be interpreted not only as an atavism, as a remnant of the days of absolute monarchy and mercantilism, when it was to the interest of the prince to increase his territory and the number of his subjects, but also as an aberration, to be classed with the extravagances of nationalism. Just as nationalism can drive individuals to the point of sacrificing their very lives for the purposes of the state, so imperialism has driven them to the utmost exertions and the extreme sacrifice, even though the stake might be only some little known and at bottom valueless part of Africa or Asia. In the days when communication and economic interdependence have made the world one in so many ways, men still interpret international relations in terms of the old cabinet policies, they are still swayed by out-moded, feudalistic ideas of honor and prestige.

In a sense, then, you can say that there is, in every people, a certain indefinable national energy, which may find expression in a variety of ways.

As a general rule great domestic crises and outbursts of expansion follow each other in the history of the world. In many of the continental countries of Europe, and for that matter in our own country, great internal problems were fought out in the period before 1870. The energies which, in Germany and Italy, went into the victory of the national cause, soon began to project themselves beyond the frontiers. While the continental nations were settling great issues between them, England sat "like a bloated Quaker, rubbing his hands at the roaring trade" he was carrying on. In those days the British cared very little for their empire. Many of them would have felt relieved if the colonies had broken away without a fuss. But, says Egerton, the best-known historian of British colonial policy, when the Germans and the French began to show an interest in colonial expansion, then the British began to think that there must be some value as yet undiscovered in the colonies. They not only started a movement to bind the colonies and the mother country more closely together, but they stretched out their hands for more. In the end they, who had the largest empire to begin with, got easily the lion's share of the yet unappropriated parts of the world. Some thought they were engaged in the fulfilment of a divine mission to abolish slavery, to spread the gospel, to clothe and educate the heathen. Others thought they were protecting the new markets from dangerous competitors, securing their supply of raw materials, or finding new fields for investment. But underlying the whole imperial outlook there was certainly more than a little misapprehension of economics, much self-delusion and self-righteousness, much misapplication of evolutionary teaching and above all much of the hoary tradition of honor, prestige, power and even plain combativeness. Imperialism always carries with it the connotation of the *Imperator* and of the tradition of rule. It is bound up with conscious or subconscious ideas of force, of brutality, of ruthlessness. It was these traits and tendencies that were so vividly expressed in the poetry and stories of Kipling, and it was his almost uncanny ability to sense the emotions of his time and people that made him the greatest apostle of imperialism.

We shall not go far wrong, then, if we stress the psychological and political factors in imperialism as well as its economic and intellectual elements. It was, of course, connected closely with the great changes in the social structure of the western world, but it was also a projection of nationalism beyond the boundaries of Europe, a projection on a world scale of the time-honored struggle for power and for a balance of power as it had existed on the Continent for centuries. The most casual perusal of the literature of imperialism will reveal the continued potency of these atavistic motives. In a recent number of this very journal a leading Italian diplomat [*Dino Grandi* —D. K.], explaining the policy of the Duce, recurred again and again to the failure of the other countries to appreciate the fact that Italy is a young and active country "animated by new spiritual values." By the much-decried Corfu episode of 1923, Mussolini, to give a concrete example, "called Europe's attention to the respect due to the new Italy and to the reawakened energies of the Italian people." In the present Ethiopian crisis there is not very much suggestion of economic or civilizing motives on the part of the Italians; rather the Duce holds before his followers the prospect of revenge for the defeat at Adua (reminiscent of Britain's thirst to avenge Gordon) and promises them a glorious future. Not long ago he spoke to a group of veterans among the ruins of ancient Rome and told them that every stone surrounding them should remind them that Rome once dominated the world by the wisdom of her rule and the might of her arms and that "nothing forbids us to believe that what was our destiny yesterday may again become our destiny tomorrow." In much the same spirit an eminent Japanese statesman expressed himself recently in FOREIGN AFFAIRS: "As soon as the Meiji Restoration lifted the ban on foreign intercourse, the long-pent-up energy of our race was released, and with fresh outlook and enthusiasm the nation has made swift progress. When you know this historical background and understand this overflowing vitality of our race, you will see the impossibility of compelling us to stay still within the confines of our little island home. We are destined to grow and expand overseas." It is the same emphasis given by the Italian diplomat to the need for an outlet for surplus energies.

It is, of course, true that both Italy and Japan have a serious population problem and that Japan, at any rate, has an economic argument to back her imperialistic enterprises in Manchuria and China. But it has been shown long ago that the acquisition of new territory has no direct bearing on the population problem and that emigrants go where their interest calls them, not where their governments would like to have them go. As for Japan's economic needs, it may at least be questioned whether she would not be better off if she avoided political and military commitments in China. Her cheap goods have made very extensive inroads in all the markets of the world, and her eventual conquest of the whole Chinese market is perhaps inevitable. Far from having gained much from her recent policy, she has had to face boycotts and other forms of hostility. In this case, certainly, one might debate whether the game is worth the candle.

Baron Wakatsuki, whose statement is quoted above, was careful to avoid mention of a factor in Japanese imperialism which, as every well-informed person knows, is probably the real explanation of Japanese policy. After the Meiji Restoration it was more the exuberance and bellicosity of the military caste in Japan than the enthusiasm of the country at large which determined the policy of the government. If one reads modern Japanese history aright one will find that from 1870 onward the military classes were constantly pressing upon the government for action in Korea. Only with the greatest difficulty did the civil authorities stave off this pressure. In 1894 the Tokyo government more or less rushed into the war with China in order to avoid a dangerous domestic crisis. In other words, the ideas of honor and patriotism were appealed to in order to divert attention from the parliamentary conflict which was then raging. After the Japanese victory it was the military men who, against the better judgment of men like Count Ito and Baron Mutsu, insisted on the cession of the Liaotung Peninsula, which netted Japan nothing but the intervention of Russia, Germany, and France. We need not pursue this subject in all its minute details. The point I want to make is that in the case of Japan, as in the case of many other countries, it is easier to show that the military and official classes are a driving force behind the movement for expansion than to show that a clique of nefarious bankers or industrialists is the determining factor. Business interests may have an interest in the acquisition of territory, or they may not. But military and official classes almost always have. War is, for the soldiers, a profession, and it is no mere chance that war and imperialism are so commonly lumped together. For officials, expansion means new territories to govern and new jobs to be filled.

Hobson, with his pronouncedly economic approach to the problem, held that "the struggle for markets, the greater eagerness of producers to sell than of consumers to buy, is the crowning proof of a false economy of distribution," of which imperialism is the fruit. The remedy, he thought, lay in "social reform." "There is no necessity to open up new foreign markets," he maintained; "the home markets are capable of indefinite expansion." These contentions sound familiar enough in this day of world depression. Whether the home markets are capable of indefinite expansion is a question on which the economic internationalists and the advocates of autarchy hold different opinions. The interesting thing for us to consider, however, is the fact that movements towards autarchy should have developed at all and that so much stress should now be laid upon the problems of redistribution of wealth, of building up purchasing power, and, in general, of domestic social reform. The current of activity has shifted distinctly from expansion to revolution, peaceful or violent. Perhaps it may be argued from this that the socialist thesis regarding imperialism is now being proved; that capitalism has already transformed the backward areas to such an extent that the markets are ruined, and that the capitalist system is rapidly choking. This view might be acceptable if it were not for the fact that the colonies and backward areas are still very far from developed and if it were not for the further fact that before the depression the colonial trade with the older countries was steadily increasing. In the last five years, to be sure, international commerce has sunk to an unbelievably low point, but the difficulty has been chiefly with the trade between the great industrial Powers themselves. It is quite conceivable that the crisis is primarily due to the special situation arising from the World War and that the root of the trouble lies in the impossibility of fitting tremendous international payments into the existing framework of trade relations. The fantastic tariff barriers which have been set up on all sides have simply aggravated a situation which has been developing since the teachings of Cobdenism first began to fall into disrepute.

But whatever the true explanation of our present difficulties, very few voices are raised in favor of a solution by the methods of imperialism. Indeed, the movement toward autarchy is in a way a negation of imperialism. Economically we have been disillusioned about imperialism. We have learned that colonies do not pay. Britain's expenditure for the defense of the empire alone is enormous, yet she has never yet devised a method by which anything like a commensurate return could be secured. The French military outlay on the colonies in 1913 was more than five hundred million francs, at a time when the entire trade of France with her colonies came to hardly three times that figure. Similar statistics could be quoted for Germany, and it is a well-known fact that the colonies of both Spain and Portugal were much more of a liability than an asset.

In the same way it has turned out that foreign investments of capital are not all that they were expected to be. The higher returns from colonial investments have often been counterbalanced by the greater insecurity that went with them. European countries had more than one opportunity to learn the lesson even before the war. We need only recall the Argentine fiasco of 1890 and the wildcat Kaffir Boom in South African securities in 1895 as classical examples of what might happen. But of course all these instances are completely dwarfed by the experiences of the postwar—or perhaps better, the pre-depression decade. Foreign investments have caused acute international tensions and have resulted in phenomena like American dollar diplomacy in Latin America. The expenditure has been immense and what has been salvaged has been unimpressive enough. The nations of the world are still on the lookout for markets, as they have been for centuries, but the peoples of the world have become more or less convinced that the markets, if they can be got at all, can be got only by the offering of better and cheaper goods and not by occupation, political control or forceful exploitation. As for foreign investments, no one has any stomach for them and most of those fortunate enough to have money to invest would be glad to learn of a safe investment at home. The assurance of needed sources for raw materials is as much if not more of a problem today than it was a generation ago, but there is little sense in taking over the expensive administration of tropical or other territory to guarantee a source of raw materials, because somehow or other it usually turns out that the other fellow has the materials that you want, and it has long since become obvious that the idea of controlling sources of all the materials you may need is a snare and a delusion.

In 1919, at the Paris Peace Conference, the struggle among the victors for the colonial spoils of the vanquished reached the proportions of the epic and the heroic. It seems like a long time ago, because so much has happened since and because we have come to see that in large measure it was a case of much ado about nothing. To meet the demands for some sort of ethics in imperialism, the German colonies and large parts of the Ottoman Empire were set up as mandates under the League, the principle being wholly in consonance with the demand already put forward by Hobson that there be an "international council" which should "accredit a civilized nation with the duty of educating a lower race." But no one will deny that the mandate-seeking nations had other than purely altruistic motives. Though they should have known better, they still proceeded on the principle that some good was to be gotten out of colonies. But the sequel has shown that, just as the more backward regions imported producers' as well as consumers' goods from Europe and thereby laid the foundation for an independent economy by no means favorable to European industrialism, so they imported from Europe the ideas of self-determination and nationalism. Since the disaster suffered by the Italians at Adua in 1896 Europe has had ample evidence of what may happen when these ideas are taken up by native populations and defended with European implements of war. The story of the last generation has been not only the story of the westernization of the world, but also the story of the revolt of Asia and Africa against the western nations. True to Hobson's prediction, the attacks of imperialism on the liberties and existence of weaker races have stimulated in them a corresponding excess of national self-consciousness. We have had much of this in India and China and we have lived to witness the rise of Mustapha Kemal and Ibn Saud, to whom, for all we know, may be added the name of Hailé Selassié. France has had her battles in Morocco and the United States has at last come to appreciate the depth of resentment and ill-feeling against her in Latin America.

That these are not matters to be trifled with has by this time penetrated not only the minds of the governing classes and of the industrial and financial magnates, but also the mind of the man in the street. Who is there in England, for example, who puts much store by the mandates? Since the war England has allowed Ireland to cut loose and she is trying, as best she can, to put India on her own. Egypt has been given her independence and the mandate over Iraq has been abandoned. It would probably not be overshooting the mark to say that the British would be glad to get out of the Palestine hornet's nest if they could, and it is whispered that they would not be averse to turning back to Germany some of the African colonies. But it is not at all clear that Hitler really wants the colonies back. There obviously are other things that he wants more and the return of the colonies is more a question of vindication and prestige than anything else. In like fashion the United States has reversed the rambunctious policy of interference and disguised control in Mexico, the Caribbean and Latin America. We are about to withdraw from the Philippines with greater haste than the Filipinos desire or than many Americans think wise or decent. Neither Britain nor America has shown much real appetite for interfering against Japan in the Far East. Public opinion would not tolerate it, and even among those who have interests at stake there seems to be a growing opinion that if the Japanese wish to make the expenditure in blood and money necessary to restore order and security in China, they ought to be given a universal blessing.

France, to be sure, has shown no inclination to give up any of her vast colonial possessions, while Italy and Japan are both on the war-path. But the case of France is a very special one. Being less industrialized than England, Germany or the United States, she never felt to the same extent as those countries the urge for markets and sources of raw material. The imperialist movement was in France always something of an artificial and fictitious thing, fanned by a small group of enthusiasts. It takes a great and splendid colonial exposition to arouse much popular interest in the Greater France. It might be supposed, therefore, that France would be among the first nations to beat the retreat. But there is a purely military consideration that holds her back. Like England, she can draw troops from her colonies in time of crisis. In the British case this is always something of a gambling proposition. England has no choice but to defend the empire so long as it exists, but whether the dominions and colonies will support England is a question which they decide in each case as they choose. They elected to support the mother country in the Boer War and in the World War, but they did not choose to support her in the Near East when Mustapha Kemal drove the Greeks from Anatolia and appeared at the Straits in 1922.

With France the situation is different. In 1896 an eminent French statesman told Tsar Nicholas II, in reply to an inquiry, that France needed her colonies if only because they could supply her with man-power. The exploitation of that man-power reached large dimensions during the World War and it is now an important and generally recognized factor in France's military establishment. So far, so good, but the French must realize, and no doubt they do realize, that this may not go on forever. Who can say how long the "Senegalese" will be willing to pour out their blood in defense of

French interests? Who can say when they will make use of the training and equipment that has been given them and turn upon their own masters? The spectacle of black troops holding down the population in the Rhineland was one which roused misgivings in the minds of many who think of western civilization in terms other than those of might and political exigency.

As for Japan and Italy, perhaps the less said the better. Japan is motivated by ideas which were current in Europe a generation ago and which are now being discarded. She has serious economic problems which have come with industrialism, and she is trying to solve them by means of territorial expansion and political control. But the peculiar thing is that, with all her progress, little headway has been made in the direction of breaking the power of the former feudal, military caste. Ideas of conquest, power and prestige are still dominant and they explain, more perhaps than economic considerations, the rampant imperialism of the present day.

The Italians, on the other hand, have involved themselves deeply in the Ethiopian affair for reasons which are hardly at all economic. If they were to conquer Abyssinia, what good would it really do them? The country is populated by some six to eight million warlike natives and it would cost a fortune in blood and treasure, poured out over a long term of years, to hold them in subjection. Can anyone seriously maintain that such an area would prove a suitable one for the settlement of very considerable numbers of Italian colonists, or that emigrants from Italy would choose Ethiopia so long as the door in Latin America is even the least bit open? It may be that there are oil reserves or gold in the country, but talk on this point is to a large extent speculation. The story of Ethiopia's wealth will, in all probability, be exploded as was the myth of Yunnan's treasure in the nineties. Taken in the large, it has been proved on many an occasion that "pegging out claims for the future" is in the long run a poor proposition. But Dino Grandi has said in so many words, in the article quoted above, that Italy's claims to empire were ignored and neglected at Paris in 1919 and that Italy must now teach the world to respect her. If that is indeed the object, Mussolini has failed to note the trend of world opinion since the war. The greatness of a nation is no longer necessarily measured by the extent of the national color on the maps of the world, and on many sides empire has come to be regarded indeed as the "white man's burden." In other words, Il Duce is behind the times. I think much of the disapproval of the Italian policy in the world at large is due to the fact that other nations have grown out of the mentality that has produced the Ethiopian crisis.

Imperialism as it existed in the last two generations will never again be possible, for the world has been definitely divided up and there are but very few unclaimed areas still to be appropriated. There may be exchanges of territory between the imperial Powers, and there will undoubtedly be aggression by one against another, but, in the large, territory has, in this age of rabid nationalism, become so sacred that its permanent transference has become more and more difficult and in many places almost impossible. The tightness of the territorial settlement in Europe long since became such that changes were possible only as the result of a great cataclysm, and the same petrifaction of the territorial *status quo* now tends to hold good of the general world settlement. If we are to give up empire, it will probably be to the natives to whom the territory originally belonged. If the tide of native resistance continues to rise, as it is likely to do, that course will become inevitable. We shall have more and more nations and more and more margin for conflict between them unless the mentality of nationalism undergoes a modification and there is some divorce of the ideas of nationalism and territory. In the interval the hope of the world would seem to be in the gradual evolution of voluntary federative combinations between groups of nations, regional pacts. The British Commonwealth, the Soviet Federation and the Pan-American bloc may point the way to a transition to some form of super-national organization for which the present League of Nations will have served as a model and a guide. But all this may be merely wishful thinking.

The Outbreak of the First World War—Who Was Responsible?

CONTENTS

The discussion of the ultimate causes of the First World War is enduring and possibly fruitless. The European system of alliances, nationalism, economic competition, imperialism—all played an important role. The fact remains that in the century between the Congress of Vienna and Sarajevo, Europe had overcome one crisis after another without recourse to a major war. Yet the assassination of the Archduke Francis Ferdinand, heir to the Austro-Hungarian Empire, in a Bosnian town on June 28, 1914, produced a crisis that led to a general and catastrophic war. It is interesting to focus attention on the crisis of July, 1914, for if we cannot apportion precise shares of the blame for the war we can at least trace the steps that turned a Balkan incident into a major disaster. We shall examine the July crisis in some detail and attempt to place it in its proper perspective. Its analysis is crucial for understanding the larger problem of responsibility for the war.

QUESTIONS FOR STUDY

1   Which documents provide evidence for the Austrian responsibility? Which for the German? Which for the Russian? Which for the English? Which for the French?

2   What is the importance of the Sarajevo affair?

3   What is the importance of the Hoyos mission?

4   Is the "blank check" appropriately named?

5   What action made war inevitable?

6   What role did the Kaiser play in bringing on the war? Lord Grey? Sazonov?

7   Which nation is most to blame? Which least?

1 The Question of Responsibility

Article 231 of the Versailles Treaty firmly placed all the blame for the war on Germany, thus opening the debate.

Article 231 of the Treaty of Versailles

THE ALLIED AND ASSOCIATED GOVERNMENTS affirm and Germany accepts the responsibility of Germany and her allies for causing all the loss and damage to which the Allied and Associated Governments and their nationals have been subjected as a consequence of the war imposed upon them by the aggression of Germany and her allies.

U. S. Department of State, *The Treaty of Versailles and After: Annotations of the Text of the Treaty* (1947), p. 413.

2 A Defense of the Central Powers

The following selection is an early and direct refutation of the war-guilt clause. Count Montgelas was an official spokesman for the German republic at the Versailles discussions of responsibility for the war. He helped draft the German answer to the charge of war guilt.

FROM *The Case for the Central Powers*

BY MAX MONTGELAS

I.

GERMANY PURSUED NO AIM either in Europe or elsewhere which could only be achieved by means of war.

Austria-Hungary's only aim was to maintain the *status quo*. Her first intention of rectifying her frontiers at Serbia's expense was immediately abandoned at Germany's instance, and even Sazonov was convinced of her territorial *désintéressement* by her definite statements . . .

France aimed at recovering Alsace Lorraine, and many leading French politicians also hoped to annex the Saar basin, whilst Russia aspired to possession of Constantinople and the Straits, both Powers knowing well that these aims could not be achieved without a European war.

2.

Germany's preparations for war were on a considerably smaller scale than those made by France, having regard to the political constellation, her geographical position, the extent of her unprotected frontiers, and the number of her population. From 1913 onwards, even her actual numerical peace

Count Max Montgelas, *The Case for the Central Powers: An Impeachment of the Versailles Verdict*, Part III, Section 15 (1925), pp. 200–3, translated by Constantine Vesey. Reprinted by permission of George Allen & Unwin Ltd., London.

strength was less, in respect of white troops, quite apart from the steadily increasing strength of the French coloured troops.

As compared with Russia's armaments, those of Austria-Hungary were absolutely inadequate.

The Franco-Russian allies were far superior to the Central Powers as regards the amount of war material, as well as of man power at their disposal.

3.

It was a political mistake to construct a German battle fleet, instead of completing the naval defences, but even in London the proportion of ten to sixteen Dreadnoughts finally proposed by Germany was not regarded as a menace.

4.

Even after Bismarck's time the German Empire repeatedly omitted to take advantage of favourable opportunities for a war of prevention.

5.

The Russian suggestion of the first Hague Conference was not based on pure love of peace. All the Great Powers, without exception, were most sceptical as regards the question of reducing armaments; the Russian proposal of 1899 was unanimously rejected, and public opinion in France strongly opposed Campbell-Bannerman's 1907 suggestion.

Neither at the first nor the second Hague Conference was any proposal to adjust serious international conflicts, affecting the honour and vital interests of a nation, brought forward or supported by any Great Power.

6.

The world war was not decided upon at Potsdam on the 5th of July, 1914; Germany merely assented to Austria's going to war with Serbia.

The possibility that the Austro-Serbian war, like others—the Boer, Moroccan, Tripolitan, and Balkan wars—might lead to further complications, was well weighed, but the risk was thought very small, in view of the special provocation.

7.

After the publication of the Serbian reply, Germany no longer thought war advisable, even against Serbia, and only favoured strictly limited military operations, which were considered justifiable, even in London.

8.

It is true that Germany did not support the proposal to extend the time limit, and rejected the idea of a conference. She not only, however, accepted every other proposal of mediation which came from London, but proposed on her own initiative the two most suitable methods of negotiation, namely, direct conversations between Vienna and St. Petersburg, and the idea of not going beyond Belgrade, which was adopted by Grey.

Sazonov's first formula was considered unacceptable, even in London, and the second was far worse than the first.

9.

An understanding had almost been reached by the methods Germany had been the first to propose, namely, direct discussions between Vienna and St. Petersburg, and limiting the military operations against Serbia, when the Russian mobilization suddenly tore the threads asunder.

10.

The leading men knew just as well in Paris and St. Petersburg as in Berlin, that this mobilization must inevitably lead to war.

Viviani telegraphed to London on the 1st of August that the one who first orders general mobilization is the aggressor, and he saddled Germany with this responsibility, knowing that the accusation was false.

11.

France did not advise moderation in St. Petersburg during the crisis. Finding that the first attempt to do so had annoyed Sazonov, the French Government refrained from taking any further steps in this direction.

12.

France not only did not advise Russia against ordering general mobilization, but gave surreptitious advice as to how she could carry on her military preparations secretly without provoking Germany to take timely counter-measures.

13.

Russia was the first Power to order general mobilization.

France was the first Power to inform another Power officially of her decision to take part in a European war.

14.

England was never as firm in advising moderation in St. Petersburg as Germany in giving this advice to Vienna.

Unlike other British diplomats, Sir Edward Grey only realized the meaning of the Russian mobilization when it was too late, and St. Petersburg was no longer willing to put a stop to it.

15.

Germany's premature declaration of war on Russia was a political error, which can be accounted for by the immense danger of the position on two fronts; her declaration of war on France was a pure formality.

The decisive event was not this or that declaration of war, but the action which made the declaration of war inevitable, and this action was Russia's general mobilization.

16.

England declared war on Germany because she did not consider it compatible with her interests that France should be defeated a second time. Belgian interests, and the treaty of 1839, which Lord Salisbury had been prepared to sacrifice in 1887, were the reasons adduced to make it popular.

Over and above this, the naval agreement of 1912 with France compelled England to abandon her neutrality before Belgium's neutrality was violated.

17.

Greater diplomatic skill was shown by the Entente than by the Triple Alliance Powers.

By her false statements regarding Germany's preparations for war, particularly regarding the alleged priority of the German mobilization, by magnifying insignificant incidents on the frontier into invasions of French territory, and by withdrawing her covering troops to a distance of ten kilometres from the frontier, France created the prior condition in London, which Benckendorff had indicated, as far back as at the end of 1912, as necessary for England's intervention. An impression was produced in London that "the opponents of the Entente were the aggressors."

3 The July Crisis

*The following Austrian account describes the setting of the
murder at Sarajevo and the Serbian response.*

FROM *Austrian Red Book*

Ritter von Storck, Secretary of Legation, to Count Berchtold [1]

Belgrade, June 29, 1914.

UNDER THE TERRIBLE SHOCK of yesterday's catastrophe it is difficult
for me to give any satisfactory judgment on the bloody drama of Serajevo
with the necessary composure and judicial calm. I must ask you, therefore, to
allow me for the moment to limit myself to putting on record certain facts.

Yesterday, the 15/28, the anniversary of the battle of the Amselfeld, was
celebrated with greater ceremony than usual, and there were celebrations in
honour of the Servian patriot, Miloš Obilić, who in 1389 with two compan-
ions treacherously stabbed the victorious Murad.

Among all Servians, Obilić is regarded as the national hero. In place of
the Turks, however, we are now looked on as the hereditary enemy, thanks
to the propaganda which has been nourished under the aegis of the Royal
Government and the agitation which has for many years been carried on in
the press.

A repetition of the drama on the field of Kossovo seems, therefore, to
have hovered before the minds of the three young criminals of Serajevo,
Princip, Čabrinović and the third person still unknown, who also threw a
bomb. They also shot down an innocent woman, and may therefore think
that they have surpassed their model.

For many years hatred against the Monarchy has been sown in Servia.
The crop has sprung up and the harvest is murder.

The news arrived at about 5 o'clock; the Servian Government at about
10 o'clock caused the Obilić festivities to be officially stopped. They continued, however, unofficially for a considerable time after it was dark. The
accounts of eye-witnesses say that people fell into one another's arms in

[1] Count Leopold von Berchtold, Austro-Hungarian Minister for Foreign Affairs, 1912–1915.

Austrian Red Book in *Collected Diplomatic Documents Relating to the Outbreak of the
European War*, No. 1 (1915), p. 448.

delight, and remarks were heard, such as: "It serves them right, we have been expecting this for a long time," or "This is revenge for the annexation."

> *This document is a note from the German ambassador, Tschirschky, at Vienna, to the German Chancellor, Beth-mann-Hollweg. The marginal remarks are by the German Emperor, Wilhelm II.*

Tschirschky's Report of Austrian Opinion

The Ambassador at Vienna [1] *to the Imperial Chancellor* [2]

Vienna, June 30, 1914.

I hope not.

Now or never. Who authorized him to act that way? That is very stupid! It is none of his business, as it is solely the affair of Austria, what she plans to do in this case. Later, if plans go wrong, it will be said that Germany did not want it! Let Tschirschky be good enough to drop this nonsense! The Serbs must be disposed of, AND *that right* SOON! *Goes without saying; nothing but truisms.*

COUNT BERCHTOLD TOLD ME today that *everything* pointed to the fact that the threads of the conspiracy to which the Archduke fell a sacrifice, *ran together at Belgrade.* The affair was so well thought out that very young men were intentionally selected for the perpetration of the crime, against whom *only a mild punishment could be decreed.* The Minister spoke very bitterly about the Serbian plots.

I frequently hear expressed here, even among serious people, the wish that *at last a final and fundamental reckoning should be had with the Serbs.* The Serbs should first be presented with a number of demands, and in case they should not accept these, energetic measures should be taken. *I take opportunity of every such occasion to advise quietly but very impressively and seriously against too hasty steps.* First of all, they must make sure what they want to do, for so far I have heard only indefinite expressions of opinion. Then the chances of every kind of action should be carefully weighed, and it should be kept in mind that Austria-Hungary does not stand alone in the world, that it is her duty to think not only of her allies, but to take into consideration the entire European situation, and especially to bear in mind the attitude of Italy and Roumania on all questions that concern Serbia.

Von Tschirschky

[1] Heinrich Leonhard von Tschirschky und Bögendorff, German Ambassador to Austria-Hungary, 1907–1916.
[2] Dr. Theobald von Bethmann-Hollweg, Chancellor of the German Empire, 1909–1917.

Max Montgelas and Walther Schücking, eds., *Outbreak of the World War: German Documents Collected by Karl Kautsky,* No. 7 (1924), p. 61, translated by Carnegie Endowment for International Peace. Reprinted by permission of Carnegie Endowment for International Peace.

On July 5 Count Ladislaus Hoyos, Secretary for Balkan Affairs at the Austro-Hungarian Ministry of Foreign Affairs, arrived in Berlin to confer with the Germans. Hoyos' version of what he learned is presented here by Luigi Albertini, an Italian historian. As there has been some doubt about the reliability of the Hoyos account, Albertini cites an interview with Alfred Zimmermann, German Undersecretary of Foreign Affairs, who took part in the talks.

FROM *The Origins of the War of 1914*
BY LUIGI ALBERTINI

WHEN QUESTIONED by the present writer Hoyos stated that at his interview with Zimmermann on the afternoon of the 5th he delivered himself of the mission entrusted to him by Berchtold, handing over a copy of Francis Joseph's letter and of the Austrian memorandum. He explained to Zimmermann that the Sarajevo outrage touched vital Austrian interests in both home and foreign affairs, that Vienna found itself compelled to arrive at a definite settlement of accounts with Serbia, but that before taking a decisive step the Austrian Government needed to be certain that its intentions met with the full approval of Berlin. Hoyos assured the present writer that he had been surprised to find Zimmermann in wholehearted agreement that Austria-Hungary could no longer tolerate Serbian provocation. The decision of the Kaiser and Bethmann-Hollweg was still awaited but there was little doubt that they would give Austria the assurance of unconditional support from Germany. Zimmermann inquired what steps Vienna proposed to take and Hoyos replied that so far no decision had been taken but that the idea was to impose severe conditions on Serbia and, if these were not accepted, go to war. Zimmermann replied that if Austria meant to act she must do so immediately without diplomatic delays which would waste precious time and give the alarm to *Entente* diplomacy.

We at Vienna—he said—have the defect of arguing too much and changing our minds. Once a decision was taken, there should be no time lost in going into action so as to take Serbia and the chancelleries of

Luigi Albertini, *The Origins of the War of 1914*, II (1953), 144–5, translated and edited by Isabella M. Massey. Reprinted by permission of The Clarendon Press, Oxford.

Europe by surprise. Austrian reprisals were amply justified by the Sarajevo crime.

Zimmermann felt sure that, if this course were pursued, the conflict would remain localized, but that, should France and Russia intervene, Germany alone with her increased military strength would be able to meet them. Hoyos told him that as soon as he was in possession of the Germany reply he would return to Vienna, and a Council of Joint Ministers would be summoned. Zimmermann replied that after the Council meeting it would be desirable that no further time should be lost.

Hoyos thus continues his narrative:

> And as Tschirschky at Vienna had advised me to be very firm and detailed in my account of Austrian plans at Berlin, I carried out Berchtold's instructions by stating that, once we had beaten Serbia, we intended to partition her territory among Austria-Hungary, Bulgaria, and Albania. Zimmermann replied with a smile of satisfaction that this was a question concerning only ourselves and that he would raise no objections. Next day Bethmann officially informed Szögyény and myself in the presence of Zimmermann that it was entirely for us to decide on the measures we were to take: in whatever circumstances and whatever our decision we should find Germany unconditionally at our side in allied loyalty. Twice over he said to me, however, that in his personal opinion, with things as they were, only "immediate action against Serbia" could solve our difficulties with her. "The international situation was entirely in our favour." When I started out from Vienna, despite all that had been said by Naumann and Ganz, I did not expect to find in Berlin such instantaneous and complete understanding of our difficulties. Our design of a decisive settlement of accounts with Serbia met with no objection. On the contrary we were told that this was also the opinion of Germany and we were advised to take "immediate action." This incitement, expressed to me first by Zimmermann and then by Bethmann, made a great impression on me and I did not fail to draw attention to it in the telegram which I sent to Vienna over Szögyény's signature after the conversation.

Zimmermann, in answer to an inquiry from the present writer, wrote on 17 June 1938:

> The Wilhelmstrasse, in coming to the conclusion that the war would remain confined to Austria-Hungary and Serbia and that its spread to Europe would be avoided, went on the assumption that the Dual Monarchy would lose no time in proceeding against Serbia. To avoid the impression of exercising constraint, we unfortunately refrained from explicitly influencing our ally in the sense of this assumption. Austria-Hungary failed to act without delay and under the powerful impression of the Sarajevo murder. She allowed precious weeks to slip by in useless

investigations; finally she sent an ultimatum to Serbia without making the necessary military preparations to invade Serbia immediately and occupy Belgrade in the event of a rejection, which was surely to be expected. This mistake gave the *Entente* Powers the welcome chance to exchange views and arrive at an understanding.

Bethmann-Hollweg's Relay of Kaiser Wilhelm's Position

The Imperial Chancellor to the Ambassador at Vienna

Telegram 113.
Confidential. For Your Excellency's personal
    information and guidance.

Berlin, July 6, 1914.

T HE A USTRO-H UNGARIAN A MBASSADOR yesterday delivered to the Emperor a confidential personal letter from the Emperor Franz Joseph, which depicts the present situation from the Austro-Hungarian point of view, and describes the measures which Vienna has in view. A copy is now being forwarded to Your Excellency.

I replied to Count Szögyény [1] today on behalf of His Majesty that His Majesty sends his thanks to the Emperor Franz Joseph for his letter and would soon answer it personally. In the meantime His Majesty desires to say that he is not blind to the danger which threatens Austria-Hungary and thus the Triple Alliance as a result of the Russian and Serbian Panslavic agitation. Even though His Majesty is known to feel no unqualified confidence in Bulgaria and her ruler, and naturally inclines more toward our old ally Roumania and her Hohenzollern prince, yet he quite understands that the Emperor Franz Joseph, in view of the attitude of Roumania and of the danger of a new Balkan alliance aimed directly at the Danube Monarchy, is anxious to bring about an understanding between Bulgaria and the Triple Alliance. His Majesty will, therefore, direct his minister at Sofia to lend the Austro-Hungarian representative such support as he may desire in any action taken to this end. His Majesty will, furthermore, make an effort at Bucharest, according to the wishes of the Emperor Franz Joseph, to influence King Carol to the fulfillment of the duties of his alliance, to the renunciation

[1] Austro-Hungarian Ambassador to Germany

Max Montgelas and Walther Schücking, eds., *Outbreak of the World War: German Documents Collected by Karl Kautsky*, No. 15 (1924), pp. 78–9, translated by Carnegie Endowment for International Peace. Reprinted by permission of Carnegie Endowment for International Peace.

of Serbia, and to the suppression of the Roumanian agitations directed against Austria-Hungary.

Finally, as far as concerns Serbia, His Majesty, of course, can not interfere in the dispute now going on between Austria-Hungary and that country, as it is a matter not within his competence. The Emperor Franz Joseph may, however, rest assured that His Majesty will faithfully stand by Austria-Hungary, as is required by the obligations of his alliance and of his ancient friendship.

Bethmann-Hollweg.

Already on July 1, Victor Naumann, a German publicist close to the German Foreign Secretary, had met with Hoyos and urged an attack on Serbia. In the following selection Albertini shows that similar views were communicated by the German ambassador.

FROM *The Origins of the War of 1914*
BY LUIGI ALBERTINI

BUT BERLIN GAVE AUSTRIA-HUNGARY not only what Lutz describes as the "curse" of a free hand. It also gave her incitement and encouragement to take action against Serbia. We have already noted Naumann's call of 1 July on Hoyos. On 4 July Forgach drafted a note stating that he had seen Ganz, the Vienna correspondent of the *Frankfurter Zeitung*, who had that day been received by Tschirschky. Ganz had said that the German Ambassador had several times repeated to him with the obvious intention that the Ballplatz should be told of it

that Germany would support the Monarchy through thick and thin in whatever it might decide regarding Serbia. The Ambassador had added that the sooner Austria-Hungary went into action the better. Yesterday would have been better than to-day, and to-day would be better than to-morrow.

To his English colleague Bunsen, as the latter on 5 July reported to the Foreign Office, Tschirschky said that relations between Austria and Serbia

Luigi Albertini, *The Origins of the War of 1914*, II (1953), 150–1, translated and edited by Isabella M. Massey. Reprinted by permission of The Clarendon Press, Oxford.

must be bad, and that nothing could mend them. He added that he had tried in vain to convince Berlin of this fundamental truth. Some people in Germany still persisted in believing in the efficacy of a conciliatory policy on the part of Austria towards Serbia. He himself knew better.

But after Sarajevo, even in Germany those in authority were converted to Tschirschky's thesis and he, in consequence, could speak a very different language to Berchtold than he had used on 2 July. This is shown by what Berchtold wrote to Tisza on 8 July:

> Tschirschky has just left after having told me that he has received a telegram from Berlin containing instructions from his Imperial master to emphasize here that Berlin expects the Monarchy to take action against Serbia and that Germany would not understand our letting the opportunity slip without striking a blow. . . . From other utterances of the Ambassador I could see that Germany would interpret any compromise on our part with Serbia as a confession of weakness, which would not remain without repercussions on our position in the Triple Alliance and the future policy of Germany.

On July 18, Dr. H. von Schoen, the Bavarian chargé d'affaires *at Berlin, wrote an account of the discussions between the Germans and Austrians based on conversations with well-informed German officials.*

Von Schoen's Account of the Austro-German Discussions

The Chargé d'Affaires at Berlin to the President of the Ministerial Council
Report 386.

Berlin, July 18, 1914.

I HAVE THE HONOR most respectfully to report as follows to Your Excellency concerning the prospective settlement between the Austro-Hungarian Government and Serbia, on the basis of conversations I have had with Under-Secretary of State Zimmermann, and further with the Foreign Office reporter for the Balkans and the Triple Alliance, and with the counselor of the Austro-Hungarian Embassy.

Max Montgelas and Walther Schücking, eds., *Outbreak of the World War: German Documents Collected by Karl Kautsky,* Supplement IV, No. 2 (1924), pp. 616–8, translated by Carnegie Endowment for International Peace. Reprinted by permission of Carnegie Endowment for International Peace.

The step which the Vienna Cabinet has decided to undertake at Belgrade, and which will consist in the presentation of a note, will take place on the twenty-fifth instant. The reason for the postponement of the action to that date is that they wish to await the departure of Messrs. Poincaré and Viviani from Petersburg, in order not to facilitate an agreement between the Dual Alliance Powers on any possible counter-action. Until then, by the granting of leave of absence simultaneously to the Minister of War and the Chief of the General Staff, the Vienna authorities will have the appearance of being peacefully inclined; and they have not failed of success in their attempts to influence the press and the exchange. It is recognized here that the Vienna Cabinet has been proceeding quite cleverly in this matter, and it is only regretted that Count Tisza, who at first is said to have been against any severe action, has somewhat raised the veil of secrecy by his statement in the Hungarian House of Deputies.

As Mr. Zimmermann told me, the note, so far as has yet been determined, will contain the following demands:

1. The issuing of a proclamation by the King of Serbia which shall state that the Serbian Government has nothing to do with the Greater-Serbia movement, and fully disapproves of it.
2. The initiation of an inquiry to discover those implicated in the murder of Serajevo, and the participation of Austrian officials in this inquiry.
3. Proceedings against all who have participated in the Greater-Serbia movement.

A respite of forty-eight hours is to be granted for the acceptance of these demands.

It is perfectly plain that Serbia can not accept any such demands, which are incompatible with her dignity as a sovereign state. Thus the result would be war.

Here they are absolutely willing that Austria should take advantage of this favorable opportunity, even at the risk of further complications. But whether they will actually rise to the occasion in Vienna, still seems doubtful to Mr. von Jagow, as it does to Mr. Zimmermann. The Under-Secretary of State made the statement that Austria-Hungary, thanks to her indecision and her desultoriness, had really become the Sick Man of Europe, as Turkey had once been, upon the partition of which, the Russians, Italians, Roumanians, Serbians and Montenegrins were now waiting. A powerful and successful move against Serbia would make it possible for the Austrians and Hungarians to feel themselves once more to be a national power, would again revive the country's collapsed economic life, and would set foreign aspirations back for years. To judge from the indignation at the bloody deed that was now dominant over the entire Monarchy, it looked as if they could even be sure of the Slav troops. In a few years, with the continuance of the operation of the Slavic propaganda, this would no longer be the case, as even General Conrad von Hötzendorf himself had admitted.

So they are of the opinion here that Austria is face to face with an hour of fate, and for this reason they declared here without hesitation, in reply to an inquiry from Vienna, that we would agree to any method of procedure which they might determine on there, even at the risk of a war with Russia. The blank power of full authority that was given to Count Berchtold's Chief of the Cabinet, Count Hoyos, who came here to deliver a personal letter from the Emperor together with a detailed memorial, went so far that the Austro-Hungarian Government was empowered to deal with Bulgaria concerning her entrance into the Triple Alliance.

In Vienna they do not seem to have expected such an unconditional support of the Danube Monarchy by Germany, and Mr. Zimmermann has the impression that it is almost embarrassing to the always timid and undecided authoritities at Vienna not to be admonished by Germany to caution and self-restraint. To what extent they waver in their decisions at Vienna is shown by the circumstance that Count Berchtold, three days after he had had inquiries made here concerning the alliance with Bulgaria, telegraphed that he still had scruples about closing with Bulgaria.

So it would have been liked even better here, if they had not waited so long with their action against Serbia, and the Serbian Government had not been given time to make an offer of satisfaction on its own account, perhaps acting under Russo-French pressure.

What attitude the other Powers will take toward an armed conflict between Austria and Serbia will chiefly depend, according to the opinion here, on whether Austria will content herself with a chastisement of Serbia, or will demand territorial compensation for herself. In the first case, it might be possible to localize the war; in the other case, on the other hand, more serious complications would probably be inevitable.

The administration will, immediately upon the presentation of the Austrian note at Belgrade, initiate diplomatic action with the Powers, in the interest of the localization of the war. It will claim that the Austrian action has been just as much of a surprise to it as to the other Powers, pointing out the fact that the Emperor is on his northern journey and that the Prussian Minister of War, as well as the Chief of the Grand General Staff are away on leave of absence. (As I take the liberty to insert here, not even the Italian Government has been taken into confidence.) It will lay stress upon the fact that it is a matter of interest for all the monarchical Governments that "the Belgrade nest of anarchists" be once and for all rooted out; and it will make use of its influence to get all the Powers to take the view that the settlement between Austria and Serbia is a matter concerning those two nations alone. The mobilization of the German Army is to be refrained from, and they are also going to work through the military authorities to prevent Austria from mobilizing her entire Army, and especially not those troops stationed in Galicia, in order to avoid bringing about automatically a counter-mobilization on the part of Russia, which would force, first ourselves, and then France, to take similar measures and thereby conjure up a European war.

The attitude of Russia will, above all else, determine the question whether the attempt to localize the war will succeed.

If Russia is not determined on war against Austria and Germany, in any case, she can, in that event—and that is the most favorable factor in the present situation—very well remain inactive, and justify herself toward the Serbs by announcing that she approves of the kind of fighting that goes to work with the throwing of bombs and with revolver shots just as little as any of the other civilized nations; this, especially, so long as Austria does not render doubtful Serbia's national independence. Mr. Zimmermann assumes that both England and France, to neither of whom a war would be acceptable at the present moment, will try to exert a pacifying influence on Russia; besides that, he is counting on the fact that "bluffing" constitutes one of the most favored requisites of Russian policy, and that while the Russian likes to threaten with the sword, he still does not like so very much to draw it in behalf of others at the critical moment.

England will not prevent Austria from calling Serbia to account; it is only the destruction of the nation that she would scarcely permit, being far more likely—true to her traditions—presumably to take a stand, even in this case, for the principles of nationality. A war between the Dual Alliance and the Triple Alliance would be unwelcome to England at the present time, if only in consideration of the situation in Ireland. Should it, however, come to that, according to all opinion here, we should find our English cousins on the side of our enemies, inasmuch as England fears that France, in the event of a new defeat, would sink to the level of a Power of the second class, and that the "balance of power," the maintenance of which England considers to be necessary for her own interests, would be upset thereby.

> *This report from Pourtalès, German ambassador to Russia, to Bethmann-Hollweg, describes the attitude of Sazonoff, Russian Minister for Foreign Affairs, to the growing crisis. The marginal remarks are by Kaiser Wilhelm.*

Pourtalès's Report of the Russian Response

The Ambassador at Petersburg to the Imperial Chancellor

St. Petersburg, July 21, 1914.

MR. SAZONOFF, who spent several days last week at his country estate in the Government of Grodno, has been quite anxious since his return from

---

Max Montgelas and Walther Schücking, eds., *Outbreak of the World War: German Documents Collected by Karl Kautsky*, No. 120 (1924), pp. 159–62, translated by Carnegie Endowment for International Peace. Reprinted by permission of Carnegie Endowment for International Peace.

there on account of the relations between Austria-Hungary and Serbia. He told me that he had received very alarming reports from London, Paris and Rome, and that Austria-Hungary's attitude was inspiring an increasing worry everywhere. Mr. Schebeko, too, who was in general a calm observer, reported that the feeling in Vienna against Serbia was constantly growing more bitter.

The Minister took the opportunity of giving his wrath at the Austro-Hungarian policy free rein, as usual. That the Emperor Franz Joseph and even Count Berchtold were friends of peace, Mr. Sazonoff was, it is true, willing to admit, but he said that there were very powerful and dangerous influences at work, which were constantly gaining ground in both halves of the Empire, and which did not hesitate at the idea of plunging Austria into a war, even at the risk of starting a general world conflagration. One anxiously asked oneself the question whether the aged Monarch and his weak Foreign Minister would always be able to successfully oppose these influences.

The picture fits Petersburg much better!

Previously the belligerent elements, among which clerical intrigues also played an especially important rôle, had set their hopes on the dead Archduke, Franz Ferdinand. The death of the Archduke had in no way discouraged them; on the other hand, they were the very ones who were inspiring [1] the dangerous policy which Austria-Hungary was pursuing at the present moment. The actual leaders in this policy were two men, particularly, whose increasing influence appeared to the highest degree dubious—namely, Count Forgach, who is "an intriguer of the basest sort," and Count Tisza, who "is half a fool."

Fool yourself, Mr. Sazonoff!

I replied to Mr. Sazonoff that his unmeasured reproaches against Austro-Hungarian policy appeared to me to be strongly influenced by his too great sympathy for the Serbs, and to be utterly unjustified. No sensible man could refuse to recognize the complete restraint observed by the Vienna Cabinet since the assassination at Serajevo. It seemed to me that to decide just how far Austria-Hungary was justified in holding the Serbian Government responsible for the Greater-Serbia agitations, as early as this, before the result of the inquiry concerning the assassination was known, was absolutely premature. But according to everything that was already known, one could scarcely doubt *that the Greater-Serbia agitation was stirred up under the very eyes of the Serbian Government, and that even the shameless assassination itself had been planned in Serbia.* No great

Yes.

[1] Exclamation-point by the Emperor in the margin.

nation, however, could possibly tolerate permanently the existence along its borders of a propaganda which directly threatened its own security. Should, therefore, as appearances now seemed to indicate, traces be discovered at the inquiry into the origin of the crime which pointed back to Serbia, and should it be proved that the Serbian Government had regrettably connived at the intrigues directed against Austria, then the Austro-Hungarian Government would unquestionably be justified in using strong language at Belgrade. I could not conceive that in such a case the representations of the Vienna Cabinet to the Serbian Government could meet with the objection of any Power whatsoever.

Right.

Yes.

Good.

The Minister met these arguments with the assertion that the support of the Greater-Serbia propaganda in Austria-Hungary by Serbia or by the Serbian Government in any way, *had in nowise been proved. A whole country could not be held responsible* for *the acts of individuals.* Furthermore, the murderer of the Archduke was not even a Serbian subject. There *certainly* was a Greater-Serbia propaganda *in Austria,* but it was the result of the *bad* methods of government by which Austria had distinguished herself for ages back. Just as there was a Greater-Serbia propaganda, one heard talk also of the Italian Irredenta and of the Free-from-Rome movement. The Vienna Cabinet had not the slightest reason for complaining of the *attitude of the Serbian Government,* which, on the contrary, *was behaving itself with entire propriety.*

Genuinely Russian.

Damnation!

I interjected here that it did not suffice for members of the Serbian Government themselves to refrain from participation in the anti-Austrian propaganda. Austria-Hungary had far more reason to require that the Serbian authorities should proceed actively against the anti-Austrian propaganda, for it was impossible that the Government should refuse responsibility for everything that was going on in the country.

Right.

According to that principle, returned Mr. Sazonoff, Russia ought to hold the Swedish Government responsible for the *anti-Russian agitation* that has been *going on in Sweden* for about a year and a half.

And Russia for her spies that are being apprehended everywhere!

I pointed out that in Sweden the matter merely concerned a political agitation, and not, as in Serbia, a propaganda of action.

Mr. Sazonoff remarked in reply that those people in Austria who were advocating proceeding against Serbia would apparently not content themselves with making rep-

resentations at Belgrade, but that their object was the annihilation of Serbia. I answered that I had never heard of any
object but one, namely, the "clarification" of Austria-Hungary's relations with Serbia.

*And the best
thing, too.*

The Minister continued excitedly, saying that in any
case, Austria-Hungary, if she was absolutely determined
to disturb the peace, ought not to forget that in that event
she would *have to reckon with Europe.* Russia could not
look indifferently on at a move at Belgrade which aimed
at the humiliation (of) Serbia. I remarked that I was able
[to] *see no humiliation* in serious representations by which
Serbia was reminded of her international obligations. Mr.
Sazonoff answered that it would all depend on how the
move was carried out; that in no case *should there be any
talk of an ultimatum.*

*No! with Russia,
yes! as the perpe-
trator and advocate
of regicide!!!*

Right.

It's already there!

The Minister repeatedly called attention in the course
of the conversation to the fact that, according to information
he had received, the situation was being very seriously regarded in Paris and London also, and he was visibly attempting to give me the impression that even in England
Austria's attitude was strongly disapproved.

He is wrong!

At the conclusion of our conversation I asked Mr.
Sazonoff what there was, in his opinion, to the alleged
plan for the union of Serbia and Montenegro, lately so
much discussed in the papers. The Minister remarked that
such a union was desired only by Montenegro, which would
of course benefit most by it. Such a union was not being
considered at all in Serbia, as the late Mr. Hartwig had
specifically emphasized in one of his last reports. At the
most, all that was wanted was a closer economic relation
with Montenegro, but a personal union was not in any
way desired.

Mr. Sazonoff has also expressed to my Italian colleague
his anxiety about the Austro-Serbian tension, and remarked
at the time that Russia would *not be able to permit* Austria-Hungary to *make any threats against Serbia* or to *take
any military measures.* "La politique de la Russie," said Mr.
Sazonoff, "*est pacifique, mais pas passive.*"

Qui vivra verra!

F. Pourtalès.

*On the afternoon of July 23 the Austrians presented a list of
demands to Serbia and the Serbs were given forty-eight*

hours to reply. The Austrian ambassador to Belgrade was instructed to leave the country and break off diplomatic relations unless the demands were met without reservations.

The Austrian Ultimatum

THE RESULTS BROUGHT OUT by the inquiry no longer permit the Imperial and Royal Government to maintain the attitude of patient tolerance which it has observed for years toward those agitations which center at Belgrade and are spread thence into the territories of the Monarchy. Instead, these results impose upon the Imperial and Royal Government the obligation to put an end to those intrigues, which constitute a standing menace to the peace of the Monarchy.

In order to attain this end, the Imperial and Royal Government finds itself compelled to demand that the Serbian Government give official assurance that it will condemn the propaganda directed against Austria-Hungary, that is to say, the whole body of the efforts whose ultimate object it is to separate from the Monarchy territories that belong to it; and that it will obligate itself to suppress with all the means at its command this criminal and terroristic propaganda.

In order to give these assurances a character of solemnity, the Royal Serbian Government will publish on the first page of its official organ of July 26/13, the following declaration:

> The Royal Serbian Government condemns the propaganda directed against Austria-Hungary, that is to say, the whole body of the efforts whose ultimate object it is to separate from the Austro-Hungarian Monarchy territories that belong to it, and it most sincerely regrets the dreadful consequences of these criminal transactions.
>
> The Royal Serbian Government regrets that Serbian officers and officials should have taken part in the above-mentioned propaganda and thus have endangered the friendly and neighborly relations, to the cultivation of which the Royal Government had most solemnly pledged itself by its declaration of March 31, 1909.
>
> The Royal Government, which disapproves and repels every idea and every attempt to interfere in the destinies of the population of whatever portion of Austria-Hungary, regards it as its duty most expressly to call the attention of the officers, officials, and the whole popula-

Max Montgelas and Walther Schücking, eds., *Outbreak of the World War: German Documents Collected by Karl Kautsky,* Supplement I (1924), pp. 604–5, translated by Carnegie Endowment for International Peace. Reprinted by permission of Carnegie Endowment for International Peace.

tion of the Kingdom to the fact that for the future it will proceed with the utmost rigor against any persons who shall become guilty of any such activities, activities to prevent and to suppress which, the Government will bend every effort.

This declaration shall be brought to the attention of the Royal army simultaneously by an order of the day from His Majesty the King, and by publication in the official organ of the army.

The Royal Serbian Government will furthermore pledge itself:

1. to suppress every publication which shall incite to hatred and contempt of the Monarchy, and the general tendency of which shall be directed against the territorial integrity of the latter;

2. to proceed at once to the dissolution of the *Narodna Odbrana,* to confiscate all of its means of propaganda, and in the same manner to proceed against the other unions and associations in Serbia which occupy themselves with propaganda against Austria-Hungary; the Royal Government will take such measures as are necessary to make sure that the dissolved associations may not continue their activities under other names or in other forms;

3. to eliminate without delay from public instruction in Serbia, everything, whether connected with the teaching corps or with the methods of teaching, that serves or may serve to nourish the propaganda against Austria-Hungary;

4. to remove from the military and administrative service in general all officers and officials who have been guilty of carrying on the propaganda against Austria-Hungary, whose names the Imperial and Royal Government reserves the right to make known to the Royal Government when communicating the material evidence now in its possession;

5. to agree to the cooperation in Serbia of the organs of the Imperial and Royal Government in the suppression of the subversive movement directed against the integrity of the Monarchy;

6. to institute a judicial inquiry against every participant in the conspiracy of the twenty-eighth of June who may be found in Serbian territory; the organs of the Imperial and Royal Government delegated for this purpose will take part in the proceedings held for this purpose;

7. to undertake with all haste the arrest of Major Voislav Tankositch and of one Milan Ciganovitch, a Serbian official, who have been compromised by the results of the inquiry;

8. by efficient measures to prevent the participation of Serbian authorities in the smuggling of weapons and explosives across the frontier; to dismiss from the service and to punish severely those members of the Frontier Service at Schabats and Losnitza who assisted the authors of the crime of Serajevo to cross the frontier;

9. to make explanations to the Imperial and Royal Government concerning the unjustifiable utterances of high Serbian functionaries in Serbia and

abroad, who, without regard for their official position, have not hesitated to express themselves in a manner hostile toward Austria-Hungary since the assassination of the twenty-eighth of June;

10. to inform the Imperial and Royal Government without delay of the execution of the measures comprised in the foregoing points.

The Imperial and Royal Government awaits the reply of the Royal Government by Saturday, the twenty-fifth instant, at 6 P.M., at the latest.

A mémoire concerning the results of the inquiry at Serajevo, as far as they concern the functionaries referred to in Points 7 and 8, is appended to this note.

> *This is a report from the German ambassador at St. Petersburg to the Foreign Office in Berlin. Marginal remarks are by Kaiser Wilhelm.*

Pourtalès's Report on Russia's Reaction to Austria's Ultimatum

The Ambassador at Petersburg to the Foreign Office

Telegram 149.

St. Petersburg, July 25, 1914.

HAVE JUST HAD LONG INTERVIEW with Sazonoff at which subject of dispatch 592 figured exhaustively. Minis-

Good.

ter, who was *very much excited* and gave vent to boundless reproaches against Austria-Hungary, stated in the most determined manner that it would be impossible for Russia to admit that the Austro-Serb quarrel could be settled between the two parties concerned. The obligations which Serbia had assumed after the Bosnian crisis and to which the Austrian note refers, were assumed toward Europe, consequently the affair was a European affair, and it was

Rot!

for *Europe* to investigate as to whether Serbia had lived up to these obligations. He therefore proposes that the documents in relation to the inquiry be laid before the Cabinets

Max Montgelas and Walther Schücking, eds., *Outbreak of the World War: German Documents Collected by Karl Kautsky,* No. 160 (1924), pp. 186-7, translated by Carnegie Endowment for International Peace. Reprinted by permission of Carnegie Endowment for International Peace.

of the six Powers. Austria could not be both accuser and judge in her own case. Sazonoff announced that he could in no way consider as proven the facts alleged by Austria in her note, that the inquiry, on the other hand, inspired him with the greatest (suspicion). He continued by saying that, in case the facts asserted should be proved to be true, Serbia could give Austria satisfaction in the purely legal questions, but not, on the other hand, in the matter of the demands of a political nature. I called attention to the fact that it was impossible to separate the legal from the political side of the matter, as the assassination was inseparably connected with the Greater-Serbia propaganda.

That's a question of the point of view!

Cannot be separated.

I promised to lay his ideas before my Government, but did not believe that we would suggest to our ally to submit the results of an inquiry conducted by her *once more to a European tribunal*. Austria would object to this suggestion just as any Great Power would have to refuse to submit itself to a court of arbitration in a case in which its vital interests were at stake.

Right.
Panslavistic.
Most certainly not!

Bravo!
Well said!

My references to the monarchical principle made little impression on the Minister. Russia *knew* what she *owed to the monarchical principle,* with which, however, this case had nothing to do. I requested Sazonoff very seriously, avoiding everything that might have the appearance of a threat, not to let himself be led astray by his hatred of Austria and *"not to defend a bad cause."* Russia could not possibly constitute herself the advocate *of regicides.*

Not since her fraternizing with the French socialist republic!

Regicide.
Very good.

In the course of the conversation Sazonoff exclaimed: "If Austria-Hungary devours Serbia, we will go to war with her." From this it may perhaps be concluded that Russia will only take up arms in the event of Austria's attempting to acquire territory at the expense of Serbia. The expressed desire to Europeanize the question also seems to point to the fact that immediate intervention on the part of Russia is not to be anticipated.

Well, go to it!

That it wants to do, it seems.

Not correct.

Pourtalès.

Here is a telegram from Sir Edward Grey, British Secretary
of State for Foreign Affairs to the British ambassador in
Vienna.

Grey's Conveyal of the British Response to Austria's Ultimatum

Grey to Bunsen

Tel. (No. 148)

Foreign Office, July 24, 1914

A USTRO-HUNGARIAN AMBASSADOR has communicated to me the note addressed to Servia with the explanation of the Austro-Hungarian Government upon it.

I said that the murder of the Archduke and some of the circumstances stated in the Austro-Hungarian note with regard to Servia naturally aroused sympathy with Austria, but I thought it a great pity that a time-limit, and such a short time-limit, had been introduced at this stage, and the note seemed to me the most formidable document I had ever seen addressed by one State to another that was independent. Demand No. 5 might mean that the Austro-Hungarian Government were to be entitled to appoint officials who should have authority in Servian territory and this would hardly be consistent with the maintenance of independent sovereignty of Servia.

I was not, however, making these comments in order to discuss the merits of the dispute between Austria-Hungary and Servia; that was not our concern. It was solely from the point of view of the peace of Europe that I should concern myself with the matter, and I felt great apprehension.

I must wait to hear the views of other Powers and no doubt we should consult with them to see what could be done to mitigate difficulties.

The Austro-Hungarian Ambassador observed that there had been so much procrastination on the part of Servia that a time-limit was essential. Some weeks had passed since the murder of the Archduke and Servia had made no sign of sympathy or help; if she had held out a hand after the murder the present situation might have been prevented.

I observed that a time-limit could have been introduced at any later stage if Servia had procrastinated about a reply; as it was, the Austro-Hungarian Government not only demanded a reply within forty-eight hours, but dictated the terms of the reply.

British Documents on the Origins of the War 1898–1914, XI, No. 91 (1926), 73–4.

Grey's Proposal for a Conference

Sir Edward Grey to Sir F. Bertie

Tel. (No. 232)

Foreign Office, July 26, 1914

ASK MINISTER FOR FOREIGN AFFAIRS if he would be disposed to instruct Ambassador here to join with representatives of Italy, Germany, France, and myself in a conference to be held here at once in order to endeavour to find an issue to prevent complications. With this view representatives at Vienna, St. Petersburg and Belgrade should be authorised in informing Governments to which they are accredited of above suggestion to request that pending results of conference all active military operations shall be suspended.

(Repeated to Vienna, St. Petersburg, and Nish.)
(Sent also to Berlin, and Rome.)

> *Prince Lichnowsky, German Ambassador to London, was in close touch with the ruling circles of England and better informed on British opinion than were his colleagues in Berlin. The following report is one of several in which he argues against war on the grounds that England would be likely to fight against Germany.*

Lichnowsky's Appraisal of the British Position

The Ambassador at London to the Foreign Office

Telegram 161.

London, July 26, 1914

HAVE JUST TALKED with Sir A. Nicolson and Sir W. Tyrrell. According to reports at hand here, a general calling to the colors of the Russian

---

British Documents on the Origins of the War 1898–1914, XI, No. 140 (1926), 101.

Max Montgelas and Walther Schücking, eds., *Outbreak of the World War: German Documents Collected by Karl Kautsky*, No. 236 (1924), pp. 230–1, translated by Carnegie Endowment for International Peace. Reprinted by permission of Carnegie Endowment for International Peace.

reservists is not projected, but only a partial mobilization far from our frontiers. Both gentlemen see in Sir E. Grey's proposal to hold a conference *à quatre* here, the only possibility of avoiding a general war, and hope that in this way it would be possible to get full satisfaction for Austria, as Serbia would be more apt to give in to the pressure of the Powers and to submit to their united will than to the threats of Austria. But the absolute prerequisite to the bringing about of the conference and the maintenance of peace would be the cessation of all military activities. Once the Serbian border was crossed, everything would be at an end, as no Russian Government would be able to tolerate this, and would be forced to move to the attack on Austria unless she wanted to see her status among the Balkan nations lost forever. Sir W. Tyrrell, who saw Sir E. Grey last evening and is fully cognizant of his views, pointed out to me repeatedly and with emphasis the immense importance of Serbia's territory remaining unviolated until the question of the conference had been settled, as otherwise every effort would have been in vain and the world war would be inevitable. The localization of the conflict as hoped for in Berlin was wholly impossible, and must be dropped from the calculations of practical politics. If we two should succeed—that is, His Majesty the Emperor or his Government and representatives in conjunction with Sir E. Grey—in preserving the peace of Europe, German-English relations would be placed on a firm foundation for time everlasting. If we did not succeed, everything would be doubtful.

I would like to offer an urgent warning against believing any further in the possibility of localization, and to express the humble wish that our policy be guided solely and alone by the need of sparing the German nation a struggle in which it has nothing to gain and everything to lose.

Sir E. Grey returns this evening.

Lichnowsky.

Serbia's Answer to the Ultimatum

THE ROYAL SERVIAN GOVERNMENT have received the communication of the Imperial and Royal Government of the 10th instant, and are convinced that their reply will remove any misunderstanding which may threaten to impair the good neighbourly relations between the Austro-Hungarian Monarchy and the Kingdom of Servia.

Conscious of the fact that the protests which were made both from the tribune of the national Skuptchina and in the declarations and actions of the responsible representatives of the State—protests which were cut short by the

British Diplomatic Correspondence in Collected Diplomatic Documents Relating to the Outbreak of the European War, No. 39 (1915), pp. 31–7.

declarations made by the Servian Government on the 18th March, 1909—have not been renewed on any occasion as regards the great neighbouring Monarchy, and that no attempt has been made since that time, either by the successive Royal Governments or by their organs, to change the political and legal state of affairs created in Bosnia and Herzegovina, the Royal Government draw attention to the fact that in this connection the Imperial and Royal Government have made no representation except one concerning a school book, and that on that occasion the Imperial and Royal Government received an entirely satisfactory explanation. Servia has several times given proofs of her pacific and moderate policy during the Balkan crisis, and it is thanks to Servia and to the sacrifice that she has made in the exclusive interest of European peace that that peace has been preserved. The Royal Government cannot be held responsible for manifestations of a private character, such as articles in the press and the peaceable work of societies—manifestations which take place in nearly all countries in the ordinary course of events, and which, as a general rule, escape official control. The Royal Government are all the less responsible, in view of the fact that at the time of the solution of a series of questions which arose between Servia and Austria-Hungary they gave proof of a great readiness to oblige, and thus succeeded in settling the majority of these questions to the advantage of the two neighbouring countries.

For these reasons the Royal Government have been pained and surprised at the statements, according to which members of the Kingdom of Servia are supposed to have participated in the preparations for the crime committed at Serajevo; the Royal Government expected to be invited to collaborate in an investigation of all that concerns this crime, and they were ready, in order to prove the entire correctness of their attitude, to take measures against any persons concerning whom representations were made to them. Falling in, therefore, with the desire of the Imperial and Royal Government, they are prepared to hand over for trial any Servian subject, without regard to his situation or rank, of whose complicity in the crime of Serajevo proofs are forthcoming, and more especially they undertake to cause to be published on the first page of the "Journal officiel," on the date of the 13th (26th) July, the following declaration:—

"The Royal Government of Servia condemn all propaganda which may be directed against Austria-Hungary, that is to say, all such tendencies as aim at ultimately detaching from the Austro-Hungarian Monarchy territories which form part thereof, and they sincerely deplore the baneful consequences of these criminal movements. The Royal Government regret that, according to the communication from the Imperial and Royal Government, certain Servian officers and officials should have taken part in the above-mentioned propaganda and thus compromised the good neighbourly relations to which the Royal Servian Government was solemnly engaged by the declaration of the 31st March, 1909, which declaration disapproves and repudiates all idea or attempt at interference with the destiny of the inhabitants of any part whatsoever of Austria-Hungary, and they consider it their duty formally to warn the officers, officials, and entire population of the kingdom that henceforth they will take the most rigorous steps against all such persons as are guilty of such acts, to prevent and to repress which they will use their utmost endeavour."

This declaration will be brought to the knowledge of the Royal Army in an order of the day, in the name of His Majesty the King, by his Royal Highness the Crown Prince Alexander, and will be published in the next official army bulletin.

The Royal Government further undertake:—

1. To introduce at the first regular convocation of the Skuptchina a provision into the press law providing for the most severe punishment of incitement to hatred or contempt of the Austro-Hungarian Monarchy, and for taking action against any publication the general tendency of which is directed against the territorial integrity of Austria-Hungary. The Government engage at the approaching revision of the Constitution to cause an amendment to be introduced into article 22 of the Constitution of such a nature that such publication may be confiscated, a proceeding at present impossible under the categorical terms of article 22 of the Constitution.

2. The Government possess no proof, nor does the note of the Imperial and Royal Government furnish them with any, that the "Narodna Odbrana" and other similar societies have committed up to the present any criminal act of this nature through the proceedings of any of their members. Nevertheless, the Royal Government will accept the demand of the Imperial and Royal Government, and will dissolve the "Narodna Odbrana" Society and every other society which may be directing its efforts against Austria-Hungary.

3. The Royal Servian Government undertake to remove without delay from their public educational establishments in Servia all that serves or could serve to foment propaganda against Austria-Hungary, whenever the Imperial and Royal Government furnish them with facts and proofs of this propaganda.

4. The Royal Government also agree to remove from military service all such persons as the judicial enquiry may have proved to be guilty of acts directed against the integrity of the territory of the Austro-Hungarian Monarchy, and they expect the Imperial and Royal Government to communicate to them at a later date the names and the acts of these officers and officials for the purposes of the proceedings which are to be taken against them.

5. The Royal Government must confess that they do not clearly grasp the meaning or the scope of the demand made by the Imperial and Royal Government that Servia shall undertake to accept the collaboration of the organs of the Imperial and Royal Government upon their territory,

but they declare that they will admit such collaboration as agrees with the principle of international law, with criminal procedure, and with good neighbourly relations.

6. It goes without saying that the Royal Government consider it their duty to open an enquiry against all such persons as are, or eventually may be, implicated in the plot of the 15th June, and who happen to be within the territory of the kingdom. As regards the participation in this enquiry of Austro-Hungarian agents or authorities appointed for this purpose by the Imperial and Royal Government, the Royal Government cannot accept such an arrangement, as it would be a violation of the Constitution and of the law of criminal procedure; nevertheless, in concrete cases communications as to the results of the investigation in question might be given to the Austro-Hungarian agents.

7. The Royal Government proceeded, on the very evening of the delivery of the note, to arrest Commandant Voislav Tankossitch. As regards Milan Ziganovitch, who is a subject of the Austro-Hungarian Monarchy and who up to the 15th June was employed (on probation) by the directorate of railways, it has not yet been possible to arrest him.

   The Austro-Hungarian Government are requested to be so good as to supply as soon as possible, in the customary form, the presumptive evidence of guilt, as well as the eventual proofs of guilt which have been collected up to the present, at the enquiry at Serajevo for the purposes of the later enquiry.

8. The Servian Government will reinforce and extend the measures which have been taken for preventing the illicit traffic of arms and explosives across the frontier. It goes without saying that they will immediately order an enquiry and will severely punish the frontier officials on the Schabatz-Loznitza line who have failed in their duty and allowed authors of the crime of Serajevo to pass.

9. The Royal Government will gladly give explanations of the remarks made by their officials whether in Servia or abroad, in interviews after the crime which according to the statement of the Imperial and Royal Government were hostile towards the Monarchy, as soon as the Imperial and Royal Government have communicated to them the passages in question in these remarks, and as soon as they have shown that the remarks were actually made by the said officials, although the Royal Government will itself take steps to collect evidence and proofs.

10. The Royal Government will inform the Imperial and Royal Government of the execution of the measures comprised under the above heads, in so far as this has not already been done by the present note, as soon as each measure has been ordered and carried out.

If the Imperial and Royal Government are not satisfied with this reply, the Servian Government, considering that it is not to the common interest to precipitate the solution of this question, are ready, as always, to accept a pacific understanding, either by referring this question to the decision of the International Tribunal of the The Hague, or to the Great Powers which took part in the drawing up of the declaration made by the Servian Government on the 18th (31st) March 1909.

Belgrade, July 12 (25), 1914

Bethmann-Hollweg's Reaction to the British Proposal

The Imperial Chancellor to the Ambassador at Vienna

Telegram 169.

Berlin, July 27, 1914.

Prince Lichnowsky has just telegraphed:

S IR E . G RE Y had me call on him just now and requested me to inform Your Excellency as follows:

The Serbian Chargé d'Affaires had just transmitted to him the text of the Serbian reply to the Austrian note. It appeared from the reply that Serbia had agreed to the Austrian demands to an extent such as he would never have believed possible; except in one point, the participation of Austrian officials in the judicial investigation, Serbia had actually agreed to everything that had been demanded of her. It was plain that this compliance of Serbia's *was to be attributed solely to the pressure exerted from Petersburg.*

Should Austria fail to be satisfied with this reply, in other words, should this reply not be accepted at Vienna as a foundation for peaceful negotiations, or should Austria even proceed to the occupation of Belgrade, which lay quite defenseless before her, it would then be absolutely evident that Austria was only seeking an excuse for crushing Serbia. And thus, that Russia and Russian influence in the Balkans were to be struck at through Serbia. It was plain that Russia could not regard such action with equanimity, and would have to accept it as a direct challenge. The result would be the most frightful war that Europe had ever seen, and no one could tell to what such a war might lead.

We had repeatedly, and even yesterday, stated the Minister, turned to him with the request that he *make a plea for moderation at Petersburg. He had always gladly complied with this request* and during the last crisis had subjected himself to reproaches from Russia to the effect that he was placing himself too much on our side and too little on theirs. Now he was turning to us with the request that we should make use of our influence at Vienna either to get them to accept the reply from Belgrade as satisfactory or as the basis for conferences. He was convinced that it lay in our hands to bring

Max Montgelas and Walther Schücking, eds., *Outbreak of the World War: German Documents Collected by Karl Kautsky*, No. 277 (1924), pp. 255–6, translated by Carnegie Endowment for International Peace. Reprinted by permission of Carnegie Endowment for International Peace.

the matter to a settlement by means of the proper representations, and he would regard it as a good augury for the future *if we two should once again succeed in assuring the peace of Europe by means of our mutual influence on our allies.*

I found the Minister irritated for the first time. He spoke with great seriousness and seemed absolutely to expect that we should successfully make use of our influence to settle the matter. He is also going to make a statement in the House of Commons today in which he is to express his point of view. In any event, I am convinced that in case it should come to war after all, we should no longer be able to count on British sympathy or British support, as every evidence of ill-will would be seen in Austria's procedure.

Since we have already refused one English proposal for a conference, it is impossible for us to waive *a limine* this English suggestion also. By refusing every proposition for mediation, we should be held responsible for the conflagration by the whole world, and be set forth as the original instigators of the war. That would also make our position impossible in our own country, where we must appear as having been forced into the war. Our situation is all the more difficult, inasmuch as Serbia has apparently yielded to a very great degree. Therefore we cannot refuse the mediator's rôle, and must submit the English proposal to the consideration of the Vienna Cabinet, especially as London and Paris continue to make their influence felt in Petersburg. I request Count Berchtold's opinion on the English suggestion, as likewise his views on Mr. Sazonoff's desire to negotiate directly with Vienna.

Bethmann-Hollweg.

Goschen was the British Ambassador to Berlin. In the following telegram he reports the German answer to the proposal for a conference to Grey.

Goschen's Transmission of the German Refusal

Sir E. Goschen to Sir Edward Grey

Tel. (No. 96)

Berlin, July 27, 1914

Your telegram No. 232 of 26th of July to Paris.

SECRETARY OF STATE FOR FOREIGN AFFAIRS says that conference you suggest would practically amount to a court of arbitration and could

not, in his opinion, be called together except at the request of Austria and
Russia. He could not therefore, desirous though he was to cooperate for the
maintenance of peace, fall in with your suggestion. I said I was sure that
your idea had nothing to do with arbitration, but meant that representatives
of the four nations not directly interested should discuss and suggest means
for avoiding a dangerous situation. He maintained, however, that such a conference as you proposed was not practicable. He added that news he had just
received from St. Petersburg showed that there was an intention on the part
of M. Sazonof to exchange views with Count Berchtold. He thought that
this method of procedure might lead to a satisfactory result, and that it would
be best, before doing anything else, to await outcome of the exchange of
views between the Austrian and Russian Governments.

In the course of a short conversation Secretary of State for Foreign
Affairs said that as yet Austria was only partially mobilising, but that if
Russia mobilised against Germany latter would have to follow suit. I asked
him what he meant by "mobilising against Germany." He said that if Russia
only mobilised in south Germany would not mobilise, but if she mobilised in
north Germany would have to do so too, and Russian system of mobilisation
was so complicated that it might be difficult exactly to locate her mobilisation. Germany would therefore have to be very careful not to be taken by
surprise.

> *In the crucial days following the rejection of the ultima-*
> *tum, France seems not to have tried to restrain Russia. The*
> *following telegram was omitted from the* Russian Orange
> Book.

French Full Support of Russia

The Russian Ambassador at Paris,   M. Isvolsky,
to the Russian Foreign Secretary,   M. Sazonov

Telegram. Secret. No. 195

Paris, July 14/27, 1914

IMMEDIATELY UPON MY RETURN to Paris, I saw the Minister of
Justice [Bienvenu-Martin] in the presence of Abel Ferry and Berthelot.
They confirmed the details of the steps taken by the German Ambassador, of
which you have been informed by Sevastopoulo's telegrams Nos. 187 and
188. This morning, Baron Schoen confirmed in writing the declaration made
by him yesterday, to wit:

1. "Austria has declared to Russia that she is not seeking territorial acquisitions and will respect the integrity of Serbia. Her only aim is to assure her own security;

2. "The prevention of war consequently rests upon Russia;

3. "Germany and France entirely united in the ardent desire to maintain peace, ought to press Russia to be moderate."

In this connection Baron Schoen particularly emphasized the expression "united" [*solidaire*] applied to Germany and France. According to the conviction of the Minister of Justice, these steps on the part of Germany are taken with the evident object of disuniting Russia and France, of inducing the French Government to make representations at St. Petersburg, and of thus compromising our ally in our eyes, and, in case of war, of throwing the responsibility not on Germany, who is ostensibly making every effort to preserve peace, but on Russia and France. Today, two hours before the steps taken by the Austrian Ambassador reported in my telegram 191, the German Ambassador paid a visit to Abel Ferry and made him, in the name of his Government, a new proposition "of intervention of France and Germany between Russia and Austria." Abel Ferry replied to him that he would bring this proposal to the attention of the Minister of Justice and merely observed that it would be opportune to leave the initiative of intervention to the four Powers, to which Baron Schoen acquiesced. The Minister of Justice has told me that he does not understand the sense of the new proposal of Baron Schoen, but that he viewed it with defiance and proposed to tell him tomorrow that a reply would be given him on the return to Paris of the Minister of Foreign Affairs on Wednesday. Altogether, I am struck by the way the Minister of Justice and his colleagues correctly understand the situation and how firm and calm is their decision to give us the most complete support and to avoid the least appearance of divergence of view between us.

Isvolsky

The Kaiser's Reaction to Serbia's Reply

The Emperor to the Secretary of State for Foreign Affairs

Your Excellency:

New Palace, July 28, 1914, 10 A.M.

AFTER READING OVER THE SERBIAN REPLY, which I received this morning, I am convinced that on the whole the wishes of the Danube

Max Montgelas and Walther Schücking, eds., *Outbreak of the World War: German Documents Collected by Karl Kautsky*, No. 293 (1924), pp. 273–4, translated by Carnegie Endowment for International Peace. Reprinted by Carnegie Endowment for International Peace.

Monarchy have been acceded to. The few reservations that Serbia makes in regard to individual points could, according to my opinion, be settled by negotiation. But it contains the announcement *orbi et urbi* of a capitulation of the most humiliating kind, and as a result, *every cause for war* falls to the ground.

Nevertheless, the piece of paper, like its contents, can be considered as of little value so long as it is not translated into *deeds*. The Serbs are Orientals, therefore liars, tricksters, and masters of evasion. In order that these beautiful promises may be turned to truth and facts, a *douce violence* must be exercised. This should be so arranged that Austria would receive a HOSTAGE (Belgrade), as a guaranty for the enforcement and carrying out of the promises, and should occupy it until the *petita* had ACTUALLY been complied with. This is also necessary in order to give the army, now UNNECESSARILY mobilized for the third time, the external *satisfaction d'honneur* of an ostensible success in the eyes of the world, and to make it possible for it to feel that it had at least stood on foreign soil. Unless this were done, the abandonment of the campaign might be the cause of a wave of bad feeling against the Monarchy, which would be dangerous in the highest degree. In case Your Excellency shares my views, I propose that we say to Austria: Serbia has been forced to retreat in a very humiliating manner, and we offer our congratulations. Naturally, as a result, EVERY CAUSE FOR WAR HAS VANISHED. But a GUARANTY that the promises WILL BE CARRIED OUT is unquestionably necessary. That could be secured by means of the TEMPORARY military occupation of a portion of Serbia, similar to the way we kept troops stationed in France in 1871 until the billions were paid. ON THIS BASIS, I am ready to MEDIATE FOR PEACE with Austria. Any proposals or protests to the contrary by other nations I should refuse regardless, especially as all of them have made more or less open appeals to me to assist in maintaining peace. This I will do in my own way, and as sparingly of Austria's NATIONALISTIC FEELING, and of the HONOR OF HER ARMS as possible. For the latter has already been appealed to on the part of the highest War Lord, and is about to respond to the appeal. Consequently it is absolutely necessary that it receive a visible *satisfaction d'honneur;* this is the *prerequisite* of my mediation. Therefore Your Excellency will submit a proposal to me along the lines sketched out; which shall be communicated to Vienna. I have had Plessen write along the lines indicated above to the Chief of the General Staff, who is entirely in accord with my views.

Wilhelm I. R.

Austria's Reception of Serbia's Reply

The Austro-Hungarian Ambassador to the Foreign Office

Memorandum

Berlin, July 27, 1914.

THE ROYAL SERBIAN GOVERNMENT has refused to agree to the demands which we were forced to make for the lasting assurance of those of our vital interests threatened by that Government, and has thus given evidence that it is not willing to desist from its destructive efforts directed toward the constant disturbance of some of our border territories and their eventual separation from the control of the Monarchy. We are therefore compelled, to our regret and much against our will, to force Serbia by the sharpest means to a fundamental alteration of her hitherto hostile attitude. That in so doing, aggressive intentions are far from our thoughts, and that it is merely in self-defense that we have finally determined, after years of patience, to oppose the Greater-Serbia intrigues with the sword, is well known to the Imperial German Government.

It is a cause of honest satisfaction to us that we find both in the Imperial German Government and in the entire German people a complete comprehension of the fact that our patience was of necessity exhausted after the assassination at Serajevo, which, according to the results of the inquiry, was planned at Belgrade and carried out by emissaries from that city; and that we are now forced to the task of securing ourselves by every means against the continuation of the present intolerable conditions on our southeastern border.

We confidently hope that our prospective difference with Serbia will be the cause of no further complications; but in the event that such should nevertheless occur, we are gratefully certain that Germany, with a fidelity long proven, will bear in mind the obligations of her alliance and lend us her support in any fight forced upon us by another opponent.

Max Montgelas and Walther Schücking, eds., *Outbreak of the World War: German Documents Collected by Karl Kautsky*, No. 268 (1924), p. 249, translated by Carnegie Endowment for International Peace. Reprinted by permission of Carnegie Endowment for International Peace.

> *The following telegrams from Bethmann-Hollweg to Tschirschky have often been taken as evidence for a change of heart at Berlin and the beginning of a policy of re-straining Austria.*

Bethmann-Hollweg's Telegrams to Tschirschky

The Imperial Chancellor to the Ambassador at Vienna

Telegram 174.
Urgent.

Berlin, July 28, 1914.

THE AUSTRO-HUNGARIAN GOVERNMENT has distinctly informed Russia that it is not considering any territorial acquisitions in Serbia. This agrees with Your Excellency's report to the effect that neither the Austrian nor the Hungarian statesmen consider the increase of the Slavic element in the Monarchy to be desirable. On the other hand, the Austro-Hungarian Government has left us in the dark concerning its intentions, despite repeated interrogations. The reply of the Serbian Government to the Austrian ultimatum, which has now been received, makes it clear that Serbia has agreed to the Austrian demands to so great an extent that, in case of a completely uncompromising attitude on the part of the Austro-Hungarian Government, it will become necessary to reckon upon the gradual defection from its cause of public opinion throughout all Europe.

According to the statements of the Austrian General Staff, an active military movement against Serbia will not be possible before the 12th of August. As a result, the Imperial Government is placed in the extraordinarily difficult position of being exposed in the meantime to the mediation and conference proposals of the other Cabinets, and if it continues to maintain its previous aloofness in the face of such proposals, it will incur the odium of having been responsible for a world war, even, finally, among the German people themselves. A successful war on three fronts cannot be commenced and carried on on any such basis. It is imperative that the responsibility for the eventual extension of the war among those nations not originally immediately concerned should, under all circumstances, fall on Russia. At Mr. Sazonoff's last conversation with Count Pourtalès the Minister already conceded that Serbia would have to receive her "deserved lesson."

Max Montgelas and Walther Schücking, eds., *Outbreak of the World War: German Documents Collected by Karl Kautsky*, No. 323 (1924), pp. 288–9, and No. 395 (1924), pp. 344–5, translated by Carnegie Endowment for International Peace. Reprinted by permission of Carnegie Endowment for International Peace.

At any rate the Minister was no longer so unconditionally opposed to the Austrian point of view as he had been earlier. From this fact it is not difficult to draw the conclusion that the Russian Government might even realize that, once the mobilization of the Austro-Hungarian Army had begun, the very honor of its arms demanded an invasion of Serbia. But it will be all the better able to compromise with this idea if the Vienna Cabinet repeats at Petersburg its distinct declaration that she is far from wishing to make any territorial acquisitions in Serbia, and that her military preparations are solely for the purpose of a temporary occupation of Belgrade and certain other localities on Serbian territory in order to force the Serbian Government to the complete fulfilment of her demands, and for the creation of guaranties of future good behavior—to which Austria-Hungary has an unquestionable claim after the experiences she has had with Serbia. An occupation like the German occupation of French territory after the Peace of Frankfurt, for the purpose of securing compliance with the demands for war indemnity, is suggested. As soon as the Austrian demands should be complied with, evacuation would follow. Should the Russian Government fail to recognize the justice of this point of view, it would have against it the public opinion of all Europe, which is now in the process of turning away from Austria. As a further result, the general diplomatic, and probably the military, situation would undergo material alteration in favor of Austria-Hungary and her allies.

Your Excellency will kindly discuss the matter along these lines thoroughly and impressively with Count Berchtold, and instigate an appropriate move at St. Petersburg. You will have to avoid very carefully giving rise to the impression that we wish to hold Austria back. The case is solely one of finding a way to realize Austria's desired aim, that of cutting the vital cord of the Greater-Serbia propaganda, without at the same time bringing on a world war, and, if the latter cannot be avoided in the end, of improving the conditions under which we shall have to wage it, in so far as is possible.

Wire report.

Bethmann-Hollweg.

The Imperial Chancellor to the Ambassador at Vienna

Telegram 192.
Urgent.

Berlin, July 30, 1914.

THE IMPERIAL AMBASSADOR at London telegraphs:

Sir E. Grey just sent for me again. The Minister was entirely calm, but very grave, and received me with the words that the situation was continuing to grow more acute. Sazonoff had stated that after the declaration of war he will no longer be in a position to negotiate with Austria direct, and *had requested them here to take up the mediation efforts again*. The Russian Government regards the cessation of hostilities for the present as a necessary preliminary to mediation.

Sir E. Grey repeated his suggestion already reported, that we take part in a mediation *à quatre,* such as we had already accepted in principle. It would seem to him to be a suitable basis for mediation, if Austria, after occupying Belgrade, for example, or other places, should announce her conditions. Should Your Excellency, however, undertake mediation, a prospect I was able early this morning to put before him, this would of course suit him equally well. But *mediation* seemed now to him to be urgently necessary, if *a European catastrophe were not to result.*

Sir E. Grey then said to me that he had a friendly and private communication to make to me, namely, that he did not want our warm personal relations and the intimacy of our talks on all political matters to lead me astray, and he would *like to spare himself later the reproach (of) bad faith.* The British Government desired now as before to cultivate our previous friendship, and it could *stand aside as long as the conflict remained confined to Austria and Russia. But if we and France* should *be involved,* the situation would immediately be altered, and the British Government would, *under the circumstances, find itself forced to make up its mind quickly.* In that event *it would not be practicable to stand aside and wait for any length of time.* "If war breaks out, it will be *the greatest catastrophe that the world has ever seen."* It was far from his desire to express any kind of a threat; he only wanted to protect me from disappointments and *himself* from the *reproach of bad faith,* and had therefore chosen the form of a private explanation.

As a result we stand, in case Austria refuses all mediation, before a conflagration in which England will be against us; Italy and Roumania to all appearances will not go with us, and we two shall be opposed to four Great Powers. On Germany, thanks to England's opposition, the principal burden of the fight would fall. Austria's political prestige, the honor of her arms, as well as her just claims against Serbia, could all be amply satisfied by the occupation of Belgrade or of other places. She would be strengthening her status in the Balkans as well as in relation to Russia by the humiliation of Serbia. Under these circumstances we must urgently and impressively suggest to the consideration of the Vienna Cabinet the acceptance of mediation on the above-mentioned honorable conditions. The responsibility for the consequences that would otherwise follow would be an uncommonly heavy one both for Austria and for us.

Bethmann-Hollweg.

At 9:15 on July 27, more than two hours before Bethmann-Hollweg sent his telegram to Tschirschky, Count Laszlo

*Szögyény, the Austrian ambassador to Berlin, sent the fol-
lowing report to Vienna. The reliability of Szögyény's account has been challenged, but Luigi Albertini defends it
and thinks that "No stronger shaft of light could fall on the
guilt and duplicity of the German Government."*

FROM *The Origins of the War of 1914*

BY LUIGI ALBERTINI

THE SECRETARY OF STATE told me very definitely in a strictly confidential form that in the immediate future mediation proposals from England will possibly (*eventuell*) be brought to Your Excellency's knowledge by
the German Government. The German Government, he says, tenders the
most binding assurances that it in no way associates itself with the proposals,
is even decidedly against their being considered, and only passes them on in
order to conform to the English request. In so doing the Government
proceeds from the standpoint that it is of the greatest importance that
England at the present moment should not make common cause with Russia
and France. Consequently everything must be avoided that might disconnect
the telegraph line between Germany and England which till now has been
in good working order. Were Germany to say flatly to Sir E. Grey that she is
not willing to pass on his wishes to Austria-Hungary, by whom England
believes these wishes will sooner find consideration if Germany is the
intermediary, then the situation would arise which, as has just been said,
must at all costs be avoided. The German Government would, moreover, in
respect of any other request of England to Vienna, assure the latter most
emphatically that it in no way supports any such demands for intervention
in regard to Austria-Hungary and only passes them on to comply with the
wish of England. For instance only yesterday the English Government
approached him, the Secretary of State, through the German Ambassador to
London and directly through its own representative here, asking him to
support the wish of England in regard to a toning down by us of the note to
Serbia. He, Jagow, gave answer that he would certainly fulfil Sir E. Grey's
wish and pass on England's desire to Your Excellency, but that he could not
support it himself, since the Serbian conflict was a question of prestige for
the Austro-Hungarian Monarchy in which Germany was also involved. He,
the Secretary of State, had therefore passed on Sir E. Grey's note to Herr von
Tschirschky, but without giving him instructions to submit it to Your

Luigi Albertini, *The Origins of the War of 1914*, II (1953), 445–6, translated and edited by
Isabella M. Massey. Reprinted by permission of The Clarendon Press, Oxford.

Excellency; thereupon he had been able to inform the English Cabinet, that he did not directly decline the English wish, and had even forwarded it to Vienna. In conclusion the Secretary of State reiterated his standpoint to me and, in order to prevent any misunderstanding, asked me to assure your Excellency that, also in the case just adduced, he, in acting as intermediary, was not in the slightest degree in favour of consideration being given to the English wish.

> *On July 28 Austria declared war on Serbia. Further at-tempts at negotiation were made, but once military mobili-zation began military considerations became paramount. Germany had always insisted that Russian mobilization would mean war, for the Schlieffen Plan demanded a quick victory before France—and particularly Russia—could be fully prepared for war. After Russia's total mobilization, the war was unavoidable. The marginal notes are once again those of the Kaiser.*

Pourtalès's Report of Russian Mobilization

The Ambassador at Petersburg to the Foreign Office

Telegram 189.
Urgent.

Petersburg, July 30, 1914.

JUST HAD ONE AND A HALF HOURS' CONFER-ENCE with Sazonoff, who sent for me at midnight. Minister's purpose was to persuade me to advocate participation by my Government in a conference of four, in order to find a way to *move Austria by friendly means to drop those de-mands which infringe on the sovereignty of Serbia.* I con-fined myself to promising to report the conversation, and took the stand that any exchange of opinions appeared to me to be a very difficult if not an impossible matter now that Russia had *decided to take the fateful step of mobiliza-tion.* Russia was demanding of us to do that to Austria which Austria was being reproached for doing to Serbia;

Is Russian mobiliza-tion a friendly means?!

Right.

Max Montgelas and Walther Schücking, eds., *Outbreak of the World War: German Documents Collected by Karl Kautsky,* No. 401 (1924), pp. 348–50, translated by Carnegie Endowment for International Peace. Reprinted by permission of Carnegie Endowment for International Peace.

to wit, *infringing upon her rights of sovereignty*. Since Austria had promised to *consider Russian interests* by her declaration of territorial disinterestedness, which, on the part of a nation at war *meant a great deal,* the Austro-Hungarian Monarchy ought to be let alone while settling her affairs with Serbia. It would be time enough to return to the question of sparing Serbia's sovereign rights when *peace* was concluded. I added very earnestly that the whole Austro-Serbian matter took a *back seat* for the moment in the face of the *danger of a European conflagration.* I took great pains to impress the magnitude of this danger upon the Minister. Sazonoff was not to be diverted from the idea that Russia could not leave Serbia in the lurch. No Government could follow such a policy here *without seriously endangering the Monarchy.*

During the course of the conversation *Sazonoff wanted to argue* the inconsistency between the telegram of His Majesty the Emperor to the Czar and Your Excellency's telegraphic instructions number 134. I decidedly denied any, and pointed out that *even if we had already mobilized,* an appeal by my Most Gracious Master to the common interests of monarchs *would not be inconsistent* with such a measure. I said that the communication I had made him this afternoon according to the instructions of Your Excellency, had been no threat, but a friendly warning in the shape of a reference to the *automatic effect that the mobilization here would have to have on us in consequence of the German-Austrian alliance.* Sazonoff stated that the order for mobilization *could no longer possibly be retracted,* and that the *Austrian mobilization was to blame for it.*

From Sazonoff's statements I received the impression that His Majesty's telegram did not fail of an effect on the Czar, but that the Minister is busily striving to make sure that the Czar stands firm.

Pourtalès.

If mobilization can no longer be retracted—WHICH IS NOT TRUE—*why, then, did the Czar appeal for my mediation three days afterward without mention of the issuance of the mobilization order? That shows plainly that the mobilization appeared to him to have been precipitate, and that after it he made this move* pro forma *in our direction for the sake of quieting his uneasy conscience, although he knew that it would no longer be of any use, as he did not feel himself to be strong enough to* STOP *the mobilization. Frivolity and weakness are to plunge the world into the most frightful war, which eventually aims at the destruction of Germany. For I have no doubt*

Marginal notes:

Very good.

Good.

Yes.
Nonsense! that sort of policy conceals within itself the greatest dangers for the Czar!

Nothing done as yet.

Right.

That was a partial mobilization of six corps for a limited purpose!

left about it: England, Russia and France have AGREED *among themselves—after laying the foundation of the* casus foederis *for us through Austria—to take the Austro-Serbian conflict for an* EXCUSE *for waging a* WAR OF EXTERMINATION *against us. Hence Grey's cynical observation to Lichnowsky "as long as the war is* CONFINED *to Russia and Austria, England would sit quiet, only when we and France* MIXED INTO IT *would he be compelled to make an active move against us(");* i.e., *either we are shamefully to betray our allies,* SACRIFICE *them to Russia—thereby breaking up the Triple Alliance, or we are to be attacked in common by the Triple Entente for our* FIDELITY TO OUR ALLIES *and punished, whereby they will satisfy their jealousy by joining in totally* RUINING *us. That is the real naked situation in* nuce, *which, slowly and cleverly set going, certainly by Edward VII, has been carried on, and systematically built up by disowned conferences between England and Paris and Petersburg; finally brought to a conclusion by George V and set to work. And thereby the stupidity and ineptitude of our ally is turned into a snare for us. So the famous "*CIRCUMSCRIPTION*" of Germany has finally become a complete fact, despite every effort of our politicians and diplomats to prevent it. The net has been suddenly thrown over our head, and England sneeringly reaps the most brilliant success of her persistently prosecuted purely* ANTI-GERMAN WORLD-POLICY, *against which we have proved ourselves helpless, while she twists the noose of our political and economic destruction out of our fidelity to Austria, as we squirm* ISOLATED *in the net. A great achievement, which arouses the admiration even of him who is to be destroyed as its result! Edward VII is stronger after his death than am I who am still alive! And there have been people who believed that England could be won over or pacified, by this or that puny measure!!! Unremittingly, relentlessly she has pursued her object, with notes, holiday proposals, scares, Haldane, etc., until this point was reached. And we walked into the net and even went into the one-ship-program in construction with the ardent hope of thus pacifying England!!! All my warnings, all my pleas were voiced for nothing. Now comes England's so-called gratitude for it! From the dilemma raised by our fidelity to the venerable old Emperor of Austria we are brought into a situation which offers England the desired pretext for annihilating us under the hypocritical cloak of justice, namely, of helping France on account of the reputed "balance of power" in Europe,* i.e., *playing the card of all the European nations in England's favor against us! This whole business must now be ruthlessly uncovered and the mask of Christian peaceableness publicly and brusquely torn from its face in public, and the pharisaical hypocrisy exposed on the pillory!! And our consuls in Turkey and India, agents, etc., must fire the whole Mohammedan world to fierce rebellion against this hated, lying, conscienceless nation of shop-keepers; for if we are to be bled to death, England shall at least lose India.*

W.

4   The Revisionist Position

*The 1920s witnessed a reassessment of the question of war
guilt. In England and America, particularly, scholars began
to revise the general opinion that Germany and Austria
were exclusively responsible. Sidney B. Fay was one of the
leaders of the revisionist movement.*

FROM *Origins of the World War* BY SIDNEY B. FAY

NONE OF THE POWERS wanted a European War. Their governing
rulers and ministers, with very few exceptions, all foresaw that it must be a
frightful struggle, in which the political results were not absolutely certain,
but in which the loss of life, suffering, and economic consequences were
bound to be terrible. This is true, in a greater or less degree, of Pashitch,
Berchtold, Bethmann, Sazonov, Poincaré, San Giuliano and Sir Edward
Grey. Yet none of them, not even Sir Edward Grey, could have foreseen that
the political results were to be so stupendous, and the other consequences so
terrible, as was actually the case.

For many of the Powers, to be sure, a European War might seem to
hold out the possibility of achieving various desired advantages: for Serbia,
the achievement of national unity for all Serbs; for Austria, the revival of her
waning prestige as a Great Power, and the checking of nationalistic tendencies which threatened her very existence; for Russia, the accomplishment of
her historic mission of controlling Constantinople and the Straits; for Germany, new economic advantages and the restoration of the European balance
which had changed with the weakening of the Triple Alliance and the
tightening of the Triple Entente; for France, the recovery of Alsace-Lorraine
and the ending of the German menace; and for England, the destruction of
the German naval danger and of Prussian militarism. All these advantages,
and many others, were feverishly striven and intrigued for, on all sides, the
moment the War actually broke out, but this is no good proof that any of the
statesmen mentioned deliberately aimed to bring about a war to secure these

Reprinted with permission of The Macmillan Company from *Origins of the World War*, II
(1930), 547–58, by Sidney B. Fay. Copyright 1928 and 1930 by The Macmillan Company.

advantages. One cannot judge the motives which actuated men before the War, by what they did in an absolutely new situation which arose as soon as they were overtaken by a conflagration they had sought to avert. And in fact, in the case of the two Powers between whom the immediate conflict arose, the postponement or avoidance of a European War would have facilitated the accomplishment of the ultimate advantages aimed at: Pashitch knew that there was a better chance for Serbian national unity after he had consolidated Serbian gains in the Balkan Wars, and after Russia had completed her military and naval armaments as planned for 1917; and Berchtold knew that he had a better chance of crushing the Greater Serbia danger and strengthening Austria, if he could avoid Russian intervention and a general European War.

It is also true, likewise, that the moment war was declared, it was hailed with varying demonstrations of enthusiasm on the part of the people in every country—with considerable in Serbia, Austria, Russia and Germany, with less in France, and with almost none in England. But this does not mean that the peoples wanted war or exerted a decisive influence to bring it about. It is a curious psychological phenomenon that as soon as a country engages in war, there develops or is created among the masses a frenzy of patriotic excitement which is no index of their pre-war desires. And in the countries where the demonstratious of enthusiasm were greatest, the political influence of the people on the Government was least.

Nevertheless, a European War broke out. Why? Because in each country political and military leaders did certain things, which led to mobilizations and declarations of war, or failed to do certain things which might have prevented them. In this sense, all the European countries, in a greater or less degree, were responsible. One must abandon the dictum of the Versailles Treaty that Germany and her allies were solely responsible. It was a dictum exacted by victors from vanquished, under the influence of the blindness, ignorance, hatred, and the propagandist misconceptions to which war had given rise. It was based on evidence which was incomplete and not always sound. It is generally recognized by the best historical scholars in all countries to be no longer tenable or defensible. They are agreed that the responsibility for the War is a divided responsibility. But they still disagree very much as to the relative part of this responsibility that falls on each country and on each individual political or military leader.

Some writers like to fix positively in some precise mathematical fashion the exact responsibility for the war. This was done in one way by the framers of Article 231 of the Treaty of Versailles. It has been done in other ways by those who would fix the responsibility in some relative fashion, as, for instance, Austria first, then Russia, France and Germany and England. But the present writer deprecates such efforts to assess by a precise formula a very complicated question, which is after all more a matter of delicate shading than of definite white and black. Oversimplification, as Napoleon once said in framing his Code, is the enemy of precision. Moreover, even supposing that a general consensus of opinion might be reached as to the relative responsibility of any individual country or man for immediate causes connected with the July crisis of 1914, it is by no means necessarily true that the same relative responsibility would hold for the underlying causes, which for years had been tending toward the creation of a dangerous situation.

One may, however, sum up very briefly the most salient facts in regard to each country.

Serbia felt a natural and justifiable impulse to do what so many other countries had done in the nineteenth century—to bring under one national Government all the discontented Serb people. She had liberated those under Turkish rule; the next step was to liberate those under Hapsburg rule. She looked to Russia for assistance, and had been encouraged to expect that she would receive it. After the assassination, Mr. Pashitch took no steps to discover and bring to justice Serbians in Belgrade who had been implicated in the plot. One of them, Ciganovitch, was even assisted to disappear. Mr. Pashitch waited to see what evidence the Austrian authorities could find. When Austria demanded cooperation of Austrian officials in discovering, though not in trying, implicated Serbians, the Serbian Government made a very conciliatory but negative reply. They expected that the reply would not be regarded as satisfactory, and, even before it was given, ordered the mobilization of the Serbian army. Serbia did not want war, but believed it would be forced upon her. That Mr. Pashitch was aware of the plot three weeks before it was executed, failed to take effective steps to prevent the assassins from crossing over from Serbia to Bosnia, and then failed to give Austria any warning or information which might have averted the fatal crime, were facts unknown to Austria in July, 1914; they cannot therefore be regarded as in any way justifying Austria's conduct; but they are part of Serbia's responsibility, and a very serious part.

Austria was more responsible for the immediate origin of the war than any other Power. Yet from her own point of view she was acting in self-defence—not against an immediate military attack, but against the corroding Greater Serbia and Jugoslav agitation which her leaders believed threatened her very existence. No State can be expected to sit with folded arms and await dismemberment at the hands of its neighbors. Russia was believed to be intriguing with Serbia and Rumania against the Dual Monarchy. The assassination of the heir to the throne, as a result of a plot prepared in Belgrade, demanded severe retribution; otherwise Austria would be regarded as incapable of action, "Worm-eaten" as the Serbian Press expressed it, would sink in prestige, and hasten her own downfall. To avert this Berchtold determined to crush Serbia with war. He deliberately framed the ultimatum with the expectation and hope that it would be rejected. He hurriedly declared war against Serbia in order to forestall all efforts at mediation. He refused even to answer his own ally's urgent requests to come to an understanding with Russia, on the basis of a military occupation of Belgrade as a pledge that Serbia would carry out the promises in her reply to the ultimatum. Berchtold gambled on a "local" war with Serbia only, believing that he could rattle the German sword; but rather than abandon his war with Serbia, he was ready to drag the rest of Europe into war.

It is very questionable whether Berchtold's obstinate determination to diminish Serbia and destroy her as a Balkan factor was, after all, the right method, even if he had succeeded in keeping the war "localized" and in temporarily strengthening the Dual Monarchy. Supposing that Russia in 1914, because of military unpreparedness or lack of support, had been ready to tolerate the execution of Berchtold's designs, it is quite certain that she would have aimed within the next two or three years at wiping out this second humiliation, which was so much more damaging to her prestige than that of 1908–09. In two or three years, when her great program of military reform was finally completed, Russia would certainly have found a pretext to reverse the balance in the Balkans in her own favor again. A further consequence of Berchtold's policy, even if successful, would have been the still closer consolidation of the Triple Entente, with the possible addition of Italy. And, finally, a partially dismembered Serbia would have become a still greater source of unrest and danger to the peace of Europe than heretofore. Serbian nationalism, like Polish nationalism, would have been intensified by partition. Austrian power and prestige would not have been so greatly increased as to be able to meet these new dangers. Berchtold's plan was a mere temporary improvement, but could not be a final solution of the Austro-Serbian antagonism. Franz Ferdinand and many others recognized this, and so long as he lived, no step in this fatal direction had been taken. It was the tragic fate of Austria that the only man who might have had the power and ability to develop Austria along sound lines became the innocent victim of the crime which was the occasion of the World War and so of her ultimate disruption.

Germany did not plot a European War, did not want one, and made genuine, though too belated efforts, to avert one. She was the victim of her alliance with Austria and of her own folly. Austria was her only dependable ally, Italy and Rumania having become nothing but allies in name. She could not throw her over, as otherwise she would stand isolated between Russia, where Panslavism and armaments were growing stronger every year, and France, where Alsace-Lorraine, Delcassé's fall, and Agadir were not forgotten. Therefore, Bethmann felt bound to accede to Berchtold's request for support and gave him a free hand to deal with Serbia; he also hoped and expected to "localize" the Austro-Serbian conflict. Germany then gave grounds to the Entente for suspecting the sincerity of her peaceful intentions by her denial of any foreknowledge of the ultimatum, by her support and justification of it when it was published, and by her refusal to Sir Edward Grey's conference proposal. However, Germany by no means had Austria so completely under her thumb as the Entente Powers and many writers have assumed. It is true that Berchtold would hardly have embarked on his gambler's policy unless he had been assured that Germany would fulfil the obligations of the alliance, and to this extent Germany must share the great responsibility of Austria. But when Bethmann realized that Russia was likely to intervene, that England might not remain neutral, and that there was danger of a world war of which Germany and Austria would appear to be the instigators, he tried to call a halt on Austria, but it was too late. He pressed mediation proposals on Vienna, but Berchtold was insensible to the pressure, and the Entente Powers did not believe in the sincerity of his pressure, especially as they produced no results.

Germany's geographical position between France and Russia, and her inferiority in number of troops, had made necessary the plan of crushing the French army quickly at first and then turning against Russia. This was only possible, in the opinion of her strategists, by marching through Belgium, as it was generally anticipated by military men that she would do in case of a European War. On July 29, after Austria had declared war on Serbia, and after the Tsar had assented to general mobilization in Russia (though this was not known in Berlin and was later postponed for a day owing to the Kaiser's telegram to the Tsar), Bethmann took the precaution of sending to the German Minister in Brussels a sealed envelope. The Minister was not to open it except on further instructions. It contained the later demand for the passage of the German army through Belgium. This does not mean, however, that Germany had decided for war. In fact, Bethmann was one of the last of the statemen to abandon hope of peace and to consent to the mobilization of his country's army. General mobilization of the continental armies took place in the following order: Serbia, Russia, Austria, France and Germany. General mobilization by a Great Power was commonly interpreted by military men in every country, though perhaps not by Sir Edward Grey, the Tsar, and some civilian officials, as meaning that the country was on the point of making war—that the military machine had begun to move and would not be stopped. Hence, when Germany learned of the Russian general mobilization, she sent ultimatums to St. Petersburg and Paris, warning that German mobilization would follow unless Russia suspended hers within twelve hours, and asking what would be the attitude of France. The answers being unsatisfactory, Germany then mobilized and declared war. It was the hasty Russian general mobilization, assented to on July 29 and ordered on July 30, while Germany was still trying to bring Austria to accept mediation proposals, which finally rendered the European War inevitable.

Russia was partly responsible for the Austro-Serbian conflict because of the frequent encouragement which she had given at Belgrade—that Serbian national unity would be ultimately achieved with Russian assistance at Austrian expense. This had led the Belgrade Cabinet to hope for Russian support in case of a war with Austria, and the hope did not prove vain in July, 1914. Before this, to be sure, in the Bosnian Crisis and during the Balkan Wars, Russia had put restraint upon Serbia, because Russia, exhausted by the effects of the Russo-Japanese War, was not yet ready for a European struggle with the Teutonic Powers. But in 1914 her armaments, though not yet completed, had made such progress that the militarists were confident of success, if they had French and British support. In the spring of 1914, the Minister of War, Sukhomlinov, had published an article in a Russian newspaper, though without signing his name, to the effect, "Russia is ready, France must be ready also." Austria was convinced that Russia would ultimately aid Serbia, unless the Serbian danger were dealt with energetically after the Archduke's murder; she knew that Russia was growing stronger every year; but she doubted whether the Tsar's armaments had yet reached the point at which Russia would dare to intervene; she would therefore run less risk of Russian intervention and a European War if she used the Archduke's assassination as an excuse for weakening Serbia, than if she should postpone action until the future.

Russia's responsibility lay also in the secret preparatory military measures which she was making at the same time that she was carrying on diplomatic negotiations. These alarmed Germany and Austria. But it was primarily Russia's general mobilization, made when Germany was trying to bring Austria to a settlement, which precipitated the final catastrophe, causing Germany to mobilize and declare war.

The part of France is less clear than that of the other Great Powers, because she has not yet made a full publication of her documents. To be sure, M. Poincaré, in the fourth volume of his memories, has made a skilful and elaborate plea, to prove *"La France innocente."* But he is not convincing. It is quite clear that on his visit to Russia he assured the Tsar's Government that France would support her as an ally in preventing Austria from humiliating or crushing Serbia. Paléologue renewed these assurances in a way to encourage Russia to take a strong hand. He did not attempt to restrain Russia from military measures which he knew would call forth German counter-measures and cause war. Nor did he keep his Government promptly and fully informed of the military steps which were being taken at St. Petersburg. President Poincaré, upon his return to France, made efforts for peace, but his great preoccupation was to minimize French and Russian preparatory measures and emphasize those of Germany, in order to secure the certainty of British support in a struggle which he now regarded as inevitable.

Sir Edward Grey made many sincere proposals for preserving peace; they all failed owing partly, but not exclusively, to Germany's attitude. Sir Edward could probably have prevented war if he had done either of two things. If, early in the crisis, he had acceded to the urging of France and Russia and given a strong warning to Germany that, in a European War, England would take the side of the Franco-Russian Alliance, this would probably have led Bethmann to exert an earlier and more effective pressure on Austria; and it would perhaps thereby have prevented the Austrian declaration of war on Serbia, and brought to a successful issue the "direct conversations" between Vienna and St. Petersburg. Or, if Sir Edward Grey had listened to German urging, and warned France and Russia early in the crisis, that if they became involved in war, England would remain neutral, probably Russia would have hesitated with her mobilizations, and France would probably have exerted a restraining influence at St. Petersburg. But Sir Edward Grey could not say that England would take the side of France and Russia, because he had a Cabinet nearly evenly divided, and he was not sure, early in the crisis, that public opinion in England would back him up in war against Germany. He could resign, and he says in his memoirs that he would have resigned, but that would have been no comfort or aid to France, who had come confidently to count upon British support. He was determined to say and do nothing which might encourage her with a hope which he could not fulfil. Therefore, in spite of the pleadings of the French, he refused to give them definite assurances until the probable German determination to go through Belgium made it clear that the Cabinet, and Parliament, and British public opinion would follow his lead in war on Germany. On the other hand, he was unwilling to heed the German pleadings that he exercise restraint at Paris and St. Petersburg, because he did not wish to endanger the Anglo-Russian Entente and the solidarity of the Triple Entente, because he felt a moral obligation to France, growing out of the Anglo-French military and naval conversations of the past years, and because he suspected that Germany was backing Austria up in an unjustifiable course and that Prussian militarists had taken the direction of affairs at Berlin out of the hands of Herr von Bethmann-Hollweg and the civilian authorities.

Italy exerted relatively little influence on the crisis in either direction.

Belgium had done nothing in any way to justify the demand which Germany made upon her. With commendable prudence, at the very first news of the ominous Austrian ultimatum, she had foreseen the danger to which she might be exposed. She had accordingly instructed her representatives abroad as to the statements which they were to make in case Belgium should decide very suddenly to mobilize to protect her neutrality. On July 29, she placed her army upon "a strengthened war footing," but did not order complete mobilization until two days later, when Austria, Russia, and Germany had already done so, and war appeared inevitable. Even after being confronted with the terrible German ultimatum, at 7 P.M. on August 2, she did not at once invite the assistance of English and French troops to aid her in the defense of her soil and her neutrality against a certain German assault; it was not until German troops had actually violated her territory, on August 4, that she appealed for the assistance of the Powers which had guaranteed her neutrality. Belgium was the innocent victim of German strategic necessity. Though the German violation of Belgium was of enormous influence in forming public opinion as to the responsibility for the War after hostilities began, it was not a cause of the War, except in so far as it made it easier for Sir Edward Grey to bring England into it.

In the forty years following the Franco-Prussian War, as we have seen, there developed a system of alliances which divided Europe into two hostile groups. This hostility was accentuated by the increase of armaments, economic rivalry, nationalist ambitions and antagonisms, and newspaper incitement. But it is very doubtful whether all these dangerous tendencies would have actually led to war, had it not been for the assassination of Franz Ferdinand. That was the factor which consolidated the elements of hostility and started the rapid and complicated succession of events which culminated in a World War, and for that factor Serbian nationalism was primarily responsible.

But the verdict of the Versailles Treaty that Germany and her allies were responsible for the War, in view of the evidence now available, is historically unsound. It should therefore be revised. However, because of the popular feeling widespread in some of the Entente countries, it is doubtful whether a formal and legal revision is as yet practicable. There must first come a further revision by historical scholars, and through them of public opinion.

5 The Case Against the Central Powers

FROM *The Struggle for the Mastery of Europe*
BY A. J. P. TAYLOR

IT HAS BEEN STRONGLY ARGUED that the Germans deliberately timed war for August 1914. There is little evidence for this, and a decisive argument against it. Bethmann and William II were incapable of consistent policy; Moltke, the chief-of-staff, could not conduct a campaign, let alone make a war. The Germans were involved in war by Austria-Hungary, but they went with her willingly. It was easy to co-operate with her; it would have needed a statesman to refuse. On 28 June Francis Ferdinand was assassinated at Sarejevo, the capital of Bosnia, by a Bosnian Serb. Berchtold was weary of being jeered at by Conrad as irresolute and feeble. Moreover, when Turkey-in-Asia took the place of the Balkans as the centre of international rivalry, Austria-Hungary was pushed aside too; and the Germans had rejected with impatience Berchtold's claim to be allotted a "sphere" in Asia Minor. The murder at Sarejevo revived the Balkan question and enabled Austria-Hungary to reappear misleadingly as a Great Power. This time she could only hold the centre of the stage if she actually provoked a war. The German talk of writing off Austria-Hungary and of somehow restoring good relations with Russia at her expense had not escaped Austrian attention: and the Habsburg monarchy brought on its mortal crisis to prove that it was still alive.

Berchtold determined to force war on Serbia, though he had no proofs of Serbian complicity and never found any. Tisza, the Hungarian prime minister, opposed him. Berchtold wanted to restore the prestige of the monarchy; Tisza cared only for great Hungary. Like Kossuth before him, he looked to Germany, not to Vienna, as Hungary's ally and would not have much regretted the collapse of the Dual Monarchy, so long as great Hungary survived. Berchtold turned Tisza's opposition by appealing to Germany for support; Tisza could not hold out if Berlin, not Vienna, urged war. Berch-

A. J. P. Taylor, *The Struggle for the Mastery of Europe 1848–1918* (1954), pp. 520–31. Reprinted by permission of The Clarendon Press, Oxford.

told took out his memorandum of 24 June, which had urged alliance with Bulgaria; added a postscript blaming Serbia for the assassination; and accompanied this with a letter from Francis Joseph to William II, which managed to blame Russian Panslavism as well. The conclusion: "Serbia must be eliminated as a political factor in the Balkans . . . friendly settlement is no longer to be thought of." These two documents were presented to William II on 5 July.

At Berlin there was no serious consultation. William II invited the Austro-Hungarian ambassador to lunch at Potsdam. At first he said that he must wait for Bethmann's opinion; then changed his mind after lunch and committed himself. Szögyény, the Austrian ambassador, reported: "Action against Serbia should not be delayed. . . . Even if it should come to a war between Austria and Russia, we could be convinced that Germany would stand by our side with her accustomed faithfulness as an ally." Bethmann arrived in the afternoon, went for a walk in the park with William II, and approved of what he had said. The next day he gave Szögyény official confirmation: "Austria must judge what is to be done to clear up her relations with Serbia; but whatever Austria's decision, she could count with certainty upon it, that Germany will stand behind her as an ally." Berchtold's plan of partitioning Serbia with Bulgaria was explained to Bethmann. He approved of it and added: "If war must break out, better now than in one or two years' time when the Entente will be stronger."

William II and Bethmann did more than give Austria-Hungary a free hand; they encouraged her to start a war against Serbia and to risk the greater consequences. They had grown used to Berchtold's irresolution during the Balkan wars and were determined not to be blamed for it. The most probable outcome of all the stir, they expected, would be an Austro-Hungarian alliance with Bulgaria. Further, both of them thought that Russia was not ready for war and that she would allow the humiliation of Serbia after some ineffective protest; then their position would be all the stronger to strike a bargain with Russia later. On the other hand, if it came to war, they were confident of winning it now and less confident of winning it later. They did not decide on war; but they did decide on 5 July to use their superior power either to win a war or to achieve a striking success. Bethmann had always said that Germany and Great Britain should cooperate to keep the peace. If he had wanted a peaceful solution of the present crisis, he would have approached the British at once. Instead he did nothing. He did not wish to alarm them. His aim, so far as he had one, was to keep them neutral in a continental war, not to enlist their support for a general peace.

The German reply gave Berchtold what he wanted: it enabled him to convert Tisza. He could now argue that Germany was urging them to war. On 14 July Tisza gave way: great Hungary had to keep German favour. He laid down one condition: Austria-Hungary should not acquire any Serbian territory. Though Berchtold accepted this condition, he meant to cheat

Tisza, once Serbia had been crushed: her southern territories would be partitioned between Albania and Bulgaria, and the rest would become a dependency of the monarchy, even if it were not directly annexed. The one chance of success for Austria-Hungary would have been rapid action. Instead Berchtold dawdled, in the usual Viennese fashion. The ultimatum to Serbia was sent on 23 July, when all Europe had forgotten its first indignation at the archduke's murder. The Serbs replied on 25 July, accepting Berchtold's conditions much more nearly than had been expected. It made no difference. The Austrians were determined on war; and the Germans encouraged them to action. On 28 July Austria-Hungary declared war on Serbia. Military reasons were not the motive: the Austro-Hungarian army could not be ready even against Serbia until 12 August. But, as Berchtold said: "the diplomatic situation will not last as long as that." He needed a declaration of war in order to reject all attempts at mediation or a peaceful solution: they had now been "outstripped by events."

The Austro-Hungarian declaration of war on Serbia was the decisive act; everything else followed from it. Diplomacy had been silent between the assassination of Francis Ferdinand on 28 June and the Austro-Hungarian note of 23 July; there was nothing it could do until the Austro-Hungarian demands were known. Then the statesmen tried to avert the crisis. The Russians advised Serbia not to resist, but to trust to the Great Powers; Grey offered to mediate between Serbia and Austria-Hungary. But the Russians had repeatedly declared that they would not allow Serbia to be crushed; they could do no other if they were to maintain the buffer of independent Balkan states. Poincaré and Viviani were in St. Petersburg just before the Austro-Hungarian note to Serbia was sent off. They emphasized again French loyalty to the alliance; but there is no evidence that they encouraged Russia to provoke a war, if a peaceful settlement could be found. When Austria-Hungary declared war on Serbia, the Russians attempted to mobilize against her alone, although they had no plans except for total mobilization. They were, in fact, still acting in terms of diplomacy; they were raising their bid, not preparing for war. The Germans now entered the field. They had assured the Austrians that they would keep Russia out of things, and they set out to do so. On 29 July they warned Sazonov that "further continuation of Russian mobilization would force us to mobilize also."

This time the Russians were determined not to retreat; they raised their bid still higher. On 30 July they resolved on general mobilization. This, too, was a diplomatic move; the Russian armies could not be ready for many weeks. But, in Jagow's words, "the German asset was speed." Their only military plan was to defeat France in six weeks and then to turn against Russia before she was fully prepared. Therefore they had to precipitate events and to force a rupture on both Russia and France. William II might still carry on a private telegraphic correspondence with Nicholas II, which was prolonged even after the declaration of war; Bethmann might still seek an impossible diplomatic success. They were both swept aside by the generals; and they had no answer to the military argument that immediate war was necessary for Germany's security. Yet even the generals did not want war; they wanted victory. When Bethmann urged caution at Vienna and Moltke at the same time urged speedier action, Berchtold exclaimed: "What a joke! Who rules at Berlin?" The answer was: nobody. German statesmen and generals alike succumbed to the demands of technique.

On 31 July the Germans took the preliminary step towards general mobilization on their side. From this moment, diplomacy ceased so far as the continental Powers were concerned. The only German concern was to get the war going as soon as possible. On 31 July they demanded from Russia the arrest of all war measures; when this was refused, a declaration of war followed on 1 August. The French were asked for a promise of neutrality in a Russo-German war; if they had agreed, they would also have been told to surrender their principal fortresses on the frontier, Toul and Verdun, as pledge of their neutrality. Viviani merely replied: "France will act in accordance with her interests." The Germans had no plausible excuse for war against France. They therefore trumped up some false stories of French violation of German territory; and with these decked out a declaration of war on 3 August.

Negotiations between Germany and Great Britain were more prolonged. Their object, on the German side, was to secure British neutrality, not to avert a continental war. All along, Bethmann had urged Berchtold to appear conciliatory in order to impress the British, not in order to find a compromise. On 29 July he offered not to annex any French territory if Great Britain remained neutral; the offer did not extend to the French colonies. As well, Germany would respect the integrity of Belgium after the war, provided that "she did not take sides against Germany." Grey stuck to his line of policy to the end. He made repeated attempts to settle the original Austro-Serb dispute by negotiation; later he tried to assemble a conference of the Great Powers. He warned the Germans not to count on British neutrality; equally he warned the French and Russians not to count on her support.

It is sometimes said that Grey could have averted the war if he had defined his policy one way or the other. This is not so. The German general staff had long planned to invade France through Belgium and would not have been deterred by any British threat. Indeed they had always assumed that Great Britain would enter the war; they did not take her military weight seriously, and naval questions did not interest them. Bethmann had wanted a British declaration of neutrality in order to discourage France and Russia; once it was clear that they would go to war in any case, British policy ceased to interest him. Emotionally he deplored the breach with Great Britain; but he did nothing to avert it and, in any case, was impotent to influence the German generals. On the other side, France and Russia decided on war without counting firmly on British support; the French believed that they could defeat Germany, and the Russians could not risk their own diplomatic defeat. A British declaration of neutrality would not have influenced their policy. Besides, Grey was resolved that they should decide their policy without encouragement from him; war must spring from their independent resolve.

Those who urged a clear British line did so from contradictory motives. Nicolson feared that Russia and France would win a complete victory and that the British empire would then be at their mercy. Eyre Crowe, more representative of official opinion, feared that France would be defeated and that Great Britain would then be at the mercy of Germany. In any case it was impossible for Grey to make any clear declaration; public opinion would not have allowed it. If there is a criticism of Grey, it must be that he had not educated the British public enough in the previous years. No doubt he had shrunk from increasing the tension in Europe; but, as well, the unity of the liberal party and the survival of the liberal government had ranked higher in his mind than a decisive foreign policy. It was common form to regret discussion of foreign issues. Eyre Crowe, for instance, "deplored all public speeches on foreign affairs"; and Grey agreed with him. As a result, in July 1914, the cabinet overruled any commitment. On 27 July Lloyd George said: "there could be no question of our taking part in any war in the first instance. He knew of no Minister who would be in favour of it."

Moreover, Grey supposed that British intervention would not carry much weight. He thought solely of naval action; it seemed impossible to him to send even an expeditionary force to France, and he certainly never imagined military intervention on a continental scale. On 2 August the cabinet authorized him to warn the Germans that their fleet would not be allowed to attack France in the Channel. Even this condition was not decisive; the Germans would have gladly agreed to it, in exchange for British neutrality. But on 3 August they sent an ultimatum to Belgium, demanding free passage to invade France; the British answered on 4 August demanding that Belgian neutrality be respected. Here again Grey has been criticised for not acting earlier; he should, it is said, have made British neutrality conditional on respect for Belgium. It would have made no difference. The German ultimatum to Belgium was drafted on 26 July, that is, even before the Austro-Hungarian declaration of war on Serbia; invasion of Belgium was an essential, indeed the essential, part of their plans. Only a French surrender could have held them from it. If Grey had acted earlier he would have achieved nothing, except perhaps the break-up of the liberal government; if he had delayed longer he would not have saved Belgium and he would have lost the inestimable value of moral superiority.

On 4 August the long Bismarckian peace ended. It had lasted more than a generation. Men had come to regard peace as normal; when it ended, they looked for some profound cause. Yet the immediate cause was a good deal simpler than on other occasions. Where, for instance, lay the precise responsibility for the Crimean war, and when did that war become inevitable? In 1914 there could be no doubt. Austria-Hungary had failed to solve her national problems. She blamed Serbia for the South Slav discontent; it would be far truer to say that this discontent involved Serbia, against her will, in Habsburg affairs. In July 1914 the Habsburg statesmen took the easy course of violence against Serbia, as their predecessors had taken it (though with more justification) against Sardinia in 1859. Berchtold launched war in 1914, as consciously as Buol launched it in 1859 or Gramont in 1870. There was this difference. Buol counted on support from Prussia and Great Britain; Gramont on support from Austria-Hungary. They were wrong. Berchtold counted rightly on support from Germany; he would not have persisted in a resolute line if it had not been for the repeated encouragements which came from Berlin. The Germans did not fix on war for August 1914, but they welcomed it when the occasion offered. They could win it now; they were more doubtful later. Hence they surrendered easily to the dictates of a military time-table. Austria-Hungary was growing weaker; Germany believed herself at the height of her strength. They decided on war from opposite motives; and the two decisions together caused a general European war.

The Powers of the Triple Entente all entered the war to defend themselves. The Russians fought to preserve the free passage of the Straits, on which their economic life depended; France for the sake of the Triple Entente, which she believed, rightly, alone guaranteed her survival as a Great Power. The British fought for the independence of sovereign states and, more remotely, to prevent a German domination of the Continent. It is sometimes said that the war was caused by the system of alliances or, more vaguely, by the Balance of Power. This is a generalization without reality. None of the Powers acted according to the letter of their commitments, though no doubt they might have done so if they had not anticipated them. Germany was pledged to go to war if Russia attacked Austria-Hungary. Instead, she declared war before Russia took any action; and Austria-Hungary only broke with Russia, grudgingly enough, a week afterwards. France was pledged to attack Germany, if the latter attacked Russia. Instead she was faced with a German demand for unconditional neutrality and would have had to accept war even had there been no Franco-Russian alliance, unless she was prepared to abdicate as a Great Power. Great Britain had a moral obligation to stand by France and a rather stronger one to defend her Channel coast. But she went to war for the sake of Belgium and would have done so, even if there had been no Anglo-French entente and no exchange of letters between Grey and Cambon in November 1912. Only then, the British intervention would have been even less effective than it was.

As to the Balance of Power, it would be truer to say that the war was caused by its breakdown rather than by its existence. There had been a real European Balance in the first decade of the Franco-Russian alliance; and peace had followed from it. The Balance broke down when Russia was weakened by the war with Japan; and Germany got in the habit of trying to get her way by threats. This ended with the Agadir crisis. Russia began to recover her strength, France her nerve. Both insisted on being treated as equals, as they had been in Bismarck's time. The Germans resented this and resolved to end it by war, if they could end it no other way. They feared that the Balance was being re-created. Their fears were exaggerated. Certainly, Russia would have been a more formidable Power by 1917, if her military plans had been carried through and if she had escaped internal disturbance—two formidable hypotheses. But it is unlikely that the three-year service would have been maintained in France; and, in any case, the Russians might well have used their strength against Great Britain in Asia rather than to attack Germany, if they had been left alone. In fact, peace must have brought Germany the mastery of Europe within a few years. This was prevented by the habit of her diplomacy and, still more, by the mental outlook of her people. They had trained themselves psychologically for aggression.

The German military plans played a vital part. The other Great Powers thought in terms of defending themselves. No Frenchman thought seriously of recovering Alsace and Lorraine; and the struggle of Slav and Teuton in the Balkans was very great nonsense so far as most Russians were concerned. The German generals wanted a decisive victory for its own sake. Though they complained of "encirclement," it was German policy that had created this encirclement. Absurdly enough, the Germans created their own problem when they annexed Alsace and Lorraine in 1871. They wanted an impregnable frontier; and they got one, as was shown in August 1914, when a small German force held its own there against the bulk of the French army. After 1871 the Germans could easily have fought Russia and stood on the defensive in the west; this was indeed the strategical plan of the elder Moltke. It was not a strategy which guaranteed final, decisive, victory; and Schlieffen therefore rejected it. In 1892 he insisted that France must be defeated first; ten years later he drew the further inevitable conclusion that the German armies must go through Belgium. If the strategy of the elder Moltke had been adhered to with all its political consequences, it would have been very difficult to persuade French and British opinion to go to the assistance of Russia; instead, it appeared in 1914 that Russia was coming to the assistance of France and even of Great Britain. Schlieffen first created the Franco-Russian alliance; and then ensured that Great Britain would enter the war as well. The Germans complained that the war could not be "localized" in 1914; Schlieffen's strategy prevented it. He would be content with nothing less than total victory; therefore he exposed Germany to total defeat.

There is a deeper explanation still. No one in 1914 took the dangers of war seriously except on a purely military plane. Though all, except a few fighting men, abhorred its bloodshed, none expected a social catastrophe. In the days of Metternich, and even afterwards, statesmen had feared that war would produce "revolution"—and revolutionaries had sometimes advocated it for that very reason. Now they were inclined to think that war would stave off their social and political problems. In France it produced the "sacred union"; in Germany William II was able to say: "I do not see parties any more; I see only Germans." All thought that war could be fitted into the existing framework of civilization, as the wars of 1866 and 1870 had been. Indeed, these wars had been followed by stabler currencies, freer trade, and more constitutional governments. War was expected to interrupt the even tenor of civilian life only while it lasted. Grey expressed this outlook in extreme form, when he said in the house of commons on 3 August: "if we are engaged in war, we shall suffer but little more than we shall suffer if we stand aside"; and by suffering he meant only the interruption of British trade with the continent of Europe. No country made serious economic preparations for war. In England the cry was raised of "business as usual" to mitigate the unemployment which war was expected to cause. The Germans so little understood the implications of total war that they abstained from invading Holland in August 1914, so as to be able to trade freely with the rest of the world.

The Balkan wars had taught a deceptive lesson. Everyone supposed that decisive battles would be fought at once, and a dictated peace would follow. The Germans expected to take Paris; the French expected to break through in Lorraine. The Russian "steam-roller" would reach Berlin; more important, from the Russian point of view, their armies would cross the Carpathians and take Budapest. Even the Austrians expected to "crush" Serbia. The British expected to destroy the German fleet in an immediate naval engagement and then to establish a close blockade of the German coast; apart from that, they had no military plans, except to applaud the victories of their allies and perhaps to profit from them.

None of these things happened. The French armies failed to make headway in Lorraine and suffered enormous casualties. The Germans marched through Belgium and saw from afar the Eiffel Tower. On 6 September they were halted on the Marne and driven back in defeat. But though the French won the battle of the Marne, they could not exploit their victory; the Germans were neither destroyed nor even expelled from French soil. By November there was a line of trenches running from Switzerland to the sea. The Russians invaded east Prussia; they were catastrophically defeated at Tannenberg on 27 August, and their armies in Galicia failed to reach the Carpathians. The Austrians occupied Belgrade, from which the Serbs had withdrawn; they were driven out again in November, and Serbian forces entered southern Hungary. The German fleet remained in harbour; and the British fleet was similarly imprisoned in order to balance it. Everywhere siege warfare superseded decisive battles. The machine-gun and the spade changed the course of European history. Policy had been silenced by the first great clash; but in the autumn of 1914 diplomacy was renewed. All the Powers sought to consolidate their alliances; to enlist new allies; and, more feebly, to shake the opposing coalition.

6 The Failure of Imagination

FROM *The Long Fuse* BY LAURENCE LAFORE

THE COURSE OF EVENTS that led to this general war are perfectly clear, though the motives and in some cases the timing are not. Austria-Hungary, at the urging of its ally, Germany, undertook strong measures against Serbia in order to protect its existence and its position as a Great Power. The exact purpose of these measures was not clearly agreed upon in Vienna, but they were of a sort to convince the Russians that Austria intended to extinguish Serbian sovereignty and to establish Austro-German predominance in the Balkans. To prevent this, and perhaps to frighten Austria into a more reasonable frame of mind, the Russians adopted military measures. The Germans felt absolutely obliged to stand by their ally, and they believed, from the moment of the assassination, that the safest course of action for Austria-Hungary to adopt would be a quick, decisive one, a *fait accompli*. They were prepared to incur the risk of fighting Russia, although they believed that it could be avoided. They urged—fruitlessly, most of the time—speed and decision in Vienna, and they continued to urge it after the Russian reaction to the ultimatum had showed that the risks were very serious. The Austrians responded by speeding up the declaration of war against Serbia; the Russians reacted, according to schedule, by mobilizing. Military considerations made it expedient that their mobilization be general, and this constituted a direct threat to Germany that could be met only by German mobilization. The French felt absolutely obliged to stand by *their* ally; it would almost certainly have been impossible for them to abstain from participation if they had wanted to, since the Germans almost certainly would have attacked them anyway as part of their plan for war against Russia. But the French did not consider abstention; instead, they gave the Russians unchanging, and sometimes provocative, assurances of their loyalty. German mobilization meant French mobilization, and German war against Russia meant a war between France and Germany. And since war between France and Germany involved the German violation of Belgium, it meant, too, war between Germany and Great Britain.

In this summary of events, stripped of the fruitless proposals for negotiation, may be discerned several elementary facts.

First, the vital interests of Germany and of France required loyalty to their respective allies; betrayal, or even a suggestion of weakness, would have incurred charges of treachery and led to a vulnerable and invidious isolation in a dangerous world. *The strength of their allies was part—an essential part —of their own strength and safety;* the preservation of that strength was deemed to demand not only loyal support but assistance in executing the policy of the ally. Prestige was part of strength; the Germans feared, rightly, a diminution of Austro-Hungarian authority; the French feared a diminution of Russian authority. Neither believed that the two were wholly incompatible, but they had very different views as to the minimum requirements of their allies' needs.

Second, the safety of each Power depended upon the execution, within very narrow time limits, of a very complicated and unalterable military plan. Not only could the plans not be changed; they must be put into effect as rapidly as possible to prevent grave military disadvantage, once the threat of war became serious.

Third, the Russians were absolutely convinced that Austria had sinister plans in the Balkans seriously menacing to their own interests, and they were convinced that the sovereignty of Serbia, however much of a nuisance they thought that nation might be, was indispensable to their own security and dignity.

Fourth, the Austrians were convinced that the sovereignty of Serbia was a serious and permanent threat to their own existence.

Fifth, the irretrievable steps were military measures, and these were taken in most cases at the urgent behest of the chiefs of staff and their advisers. The generals appear in a very unfavorable light in most narratives of events. There is no doubt that some of them—most conspicuously, Conrad —inclined to rabid bellicosity. But none of them acted except when ordered by civilian ministers. And the advice of most of them, of Janushkevich, of Moltke, of Joffre, was given as a matter of duty when facts drove them, correctly, to the conclusion that they could not safeguard their countries without preparing for war. This had nothing to do with their views as to whether war was or was not wise. They, like the ministers they advised, were merely performing their necessary function. As Winston Churchill was to say some twenty years later, "The responsibility of ministers for the public safety is absolute and needs no mandate."

But this is not to suggest that the course of events was preordained or that nothing could have been done to prevent its developing as it did. There are hundreds of supposititious changes that might have prevented the war from taking place when it did and on the terms it did. To discuss them is profitless, but to suggest a few possibilities, chosen at random, may be instructive.

For one thing, the French Ambassador at Saint Petersburg, Maurice

Paléologue, repeatedly pressed on Sazonov the need for a "firm policy." His position was very influential—both because he represented Russia's ally and because, since his chiefs were inaccessible, it was necessary for him to act on his own responsibility. He was, for a time, *making* French policy toward Russia, and the policy he made was incitement to war. A different ambassador might well have altered the course of events. Paléologue went far beyond the terms of the alliance, beyond the need to show diplomatic solidarity, beyond the limits of previous French policy. His actions and influences offer a precise counterpart to those of Tschirschky in Vienna.

To take another example, it has frequently been said by both sides that a clearer stand by Sir Edward Grey would have saved the peace. If the Germans had been told, early and with conviction, that Britain would take part in the war, they would very probably have averted instead of encouraging the Austrian ultimatum and declaration of war. There is strong evidence for this; some Germans have even taken the weird moral stand that Grey was responsible for starting the war because if he had made his position clear the Germans would never have permitted it to start. The ethics of this attitude are not convincing, but the facts are. A less fastidious, conciliatory, and correct statesman might have acted more effectively. A modest measure of duplicity, such as many diplomats regard as a proper tool of their trade, would have permitted him to make much stronger representations much sooner than he did. No absolute commitment was necessary; he could have told both Lichnowsky and his own Ambassador at Berlin that Great Britain *did* regard the Austro-Serbian problem as of European and British concern (that would have been a matter of judgment, not of propriety) and that if war broke out Great Britain would almost certainly take part in it on the allied side. This would have been tricky, in both senses of the word, but experienced diplomats of the utmost rectitude like Nicolson and Eyre Crowe were urging something like it. Sir Edward suffered from an excess of scruples and perhaps an insufficiency of grasp; his case is a demonstration for the argument that there is at times nothing so dangerous as pacific punctilio.

If either Sazonov or Berchtold had behaved differently, on any of several occasions, the course of events would certainly have been different. A less volatile and more judicious statesman than Sazonov, and one surer of his own ground, might not have reacted with so much emotion and so little regard for political realities as he did on hearing of the Austrian ultimatum. A smaller concern for Russia's prestige and his own might have prevented his urging the Serbs to reject the ultimatum, and it might have delayed the Period Preparatory to War and given time for fruitful negotiation. A less indecisive statesman than Berchtold, and one with a clearer vision of the future, might have formulated concrete demands for Serbia that would secure Austria's ends without leaving so much scope for uncertainty, even apparently in his own mind, about what really was intended as an objective. The problem of Austria-Hungary was in some ways comparable to that of Great Britain: there were too many disagreements and cross-currents and deterrents to clear-cut action. But a different sort of statesman in either country might have overcome them and produced a definite and rapid solution to the difficulties.

Most important, there were in Germany many occasions when different events would have followed if even slightly different decisions had been made. At all times the Germans treated the prospective war as if it were a rather inviting prospect. From July 5 on, the Germans behaved unwisely in regard to Austria; they first pressed for decisive action and, when it was not forthcoming, continued to press for it without regard to changing circumstances. They seem to have been wildly optimistic about the chances of French and British pressure being exerted at Saint Petersburg. They were certainly wildly irresponsible in acting on the belief that they could win a European war if one broke out. Such unwisdom was an understandable but not a necessary component of German policy. If the German leaders had not been widely dispersed around the middle of July, if the Emperor had returned a few days earlier from his cruise, if Bethmann-Hollweg and Jagow had not been caught up in the established policy that a *fait accompli* was possible, Austria-Hungary might not have rejected out of hand the Serbian reply, might not have broken diplomatic relations with Serbia, might not have declared war, might not have provoked the Russian mobilization.

All these involve reproaches to the statesmen for deficiencies in their stature. But the basic reproach must be the failure of imagination; the statesmen were thinking of the defense of visible interests that seemed vital; they failed to discern that invisible and much larger interests were involved in their decisions. There were, in Russia, those who foresaw a threat to the regime in the war, but the defense of the regime seemed to Sazonov and the Emperor Nicholas to demand not peace but prestige. No one, let it be said again, realized that the war they were consciously risking would be the first World War.

Two things happened to turn war into cataclysm. First, the breakdown of the German strategy in France and the establishment of stable lines in early September, 1914: instead of a decision there was an indecision, made perennial by the peculiar equilibrium of military technology. Second, the accumulated tensions and conflicts of the European State System, long repressed or stabilized, all broke out the moment that war was a fact; the war could not be ended until they were resolved. Most of these tensions had nothing to do with the events that caused the war to break out; they were buried at the bottom of the rivalries and the institutions that made it possible. There was Alsace-Lorraine: once a Franco-German war had started, France could not make peace until Alsace-Lorraine was restored, except after a military disaster; without a military disaster, Germany would never concede the loss of the provinces. There was the Anglo-German naval rivalry: once war had started, Great Britain would not make peace until the threat of a strong German Navy had been permanently dispersed. There was Constantinople: once war broke out, the Russian government could not make peace until it was assured that the centuries-old ambition for Constantinople would be satisfied. There was Germany's encirclement: once war broke out, Germany could not, short of military disaster, make peace until the encirclement had been broken, which meant the decisive crushing of both France and Russia.

These needs and ambitions had underlaid the tensions of Europe and had shaped the alliance system and the policies of the Powers. But they none of them had led to actions that produced war. They were either negotiable or repressible. The one problem that was neither negotiable nor repressible was that raised by threats to the integrity of Austria-Hungary. The composition of the Habsburg Monarchy made it fatally vulnerable to the activities of the Serbs; at the same time, it made it difficult to eliminate those activities by rapid and resolute action; and it made it difficult for the government of Austria-Hungary—or its ally, Germany—to retreat, to equivocate, to delay, once the decision to take action had been made, ill defined and unsatisfactory as the decision was. It was this problem that caused the war which became the first World War.

The Fall of the Russian Monarchy—Inherent Failure or Planned Revolution?

CONTENTS

QUESTIONS FOR STUDY

1 *What are the differences between the accounts of Heald and Paléologue?*

2 *How do you account for them?*

3 *Which of the accounts emphasizes the role of the individual?*

4 *Which emphasizes impersonal forces?*

5 *Does Trotsky's account fall neatly into either category?*

6 *Do the varying interpretations rest on different factors?*

The Russian Revolution was one of those striking events that decisively change the course of history. Much of what has happened in the world since 1917 has been a response to that great upheaval. There were of course, two revolutions. One overthrew the Czar and the monarchy, established a liberal regime, and tried to prosecute the war. A second overthrew the Kerensky government by coup d'état, *established an oligarchy of the Bolsheviks, and later evolved into the Stalinist dictatorship. It is the former revolution that will be considered here. The destruction of a monarchy dating back to the sixteenth century, the most autocratic government in Europe, has given rise to much controversy. We want to know how it came about, whether or not it was planned, and who were its leaders.*

1   Descriptions of the Revolutionary Days

The following account is taken from a letter written by Edward T. Heald, an American who was working for the Y.M.C.A. in Petrograd in 1917. It gives a lively sense of how the revolution looked to an ordinary man on the street. The introduction is by W. B. Walsh.

FROM *Edward T. Heald's Letter to Mrs. Heald*

The value of the following lies in the fact that Mr. Edward T. Heald, who wrote it, was not seeking to make a case for any side. The letter was written to Mrs. Heald and was not intended for publication. It does not pretend to be an analysis but only an informal description of what Mr. Heald saw, heard and thought during the stirring first week of the first 1917 Revolution. At that time, Mr. Heald had been a Y.M.C.A. secretary in Petrograd for about nine months.

MONDAY, MARCH 12TH, was the great day that suddenly sounded the knell of the old regime, though we were slow to realize what was taking place. It was quieter on the Nevsky than the day before. I walked up the Prospect to the Sadovaya at noon, and saw nothing exciting though the banks and most of the business places were closed. The center of action Monday was on the other side of the city. . . .

Mr. Harte, who always treated our predictions of a revolution with a smile saying that nothing of the sort would happen, was still planning to go to Sweden the next morning. His secretary, Penn Davis, had to go through the trouble zone this Monday morning to complete passport arrangements and secure documents for Mr. Harte and himself. When he arrived at the Liteiny Prospect he found barricades, and was stopped by the strikers who

W. B. Walsh, "Petrograd, March–July, 1917. The Letters of Edward T. Heald," *American Slavic and East European Review*, VI, Nos. 16–17, 120–133. Reprinted, with omission of footnotes, by permission of *Slavic Review* and W. B. Walsh.

had some student soldiers with them. After showing his American passport and explaining his business he was allowed to go on, and got back alright.

During the day the sound of firing became louder in our part of the city. Neither Baker nor I understood what was taking place when we started over to the Narodni Dom after tea that evening to hear Shaliapin in *The Roussalkas*. There was an atmosphere everywhere of excitement, uncertainty, and danger. Volleys and shots started at every crossing and corner. Around the Winter Palace Square people clung to sides of buildings, and if they came to street intersections where they had to cross they darted across. The gloomy sombre red buildings seemed to be sitting in judgment on the country's doom.

When we reached the middle of the New Nicholaievsky Bridge over the Neva we stopped on the high middle and looked back over the city. We saw flames rising over the Liteiny region, which we afterwards learned were burning law courts. Machine guns were keeping up an incessant rat-atat-tat in a dozen different quarters of the city, and particularly loud in the direction of the Narodni Dom. At the further end of the bridge was a squad of soldiers forming a line across. I went up to the officer and asked if there was any objection to our proceeding on to the Narodni Dom. He asked for passports and when I showed them he said "Alright." As we neared the bridge over the Little Neva a little further on, another squad of soldiers stood facing us. When we were about fifty paces off the crowd of women and working people in front of us broke and ran, and looking ahead we saw the guns raised in our direction. We immediately reversed our direction, and while we didn't run, we never walked faster until we put a building between us and the raised guns. We decided to hear Shaliapin some other evening. Later we learned that no performance was held at the Narodni Dom that night.

We saw no policemen during this walk. It was the first time that they had not been on the streets in the center of the city. We haven't seen any since. They disappeared from the streets late that afternoon.

The real surprise awaited Baker and me when we got back to Mr. Harte's room at the Grand Hotel. He had given up his trip to Sweden the next morning. But not until he and Day had taken a trip to the station that had been full of thrillers. They had loaded the trunks and baggage on one of the high Russian sleds known as lamovois, to take to the station for checking purposes the night before the train leaves according to the Russian custom. As their lamovois passed the big square in front of the Winter Palace they were fired upon. As they continued down the narrow Millionaya Ulitza they were fired upon again. They ducked their heads and Mr. Harte prayed while George used his Russian on the driver to speed him up. The driver didn't need any coaxing. They arrived at the Liteiny Bridge only to be surrounded and held up by a crowd of about a hundred and fifty strikers, students and soldiers. The leader was a student. The strikers thought that Harte and Day were trying to take ammunition over the river to the enemy, and demanded that the trunks be opened for search. There were these two Americans standing up on the high sled, with the crowd of revolutionists thronging around them from every side. What Mr. Harte feared most was that some of the Tsar's cavalry or police would suddenly appear on the scene and proceed to fire upon them, in which case Mr. Harte and George, standing high above the crowd, would be the best targets.

Another thing was troubling Mr. Harte. He had forgotten to bring one of the trunk keys which he had left with Penn Davis at the Hotel. What would the strikers think when he told them that he did not have the key? But he had one of the keys and opened the trunk it fitted. After carefully searching it, the mob was satisfied and did not ask to look in the other trunk. They provided an escort of soldiers to conduct him to the station. As soon as they got their trunks off the lamovois at the station, the driver disappeared with his horses and sled. Then Mr. Harte could find no one to take charge of their baggage. The customary crowd of porters was nowhere in sight. No officials were to be seen. The platform was almost deserted. Finally a lone official appeared who looked at the Americans in wonderment, and told them that there would be no train in the morning; that the officials had been unarmed by the strikers; that no one was in authority; and that there was no one to look after their trunks.

It was in vain that Mr. Harte and Day searched for another vehicle of any kind to take them and their baggage back to the Hotel. They were almost giving up hope of finding a place to store their baggage when a man appeared who showed them a closet where they could lock their things up. It was characteristic of Mr. Harte that the excitement did not keep him from seeing to it carefully that his wardrobe trunk was set up in the right position, doubtful though it was that he would ever see it again. Then he and Day walked the four miles back to the Hotel, arriving there shortly before we returned. Mr. Harte was ready to acknowledge that the situation was serious. Half of the city that he had been through was in the hands of the strikers.

The next big surprise awaited us at ten o'clock when Day and I returned to our apartments. A Russian sailor was there, who was a friend of Madame Stepan. He gave us the astounding news that the old government was overthrown, that a new government had been established with a committee of twelve at its head responsible to the Duma, and that the entire city was in the hands of the revolutionists, excepting the Police Districts which were all under the fire of the revolutionists. He lived in the Morskaya Police District. Most of the soldiers had already gone over to the strikers and the people and the others were rapidly following suit. Not until then did we realize that we were in the midst of a great revolution that so many of our friends had talked about and dreaded.

One of the pieces of information which our marine friend gave us, which was later verified, was that the same Monday morning the Tsar had appointed Minister Protopopov dictator, ordering the dissolution of the Duma. But the Duma ignored the orders of the Tsar and immediately went into executive session thus defying the Tsar and his government. That was the point were the real revolution began.

Our marine friend said that he could not get home on account of the siege against the Police District near his home. He said that most of the firing then going on in the city was at the Police Districts, and also by boys who had secured fire-arms and were shooting them off in the air for sport. Crowds of soldiers and strikers were holding jubilee meetings over the city, as comrades in a common cause, adopting the red flag of the revolution. Officers who stood by their oath of loyalty to the Tsar were being arrested.

One of the first efforts of the revolutionists was to clean out the Police Department, and the lives of the police were unsafe if seen on the streets. The wrath of the movement seemed directed chiefly towards this instittion, the records of which were dumped out of the windows on to the streets and sidewalks below and burned. Russians with whom we talked called the police system a treacherous German institution that had been foisted upon the people back in the time of Peter the Great, and that it had been used as an instrument to keep the masses in ignorance and bondage ever since.

The next piece of news came when B. . . . arrived home at midnight. He and G. . . . met an officer in the same block that our apartments are located. Across the street is the building of the War Ministry. This officer asked B. . . . and G. . . . if they were English. They replied that they were Americans. The officer replied "Good, I also foreigner. I Finnlandsky. To-morrow that building is ours," pointing to the war ministry. He spoke in Russian and B. . . . and G. . . . knew just enough of the language to guess that he said that they were going to blow up the building. We accordingly wondered as we turned in that night whether we would be awakened by an explosion. The Finn was as happy as a boy. Immediately after talking with B. . . . and G. . . . he went over to the building and passed into the court between lines of soldiers who evidently held the building for the revolutionists.

A half hour after midnight Eric Christensen, our big Dane secretary, came home. Ordinarily he is very calm, but this time he was dancing and shouting with excitement. He had just shaken hands with a couple of men who had been released from the famous Peter and Paul Fortress. Both the prisoners were Finns, and had a thousand rubles each furnished by some Finnish revolutionary committee, to pay their expenses home. The Fortress had been taken by the soldiers that evening, and all the prisoners, who were there for political and religious reasons, were released, including nineteen soldiers who had been imprisoned during the last few days.

It was hard to shake off enough of the excitement that night to get to sleep.

Tuesday March 13th dawned a beautiful clear day. We were awakened by volleys and artillery fire at an early hour, which increased in intensity. People hugged the courtways in the street below us, and if they crossed the streets they did so with a dash. If they began to take to the sidewalks a sudden volley would send them scattering for shelter. Our soldat told us that the Dvornik (house-porter) gave orders to stay in that day.

At nine o'clock, however, I started out as usual for the office planning to stop at Mr. Harte's room in the Grand Hotel on the way. As I reached the end of the block, at the corner of Gogol Street and Vosnesensky Prospect, an imposing sight was before me. Directly ahead, a block away, the square opposite the Astoria Hotel (headquarters for the officers) was full of soldiers. Down the Morskaya came column after column of soldiers, in martial order, greeted with the rousing shouts of the people assembled in the square in front of St. Isaac's Cathedral. The sun shining on the masses of soldiers made a brilliant spectacle. The soldiers stopped short when they came even with the statue of Nicholas, where they faced the Astoria Hotel.

Suddenly there was a tremendous volley and the sidewalks and squares were emptied of people in the twinkling of an eye. I was half way across Gogol Street when the volleys came, and I had that naked feeling the soldiers are said to have when they go over the top. I wasted no time covering the remaining half of the street and was soon in Mr. Harte's room. While we stood at his window looking out on the street, soldiers began to come along the middle of the street leading officers to the Duma to swear allegiance to the new government. These were the officers who surrendered and said they were willing to swear allegiance to the new order. Some of them looked downcast and others happy.

During a lull in the fighting I crossed the street to our office building, and with some of the other secretaries looked down from our sixth floor directly on top of the Astoria Hotel roof at the end of the block on the opposite side of the street, and on the fighting in the street and square in front of the hotel. We could see the marines lying on Gogol Street in front of St. Isaac's shooting at the hotel. We saw several men fall, and some of them afterwards crawled off dragging a wounded arm or leg. The Red Cross automobiles came and went rapidly. The famous storming of the officer's headquarters was in full swing. More and more detachments of soldiers came along leading officers to the Duma. Some of the officers offered resistance and were killed on the spot. Others shouted "We're for you" and were allowed to keep their swords and arms and often given commands. At the height of the fighting we noticed a commotion on top of the Astoria Hotel roof. A machine gun had been placed there and the officers had begun firing down on the sidewalk below. It did not take long for the soldiers to spot the mischief and put an end to it with short shrift for the unfortunate officers.

While we were watching this affair from our window B. . . . and G. . . . had an exciting time down on the street. They were on the Morskaya under the Astoria Hotel when the machine gun began its work from the roof. In the rush for shelter, B. .   . fell and had many a kick and cuff before he regained his feet. He said he got all the excitement he wanted that time.

We saw the soldiers smashing bottles of liquor on the sidewalks, and we saw the contents running down the street. We saw only a few soldiers carrying off or drinking the liquor.

The battle lasted about a half hour, and by that time the soldiers had everything in their own hands, and the officers had flung out the white flag. This was the day of the private soldier. They told their officers to go home and stay out of sight until things were quiet again. The officers, having taken their individual oath of allegiance to the Tsar, considered themselves more bound to it than the soldiers who took allegiance in groups. For the officers it was a great moral struggle, many[?] of them being in sympathy with the revolution. Caught as they were in a situation where they had to make instant decision, there was a variety of reactions on their part, many paying with their lives for their hesitation.

The way the soldiers took things in their own hands was a revelation. They showed perfect confidence, tackled most difficult tasks with a practical efficiency and did all with a buoyant, smiling assurance and mastery that gave everyone confidence that they knew what they were doing. The "children of the Tsar" this day stepped forth as their own men and masters.

Probably the predominant impression that an American received from the events of the day was the self-restraint and order of the soldiers, as well as of the workingmen. There were cases of killing and bloodshed, and during the day many were taken to the hospitals, but considering the size of the revolution, the number of men and soldiers engaged in the struggle, the amount of bloodshed was small. Outside of the destruction of property in the police districts, the officers' quarters, and the homes of the suspected aristocracy, there was little looting. And this order was maintained despite the fact that there was an indiscriminate distributing of firearms to working men and boys. This was one time when prohibition was a blessing to Russia. If vodka could have been found in plenty, the revolution could easily have had a terrible ending.

One of the problems of this day was the snipers. The soldiers quickly handled such cases by bringing up an armored car or tank against the building from which the shots came, and playing the machine gun upon it. Many of the police were in hiding, concealed often through the connivance of dvorniks, who formed a part of the old police system. The H. . . . 's had an exciting experience in their apartments. Shots were fired into the court from some upper floors. A group of fifty or sixty soldiers immediately came in and made a thorough search of every room at the point of a gun. The starshy (head) dvornik was almost shot, but was saved at the last moment by one of the captors who had an argument that had an effect upon the other soldiers.

The center of action was transferred from the Liteiny District to the Gogol and Morskaya District. We had the full benefit of it. In the afternoon the magnificent palace of Baron Friederichs, the German sympathizer, who was the Tsar's personal advisor and Chamberlin, was in flames. It was in plain view up the Gogol from our office and was completely burned out.

Towards evening of this day I picked up on the streets a news-sheet entitled *"Izvestiya Petrogradskago Soveta Rabochikh deputatov"* dated 28 February [OS] 1917, and calling upon the workingmen of all lands to unite. It announced that the bourgeois system had been overthrown, the capitalistic class destroyed, and urged the workingmen and soldiers to elect deputies for a central labor council or soviet. This was the first printed matter that had appeared in the capital for several days. It was also the first announcement of or by the Soviet. The newspapers had all been closed since Friday. We didn't know what was going on in the rest of the world or Empire. The wildest rumors were afloat.

One rumor had the Kaiser overthrown and a revolution successful in Germany. Another had the Tsar's army on the way from the front to put down the revolution. The discovery of five hundred machine guns on the roofs of the buildings in Petrograd, carrying an apparent threat of a St. Bartholomew's Eve massacre to put down the revolution if necessary, did not dispel our nervousness. The minister Protopopov, had ordered one thousand machine guns placed, according to report, but had only succeeded in getting five hundred up when the plan was discovered. The plan was for all the machine guns to begin playing upon the multitudes at the same instant, signal for which was to be an airplane that would come over the city from Tsarskoe Selo. Rumor had it that the Tsarina was to give the fatal order that would start the airplane, but that she lost her nerve at the last moment. Well, to pick up this red revolutionary bulletin on top of these rumors did not quiet our nerves. All restaurants and stores were closed, at night the streets were pitch dark, the street lamps not being lighted. It was a disquieting evening.

Wednesday [the 14th] conditions became more normal. At ten-thirty I started afoot for the American Embassy. Cheering on the Morskaya attracted my attention, and when I arrived on the street I found a great parade in progress, all revolutionists carrying the red flag and the bands playing the Marseillaise. I followed the parade along the Nevsky and shall never forget the wonderful sight. From the Morskaya to the Liteiny, over a mile and a half, the great Nevsky Prospect was packed with people from the buildings on one side to the buildings on the other side.

The parade itself consisted of soldiers, officers, marines, workingmen all marching in order, and every division hoisting the big red banners. The marching columns stretched from the curb-stone to the middle of the broad Prospect. The spectators packed the rest of the street, a continuous deafening cheer greeting the marching columns along the whole route. Now and then armored cars darted along with soldiers armed to the teeth. I never expect to see a more thrilling sight in my life.

During the whole time I saw only one drunken man, and heard only two shots fired. The order was wonderful. The people were not so much wild with enthusiasm as they were joyously, freely, intensely, spiritually happy. There was an exhilaration to it that was thrilling and indescribable. One felt that it must be a dream; that it was impossible that such things were happening in Russia. Well dressed people were in evidence and apparently as happy as the bent gray-haired working men who looked about with a dazed sort of happiness, while their faces shone with a rapturous glow. There seemed to be the best of feeling between the officers and soldiers.

When I reached the Embassy I learned that the Tsar was expected to be at the Duma that afternoon to proclaim a new constitution. The people at the Embassy thought he could still save his dynasty if he would grant the constitution and appoint new ministers who would represent the people. But the Tsar never appeared. He let this last chance slip by. Sixty thousand soldiers at Peterhof this day have their allegiance to the Duma. This same day Grand Duke Cyril went out to the Duma and tendered his allegiance and the service of the marines under his command to the new government. We also got our first outside telegraph news this day, to the effect that Moscow was also in the hands of the revolutionists. The struggle there had been brief and an easy victory for the revolutionists. The Mayor of the city was a liberal. The police took refuge in the Kremlin but had to surrender speedily.

While I was at the Embassy word came that Protopopov, the former Minister of the Interior, had surrendered. He had been in hiding with the other ministers of the old regime at the Admiralty since Monday. At eleven-fifteen Wednesday he appeared at the Tauride Palace, where the Duma meets. A student was at the entrance. Protopopov went up to the student and said, "You are a student?" "I am," was the reply. "I have always been interested in the welfare of our country," said Protopopov, "and therefore I come and give myself voluntarily. I am former Minister of the Interior Protopopov. Lead me to whatever person is necessary." The student led him to the Temporary Executive Committee. On the way the soldiers, recognizing him, gave vent to their indignation, and threatened him, and when he arrived at the committee, he was pale and tottering. Kerensky, the new Minister of Justice, pacified the crowd and prevented violence.

At noon this day the Admiralty passed into the hands of the revolutionary soldiers, and the ministers who had been in hiding either fled or gave themselves up.

On my way home from the Embassy I saw armored cars racing through the streets filled with armed soldiers who were scattering bulletins. I picked one up. It was called *Prikaz No. 1*, was dated March 1, and was signed by the Soviet of the Workers' and Soldiers' Deputies, the uniting of these two groups apparently having taken place during the preceding twenty-four hours. This order called upon the soldiers not to salute their officers except when on duty. All titles were to be dropped. Soldiers could no longer be addressed by their officers with the familiar "Thou" but only by "Sir" and the polite "You." The day before (Tuesday) there had been no saluting, but during the big parade Wednesday morning saluting was general. With the appearance of Prikaz No. 1 however, saluting stopped. Trouble brewed in the atmosphere.

Thursday noon Zemmer showed up at the office. All his enthusiasm for the new regime was gone. "Everybody is out for what he can get for his own profit," said Zemmer. "There is no patriotism. Everything was beautiful the first two days, then differences arose and harmony disappeared." Zemmer had been at the Duma the preceding day to swear allegiance to the new government, along with two thousand other officers. He was worried as to the outcome, as out of eight thousand officers in the city only two thousand had shown up at the Duma. It was reported that a large number had gone out to Tsarskoe Selo to the Tsar. Others were in hiding. Moreover there was a serious struggle going on between the radical revolutionists who wanted a social revolution, and the conservative liberals, who wanted a constitutional monarchy. Zemmer was afraid that they might split and give the old regime its opportunity to regain control. It was reported that a large army loyal to the Tsar was on the way from the front to put down the revolution. Regarding Prikaz No. 1, Zemmer said that it had been dispatched with haste by the truck-load to the front, and that it would ruin the discipline of the whole army.

Banks opened up until one o'clock Thursday. Many stores of provisions were brought to light. Butter, which had been selling at three rubles and twenty kopeks (about $1.00) per pound, dropped to eighty kopeks by revolutionary order. Soldiers were on hand to see that no more than that was charged. Sugar, which had been issued only on tickets, could now be secured without tickets. Great stores of meat were brought forth from cold storage and placed on the market. Out at Nevsky Monastery a couple of thousand tons of sugar were seized by the revolutionists and placed at the disposal of the government. There was a rush for provisions from every hand all day.

In the evening we heard that the Tsar's army had arrived from the front and was engaging the revolutionists in a great battle at the edge of the city near the Baltsky Station. We walked over that way, but heard and saw nothing out of the ordinary and concluded that the rumor was false.

Friday morning [the 16th] we were thrilled to see in the windows of the *Novoye Vremya* newspaper a bulletin reading that Nicolai Romanov (all titles removed) had abdicated at three o'clock that morning for himself and his heir, Alexei, in favor of Michael Alexandrovitch, the next in line. Alongside it another bulletin read that Michael Alexandrovitch declined to accept the throne, stating that the people wanted a Republic, and that he wanted to get back to the front where he belonged. The abdication of the Tsar had been written on his special train near Pskov, after it had been shunted back and forth in vain efforts to elude the revolutionists.

The story of the worries and remarks of the Tsar during those last hours, as reported in the newspapers, reads like a chapter from the Middle Ages. When it was all over and he had signed the abdication he sighed,

"How I long to be with my roses in the Crimea." Baron Friederichs, whose palace was burned, was with him to the last.

With the appearance of the morning bulletins the new Cabinet was announced. The new Minister of Justice is Kerensky, a Socialist, and his first order was that any important papers or documents which were found in the Police Headquarters and were worthy of saving were to be transferred to the Academy of Science. He seems to know how to attract the attention and seize the imagination of the people. There was also appointed a new Minister, one for Finnish Affairs, to take the place of the old Governor General of Finland, who has been arrested. Also the man who was responsible for the new restrictive and repressive measures in Finland in 1905 is in custody.

In the same bulletins the Cabinet announces that it will be guided by the following principles: (1) Full and immediate amnesty in all political and religious affairs; (2) Liberty of word, press, assembly, unions and strikes with extension of political liberty to those in military service within the confines permissible by military technical conditions; (3) Abolition of all class, religious and national limitations; (4) Immediate preparations to convoke on the basis of universal, equal, direct, and secret suffrage, a Constitutional Assembly, which will establish the form of administration and constitution; (5) Substitution of national militia in the place of police, with elected leaders and subject to local administration; (6) Elections to local administration on the basis of universal suffrage. On the following day a proclamation was issued removing all restrictions from the Jews.

On Friday [the 16th] the old flag of Russia was replaced by the red flag in all quarters of the city. Soldiers were busy all day pulling down the coats of arms of the old regime, including those on the Winter Palace. The Singer Sewing Machine Building protected the American Eagle on its top by having it wrapped in the American flag, but all other eagles in the city came down.

Little Alexander, our office boy, when asked what he thought of the revolution, said "Tsar ne nado." (No need of a Tsar.)

One of Mr. Harte's friends, Count Stackelburg, was killed Monday. Revolutionists came to his palace on the Millionaya, and when he refused to open the doors, he was shot down. Sturmer is reported dead in prison. Count Pallen has not been heard of since Monday. He went down to one of his estates in the country near Moscow just before the revolution, and his life is feared for. The girls in our office are back at work, and all seem happy at the new day.

We now feel that we can draw a full breath; that what we see is no longer a dream but a reality; that a new era has opened with consequences beyond imagination. We are thrilled with the new energy, purpose, and enthusiasm that has taken hold everywhere. It has been good to be alive these marvelous days. We can take our hats off to the Russian people; they know how to put great things across. Their good-nature is impressive; even in the course of the fighting they seemed to retain their good-nature. They don't seem to have the natures that would lead to the excesses of the French Revolution. They handle the most exciting emergencies in a cool matter-of-fact way. And I am struck with their continued loyalty to the Allies. I talked with a number of the soldiers during the week. "Give us a week to clean this up," they said, "and then we'll go back and clean up the Germans so quick no one can stop us."

> *Maurice Paléologue was the French Ambassador to Russia during the revolutionary period. Unlike Heald he had access to politicians and foreign diplomats during the troubled days of March, 1917, and his remarks are more analytical and better informed. On the other hand, his memoirs were written for publication years after the event.*

FROM *An Ambassador's Memoirs*
BY MAURICE PALÉOLOGUE

Tuesday, March 6, 1917.

PETROGRAD IS SHORT OF BREAD AND WOOD, and the public is suffering want.

At a bakery on the Liteïny this morning I was struck by the sinister expression on the faces of the poor folk who were lined up in a queue, most of whom had spent the whole night there.

Pokrovski, to whom I mentioned the matter, did not conceal his anxiety. But what can be done! The transport crisis is certainly worse. The extreme cold (43°) which has all Russia in its grip has put more than twelve hundred engines out of action, owing to boiler tubes bursting, and there is a shortage of spare tubes as a result of strikes. Moreover, the snowfall of the last few weeks has been exceptionally heavy and there is also a shortage of labor in the villages to clear the permanent way. The result is that at the present moment fifty-seven thousand railway wagons cannot be moved.

Thursday, March 8, 1917.

There has been great agitation in Petrograd all day. Processions have been parading the main streets. At several points the mob shouted for "Bread and peace!" At others it sang the Working Man's *Marseillaise*. In the Nevsky Prospekt there have been slight disorders.

From *An Ambassador's Memoirs* by Maurice Paléologue (1924), pp. 213–6, 221–5, 228, 230–1, 233–4, 236–41. Reprinted by permission of Doubleday & Company, Inc., and Hutchinson Publishing Group Ltd., London.

I had Trepov, Count Tolstoï, Director of the Hermitage, my Spanish colleague, Villasinda, and a score of my regular guests to dinner this evening.

The occurrences in the streets were responsible for a shade of anxiety which marked our faces and our conversation. I asked Trepov what steps the Government was taking to bring food supplies to Petrograd, as unless they are taken the situation will probably soon get worse. His replies were anything but reassuring.

When I returned to my other guests, I found all traces of anxiety had vanished from their features and their talk. The main object of conversation was an evening party which Princess Leon Radziwill is giving on Sunday: it will be a large and brilliant party, and everyone was hoping that there will be music and dancing.

Trepov and I stared at each other. The same words came to our lips: "What a curious time to arrange a party!"

In one group, various opinions were being passed on the dancers of the Marie Theatre and whether the palm for excellence should be awarded to Pavlova, Kchechinskaïa or Karsavina, etc.

In spite of the fact that revolution is in the air in his capital, the Emperor, who has spent the last two months at Tsarskoïe-Selo, left for General Headquarters this evening.

Friday, March 9, 1917.

This morning the excitement in industrial circles took a violent form. Many bakeries were looted, especially in the Viborg Quarter and Vassili-Ostrov. At several points the Cossacks charged the crowd and killed a number of workmen.

Pokrovski has been confiding his anxieties to me:

"I should regard these disorders as of minor importance if my dear colleague at the Interior still retained a shred of common sense. But what can you do with a man who has lost all idea of reality for weeks, and confers with the shade of Rasputin every night? This very evening he's been spending hours in conjuring up the ghost of the *staretz!*" [*the holy man, i.e., Rasputin—D.K.*]

Saturday, March 10, 1917.

The hair-raising problem of food supplies has been investigated to-night by an "Extraordinary Council," which was attended by all the ministers (except the Minister of the Interior), the President of the Council of Empire, the President of the Duma and the Mayor of Petrograd. Protopopov did not condescend to take part in the conference; he was no doubt communing with the ghost of Rasputin.

Gendarmes, Cossacks and troops have been much in evidence all over the city. Until four o'clock in the afternoon the demonstrations gave rise to no untoward event. But the public soon began to get excited. The *Marseillaise* was sung, and red flags were paraded on which was written: *Down*

With the Government! . . . Down with Protopopov! . . . Down with the war! . . . Down with Germany! . . . Shortly after five disorders began in the Nevsky Prospekt. Three demonstrators and three police officers were killed and about a hundred persons wounded.

Sunday, March 11, 1917.

The ministers sat in council until five o'clock this morning. Protopopov condescended to join his colleagues and reported to them the strong measures he had prescribed to preserve order "at any cost." The result is that General Khabalov, Military Governor of Petrograd, has had the city placarded with the following warning this morning:

All meetings or gatherings are forbidden. I notify the civil population that I have given the troops fresh authority to use their arms and stop at nothing to maintain order.

Monday, March 12, 1917.

At half-past eight this morning, just as I finished dressing, I heard a strange and prolonged din which seemed to come from the Alexander Bridge. I looked out: there was no one on the bridge, which usually presents such a busy scene. But, almost immediately, a disorderly mob carrying red flags appeared at the end which is on the right bank of the Neva, and a regiment came towards it from the opposite side. It looked as if there would be a violent collision, but on the contrary the two bodies coalesced. The army was fraternizing with revolt.

Shortly afterwards, someone came to tell me that the Volhynian regiment of the Guard had mutinied during the night, killed its officers and was parading the city, calling on the people to take part in the revolution and trying to win over the troops who still remain loyal.

At ten o'clock there was a sharp burst of firing and flames could be seen rising somewhere on the Liteïny Prospekt which is quite close to the embassy. Then silence.

Accompanied by my military attaché, Lieutenant-Colonel Lavergne, I went out to see what was happening. Frightened inhabitants were scattering through the streets. There was indescribable confusion at the corner of the Liteïny. Soldiers were helping civilians to erect a barricade. Flames mounted from the Law Courts. The gates of the arsenal burst open with a crash. Suddenly the crack of machine-gun fire split the air: it was the regulars who had just taken up position near the Nevsky Prospekt. The revolutionaries replied. I had seen enough to have no doubt as to what was coming. Under a hail of bullets I returned to the embassy with Lavergne who had walked calmly and slowly to the hottest corner out of sheer bravado.

About half-past eleven I went to the Ministry for Foreign Affairs, picking up Buchanan on the way.

I told Pokrovski everything I had just witnessed.

"So it's even more serious than I thought," he said.

But he preserved unruffled composure, flavoured with a touch of scepticism, when he told me of the steps on which the ministers had decided during the night:

"The sitting of the Duma has been prorogued to April and we have sent a telegram to the Emperor, begging him to return at once. With the exception of M. Protopopov, my colleagues and I all thought that a dictatorship should be established without delay; it would be conferred upon some general whose prestige with the army is pretty high, General Russky for example."

I argued that, judging by what I saw this morning, the loyalty of the army was already too heavily shaken for our hopes of salvation to be based on the use of the "strong hand," and that the immediate appointment of a ministry inspiring confidence in the Duma seemed to me more essential than ever, as there is not a moment to lose. I reminded Pokrovski that in 1789, 1830 and 1848, three French dynasties were overthrown because they were *too late* in realizing the significance and strength of the movement against them. I added that in such a grave crisis the representative of *allied* France had a right to give the Imperial Government advice on a matter of internal politics.

Buchanan endorsed my opinion.

Pokrovski replied that he personally shared our views, but that the presence of Protopopov in the Council of Ministers paralyzed action of any kind.

I asked him:

"Is there no one who can open the Emperor's eyes to the real situation?"

He heaved a despairing sigh.

"The Emperor is blind!"

Deep grief was writ large on the face of the honest man and good citizen whose uprightness, patriotism and disinterestedness I can never sufficiently extol.

He asked us to call in again at the end of the day.

When I returned to the embassy the situation had become much worse.

One piece of bad news followed another. The Law Courts had become nothing but an enormous furnace; the Arsenal on the Liteïny, the Ministry of the Interior, the Military Government building, the Minister of the Courts' offices, the headquarters of the Detective Force, the too, too, famous *Okhrana,* and a score of police-stations were in flames; the prisons were open and all the prisoners had been liberated; the Fortress of SS. Peter and Paul was undergoing a siege and the Winter Palace was occupied. Fighting was in progress in every part of the city.

At half-past six I returned with Buchanan to the Ministry for Foreign Affairs.

Pokrovski told us that in view of the gravity of the situation the Council of Ministers had decided to remove Pokrovski from the Ministry of the Interior and appoint General Makarenko "provisional director." The Council at once reported accordingly to the Emperor and also begged him to confer extraordinary powers immediately on some general, authorizing him to take all the exceptional measures the situation requires, and particularly to appoint other ministers.

He also informed us that in spite of the *ukase* of prorogation, the Duma met at the Tauris Palace this afternoon. It has set up a permanent committee with the object of serving as intermediary between the Government and the mutinous troops. Rodzianko, who is president of this committee, has telegraphed to the Emperor that the dynasty is in the greatest danger and the slightest hesitation will be fatal to it.

It was pitch dark when Buchanan and I left the Ministry for Foreign Affairs; not a lamp was lit. Just as my car was emerging from the Millionaïa, opposite the Marble Palace, we were stopped by a military mob. Something was happening in the barracks of the Pavlovski Regiment. Infuriated soldiers were shouting, yelling and fighting on the square. My car was surrounded. There was a violent demonstration against us. It was in vain that my chasseur and chauffeur tried to explain that we were the ambassadors of France and England. The doors were opened and our position was on the point of becoming dangerous when a non-commissioned officer, perched on a horse, recognized us and in a voice of thunder proposed a "cheer for France and England!" We came out of this unpleasant predicament to the accompaniment of a storm of cheering.

I spent the evening trying to obtain information as to what the Duma was doing. It was a very difficult matter as shooting and burning were in progress in all quarters.

At length certain reports came in which substantially agreed.

The Duma, I was told, was doing everything in its power to organize a Provisional Government, restore order to some extent and secure the food supplies of the capital.

The swift and complete defection of the army has been a great surprise to the leaders of the liberal parties and even the working-class party. As a matter of fact, it faces the moderate deputies, who are trying to direct and control the popular movement (Rodzianko, Miliukov, Shingarev, Maklakov, etc.) with the question whether it is not too late to save the dynastic *régime*. It is a formidable problem, as the republican idea, which is favoured in labour circles in Petrograd and Moscow, is foreign to the spirit of the country and it is impossible to foretell how the armies at the front will receive the occurrences in the capital.

Tuesday, March 13, 1917.

*   *   *

I have successively learned that Prince Golitizin (President of the Council), the Metropolitan Pitirim, Sturmer, Dobrovolsky, Protopopov, etc., have been arrested. The livid glow of fresh fires can be seen at various points. The Fortress of SS. Peter and Paul has become the headquarters of the revolt. Fierce fighting is taking place around the Admiralty, where the War Minister, the Naval Minister and several high officials have taken refuge. In all other parts of the city the insurgents are ruthlessly tracking down "traitors," police officials and gendarmes. The shooting has sometimes been so brisk in the streets round the embassy that my *dvorniks* have refused to take my telegrams to the General Post Office, the only one which is still working; I have had to rely on a petty officer of the French Navy who is on leave in Petrograd and is not afraid of bullets.

About five o'clock, a high official, K———, came to tell me that the executive committee of the Duma is trying to form a "provisional government," but that President Rodzianko, Gutchkov, Shulgin and Maklakov are utterly taken aback by the anarchical behaviour of the army.

"They never imagined a revolution like this," my informer added; "they hoped to direct it and keep it within bounds through the army. The troops recognize no leader now and are spreading terror throughout the city."

Wednesday, March 14, 1917.

There has been much fighting and burning again in Petrograd this morning. The soldiers are hunting down officers and gendarmes—a ruthless and savage chase which betrays all the barbarous instincts still latent in the *moujik* nature.

In the general anarchy which is raging in Petrograd, three directing bodies are in process of formation:

(1) The "Executive Committee of the Duma," with Rodzianko as its president and comprising twelve members, including Miliukov, Shulgin, Konovalov, Kerensky and Cheidze. It is thus representative of all parties of the progressive group and the Extreme Left. It is trying to secure the necessary reforms immediately in order to maintain the existing political system, at the cost of proclaiming another emperor, if need be. But the Tauris Palace is occupied by the insurgents so that the committee has to confer amidst general uproar, and is exposed to the bullying of the mob; (2) The "Council of Working-Men and Soldier Deputies," the *Soviet*. It holds its sittings at the Finland station. Its password and battlecry is "Proclaim the social Republic and put an end to the war." Its leaders are already denouncing the members of the Duma as traitors to the revolution, and openly adopting the same attitude towards the legal representative body as the Commune of Paris adopted towards the Legislative Assembly in 1792; (3) The "Headquarters of the Troops." This body sits in the Fortress of SS. Peter and Paul. It is composed of a few junior officers who have gone over to the revolution and several N.C.O.'s or soldiers who have been promoted to officer rank. It is endeavouring to introduce a little system into the business of supplying the combatants and is sending them food and ammunition. In particular it is keeping the Duma in a state of subjection. Through it the

soldiery is all-powerful at the present moment. A few battalions, quartered in and around the Fortress, are the only organized force in Petrograd; they are the praetorians of the revolution and as determined, ignorant and fanatical as the famous battalions of the Faubourg Saint-Antoine and the Faubourg Saint-Marcel in that same year 1792.

Since the Russian revolution, memories of the French revolution have often passed through my mind. But the spirit of the two movements is quite dissimilar. By its origins, principles and social, rather than political character, the present upheaval has a much stronger resemblance to the Revolution of 1848.

*　　*　　*

The Emperor left Mohilev this morning. His train proceeded towards Bologoïe, which is half-way between Moscow and Petrograd. It is presumed that the Emperor intends to return to Tsarskoïe-Selo but some people are wondering whether he is not thinking of going to Moscow to organize resistance to the revolution.

*　　*　　*

Just before midnight I was told that the leaders of the liberal parties held a secret conference this evening—in the absence of the socialists and without their knowledge—with a view to arriving at an agreement about the future form of government.

They were of one accord that the monarchy must be retained, but Nicholas II, who is responsible for the present disasters, must be sacrificed to the salvation of Russia. The former president of the Duma, Alexander Ivanov Gutchkov, who is now sitting in the Council of Empire, then expressed the following opinion: "It is of vital importance that Nicholas II should not be overthrown by violence. The only thing which can secure the permanent establishment of a new order, without too great a shock, is his voluntary abdication. The spontaneous renunciation of Nicholas II is the only means of saving the imperial system and the dynasty of the Romanovs." This view, which seems to me very sound, was unanimously adopted.

*　　*　　*

The liberal leaders closed their conference by deciding that Gutchkov and Shulgin, the deputy from the Nationalist Right, shall go straight to the Emperor and beg him to abdicate in favour of his son.

Thursday, March 15, 1917.

Gutchkov and Shulgin left Petrograd at nine o'clock this morning. Thanks to the aid of an engineer attached to the railway service, they were able to get a special train without arousing the suspicions of the socialist committees.

Discipline is gradually being re-established among the troops. Order has been restored in the city and the shops are cautiously opening their doors again.

The Executive Committee of the Duma and the Council of Workmen's and Soldiers' Deputies have come to an agreement on the following points:

(1) Abdication of the Emperor; (2) Accession of the Tsarevitch; (3) The Grand Duke Michael (the Emperor's brother) to be regent; (4) Formation of a responsible ministry; (5) Election of a constituent assembly by universal suffrage; (6) All races to be proclaimed equal before the law.

The young deputy Kerensky, who has gained a reputation as an advocate in political trials, is coming out as one of the most active and strong-minded organizers of the new order. His influence with the *Soviet* is great. He is a man we must try to win over to our cause. He alone is capable of making the *Soviet* realize the necessity of continuing the war and maintaining the alliance. I have therefore telegraphed to Paris, suggesting to Briand that an appeal from the French socialists to the patriotism of the Russian socialists should be sent through Kerensky.

* * *

During the evening, the leaders of the Duma have at last succeeded in forming a Provisional Government with Prince Lvov as president; he is taking the Ministry of the Interior. The other ministers are Gutchkov (War), Miliukov (Foreign Affairs), Terestchenko (Finance), Kerensky (Justice), etc.

The first cabinet of the new *régime* was only formed after interminable wrangling and haggling with the *Soviet*. The socialists have certainly realized that the Russian proletariat is still too inorganic and ignorant to shoulder the practical responsibilities of power; but they are anxious to be the power behind the scenes, so they have insisted on the appointment of Kerensky as Minister for Justice in order to keep an eye on the Provisional Government.

Friday, March 16, 1917.

Nicholas II abdicated yesterday, shortly before midnight.

When the emissaries of the Duma, Gutchkov and Shulgin, arrived at Pskov about nine o'clock in the evening, the Emperor gave them his usual simple and kindly reception.

In very dignified language and a voice which trembled somewhat, Gutchkov told the Emperor the object of his mission and ended with these words:

"Nothing but the abdication of Your Majesty in favour of your son can still save the Russian Fatherland and preserve the dynasty."

The Emperor replied very quickly, as if referring to some perfectly commonplace matter:

"I decided to abdicate yesterday. But I cannot be separated from my son; that is more than I could bear; his health is too delicate; you *must* realize what I feel . . . I shall therefore abdicate in favour of my brother, Michael Alexandrovitch."

Gutchkov at once bowed to the argument of fatherly affection to which the Tsar appealed and Shulgin also acquiesced.

The Emperor then went into his study with the Minister of the Court; he came out ten minutes later with the act of abdication signed. Count Fredericks handed it to Gutchkov.

This memorable document is worded as follows:

By the grace of God, we, Nicholas II, Emperor of all the Russias, Tsar of Poland, Grand Duke of Finland, etc., etc., to all our faithful subjects make known:

In these days of terrible struggle against the foreign enemy who has been trying for three years to impose his will upon Our Fatherland, God has willed that Russia should be faced with a new and formidable trial. Troubles at home threaten to have a fatal effect on the ultimate course of this hard-fought war. The destinies of Russia, the honour of Our heroic army, the welfare of the nation and the whole future of our dear country require that the war shall be continued, cost what it may, to a victorious end.

Our cruel enemy is making his final effort and the day is at hand when our brave army, with the help of our glorious allies, will overthrow him once and for all.

At this moment, a moment so decisive for the existence of Russia, Our conscience bids Us to facilitate the closest union of Our subjects and the organization of all their forces for the speedy attainment of victory.

For that reason We think it right—and the Imperial Duma shares Our view—to abdicate the crown of the Russian State and resign the supreme power.

As We do not desire to be separated from Our beloved son, We bequeath Our inheritance to Our brother, the Grand Duke Michael Alexandrovitch, and give him Our blessing on his accession to the throne. We ask him to govern in the closest concert with the representatives of the nation who sit in the legislative assemblies and to pledge them his inviolable oath in the name of the beloved country.

We appeal to all the loyal sons of Russia and ask them to do their patriotic and sacred duty by obeying their Tsar at this moment of painful national crisis and to help him and the representatives of the nation to guide the Russian State into the path of prosperity and glory.

May God help Russia!

Nicholas.

The accession of the Grand Duke Michael to the throne has aroused the fury of the *Soviet*: "No more Romanovs!" is the cry in all quarters: "We want a republic!"

For one moment the harmony was shattered which was established with such difficulty between the Executive Committee of the Duma and the *Soviet* yesterday evening. But fear of the gaol-birds who are in command at the Finland Station and the Fortress has compelled the representatives of the Duma to give way. A delegation from the Executive Committee went to see the Grand Duke Michael who made no sort of objection and consented to accept the crown only if it should be offered to him by the constituent assembly. Perhaps he would have submitted less tamely if his wife, the clever and ambitious Countess Brassov, had been at his side and not at Gatchina.

The *Soviet* is now master.

Saturday, March 17, 1917.

One of those who were present gives me the following detailed account of the meeting at the conclusion of which the Grand Duke Michael signed his provisional abdication yesterday.

It took place at ten o'clock in the morning at Prince Paul Putiatin's house, No. 12, Millionaïa.

In addition to the Grand Duke and his secretary, Matveïev, there were present Prince Lvov, Rodzianko, Miliukov, Nekrassov, Kerensky, Nabokov, Shingarev and Baron Nolde; about half-past ten they were joined by Gutchkov and Shulgin, who had come straight from Pskov.

As soon as the discussion began, Gutchkov and Miliukov boldly asserted that Michael Alexandrovitch had no right to evade the responsibility of supreme power. Rodzianko, Nekrassov and Kerensky argued *contra* that the accession of a new Tsar would release a torrent of revolutionary passion and bring Russia face to face with a frightful crisis; their conclusion was that the monarchical question should be reserved until the meeting of the constituent assembly which would make its sovereign will known. The argument was pressed with such force and stubbornness, particularly by Kerensky, that all those present came round to it with the exception of Gutchkov and Miliukov. With complete disinterestedness the Grand Duke himself agreed.

Gutchkov then made a final effort. Addressing the Grand Duke in person and appealing to his patriotism and courage he pointed out how necessary it was that the Russian people should be presented at once with the living embodiment of a national leader:

"If you are afraid to take up the burden of the imperial crown *now*, Monseigneur, you should at least agree to exercise supreme authority as 'Regent of the Empire during the vacancy of the throne,' or, to take a much finer title, 'Protector of the Nation,' as Cromwell styled himself. At the same time you would give a solemn undertaking to the nation to surrender your power to a constituent assembly as soon as the war ends."

This ingenious idea, which might have saved the whole situation, made Kerensky almost beside himself with passion and provoked him to a torrent of invective and threats which terrified everyone there.

In the general confusion the Grand Duke rose with the remark that he would like to think things over by himself for a minute or two. He was making for the next room when Kerensky leaped in front of him as if to keep him back:

"Promise us not to consult your wife, Monseigneur!"

His thoughts had at once gone to the ambitious Countess Brassov whose empire over her husband's mind was complete. With a smile the Grand Duke replied:

"Don't worry, Alexander Feodorovitch, my wife isn't here at the moment; she stayed behind at Gatchina!"

Five minutes later the Grand Duke returned. In very calm tones he declared:

"I have decided to abdicate."

The triumphant Kerensky called out:

"Monseigneur, you are the noblest of men!"

2 The Collapse of the Monarchy

*Not all scholars have seen the Russian Revolution to be
inevitable. Some scholars consider the failure of the Russian
monarchy to govern with even minimal intelligence and
skill a major cause of the revolution. Sir Bernard Pares
emphasizes the role of the Empress and Rasputin in bringing on the catastrophe.*

FROM *Rasputin and the Empress* BY BERNARD PARES

THE PUBLICATION OF THE LETTERS of the Tsaritsa to her husband for the first time showed in black and white Rasputin's enormous political significance. But those who took the trouble to wade through that
mass of loose English were probably too overcome by the sweep of the vast
tragedy to realize at first the unique importance of the letters as historical
material. It is to this aspect of the subject that this article is devoted.

The Rasputin tragedy passed at the time behind closed doors, except for
Rasputin's own entire indifference to public scandal. By now almost every
one of the persons who could give valuable first-hand evidence on the subject
has said his word. M. Gilliard, tutor to the Tsarevich, a man of great good
sense and good feeling, has given a beautiful picture of the home life of the
Imperial family, the accuracy of which has been confirmed both by the
Provisional and the Soviet Governments. We have for what it is worth the
Apologia of Madame Vyrubov, the only person who was with the family
continually, and Rasputin's chosen go-between for his communications with
the Empress. A slighter record is given by another friend of the Empress,
Madame Lili Dehn. The Head of the Police Department, Beletsky, has told
a typical story of ministerial intrigue centered round Rasputin. The French
Ambassador, M. Paléologue, has issued a current record of events, evidently
touched up for publication, which gives the atmosphere of grand ducal and
higher society, but also connects Rasputin at point after point with political

Sir Bernard Pares, "Rasputin and the Empress: Authors of the Russian Collapse," *Foreign
Affairs*, VI, No. 1 (October, 1927), 140–55. Copyright by The Council on Foreign Relations,
Inc., New York. Some footnotes have been omitted.

events of the most critical importance. Now we have also the important record of the President of the Third and Fourth Dumas, Mr. Michael Rodzianko, prepared in exile without many materials but preserving the details of his various conversations with the Emperor, which were evidently written down with care at the time.

Rasputin, who was under fifty at the time of his death, was born in the village of Pokrovskoe on the Tura, near Tobolsk in Siberia. Like many peasants he had no surname; Rasputin, which means "dissolute," was a nickname early given him by his fellow peasants. He suddenly went off to the Verkhne-Turski Monastery near his home, where were several members of the *Khlysty,* a sect who mingled sexual orgies with religious raptures and who were emphatically condemned by the Orthodox Church. On his return he became a *strannik,* or roving man of God, not a monk, not in orders, but one with a self-given commission from heaven, such as have often appeared in Russian history, especially at critical times. Meanwhile, he lived so scandalous a life that his village priest investigated it with care. That he habitually did much the same things as the *Khlysty* is conclusively proved; but that he was actually one of the sect has not been definitely established. Certainly to the end of his life he alternated freely between sinning and repenting, and professed the view that great sins made possible great repentances. He seduced a large number of women, several of whom boasted of the fact, or repented and confessed it to others. The village priest reported him to Bishop Antony of Tobolsk, who made a more thorough enquiry and found evidence which he felt bound to hand over to the civil authorities. During the enquiry Rasputin disappeared. He went to St. Petersburg, and as a great penitent secured the confidence of Bishop Theophan, head of the Petersburg Religious Academy, and Confessor to the Empress, a man whose personal sanctity has been recognized by everyone. He secured also the patronage of the Grand Duchess Militsa, daughter of King Nicholas of Montenegro, a lady with a strong taste for the sensational, and also that of her future brother-in-law, the Grand Duke Nicholas. It was these who introduced him to the Palace.

The Empress Alexandra, formerly Princess Alix of Hesse Darmstadt, was a daughter of the English Princess Alice and a favorite granddaughter of Queen Victoria, from whom she may be said to have taken all the ordinary part of her mental environment. The unusual feature in her character was her strong mysticism. Her family was scourged with the haemiphilic ailment; all the male children of her sister Princess Irene of Prussia suffered from it. It does not appear in females, but is transmitted by them to males. Its effect is that the slightest accident may set up internal bleeding, which there is no known way of arresting. Children suffering from it may die at any moment, and on almost any occasion, though if they live to the age of 13 they may in some measure overcome it; Rasputin prophesied such an issue for the Tsarevich Alexis. Much of the tragedy in the position of the Empress lay in the fact that after she had given birth to four charming and healthy daughters, her only son, the long desired heir to the throne, suffered from this scourge, and that she well knew that his disease came through herself.

In every other domestic respect the family was ideally happy. Husband and wife literally adored each other; the children were equally united with them and with each other. The Empress was the pillar of the house, their actual nurse and attendant in time of sickness. She brought them up entirely in English ideas; they had cold baths and slept on camp beds; they talked largely in English. The family as a whole, in its clean-minded life, represented a veritable oasis in the corruption which was so prevalent in higher Russian society, and we may imagine that with that world this aspect of their isolation was one of their chief offenses. They lived almost as much apart from it as if they were settlers in Canada.

The Empress's nature was singularly narrow and obstinate; Rodzianko rightly describes her as "essentially a creature of will." She had a fondness for her first "little home" at Hesse Darmstadt, but a strong antipathy for the Emperor William; indeed the Prussian monarchy found many of its bitterest critics among the smaller reigning German families. She regarded herself as essentially English, but she had frankly embraced the country of her adored husband, and more than that, she had embraced the Russian autocracy. She repeatedly speaks of herself as "anointed by God," and once as "Russia's mother." There is on record a conversation between her and Queen Victoria in which she put very strongly this difference between the English monarchy and the Russian. For her, Russia was the Russian people, above all the peasantry. Society she identified with the general corruption which she saw around her. She was always, we may be sure, entirely against the Duma and against the concession of a Russian constitution. Any such suggestion she regarded as a direct wrong to her son, and denounced in the strongest language.

When she married, three of her husband's last five ancestors had perished by assassination. Her first appearance before the Russian public was in the funeral procession of her father-in-law, and the reign from start to finish was soaked in an atmosphere of fatality. She had an antipathy to all Court ceremonies. The slightest accident filled her with apprehension. In the period when her most ardent desire was to give an heir to the throne, she met in France a charlatan soul doctor, Philippe, who was brought to Russia but expelled, despite her protection, for meddling in politics during the Japanese War. Philippe gave her a bell as a token that she was to scare away all other counsellors from her husband. She refers to this several times in her letters. Bishop Theophan, when he introduced Rasputin to the Court, appears only to have thought that he was substituting a Russian influence for a foreign.

Rasputin at first kept quiet and studied his ground. He saw the Imperial family infrequently, and his presence was sought only to comfort the nerves of the Empress and her husband, and to re-assure them as to the health of their son. M. Gilliard, who was nearly all day with his charge, saw him but once. The meetings ordinarily took place at the little house of Madame

Vyrubov outside the Palace. Soon, however, Rasputin went on openly with his earlier scandalous life. Towards the end of 1911 sensational happenings attracted public attention to him. Among his former supporters had been the robust Bishop of Saratov, Hermogen, a very strong monarchist, and the Monk Heliodor, a notable and popular preacher, also very conservative. An attempt was made to push through the Synod an authorization to ordain Rasputin a priest. This was defeated in view of his well-known dissoluteness. Hermogen was one of its most vigorous opponents. Direct interference from the Court obtained at least a partial reversion of the decision of the Synod. Hermogen again was most vigorous in his protests. He and Heliodor, acting together, arranged a meeting with Rasputin which resulted in threats on both sides; Rasputin threw himself on the Bishop as if to strangle him, and when pulled off departed threatening vengeance. Hermogen was than banished to his diocese by order of the Emperor and, as he still refused to submit, both he and Heliodor were ultimately relegated to monasteries. The Emperor had acted illegally in imposing such a sentence on a bishop without trial by a church court.

This was not the end. Shortly afterwards one Novoselov, a specialist on Russian sects who lectured at the Religious Academy near Moscow, issued a pamphlet giving full details of Rasputin's seductions, which seemed to be numberless. The book was immediately suppressed, but was widely quoted by Russian newspapers beginning with "The Voice of Moscow," the organ of Guchkov. He was leader of the Duma, and for a short time its President, and he had at first hoped to play the part of tribune of the people at the palace and to carry the Emperor with him for reform. But he had been severely rebuffed, and chose this ground for attack. The papers were now forbidden to speak of Rasputin. At this time the preliminary censorship no longer existed, and such orders by the government were therefore illegal. Fines could be imposed after publication, but fines in this case the newspapers were ready to pay. Guchkov led a debate in the Duma on this infraction of the law. Rodzianko, who tried to limit and moderate the debate as much as possible, obtained an audience from the Emperor, and speaking with absolute plainness laid a number of data before him. "I entreat you," he ended, "in the name of all that is holy for you, for Russia, for the happiness of your successor, drive off from you this filthy adventurer, disperse the growing apprehensions of people loyal to the throne." "He is not here now," said the Emperor. Rodzianko took him up, "Let me tell everyone that he will not return." "No," said Nicholas, "I cannot promise you that, but I fully believe all you say. I feel your report was sincere, and I trust the Duma because I trust you." Next day he authorized Rodzianko to make a full investigation, and the plentiful material in the possession of the Synod was handed over to him. The Empress tried to get these papers back, but Rodzianko gave a stout refusal to her messenger, saying that she was as much the subject of the Emperor as himself. When he was ready with his conclusions he asked for another audience, but Nicholas put him off. He threatened to resign, and was invited to send in a report. Later he heard that it had been studied by Nicholas and the Grand Duke of Hesse, brother of the Empress, while they were together at Livadia in Crimea. The Grand Duke, as is known, in no way supported the attitude of the Empress.

For the time Rasputin disappeared. In the summer of 1912, while the Imperial family was at a hunting box in Poland, the Tsarevich fell on the gunwale of a boat; the bruise set up internal bleeding and for some weeks his life was despaired of. All the family were distracted with grief. The best doctors declared themselves impotent. The Empress then ordered a telegram to be sent to Rasputin, who replied: "This illness is not dangerous; don't let the doctors worry him." From the time of the reception of the telegram the boy rapidly recovered. There is no doubt as to these facts, which were testified to unanimously by various witnesses. Nor is there evidence of any kind for the supposition that the illness was artificially created.

Stolypin before his death in 1911 had reported in the strongest language against Rasputin. The attitude of his successor, Count Kokovtsev, was practically the same. The Empress when she met him turned her back on him, and he was curtly dismissed from the post of Premier in January, 1914. The aged Goremykin who succeeded him, and who possessed throughout the complete confidence of the Empress, summed up the question to Rodzianko in the words, "C'est une question clinique."

When war broke out, Rasputin was lying dangerously ill at Tobolsk, where one of his female victims had tried to assassinate him. He sent a telegram to Madame Vyrubov, "Let Papa (the Emperor) not plan war. It will be the end of Russia and of all of us. We shall be destroyed to the last man." The Emperor was very annoyed at this, and never was he more at one with his people than when he appeared on the balcony of the Winter Palace and the vast crowd kneeled in front of him. For the first period of the war the Empress devoted herself to hospital work, and spared herself no labor or unpleasantness in the care of the sick; on matters of administration she only ventured tentative and timid opinions.

The discovery of gross munition scandals in the early summer of 1915 roused a wave of national indignation, and seemed at first to bring Russia nearer to an effective constitution than ever before. It must be understood that the constitutional question was still unsettled. The Duma had come to stay, as even the Empress at this time admitted. In spite of a manipulated and limited franchise, it had more and more come to represent the nation. The limits on its competence, however, remained; it had once succeeded by moral pressure in removing a Minister (Timiriazev), but the Ministers were not responsible to it. As is clear from the Emperor's talks with Rodzianko, he certainly did not recognize his famous edict of October 30, 1905, which gave full legislative powers to the Duma, as the grant of a Constitution, and the Duma's rights had been whittled down since then both by limitations imposed at the outset in the fundamental laws of 1906, and also in practice ever since.

The Emperor was in entire agreement with his people as to the needs of his army. He appealed for the utmost efforts, and at Rodzianko's request he established a War Industries Committee on which the Duma was to be represented. The Alliance itself worked in the same direction, for democratic France and England desired to see as hearty as possible a coöperation of the Russian people in the prosecution of the war. The War Minister, Sukhomlinov, who had been at least criminally negligent, was dismissed; the Emperor also got rid of those of his Ministers who were at best half-hearted about the war, Nicholas Maklakov, Shcheglovitov and Sabler, and replaced them by men who had the confidence of the country. It looked as if the movement would go a good deal further. The bulk of the Duma, containing nearly all its best brains, had practically formed into one party under the name of the Progressive Bloc, and it asked for the definite adoption of the principle that the Ministry as a whole should be such as to possess the public confidence. Those of the Ministers who were of the same view, at this time a majority in the Cabinet, went even further; they wrote a letter to the Sovereign asking that the aged and obviously incompetent Prime Minister should be changed. If things had not stopped here, Russia would have done what all her Allies were doing at the same time, namely have formed a national and patriotic Coalition Ministry; but, beyond that, she would also have completed the process towards a Constitution which, though often interrupted, had been going on since the Emancipation of the Serfs in 1861.

It was here that the Empress intervened, with the assistance and advice of Rasputin. She got the Emperor back to Tsarskoe Selo for several weeks and persuaded him to dismiss from the Chief Command the Grand Duke Nicholas, who was popular with the Duma and the country. This both she and Rasputin regarded as the most essential victory of all. She then obtained the prorogation of the Duma, and its President and the delegates of other public bodies who begged the Emperor to reverse this decision were met with the most chilling refusal. She then persuaded her husband that all the Ministers who had, so to speak, struck work against Premier Goremykin should be replaced as soon as possible. We thus enter the critical period which changed the war from being an instrument for producing a Russian Constitution into the principal cause of the Russian Revolution. From now till the final collapse Russia was governed by the Empress, with Rasputin as her real Prime Minister.

Two incidents in the summer and autumn sharpened the conflict between the Court and the public over the influence of Rasputin. In the summer Rasputin varied his dissolute orgies with a severe course of repentance and visited the tombs of the Patriarchs in Moscow. Presumably he overdid the repentance, for he followed it up with a visit to a notorious resort, the Yar, where he got drunk and behaved in the most scandalous way. His proceedings were recorded in detail by the police, who were present, and were reported by them to one of the most loyal servants of the Emperor, General Dzhunkovsky, at this time Commander of the Palace Guard.

Dzhunkovsky presented the report without comment to the Emperor. Next day he was dismissed from all appointments, and the protest of another intimate friend of the Emperor, Prince Orlov, had the same result. The Empress flatly refused to believe such reports and persisted in regarding them as machinations of the police.

In 1915 the Emperor was starting with his son for the front when the Tsarevich was taken violently ill in the train, which thereupon returned to Tsarskoe Selo. Rasputin was summoned at once and from the time of his visit the boy recovered, as in 1912. Rasputin often played on this theme. Once he fell into fervent prayer and when he had ended declared that he had saved the Emperor from assassination. He made many happy guesses, some of which were almost uncanny. On the other hand, the Empress herself gives several instances, some of them conspicuous, of predictions which went all wrong.

Neither the Emperor nor the Empress had at this time any thought whatsoever of a separate peace; the Emperor, we know, never entertained such an idea even after abdication. Up till December 30, the date of the last of the Empress's letters, we know that she regarded victory in the war as a foregone conclusion, that her chief anxiety was that Russian influence might be overshadowed by British when the victorious peace was made, and that her main desire was that the victory of Russia should be entirely the triumph of her husband. Nicholas at times spoke tentatively of reforms, but through-out this period insisted that they could only follow after the war.

In going to the front the Emperor had *ipso facto* more or less abandoned the administration to his wife, who definitely describes herself as his "wall in the rear," speaks even of "wearing the trousers" in the struggle against internal enemies, recalls the time when Catherine the Great (who had much more drastically disposed of her husband) received the Ministers, and in the end is absolutely certain that she is "saving Russia." Rasputin who had on several occasions pushed suggestions as to the war, gradually became the ultimate factor in all decisions. Practically no Minister could be appointed except on his recommendation or after accepting allegiance to him.

He initiated the period of his power by making himself absolutely supreme in all Church affairs. Let me sum up his principal achievements in this domain. He dismisses an adverse Minister of Religion, Samarin, who had been the elected Marshal of the Moscow Nobility; he dismisses his successor, Volzhin, appointed at his own desire; he practically appoints a third Minister, Raiev; he commands a public prayer-giving throughout the country, insisting that the order should not pass through the Synod; he appoints as Metropolitan of Petrograd, Pitirim, a contemptible sycophant of his own; he negatives a project of the Synod to create seven Metropolitan Sees in Russia; through one of his subordinates and in violation of all rules he creates a new Saint, St. John of Tobolsk.

But there was hardly any other department of administration with which he did not interfere. He settles at various times and in various ways the administration of the food supply; he orders an absurdly simplified way of dealing with the question of rations; he confers repeatedly with the Minister of Finance, whose resignation he at first demands and then defers, and he insists on the issue of an enormous loan. He secures that the whole passenger transport of the country should be suspended for six days for the passage of food—a measure which is made futile by the failure to collect the food supplies at the proper places for transport. He repeatedly interferes both in military appointments and in military operations; he secures the suspension of Sukhimlinov's trial; he secures the dismissal of his successor, Polivanov, who according to all military evidence, including that of Hindenburg, in his few months of office brought about a wonderful recovery of the efficiency of the Russian army; he orders an offensive; he countermands an offensive; he dictates the tactics to be followed in the Carpathians; he even demands to be informed in advance of all military operations, and to know the exact day on which they are to begin, in order that he may decide the issue by his prayers; he arranges the details of the future military entry into Constantinople. He removes the Foreign Minister, Sazonov, who in Russia was the main arch of the alliance, the trusted friend of the British and French Ambassadors. He adjourns and opposes any execution of the Emperor's promise to give autonomy to Poland. He dictates telegrams to the King of Serbia and to the King of Greece.

The following are extracts from letters of the Empress which refer to this period:

1915

Apr. 4 "Our Friend is shocked at the style of N.N." (the Grand Duke).

6 He thought the Tsar should not have visited Galicia till after the War.

10 He is "rather disturbed about the meat stores."

May 11 He spends two hours with Bark (Minister of Finance).

Jun. *10* He says the second class of recruits should not be called in. The Empress adds, "Hearken unto Our Friend."

11 He is against the assembling of the Duma.

12 She objects to Polivanov, the new War Minister. "Is he not Our Friend's enemy? That brings bad luck." Rasputin likes Shakhovskoy (Minister of Trade). "Can influence him for good." He "begs most incessantly" for a one-day's prayer-giving to be ordered by the Tsar without the Synod. She adds "Be more autocratic, my very own sweetheart."

15 Message from Rasputin to the Tsar: "You are to pay less attention to what people say to you, not let yourself be influenced by them. They know much less than you . . ." The Empress adds: "He regrets you did not speak to him more about all you think and were intending to do."

16 "Think more of Gr. (Gregory): ask Him to intervene before God to guide you right."

17 Rasputin begs to postpone the Duma.

18 Of Samarin, Procurator of the Holy Synod: "He is an enemy of Our Friend's and that is the worst thing there can be."

24 The Premier (Goremykin) is to tell Samarin and Shcherbatov (Minister of Interior) how they are to behave to Rasputin.

Aug. 22 Rasputin, after the replacement of the Grand Duke: "The worst is over."

28 He tells the Tsar to set free criminals and send them to the front.

29 He desires more munition factories. "Khvostov (candidate for Minister of Interior) spoke justly and well about Our Friend" (Khvostov told Rodzianko he intended to discredit Rasputin by making him drunk).

Sep. 7 She sends a list of possible successors to Samarin. Guriev (one of them) "likes Our Friend."

8 She asks to put Pitirim on the Synod. "He venerates Our Friend."

15 "Comb your hair with His comb" when about to receive the Ministers.

17 She recommends General Shvedov for Procurator, "He calls Our Friend Father Gregory."

Oct. 3 Rasputin begs the Tsar to telegraph to the King of Serbia. She adds "so I enclose a paper . . . put the sense in your words." Rasputin condemns the new stamp money. She will tell Bark.

8 Rasputin says the Grand Duke cannot be successful (in the Caucasus) "for going against Him." (On Sept. 19 Rasputin sent a message "There is little sunshine in the Caucasus.")

10 "He says you must give an order that waggons with flour, butter and sugar should be allowed to pass": no other trains for 3 days. He "saw the whole thing in the night in a vision." This is done.

Nov. 1 Rasputin is "very grieved at Trepov's nomination" (as Minister of Commerce) "as He knows he is very against Him." "Our Friend was always against the war, saying the Balkans were not worth troubling to fight about."

8 "Our Friend is anxious to know . . . about your plans for Rumania." He dictates the course to be followed with Rumania and Greece, walking about and crossing himself. Gives his plans for the march into Constantinople.

10 Rasputin has recommended the dismissal of the Premier (Goremykin). Now he asks the Tsar to wait till He has seen the elder Khvostov "to form his impressions" of him as a possible successor.

12 He pushes Pitirim "as the only suitable man" for Metropolitan. He proposes Zhivakhov as Assistant Procurator of the Synod.

13 He spends 1½ hours with the Empress: tells the Tsar to wait as to the Premier "according to God." He suggests a surprise visit of the Tsar to the Duma to avert scandals (this is done later).

15 "Prompted by what He saw in the night," he bids an advance near Riga. He "says it is necessary: begs you seriously; says we can and we must." He bids summon the Duma if there is no victory at the front. Tell the Premier to feign illness and let the Tsar make a surprise visit, though "He loathes their existence as I do for Russia." The Empress adds: "I feel sure you will agree to Gregory sooner than to the old man" (the Premier, who is her own choice).

Dec. 2 Among his instructions is one that "He cannot exactly remember, but He says that one must always do what He says."

16 "Always the first place for Gregory" (when entertained at Pitirim's).

19 She suggests Tatishchev as successor to Bark; he "knows and venerates Our Friend: hates Guchkov and those Moscow types."

22 Rasputin says "no more fogs would disturb."

31 He says, "always pay attention to the weather."

1916

Jan. 4 She recommends Stürmer for Premier (done).

6 Rasputin "regrets you began that movement (at the front) without asking Him." She sends "a petition from Our Friend, it is a military thing."

7 Rasputin says Stürmer (his protégé) is not to change his German name. She sends a budget of his requests.

30 Rasputin and the Empress urge Ivanov for Minister of War *vice* Polivanov.

Feb. 1 Rasputin objects to Obolensky (in charge of food supplies).

5 The Tsarevich ill. He says "it will pass in two days."

Mar. 4 "Remember about (dismissing) Polivanov."

6 Rasputin on a responsible Ministry: "It would be the ruin of everything."

12 She writes imploring the dismissal of Polivanov, "Lovey, don't dawdle." She receives the Tsar's consent and adds: "Oh, the relief." She objects to Ignatiev, Minister of Education.

13 She questions the Tsar's new choice for War Minister, Shuvaiev.

14 Rasputin is for Ivanov. She adds "In that He is certainly right." The Synod has proposed to create 7 Metropolitan Sees. "Our Friend begs you not to agree."

15 "I wish you could shut up that rotten War Industries Committee."

Apr. 1 Ivanov appointed as military adviser at headquarters. Rasputin is pleased.

25 Rasputin on the trial of Sukhomlinov: "It is a bit not well."

May 23 He "begs very much not to name Makarov Minister of Interior."

Jun. 4 He "begs not yet strongly advance in the North."

5 "Our Friend says it is good for us that Kitchener died . . . as later he might have done Russia harm."

9 Rasputin wishes the Tsar to come for two days to Petrograd. She forwards 5 first-class requests transmitted to her from him: prorogue the Duma; dismiss Obolensky; give the food supply to the Minister of Interior: don't thank the zemstvo Red Cross; the fifth request Mme. Vyrubov has forgotten. The Empress asks for a telegram, "Agree to your questions." She proposes a milder judge to try Sukhomlinov. Rasputin hopes "there will be a great victory, perhaps at Kovel," and wants Sukhomlinov then amnestied.

16 Rasputin is against the augmented tram prices. He wishes the Empress to take Mme. Vyrubov with her to headquarters (she does so).

17 He "predicts fatal results" if the 7 Metropolitan Sees are created.

18 He begs the Tsar to be "very firm with the Ministers."

25 The Empress wants Raiev as Procurator of the Synod.

Jul. 16 She protests at the nomination of Makarov (Minister of Justice: the Tsar's choice). "I must have Our Friend guaranteed against them."

July 24 Rasputin is against further advance.

Aug. 4 He objects to the liberation of the Slavonic prisoners of war (Poles, Czechs, Serbs, etc.). He "begs you to be very severe with the Generals," and to put off calling the recruits till September 1. He intervenes as to the supply of aeroplanes.

8 He warns against advance over the Carpathians.

9 He has a long talk with the Premier (Stürmer), and tells him to report to the Empress weekly.

13 The Empress recommends Raiev for Procurator and Beliayev for Minister of War (both done later).

18 Message from Rasputin: "A bad tree will fall whatever be the axe that cuts it."

Sep. 4 "Do not hurry with the Polish affair (the promised autonomy) . . . our full trust in Our Friend's wisdom endowed by God." (This advice is followed.)

6 "Our Friend would have liked to take the Rumanian troops in hand to be surer of them."

7 He says "all will be right." He "begs very earnestly to name Protopopov as Minister of Interior." She adds "He likes Our Friend at least 4 years." He wishes an announcement of the promise of the Allies as to Constantinople: "then they must keep their word after." "About Poland he begs you to wait. Do listen to Him: He has more insight than all of them."

9 "Please take Protopopov."

14 "God bless your new choice of Protopopov."

15 He says, change Obolensky.

16 He tells the Tsar not to worry if he finds he has dismissed Generals wrongly.

17 He is given the military plans so as to pray over them. He sends a "paper."

18 The Empress asks the exact date of attack for the above reason.

19 She rejects all the Premier's (Stürmer's) candidates for Chief of Police; she tells him to "hurry up and think again."

21 "Since Catherine no Empress has received the Ministers . . . Gregory is delighted." "God inspires him and to-morrow I'll write what He said."

22 He says the food supply will go right. He advises to call up the Tartars to the army. Sukhomlinov "should not die in jail. . . . Otherwise things will not be smooth."

23 Rasputin is "very satisfied with Father's orders (i.e. from the Tsar to Brusilov)."

28 Obolensky abases himself to Rasputin and begs to be Governor-General of Finland.

29 "Did you remember about mobilising the Tartars?"

Oct. 14 "Tell him (Protopopov) to go on seeing Gregory."

16 Rasputin advises to call up young men, not old.

26 He says that when asked about Polish autonomy the Tsar is to answer, "I do all for my son, will be pure before my son."

Oct. 30 She countermands, on her own authority, an order of Protopopov (on the food supply) because "Our Friend said it was absolutely necessary." Rasputin says: "Protopopov will finish off the Unions (zemstvo and town Red Cross) and by that save Russia." She describes their wish for a responsible ministry as "colossal impudence."

31 He says the Sukhomlinov trial must be "absolutely stopped." "All my trust lies in Our Friend." The profiteer Rubinstein must be "at once" released.

Nov. 3 Message from Rasputin. "Calm papa. Write that everything will be right." She asks again for Rubinstein.

7 Rasputin and Protopopov want the Premier (Stürmer) to be "rested."

9 Rasputin says Stürmer can go on.

10 The Tsar, however, has dismissed Stürmer altogether. She is shocked. "Thanks for Sukhomlinov." Rasputin wants a new Minister of Communications (Trepov is now Premier).

11 Trepov has asked for the dismissal of Protopopov. The Empress writes to save Protopopov. "He venerates Our Friend and will be blessed."

12 "It is the question of the monarchy and your prestige . . . You were alone with us two" (herself and Rasputin).

Dec. 4 Rasputin has prophesied great times coming for the Tsar and Russia. "Our Friend's dreams mean so much."

5 "He has kept you where you are." "He entreats for Makarov (Minister of Justice) to be quicker changed." "The good is coming—the turn has begun."

8 She urges Shcheglovitov for President of the Council of State (done later). "Only have the Duma cleverly shut."

10 She begs to withdraw the case against the swindler Manuilov which is brought "to harm Our Friend." "Change Makarov." She has seen Dobrovolsky.

13 He "entreats you to be firm, to be the master, and we must give a strong country to Baby . . . I your wall am behind you . . . It is all getting calmer and better . . . Russia loves to feel the whip. . . . I am strong, but listen to me which means Our Friend."

14 "Be Peter the Great, John the Terrible, Emperor Paul, crush them all under you . . . now don't you laugh, naughty one . . . I could hang Trepov (the Premier) . . . Disperse the Duma at once. Milliukov,

Guchkov, and Polivanov also to Siberia. My duty as wife and mother, and Russia's mother, blessed by Our Friend."

15 "Thanks so much for Manuilov."

16 "They touch all near me. Sweep away the dust and dirt" (the Opposition majority in the very Conservative Council of State).

17 "Our Friend has disappeared. Such utter anguish. Am calm and can't believe it." (Rasputin had been assassinated.)

While the Empress's letters wipe clean away all the scandalous charges made against her personal character, while they show that up to Rasputin's death she was a fervent Russian patriot who had no thought of a separate peace with Germany, they also prove that she and, through her, Rasputin were the prime authors of the collapse of the Empire and of Russia.

The Boshevist leaders were far away in Switzerland or Canada,[1] and their not numerous followers were out of the picture. The leaders of the Duma, largely in answer to the pressure of Russia's Allies, were doing all that they could to postpone the explosion till after the War. Up to the intervention of the fatal pair in the late Summer of 1915, it seemed that the war itself was only bringing nearer what practically all Russia desired. Apart from the terrible depression that followed on the disillusionment of 1915, Russia was then confronted with a monstrous régime which would have seemed impossible in some small duchy in the Middle Ages. In the midst of a world-wide struggle, in a time of the closest collaboration with the best brains of Western statesmanship, the Russian Ministers were selected by an ignorant, blind and hysterical woman on the test of their subservience to an ignorant, fantastic and debauched adventurer, a test which they could only satisfy by open-eyed self-abasement or at the best by cynical passivity, and the supreme commands of the adventurer permeated every detail of government in every branch of the administration. Meanwhile, in his drunken revels he babbled publicly of his influence over the Empress, held a daily *levée* attended by the worst financial swindlers, and preached views both on the war and on the government of the country, which were shared only by the avowed friends of Germany, who evidently had easier access to him than any one else.

It was under the leadership of such a government that the lives of millions of peasants were thrown into the furnace of the World War.

---

[1] Lenin and his chief lieutenants reached Petrograd on April 16, 1917, a month after the Emperor's abdication.

3   Trotsky's View on Who Led the Revolution

FROM *The History of the Russian Revolution*

BY LEON TROTSKY

LAWYERS AND JOURNALISTS belonging to the classes damaged by
the revolution wasted a good deal of ink subsequently trying to prove that
what happened in February was essentially a petticoat rebellion, backed up
afterwards by a soldiers' mutiny and given out for a revolution. Louis XVI in
his day also tried to think that the capture of the Bastille was a rebellion, but
they respectfully explained to him that it was a revolution. Those who lose
by a revolution are rarely inclined to call it by its real name. For that name,
in spite of the efforts of spiteful reactionaries, is surrounded in the historic
memory of mankind with a halo of liberation from all shackles and all prejudices. The privileged classes of every age, as also their lackeys, have always
tried to declare the revolution which overthrew them, in contrast to past
revolutions, a mutiny, a riot, a revolt of the rabble. Classes which have outlived
themselves are not distinguished by originality.

Soon after the 27th of February attempts were also made to liken the
revolution to the military coup d'état of the Young Turks, of which, as we
know, they had been dreaming not a little in the upper circles of the Russian
bourgeoisie. This comparison was so hopeless, however, that it was seriously
opposed even in one of the bourgeois papers. Tugen-Baranovsky, an economist who had studied Marx in his youth, a Russian variety of Sombart, wrote
on March 10 in the *Birzhevoe Vedomosti*:

"The Turkish revolution consisted in a victorious uprising of the army,
prepared and carried out by the leaders of the army; the soldiers were merely
obedient executives of the plans of their officers. But the regiments of the
Guard which on February 27 overthrew the Russian throne, came without
their officers . . . Not the army but the workers began the insurrection; not
the generals but the soldiers came to the State Duma. The soldiers supported
the workers not because they were obediently fulfilling the commands of their
officers, but because . . . they felt themselves blood brothers of the workers

Leon Trotsky, *The History of the Russian Revolution*, I (1932), 136–7, 142–52, translated by
Max Eastman.

as a class composed of toilers like themselves. The peasants and the workers —those are the two social classes which made the Russian revolution."

Tugan-Baranovsky is right when he says that the February revolution was accomplished by workers and peasants—the latter in the person of the soldiers. But there still remains the great question: Who led the revolution? Who raised the workers to their feet? Who brought the soldiers into the streets? After the victory these questions became a subject of party conflict. They were solved most simply by the universal formula: Nobody led the revolution, it happened of itself. The theory of "spontaneousness" fell in most opportunely with the minds not only of all those gentlemen who had yesterday been peacefully governing, judging, convicting, defending, trading, or commanding, and today were hastening to make up to the revolution, but also of many professional politicians and former revolutionists, who having slept through the revolution wished to think that in this they were not different from all the rest.

In his curious *History of the Russian Disorders,* General Denikin, former commander of the White Army, says of the 27th of February: "On that decisive day there were no leaders, there were only the elements. In their threatening current there were then visible neither aims, nor plans, nor slogans." The learned historian Miliukov delves no deeper than this general with a passion for letters. Before the revolution the liberal leader had declared every thought of revolution a suggestion of the German Staff. But the situation was more complicated after a revolution which had brought the liberals to power. Miliukov's task was now not to dishonor the revolution with a Hohenzollern origin, but on the contrary to withhold the honor of its initiation from revolutionists. Liberalism therefore has whole-heartedly fathered the theory of a spontaneous and impersonal revolution. Miliukov sympathetically cites the semi-liberal, semi-socialist Stankevich, a university instructor who became Political Commissar at the headquarters of the Supreme Command: "The masses moved of themselves, obeying some unaccountable inner summons . . ." writes Stankevich of the February days. "With what slogans did the soldiers come out? Who led them when they conquered Petrograd, when they burned the District Court? Not a political idea, not a revolutionary slogan, not a conspiracy, and not a revolt, but a spontaneous movement suddenly consuming the entire old power to the last remnant." Spontaneousness here acquires an almost mystic character.

This same Stankevich offers a piece of testimony in the highest degree valuable: "At the end of January, I happened in a very intimate circle to meet with Kerensky. . . . To the possibility of a popular uprising they all took a definitely negative position, fearing lest a popular mass movement once aroused might get into an extreme leftward channel and this would create vast difficulties in the conduct of the war." The views of Kerensky's circle in nowise essentially differed from those of the Kadets. The initiative certainly did not come from there.

"The revolution fell like thunder out of the sky," says the president of the Social Revolutionary Party, Zenzinov. "Let us be frank: it arrived joyfully unexpected for us too, revolutionists who had worked for it through long years and waited for it always."

It was not much better with the Mensheviks. One of the journalists of the bourgeois emigration tells about his meeting in a tramcar on February 21 with Skobelev, a future minister of the revolutionary government: "This Social Democrat, one of the leaders of the movement, told me that the disorders had the character of plundering which it was necessary to put down. This did not prevent Skobelev from asserting a month later that he and his friends had made the revolution." The colors here are probably laid on a little thick, but fundamentally the position of the legal Social Democrats, the Mensheviks, is conveyed accurately enough.

Finally, one of the most recent leaders of the left wing of the Social Revolutionaries, Mstislavsky, who subsequently went over to the Bolsheviks, says of the February uprising: "The revolution caught us, the party people of those days, like the foolish virgins of the Bible, napping." It does not matter how much they resembled virgins, but it is true they were all fast asleep.

How was it with the Bolsheviks? This we have in part already seen. The principal leaders of the underground Bolshevik organization were at that time three men: the former workers Shliapnikov and Zalutsky, and the former student Molotov. Shliapnikov, having lived for some time abroad and in close association with Lenin, was in a political sense the most mature and active of these three who constituted the Bureau of the Central Committee. However, Shliapnikov's own memoirs best of all confirm the fact that the events were too much for the trio. Up to the very last hour these leaders thought that it was a question of a revolutionary manifestation, one among many, and not at all of an armed insurrection. Our friend Kayurov, one of the leaders of the Vyborg section, asserts categorically: "Absolutely no guiding initiative from the party centers was felt . . . the Petrograd Committee had been arrested and the representative of the Central Committee, Comrade Shliapnikov, was unable to give any directives for the coming day."

The weakness of the underground organizations was a direct result of police raids, which had given exceptional results amid the patriotic moods at the beginning of the war. Every organization, the revolutionary included, has a tendency to fall behind its social basis. The underground organization of the Bolsheviks at the beginning of 1917 had not yet recovered from its oppressed and scattered condition, whereas in the masses the patriotic hysteria had been abruptly replaced by revolutionary indignation.

In order to get a clear conception of the situation in the sphere of revolutionary leadership it is necessary to remember that the most authoritative revolutionists, the leaders of the left parties, were abroad and, some of them, in prison and exile. The more dangerous a party was to the old régime, the more cruelly beheaded it appeared at the moment of revolution. The Narodniks had a Duma faction headed by the non-party radical Kerensky. The official leader of the Social-Revolutionaries, Chernov, was abroad.

The Mensheviks had a party faction in the Duma headed by Cheidze and Skobelev; Martov was abroad; Dan and Tseretelli, in exile. A considerable number of socialistic intellectuals with a revolutionary past were grouped around these left factions—Narodnik and Menshevik. This constituted a kind of political staff, but one which was capable of coming to the front only after the victory. The Bolsheviks had no Duma faction: their five worker-deputies, in whom the tzarist government had seen the organizing center of the revolution, had been arrested during the first few months of the war. Lenin was abroad, Zinoviev with him; Kamenev was in exile; in exile also, the then little known practical leaders: Sverdlov, Rykov, Stalin. The Polish social-democrat, Dzerzhinsky, who did not yet belong to the Bolsheviks, was at hard labor. The leaders accidentally present, for the very reason that they had been accustomed to act under unconditionally authoritative supervisors, did not consider themselves and were not considered by others capable of playing a guiding rôle in revolutionary events.

But if the Bolshevik Party could not guarantee the insurrection an authoritative leadership, there is no use talking of other organizations. This fact has strengthened the current conviction as to the spontaneous character of the February revolution. Nevertheless the conviction is deeply mistaken, or at least meaningless.

The struggle in the capital lasted not an hour, or two hours, but five days. The leaders tried to hold it back; the masses answered with increased pressure and marched forward. They had against them the old state, behind whose traditional façade a mighty power was still assumed to exist, the liberal bourgeoisie with the State Duma, the Land and City Unions, the military-industrial organizations, academies, universities, a highly developed press, and finally the two strong socialist parties who put up a patriotic resistance to the assault from below. In the party of the Bolsheviks the insurrection had its nearest organization, but a headless organization with a scattered staff and with weak illegal nuclei. And nevertheless the revolution, which nobody in those days was expecting, unfolded, and just when it seemed from above as though the movement was already dying down, with an abrupt revival, a mighty convulsion, it seized the victory.

Whence came this unexampled force of aggression and self-restraint? It is not enough to refer to bitter feelings. Bitterness alone is little. The Petersburg workers, no matter how diluted during the war years with human raw material, had in their past a great revolutionary experience. In their aggression and self-restraint, in the absence of leadership and in the face of opposition from above, was revealed a vitally well-founded, although not always expressed, estimate of forces and a strategic calculation of their own.

On the eve of the war the revolutionary layers of the workers had been following the Bolsheviks, and leading the masses after them. With the beginning of the war the situation had sharply changed: conservative groups lifted their heads, dragging after them a considerable part of the class. The revolutionary elements found themselves isolated, and quieted down. In the course of the war the situation began to change, at first slowly, but after the defeats faster and more radically. An active discontent seized the whole working class. To be sure, it was to an extent patriotically colored, but it had nothing in common with the calculating and cowardly patriotism of the possessing classes, who were postponing all domestic questions until after the victory. The war itself, its victims, its horror, its shame, brought not only the old, but also the new layers of workers into conflict with the tzarist régime. It did this with a new incisiveness and led them to the conclusion: we can no longer endure it. The conclusion was universal: it welded the masses together and gave them a mighty dynamic force.

The army had swollen, drawing into itself millions of workers and peasants. Every individual had his own people among the troops: a son, a husband, a brother, a relative. The army was no longer insulated, as before the war, from the people. One met with soldiers now far oftener; saw them off to the front, lived with them when they came home on leave, chatted with them on the streets and in the tramways about the front, visited them in the hospitals. The workers' districts, the barracks, the front, and to an extent the villages too, became communicating vessels. The workers would know what the soldiers were thinking and feeling. They had innumerable conversations about the war, about the people who were getting rich out of the war, about the generals, government, tzar and tzarina. The soldier would say about the war: To hell with it! And the worker would answer about the government: To hell with it! The soldier would say: Why then do you sit still here in the center? The worker would answer: We can't do anything with bare hands; we stubbed our toe against the army in 1905. The soldier would reflect: What if we should all start at once! The worker: That's it, all at once! Conversations of this kind before the war were conspirative and carried on by twos; now they were going on everywhere, on every occasion, and almost openly, at least in the workers' districts.

The tzar's intelligence service every once in a while took its soundings very successfully. Two weeks before the revolution a spy, who signed himself with the name Krestianinov, reported a conversation in a tramcar traversing the workers' suburb. The soldier was telling how in his regiment eight men were under hard labor because last autumn they refused to shoot at the workers of the Nobel factory, but shot at the police instead. The conversation went on quite openly, since in the workers' districts the police and the spies preferred to remain unnoticed. " 'We'll get even with them,' the soldier concluded." The report reads further: "A skilled worker answered him: 'For that it is necessary to organize so that all will be like one.' The soldier answered: 'Don't you worry, we've been organized a long time. . . . They've drunk enough blood. Men are suffering in the trenches and here they are fattening their bellies!'. . . No special disturbance occurred. February 10, 1917. Krestianinov." Incomparable spy's epic. "No special disturbance occurred." They will occur, and that soon: this tramway conversation signalizes their inexorable approach.

The spontaneousness of the insurrection Mstislavsky illustrates with a curious example: When the "Union of Officers of February 27," formed just after the revolution, tried to determine with a questionnaire who first led out the Volynsky regiment, they received seven answers naming seven initiators of this decisive action. It is very likely, we may add, that a part of the initiative really did belong to several soldiers, nor is it impossible that the chief initiator fell in the street fighting, carrying his name with him into oblivion. But that does not diminish the historic importance of his nameless initiative. Still more important is another side of the matter which will carry us beyond the walls of the barrack room. The insurrection of the battalions of the Guard, flaring up a complete surprise to the liberal and legal socialist circles, was no surprise at all to the workers. Without the insurrection of the workers the Volynsky regiment would not have gone into the street. That street encounter of the workers with the Cossacks, which a lawyer observed from his window and which he communicated by telephone to the deputy, was to them both an episode in an impersonal process: a factory locust stumbled against a locust from the barracks. But it did not seem that way to the Cossack who had dared wink to the worker, nor to the worker who instantly decided that the Cossack had "winked in a friendly manner." The molecular interpenetration of the army with the people was going on continuously. The workers watched the temperature of the army and instantly sensed its approach to the critical mark. Exactly this was what gave such inconquerable force to the assault of the masses, confident of victory.

Here we must introduce the pointed remark of a liberal official trying to summarize his February observations: "It is customary to say that the movement began spontaneously, the soldiers themselves went into the street. I cannot at all agree with this. After all, what does the word 'spontaneously' mean? . . . Spontaneous conception is still more out of place in sociology than in natural science. Owing to the fact that none of the revolutionary leaders with a name was able to hang his label on the movement, it becomes not impersonal but merely nameless." This formulation of the question, incomparably more serious than Miliukov's references to German agents and Russian spontaneousness, belongs to a former Procuror who met the revolution in the position of a tzarist senator. It is quite possible that his experience in the courts permitted Zavadsky to realize that a revolutionary insurrection cannot arise either at the command of foreign agents, or in the manner of an impersonal process of nature.

The same author relates two incidents which permitted him to look as through a keyhole into the laboratory of the revolutionary process. On Friday, February 24, when nobody in the upper circles as yet expected a revolution in the near future, a tramcar in which the senator was riding turned off quite unexpectedly, with such a jar that the windows rattled and one was broken, from the Liteiny into a side street, and there stopped. The conductor told everybody to get off: "The car isn't going any farther." The passengers objected, scolded, but got off. "I can still see the face of that unanswering conductor: angrily resolute, a sort of wolf look." The movement of the tramways stopped everywhere as far as the eye could see. That resolute conductor, in whom the liberal official could already catch a glimpse of the "wolf look," must have been dominated by a high sense of duty in order all by himself to stop a car containing officials on the streets of imperial Petersburg in time of war. It was just such conductors who stopped the car of the monarchy and with practically the same words—this car does not go any farther!—and who ushered out the bureaucracy, making no distinction in the rush of business between a general of gendarmes and a liberal senator. The conductor on the Liteiny boulevard was a conscious factor of history. It had been necessary to educate him in advance.

During the burning of the District Court a liberal jurist from the circle of that same senator started to express in the street his regret that a roomful of judicial decisions and notarial archives was perishing. An elderly man of somber aspect dressed as a worker angrily objected: "We will be able to divide the houses and the lands ourselves, and without your archives." Probably the episode is rounded out in a literary manner. But there were plenty of elderly workers like that in the crowd, capable of making the necessary retort. They themselves had nothing to do with burning the District Court: why burn it? But at least you could not frighten them with "excesses" of this kind. They were arming the masses with the necessary ideas not only against the tzarist police, but against liberal jurists who feared most of all lest there should burn up in the fire of the revolution the notarial deeds of property. Those nameless, austere statesmen of the factory and street did not fall out of the sky: they had to be educated.

In registering the events of the last days of February the Secret Service also remarked that the movement was "spontaneous," that is, had no planned leadership from above; but they immediately added: "with the generally propagandized condition of the proletariat." This appraisal hits the bull's-eye: the professionals of the struggle with the revolution, before entering the cells vacated by the revolutionists, took a much closer view of what was happening than the leaders of liberalism.

The mystic doctrine of spontaneousness explains nothing. In order correctly to appraise the situation and determine the moment for a blow at the enemy, it was necessary that the masses or their guiding layers should make their examination of historical events and have their criteria for estimating them. In other words, it was necessary that there should be not masses in the abstract, but masses of Petrograd workers and Russian workers in general, who had passed through the revolution of 1905, through the Moscow insurrection of December 1905, shattered against the Semenovsky Regiment of the Guard. It was necessary that throughout this mass should be scattered workers who had thought over the experience of 1905, criticized the constitutional illusions of the liberals and Mensheviks, assimilated the perspectives of the revolution, meditated hundreds of times about the question of the army, watched attentively what was going on in its midst—workers capable of making revolutionary inferences from what they observed and communicating them to others. And finally, it was necessary that there should be in the troops of the garrison itself progressive soldiers, seized, or at least touched, in the past by revolutionary propaganda.

In every factory, in each guild, in each company, in each tavern, in the military hospital, at the transfer stations, even in the depopulated villages, the molecular work of revolutionary thought was in progress. Everywhere were to be found the interpreters of events, chiefly from among the workers, from whom one inquired, "What's the news?" and from whom one awaited the needed words. These leaders had often been left to themselves, had nourished themselves upon fragments of revolutionary generalizations arriving in their hands by various routes, had studied out by themselves between the lines of the liberal papers what they needed. Their class instinct was refined by a political criterion, and though they did not think all their ideas through to the end, nevertheless their thought ceaselessly and stubbornly worked its way in a single direction. Elements of experience, criticism, initiative, self-sacrifice, seeped down through the mass and created, invisibly to a superficial glance but no less decisively, an inner mechanics of the revolutionary movement as a conscious process. To the smug politicians of liberalism and tamed socialism everything that happens among masses is customarily represented as an instinctive process, no matter whether they are dealing with an anthill or a beehive. In reality the thought which was drilling through the thick of the working class was far bolder, more penetrating, more conscious, than those little ideas by which the educated classes live. Moreover, this thought was more scientific: not only because it was to a considerable degree fertilized with the methods of Marxism, but still more because it was ever nourishing itself on the living experience of the masses which were soon to take their place on the revolutionary arena. Thoughts are scientific if they correspond to an objective process and make it possible to influence that process and guide it. Were these qualities possessed in the slightest degree by the ideas of those government circles who were inspired by the Apocalypse and believed in the dreams of Rasputin? Or maybe the ideas of the liberals were scientifically grounded, who hoped that a backward Russia, having joined the scrimmage of the capitalist giants, might win at one and the same time victory and parliamentarism? Or maybe the intellectual life of those circles of the intelligentsia was scientific, who slavishly adapted themselves to this liberalism, senile since childhood, protecting their imaginary independence the while with long-dead metaphors? In truth here was a kingdom of spiritual inertness, specters, superstition and fictions, a kingdom, if you will, of "spontaneousness." But have we not in that case a right to turn this liberal philosophy of the February revolution exactly upside down? Yes, we have a right to say: At the same time that the official society, all that many-storied superstructure of ruling classes, layers, groups, parties and cliques, lived from day to day by inertia and automatism, nourishing themselves with the relics of worn-out ideas, deaf to the inexorable demands of evolution, flattering themselves with phantoms and foreseeing nothing—at the same time, in the working masses there was taking place an independent and deep process of growth, not only of hatred for the rulers, but of critical understanding of their impotence, an accumulation of experience and creative consciousness which the revolutionary insurrection and its victory only completed.

To the question, Who led the February revolution? we can then answer definitely enough: Conscious and tempered workers educated for the most part by the party of Lenin. But we must here immediately add: This leadership proved sufficient to guarantee the victory of the insurrection, but it was not adequate to transfer immediately into the hands of the proletarian vanguard the leadership of the revolution.

4 The Revolution Was Unplanned and Unled

FROM *The Russian Revolution 1917–1921*

BY WILLIAM H. CHAMBERLIN

THE COLLAPSE OF THE ROMANOV AUTOCRACY in March 1917 was one of the most leaderless, spontaneous, anonymous revolutions of all time. While almost every thoughtful observer in Russia in the winter of 1916–1917 foresaw the likelihood of the crash of the existing regime no one, even among the revolutionary leaders, realized that the strikes and bread riots which broke out in Petrograd on March 8 would culminate in the mutiny of the garrison and the overthrow of the government four days later.

The Tsarina was not distinguished by political perspicacity; and it is not surprising that she should write to her husband, who was at the Headquarters of the General Staff in Moghilev, on March 10, when the capital was in the grip of a general strike: "This is a hooligan movement, young people run and shout that there is no bread, simply to create excitement, along with workers who prevent others from working. If the weather were very cold they would all probably stay at home. But all this will pass and become calm, if only the Duma will behave itself."

But it was not only the Tsarina who failed to see the impending storm. The Socialist Revolutionary Zenzinov declared: "The Revolution was a great and joyous surprise for us, revolutionaries, who had worked for it for years and had always expected it." The Menshevik Internationalist Sukhanov observes: "Not one party was prepared for the great overturn." The Bolshevik worker Kaourov, who took an active part in the Revolution, testifies that on March 8 "no one thought of such an imminent possibility of revolution." As for the leaders of the Duma, they might whisper among each other about the possibility of a palace *coup d'état;* but the last thing they desired was an uncontrolled movement from below.

Wartime circumstances alone made any effective guidance of a mass uprising impossible. The men who afterwards distinguished themselves in the Bolshevik Revolution were either living abroad, like Lenin and Trotzky

Reprinted with permission of The Macmillan Company from *The Russian Revolution 1917–1921*, pp. 73–89, 97–8, by William Henry Chamberlin. Copyright 1935 by The Macmillan Company. Copyright renewed 1963 by William Henry Chamberlin.

and Zinoviev, or in prison or in Siberian exile, like Stalin, Kamenev and Dzerzhinsky. The more prominent leaders of other revolutionary parties were also absent from Petrograd in the decisive days. The Bolshevik members of the Duma had been exiled to Siberia in the first months of the War, and the Menshevik members of the War Industries Committee were arrested by the zealous Minister of the Interior, Protopopov, early in the year. There was a skeleton underground Bolshevik organization in Russia; but its activities were narrowly circumscribed by lack of experienced professional revolutionaries, lack of funds, and the all-pervading espionage. Indeed most of the members of the Bolshevik Petrograd Party Committee were arrested at a critical moment in the development of the movement, on the morning of March 11.

So the police measures for the protection of the Tsarist regime were almost perfect. At first sight and on paper the military measures seemed equally imposing. Petrograd had a huge garrison of about 160,000 soldiers. To be sure the fighting quality of this garrison, as subsequent events were to prove, was in inverse ratio to its size. The original Guard regiments had been sent to the front (a grave strategic error, from the standpoint of the internal security of the old regime); and the troops quartered in Petrograd consisted mainly of new recruits, untrained, housed in crowded barracks, often poorly fed.

But the Tsarist authorities did not rely primarily on the unwieldy garrison for the suppression of any possible uprising. The Minister of the Interior, Protopopov, proposed to operate against insurgent throngs first with police, then with Cossack cavalry units, bringing troops into operation only in the last resort. An elaborate plan for the suppression of disorder in the capital had been submitted to the Tsar in January. A combined force of 12,000 troops, gendarmes and police was created for this specific purpose; and a military commander was appointed in each of the six police districts into which the city was divided.

Military preparations, therefore, had not been neglected, even if there were serious omissions, quite consistent with the frequently slipshod character of Tsarist administration, in paying little attention to the morale of the troops in the capital and in selecting as commander of the Petrograd Military District, General Khabalov, a man of little experience in commanding troops in actual military operations. The unforeseen circumstances that upset all the governmental calculations were the stubbornness of the demonstrators and the ultimate unreliability of the garrison.

The atmosphere of Petrograd was so charged with discontent in this third winter of an unsuccessful war that very slight causes were sufficient to bring about a formidable explosion. There had been intermittent strikes throughout January and February. Although there was not an absolute shortage of bread poor transportation and faulty distribution made it necessary for the workers and their wives, in many cases, to stand in long queues for bread and other products. The poorer classes of the city were not apathetic from actual hunger; but they were angry and annoyed at the growing cost of living and the other deprivations which the War brought with it. Something of a sense of crowd psychology, of a sense of massed power must have developed also, from the noteworthy growth in the number of industrial workers up to approximately 400,000 as a result of the presence of many war industry plants in the capital.

The movement that was to end in the overthrow of the Romanov dynasty started on March 8, which is observed by Socialist parties as Women's Day. After speeches in the factories crowds of women poured out on the streets, especially in the workingclass Viborg section of the city, clamoring for bread. Here and there red flags appeared with inscriptions: "Down with Autocracy." There were occasional clashes with the police; but the day passed off without serious conflicts. Almost ninety thousand workers struck and fifty factories were closed. A circumstance that enhanced the militant mood of the demonstrators was a lockout at the large Putilov metal works. The workers of this plant were proverbially turbulent, with a long record of strikes; and when a wage dispute had come up in one department the management on March 7 declared a general lockout. So a coincidence of three factors—the dissatisfaction with the food situation, the celebration of Women's Day and the Putilov labor dispute, which let loose over twenty thousand workers for active participation in the demonstration—combined to give the first impetus to the Revolution.

The movement gained in scope and intensity on March 9, when the number of strikers was estimated at 197,000. There was a concerted drive by the workers to reach the central part of the city. Although the police guarded the bridges over the Neva, which was to some extent a boundary between the workingclass and the governmental parts of the city, it was relatively easy to cross the river on the ice, and meetings and demonstrations were held in the centre of the capital. An ominous symptom for the government appeared: the Cossacks showed little energy in breaking up the crowds. So a Cossack squadron rode off, amid loud cheers, leaving undisturbed a revolutionary gathering on the Nevsky Prospect, the main boulevard of Petrograd; and the police reports of the day note an incident on Znamenskaya Square, when the Cossacks responded with bows to the applause of a throng which they did not disperse.

Attacks on the police became more common on this second day of the movement, the mobs using as weapons lumps of ice, cobblestones, heavy sticks. However, firearms were not used in suppressing the disorder and there was still no general conviction of an impending crisis. The British Ambassador, Sir George Buchanan, telegraphed to Foreign Minister Balfour: "Some disorders occurred to-day, but nothing serious."

The 10th witnessed to a large extent a repetition of the events of the 9th, but on a larger scale. The strike became general; newspapers ceased to appear; the students in the universities abandoned their studies. The numbers both of the demonstrators and of the forces employed by the government increased; and there was a longer casualty list on both sides. Although there was still no mutiny, insubordination and passivity on the part of the troops, especially of the Cossacks, were more noticeable. On Znamenskaya Square a Cossack even cut down a police lieutenant, Krilov, with his sabre. The instinctive strategy of the crowd adapted itself to the mood of the troops. While there were fierce attacks on the police (by this time the police in the riotous Viborg district no longer ventured to appear on the streets, but were barricaded in their stations) there was an attempt to conciliate the troops and to avoid provoking them.

So far as there was organized leadership in the movement it aimed at winning over the troops, rather than at arming the workers. So the Bolshevik Shlyapnikov, one of the three members of the Bureau of the Central Committee of the Party, tells how he opposed the more hotheaded workers who continually demanded arms, or at least revolvers: "I decisively refused to search for arms at all and demanded that the soldiers should be drawn into the uprising, so as to get arms for all the workers. This was more difficult than to get a few dozen revolvers; but in this was the whole programme of action."

These three days of turmoil naturally affected the national and local legislative bodies, the Duma and the Petrograd City Council; and speeches were made demanding the appointment of a ministry responsible to the Duma. The Laborite deputy and radical lawyer Alexander Kerensky, destined to play a leading part in subsequent months, attacked the government so sharply in the Duma on the 9th that the Tsarina expressed a fervent desire that he should be hanged. These speeches, however, had little effect on the movement, because the War Minister forbade their publication, and after the morning of March 10, newspapers ceased to appear as a result of the general strike.

General Khabalov on March 10 received a peremptory telegram from the Tsar worded as follows: "I command you to suppress from to-morrow all disorders on the streets of the capital, which are impermissible at a time when the fatherland is carrying on a difficult war with Germany." This imperial order caused a sharp change in the tactics of the Petrograd authorities. Hitherto the use of firearms had been avoided. On the night of the 10th Khabalov gave his subordinate officers instructions to fire on crowds which refused to disperse after warning. This was the decisive stake of the old regime. If the troops obeyed, the revolutionary movement would be crushed. If they did not obey . . . But this alternative was apparently not considered very seriously.

As a further sign of resolute action the police on the night of the 10th arrested about a hundred persons suspected of holding seditious views, including five members of the Petrograd Committee of the Bolshevik Party. On the surface the course of events on the 11th, which was a Sunday, represented a victory for the government. There was firing on the crowds in four separate places in the central part of the city; and on Znamenskaya

Square the training detachment of the Volinsky regiment used machine-guns as well as rifles, with the result that about forty persons were killed and an equal number were wounded. Toward evening there was an outburst of rebellion in one company of the Pavlovsk regiment; but it was put down with the aid of other troops, and the ringleaders were imprisoned in the fortress of Peter and Paul. The government, which was headed by Prince Golitzin as Premier, apparently felt in a stronger position, because in the evening it adopted a decision to dissolve the Duma, thereby breaking off the half-hearted negotiations which had hitherto been carried on with the President of the Duma, Rodzianko, about possible coöperation between the Ministry and the Duma.

Rodzianko decided to try the effect of a personal appeal to the Tsar and despatched a telegram containing the following gravely warning phrases: "The situation is serious. There is anarchy in the capital. The government is paralyzed. It is necessary immediately to entrust a person who enjoys the confidence of the country with the formation of the government. Any delay is equivalent to death. I pray God that in this hour responsibility will not fall on the sovereign."

But neither this telegram, nor the still more urgent message which Rodzianko sent on the following morning, when the mutiny of the garrison was an accomplished fact, produced any impression on Nicholas II. Rodzianko's second telegram described the growing revolt and ended: "The situation is growing worse. Measures must be adopted immediately, because to-morrow will be too late. The last hour has come, when the fate of the fatherland and the dynasty is being decided."

After reading this message the Tsar impatiently remarked to his Minister of the Court, Count Fredericks: "This fat Rodzianko has written me some nonsense, to which I will not even reply."

There is a double significance in these last urgent appeals of the President of the Duma to the Tsar and especially in his instinctive employment of the phrase "The situation is growing worse," at a moment when the revolution was moving to victory. Like the great majority of the members of the Duma Rodzianko, who was himself a well-to-do landowner, desired to see the monarchy reformed, but not abolished. All Rodzianko's actions in these turbulent days were motivated by two factors: his hope, up to the last moment, that the Tsar would save himself and the monarchical principle by making necessary concessions, and his fear that the revolutionary movement would get out of hand.

The decisive hour of the Revolution struck on the morning of March 12, when the centre of attention shifts from rebellious workers with sticks and stones and bottles to insurgent soldiers with rifles and machine-guns. The firing on the crowds on Sunday, the 11th, was the snapping point in the frail cord of discipline that held the garrison of the capital. The mutiny that was to transform the prolonged street demonstrations into a genuine revolution started in the very unit which had inflicted the heaviest losses in the demonstrating crowds: the training detachment of the Volinsky regiment. During the night the soldiers discussed their impressions of the day's shooting and agreed that they would no longer fire on the crowds. When Captain Lashkevitch appeared in the barracks of the detachment on the morning of the 12th he was greeted with shouts: "We will not shoot." He read the telegram of the Tsar, demanding the suppression of the disorders; but this only aggravated the situation. Ultimately Lashkevitch either was shot by the insurgent soldiers or committed suicide; and the troops poured out into the streets under the command of Sergeant Kirpichnikov, one of the many obscure leaders of this unplanned upheaval. They soon aroused the soldiers of the Preobrazhensky and Litovsky regiments, who were quartered in nearby barracks.

Quickly brushing aside the resistance which some officers of the Moscow Regiment endeavored to offer and gaining new recruits among the soldiers of the Moscow regiment for their ranks, the swollen mass of soldiers made for the Viborg District, where they quickly fraternized with the throngs of workers and joined them in hunting down the police and breaking into arsenals, where the workers quickly secured the desired arms.

Khabalov, a weak and incompetent man at best, was thunderstruck as the news of one mutiny after another poured in on him. He formed a supposedly loyal force of six companies under the command of Colonel Kutepov, but it simply melted away as soon as it came into contact with the revolutionary mobs. This largely psychological process of "melting away" recurred, incidentally, whenever there was an attempt to send "reliable" troops against the revolutionary capital. It explains why a movement without organized leadership was nevertheless invincible. This breakdown of normal military discipline cannot be attributed to any single precise cause. It was a compound of many things: war-weariness, hatred of the hard and often humiliating conditions of Russian army service, responsiveness to the general mood of discontent in the country,—all explosive stuff that was ignited by the stubborn demonstrations of the workingclass population of Petrograd.

There are two features of the March Revolution that strike the observer again and again. There is the lack of planned leadership, and there is the action of the soldiers independently of their officers. The latter, with very few exceptions, simply disappeared during the decisive hours of the uprising. This fact inevitably exerted a profound effect on the subsequent morale and psychology of the soldiers, who followed leaders from their own ranks, often sergeants and corporals.

Khabalov, with the rapidly thinning remnant of his loyal troops, took refuge in the Winter Palace, where his forces on the afternoon of the 12th were reduced to "fifteen hundred or two thousand men, with a very small reserve of bullets." At the insistence of the Grand Duke Michael, the Tsar's brother, the Winter Palace was evacuated and the last defenders of the old regime took refuge in the neighboring Admiralty, whence they quietly dispersed on the following morning.

So the city passed completely into the hands of the revolutionaries. The accounts of many eyewitnesses of the upheaval are pervaded with a spirit of chaotic exaltation. The monarchy had fallen; and in the masses of the population there were few who mourned it. Vast throngs gathered to watch the burning of the large District Court building and the adjoining prison; and the Tauride Palace, where the Duma held its sessions, was a magnet for endless throngs of soldiers, workers, students and curious spectators of all classes. Red bands and ribbons appeared as if by magic; and trucks filled with soldiers raced through the city, with their guns levelled against non-existent enemies. Except for the police, who were given short shrift when they were discovered hiding in garrets or firing from roofs on the crowds, the Revolution, although tumultuous, was, in the main, good-natured. There were relatively few excesses, surprisingly few, if one considers that common criminals were released indiscriminately with political offenders in the prisons which were stormed by the mobs. Class lines had not begun to assume their subsequent sharpness. An atmosphere of vague, formless good-fellowship was prevalent; and the nationalist speeches of Shulgin or Rodzianko evoked the same hearty "Hurrah" as the exhortations of the revolutionary orators. The great mass of the mutinous soldiers scarcely realized what they were doing and were uncertain whether in the end they would be treated as heroes or as criminals.

The anonymous host of workers in collarless blouses and soldiers in grey uniforms overthrew the Romanov dynasty, with its three centuries of absolute rule behind it. But the rebellious mass had nothing concrete to put in the place of the old order. The efforts to form a new government inevitably revolved around the Duma, which, despite its lack of representative character and the timidity which it displayed in its dealings with the monarchy, was the sole national assembly in existence at the time of the Revolution.

The members of the Duma on the morning of the 12th found themselves confronted with a difficult dilemma. On one hand was the Tsarist order to dissolve; on the other were the first echoes of the formidable mutiny of the garrison. Even with this last circumstance in view the Duma did not venture to defy the Tsar's order and place itself definitely at the head of the revolutionary movement. It accepted formally the decree of dissolution and moved from its customary hall of assembly into another chamber of the Tauride Palace, where it could be technically regarded as a gathering of private citizens. At the same time the delegates adopted a resolution not to leave Petrograd and commissioned the Council of Elders to elect a Temporary Committee, the functions of which were somewhat narrowly defined as the restoration of order in the capital and the establishment of relations with public organizations and institutions. The Temporary Committee included representatives of all parties in the Duma except the extreme Right and the Bolsheviki, whose deputies were in Siberian exile.

Before the members of the Temporary Committee were chosen Rodzianko made another effort, with the coöperation of the Tsar's brother, the

Grand Duke Michael, to obtain the concession of a responsible ministry from the Tsar. Michael communicated with the Chief of Staff, General Alekseev, informing him of the seriousness of the situation and suggesting that either Prince G. Lvov, head of the All-Russian Union of Zemstvos, or Rodzianko himself should be placed at the head of the ministry. When Alekseev laid this suggestion before the Tsar the latter coldly replied that he thanked the Grand Duke for his advice, but that he knew himself how to act. A message from the Premier, Prince Golitzin, pointing out that affairs had taken a catastrophic turn and imploring the Tsar to relieve him of office elicited a reply, extraordinarily unrealistic under the circumstances which prevailed in Petrograd at the time, demanding the most vigorous measures for the suppression of the uprising and characterizing as impermissible any change in the composition of the Cabinet. The seriousness of the situation was greatly underestimated in the Stavka. As late as 1.45 in the afternoon of the 12th, when the capital was already almost entirely in the hands of the revolutionaries, War Minister Byelaev sent an absurdly optimistic telegram to the effect that the disturbances in some military units were being suppressed and that tranquillity would soon be restored.

While it was decided on the 12th to send General Ivanov with a force of Cavaliers of St. George (recipients of the highest Russian military decoration) to pacify Petrograd, Ivanov took his commission rather lightly, sending his adjutant to buy provisions in Moghilev, which he proposed to take to friends in the capital. And there was no haste in sending troops from the fronts nearest to Petrograd, the northern and western, to reinforce Ivanov, because serious importance was not attached to the events in the capital.

Throughout the few decisive days of the Revolution there was a noteworthy time-lag between the Duma and the popular movement, on one hand, and between the Tsar and the Duma, on the other. If the Duma was always behind the street crowds of Petrograd the Tsar, in his decisions, was still further behind the Duma. By the time the Tsar, on the evening of March 14, had reached the conclusion that he should commission Rodzianko with the formation of a ministry (reserving for himself, however, the appointment of War and Navy Ministers) a full-fledged provisional government was already functioning in Petrograd, and it had become too late to carry out the cherished dream of many of the Duma leaders: to save the monarchy by bringing about the abdication of Nicholas II in favor of his young son, with his brother Michael as Regent.

Events were rushing at whirlwind speed in the capital; and the Duma Committee, which set out in the afternoon with the modest functions of restoring order in the capital and establishing communication with public organizations and institutions, found itself by evening obliged to "take into its hands the restoration of state and public order and the creation of a government corresponding to the desires of the population and capable of enjoying its confidence."

When Rodzianko was still hesitating about the assumption of power the brilliant and outspoken conservative deputy of the Duma, V. V. Shulgin, offered a convincing argument in favor of prompt and decisive action: "If we don't take power, others will take it, those who have already elected some scoundrels in the factories."

Whatever one may think of Shulgin's characterization of his political opponents, another force, a counterpoise to the Duma, had already come into existence in the shape of the Soviet of Workers' and Soldiers' Deputies. The rôle of the Soviet in the 1905 Revolution had not been forgotten, and it was quite natural that one of the first acts of the 1917 Revolution should be its revival. Early in the afternoon the members of the labor group of the War Industries Committee, who had been released from prison, together with the deputies of the Left parties in the Duma and some representatives of trade-unions and coöperatives constituted themselves a Temporary Executive Committee of the Soviet of Workers' Deputies and convened a session of the Soviet in the Tauride Palace on the same evening. About two hundred and fifty delegates from factories and regiments were present at the evening session; and it was decided to fuse the representation of the workers and soldiers by creating a united organization under the name: Soviet of Workers' and Soldiers' Deputies. Although the Soviet was elected in rather haphazard fashion and suffered from the fact that most of the prominent leaders of the revolutionary parties were not in Petrograd it immediately began to assume some of the functions of power, creating a food commission to regulate the supply of the capital, organizing a workers' militia as a temporary substitute for the police and deciding which newspapers should be allowed to appear. From the beginning the Soviet was closer to the masses and enjoyed more genuine authority than did the Duma.

Beginning with March 12 the halls of the Tauride Palace began to resound to the heavy tread of soldiers' boots; and the former seat of the predominantly aristocratic and middleclass Duma witnessed wave after wave of an inundation of the masses. The members of the Duma could scarcely make their way about amid the throngs which pressed into the Palace; and if few of them, perhaps, shared the bitterness of Shulgin, whose one desire, as he tells us, was for machine-guns to drive the hateful mob away, few members of the Duma felt altogether at ease among the raw masses which suddenly poured in on them.

An exception in this respect was Kerensky, who felt quite in his element, speaking everywhere, now saving an arrested Tsarist Minister from rough handling or possible lynching by a dramatic gesture, now rushing in to throw down before his perplexed colleagues a packet containing Russia's secret treaties or a sum of two million rubles which had been saved from some institution that was in danger of being plundered. The other outstanding figure among the Duma leaders in those days was Professor Paul Milyukov, leader of the Cadet Party, who seems to have contributed more than any other individual to the formation of the First Provisional Government. Strongly different in personality from the dashing, expansive, exuberant Kerensky, Milyukov was cold, precise, logical, slightly academic. At a time when many politicians could not orient themselves in the midst of the new chaotically changing conditions Milyukov retained to the full his powers of judgment; and it was no accident that he played the leading rôle in the negotiations which finally led to the support of the Provisional Government by the Soviet.

The leaders of the Soviet in its early days were rather accidental and haphazard figures; and it is significant that not one of them played a very distinguished part in the subsequent course of the Revolution. The large tumultuous mass of rank-and-file Soviet members, workers from factories and soldiers from the barracks, could feel and cheer, but was quite incapable of orderly deliberation; and the shaping of the Soviet decisions was in the hands of the Executive Committee, which first consisted of fifteen members, later enlarged by the inclusion of nine representatives of the soldiers, and ultimately still further supplemented when more of the revolutionary party leaders returned from prison and exile. The guiding figures in the Soviet in the first days of the Revolution were radical lawyers like N. D. Sokolov, journalists and publicists like Steklov and Sukhanov, while Chkheidze, the President of the Soviet, a Duma deputy of the Menshevik Party, was a Caucasian schoolteacher who spoke Russian with a heavy rasping Caucasian accent.

Party lines were rather obscure in the first period of the existence of the Soviet; but there were three marked tendencies in the Executive Committee. The few Bolshevik members of the Executive Committee, with one or two allies from other left-wing groups, favored a temporary revolutionary government up to the election of a Constituent Assembly. The Bolsheviki had not yet reached their ultimate theory that the Soviets should be organs of power. At the other extreme were the advocates of a coalition government, in which the Soviet should have its representatives along with those of the middleclass parties. The majority, however, adhered to the idea that the Revolution was bourgeois in character, that it would be improper for socialists to take part in the Provisional Government, but that the Soviet should not take power itself. It should give grudging and very conditional support to the government for which the middleclass parties should have full responsibility. Of the three theories this last was perhaps least calculated to create a strong and stable government, especially in view of the influence which the Soviet enjoyed with the masses from the first days of its existence. This placed the Provisional Government from the start in the unenviable position of possessing responsibility without real authority. It corresponded, however, with the academic theories of the left-wing Mensheviki who predominated in the first Executive Committee, and it guided the subsequent course of events.

The Duma Committee on March 13 extended the scope of its authority by appointing commissars to administer the vacant ministries. A Military Commission under the presidency of Colonel Engelhardt was created for the double purpose of safeguarding the new regime against any attempts at restoration of Tsarism and endeavoring to restore some measure of order and discipline in the garrison of the capital. Arrests of former Tsarist Ministers and members of the police began, and the prisoners were brought to the Tauride Palace, whence a number of them were ultimately transferred to the Fortress of Peter and Paul. Some, including the hated Minister of the Interior, Protopopov, surrendered themselves for arrest voluntarily; and a feature of the Palace on this day was the appearance of long queues of police, eager to be arrested to save themselves from a worse fate at the hands of the revolutionary throngs.

The victory of the Revolution, already assured in Petrograd, became more evident throughout the whole country on the 14th. Moscow, second largest city in the country, passed into the hands of the revolutionaries much more bloodlessly than Petrograd, the situation being laconically summed up in a telegram which the governor-general, Mrozovsky, despatched to the Stavka at midday: "In Moscow there is complete revolution. The military units pass over to the side of the revolutionaries."

Petrograd bore all the brunt of the fighting in the March revolution. The number of persons killed, wounded and injured was reckoned at 1315, of whom 53 were officers, 602 soldiers, 73 policemen and 587 other citizens of both sexes. In the rest of the country the Revolution may almost be said to have been made by telegraph, practically without resistance and with serious excesses only in such naval centres as Kronstadt and Helsingfors, where the traditional hatred of the sailors for their officers flared up in a number of killings. Admiral Viren in Kronstadt and Admiral Nepenin in Helsingfors, together with a number of other officers, were put to death; and the sailors in Kronstadt, which from the beginning was a centre of extreme revolutionary sentiment, lodged the more unpopular officers in the local dungeons. A brigadier-general perished during a soldiers' demonstration in Penza and Governor Bunting was killed in Tver, where the overturn was marked by rioting and looting of liquor stores. But such incidents were exceptional rather than typical. The change was accepted too easily and too generally to involve serious bloodshed.

The futility of any attempts to crush the revolutionary capital by sending troops from the front was already pretty obvious by the night of the 14th. General Ivanov with his detachment of Georgian Cavaliers arrived in Tsarskoe Syelo, only a few miles from Petrograd, where the Tsarina was in residence at one of the Imperial palaces with her children, who were suffering from measles. Ivanov rather mysteriously obtained permission from the Duma Committee to move with his troops over the last stretch of railroad line before Tsarskoe Syelo—a fact which suggests that at least some of the Duma leaders felt that a General with reliable troops might be an asset in dealing with the turbulent workers and insurgent soldiers of the capital. But, if there was any such calculation, it was doomed to failure, because as soon as Ivanov's troops came into contact with the revolutionized Tsarskoe Syelo garrison their "reliability" began to dissolve; and the General, after a brief stay in Tsarskoe Syelo, withdrew to Viritsa, where he remained until he received instructions to return to the Stavka. Much the same experience befell some troops which General Ruzsky sent from the northern front. As soon as they arrived in Luga they began to fraternize with the local soldiers and refused to proceed further. By the 15th the Stavka, recognizing the uselessness of further efforts of this kind, issued orders to stop sending troops from the front to Petrograd.

On the night of the 14th, in one of the rooms of the crowded, noisy, smoke-filled Tauride Palace the radical lawyer, N. D. Sokolov, suddenly elevated by the Revolution to the post of a Soviet leader, sat at a writing desk, surrounded by a throng of soldiers. First one soldier, then another threw out suggestions, all of which Sokolov obediently wrote down. When the suggestions were exhausted the paper received the heading: "Order Number One." When the monarchist Shulgin read the contents of this extraordinary document he exclaimed to himself, "This is the end of the army"; and this view was widely shared in conservative military circles. Order Number One certainly dealt a severe blow to traditional conceptions of military discipline, and its influence was profound and far-reaching. At the same time it may be considered an effect as much as a cause. The Petrograd garrison was completely out of hand at this time; and the soldiers were the masters of the situation. The contents of this collective handiwork of a group of soldiers may be summarized as follows:

Committees were to be elected by the soldiers and sailors of all companies, battalions and other military and naval units. Every military unit was to obey the Soviet of Workers' and Soldiers' Deputies in political demonstrations. Orders of the Military Commission of the Duma were to be executed, except in cases when they contradicted the orders of the Soviet. The company and battalion committees must control all forms of arms and not give them out to officers, even on their demand. Soldiers, while obligated to maintain strict discipline in service, were to be given the same political and civil rights as other citizens outside of service. Standing at attention and compulsory saluting outside of service were abolished along with the sonorous titles, "Your Excellency," "Your Honor," etc. with which soldiers were formerly supposed to greet officers of the higher ranks. Officers were forbidden to use the familiar "thou" in addressing their soldiers.

Although this Order, according to the eyewitness Sukhanov, was written under the direct dictation of a group of soldiers, it corresponded closely with several resolutions which had been adopted at a session of the Petrograd Soviet; and it appeared in the Soviet official organ *Izvestia* under the signature of the Soviet. Its publication enhanced the popularity of the Soviet among the soldiers. While some parts of the Order might be regarded as harmless and reasonable modifications of the caste discipline of the old army the clause which took away the control of the arms from the officers could scarcely be reconciled with any kind of military efficiency; and the general spirit of the Order was permeated with distrust of the officers as a class. It was at once a symptom and a cause of the rapid disintegration of the military capacity of the Russian Army (already badly shaken by the disasters of poor generalship and inadequate preparedness which marked the conduct of the War) which set in after the March upheaval and was a main contributory factor in the leftward sweep of the Revolution.

Almost simultaneously with the publication of Order Number One the representatives of the Soviet reached a tentative agreement with the Duma Committee as to the conditions on which the Soviet would support the Provisional Government which the Duma Committee was now preparing to create. There was, of course, a wide gulf between the social and economic views of these two bodies; but there was a fairly wide common ground of agreement as to the establishment of democratic institutions and civil liberties. After prolonged discussion Milyukov, who proved a hard and stubborn bargainer on behalf of the Duma, persuaded the Soviet negotiators to abandon their original demands that army officers should be elected and that the Provisional Government should abstain from any action which would predetermine the future form of the state. Milyukov still hoped that the monarchy could be saved through the abdication of Nicholas II. The points on which agreement was reached and which constituted the essential part of the declaration of the Provisional Government when it formally assumed office on March 16 were as follows:

Complete amnesty for all political and religious offenses. Freedom of speech, press, assembly, strikes and trade-union association. Abolition of all caste, religious and national limitations. Immediate preparation for the holding of a constituent assembly, chosen by the method of general, direct, equal, secret ballot, which should establish the form of government and the constitution of the country. Replacement of the police by a people's militia, with an elected administration, subordinated to the organs of local self-government. Election of local administrative bodies by direct, equal, general and secret ballot. No disarming and no removal from Petrograd of the military units which took part in the revolutionary movement. Abolition of all restrictions on the enjoyment by soldiers—a general civil rights—on condition of the maintenance of the strictest discipline in service.

It is noteworthy that such really vital problems of the immediate future as the war and the land question were left unmentioned in the programme of the Provisional Government. Here the differences of viewpoint between the Soviet and the Duma Committee would have been too wide to be bridged over. Milyukov insisted that the Soviet should give some expression of support to the newly constituted government and wrote himself some parts of the Soviet declaration, which appeared along with the programme of the Provisional Government on March 16, condemning illegal searches of private apartments, decline of discipline in the army, robbery and destruction of property. It cannot be said, however, that the statement of the Soviet Executive Committee about the Provisional Government was especially hearty in its assurances of sympathy and support. It is promised support only "in the measure in which the newborn government will act in the direction of fulfilling its obligations and struggling decisively with the old government."

After assuring the indispensable support, or at least toleration, of the Soviet the Duma leaders proceeded to form the first Cabinet of the new regime. It was headed by Prince G. E. Lvov, a somewhat colorless liberal, head of the Union of Zemstvos, a man whose name, along with Rodzianko's, had often been mentioned as a suitable head of a "responsible government," had the Tsar ever been willing to grant one. Milyukov assumed the office of Minister for Foreign Affairs. The War Ministry was assigned to Guchkov, an active member of the Octobrist Party and a well-to-do Moscow merchant, who had been an advocate of military reform and modernization in pre-war years. Shingarev, a physician and a prominent member of the Cadet Party, became Minister of Agriculture and the Cadet Professor Manuilov, who had been persecuted on account of his liberal views, was appointed Minister for Education. A wealthy young Ukrainian sugar manufacturer, Tereschenko, filled the post of Minister for Finance; the progressive industrialist Konovalov, who had played an active part in the War Industries Committee, was Minister for Trade; the Left Cadet Nekrasov, Minister for Communication. The more conservative parties of the Duma had two representatives; State Controller Godnev and the Procurator of the Holy Synod, V. N. Lvov, who was subsequently to play a blundering rôle that helped to discomfit the conspiracy of General Kornilov. The Duma leaders were anxious to include representatives of the Soviet in the Cabinet; and offered the posts of Minister for Labor to Chkheidze and of Minister for Justice to Kerensky. Chkheidze, in conformity with the resolution of the Soviet Executive Committee, which by thirteen votes against eight had pronounced against the participation of its members in the new government, declined the suggestion. Kerensky, however, accepted the offer and simultaneously kept his footing in the Soviet by delivering a typical emotional speech, in which he declared, amid applause, that he could not let the representatives of the old regime out of his hands and that his first act would be the bringing back, with honor, of the exiled Bolshevik Duma deputies. Nothing was easier in those days than for a popular orator to win a rousing round of applause; and Kerensky, ignoring the frowns of some of the Soviet leaders, took the cheers of the more unsophisticated rank-and-file members as sanction for his action.

With a new government formed and a programme of adjustment, however fragile, concluded between the Duma and the Soviet, only one act in the revolutionary drama remained to be played: the elimination of the Tsar and the solution of the problem of future government. It was in Pskov, one of the oldest Russian cities, that the formal end of the sovereignty of the Romanov dynasty, which had endured more than three centuries, was destined to occur.

The former Tsar's nomination of the Grand Duke Nicholas Nicholaevitch as commander-in-chief of the army remained as ineffectual as his abdication in favor of his brother Michael. As early as the evening of March 19 Prince Lvov, significantly commenting, "Events carry us along; we don't guide events," informed Alekseev that the tide of popular animosity to the Romanovs was too strong to make it possible for the Grand Duke to assume command of the army. Alekseev, who was already dismayed by symptoms of declining discipline in the army and navy and especially by the appearance, in the immediate rear zone, of what he characterized as "undisciplined bands" of revolutionary agitators, argued strongly for the retention of the Grand Duke, in whose appointment he saw a guaranty for the discipline and unity of the army. But Lvov and Guchkov were adamant; and Alekseev himself very reluctantly, on account of his poor health and his pessimistic appraisal of the situation, agreed to take over the supreme command. The Grand Duke would indeed have been an impossible candidate in view of the fact that the Soviet had already passed a resolution calling for his arrest.

As a result of a misunderstanding the Grand Duke was not notified of the Government's change of intention; and on March 24 actually arrived in Moghilev and formally took over the command. He was quickly notified of the changed situation and was sent under house arrest to his Crimean estate.

The Romanov autocracy, with three centuries of traditional absolutism behind it, fell not as a result of any carefully planned conspiracy or *coup d'état*, but as a result of an unorganized, almost anarchical popular movement, the success of which was the measure of the inner weakness and decadence of the old order. So completely discredited was the fallen dynasty that during the subsequent civil war no outstanding leader of the anti-Bolshevik forces dared to write "Restoration of the Romanovs" on his banner. But although the old order had passed forever the outlines of the new were uncommonly vague in these confused and hectic March days. The Provisional Government was but a pale ghost of authority; the Soviet, although it possessed more real power, was still very uncertain both as to the extent of its strength and as to the use to which this strength should be put. Vladimir Ilyitch Lenin, the man who was to impose on the Russian Revolution its final form, was still pacing the streets of dull, respectable, middleclass Zürich, conjuring up one scheme after another for crossing the inhospitable battle-fronts that separated him from his native country, which, as he instinctively realized, was ripe as never before for social upheaval on the grand scale.

The Origins of Nazi Germany—
German History or
Charismatic Leadership?

CONTENTS

QUESTIONS FOR STUDY

1 What elements of German history and tradition contributed to the Nazi victory?

On January 30, 1933, Adolf Hitler took office as Chancellor of Germany. In March of the same year a compliant Reichstag voted an Enabling Act, which suspended the constitution, established Hitler's dictatorship and put an end to Germany's attempt at democratic republican government. It also introduced a reign of terror, a policy of racism and military adventurism, the like of which the world had never seen. Our problem is to decide why this disaster befell Germany. Some scholars have thought that the evil aspects and consequences of Nazism are inherent in the German character, which was created by the unique course of German history. Others find the causes of the Nazi rise to power in the peculiar problems faced by the Weimar Republic and suggest that any nation faced by such conditions and problems might well succumb. Still another view is that Nazism was largely the product of the evil genius of Adolf Hitler himself. The documents that follow illustrate some of the difficulties that Germany faced after World War I and the nature of the solutions offered by Hitler and the Nazis. They also indicate which elements of the German people helped Hitler to power.

2 *What external forces were responsible?*

3 *How did the Nazi program and propaganda exploit these elements and forces?*

4 *What was the importance of anti-Semitism to the Nazi victory?*

5 *How and why did the Communists and businessmen aid the Nazis?*

6 *Was the destruction of the Weimar Republic inevitable?*

1 Hitler, the Greatest Demagogue in History

Alan Bullock presents a sophisticated version of a widely held opinion that Nazism was the product of the demagogic genius of Adolf Hitler.

FROM *Hitler* BY ALAN BULLOCK

HITLER LIVED THROUGH the exciting days of April and May 1919 in Munich itself. What part he played, if any, is uncertain. According to his own account in *Mein Kampf,* he was to have been put under arrest at the end of April, but drove off with his rifle the three men who came to arrest him. Once the Communists had been overthrown, he gave information before the Commission of Inquiry set up by the 2nd Infantry Regiment, which tried and shot those reported to have been active on the other side. He then got a job in the Press and News Bureau of the Political Department of the Army's VII (Munich) District Command, a centre for the activities of such men as Röhm. After attending a course of "political instruction" for the troops, Hitler was himself appointed a *Bildungsoffizier* (Instruction Officer) with the task of inoculating the men against contagion by socialist, pacifist, or democratic ideas. This was an important step for Hitler, since it constituted the first recognition of the fact that he had any political ability at all. Then, in September, he was instructed by the head of the Political Department to investigate a small group meeting in Munich, the German Workers' Party, which might possibly be of interest to the Army.

The German Workers' Party had its origins in a Committee of Independent Workmen set up by a Munich locksmith, Anton Drexler, on 7 March 1918. Drexler's idea was to create a party which would be both

Hitler: A Study in Tyranny, Completely Revised Edition, pp. 63–71, 805–8, by Alan Bullock. Copyright © 1962 by Alan Bullock. Reprinted by permission of Harper & Row, Publishers, and Odhams Books Ltd., London.

working class and nationalist. He saw what Hitler had also seen, that a middle-class movement like the Fatherland Front (to which Drexler belonged) was hopelessly out of touch with the mood of the masses, and that these were coming increasingly under the influence of anti-national and anti-militarist propaganda. Drexler made little headway with his committee, which recruited forty members, and in October 1918 he and Karl Harrer, a journalist, founded the Political Workers' Circle which, in turn, was merged with the earlier organization in January 1919 to form the German Workers' Party. Harrer became the Party's first chairman. Its total membership was little more than Drexler's original forty, activity was limited to discussions in Munich beer-halls, and the committee of six had no clear idea of anything more ambitious. It can scarcely have been a very impressive scene when, on the evening of 12 September 1919, Hitler attended his first meeting in a room at the Sterneckerbräu, a Munich beer-cellar in which a handful of twenty or twenty-five people had gathered. One of the speakers was Gottfried Feder, an economic crank well known in Munich, who had already impressed Hitler at one of the political courses arranged for the Army. The other was a Bavarian separatist, whose proposals for the secession of Bavaria from the German Reich and a union with Austria brought Hitler to his feet in a fury. He spoke with such vehemence that when the meeting was over Drexler went up to him and gave him a copy of his autobiographical pamphlet, *Mein politisches Erwachen.*[1] A few days later Hitler received a postcard inviting him to attend a committee meeting of the German Workers' Party.

After some hesitation Hitler went. The committee met in an obscure beer-house, the Alte Rosenbad, in the Herrnstrasse. "I went through the badly lighted guest-room, where not a single guest was to be seen, and searched for the door which led to the side room; and there I was face to face with the Committee. Under the dim light shed by a grimy gas-lamp I could see four people sitting round a table, one of them the author of the pamphlet."[2]

The rest of the proceedings followed in the same key: the Party's funds were reported to total 7.50 marks, minutes were read and confirmed, three letters were received, three replies read and approved.

Yet, as Hitler frankly acknowledges, this very obscurity was an attraction. It was only in a party which, like himself, was beginning at the bottom that he had any prospect of playing a leading part and imposing his ideas. In the established parties there was no room for him, he would be a nobody. After two days' reflection he made up his mind and joined the Committee of the German Workers' Party as its seventh member.

The energy and ambition which had been hitherto unharnessed now found an outlet. Slowly and painfully he pushed the Party forward, and prodded his cautious and unimaginative colleagues on the committee into bolder methods of recruitment. A few invitations were multigraphed and

[1] *My Political Awakening.*   [2] *Mein Kampf,* p. 189.

distributed, a small advertisement inserted in the local paper, a larger hall secured for more frequent meetings. When Hitler himself spoke for the first time in the Hofbräuhaus in October, a hundred and eleven people were present. The result was to confirm the chairman, Karl Harrer, in his belief that Hitler had no talent for public speaking. But Hitler persisted and the numbers rose. In October there were a hundred and thirty when Hitler spoke on Brest-Litovsk and Versailles, a little later there were two hundred.

At the beginning of 1920 Hitler was put in charge of the Party's propaganda and promptly set to work to organize its first mass meeting. By the use of clever advertising he got nearly two thousand people into the *Festsaal* of the Hofbräuhaus on 24 February. The principal speaker was a Dr Dingfelder, but it was Hitler who captured the audience's attention and used the occasion to announce the Party's new name, the National Socialist German Workers' Party, and its twenty-five point programme. Angered by the way in which Hitler was now forcing the pace, Harrer resigned from the office of chairman. On 1 April 1920, Hitler at last left the Army and devoted all his time to building up the Party, control of which he now more and more arrogated to himself.

Hitler's and Drexler's group in Munich was not the only National Socialist party. In Bavaria itself there were rival groups, led by Streicher in Nuremberg and Dr Otto Dickel in Augsburg, both nominally branches of the German Socialist Party founded by Alfred Brunner in 1919. Across the frontier in Austria and in the Sudetenland the pre-war German Social Workers' Party had been reorganized and got in touch with the new Party in Munich. A number of attempts had been made in Austria before 1914 to combine a working-class movement with a Pan-German nationalist programme. The most successful was this Deutsch Arbeiterpartei which, led by an Austrian lawyer, Walther Riehl, and a railway employee named Rudolf Jung, won three seats in the Reichsrat at the Austrian elections of 1911. The Party's programme was formulated at the Moravian town of Iglau in 1913, and reflected the bitterness of the German struggle with the Czechs as well as the attraction of Pan-German and anti-Semitic ideas.

In May 1918, this Austrian party took the title of D.N.S.A.P.—the German National Socialists Workers' Party—and began to use the Hakenkreuz, the swastika, as its symbol. When the Austro-Hungarian monarchy was broken up, and a separate Czech State formed, the National Socialists set up an inter-State bureau with one branch in Vienna, of which Riehl was chairman, and another in the Sudetenland. It was this inter-State bureau which now invited the cooperation of the Bavarian National Socialists, and a Munich delegation attended the next joint meeting at Salzburg in August 1920. Shortly afterwards the Munich Party, too, adopted the name of the National Socialist German Workers' Party.

Up to August 1923, when Hitler attended the last of the inter-State meetings at Salzburg, there were fairly frequent contacts between these different National Socialist groups, but little came of them. Hitler was too jealous of his independence to submit to interference from outside, and the last meeting of the conference, at Salzburg in 1923, led to Riehl's resignation.

Much more important to Hitler was the support he received from Captain Röhm, on the staff of the Army District Command in Munich. Röhm, a tough, scar-faced soldier of fortune with real organizing ability, exercised considerable influence in the shadowy world of the Freikorps, Defence Leagues, and political conspiracies. He had actually joined the German Workers' Party before Hitler, for, like Hitler, he saw that it would be impossible to re-create a strong, nationalist Germany until the alienation of the mass of the people from their old loyalty to the Fatherland and the Army could be overcome. Any party which could recapture the working classes for a nationalist and militarist allegiance interested him. He admired the spirit and toughness of the Communists, who were prepared to fight for what they believed in: what he wanted was working-class organizations with the same qualities on his own side.

Röhm had little patience with the view that the Army should keep out of politics. The Army, he believed, had to go into politics if it wanted to create the sort of State which would restore its old privileged position, and break with the policy of fulfilling the terms of the Peace Treaty. This was a view accepted by only a part of the Officer Corps; others, especially among the senior officers, viewed Röhm's activities with mistrust. But there was sufficient sympathy with his aims to allow a determined man to use the opportunities of his position to the full.

When Hitler began to build up the German Workers' Party, Röhm pushed in ex-Freikorps men and ex-servicemen to swell the Party's membership. From these elements the first "strong-arm" squads were formed, the nucleus of the S.A. In December 1920, Röhm had persuaded his commanding officer, Major-General Ritter von Epp—himself a former Freikorps leader and a member of the Party—to help raise the sixty thousand marks needed to buy the Party a weekly paper, the *Völkischer Beobachter*. Dietrich Eckart provided half, but part of the rest came from Army secret funds. Above all, Röhm was the indispensable link in securing for Hitler the protection, or at least the tolerance, of the Army and of the Bavarian Government, which depended on the local Army Command as the ultimate arbiter of public order. Without the unique position of the Army in German, and especially in Bavarian, politics—its ability to extend powerful support to the political groups and activities it favoured—Hitler would never have been able to exercise with impunity his methods of incitement, violence and intimidation. At every step from 1914 to 1945 Hitler's varying relationship to the Army was of the greatest importance to him: never more so than in these early years in Munich when, without the Army's patronage, Hitler would have found the greatest difficulty in climbing the first steps of his political career. Before his death the Army was to learn the full measure of his ingratitude.

Yet however important this help from outside, the foundation of Hitler's success was his own energy and ability as a political leader. Without this, the help would never have been forthcoming, or would have produced insignificant results. Hitler's genius as a politician lay in his unequalled grasp of what could be done by propaganda, and his flair for seeing how to do it. He had to learn in a hard school, on his feet night after night, arguing his case in every kind of hall, from the smoke-filled back room of a beer cellar to the huge auditorium of the Zirkus Krone; often, in the early days, in the face of opposition, indifference or amused contempt; learning to hold his audience's attention, to win them over; most important of all, learning to read the minds of his audiences, finding the sensitive spots on which to hammer. "He could play like a virtuoso on the well-tempered piano of lower-middle-class hearts," says Dr Schacht. Behind that virtuosity lay years of experience as an agitator and mob orator. Hitler came to know Germany and the German people at first hand as few of Germany's other leaders ever had. By the time he came to power in 1933 there were few towns of any size in the Reich where he had not spoken. Here was one great advantage Hitler had over nearly all the politicians with whom he had to deal, his immense practical experience of politics, not in the Chancellery or the Reichstag, but in the street, the level at which elections are won, the level at which any politician must be effective if he is to carry a mass vote with him.

Hitler was the greatest demagogue in history. Those who add "only a demagogue" fail to appreciate the nature of political power in an age of mass politics. As he himself said: "To be a leader, means to be able to move masses."

The lessons which Hitler drew from the activities of the Austrian Social Democrats and Lueger's Christian Socialists were now tried out in Munich. Success was far from being automatic. Hitler made mistakes and had much to learn before he could persuade people to take him seriously, even on the small stage of Bavarian politics. By 1923 he was still only a provincial politician, who had not yet made any impact on national politics, and the end of 1923 saw the collapse of his movement in a fiasco. But Hitler learned from his mistakes, and by the time he came to write *Mein Kampf* in the middle of the 1920s he was able to set down quite clearly what he was trying to do, and what were the conditions of success. The pages in *Mein Kampf* in which he discusses the technique of mass propaganda and political leadership stand out in brilliant contrast with the turgid attempts to explain his entirely unoriginal political ideas.

The first and most important principle for political action laid down by Hitler is: Go to the masses. "The movement must avoid everything which may lessen or weaken its power of influencing the masses . . . because of the simple fact that no great idea, no matter how sublime or exalted, can be realized in practice without the effective power which resides in the popular masses."

Since the masses have only a poor acquaintance with abstract ideas, their reactions lie more in the domain of the feelings, where the roots of their positive as well as their negative attitudes are implanted. . . . The emotional grounds of their attitude furnish the reason for their extraordinary stability. It is always more difficult to fight against faith than against knowledge. And the driving force which has brought about the most tremendous revolutions on this earth has never been a body of scientific teaching which has gained power over the masses, but always a devotion which has inspired them, and often a kind of hysteria which has urged them into action. Whoever wishes to win over the masses must know the key that will open the door to their hearts. It is not objectivity, which is a feckless attitude, but a determined will, backed up by power where necessary.

Hitler is quite open in explaining how this is to be achieved. "The receptive powers of the masses are very restricted, and their understanding is feeble. On the other hand, they quickly forget. Such being the case, all effective propaganda must be confined to a few bare necessities and then must be expressed in a few stereotyped formulas." Hitler had nothing but scorn for the intellectuals who are always looking for something new. "Only constant repetition will finally succeed in imprinting an idea on the memory of a crowd." For the same reason it is better to stick to a programme even when certain points in it become out of date: "As soon as one point is removed from the sphere of dogmatic certainty, the discussion will not simply result in a new and better formulation, but may easily lead to endless debates and general confusion."

When you lie, tell big lies. This is what the Jews do, working on the principle, "which is quite true in itself, that in the big lie there is always a certain force of credibility; because the broad masses of a nation are always more easily corrupted in the deeper strata of their emotional nature than consciously or voluntarily, and thus in the primitive simplicity of their minds they more readily fall victims to the big lie than the small lie, since they themselves often tell small lies in little matters, but would be ashamed to resort to large-scale falsehoods. It would never come into their heads to fabricate colossal untruths and they would not believe that others could have the impudence to distort the truth so infamously. . . . The grossly impudent lie always leaves traces behind it, even after it has been nailed down."

Above all, never hesitate, never qualify what you say, never concede an inch to the other side, paint all your contrasts in black and white. This is the "very first condition which has to be fulfilled in every kind of propaganda: a systematically one-sided attitude towards every problem that has to be dealt with. . . . When they see an uncompromising onslaught against an adversary, the people have at all times taken this as proof that right is on the side of the active aggressor; but if the aggressor should go only halfway and fail to push home his success . . . the people will look upon this as a sign that he is uncertain of the justice of his own cause."

Vehemence, passion, fanaticism, these are "the great magnetic forces which alone attract the great masses; for these masses always respond to the compelling force which emanates from absolute faith in the ideas put forward, combined with an indomitable zest to fight for and defend them. . . . The doom of a nation can be averted only by a storm of glowing passion; but only those who are passionate themselves can arouse passion in others."

Hitler showed a marked preference for the spoken over the written word. "The force which ever set in motion the great historical avalanches of religious and political movements is the magic power of the spoken word. The broad masses of a population are more amenable to the appeal of rhetoric than to any other force." The employment of verbal violence, the repetition of such words as "smash," "force," "ruthless," "hatred," was deliberate. Hitler's gestures and the emotional character of his speaking, lashing himself up to a pitch of near-hysteria in which he would scream and spit out his resentment, had the same effect on an audience. Many descriptions have been given of the way in which he succeeded in communicating passion to his listeners, so that men groaned or hissed and women sobbed involuntarily, if only to relieve the tension, caught up in the spell of powerful emotions of hatred and exaltation, from which all restraint had been removed.

It was to be years yet before Hitler was able to achieve this effect on the scale of the Berlin Sportpalast audiences of the 1930s, but he had already begun to develop extraordinary gifts as a speaker. It was in Munich that he learned to address mass audiences of several thousands. In *Mein Kampf* he remarks that the orator's relationship with his audience is the secret of his art. "He will always follow the lead of the great mass in such a way that from the living emotion of his hearers the apt word which he needs will be suggested to him and in its turn this will go straight to the hearts of his hearers." A little later he speaks of the difficulty of overcoming emotional resistance: this cannot be done by argument, but only by an appeal to the "hidden forces" in an audience, an appeal that the orator alone can make.

Many attempts have been made to explain away the importance of Hitler, from Chaplin's brilliant caricature in *The Great Dictator* to the much less convincing picture of Hitler the pawn, a front man for German capitalism. Others have argued that Hitler was nothing in himself, only a symbol of the restless ambition of the German nation to dominate Europe; a creature flung to the top by the tides of revolutionary change, or the embodiment of the collective unconscious of a people obsessed with violence and death.

These arguments seem to me to be based upon a confusion of two different questions. Obviously, Nazism was a complex phenomenon to which many factors—social, economic, historical, psychological—contributed. But whatever the explanation of this episode in European history—and it can be no simple one—that does not answer the question with which this book has been concerned, what was the part played by Hitler. It may be true that a mass movement, strongly nationalist, anti-Semitic, and radical, would have sprung up in Germany without Hitler. But so far as what actually happened is concerned—not what might have happened—the evidence seems to me to leave no doubt that no other man played a role in the Nazi revolution or in the history of the Third Reich remotely comparable with that of Adolf Hitler.

The conception of the Nazi Party, the propaganda with which it must appeal to the German people, and the tactics by which it would come to power—these were unquestionably Hitler's. After 1934 there were no rivals left and by 1938 he had removed the last checks on his freedom of action. Thereafter, he exercised an arbitrary rule in Germany to a degree rarely, if ever, equalled in a modern industrialized state.

At the same time, from the re-militarization of the Rhineland to the invasion of Russia, he won a series of successes in diplomacy and war which established an hegemony over the continent of Europe comparable with that of Napoleon at the height of his fame. While these could not have been won without a people and an Army willing to serve him, it was Hitler who provided the indispensable leadership, the flair for grasping opportunities, the boldness in using them. In retrospect his mistakes appear obvious, and it is easy to be complacent about the inevitability of his defeat; but it took the combined efforts of the three most powerful nations in the world to break his hold on Europe.

Luck and the disunity of his opponents will account for much of Hitler's success—as it will of Napoleon's—but not for all. He began with few advantages, a man without a name and without support other than that which he acquired for himself, not even a citizen of the country he aspired to rule. To achieve what he did Hitler needed—and possessed—talents out of the ordinary which in sum amounted to political genius, however evil its fruits.

His abilities have been sufficiently described in the preceding pages: his mastery of the irrational factors in politics, his insight into the weaknesses of his opponents, his gift for simplification, his sense of timing, his willingness to take risks. An opportunist entirely without principle, he showed both consistency and an astonishing power of will in pursuing his aims. Cynical and calculating in the exploitation of his histrionic gifts, he retained an unshaken belief in his historic role and in himself as a creature of destiny.

The fact that his career ended in failure, and that his defeat was pre-eminently due to his own mistakes, does not by itself detract from Hitler's claim to greatness. The flaw lies deeper. For these remarkable powers were combined with an ugly and strident egotism, a moral and intellectual cretinism. The passions which ruled Hitler's mind were ignoble: hatred, resentment, the lust to dominate, and, where he could not dominate, to destroy. His career did not exalt but debased the human condition, and his twelve years' dictatorship was barren of all ideas save one—the further extension of his own power and that of the nation with which he had identified himself. Even power he conceived of in the crudest terms: an endless vista of military roads, S.S. garrisons, and concentration camps to sustain the rule of the Aryan "master race" over the degraded subject peoples of his new empire in the east.

The great revolutions of the past, whatever their ultimate fate, have been identified with the release of certain powerful ideas: individual conscience, liberty, equality, national freedom, social justice. National Socialism produced nothing. Hitler constantly exalted force over the power of ideas and delighted to prove that men were governed by cupidity, fear, and their baser passions. The sole theme of the Nazi revolution was domination, dressed up as the doctrine of race, and, failing that, a vindictive destructiveness, Rauschning's *Revolution des Nihilismus*.

It is this emptiness, this lack of anything to justify the suffering he caused rather than his own monstrous and ungovernable will which makes Hitler both so repellent and so barren a figure. Hitler will have his place in history, but it will be alongside Attila the Hun, the barbarian king who was surnamed, not "the Great," but "the Scourge of God," and who boasted "in a saying," Gibbon writes, "worthy of his ferocious pride, that the grass never grew on the spot where his horse had stood." [3]

The view has often been expressed that Hitler could only have come to power in Germany, and it is true—without falling into the same error of racialism as the Nazis—that there were certain features of German historical development, quite apart from the effects of the Defeat and the Depression, which favoured the rise of such a movement.

This is not to accuse the Germans of Original Sin, or to ignore the other sides of German life which were only grossly caricatured by the Nazis. But Nazism was not some terrible accident which fell upon the German people out of a blue sky. It was rooted in their history, and while it is true that a majority of the German people never voted for Hitler, it is also true that thirteen millions did. Both facts need to be remembered.

From this point of view Hitler's career may be described as a *reductio ad absurdum* of the most powerful political tradition in Germany since the Unification. This is what nationalism, militarism, authoritarianism, the worship of success and force, the exaltation of the State, and *Realpolitik* lead to, if they are projected to their logical conclusion.

There are Germans who reject such a view. They argue that what was wrong with Hitler was that he lacked the necessary skill, that he was a bungler. If only he had listened to the generals—or Schacht—or the career diplomats—if only he had not attacked Russia, and so on. There is some point, they feel, at which he went wrong. They refuse to see that it was the

[3] Gibbon: *Decline and Fall of the Roman Empire*, c. 34.

ends themselves, not simply the means, which were wrong: the pursuit of unlimited power, the scorn for justice or any restraint on power; the exaltation of will over reason and conscience; the assertion of an arrogant supremacy, the contempt for others' rights. As at least one German historian, Professor Meinecke, has recognized, the catastrophe to which Hitler led Germany points to the need to re-examine the aims as well as the methods of German policy as far back as Bismarck.

The Germans, however, were not the only people who preferred in the 1930s not to know what was happening and refused to call evil things by their true names. The British and French at Munich; the Italians, Germany's partners in the Pact of Steel; the Poles, who stabbed the Czechs in the back over Teschen; the Russians, who signed the Nazi–Soviet Pact to partition Poland, all thought they could buy Hitler off, or use him to their own selfish advantage. They did not succeed, any more than the German Right or the German Army. In the bitterness of war and occupation they were forced to learn the truth of the words of John Donne which Ernest Hemingway set at the beginning of his novel of the Spanish Civil War:

> No man is an Iland, intire of it selfe; every man is a peece of the Continent, a part of the maine; If a clod bee washed away by the Sea, Europe is the lesse, as well as if a Promontorie were, as well as if a Mannor of thy friends or of thine own were; Any man's death diminishes me, because I am involved in Mankinde; And therefore never send to know for whom the bell tolls; It tolls for thee.

Hitler, indeed, was a European, no less than a German phenomenon. The conditions and the state of mind which he exploited, the *malaise* of which he was the symptom, were not confined to one country, although they were more strongly marked in Germany than anywhere else. Hitler's idiom was German, but the thoughts and emotions to which he gave expression have a more universal currency.

Hitler recognized this relationship with Europe perfectly clearly. He was in revolt against "the System" not just in Germany but in Europe, against the liberal bourgeois order, symbolized for him in the Vienna which had once rejected him. To destroy this was his mission, the mission in which he never ceased to believe; and in this, the most deeply felt of his purposes, he did not fail. Europe may rise again, but the old Europe of the years between 1789, the year of the French Revolution, and 1939, the year of Hitler's War, has gone for ever—and the last figure in its history is that of Adolf Hitler, the architect of its ruin. *"Si monumentum requiris, circumspice"*—"If you seek his monument, look around."

2   The Weaknesses of Weimar

*Article 231 of the Treaty of Versailles, which assigned all
responsibility for the recent war to Germany and her allies,
was a thorn in the side of those Germans who defended the
Weimar democracy. The clause was widely rejected by the
Germans, and enemies of the republic used it to fix the
blame for all Germany's troubles on the republican officials
who had signed the treaty. The following remarks of Adolf
Hitler are examples of the rhetoric that was employed.*

FROM *Hitler's Speeches on War Guilt*

In a speech delivered at Munich on 13 April 1923 Hitler said:

"IN THE WINTER OF THE YEAR 1919–20 we National Socialists publicly for the first time put to the German people the question, whose is the
guilt for the War? . . . And we received pat from all sides the stereotyped
answer of despicable self-humiliation: 'We confess it: the guilt for the War is
ours!' . . . Yes, the whole Revolution was made artificially on the basis of
this truly monstrous lie. For if it had not been possible to bring this lie into
the field as a propaganda formula against the old Reich, what sense could
one give at all to the November treason? They needed this slander of the
existing system in order to justify before the people their own deed of shame.
The masses, under the influence of a criminal incitement, were prepared
without any hesitation to believe whatever the men of the new Government
told them."

*In his speech delivered in Munich on 17 April 1923 Hitler discussed "The
Peace Treaty of Versailles as the perpetual curse of the November-Republic."*

Who, *he asked,* were the real rulers of Germany in 1914 to whom war guilt
might be attributed: not the Kaiser, not the Pan-Germans, but Messrs.

The Speeches of Adolf Hitler, I (1942), 54–7, translated and edited by Norman Baynes,
published by Oxford University Press under the auspices of the Royal Institute of International
Affairs, London.

Ballin, Bleichröder, Mendelssohn, &c., a whole brood of Hebrews who formed the unofficial Government. And in 1914 the real ruler of the Reich was Herr Bethmann-Hollweg, "a descendant of a Jewish family of Frankfurt—the genuine article, and in his every act the Yiddish philosopher all over. Those were the leaders of the State, not the Pan-Germans."

*   *   *

After discussing the mistakes of German politicians during the course of the War Hitler continued:

"With the armistice begins the humiliation of Germany. If the Republic on the day of its foundation had appealed to the country: 'Germans, stand together! Up and resist the foe! The Fatherland, the Republic expects of you that you fight to your last breath,' then millions who are now the enemies of the Republic would be fanatical Republicans. To-day they are the foes of the Republic not because it is a Republic but because this Republic was founded at the moment when Germany was humiliated, because it so discredited the new flag that men's eyes must turn regretfully towards the old flag."

"It was no Treaty of Peace which was signed, but a betrayal of Peace."

"The Treaty was signed which demanded from Germany that she should perform what was for ever impossible of performance. But that was not the worst: after all that was only a question of material values. This was not the end: Commissions of Control were formed! For the first time in the history of the modern world there were planted on a State agents of foreign Powers to act as hangmen, and German soldiers were set to serve the foreigner. And if one of these Commissions was 'insulted,' a company of the German army (*Reichswehr*) had to defile before the French flag. We no longer feel the humiliation of such an act; but the outside world says, 'What a people of curs!'"

"So long as this Treaty stands there can be no resurrection of the German people: no social reform of any kind is possible! The Treaty was made in order to bring 20 million Germans to their deaths and to ruin the German nation. But those who made the Treaty cannot set it aside. At its foundation our Movement formulated three demands:

1. Setting aside of the Peace Treaty.
2. Unification of all Germans.
3. Land and soil (*Grund und Boden*) to feed our nation.

Our Movement could formulate these demands, since it was not our Movement which caused the War, it has not made the Republic, it did not sign the Peace-Treaty."

"There is thus one thing which is the first task of this Movement: it desires to make the German once more National, that his Fatherland shall stand for him above everything else. It desires to teach our people to understand afresh the truth of the old saying: He who will not be a hammer must be an anvil. An anvil are we today, and that anvil will be beaten until out of the anvil we fashion once more a hammer, a German sword!"

A major role in the weakening of the republic and in the destruction of the German people's confidence in it was played by the severe inflation that struck between 1921 and 1923. It wreaked havoc on the economy and wiped out the savings of the middle class. The following account is from the autobiography of a woman who lived through that difficult time in Germany.

FROM *Restless Days* BY LILO LINKE

THE TIME FOR MY FIRST EXCURSIONS into life was badly chosen. Rapidly Germany was precipitated into the inflation, thousands, millions, milliards of marks whirled about, making heads swim in confusion. War, revolution, and the wild years after had deprived everyone of old standards and the possibility of planning a normal life. Again and again fate hurled the helpless individual into the boiling kettle of a wicked witch. Now the inflation came and destroyed the last vestige of steadiness. Hurriedly one had to make use of the moment and could not consider the following day.

The whole population had suddenly turned into maniacs. Everyone was buying, selling, speculating, bargaining, and dollar, dollar, dollar was the magic word which dominated every conversation, every newspaper, every poster in Germany. Nobody understood what was happening. There seemed to be no sense, no rules in the mad game, but one had to take part in it if one did not want to be trampled underfoot at once. Only a few people were able to carry through to the end and gain by the inflation. The majority lost everything and broke down, impoverished and bewildered.

The middle class was hurt more than any other, the savings of a lifetime and their small fortunes melted into a few coppers. They had to sell their most precious belongings for ten milliard inflated marks to buy a bit of food or an absolutely necessary coat, and their pride and dignity were bleeding out of many wounds. Bitterness remained for ever in their hearts. Full of hatred, they accused the international financiers, the Jews and Socialists—their old enemies—of having exploited their distress. They never forgot and never forgave and were the first to lend a willing ear to Hitler's fervent preaching.

In the shop, notices announced that we should receive our salaries in weekly parts, after a while we queued up at the cashier's desk every evening, and before long we were paid twice daily and ran out during the lunch hour to buy a few things, because as soon as the new rate of exchange became known in the early afternoon our money had again lost half its value.

In the beginning I did not concern myself much with these happenings. They merely added to the excitement of my new life, which was all that mattered to me. Living in the east of Berlin and in hard times, I was long accustomed to seeing people around me in hunger, distress, and poverty. My mother was always lamenting that it was impossible for her to make both ends meet, my father—whenever he was at home—always asking what the deuce she had done with all the money he had given her yesterday. A few tears, a few outbreaks more did not make a difference great enough to impress me deeply.

Yet, in the long run, the evil influence of the inflation, financially as well as morally, penetrated even to me. Berlin had become the centre of international profiteers and noisy new rich. For a few dollars they could buy the whole town, drinks and women, horses and houses, virtue and vice, and they made free use of these possibilities. The evening when I had gone with the Count to the restaurant and the Pacific Bar I had watched them with surprised eyes, although certainly my lack of experience exaggerated the impression, as it had done many years before on the Rummel, and although the bar and the people there would in any circumstances have seemed luxurious and astonishing to me. During the next months I had many opportunities of witnessing their lavish life because I went often to expensive places, a modest grey sparrow, watching in a crowd of radiant peacocks.

The following remarks were made by Hitler in 1923 at the height of the inflation.

FROM *Hitler's Speeches*

It was the height of the inflation period and of the manufacture of paper money:

''GERMANY IS A PEOPLE OF CHILDREN; a grown-up people would say: 'We don't care a fig for your paper-money. Give us something of value—

The Speeches of Adolf Hitler, I (1942), 72–3, translated and edited by Norman Baynes, published by Oxford University Press under the auspices of the Royal Institute of International Affairs, London.

gold! What have you after all to give us? Nothing? Thus have you defrauded us, you rogues and swindlers!" An awakened people with its last thirty marks—all that is left of the millions of its glory—would buy a rope and with it string up 10,000 of its defrauders!" Even the farmer will no longer sell his produce. "When you offer him your million scraps of paper with which he can cover the walls of his closet on his dung-heap, can you wonder that he says, 'Keep your millions and I will keep my corn and my butter.'" "The individual and the nation are delivered over to the international capital of the banks; despair seizes the whole people. We are on the eve of a second revolution. Some are setting their hopes on the star of the Soviet: that is the symbol of those who began the Revolution, to whom the Revolution has brought untold wealth, who have exploited it until to-day. It is the star of David, the sign of the Synagogue. The symbol of the race high over the world, of a lordship which stretches from Vladivostok to the West—the lordship of Jewry. The golden star which for the Jew means the glittering gold."

"And when the people in its horror sees that one can starve though one may have milliards of marks, then it will perforce make up its mind and say: 'We will bow down no longer before an institution which is founded on the delusory majority principle, we want a dictatorship.' Already the Jew has a premonition of things to come: . . . he is saying to himself: If there must be a dictatorship, then it shall be a dictatorship of Cohen or Levi."

The payment of reparations by Germany to the victorious powers was disruptive in several ways. It was based on the war-guilt clause and therefore was a tangible reminder of Germany's defeat and the shameful peace; it slowed economic recovery; it was a device that enabled France to occupy the Saar and the Rhineland and thus a weapon that could be used by Nationalists against the republic. In 1929 a group of international experts met at Paris to resolve the reparations problem and produced the relatively lenient Young Plan. This plan was adopted by the powers and Germany at a conference at the Hague. The plan evoked great hostility on the right, and a committee, headed by the Nationalist Hugenberg; Hitler; Seldte, the leader of the Stahlhelm; and Class, the leader of the Pan-German League, was organized to fight it. They proposed a plebiscite to give the people a chance to repudiate the reparations settlement. In September, 1929, they published the following draft of a law. The bill was defeated, but its language shows the intensity of the animosity felt toward reparations in some quarters.

Law Against the Enslavement of the German People

1. THE GOVERNMENT OF THE REICH must immediately give notice to the foreign powers that the forced acknowledgment of war guilt in the Versailles Treaty contradicts historical truth, rests on false assumptions, and is not binding in international law.
2. The government of the Reich must work toward the formal abrogation of the war-guilt clause of Article 231 as well as Articles 429 and 430 of the Versailles Treaty. It must further work toward immediate and unconditional evacuation of the occupied territories and the removal of all control over German territory independent of the acceptance or rejection of the resolutions of the Hague Conference.
3. New burdens and obligations toward foreign powers which rest on the war-guilt clause must not be undertaken. Under this category fall the burdens and obligations that may be taken by Germany on the basis of the experts at Paris and according to the agreements coming from them.
4. Reichschancellors and Reichsministers as well as plenipotentiaries of the German Reich who sign treaties with foreign powers contrary to the prescription of clause number three are subject to the penalties of clause ninety-two, section three of the civil code [*dealing with treason—D.K.*].
5. This law goes into effect at the time of its proclamation.

Part of the reason for the failure of the Weimar Republic may be found in its constitution. The following selections from it are translated, edited, and introduced by Louis Snyder.

FROM The Constitution of the German Republic

AFTER THE GERMAN IMPERIAL GOVERNMENT had been overthrown and the Communist Spartacist revolt put down by force, Germans over nineteen years of age went to the polls on January 19, 1919, to elect a Na-

---

Deutsche Allgemeine Zeitung, No. 422 (September 12, 1929), translated by Donald Kagan.

Louis L. Snyder, ed., *Documents of German History,* pp. 385–92. Copyright 1958 by Rutgers, the State University. Reprinted by permission of Rutgers University Press.

tional Constituent Assembly. More than thirty million men and women elected 423 representatives, with the Majority Socialists leading with 165 seats, the Centrists second with 91 seats, and the Democrats third with 75 seats. The Assembly was controlled by these three top groups (the "Weimar Coalition") out of a dozen or more parties.

The National Constituent Assembly convened at Weimar on February 6, 1919. Weimar was chosen for sentimental reasons: It was believed that the spirit of Goethe had triumphed finally over that of Frederick the Great's Potsdam. The Assembly's sessions were turned by the German nationalists into riotous brawls. After electing Friedrich Ebert as President of the Republic (February 11th), the Assembly began to discuss the Constitution drafted by Dr. Hugo Preuss, a professor of constitutional law and Minister of the Interior. The article causing most heated discussion, that relating to the national colors, was settled by a compromise. The document, passed on July 31st at its third reading, went into effect on August 11, 1919, as the fundamental law of the German Republic.

The Weimar Constitution was a letter-perfect document, seemingly embodying the best features of the British Bill of Rights, the French Declaration of the Rights of Man, and the first Ten Amendments of the American Constitution. However, this magnificent Constitution planned for every contingency except that of preserving itself. Article 48, the "suicide clause," empowered the President to assume dictatorial powers in an emergency. This escape clause proved to be of inestimable value to Hitler later on.

The Weimar Constitution, "the formulation of a stalemate," was a compromise that accepted the outward forms of democracy but breathed no life into the form that had been created. It was attacked bitterly from both the Right and the Left.

The Weimar Republic was burdened by difficulties from its inception. The Social Democratic party had a program, but, in action, it was pitifully impotent. Its leaders, though undeniably men of good intentions, were unable adequately to meet the responsibilities placed upon them: the liquidation of the war, the Treaty of Versailles, reparations, the Ruhr invasion, the collapse of the mark, and the catastrophic decline of the middle class. These men were ruined in public opinion because they had been forced to accept the mission of advocating the conditions that had been imposed upon their fellow citizens. The victorious Allies, who had demanded a German democratic state, now gave but grudging assistance to the fledgling republic. In the Allied countries the suspicion persisted that the Germans had not willingly broken with their imperialist and militaristic past and that the Weimar Republic was devised merely as a necessary expedient in troublous times.

Preamble:

The German people, united in all their racial elements, and inspired by the will to renew and strengthen their Reich in liberty and justice, to preserve peace at home and abroad and to foster social progress, have established the following Constitution:

CHAPTER I: STRUCTURE AND FUNCTIONS OF THE REICH

SECTION I: REICH AND STATES

ARTICLE 1. The German Reich is a Republic. Political authority emanates from the people.

ARTICLE 2. The territory of the Reich consists of the territories of the German member states. . . .

ARTICLE 3. The Reich colors are black, red, and gold. The merchant flag is black, white, and red, with the Reich colors in the upper inside corner.

ARTICLE 4. The generally accepted rules of international law are to be considered as binding integral parts of the German Reich.

ARTICLE 5. Political authority is exercised in national affairs by the national government in accordance with the Constitution of the Reich, and in state affairs by the state governments in accordance with state constitutions. . . .

ARTICLE 12. Insofar as the Reich does not exercise its jurisdiction, such jurisdiction remains with the states . . . with the exception of cases in which the Reich possesses exclusive jurisdiction. . . .

ARTICLE 17. Every state must have a republican constitution. The representatives of the people must be elected by universal, equal, direct, and secret suffrage of all German citizens, both men and women, in accordance with the principles of proportional representation.

SECTION II: THE REICHSTAG

ARTICLE 20. The Reichstag is composed of the delegates of the German people.

ARTICLE 21. The delegates are representatives of the whole people. They are subject only to their own conscience and are not bound by any instructions.

ARTICLE 22. The delegates are elected by universal, equal, direct, and secret suffrage by men and women over twenty years of age, according to the principle of proportional representation. Election day must be a Sunday or a public holiday.

ARTICLE 23. The Reichstag is elected for four years. New elections must take place at the latest on the sixtieth day after this term has run its course. . . .

ARTICLE 32. For decisions of the Reichstag a simple majority vote is necessary, unless the Constitution prescribes another proportion of votes. . . .

ARTICLE 33. The Reichstag and its committees may require the presence of the Reich Chancellor and every Reich Minister. . . .

SECTION III: THE REICH PRESIDENT AND THE REICH CABINET

ARTICLE 41. The Reich President is elected by the whole German people. Every German who has completed his thirty-fifth year is eligible for election. . . .

ARTICLE 42. On assuming office, the Reich President shall take the following oath before the Reichstag:

> I swear to devote my energies to the well-being of the German people, to further their interests, to guard them from injury, to maintain the Constitution and the laws of the Reich, to fulfill my duties conscientiously, and to administer justice for all.

It is permissible to add a religious affirmation.

ARTICLE 43. The term of office of the Reich President is seven years. Re-election is permissible.

Before the expiration of his term, the Reich President, upon motion of the Reichstag, may be recalled by a popular vote. The decision of the Reichstag shall be by a two-thirds majority. Through such decision the Reich President is denied any further exercise of his office. The rejection of the recall motion by the popular referendum counts as a new election and results in the dissolution of the Reichstag.

ARTICLE 48. If any state does not fulfill the duties imposed upon it by the Constitution or the laws of the Reich, the Reich President may enforce such duties with the aid of the armed forces.

In the event that the public order and security are seriously disturbed or endangered, the Reich President may take the measures necessary for their restoration, intervening, if necessary, with the aid of the armed forces. For this purpose he may temporarily abrogate, wholly or in part, the fundamental principles laid down in Articles 114, 115, 117, 118, 123, 124, and 153.

The Reich President must, without delay, inform the Reichstag of all measures taken under Paragraph 1 or Paragraph 2 of this Article. These measures may be rescinded on demand of the Reichstag. . . .

ARTICLE 50. All orders and decrees of the Reich President, including those relating to the armed forces, must, in order to be valid, be countersigned by the Reich Chancellor or by the appropriate Reich Minister. Responsibility is assumed through the countersignature. . . .

ARTICLE 52. The Reich Cabinet consists of the Reich Chancellor and the Reich Ministers.

ARTICLE 53. The Reich Chancellor and, on his recommendation, the Reich Ministers, are appointed and dismissed by the Reich President.

ARTICLE 54. The Reich Chancellor and the Reich Ministers require for the exercise of their office the confidence of the Reichstag. Any one of them must resign if the Reichstag by formal resolution withdraws its confidence.

ARTICLE 55. The Reich Chancellor presides over the government of the Reich and conducts its affairs according to the rules of procedure laid down by the government of the Reich and approved by the Reich President.

ARTICLE 56. The Reich Chancellor determines the political program of the Reich and assumes responsibility to the Reichstag. Within this general policy each Reich Minister conducts independently the office entrusted to him and is held individually responsible to the Reichstag.

SECTION IV: THE REICHSRAT

ARTICLE 60. A Reichsrat is formed to give the German states representation in the law-making and administration of the Reich.

ARTICLE 61. Each state has at least one vote in the Reichsrat. In the case of the larger states one vote shall be assigned for every million inhabitants. . . . No single state shall have more than two fifths of the total number of votes. . . .

ARTICLE 63. The states shall be represented in the Reichsrat by members of their governments. . . .

SECTION V: REICH LEGISLATION

ARTICLE 68. Bills are introduced by the Reich cabinet, with the concurrence of the Reichsrat, or by members of the Reichstag. Reich laws shall be enacted by the Reichstag. . . .

ARTICLE 73. A law of the Reichstag must be submitted to popular referendum before its proclamation, if the Reich President, within one month of its passage, so decides. . . .

ARTICLE 74. The Reichsrat may protest against laws passed by the Reichstag. In case of such protest, the law is returned to the Reichstag, which may override the objection by a two-thirds majority. The Reich President must either promulgate the law within three months or call for a referendum. . . .

ARTICLE 76. The Constitution may be amended by law, but acts . . . amending the Constitution can only take effect if two thirds of the legal number of members are present and at least two thirds of those present consent. . . .

SECTION VI: THE REICH ADMINISTRATION

[Articles 78–101 cover the jurisdiction of the Reich Administration in such matters as foreign affairs, national defense, colonial policies, customs, national budgets, postal and telegraph services, railroads, and waterways.]

SECTION VII: ADMINISTRATION OF JUSTICE

[Articles 102–108 provide for a hierarchy of Reich and state courts, with judges appointed by the Reich President for life.]

CHAPTER II: FUNDAMENTAL RIGHTS AND DUTIES OF THE GERMANS

SECTION I: THE INDIVIDUAL

ARTICLE 109. All Germans are equal before the law. Men and women have the same fundamental civil rights and duties. Public legal privileges or disadvantages of birth or of rank are abolished. Titles of nobility . . . may be bestowed no longer. . . . Orders and decorations shall not be conferred by the state. No German shall accept titles or orders from a foreign government.

ARTICLE 110. Citizenship of the Reich and the states is acquired in accordance with the provisions of a Reich law. . . .

ARTICLE 111. All Germans shall enjoy liberty of travel and residence throughout the whole Reich. . . .

ARTICLE 112. Every German is permitted to emigrate to a foreign country. . . .

ARTICLE 114. Personal liberty is inviolable. Curtailment or deprivation of personal liberty by a public authority is permissible only by authority of law.

Persons who have been deprived of their liberty must be informed at the latest on the following day by whose authority and for what reasons they have been held. They shall receive the opportunity without delay of submitting objections to their deprivation of liberty.

ARTICLE 115. The house of every German is his sanctuary and is inviolable. Exceptions are permitted only by authority of law. . . .

ARTICLE 117. The secrecy of letters and all postal, telegraph, and telephone communications is inviolable. Exceptions are inadmissible except by national law.

ARTICLE 118. Every German has the right, within the limits of the general laws, to express his opinion freely by word, in writing, in print, in picture form, or in any other way. . . . Censorship is forbidden. . . .

SECTION II: THE GENERAL WELFARE

ARTICLE 123. All Germans have the right to assembly peacefully and unarmed without giving notice and without special permission. . . .

ARTICLE 124. All Germans have the right to form associations and societies for purposes not contrary to the criminal law. . . .

ARTICLE 126. Every German has the right to petition. . . .

SECTION III: RELIGION AND RELIGIOUS SOCIETIES

ARTICLE 135. All inhabitants of the Reich enjoy full religious freedom and freedom of conscience. The free exercise of religion is guaranteed by the Constitution and is under public protection. . . .

ARTICLE 137. There is no state church. . . .

SECTION IV: EDUCATION AND THE SCHOOLS

ARTICLE 142. Art, science, and the teaching thereof are free. . . .

ARTICLE 143. The education of the young is to be provided for by means of public institutions. . . .

ARTICLE 144. The entire school system is under the supervision of the state. . . .

ARTICLE 145. Attendance at school is compulsory. . . .

SECTION V: ECONOMIC LIFE

ARTICLE 151. The regulation of economic life must be compatible with the principles of justice, with the aim of attaining humane conditions of existence for all. Within these limits the economic liberty of the individual is assured. . . .

ARTICLE 152. Freedom of contract prevails . . . in accordance with the laws. . . .

ARTICLE 153. The right of private property is guaranteed by the Constitution. . . . Expropriation of property may take place . . . by due process of law. . . .

ARTICLE 159. Freedom of association for the preservation and promotion of labor and economic conditions is guaranteed to everyone and to all vocations. All agreements and measures attempting to restrict or restrain this freedom are unlawful. . . .

ARTICLE 161. The Reich shall organize a comprehensive system of [social] insurance. . . .

ARTICLE 165. Workers and employees are called upon to cooperate, on an equal footing, with employers in the regulation of wages and of the conditions of labor, as well as in the general development of the productive forces. . . .

CONCLUDING PROVISIONS

ARTICLE 181. . . . The German people have passed and adopted this Constitution through their National Assembly. It comes into force with the date of its proclamation.

Schwarzburg, August 11, 1919.

The Reich President
EBERT
The Reich Cabinet
BAUER

ERZBERGER   HERMANN MÜLLER   DR. DAVID
NOSKE   SCHMIDT
SCHLICKE   GIESBERTS   DR. BAYER
DR. BELL

One of the advantages held by the Nazis was that their opponents were badly divided. The left was particularly weakened by the split between the Social Democrats and the Communists. In the following statement Ernst Thäl-mann, head of the Communist Party, expresses the party's position in respect to the Nazis and the Socialists.

The Revolutionary Alternative and the KPD
BY ERNST THÄLMANN

WHAT IS THE CURRENT RELATIONSHIP between the policy of Hitler's party and Social Democracy? The eleventh plenum [*of the German Communist Party—D.K.*] has already spoken of an involvement of both these factors in the service of finance capital. Already in 1924 Comrade Stalin most clearly characterized the role of both these wings when he spoke of them as twins who supplement each other.

Ernst Thälmann, "Der Revolutionäre Ausweg und die KPD," in Hermann Weber, *Der Deutsche Kommunismus Dokumente* (1963), pp. 185–6. Translated by Donald Kagan by permission of Verlag Kiepenheuer & Witseh, Cologne.

At present this development is revealed unmistakably in Germany. . . . In the question of terror organizations, too, the SPD [*German Socialist Party—D.K.*] increasingly copies Hitlerism. In this respect one need only think of the creation of the Reichsbanner or, more recently, of the so-called "hammer units" of the Iron Front, which were to be used as instruments to help the capitalist dictatorship in the defense of the capitalistic system against the revolutionary proletariat.

But above all it is the Prussian government of the SPD and the ADGB [*Free Trade Unions—D.K.*] that, through their actions, fully and completely confirm the role of the Social Democracy as the most active factor in making Germany Fascistic, as the eleventh plenum has stated.

Thus, while the Social Democrats increasingly approach Hitlerite Fascism, Fascism, in turn, emphasizes its legality and lately even steps onto the platform of Brüning's foreign policy. . . .

All these points reveal the far-reaching mutual rapprochement of the SPD and the National Socialists toward the line of Fascism.

WHY MUST WE DIRECT THE CHIEF BLOW AGAINST THE SOCIAL DEMOCRATS?

Our strategy, which directs the chief blow against the Social Democrats without thereby weakening the struggle against Hitlerite Fascism; our strategy, which provides the first assumption of an effective fight against Hitlerite Fascism precisely through the chief blow against the Social Democrats—this strategy is not comprehensible if one has not clearly understood the role of the proletarian classes as the only class that is revolutionary to the end. . . .

The practical application of this strategy in Germany calls for the chief blow against the Social Democracy. With its "left" branches it is the most dangerous support of the enemy of the revolution. It is the major social support of the bourgeoisie; it is the most active factor in creating Fascism, as the eleventh plenum has correctly declared. At the same time it understands in the most dangerous way, as the "more moderate wing of Fascism," how to capture the masses, by its fraudulent maneuvers, for the dictatorship of the bourgeoisie and for its Fascistic methods. To strike the Social Democrats is the same as to conquer the majority of the proletariat and to create the preconditions for the proletarian revolution. . . .

WHAT DOES A POLICY OF A UNITED FRONT MEAN?

To carry out a policy of the revolutionary united front means to pursue a merciless struggle against Social Fascists of every shade, especially against the most dangerous "left" variety of Social Fascism, against the SAPD [*Socialist Workers Party—D.K.*], against the Brandler Group and similar cliques and tendencies.

To pursue a policy of the revolutionary united front means to mobilize the masses for the struggle really from below, in the factories and in the unemployment offices.

A policy of a revolutionary united front cannot come to pass through parliamentary negotiations. It cannot happen through accommodation with other parties or groups, but it must grow from the movement of the masses and be supported by that movement and present a really living fighting front.

There is no negotiation of the KDP with the SDP, SAPD, or Brandler Group; there must be none!

One important source of support for Hitler came from the German business community, which helped him both politically and financially. The following documents illustrate the nature of their support.

Poechlinger's Letter to Krupp

Director of the Leading Department,
Certified Engineer JOSEF POECHLINGER
Press Representative of the Reichs
    Minister, Dr. TODT.

Berlin, W.8.   12.3.41.
Pariser Place, 3,
Telephone No. 11 6481.
[note in pencil: For attention of Mr. Goerferns]
[Stamp: Reply given as per enclosure, 14.3.41].

Dr Krupp von Bohlen und Halbach,
Essen.
at the Huegel.

Dear Dr. Krupp,

BY REQUEST OF THE REICHS MINISTER, Dr. Todt, I am preparing to publish a presentation book for the German armament worker, in which he will be honoured on the account of his hard work for the German armament industry.

Office of United States Chief Counsel for Prosecution of Axis Criminality, *Nazi Conspiracy and Aggression,* VI (1946), 1030–1.

The structure of the book is as follows:—

1. Dr. Todt Introduction.
2. Josef Weinheber. Ode to the German Armaments Worker.
3. Josef Poechlinger. "The Meaning of Work."
4. M. Schulze-Fielitz (Reichs Ministry for Arms and Munitions), "The Organization of the German Armament Industry."
5. Reichs Department Leader Fuehrer (Chief Department of Technology, NSDAP). "The Employment of the Parties for the German Armament Industry."
6. —— "Works Leader and Armament Worker."
7. Maier-Dorn, Reichs School Trustee of the National Socialist Union of German Technology. "Front Line Soldier and Armament Worker."
8. Gauleiter Krebs. "Your Contribution to the Great Reich."

May I ask whether you would be prepared to compile the chapter "Works Leader and Armament Worker"? A work of approximately twenty typewritten pages would be sufficient, in which you would briefly and pleasantly describe, in your capacity of the best-known and most authoritative representative of the German armament industry, the relationship between the works leader and armament worker, as well as your observations, adventures and experiences in connection with the workers.

The article would have to reach me in about four weeks.

I shall be grateful for a brief notification whether you are prepared to take on this work.

> Heil Hitler:
> Yours very sincerely,
> (Sgd.) POECHLINGER.

FROM *Draft of Works Leader and Armaments Works* BY GUSTAV KRUPP

EVERYONE CAN GATHER the significance of the outcome of the war for the Krupp works as well as for my wife and myself, without my writing about it at great length. It is general knowledge that hardly any works were so badly hit by the Treaty of Versailles as Krupp. At this point, once more, I should like to reiterate a few shattering figures. After the signing of the peace, values amounting to 104 million goldmarks were destroyed at our works. Nine thousand three hundred machines, with a total weight of 60,000

Office of United States Chief Counsel for Prosecution of Axis Criminality, *Nazi Conspiracy and Aggression*, VI (1946), 1031–4.

tons were demolished or destroyed amounting to nearly half of our entire machinery of November 1918. Eight hundred and one thousand, four hundred and twenty pieces of gauges, moulds, jigs and tools, with a total weight of 9588 tons were destroyed. Three hundred and seventy-nine plants, such as presses, hardening ovens, oil and water tanks, cooling plants and cranes were smashed.

In those days the situation seemed hopeless at times. It appeared even more desperate if one remained as firmly convinced as I was that "Versailles" could not represent the end.

Everything in me revolted against believing, and many many Germans felt likewise, that the German people should remain enslaved forever.

I knew German history only too well, and I believed, particularly with my experiences in other parts of the world, that I knew the German people. For that reason, I never believed that, in spite of all existing evidence to the contrary, a change would come one day; I did not know, nor did I ask myself that question, but I believed in it; but owing to this—and today I can talk about these things, and this is the first time that I do so publicly and at length—owing to this, I emphasize, I, as the responsible leader of the Krupp Works, had to come to conclusions of great significance. If ever there should be a resurrection for Germany, if ever she were to shake off the chains of Versailles, then Krupp would have to be prepared.

The machines were demolished; the tools were destroyed; but one thing had remained—the men, the men at the drawing boards and in the workshops, who, in happy co-operation had brought the manufacture of guns to its last perfection. Their skill would have to be saved, these immense resources of knowledge and experience. The decisions of that period were, probably, amongst the most difficult ones of my life. Even though camouflaged I had to maintain Krupps as an armament factory for the distant future, in spite of all obstacles. Only in a very small and most trustworthy circle could I speak about the actual reasons which caused me to pursue this intention of reorganizing the works for the production of certain definite articles. I had to be prepared, therefore, to be generally misunderstood, probably have ridicule heaped upon myself—as it promptly occurred, of course—but never in my life have I felt the inner urge for my actions as strongly as in those fateful weeks and months of the years 1919-20. Just then I felt myself fully part of the magic circle of the solid community of the workers. I understood the sentiments of my workers, who until now had so proudly worked for Germany's defense and who now were suddenly to undergo what, from their point of view, meant some sort of degradation. I owed it to them, too, to keep my chin up, and think of a better future. Without losing time or skilled men the necessary preparations were made and measures taken. Thus, to the surprise of many people, Krupps concentrated on the manufacture of articles which seemed to be particularly remote from the activities of the weapon-smithy. Even the Allied spying commission was fooled. Padlocks, milk cans, cash registers, rail mending machines, refuse carts and similar rubbish appeared really innocent, and locomotives and motor cars appeared perfectly "peaceful."

In this manner, during years of unobtrusive work, we created the scientific and material conditions which were necessary in order to be ready to work for the Armed Forces of the Reich at the right hour, and without loss of time and experience. Many a fellow worker will have had his own private thoughts and often have been without a clue, just why he was employed in this and that manner.

The whole reorganization, furthermore, was not only a personnel problem and of a purely technical character, but was also of immense economic significance. Our new production had to meet competition, far superior because of its considerable start.

It was my aim at all times, even when measures for the reduction of personnel were simply unavoidable, to maintain the nucleus of the workers at Krupp, whom we would need one day,—and nothing could deter me from that contention—for the purpose of rearmament.

After the assumption of power by Adolf Hitler I had the satisfaction of being able to report to the Fuehrer that Krupp needed only a short period to get ready for the re-arming of the German people and that there were no gaps in our experience. The blood of our comrades had not been shed in vain on that Passion Saturday of 1923. Thus, many a time I was able to walk through the old and new work-shops with him and to experience the gratitude expressed in the cheers of the workers of Krupps.

We worked with incredible zeal during those years after 1933, and finally when war broke out, speed and output increased still further. We are, all of us, proud that we have thus been able to contribute to the tremendous successes of our Forces.

It may appear that this record of mine is of too personal a character. But when I spoke of myself and the business concern in my trust, when I spoke of my experiences and impressions during a long life, I only did so to make the subject "Works Leader and Armament Worker" more colourful and descriptive, in preference to treating it under general headings.

I am standing here not wanting to make myself an example, for many another man who has been put into his key position in the German armament industry through fate, and, I think, his suitability. Like the workers of Krupps, these workers, too, are doing their duty faithfully in many other works. I have always considered it an honour, as well as an obligation, to be the leader of an armaments plant, and I know that the workers of Krupps share these sentiments.

This, thanks to the educational work of the National Socialist Leaders of the State, this is the same everywhere in Germany. What I have said especially about the armament worker applies, and this I know, to simply every German worker; with the help of these men and women, working with all their hearts, cool heads and skilled hands for the great whole, we shall succeed whatever our fate may be.

FROM *Interrogation of Dr. Hjalmar Schacht at "Dustbin"*

INTERROGATOR: C. J. HYNNING

Q. When did you next see Goering?

A. He invited me to a party in his house for the first of January 1931, where I met Hitler.

Q. Did you meet anybody else?

A. At that party Fritz Thyssen was also present, and that evening Hitler made a long speech, for almost two hours, although the company was a small one.

Q. Was that a monologue?

A. An entire monologue and everything that he said was reasonable and moderate that night.

Q. What did he say?

A. Oh, ideas he expressed before, but it was full of will and spirit.

Q. What did he say?

A. He elaborated his program as it was outlined more extensively in his book.

Q. And in the party platform?

A. Yes, also the party platform. But the platform is very short and brief, it is not so full of general phrases.

Q. Were there any prominent officers present?

A. No.

Q. Any industrialists like Fritz Thyssen?

A. No.

Q. What was your impression at the end of that evening?

A. I thought that Hitler was a man with whom one could cooperate.

Office of the United States Chief Counsel for Prosecution of Axis Criminality, *Nazi Conspiracy and Aggression*, VI (1946), 464–5.

Q. Did you think he was a man of the future and that you had to deal with him as a man of the future?

A. Well, I could not know that at the time.

Q. Did you think it desirable to join the Nazi Party at that time?

A. I can't tell you as to that time, but if his ideas, which he developed that night, were backed by a big party, as it seemed to be, I think that one could join that group for public purposes.

Q. Let us then direct our attention to February and March 1933. I have been told by Goering and by Funk and Baron von Schnizler and also by Thyssen, that there was a meeting held in the house of Goering of certain prominent German industrialists at which you were also present in 1933. This was after Hitler became chancellor but before the elections of that spring. Hitler came into the meeting and made a short speech and left. Then, according to the testimony of Funk, you passed the hat. You asked the industrialists to support the Nazi Party financially to the tune of approximately 7, 8, 9 or 10 million marks. Do you recall that?

A. I recall that meeting very well. And I have answered the same question to Major Tilley. It must be in one of my former memorandums or in the hearings done by Major Tilley. As far as I remember, the meeting was not in Goering's house, but in some hotel room I think, or some other more public room. After Hitler had made his speech the old Krupp von Bohlen answered Hitler and expressed the unanimous feeling of the industrialists to support Hitler. After that I spoke for the financial part only, not on political principles or intentions. And the amount which I collected was 3 million marks. The apportionment amongst the industrialists was made not by me but by they themselves and the payments afterwards were made to the bank of Delbruck Schickler. The books will certainly show the amounts which were paid in and which went to the party. I had nothing to do with that account. I just played the role of cashier or financial treasurer at the meeting itself.

3 The Democratic Spirit in Germany

It is important to remember that many Germans were loyal to the republic and its constitution and determined to make German democracy a success and a reality. The following exerpt from Lilo Linke's account of her youth illustrates the enthusiasm some Germans felt for the new German state.

FROM *Restless Days* BY LILO LINKE

THE UNIVERSITY WAS ONE OF THE CENTRES of liberal thought and welcomed us heartily. So did half a dozen high officials from the Republic of Baden, the town, the Reichsbanner, the Democratic Party. In their united opinion we were the hope of Germany, born into a nation which our fathers had freed and refounded seven years ago on the principles of liberty and democracy. In this new Germany there was room for all, the hand of brotherhood was stretched out and encouragement was given to those who were full of goodwill. Our task, the task of the young, was to grow up as true and worthy citizens of this free Republic.

When the last speaker had concluded his address, the signal for the fireworks was given, and a few minutes later the ruins seemed to be burning again in red flames and smoke, golden stars shot up into the air, silver waterfalls sparkled, orange-coloured wheels rolled over the sky, rising and descending to make room for the next. But before the final cascade had died away, torch-bearers ran over the courtyard to kindle the two thousand torches which meanwhile had been distributed among all of us, rousing a waving ocean of light.

A procession was formed, headed by the military band with triangles and drums and clarinets and followed by the members of the movement, two abreast, holding their torches in their upraised hands. We marched through the town, our ghostly magnified shadows moving restlessly over the fronts of the houses.

Never before had I followed the flag of the Republic, which was now waving thirty yards in front of me, spreading its colours overhead, the black melting in one with the night, the red glowing in the light of the torches, and the gold overshining them like a dancing sun. It was not just a torchlight march for me, it was a political confession. I had decided to take part in the struggle for German democracy, I wanted to fight for it although I knew that this meant a challenge to my parents and my whole family, who all lived with their eyes turned towards the past and thought it disloyal and shameful to help the Socialists.

From the band a song floated back through the long columns, a defiant determined song:

> We do not call it liberty
> When mercy grants us right,
> When our cunning enemy
> Is checked today by fright.
> Not king alone and army,
> But strong-box we must fight.
> Powder is black,
> Blood is red,
> Golden flickers the flame.

We marched out of the town to the cemetery, where the first President of the Republic, Fritz Ebert, had been buried. Silently we assembled round the grave. Wilhelm Wismar, national leader of the Young Democrats and youngest member of the Reichstag, stepped forward and spoke slowly the oath:

"We vow to stand for the Republic with all our abilities and strength.

"We vow to work for the fulfilment of the promises given to the German people in the Weimar Constitution.

"We vow to shield and defend democracy against all its enemies and attackers whoever they might be."

And out of the night in a rolling echo two thousand citizens of tomorrow answered, repeating solemnly word for word:

"We vow to stand for the Republic with all our abilities and strength.

"We vow to work for the fulfilment of the promises given to the German people in the Weimar Constitution.

"We vow to shield and defend democracy against all its enemies and attackers whoever they might be."

4 *The Nazi Program*

FROM *National Socialistic Yearbook 1941*

THE PROGRAM OF THE NSDAP

THE PROGRAM is the political foundation of the NSDAP and accordingly the primary political law of the State. It has been made brief and clear intentionally.

All legal precepts must be applied in the spirit of the party program.

Since the taking over of control, the Fuehrer has succeeded in the realization of essential portions of the Party program from the fundamentals to the detail.

The Party Program of the NSDAP was proclaimed on the 24 February 1920 by Adolf Hitler at the first large Party gathering in Munich and since that day has remained unaltered. Within the national socialist philosophy is summarized in 25 points:

1. We demand the unification of all Germans in the Greater Germany on the basis of the right of self-determination of peoples.
2. We demand equality of rights for the German people in respect to the other nations; abrogation of the peace treaties of Versailles and St. Germain.
3. We demand land and territory (colonies) for the sustenance of our people, and colonization for our surplus population.
4. Only a member of the race can be a citizen. A member of the race can only be one who is of German blood, without consideration of creed. Consequently no Jew can be a member of the race.
5. Whoever has no citizenship is to be able to live in Germany only as a guest, and must be under the authority of legislation for foreigners.
6. The right to determine matters concerning administration and law belongs only to the citizen. Therefore we demand that every public office, of any sort whatsoever, whether in the Reich, the county or municipality, be filled only by citizens. We combat the corrupting parliamentary economy, office-holding only according to party inclinations without consideration of character or abilities.

Office of United States Counsel for Prosecution of Axis Criminality, *Nazi Conspiracy and Aggression,* IV (1946), 208–11.

7. We demand that the state be charged first with providing the opportunity for a livelihood and way of life for the citizens. If it is impossible to sustain the total population of the State, then the members of foreign nations (non-citizens) are to be expelled from the Reich.
8. Any further immigration of non-citizens is to be prevented. We demand that all non-Germans, who have immigrated to Germany since the 2 August 1914, be forced immediately to leave the Reich.
9. All citizens must have equal rights and obligations.
10. The first obligation of every citizen must be to work both spiritually and physically. The activity of individuals is not to counteract the interests of the universality, but must have its result within the framework of the whole for the benefit of all.

Consequently we demand:

11. Abolition of unearned (work and labour) incomes. Breaking of rent-slavery.
12. In consideration of the monstrous sacrifice in property and blood that each war demands of the people personal enrichment through a war must be designated as a crime against the people. Therefore we demand the total confiscation of all war profits.
13. We demand the nationalization of all (previous) associated industries (trusts).
14. We demand a division of profits of all heavy industries.
15. We demand an expansion on a large scale of old age welfare.
16. We demand the creation of a healthy middle class and its conservation, immediate communalization of the great warehouses and their being leased at low cost to small firms, the utmost consideration of all small firms in contracts with the State, county or municipality.
17. We demand a land reform suitable to our needs, provision of a law for the free expropriation of land for the purposes of public utility, abolition of taxes on land and prevention of all speculation in land.
18. We demand struggle without consideration against those whose activity is injurious to the general interest. Common national criminals, usurers, Schieber and so forth are to be punished with death, without consideration of confession or race.
19. We demand substitution of a German common law in place of the Roman Law serving a materialistic world-order.
20. The state is to be responsible for a fundamental reconstruction of our whole national education program, to enable every capable and industrious German to obtain higher education and subsequently introduction into leading positions. The plans of instruction of all educational institutions are to conform with the experiences of practical life. The comprehension of the concept of the State must be striven for by the school [Staatsbuergerkunde] as early as the beginning of understanding. We demand the education at the expense of the State of outstanding

intellectually gifted children of poor parents without consideration of position or profession.

21. The State is to care for the elevating of national health by protecting the mother and child, by outlawing child-labor, by the encouragement of physical fitness, by means of the legal establishment of a gymnastic and sport obligation, by the utmost support of all organizations concerned with the physical instruction of the young.

22. We demand abolition of the mercenary troops and formation of a national army.

23. We demand legal opposition to known lies and their promulgation through the press. In order to enable the provision of a German press, we demand, that: a. All writers and employees of the newspapers appearing in the German language be members of the race: b. Non-German newspapers be required to have the express permission of the State to be published. They may not be printed in the German language: c. Non-Germans are forbidden by law any financial interest in German publications, or any influence on them, and as punishment for violations the closing of such a publication as well as the immediate expulsion from the Reich of the non-German concerned. Publications which are counter to the general good are to be forbidden. We demand legal prosecution of artistic and literary forms which exert a destructive influence on our national life, and the closure of organizations opposing the above made demands.

24. We demand freedom of religion for all religious denominations within the state so long as they do not endanger its existence or oppose the moral senses of the Germanic race. The Party as such advocates the standpoint of a positive Christianity without binding itself confessionally to any one denomination. It combats the Jewish-materialistic spirit within and around us, and is convinced that a lasting recovery of our nation can only succeed from within on the framework: common utility precedes individual utility.

25. For the execution of all of this we demand the formation of a strong central power in the Reich. Unlimited authority of the central parliament over the whole Reich and its organizations in general. The forming of state and profession chambers for the execution of the laws made by the Reich within the various states of the confederation. The leaders of the Party promise, if necessary by sacrificing their own lives, to support by the execution of the points set forth above without consideration.

Adolf Hitler proclaimed the following explanation for this program on the 13 April 1928:

EXPLANATION

Regarding the false interpretations of Point 17 of the Program of the NSDAP on the part of our opponents, the following definition is necessary:

"Since the NSDAP stands on the platform of private ownership it happens that the passage" gratuitous expropriation concerns only the creation of legal opportunities to expropriate if necessary, land which has been illegally acquired or is not administered from the view-point of the national welfare. This is directed primarily against the Jewish land-speculation companies.

5 *The Influence of Germany's Past*

*Some scholars have suggested that one of the great appeals
of Nazism was its ardent militarism and war spirit, which
corresponded with similar sentiments embedded in the history and character of Germany. In the following selection
Louis Snyder introduces evidence of the cultivation of such
notions in both Weimar and Hitler Germany.*

FROM *Documents of German History*

ALL NATIONS HAVE AT ONE TIME OR ANOTHER been victims of
the diseases of jingoism and chauvinism. The glorification of war has been the
prime aim of super-patriots everywhere. But in Germany the phenomenon has
been so persistent that it merits the special attention of the historian. Such historians as Heinrich von Treitschke ("Those who preach the nonsense of eternal peace do not understand Aryan national life"), such militarists as
Friedrich von Bernhardi ("War is a biological necessity"), and such leaders
as Adolf Hitler ("In eternal peace, mankind perishes") expressed a point of
view that was not unique but widespread. In both world wars, Allied
propagandists published bulky collections of German quotations glorifying
war, which were strongly effective in solidifying world public opinion against
Germany.

The war spirit infected institutions both of higher and lower education.
In the first extract quoted here, a superintendent of schools during the era of
the Weimar Republic gave his suggestion for a student's composition on the
advantages of war. The following two poems show how first-grade children
during the Hitler regime were encouraged to imbibe the war spirit.

DRAFT FOR A STUDENT COMPOSITION ON THE ADVANTAGES OF WAR, 1927

I. FOR THE NATION:

1. War is the antidote for the weeds of peace, during which intellectualism
takes precedence over idealism and puts everything to sleep.

Louis L. Snyder, ed., *Documents of German History*, pp. 408–10. Copyright 1958 by Rutgers,
the State University. Reprinted by permission of Rutgers University Press.

2. Patriotism is stimulated, and a sacred enthusiasm for the Fatherland is awakened.
3. The triumphant nation obtains a position of power, as well as the prestige and influence it deserves; the honor of the defeated nation is not affected at all if it has defended itself with courage.
4. Peoples learn to know each other better and to respect one another. There is an exchange of ideas, opinions, points of view.
5. Trade finds new routes, often favorable ones.
6. The arts, especially poetry and painting, are given excellent subjects.

II. FOR THE CITIZENS:

1. War gives them the opportunity to develop their talents. Without war the world would have fewer great men.
2. War enables many virtues to assert themselves.
3. Many active persons get the opportunity to make great fortunes.
4. It is sweet to die for the Fatherland. The dead of the enemy live in the memory of the victor.

POEMS FROM FIRST-YEAR READERS, 1940

A

Trum, trum, trum!
There they march,
Always in step,
One, two, one, two,
Teo is also there.
Dieter plays the drums.
Trum, trum, trum!

B

He who wants to be a soldier,
That one must have a weapon,
Which he must load with powder,
And with a good hard bullet.
Little fellow, if you want to be a recruit,
Take good care of this little song!

Both racism and anti-Semitism had roots in German history and were not confined to the Nazis. Hitler, however, made brilliant use of these sentiments to win support for his own party.

FROM *Hitler's Speeches*

THE GERMAN PEOPLE was once clear thinking and simple: why has it lost these characteristics? Any inner renewal is possible only if one realizes that this is a question of race: America forbids the yellow peoples to settle there, but this is a lesser peril than that which stretches out its hand over the entire world—the Jewish peril. "Many hold that the Jews are not a race, but is there a second people anywhere in the wide world which is so determined to maintain its race?"

"As a matter of fact the Jew can never become a German however often he may affirm that he can. If he wished to become a German, he must surrender the Jew in him. And that is not possible: he cannot, however much he try, become a German at heart, and that for several reasons: first because of his blood, second because of his character, thirdly because of his will, and fourthly because of his actions. His actions remain Jewish: he works for the 'greater idea' of the Jewish people. Because that is so, because it cannot be otherwise, therefore the bare existence of the Jew as part of another State rests upon a monstrous lie. It is a lie when he pretends to the peoples to be a German, a Frenchman, &c."

"What then are the specifically Jewish aims?"

"To spread their invisible State as a supreme tyranny over all other States in the whole world. The Jew is therefore a disintegrator of peoples. To realize his rule over the peoples he must work in two directions: in economics he dominates peoples when he subjugates them politically and morally: in politics he dominates them through the propagation of the principles of democracy and the doctrines of Marxism—the creed which makes a Proletarian a Terrorist in the domestic sphere and a Pacifist in foreign policy. Ethically the Jew destroys the peoples both in religion and in morals. He who wishes to see that can see it, and him who refuses to see it no one can help."

"The Jew, whether consciously or unconsciously, whether he wishes it or not, undermines the platform on which alone a nation can stand."

"We are now met by the question: Do we wish to restore Germany to

The Speeches of Adolf Hitler, I (1942), 59–61, translated and edited by Norman Baynes, published by Oxford University Press under the auspices of the Royal Institute of International Affairs, London.

freedom and power? If 'yes': then the first thing to do is to rescue it from him who is ruining our country. Admittedly it is a hard fight that must be fought here. We National Socialists on this point occupy an extreme position: but we know only one people: it is for that people we fight and that is our own people. . . . We want to stir up a storm. Men must not sleep: they ought to know that a thunder-storm is coming up. We want to prevent our Germany from suffering, as Another did, the death upon the Cross."

"We may be inhumane, but if we rescue Germany we have achieved the greatest deed in the world! We may work injustice, but if we rescue Germany then we have removed the greatest injustice in the world. We may be immoral, but if our people is rescued we have once more opened up the way for morality!"

In a speech on "Race and Economics: the German Workman in the National Socialist State," delivered on 24 April 1923 Hitler said:

"I reject the word 'Proletariat.' The Jew who coined the word meant by 'Proletariat,' not the oppressed, but those who work with their hands. And those who work with their intellects are stigmatized bluntly as 'Bourgeois.' It is not the character of a man's life which forms the basis of this classification, it is simply the occupation—whether a man works with his brain or with his body. And in this turbulent mass of the hand-workers the Jew recognized a new power which might perhaps be his instrument for the gaining of that which is his ultimate goal: World-supremacy, the destruction of the national States."

"And while the Jew 'organizes' these masses, he organizes business (*Wirtschaft*), too, at the same time. Business was depersonalized, i.e., Judaized. Business lost the Aryan character of work: it became an object of speculation. Master and man (*Unternehmer und Arbeiter*) were torn asunder . . . and he who created this class-division was the same person who led the masses in their opposition to this class-division, led them not against his Jewish brethren, but against the last remnants of independent national economic life (*Wirtschaft*)."

"And these remnants, the *bourgeoisie* which also was already Judaized, resisted the great masses who were knocking at the door and demanding better conditions of life. And so the Jewish leaders succeeded in hammering into the minds of the masses the Marxist propaganda: 'Your deadly foe is the *bourgeois,* if he were not there, you would be free.' If it had not been for the boundless blindness and stupidity of our *bourgeoisie* the Jew would never have become the leader of the German working-classes. And the ally of this stupidity was the pride of the 'better stratum' of society which thought it would degrade itself if it condescended to stoop to the level of the 'Plebs.' The millions of our German fellow-countrymen would never have been alienated from their people if the leading strata of society had shown any care for their welfare."

It has been suggested that the Germans have always been peculiarly susceptible to autocratic government. Whatever truth there may be in that, there is no question that Hitler openly announced and advertised the dictatorial and autocratic nature of his proposed regime and contrasted it to the weak and inefficient democratic republic of Weimar.

FROM *Organization Book of the NSDAP*

THE ORGANIZATION OF THE NSDAP AND ITS AFFILIATED ASSOCIATIONS

THE PARTY WAS CREATED by the Fuehrer out of the realization that if our people were to live and advance towards an era of prosperity they had to be led according to an ideology suitable for our race. They must have as supporters men above average, that means, men who surpass others in self-control, discipline, efficiency, and greater judgment. The party will therefore always constitute a minority, the order of the National Socialist ideology which comprises the leading elements of our people.

Therefore the party comprises only fighters, at all times prepared to assume and to give everything for the furtherance of the National Socialist ideology. Men and women whose primary and most sacred duty is to serve the people.

The NSDAP as the leading element of the German people control the entire public life, from an organizational point of view, as well as from that of affiliates, the organizations of the State administration, and so forth.

In the long run it will be impossible to let leaders retain responsible offices if they have not been recognized by the Party.

Furthermore, the party shall create the prerequisites for a systematic selection of potential "Fuehrers."

The reconstruction of the National Socialist organizational structure itself is demonstrated by the observation of the following principles:

The Fuehrer Principle.
The subordination and coordination within the structure of the entire organization.
The regional unity.
The expression of the practical community thought.

Office of United States Chief Counsel for Prosecution of Axis Criminality, *Nazi Conspiracy and Aggression*, IV (1946), 411–4.

I. FUEHRER PRINCIPLE [FUEHRERPRINZIP]

The Fuehrer Principle requires a pyramidal organization structure in its details as well as in its entirety.

The Fuehrer is at the top.

He nominates the necessary leaders for the various spheres of work of the Reich's direction, the Party apparatus and the State administration.

Thus a clear picture of the tasks of the party is given.

The Party is the order of "Fuehrers." It is furthermore responsible for the spiritual-ideological National Socialist direction of the German people. The right to organize people for their own sake emanates from these reasons.

This also justifies the subordination to the party of the organizations concerned with the welfare of the people, besides the inclusion of people in the affiliates of the party, the SA, SS, NSKK, the Hitler Youth, the NS Womanhood, the NS German Student Association and the NS German "Dozentenbund" [University teachers association].

This is where the National Socialist Fuehrer structure becomes more strongly apparent.

Every single affiliate is cared for by an office of the NSDAP.

The leadership of the individual affiliates is appointed by the Party.

The Reich Organization Leader [Reichsorganisationsleiter] of the NSDAP is simultaneously leader of the DAF. The NSBO is the organization bearer of the DAF.

The Leader of the Head-Office for Public Welfare also handles within the "Personalunion" the National Socialist Welfare and the Winter Relief. The same applies to:

The Reich Justice Office [Reichsrechtsamt] for the NS "Rechtswahrerbund,"

The head office for public health for the NS. German Medical Association,

The head office for educators for the NS Teachers Association,

The head office for civil servants for the Reich Association of Civil Servants,

The head office for war victims for the NS. War Victim Relief,

The head office for technology for the NS. Association of German Technology.

The Racial Political Office handles the Reich Association of families with many children, the NS Womanhood [Frauenschaft] and the "Deutches Frauenwerk."

The Reich Office for agrarian politics of the NSDAP remains furthermore in closest touch with the "Reichnaehrstand" [Reich Nutrition Office] which is anchored in the State. Direct handling and personal contact of the leaders is also provided in this manner.

All attached affiliates, as well as the offices of the Party, have their foundation, in the same manner as in the Reich direction, in the sovereign territories, in the "Gaue" and furthermore in the districts (Kreise) and if required in the local groups of the NSDAP. This applies also to cells and blocks in the case of the NS Womanhood, the DAF, and the NSV. The members of the attached affiliates will be included in local administrations, respectively district sectors or district comradeships which correspond geographically to local groups of the Party.

II. FUEHRER PRINCIPLE. SUBORDINATION AND COORDINATION WITHIN THE TOTAL ORGANIZATIONAL STRUCTURE

The Fuehrer structure would be split, though, if all subdivisions, including attached affiliates were completely independent in their structure from the smallest unit up to the "Reichsfuehrung" and were they to come only at the top directly under the Fuehrer.

Like a four-story building, if we consider the four Sovereign territories [Reich, Gau, etc.] whose pillars and walls go up to the roof without having supporting joists (wooden stays) or connections on the various floors. Furthermore, it would not be reconcilable with the Fuehrer principle, which assumes complete responsibility, to assume that the Leader of a sub-division, as well as of an affiliated organization, would be in the position to guarantee beyond a professional and factual responsibility the political and ideological attitude of *all* the sub-leaders down to the smallest unit on the basis of his Reich leadership. The total independence of individual organizations would necessitate furthermore, the creation of an organizational, personal and educational apparatus for each one of them. This, in turn, would create eventually, in spite of the best will of the responsible "Reichsleiters" [Reich Leaders], central offices and office leaders in the Reich Leadership [Reichsfuehrung] of the party, differences in the various organizations. Those differences would later on of necessity take the shape of completely different systems in regional, vertical, and personal respects, etc. within the National Socialist regime.

The Subdivisions NS German Student Association, NS Womanhood Association, NSD [Dozentenbund] and the affiliates and their leaders come therefore under the authority of the competent sovereign leaders of the NSDAP. At the same time their structure is professionally effectuated from the bottom up and they are subordinated to their immediately superior organization in the sovereign divisions of the Party, from a disciplinary point of view, that is to say insofar as organization, ideology, politics, supervision and personal questions are concerned.

Thus a solid anchorage for all the organizations within the party structure is provided and a firm connection with the sovereign leaders of the NSDAP is created in accordance with the Fuehrer Principle.

6   The Burden of Germany's Past

A. J. P. Taylor argues that the destruction of the republic and the coming of Nazism was inherent in the history of Germany.

FROM *The Course of German History*

BY A. J. P. TAYLOR

IN 1930 PARLIAMENTARY RULE ceased in Germany. There followed, first, temporary dictatorship, then permanent dictatorship. Technically the Reichstag remained sovereign (as it does to the present day); actually Germany was ruled by emergency decrees, which the democratic parties tolerated as the "lesser evil"—the greater evil being to provoke a civil conflict in defence of democracy. Unemployment, the result of the economic crisis, sapped the spirit of the skilled workers, who were the only reliable republicans. Their skill had been the one secure possession to survive the inflation; unemployment made it as worthless as the paper savings of the middle classes. Therefore, though still loyal to the republic, they became half-hearted, indifferent to events, feeling that they stood for a cause which was already lost, ready to respond, though with shame, to a "national" appeal. The depression, too, completed the demoralization of the respectable middle class. The brief period of prosperity had stimulated a tendency, or its beginning, to postpone "revenge" to a distant future—just as French pacificism after 1871 began as a very temporary affair. Of course Versailles had to be destroyed, but not while profits were mounting, not while salaries were good, not while more and more bureaucratic posts were being created; the German bourgeoisie felt that their generation had done enough for Germany. But in 1930, with the ending of prosperity, the distant future of "revenge" arrived: the crisis seemed almost a punishment for the wickedness of neglecting the restoration of German honour and power. As for the great capitalists, they welcomed the depression, for it enabled them to carry still further the process of rationalization, which had been its cause. As one of them exclaimed:

"This is the crisis we need!" They could shake off both the remnants of Allied control and the weak ineffective brake of the republic, could make their monopolies still bigger, could compel even the Allies to welcome German rearmament as the only alternative to social revolution.

The republic had been an empty shell; still its open supersession in 1930 created a revolutionary atmosphere, in which projects of universal upheaval could flourish. Now, if ever, was the time of the Communists, who saw their prophecies of capitalist collapse come true. But the Communists made nothing of their opportunity: they still regarded the Social Democrats as their chief enemy, still strove to increase confusion and disorder in the belief that a revolutionary situation would carry them automatically into power. The German Communists, with their pseudo-revolutionary jargon, were silly enough to evolve this theory themselves; but they were prompted on their way by the orders of the Comintern, which was still obsessed with the fear of a capitalist intervention against the Soviet Union and so desired above everything else to break the democratic link between Germany and western Europe. The Soviet leaders, with their old-fashioned Marxist outlook, thought that the German army leaders were still drawn exclusively from the Prussian Junkers and therefore counted confidently on a renewal of the old Russo-Prussian friendship. In 1930 German democracy was probably too far gone to have been saved by any change of policy; still the Communist line prevented the united front of Communist and Social Democratic workers which was the last hope of the republic. The Communists were not very effective; so far as they had an effect at all it was to add to the political demoralization, to act as the pioneers for violence and dishonesty, to prepare the way for a party which had in very truth freed itself from the shackles of "bourgeois morality," even from the morality devised by the German bourgeois thinker, Karl Marx.

To talk of a "party," however, is to echo the misunderstandings of those lamentable years. The National Socialists were not a party in any political sense, but a movement: they were action without thought, the union of all those who had lost their bearings and asked only a change of circumstances no matter what. At the heart of the National Socialists were the Free Corps, the wild mercenaries of the post-war years, whose "patriotism" had taken the form of shooting German workers. The Munich rising in November 1923 had been the last splutter of their Free Corps days. Since then they had been taught discipline by a ruthless gangster leader, Hitler, a man bent on destruction, "the unknown soldier of the last war," but unfortunately not buried, expressing in every turn of his personality the bitter disillusionment of the trenches; and a greater master of hysteric oratory than either Frederick William IV or William II. The National Socialists had no programme, still less a defined class interest; they stood simply for destruction and action, not contradictory but complementary. They united in their ranks the disillusioned of every class: the army officer who had failed to find a place in civil life; the ruined capitalist; the unemployed worker; but, most of all, the "white collar" worker of the lower middle class, on whom the greatest burden of the post-war years had fallen. The unemployed clerk; the university student who had failed in his examinations; the incompetent lawyer and the blundering doctor: all these could exchange their shabby threadbare suits for the smart uniforms of the National Socialist army and could find in Hitler's promise of action new hope for themselves. In England they would have been shipped off to the colonies as remittance men: their presence in Germany was the high price which the victors of 1918 paid for the worthless tracts of German colonial territory.

The failure of the Munich rising in 1923 had taught Hitler a bitter lesson: he must not run head on against the army and the possessing classes. From that moment until September 1933 he used the method of intrigue, of terror and persuasion, not the method of open assault. Just as the Communists had tried to outbid the "national" parties in whipping up nationalist passion, so now Hitler outbid the Communists, but with the added attraction, for the upper classes, that this nationalist passion would be turned against the German working classes as well. He was at once everyone's enemy and everyone's friend: his programme of contradictory principles could succeed only in a community which had already lost all unity and self-confidence. To the workers he offered employment; to the lower-middle classes a new self-respect and importance; to the capitalists vaster profits and freedom from trade union restraints; to the army leaders a great army; to all Germans German supremacy; to all the world peace. In reality it mattered little what he offered: to a Germany still bewildered by defeat he offered action, success, undefined achievement, all the sensations of a revolution without the pains. In September 1930, when the economic crisis had hardly begun, but when the French had evacuated the Rhineland, the National Socialists were already hot on the heels of the Social Democrats as the largest party in the Reichstag; the "national" card was irresistible.

This moral was drawn too by Brüning, who, in his hatred of National Socialist paganism, adopted in succession almost every item of the National Socialist creed. Called in to save German capitalism and to promote German rearmament, Brüning went further on the path already marked out by Stresemann. Stresemann had tried to make the republic popular by winning concessions in foreign affairs. Brüning demanded concessions in foreign affairs in order to win support for his system of presidential dictatorship. If Germany was allowed to rearm, the Germans might not notice the reductions in their wages. More than that, if Germans were brought together in a campaign of hatred against Poland, the disparities between rich and poor would be overlooked. Where Stresemann had tried to conciliate the Allies, Brüning blackmailed them: if they did not make concessions to him, they would have to deal with Hitler and the National Socialists. Brüning knew that the economic crisis was due to deflation, the decline of prices and wages; still, far from attempting to arrest or even alleviate this deflation, he drove it on—forced wages and, less effectively, prices, still lower—perhaps to get the crisis over all the sooner, perhaps to threaten the Allies with the prospect of German ruin. For the Brüning Cabinet was primarily a cabinet of "front-line fighters," officers of the Four Years' War, who were dominated by the resolve to reverse the verdict of 1918. Stresemann too had desired to liquidate Versailles, but he had cared also for democracy; Brüning was for the undoing of Versailles pure and simple, hoping, no doubt, to win popularity with the German people, satisfying still more his own deepest feelings. For him, as much as for the great capitalists, the crisis was welcome, the crisis he needed. His most ambitious effort was the customs union with Austria in March 1931, ostensibly a measure against the depression, though it is difficult to see the use of a customs union between two countries both suffering from unemployment and impoverishment. In reality the purpose of the customs union was not economic, but demagogic, an evocation of the programme of Greater Germany, and, so far as it had any sense, a move of economic war against Czechoslovakia, exposed outpost of the system of Versailles. France and her central European allies protested and, almost for the last time, got their way: the separation of Austria from Germany was the only remaining guarantee against an overwhelming German power, and this last fragment of victory was shored up for a few more years.

The Brüning policy of combating evil by taking homoeopathic doses of the same medicine, far from checking the National Socialists, aided their advance. If the Allies trembled before Brüning's blackmail, they would collapse altogether before the blackmail of Hitler. Brüning made everyone in Germany talk once more of rearmament, of union with Austria, of the injustice of the eastern frontier; and every sentence of their talk made them turn, not to Brüning, but to the movement of radical revision. Above all, Brüning had overlooked the lesson of the Four Years' War which Ludendorff had learnt too late—that a programme of German power must rest on a demagogic basis. Austria, Poland, Bohemia, could not be conquered, and Versailles defied, by a Chancellor supported only by a section of the Centre party; for that, a united German will was needed. Captain Brüning was halfway between General Ludendorff and Corporal Hitler, with the weaknesses of both, the advantages of neither. Brüning, the defender of the Roman Catholic Church, shared the error of Stresemann, the defender of the republic: both thought to draw the sting of nationalism by going with it, to silence demagogy by trying to capture its tone. Neither grasped that his every step strengthened his enemy; neither understood that the only security for German democracy, or for German Christian civilization, lay in a full and sincere acceptance of the Treaty of Versailles. Only if Germany made reparation; only if Germany remained disarmed; only if the German frontiers were final; only, above all, if the Germans accepted the Slav peoples as their equals, was there any chance of a stable, peaceful, civilized Germany. No man did more than Brüning to make this Germany impossible.

The decay, disappearance indeed, of peaceful Germany was openly revealed in 1932 when the time came to elect a new President. The candidate

of upheaval and violence was Hitler; the candidate of the peaceful constitutional Left was Hindenburg, hero of the Four Years' War and candidate in
1925 of the "national" parties. The "left" had moved immeasurably to the
"right" in the last seven years: what was then a defeat would now rank as a
dazzling victory—for it could not be supposed that a senile soldier of over
eighty and never mentally flexible had changed his outlook since 1925, or for
that matter since 1918. The German people had accepted militarism: the only
dispute was between the orderly militarism of a field-marshal and the
unrestrained militarism of a hysterical corporal. Hindenburg carried the day,
evidence that the Germans still craved to reconcile decency and power,
militarism and the rule of law. Yet Hindenburg's victory, strangely enough,
was the prelude to National Socialist success. Brüning drew from the presidential election the moral that his government must win greater popularity
by some demagogic stroke; and, as a stroke in foreign policy was delayed, he
sought for achievement in home affairs. His solution was his undoing. He
planned to satisfy Social Democratic workers and Roman Catholic peasants
by an attack on the great estates of eastern Germany, breaking them up for
the benefit of ex-servicemen; and as a first step he began to investigate the
affairs of the *Osthilfe*, the scheme of agrarian relief inaugurated in 1927 by
which tens of millions of pounds had been lavished on the Junker landowners. This was a programme of social revolution, and it could be
carried out only with the backing of enthusiastic and united democratic
parties. But Brüning's solution of Germany's ills was the restoration of the
monarchy, and he would not condescend to democracy by a single gesture;
he relied solely on Hindenburg, and this reliance was his undoing. For
Hindenburg, once himself the patron of land settlement for ex-servicemen,
had been long won over by the Junker landowners, who in 1927 had
launched a plan for presenting Hindenburg with an estate at Neudeck, once
a Hindenburg property, but long alienated. It was characteristic of the
Junkers that even for their own cause they would not pay: all the estate
owners of eastern Germany only subscribed 60,000 marks, the rest of the
required million was provided by the capitalists of the Ruhr—principally by
Duisberg, manufacturer of paints and cosmetics. But thereafter Hindenburg
counted himself a Junker landowner; and he turned against Brüning the
moment that he was persuaded that Brüning's plans threatened the great
estates. On May 29th, 1932, Brüning was summarily dismissed.

With the dismissal of Brüning there began eight months of intrigue and
confusion, in which the old order in Germany, which had now come into its
own, struggled to escape from the conclusion that, to achieve its ends, it must
strike a bargain with the gangsters of National Socialism. Fragments of past
policies were resurrected haphazard, as a dying man recalls chance echoes of
his life. First device was the Roman Catholic cavalry officer, Papen, and his
"cabinet of barons," a collection of antiquarian conservatism unparalleled
since the days of Frederick William IV, the sort of government which might
have existed for a day if a few romantic officers had refused to acknowledge

the abdication of William II in 1918. Papen's great achievement in the eyes of the Prussian landowners was to end constitutional government in Prussia: the Socialist ministers were turned out without a murmur. It was both curious and appropriate that Prussian constitutionalism, which had originated in the Junkers' selfish interest in the *Ostbahn,* should owe its death to the Junkers' selfish interest in the *Osthilfe.* Papen, in his daring, blundering way, continued, too, Brüning's undoing of Versailles, and accomplished the two decisive steps: reparations were scrapped in September 1932; German equality of armaments recognized in December. But it was impossible for a government of frivolous aristocrats, which would have been hard put to it to survive in 1858, to keep Germany going in 1932. Even the Centre, with its readiness to support any government, dared not offend its members by supporting Papen and expelled him from the party. The Germans, divided in all else, were united against the "cabinet of barons."

The army was forced to the last expedient of all: it took over the government itself. In December, Papen in his turn was ordered out of office and succeeded by General Schleicher, forced into office by his own intrigues. Schleicher, too, intended to do without the National Socialists, though he had often flirted with them in the past. He was the first professional soldier to rule Germany without an intermediary since Caprivi. Like Caprivi he was a "social general," intelligent enough to see the advantages of an alliance between the army and the Left, not intelligent enough to see its impossibility. To win over the Social Democrats, he revived the proposal for agrarian reform in eastern Germany and proposed to publish the report of the Reichstag committee on the *Osthilfe* at the end of January; in return he asked the trade union leaders to stand by him in his quarrel with the National Socialists. The prospect of the publication of the *Osthilfe* report made the Junkers around Hindenburg abandon all caution. The agent of reconciliation between the conservatives of the old order and the demagogic National Socialists was none other than Papen, who now hoped somehow to manoeuvre himself into the key position of power. Papen not only swung the Junkers behind Hitler. Early in January 1933 he negotiated an alliance between Hitler and the great industrialists of the Ruhr: Hitler was to be made Chancellor; the debts of the National Socialists were to be paid; and in return Hitler promised not to do anything of which Papen or the Ruhr capitalists disapproved. Papen's sublime self-confidence had already landed him in many disasters; but even he never made a more fantastic mistake than to suppose that Hitler's treachery and dishonesty, immutable as the laws of God, would be specially suspended for Franz von Papen. Against this combination Schleicher was helpless. He could not even count on the support of the Reichswehr; for though the army leaders had often acted independently of the Junkers and sometimes gone against them in great issues of foreign policy, they were not prepared to become the agents of agrarian revolution. They returned to the union of generals and landowners from which Bismarck had started. The *Osthilfe* report was to be published on January 29th. On January 28th Schleicher was dismissed and publication held up; and on January 30th Hindenburg, a field-marshal and a Prussian landowner, made Hitler Chancellor.

It was a symbolic act. The privileged classes of old Germany—the landowners, the generals, the great industrialists—made their peace with demogogy: unable themselves to give "authority" a popular colour, they hoped to turn to their own purposes the man of the people. In January 1933 the "man from the gutter" grasped the "crown from the gutter" which Frederick William IV had refused in April 1849. The great weakness of the Bismarckian order, the weakness which caused its final liquidation in January 1933, was that the interests of the "national" classes could never correspond to the deepest wishes of the German people. It was the Centre and the Social Democrats, not the Conservatives and still less the National Liberals, who had gained mass support. There was no need for a new party or a new leader to carry out the wishes of the landowners and the industrialists; but there was need for a new party and a new leader who would capture the mass enthusiasm, formerly possessed by the Centre and the Social Democrats, for the "national" programme. This was Hitler's achievement, which made him indispensable to the "national" classes, and so ultimately their master. He stole the thunder of the two parties which even Bismarck had never been able to master. The sham Socialism of his programme captured the disillusioned followers of the Social Democrats; the real paganism of his programme rotted the religious basis of the Centre.

There was nothing mysterious in Hitler's victory; the mystery is rather that it had been so long delayed. The delay was caused by the tragic incompatibility of German wishes. The rootless and irresponsible, the young and the violent embraced the opportunity of licensed gangsterdom on a heroic scale; but most Germans wanted the recovery of German power, yet disliked the brutality and lawlessness of the National Socialists, by which alone they could attain their wish. Thus Brüning was the nominee of the Reichswehr and the enemy of the republic, the harbinger both of dictatorship and of German rearmament. Yet he hated the paganism and barbarity of the National Socialists and would have done anything against them— except breaking with the generals. Schleicher, in control of the Reichswehr, was obsessed with German military recovery; yet he contemplated an alliance with the trade unions against the National Socialists and, subsequently, paid for his opposition with his life. The generals, the judges, the civil servants, the professional classes, wanted what only Hitler could offer— German mastery of Europe. But they did not want to pay the price. Hence the delay in the National Socialist rise to power; hence their failure to win a clear majority of votes even at the general election in March 1933. The great majority of German people wanted German domination abroad and the rule of law at home, irreconcilables which they had sought to reconcile ever since 1871, or rather ever since the struggles against Poles, Czechs, and Danes in 1848.

In January 1933 the German upper classes imagined that they had taken Hitler prisoner. They were mistaken. They soon found that they were in the position of a factory owner who employs a gang of roughs to break up a strike: he deplores the violence, is sorry for his workpeople who are being beaten up, and intensely dislikes the bad manners of the gangster leader whom he has called in. All the same, he pays the price and discovers, soon enough, that if he does not pay the price (later, even if he does) he will be shot in the back. The gangster chief sits in the managing director's office, smokes his cigars, finally takes over the concern himself. Such was the experience of the owning classes in Germany after 1933. The first act of the new dictators won the game. When the terror of their private armies looked like failing, the National Socialists set fire to the Reichstag, proclaimed the discovery of a Communist plot, and so suspended the rule of law in Germany. The Reichstag fire, burning away the pretentious home of German sham-constitutionalism, was the unexpected push by which the old order in Germany, hesitating on the brink, was induced to take the plunge into gangster rule. The new Reichstag, still, despite the outlawing of the Communists, with no clear National Socialist majority, met under open terror. Hitler asked for an Enabling Bill, to make him legal dictator. He was supported by the "national" parties, and the Centre, faithful to its lack of principles to the last, also voted for Hitler's dictatorship, in the hope of protecting the position of the Roman Catholic Church; impotent to oppose, they deceived themselves with the prospect of a promise from Hitler, which was in fact never given. Only the Social Democrats were loyal to the republic which they had failed to defend and by a final gesture, impotent but noble, voted unitedly against the bill. But even the Social Democrats went on to show the fatal weakness which had destroyed German liberties. When in May 1933 the Reichstag was recalled to approve Hitler's foreign policy, the Social Democrats did not repeat their brave act: some abstained, most voted with the National Socialists. This was an absurdity. If Germany intended to undo the system of Versailles, she must organize for war, and she could organize for war only on a totalitarian basis. Only by renouncing foreign ambitions could Germany become a democracy; and as even the Social Democrats refused to make this renunciation the victory of the National Socialists was inevitable.

This is the explanation of the paradox of the "Third Reich." It was a system founded on terror, unworkable without the secret police and the concentration camp; but it was also a system which represented the deepest wishes of the German people. In fact it was the only system of German government ever created by German initiative. The old empire had been imposed by the arms of Austria and France; the German Confederation by the armies of Austria and Prussia. The Hohenzollern empire was made by the victories of Prussia, the Weimar republic by the victories of the Allies. But the "Third Reich" rested solely on German force and German impulse; it owed nothing to alien forces. It was a tyranny imposed upon the German people by themselves. Every class disliked the barbarism or the tension of

National Socialism; yet it was essential to the attainment of their ends. This is most obvious in the case of the old "governing classes." The Junker landowners wished to prevent the expropriation of the great estates and the exposure of the scandals of the *Osthilfe;* the army officers wanted a mass army, heavily equipped; the industrialists needed an economic monopoly of all Europe if their great concerns were to survive. Yet many Junkers had an old-fashioned Lutheran respectability; many army officers knew that world conquest was beyond Germany's strength; many industrialists, such as Thyssen, who had financed the National Socialists, were pious and simple in their private lives. But all were prisoners of the inescapable fact that if the expansion of German power were for a moment arrested, their position would be destroyed.

But the National Socialist dictatorship had a deeper foundation. Many, perhaps most, Germans were reluctant to make the sacrifices demanded by rearmament and total war; but they desired the prize which only total war would give. They desired to undo the verdict of 1918; not merely to end reparations or to cancel the "war guilt" clause, but to repudiate the equality with the peoples of eastern Europe which had then been forced upon them. During the preceding eighty years the Germans had sacrificed to the Reich all their liberties; they demanded as reward the enslavement of others. No German recognized the Czechs or Poles as equals. Therefore every German desired the achievement which only total war could give. By no other means could the Reich be held together. It had been made by conquest and for conquest; if it ever gave up a career of conquest, it would dissolve. Patriotic duty compelled even the best of Germans to support a policy which was leading Germany to disaster.

7 *Against a Fatalistic View of German History*

Anderson takes a view different from that of Taylor.

FROM *Freedom and Authority in German History*

BY EUGENE N. ANDERSON

BY A KIND OF INVERTED RACIALISM, the German people are often branded as irretrievably authoritarian in government and politics and in the manifestations of social life. The father of the family and the labor leader, the social worker and the school teacher, all are accused of conforming to a pattern of authoritarianism set by the long domination of monarchism and militarism and of their servant, bureaucracy. The goose step is regarded as the normal manner of walking, thinking, and acting; and the sharp and rude precision of its jerky progress is found to be reflected in the gruff, staccato accents of the German language. The conclusion from this view follows illogically but inevitably: the Germans cannot be trusted to live peaceably with the rest of the world; they will succumb to the violent promises and deeds of another *Führer;* one must either reduce them to a harmless number or prevent the rise of another Hitler by assuming over them authoritarian power.

Since both prospects are repulsive to the Western world, it is essential that the premises on which such conclusions rest be re-examined. Are the German people congenitally authoritarian? Do elements of freedom find any support among them? The definitive answer cannot be found by turning to the study of the past alone; but as history supplies one of the few available sources of evidence, an analysis of German past experience with respect to freedom and authority should indicate the degree of permanence of National Socialist behavior and the dimensions of the German problem.

Taken as a whole, German historical tradition is rich enough to supply

Eugene N. Anderson, "Freedom and Authority in German History," in Gabriel A. Almond, ed., *The Struggle for German Democracy* (1949), pp. 3–5, 22–32. Reprinted by permission of University of North Carolina Press.

evidence in support of any thesis about the German people. It seems irrelevant and unnecessary for the purpose in hand, however, to explore any period prior to that which has exercised an immediate influence upon the present day. There are times in the history of every country when habits are formed, institutions are established, social classes and groups are fixed in relation to one another, legal systems and norms are created, and ideals are accepted which inaugurate a new period in the life of the country. These changes fundamentally condition the character of that period and incorporate into its living forms all that is relevant from earlier times. This period of history, with its particular institutions and ways, then endures until the course of time changes the foundations and evolves a new age.

In the case of Germany the present evidence indicates that the years between the unification of the country in the third quarter of the nineteenth century and the overthrow of Nazism may be called a historical period with a particular life of its own. It is the period of the rise and fall of the second German Reich, and its essential characteristics were developed during the unification of the country. That Nazism would actually be the climax of the period no one could foresee. Even though certain German nationalistic writers envisaged such a future occurrence, it would be attributing to Germany an omnipotence which neither it nor any other country ever possessed to assume that Nazism grew inevitably out of Bismarckian Germany. Since hindsight is not difficult, the historian can find many origins and a superficially convincing logical course for the degeneration of modern Germany into National Socialism. However, the interplay, particularly of international power politics, has been so sharp during the past three quarters of a century, not merely at Germany's instigation but at that of all the great Powers, and the course of economic life has been subject to such unexpected and violent depressions, that no one country can be credited with the full responsibility for its own history. One can at most state that, without being able to control the course of events in all its richness, Germany received through Bismarck's actions the social and political organization and ways out of which under favorable circumstances Nazism could develop. For Bismarck's work of national unification fixed the political, social, and institutional framework within which or against which German events have since then moved.

The three wars of German unification, in common with all other European wars after the French Revolution, affected both international and internal affairs. A unified Germany pushed her way authoritatively into the family of nations and assumed a position of power. At the same time a hierarchical relationship of social groups in Germany, in contrast to the free relationship in a democracy, became fixed for decades to come, and the governmental institutions of authoritarianism were firmly established. In 1914–18 it required the combined power of the rest of the world to undermine these dominant social groups and institutions, and even then the social groups escaped destruction. Able to revive and exploit the general despair of the economic crisis of 1930–31, these groups assisted National Socialism to power and without entirely identifying themselves with Nazism contributed elements essential for enabling it to wreck Germany and Europe and to menace the world.

The effect of World War I upon the relative strength of freedom and authoritarianism in Germany cannot be summed up in a formula. The concentration of power incident upon the necessities of fighting set precedents in new institutions and habits for authoritarian rule which were essential as a basis for the rise of National Socialism. The war blended military and civilian methods and ideals to a degree not before experienced in German history and supplied the future Nazis with the pattern of a society organized exclusively for war. At the same time the growing aversion to the war aroused the proletariat and increasingly large elements of the middle classes and bourgeoisie to new recognition of the value of freedom from authoritarian control.

The postwar (1918–33) course of German history does not lend itself to adequate explanation in terms of class conflicts and material interests. The psychological effects of war, defeat, and revolution cut across class and occupational lines and left tensions which within a short time transformed the acceptance of freedom and democracy into a furious endeavor on the part of the old conservative forces and the lower middle class to destroy them. Groups picked up extreme ideals, of which German history had a copious variety, as a means of solving their problems; and the period is full of ists and isms, crisscrossing, merging, fighting, each with its own troubled history.

The Social Democrats, who supplied the force of the revolution, stopped with a transformation of government. Their leaders wished to establish a constitutional regime based on parliamentary control and the rule of law, and operating by way of political parties. They used these means to develop model instruments for handling labor-management relations and to transform the authoritarian state into a state concerned with the welfare of all its members. They established the conditions of intellectual and spiritual freedom, to which the response was immediate. The theatre, literature, and the arts flourished during the short life of the Weimar Republic as nowhere else in Europe. Educational reforms were vigorously discussed and experimental schools of a progressive type emerged. In spite of the recent war, the cultural ties with the rest of the world were closer than in any age since the time of Goethe. In internal organization and policy the Weimar Republic was endeavoring to align with Western democracies, and in its international relations it was striving to overcome German nationalism in favor of world cooperation and understanding. Democratic Catholics in the Centrist party and many of the middle classes and bourgeoisie supported this policy, and the world witnessed the extraordinary sight of political cooperation between Marxian Socialists and Catholic Centrists in the government of a democratic republic.

The Social Democrats and their new allies opposed a thorough social revolution with a fundamental change in the ownership of property and in the distribution of social power. Social Democrats in the revolutionary government used the old military leaders and forces to prevent the feeble attempts at the kind of revolution which, in theory, the workers had advocated for decades. The standards and ideals of the authoritarian groups had affected Socialist leaders like Ebert and Noske to the extent that they agreed on the necessity of preserving order. The war had not diminished the Social Democrats' faith in the essential reasonableness of man, and they apparently expected the former ruling elements suddenly to become converted to the same belief and to practice it. A democratic government thus established itself in a society which had little experience with democracy, which had suffered through four years of war and an accentuated form of authoritarian rule, and which was neither morally nor politically prepared for defeat. This society teemed with bitterness, inner conflicts, and fear. A majority was willing to accept democracy if it brought peace, full employment, and a high standard of living; that is, if it immediately established better living conditions than had obtained under the empire. The people, trained to look to others for leadership and to throw responsibility on them, expected a miracle to occur by the grace of the victorious and occupying Powers, with no more effort on their part than the formulation of a constitution and the erection of a new government. They did not know that they had to earn democracy; that they must practice democracy in every-day life, where it meant more than a formal structure of government and the secret ballot.

The Weimar Republic failed to teach all Germans that political parties, as well as all other organized groups, can live together in peace only by learning the ways of compromise, of respecting the views of others, of accepting defeat without recourse to violence. The Social Democrats and the Catholic Centrist party, and even certain middle class and bourgeois parties, had learned this elementary lesson; but the extreme groups on left and right, the Communists, the Nationalists, and all those elements rapidly turning to Nazism and similar organizations, never were willing to admit that their opponents might have some justice and truth on their side.

The course of developments during the Weimar Republic sadly disappointed almost everyone. When the miracle failed to appear, a large number of voters, especially from the lower middle classes, wandered from party to party, seeking a panacea, landing finally in National Socialism. The forces of conservatism and reaction revived and fought with their accustomed bitterness and ruthlessness to restore their control. Political freedom permitted them to do so. Economic interests re-established their affiliation with political groups. The Junkers and the big landowners remained as powerful economically as before and determined to regain through ardent nationalism their social and political dominance. In comparison with their prewar position they suffered under the handicap of having a Social Democratic laborer in place of the Kaiser and his court; but they soon found a thoroughly satisfactory substitute in Field Marshal von Hindenburg, president after 1925 of the German Republic. Loss of control by an authoritarian government and the lack of a disproportionate influence in the representative assemblies could not yet be overcome; but the bureaucracy, with the exception of a few departments, remained loyal to conservative ideals and never operated in a democratic way. Whenever a former army officer or other reactionary nationalist assassinated a democratic member of the Cabinet or political leader, or instigated a rebellion, the judges could be relied upon to free him entirely or impose a gentle sentence; after all, it would be said, he had killed from the finest patriotic motives. Most of the upper bourgeoisie, except for the Catholics, sided with the conservatives and financed the many patriotic groups bent on undermining or overthrowing the Weimar regime. The bourgeoisie disliked the so-called workers' republic, imposed, as most Germans believed, by the victorious Powers and alien to true Germanism. The numerous professional army officers, unemployed because of the Treaty of Versailles, provided invaluable men of action for these authoritarian groups and served efficiently as private and illegal adjuncts to the small professional army left to Germany. The educational system continued to be organized mainly on a class basis, and teachers and professors remained on the whole as staunchly conservative and nationalistic as before the war.

The democratic forces had to contend not merely with these authoritarian powers. They confronted the problem common to every state, whether victor or vanquished, in the postwar period; namely, how to balance the necessity for large-scale governmental planning and action in order to cope with the numerous and unprecedented difficulties in economic and cultural life with the necessity for leaving an equally wide area for freedom of action on the part of individuals and private groups in order to allow the people the opportunity for training themselves in the ways of freedom and democracy. The Germans had to learn not to look to the state for guidance on all matters; they had to learn to rely on individual and private activities in civic affairs; they had to transform the bureaucracy into a servant, tolerant, at the least, of cordial relations with a respected and confident public; they had to overcome an awesome deference toward officialdom and to bring themselves to the point of taking the initiative or participating vigorously in affairs which they had formerly left to the government and bureaucracy. The problem acquired enhanced significance in Germany where statesmanship of rare quality would have been needed to prevent the powerful authoritarian elements from exploiting present needs for the revival and accentuation of traditional authoritarian forms of control as the sole means of salvation. The war, defeat, and revolution left vast difficulties on a national scale which an authoritarian government seemed most competent to handle. Every inducement, reasonable as well as emotional, seemed to lead the Germans, unaccustomed to self-government, to throw all their pressing burdens upon the state. Taxes were high while wages and salaries were low; the Weimar Republic was blamed. Social Security was expensive; the state was blamed. Foreign markets did not materialize; the state had failed to do its duty. Labor conflicts arose; if the state interfered it did not settle them properly or fairly, if it did not interfere, it should have. Credit was tight; the state should help out. Bankruptcy threatened; the state must save the firm. The schools must be left alone, the schools must be reformed; the state was blamed for doing one or the other. Newspapers published too much scandal; the state should forbid it. And so on and on. The times were full of uncertainty—as to economic conditions, markets, sources of raw materials, credit; as to social standards and social power; as to political control; as to governmental structure. It seems true that the majority of Germans disliked with more or less intensity the Weimar government and constitution and all that they stood for; but the opponents of Weimar could not go back to the old regime, and they did not know what kind of a new order they wanted. The realistic and immediate problems caused them to fight for control of the powerful machinery of government in order to use it for special interests. Those who thought that they had most to gain from reconquering the government, namely, the authoritarian groups, most loudly asserted their nationalism. The supporters of a democratic Germany had increasing difficulty in maintaining themselves.

The emotional currents of the Weimar period were rich and varied, with moral standards in flux. The war had brutalized many groups and individuals ready for any sadistic action. It had accustomed even the rest of society to acquiesce in legal arbitrariness and murder in times of stress, and, although most were appalled at the thought of another war and wished the lawlessness to stop, the odor of blood remained in the air. Almost all Germans believed that they had lost the war unjustly. Even more of them refused to accept the thesis of German guilt and regarded the Treaty of Versailles as a wicked imposition. When the inflation wiped out the savings of a lifetime, made some unjustly rich and others unjustly poor overnight, the economic order of life seemed shattered. The economic depression of 1930–31 completed the work of disillusionment. Germans came to believe that this was a world of hazard, of no fixed principles, a world in which the individual confronted overwhelming, arbitrary powers. Forces beyond one's control appeared too strong. The moral order seemed to have degenerated into moral chaos. The rule of law had given way to arbitrariness. Reason could not be trusted as a guide, for it had succumbed to the forces of blind and cruel chance. Intelligence offered no salvation. Compromise failed when others would not compromise; or if agreement was reached, some alien force or unpredictable economic crisis might nullify the result. Democracy meant, therefore, so it seemed, the continued shackling of Germany for the advantage of mean, selfish foreign Powers. Millions of Germans came to believe that the country could be saved only by repudiating the Weimar system and turning to a new messiah, a man of miracles, a leader, arbitrary and cruel, determined and ruthless, like the rest of the world. The problems of the Germans as individuals and as a people seemed insoluble without such a leader. Nationalism arose like a flame to help the Germans escape from freedom, to guide them into the hysteria of Nazism.

The Germans accepted National Socialism as a last act of desperation. A nation which appreciated its own excellent qualities and high abilities thought its existence menaced by chaos. It could not understand the reason for this plight and refused to acquiesce. Millions of Germans from all classes and occupations felt the crisis to be so acute that the Nazis were quickly transformed from a small group of crackpots into a mass party led by a messiah determined upon action to restore the vigor and the rightful glory of the German people. The ingredients of National Socialism were derived in sufficient strength from the German past to be acceptable as German. The *Führerprinzip* enjoyed the traditional prestige of centuries of absolute or strong monarchism, of Bismarckian authoritarianism, and of the traditions and habits of military and even bureaucratic command. It had been practiced, in an appropriate form, by Krupp, Stumm, and many other big industrialists. The new popular element in it was exalted as a sign of democratic equality and became immediately a powerful asset accepted even by the upper classes. The Germans also knew that in every crisis among every people the executive head becomes increasingly important as the instrument for quick and effective action. The relegation of parliament to an insignificant position seemed necessary and was fully approved by the millions of conservatives who had never liked representative government and by the middle classes and even many of the workers who cared less about it than about steady employment. Responsible representative government had had a short history, from 1919 to 1933, and had scarcely been crowned with success. The Germans were accustomed to a wide range of governmental authority, and in the crisis the individual wished the state to take even more responsibility away from him. The absence of tradition of private initiative and responsibility in civic affairs among most of the people and the dislike of politics and political parties as degrading influences led them to reject the potentialities of the Weimar Republic in favor of the wild promises of Nazism. They lacked democratic safeguards in the habits and standards of their private lives against the enticement of a seemingly easy way out of an unexpected and overwhelming crisis like that of the world economic depression. Certainly for some years until the destructive qualities of Nazism became apparent, few manifested any interest in defending moral principles against the nihilism of the National Socialist.

The qualities which German tradition regarded as the highest virtues became means of totalitarian domination. The Germans made a fetish of order, cleanliness, performance of duty, efficiency in craft or profession, concentration on the business in hand without interference in affairs about which they knew little, being obedient to officers and officials and to the law irrespective of the validity or morality of the order, ardent love of the nation and supreme loyalty to it. All peoples of our civilization have these traits in varying degrees, but in Western democracies they are balanced by a strong sense of civic responsibility and of individual worth as a citizen. In no other country than Germany did such a combination of qualities obtain on such a broad scale, qualities which in favorable circumstances could be exploited to the ruin of a people.

One important line of German political and social philosophy for at least a century and a half had been basically concerned with the problem of the relation of the individual and the state. Scholars and popular writers at all levels of intelligence had discussed the subject. It permeated the cheap pamphlet literature which Hitler read as an embittered, unemployed ex-soldier. At times of prosperity the rights of the individual might be emphasized; but at every period of crisis—the Napoleonic era, 1848, the 1860's, the Bismarckian era, World War I, the economic depression of 1930–31, the Nazi seizure of power—the belief in the subordination of the individual to the welfare of the nation-state became widespread. This exaggeration seems logical and understandable for a crisis situation where the individual finds no way to solve his problems alone and throws himself upon the mercy of the state. The view forms the core of nationalistic thought in every country, France, England, Italy, Russia, Germany, or any other. It is the peculiar fate of German history, however, that the idea, derived easily from a class society struggling to maintain hierarchy, suited nicely the needs of the upper classes, especially the monarchy and the aristocrats, in their effort to keep control over the rest of the population. Since they dominated, or believed that with a little more action they could restore their domination over the lower classes, they kept alive the ideal of the superior interests of the state over those of the individual.

When National Socialism arose, it adopted for its own purposes this rich tradition. For the first time in history a nation sought to organize and run itself according to the ideals of nationalism. The process of nationalism which characterized European history after the French Revolution thereby reached its culmination. As stated above, the National Socialists could have found most of their ideals in the nationalistic writings of any country; there is nothing peculiarly German in them. No other people, however, has attempted to realize these ideals, for in no other country has the combination of conditions, inherited and present, been comparable to that which gave National Socialism its opportunity. Only one further step is possible in the unfolding of nationalism and of authoritarianism. That step may be described as national bolshevism. Although one strong faction wished to go so far, the National Socialists were unable to force the German people into the final act of destruction of their social and institutional heritage.

It would be wrong to conclude that Nazism grew inevitably from the German past. This theory would imply a fatalism which is entirely out of place in any serious study of history. A careful analysis of the events of 1932–33 shows that at that time a substantial majority of the German people favored an extraordinary increase in governmental authority necessary to solve their problems but opposed National Socialism, that this majority was increasing, and that the recession of the economic crisis would have entailed further losses of Nazi popular support. A relatively small group of Junkers, industrialists, and militarists actually achieved Hitler's appointment as Chancellor and utilized the senility of President von Hindenburg to accomplish its purpose. The group expected to control the Nazis and to exploit the Nazi power for its own purposes; but the National Socialists proved too clever and too ruthless for it, giving the next twelve years their own imprint. It would also be wrong to equate the conservative authoritarianism of the Hohenzollerns, Bismarck, the Junkers, the big industrialists, and the army officers with National Socialist authoritarianism. The conservatives believed in and practiced authoritarianism as a means of preserving their social, economic, and political status, a status quite different from that of Nazism. Their way of life included respect for at least some of the Christian virtues and for the qualities of their own type of cultured personality. It implied a certain reasonableness and a disinclination on the whole to run desperate risks. Perhaps one may counter by asserting that totalitarianism in all its fulness and with its extreme ruthlessness lay dormant in these groups and awaited the utilization of a Hitler. The growing evidence does not bear out this accusation. Rather it points to a milder view that these conservatives sympathized strongly with a popular totalitarian movement, the full import of which they did not understand, that their nationalism and their craving for power induced them to take a chance with Hitler, and that the authoritarian forms of their own thinking and acting and of those of the German people made possible the easy acceptance of National Socialism. The obedience of the German conservatives and all other elements to the Nazis through twelve years of hell does not prove the identity of all the German people with National Socialism. It merely reveals how politically irresponsible two generations of conservative authoritarianism had left a great nation and how susceptible the people were to nationalistic and military success, how unable they were to distinguish between a form of authoritarianism in the old Christian tradition which might have helped to solve their problems without violating the ideals and standards of Western culture and the violent, sadistic ultra-nationalism of Nazi nihilism.

Few Germans seemed to regret the disappearance of freedom after 1933. The overwhelming majority of the population either joyfully accepted dictatorship or acquiesced in it. While history helps to explain this fact, it also offers the assurance that the Germans have not always approved authoritarianism, that they have not always been nationalistic, indeed, that a large percentage opposed vigorously the Hohenzollern authoritarianism and militarism and preferred the ideals of freedom. History shows that on several occasions the adherents to freedom were powerful enough almost to gain a decisive victory. Historical conditions differed markedly in Germany's development over the past century from those of Britain and France and produced the peculiar mixture of elements from the *ancien régime,* modern industrial capitalism, and mass social movements which reached its fullest authoritarian form in National Socialism. History offers the assurance that under new and favorable conditions the Germans have the elements of a liberal and even democratic tradition of sufficient strength to encourage and assist them in turning toward democracy. There is no historical reason to doubt that they are able and would be willing to learn the ways of living in social and political freedom; but it is equally clear that their experience since national unification does not offer them much positive guidance. Conservative authoritarianism provides no assurance against a resurgence of totalitarianism. The fate of the Weimar Republic demonstrates that democracy depends upon more than a free constitution and free political instruments; it must permeate likewise individual conduct and social relations. It is this conception of democracy that the Germans must for the first time and on a national scale learn how to practice.

The Cold War—

Who Is To Blame?

CONTENTS

QUESTIONS FOR STUDY

1 In what ways do Fleming and Bailey disagree on the facts of the Cold War?

2 What was the part played by the Baruch plan in the Cold War?

3 Why did Russia reject it?

During the Second World War the United States, Great Britain, and the Soviet Union were allied in a fight for survival against the Axis powers. From the beginning there were differences in strategy, aims, and ideology, accompanied by mutual distrust. Nevertheless the alliance held together; at Teheran and Yalta conferences were held and joint plans made for the conduct of the war and for the shape of the peace to come. A United Nations organization was envisaged in which all would participate to maintain peace and harmony. But within a few years hopes for friendship and cooperation had been dashed and the world was divided into two hostile armed camps; the Cold War had begun. It is the aim of this chapter to investigate the problem of how this reversal came about.

---

4   *What was the beginning of the breach between Russia and the United States?*

5   *What is the importance of the coup in Czechoslovakia?*

6   *Compare the views of Fleming, Bailey, and Lukacs on the importance of the Truman Doctrine, the Marshall Plan, and NATO.*

1 America's Responsibility

In the following selection D. F. Fleming presents the view that the United States was largely responsible for the coming of the Cold War and establishes the nature of the controversy.

FROM *The Cold War and Its Origins*
BY D. F. FLEMING

THE CHRONOLOGY OF THE COLD WAR

THERE CAN BE NO REAL UNDERSTANDING of the Cold War unless chronology is kept in mind. What came first? What was action and what reaction? Not everything that came after a given act was due to that act, but a later event could not be the cause of an earlier one.

Below are the principal events of the Cold War in the order in which they occurred.

1 September 1938—Control of East Europe achieved by Hitler at Munich.

2 December 5, 1941 to February 4, 1942—State Department decisions not to make any wartime agreements about Russia's western boundaries.

3 April 1942 to June 1944—The second front postponed. Peripheral war conducted in Africa and Italy.

4 October 9, 1944—Churchill and Stalin agreed on spheres of influence in the Balkans: Greece to Britain; Bulgaria and Rumania to Russia; Yugoslavia 50–50.

5 December 3, 1944 to January 15, 1945—The British crushed the Greek leftists in heavy fighting.

6 December 24, 1944 to May 14, 1945—Bulgarian purge trials executed 2000 rightists and imprisoned 3000.

7 March 29, 1944 to February 1945—Soviet armies occupied East Europe.

From *The Cold War and Its Origins, 1917–1960*, II (1961), 1038–51, by D. F. Fleming. Reprinted by permission of Doubleday & Company, Inc., and George Allen & Unwin Ltd., London.

8 February 1945—The Yalta Conference conceded friendly governments in East Europe to Russia, but with free elections and a reorganization of the Polish Government.

9 March 6, 1945—Russia imposed a communist-led coalition in Rumania.

10 March 1945—Friction with Russia over German surrender negotiations in Italy.

11 April 12, 1945—Franklin D. Roosevelt's death, four months after Cordell Hull's resignation.

12 April 23, 1945—Truman's White House lecture to Molotov on the Polish Government.

13 July 17-25, 1945—The Potsdam Conference failed to alter Russian arrangements in East Europe.

14 August 6, 1945—The first American A-bomb upset the expected world strategic balance.

15 August 18, 1945—Beginning of the Byrnes-Bevin diplomatic drive to force free elections in East Europe.

16 September 1945—First Council of Foreign Ministers deadlocked over East Europe.

17 March 5, 1946—Churchill's Fulton speech demanded an Anglo-American preponderance of power against Russia, with reference to East Europe.

18 April 1946—Russian troops forced from Iran through the United Nations.

19 August 1946—Soviet demands upon Turkey for the return of two provinces and for a base in the Straits.

20 July to December 1946—Peace treaties for Italy, Hungary, Rumania, Bulgaria and Finland hammered out.

21 November 1946—The Republicans won control of the Congress, aided by charges of widespread communist infiltration in the United States.

22 Late December 1946—General relaxation and expectation of peace.

23 March 12, 1947—The Truman Doctrine, calling for the containment of the Soviet Union and communism.

24 March 23, 1947—Truman's order providing for the loyalty investigation of *all* government employees.

25 March to August 1947—The freely elected Smallholder's Party Government of Hungary disintegrated by communist pressure.

26 June 5, 1947—The Marshall Plan announced. Rejected by Russia August 2, 1947.

27 November 1947—The Cominform organized, uniting all the principal communist parties of Europe, including those of France and Italy.

28 January 22, 1948—A plan for a Western Union in Europe announced by Bevin.

29 February 25, 1948—A communist coup seized control of Czechoslovakia.

30 March 25, 1948—Western Union treaty signed. Devil theory address by President Truman.

31 June 28, 1948—Yugoslavia expelled by the Cominform. Received help from the West.

32 June 1948 to May 1949—The Berlin blockade.

33 March to August 1949—The signing and ratification of the North Atlantic Treaty creating NATO.

34 September 23, 1949—The first Soviet A-bomb hung the threat of total destruction over West Europe.

35 February 1, 1950—Drive for the H-bomb announced by Truman.

36 February 9, March 9 and 16, 1950—Acheson explained the policy of no negotiation with the Russian river of aggression until strength had been accumulated.

37 October 1948 to January 1950—The Chinese Nationalist armies captured or destroyed by the Communists.

38 February to May 1950—The first explosion of McCarthyism.

39 June 25, 1950—The outbreak of the Korean War.

40 September 12, 1950—The United States demanded the rearmament of Germany and began a vast rearmament.

41 October 1950—Having liberated South Korea, we decided to conquer the North Korean Republic.

42 February 1952—Acheson's Lisbon NATO arms goals overstrained our allies.

43 May to November 1952—Our allies escaped from control during the long American election campaign.

44 November 1952—The first American H-bomb exploded, on the ground.

45 March 6, 1953—The death of Stalin created uncertainty and a desire for relaxation in Russia.

46 May 11, 1953—Churchill repealed his Fulton address and called for an end of the Cold War on the basis of guaranteeing Russia's security in East Europe.

47 July 26, 1953—Korean cease-fire signed.

48 August 9, 1953—The first air-borne H-bomb achieved by Russia, and growing Russian air power brought the threat of incineration to all large American cities.

49 November 6, 1953—Ex-President Truman officially charged with knowingly harboring a communist spy.

50 May 1952 to January 1954—A growing realization that the world power struggle had become a stalemate.

51 April 22 to June 15, 1954—The crest of McCarthyism.

52 July 18–24, 1955—The First Summit Conference recognized the atomic arms stalemate and the inevitability of competitive coexistence.

53 February 15–20, 1956—Khrushchev's denunciation of Stalin accelerated a wave of reforms behind the iron curtain, relaxing police state controls and giving greater incentives to individuals.

54 March 7, 1956—President Eisenhower urged that we counter the threat to us "more by positive measures that people throughout the world will trust, than just by trying to answer specific thrusts."

55 October-November 1956—Revolution in Poland and Hungary against Soviet control and Communism.

56 November 1956—Attacks upon Egypt by Israel, France and Britain.

57 August 26, 1957—The first intercontinental ballistic rocket claimed by the Soviet Union.

58 October 4, 1957—The first of the increasingly heavy Sputniks demonstrated Russia's ability to lay down large pay-loads accurately across great distances.

59 April 1958—The pro-American Liberal Party ousted in Canada by the strongly nationalistic Conservatives.

60 May 1958—Vice President Nixon mobbed in Peru and Venezuela.

61 July 1958—Revolution in Iraq and the sending of American troops to Lebanon.

62 August-October 1958—The second Quemoy crisis, ending in China's defeat.

63 November 1958 to July 1959—The second Berlin crisis.

64 April 16, 1959—The resignation of Secretary of State John Foster Dulles.

65 September 1959—Khrushchev's visit to the United States, inaugurating President Eisenhower's effort to move toward making peace and ending the Cold War.

66 September-October 1959—A Soviet *Lunik* rocket hit the moon and another went around it relaying to earth pictures of its hidden side, emphasizing Russia's continued leadership in rocketry and the conquest of space.

67 November 16, 1959—Secretary of State Herter's appeal for keeping the great competition of our time with communism "within the bounds set by the conditions of co-survival."

68 December 1959—Eisenhower's eleven nation crusade for a new international climate and peace, climaxed by his statement to the Parliament of India on December 10 that the mistrusts, fixations and tensions that exist in the world "are the creations of Governments, cherished and nourished by Governments. Nations would never feel them if they were given freedom from propaganda and pressure."

69 October 1955 to May 1960—The Second Summit Conference frustrated by the steady erosion in the West of the expectation of serious negotiations about West Berlin and by the U-2 spy plane incident at Sverdlovsk.

70 June 16, 1960—President Eisenhower turned back from a visit to Japan by the inability of the Japanese Government to protect him from great hostile demonstrations.

It is of cardinal importance to remember that East Europe was given away not at Yalta but at Munich. Before that the curbing of Hitler might have cost the West the same territories which Hitler yielded to Russia. After

Munich the marching armies would grind back and forth across the face of Europe until the Red armies came to rest in Berlin and Vienna.

DECISIONS DURING THE WAR

This was not foreseen in the State Department as late as December 5, 1941 and February 1942 when the Atherton-Dunn memoranda reasoned that Stalin might not be able to recover all of his lost territories and ruled against recognizing his seizure of the Baltic states and half of Poland. Our fear of another uproar in this country over "secret treaties," such as had been raised after World War I, and of the outcry of Polish and other citizens, combined with aversion to any extension of the area of communism to prevent the British from making a more realistic agreement with Russia in April 1942.

Then the British managed to lead Western war operations through peripheral warfare in North Africa, Sicily, and Italy until May 1944. This was justifiable strategy for us, but it left the main brunt of the land war on the Russians to the end and created in their minds lasting suspicions of being deliberately sacrificed. More important, it gave the Russian armies time to come into Central Europe, at the cost of many hundreds of thousands of casualties, losses which we would have suffered had we struck sooner and directly at Germany.

All during the war years Churchill sought manfully to retrieve in East Europe what Chamberlain had given away. His eyes were always on the non-existent "soft underbelly" of Europe, then in the late stages of the war on an invasion through Trieste, and finally for lunges into Germany to seize areas beyond the agreed zones of occupation for bargaining purposes. But always the actual balance of forces defeated him. The Russians were required to maul the bulk of the German forces to the last day of the war. Allied forces thrown through Trieste might well have enabled the Russians to skirt the Baltic Sea and appear on the English Channel. Furthermore, attempts to change the zones of occupation against the Russians would have been rejected by allied public opinion. Long afterward General Bedell Smith, one of General Eisenhower's most trusted generals, recorded his conviction that it "would have been quite impossible in the light of world public opinion in our own country," and his advice to Churchill at the time was "that I didn't think his own public opinion would permit it."

Soviet control of East Europe was the price we paid for the years of appeasement of Hitler, and it was not a high price. In Toynbee's judgment "the Nazis would have conquered the world," if we and the Soviets had not combined our efforts. They would eventually have crossed the narrow gap of the South Atlantic to Brazil and the rest of South America, where strong fifth columns could have been organized in more than one country. By our war alliance with the Soviets we prevented the unification of the world by the Nazis. That was a victory beyond price, but, says Toynbee, we "could not have put down Hitler without consequently producing the situation with which all of us now find ourselves confronted."

All this was fully evident during the war and it is still true. C. B. Marshall has reminded us that we do not have to guess what the Axis powers would have done had they won. They set it down plainly in their Tripartite Alliance on September 27, 1940—"a pattern for the conquest of the rest of the world and the beleaguerment of the United States." Why then did we have ten years of cold war over Russia's control of East Europe and over her desire to have a military base on the Turkish Straits?

EAST EUROPE DIVIDED BY CHURCHILL AND STALIN

Early in October 1944 Churchill sought to come to terms with the inevitable. Over the strong opposition of our State Department, but with Roosevelt's permission, he went to Moscow to make a temporary agreement for three months concerning the Balkans.

On October 9 he proposed to Stalin that Russia have 90 per cent predominance in Rumania, others 10 per cent, and 75 per cent predominance in Bulgaria, others 25 per cent. In Greece Britain would have 90 per cent predominance, and others 10 per cent. The "predominance" was to be divided 50–50 in Hungary and Yugoslavia. Nothing was said about this division of influence being temporary.

Stalin accepted this proposal without a word. He permitted a really free election in Hungary, which the old ruling classes duly won, and he did his best to force Tito to honor the bargain about Yugoslavia. Also he held his hand completely while Churchill promptly crushed the left forces in Greece, thereby sealing his agreement with Churchill and committing Roosevelt to it, before Yalta.

The communist revolution in Bulgaria was already in full cry when the Yalta conference met. The overthrow in the preceding December of the mighty ELAS movement in Greece by the British army and the Greek officer caste had suggested to the Russians that something very similar could occur in Bulgaria, where the Bulgarian army officers used the coup d'état "as a normal political instrument." "People's Court" trials began on December 24, 1944, and cut down the Bulgarian army officers as with a scythe until the end of February 1945.

On March 6 the Soviet Government imposed a communist-led government upon Rumania, deposing the Rumanian conservatives. It was "very hard to think of any constructive alternative," since free elections in Rumania under their control would have been "an invitation to Fascism here more than elsewhere."

The situation was worst in Rumania, where government was notoriously "so corrupt that it is a synonym for corrupt government," but there was no country in East Europe, with the exception of Greece, where the kind of free elections we wanted would not have been controlled by the old ruling classes. They had manipulated the elections for generations. No free election had ever been held. The Hungarian landlords had been ruthless rulers for a thousand years, and elsewhere the cliques which ruled for their own benefit had virtually all of the knowledge of political manipulations. The Hungarian and Rumanian ruling groups had also sent two million conscripted troops deep into Russia, behind Hitler's armies.

FREE ELECTIONS

In these circumstances the question arises, why did Stalin agree at Yalta to conduct "free elections" in Eastern Europe? Why we demanded them was clear. That is the American way of doing things, subject to the operations of political machines, and we wanted very much to prevent East Europe from being communized. No one at Yalta dreamed of denying that the region must cease to be a hostile *cordon sanitaire* against the Soviet Union and become "friendly" politically to the Soviet Union. No one could deny that, with the Red armies at that moment across Poland, within thirty miles of Berlin, and beyond Budapest sweeping up the Danube, while the Western allies were still in France, set back by the Ardennes offensive.

But could governments friendly to Russia be obtained in this region by "free elections" in which the ruling groups participated freely? It was inconceivable that these groups could be friendly to Russia, or that communist Russia could think of depending on them. That was as incredible as that we should freely arrange for a communist government in France or Italy. The Soviets also happened to believe that their system of government was as valid as ours, and that they could really depend only upon it to stop East Europe from being used as an invasion corridor into the Soviet Union.

If the Americans at Yalta committed a fault, it was not in "giving away" East Europe. That had been done at Munich long before. It was in trying to achieve the impossible under the formula of "free elections." Yet free elections were in their blood and they could do no other than to believe that this was a solution which all must accept. On his side, it is not likely that Stalin thought the formula would prevent him from purging the long dominant elements in East Europe, whose hostility to Red Russia needed no further demonstration. These elections might be managed and "people's democracies" set up which would be acceptable to the Americans. He knew that the decisive settlement for the area had been made in his gentleman's agreement with Churchill, on October 9, 1944, and that its execution was already far advanced on both sides.

He was loyally holding to his side of the bargain with Churchill and he could hardly have believed that the Yalta formulas would disrupt allied relations as soon as the war was over and lead to long years of bitter cold war.

TRUMAN'S REVERSAL OF THE ROOSEVELT–HULL POLICY

It is possible that if Roosevelt had lived the same deadly quarrel would have developed, though it is far more likely that he already understood the deeper forces involved and the impossibility of frustrating them. What made a clash

certain was the accession of Truman just at the close of the war. He intended
to carry out Roosevelt's engagements, loyally and fully, and to exact from
Stalin the same complete fulfilment, including free elections in East Europe.
This theme runs through the first volume of his memoirs.

However his methods were poles apart from those of Roosevelt and
Hull. All through 1944, his last year in office, Hull had conducted off-the-
record conferences with groups of editors, clergymen, and members of
Congress, to explain to them how far the Russians had come with us, how
they had been "locked up and isolated for a quarter of a century," used to
receiving violent epithets. It would "take time for them to get into step," but
they would do it. He urged that "we must be patient and forbearing. We
cannot settle questions with Russia by threats. We must use friendly methods."

No one was more opposed than Hull to Soviet control of East Europe,
"interfering with her neighbors," but as he left office his policy rested on two
bases: to show the Russians by example how a great power should act and to
continue in constant friendly discussion with them. "Consult them on every
point. Engage in no 'cussin matches' with them."

Nothing could have been further from President Truman's approach.
He quickly read all the dispatches about friction with Russia over German
surrenders, listened to everybody who wanted to get tough with the Russians, and when Molotov came by on April 23, 1945, to pay his respects to the
new President, he received such a dressing down that he complained at the
end of it that no one had ever talked like that to him before.

This was exactly eleven days after Roosevelt's death. It took Truman
just that long to reverse the entire Roosevelt-Hull approach to Russia and to
inaugurate an era of toughness and ever greater toughness in our dealings
with her. Then on August 6, 1945, the Hiroshima explosion gave him the
means to back insistence on free elections in East Europe and when the
London Conference of September 1945 deadlocked over this issue he made
up his mind at once to contain Russia. It was at this moment that Lippmann,
noting that we had terminated lend-lease "abruptly and brutally" and had
drifted into an arms race with the Soviet Union, warned: "Let no one
deceive himself. We are drifting toward a catastrophe."

To the already deep fears of Russia for her own security, thrice justified
since 1914, was added a new and dreadful fear of a fourth Western attack,
backed by the atomic bomb. From the psychological point of view the policy
of toughness was "the worst treatment" that could have been devised. "If a
patient is suffering from genuine fear, you do not cure his fears and establish
a rational relationship with him by making him more afraid. You endeavor
to show him patiently and by your actions toward him that he has nothing to
fear."

Exactly the opposite course was followed, with increasing momentum.
In the following spring of 1946 Churchill issued at Fulton, Missouri, and in
President Truman's applauding presence, his call for an overwhelming

preponderance of power against Russia, hinting broadly at later forcible interventions in East Europe. Nevertheless, peace was made in Europe during the remainder of 1946. In three sessions of the Council of Foreign Ministers and a conference of 21 nations in Paris, peace treaties were hammered out in substantially the terms established by the various armistices. Really free elections had been held in Hungary and there were many signs of relaxation of tension as the year closed.

RESULTS OF THE TRUMAN DOCTRINE

However, in February the British turned the burden of supporting Greece over to us and Truman seized the occasion to proclaim the doctrine of containment, on March 12, 1947, which George F. Kennan spelled out fully in the July issue of *Foreign Affairs* as "long term, patient but firm and vigilant containment of Russian expansive tendencies." Otherwise the Kremlin would take its time about filling every "nook and cranny available to it in the basin of world power."

On its face this was the rashest policy ever enunciated by any American leader. For the first time in history the encirclement of a great power was openly proclaimed. This power, too, was in firm possession of the great heartland of Eurasia. It had already demonstrated that it could industrialize itself quickly and enough to defeat Hitler's armies. What it would do, after the Cold War was declared by Churchill and Truman, was easily predictable by any average man. The Soviet Union would put up a bold front to cover its frightening post-war weakness and work mightily to gain strength to hold what it had and then break the encirclement.

This was a difficult undertaking, for not only was the Soviet Union frightfully devastated, but Eastern Europe was in nearly as bad shape. However, what the Soviet peoples had done twice already they could do again under the lash of containment. After the two gruelling forced marches, before 1941 and after the German invasion, they undertook still a third and within eleven years from 1946 they had achieved first their A-bomb in 1949, then the H-bomb in 1953 and the first ICBM in 1957. In all other vital respects also they had gained that position of strength which was our announced goal after March 1950.

In the course of containment, "negotiation from strength" and liberation, we revivified fully the machinery of totalitarian rule in Russia. As William A. Williams has pointed out: "Appearing as a classic and literal verification of Marx's most apocalyptic prophecy, the policy of containment strengthened the hand of every die-hard Marxist and every extreme Russian nationalist among the Soviet leadership."

Containment also gave Stalin total power over the Soviet peoples. Williams continues: Armed with the language and actions of containment, which underwrote and extended his existing power, Stalin could and did drive the Soviet people to the brink of collapse and, no doubt, to the thought of open resistance. But the dynamic of revolt was always blocked, even among those who did have access to the levels of authority, by the fact of containment and the open threat of liberation. Thus protected by his avowed enemies, Stalin was able to force his nation through extreme deprivations and extensive purges to the verge of physical and psychological exhaustion. But he also steered it through the perils of reconstruction to the security of nuclear parity with the United States."

Stalin's first reply to containment was the destruction of the Smallholder's Party in Hungary, between March and August 1947, into which he had allowed the dispossessed landlords to go, and to take over the Hungarian government in its first free elections. The ending of this government was not difficult, since a topnotch American newsman found in Hungary that the "political sterility" of these elements was so great and their inclinations toward corruption so "incorrigible" that an astonishing number of anticommunists accepted the communist claim to represent the people. The kind of democracy for which we had fought throughout East Europe might have been destroyed in Hungary anyway, but the Truman Doctrine made it a matter of life and death for the Hungarian Reds to end it.

FROM THE MARSHALL PLAN TO TOTAL DIPLOMACY

THE MARSHALL PLAN

Meanwhile the yawning economic void in West Europe had led to the American Marshall Plan, and offer of economic help to all the nations of Europe, a "policy not directed against any country or doctrine, but against hunger, poverty, desperation and chaos."

If this magnificent conception had come earlier, while the Russians were asking in vain for a six billion dollar loan, before UNRRA was abolished and before the Truman Doctrine had drawn the lines of conflict tightly, there would have been no Cold War. In the context of the declared Cold War, Russia not only rejected the Marshall Plan for herself but forbade her East European satellites to participate, foreseeing that the American largesse would dissolve shaky loyalties to her satellite governments in more than one East European quarter.

Molotov's angry departure from the Marshall Plan conference in Paris, on August 2, 1947, convinced much of Western opinion that Russia was hostile to the West and that she had deliberately split the world in two. Three months later Russia created the Cominform, an organization of all the Communist parties in East Europe, plus those of France and Italy, to back the Molotov Plan for East European reconstruction, to oppose the Marshall Plan and to fight the Cold War generally. This response to the Truman Doctrine and the Marshall Plan convinced many people throughout the West that the Russians had reverted to the world revolution and were plotting to take over the earth.

Then the Communist seizure of Czechoslovakia hardened this fear into frightened certainty. This high peak of the Cold War, in late February 1948, had been preceded by the announcement on January 22 of a plan for a Western Union in Europe, which the London *Times* later thought might have "provoked the Soviet Union to hurry forward its own plans" for the consolidation of the Communist bloc.

CZECHOSLOVAKIA

But Czechoslovakia had been lost to the West at Munich, and in the successive events of the German occupation, which had destroyed most of the conservative classes and made it impossible for the Czechs to wish to oppose Russia. Both the Truman Doctrine and the Marshall Plan had also made it certain that Russia would bring Czechoslovakia behind the Iron Curtain before long. When this happened, the West lost nothing from the power standpoint. On broader grounds it was a time for sorrow and remorse that big power politics had twice deprived the Czechs of the democracy and freedom they did not deserve to lose either time.

However, all this was forgotten in the wave of shock, alarm and anger which swept over the West. Within a month the five power Western Union treaty was signed and on the same day, March 25, 1948, President Truman made an address in which he developed the devil theory fully. One nation, and one alone, had refused to cooperate in making peace, had broken the agreements it did make, had obstructed the United Nations and destroyed both the independence and the democratic character of a whole series of nations in Central and East Europe. To stop this nation Truman demanded prompt passage of ERP, more funds for Greece, Turkey and Chiang Kai-shek, and universal military training.

Thereafter the United States proceeded rapidly along an essentially negative course, in which we rushed to counter each communist move, tied up our resources in blocking efforts, selected our friends on one test alone, and rapidly adopted at home the methods and weapons of "the enemy."

BERLIN BLOCKADE

There is more cause for satisfaction in our handling of the Berlin blockade from June 1948 to May 1949. The Russians had a strong case for terminating the four power occupation of Berlin, because the West had announced plans on June 7 for the creation of a West German government. Since the four power occupation of Berlin was based on the assumption that Berlin would be the capital of a united Germany, the quadripartite occupation did become an anomaly when the assumption was destroyed. Thereafter West Berlin became from the Russian standpoint only a listening post and spy center for the West in the center of East Germany, and an ideological thorn in her side.

The announcement of a new currency for West Germany, imperatively needed, also created urgent problems for East Germany, since it would circulate in Berlin.

These were real grievances, but from the Western standpoint they did not justify an attempt to starve out 2,000,000 West Berliners. The crisis was grave and it was met by the West imaginatively, boldly and resolutely. The advocates of sending an army of tanks to Berlin were silenced and the air-lift did the job, dramatically lifting allied prestige to new heights. In this engagement of the Cold War the action of the West was a model of combined courage and restraint, and President Truman deserves his large share of the credit for it.

''TOTAL DIPLOMACY''

The Cold War as proclaimed by Churchill and Truman would have been impractical from the start had it not been for the American A-bomb monopoly, in which both leaders took the deepest satisfaction. When it was abruptly ended in September 1949, long before the expected time, a severe crisis of confidence shook Washington, a crisis which was ended by the decision to produce H-bombs and rearm further for the successful prosecution of the Cold War. It would be a long pull and take very steady nerves, Secretary of State Acheson explained on three occasions early in 1950, but the Russian river of aggression would be contained.

Restored confidence was expressed in Acheson's Berkeley speech of March 16, 1950, in which he laid down seven pre-conditions for negotiation with Russia amounting to Soviet surrender of its positions before negotiation.

KOREA

Then on June 25, 1950, the Russian river of aggression actually moved into Western held territory for the first time when the North Koreans invaded South Korea. Hardly anyone in the West questioned this verdict. Yet there were two other equally strong probabilities: that the North Koreans plunged southward on their own initiative, and that Syngman Rhee provoked them to do so by taking the initiative along the border in the day or two after the UN observers returned to Seoul. That he would be wholly capable of precipitating a war for the unification of Korea has been amply demonstrated several times since. Both sides in Korea were highly keyed for civil war, each intent on unification its way.

Ingram's conclusion is sound when he says: "Nor are we in possession of any positive proof that in Korea or elsewhere she (Russia) has conspired to instigate minor war against the Western allies through one of her satellites." He adds that "suspicions are not proof" and doubts that any evidence can be found later to sustain the charge that the Korean trouble arose as the result of a plot by China, or the Soviet Union, or both, to embarrass the West.

No doubts on this score entered the minds of our leaders in June 1950. It was assumed at once that the Kremlin had ordered the invasion and that this was the first of a series of satellite wars which would stampede both Asia and eventually West Europe into the Soviet camp, unless this attempt were promptly scotched. The United Nations was instantly mobilized, to minimize the shock of our intervention in an Asiatic civil war.

If our cold war purpose had not been predominant, the defeat of the North Korean aggression would have been a great victory for collective security and the United Nations. As the crisis did develop the UN Security Council approved our military action before it had heard the North Koreans, and it never did hear them—a serious breach of normal, fair procedure.

Then when the 38th Parallel was recovered, within three months and relatively painlessly, the monumental error was committed of trying to abolish the North Korean state. This mistake ranks close behind our failure to lead the League of Nations and our enunciation of the Truman Doctrine among the foreign policy errors committed by the United States. It was a political mistake of the first magnitude because it challenged both China and Russia in the North Korean triangle, a strategic area of the utmost importance to them. Moreover, it challenged them as communist powers to permit the Americans to destroy a communist state in their own front yards and set up a model capitalist democracy. It was a military gamble because it launched our armies precipitately into untenable territory. It was a moral blunder because it invalidated the central idea of the United Nations that it is a police force and not a partisan belligerent. When the United Nations invaded North Korea "they were no longer acting as police, but as co-belligerents on the side of the South Koreans."

Consequently, when China intervened on behalf of the North Koreans "the United Nations by becoming belligerents instead of a police force were no longer morally entitled to indict China." But she was indicted as an aggressor, under total pressure from Washington, and is still excluded from the United Nations on that ground.

Thus what should have been a brief, successful UN police operation was converted into a full-scale war which dragged on for three more years, always on the edge of a world war, until neutralism had been made a world movement, until the whole idea of the United Nations being a policeman had been made highly doubtful, and until President Truman and his party had been driven from office, more because of "Truman's war," never declared by Congress, than for any other reason. The war had become to the American people a never ending horror in a far country, for veiled cold war reasons.

TRUMAN'S LEADERSHIP

The tragedy of the second war in Korea brought out sharply both the defects and the good qualities of President Truman's leadership. His ability to make up his mind and act is a great quality in a ruler. Without it he is lost. But it is not the only quality necessary. There are occasions, perhaps more of them, when restraint is what is needed. There are even times when a President must have "the courage to be timid" or to seem so. Restraint is a far greater virtue than rashness. Truman could plunge in easily and too far, but he did not expand the second Korean war into World War III, as so many urged him to do, and he finally recalled General MacArthur who had flagrantly exceeded his instructions and was leading the cry for a greater war. Thus Truman did not compound his great Korean error into an irretrievable one, even when there was a widespread, angry belief that the Kremlin planned to bleed us white in a series of satellite wars around Russia's vast perimeter— accepting the challenge and logic of the Truman Doctrine.

On the great issue of the Chinese Revolution Truman also avoided disaster. His Doctrine was breached in gigantic fashion by the Communist Revolution in China, and his political enemies pushed him relentlessly to enforce it there, but he had the good sense to send his greatest lieutenant, General Marshall, to China for a long effort to mediate the Chinese civil war, and afterwards he accepted Marshall's report that we could not settle that gigantic conflict. It must have been difficult to put his Doctrine into abeyance, in the place where it was violated on the greatest scale, but he did it and avoided inaugurating a third world war by that route.

By 1950, an experienced editor and biographer could write of Truman: "In 1945 the moral hegemony of the world was within his grasp, but it has slipped from his fingers."

At the close of his presidency the moral leadership of the world had passed in large part to Nehru, the neutral opponent of the Cold War, but much of it went begging for lack of a truly powerful voice. Truman, who might have voiced it, had become only the belligerent leader of an anti-Soviet, anti-communist crusade.

2 The Development of the Cold War

Not long after the Yalta conference it became clear that the allies disagreed on the interpretation of its terms. The Russians had promised self-determination and free elections in Eastern Europe. It soon became apparent that by Western standards these promises were not being kept. In the following letter written shortly before his death Roosevelt complains to Stalin.

President Roosevelt's Letter to Marshal Stalin

Received on April 1, 1945

Personal and Top Secret for Marshal Stalin
from President Roosevelt

I CANNOT CONCEAL FROM YOU the concern with which I view the developments of events of mutual interest since our fruitful meeting at Yalta. The decisions we reached there were good ones and have for the most part been welcomed with enthusiasm by the peoples of the world who saw in our ability to find a common basis of understanding the best pledge for a secure and peaceful world after this war. Precisely because of the hopes and expectations that these decisions raised, their fulfillment is being followed with the closest attention. We have no right to let them be disappointed. So far there has been a discouraging lack of progress made in the carrying out, which the world expects, of the political decisions which we reached at the conference particularly those relating to the Polish question. I am frankly puzzled as to why this should be and must tell you that I do not fully understand in many respects the apparent indifferent attitude of your Gov-

Ministry of Foreign Affairs of the U.S.S.R., *Correspondence Between the Chairman of the Council of Ministers of the U.S.S.R. and the Presidents of the U.S.A. and the Prime Ministers of Great Britain During the Great Patriotic War of 1941–1945,* II (1957), 201–4.

ernment. Having understood each other so well at Yalta I am convinced that the three of us can and will clear away any obstacles which have developed since then. I intend, therefore, in this message to lay before you with complete frankness the problem as I see it.

Although I have in mind primarily the difficulties which the Polish negotiations have encountered, I must make a brief mention of our agreement embodied in the Declaration on Liberated Europe. I frankly cannot understand why the recent developments in Roumania should be regarded as not falling within the terms of that Agreement. I hope you will find time personally to examine the correspondence between our Governments on this subject.

However, the part of our agreements at Yalta which has aroused the greatest popular interest and is the most urgent relates to the Polish question. You are aware of course that the Commission which we set up has made no progress. I feel this is due to the interpretation which your Government is placing upon the Crimea decisions. In order that there shall be no misunderstanding I set forth below my interpretations of the points of the Agreement which are pertinent to the difficulties encountered by the Commission in Moscow.

In the discussions that have taken place so far your Government appears to take the position that the new Polish Provisional Government of National Unity which we agreed should be formed should be little more than a continuation of the present Warsaw Government. I cannot reconcile this either with our agreement or our discussions. While it is true that the Lublin Government is to be reorganized and its members play a prominent role, it is to be done in such a fashion as to bring into being a new government. This point is clearly brought out in several places in the text of the Agreement. I must make it quite plain to you that any such solution which would result in a thinly disguised continuance of the present Warsaw régime would be unacceptable and would cause the people of the United States to regard the Yalta agreement as having failed.

It is equally apparent that for the same reason the Warsaw Government cannot under the Agreement claim the right to select or reject what Poles are to be brought to Moscow by the Commission for consultation. Can we not agree that it is up to the Commission to select the Polish leaders to come to Moscow to consult in the first instance and invitations be sent out accordingly. If this could be done I see no great objection to having the Lublin group come first in order that they may be fully acquainted with the agreed interpretation of the Yalta decisions on this point. It is of course understood that if the Lublin group come first no arrangements would be made independently with them before the arrival of the other Polish leaders called for consultation. In order to facilitate the agreement the Commission might first of all select a small but representative group of Polish leaders who could suggest other names for the consideration of the Commission. We have not and would not bar or veto any candidate for consultation which Mr. Molotov might propose, being confident that he would not suggest any Poles who would be inimical to the intent of the Crimea decision. I feel that it is not too much to ask that my Ambassador be accorded the same confidence and that any candidate for consultation presented by any one of the Commission be accepted by the others in good faith. It is obvious to me that if the right of the Commission to select these Poles is limited or shared with the Warsaw Government the very foundation on which our agreement rests would be destroyed.

While the foregoing are the immediate obstacles which in my opinion have prevented our Commission from making any progress in this vital matter, there are two other suggestions which were not in the agreement but nevertheless have a very important bearing on the result we all seek. Neither of these suggestions has been as yet accepted by your Government. I refer to:

(1) That there should be the maximum of political tranquility in Poland and that dissident groups should cease any measures and counter-measures against each other. That we should respectively use our influence to that end seems to me eminently reasonable.

(2) It would also seem entirely natural in view of the responsibilities placed upon them by the Agreement that representatives of the American and British members of the Commission should be permitted to visit Poland. As you will recall Mr. Molotov himself suggested this at an early meeting of the Commission and only subsequently withdrew it.

I wish I could convey to you how important it is for the successful development of our program of international collaboration that this Polish question be settled fairly and speedily. If this is not done all of the difficulties and dangers to Allied unity which we had so much in mind in reaching our decisions at the Crimea will face us in an even more acute form. You are, I am sure, aware that the genuine popular support in the United States is required to carry out any government policy, foreign or domestic. The American people make up their own mind and no government action can change it. I mention this fact because the last sentence of your message about Mr. Molotov's attendance at San Francisco made me wonder whether you give full weight to this factor.

One of the Russian grievances was America's cessation of lend-lease shipments after the end of the European War. In the following selection, Secretary of State Byrnes reports Stalin's complaint and the American response.

FROM *Speaking Frankly* BY JAMES F. BYRNES

H E [*Stalin—D. K.*] W A S P A R T I C U L A R L Y I R R I T A T E D by the manner in which lend-lease shipments had been suspended at the end of the European war. The fact that ships with supplies bound for Russia even had been unloaded indicated to him that the cancellation order was an effort to put pressure on the Soviet Union. This, he declared, was a fundamental mistake and the United States should understand much could be gained from the Russians only if they were approached on a friendly basis.

In the case of the German Navy and merchant fleet, he had sent a message to the President and the Prime Minister suggesting that one-third be turned over to the Soviets. Not only had he received no reply, he said, but he had acquired instead an impression that the request was to be rejected.

These complaints were surprising to us at home. They revealed an extreme sensitivity and an amazing degree of almost instinctive suspicion.

Mr. Hopkins forcefully and tactfully presented the position of the United States. As for the German ships, it was our intention that they should be divided equally among the three and we thought that the matter could be settled at the forthcoming meeting of the Big Three. He explained that the cancellation of lend-lease was necessary under the law because lend-lease was authorized only for the purpose of prosecuting the war. With the German war ended and with the Soviet Union not yet a participant in the Japanese war, further shipment could not be justified. The order to unload the ships was the mistake of an official who had nothing to do with policy, and the order had been withdrawn quickly. He reminded the Marshal of how liberally the United States had construed the law in sending foodstuffs and other nonmilitary items to their aid.

Stalin readily acknowledged the accuracy of Hopkins' statement. If proper warning had been given there would have been no feeling about the matter, he said, pointing out that advance notice was important to them because their economy is based on plans. The way in which the shipments had been halted made it impossible for him to express, as he had intended, the great appreciation of the Soviets for the lend-lease aid given to them.

James F. Byrnes, *Speaking Frankly* (1947), pp. 62–3. Reprinted by permission of James F. Byrnes Foundation.

Hopkins told the Marshal that what disturbed him most was the revelation that Stalin believed the United States would use lend-lease as a pressure weapon. The United States, he asserted, is a strong nation and does not need to indulge in such methods. With this, Stalin said he was fully satisfied with our explanation.

It is sometimes alleged that America's use of the atomic bomb to end the war in Asia was politically motivated and is evidence of American suspicion and hostility toward Russia even during the war. In the following selection, Norman Cousins and Thomas Finletter argue for such an interpretation.

FROM *A Beginning for Sanity*

BY NORMAN COUSINS AND THOMAS K. FINLETTER

SUMMING UP, the scientists expressed their conviction that a unilateral approach to the dropping of the bomb, even apart from moral considerations, however overwhelming, would almost inevitably result in unilateral action by other nations. And unilateralism in an atomic age was not merely a problem but a fatal disease. We would be undermining a possible common ground upon which common controls might later be built. As a corollary, we would be destroying whatever stand we might later decide to take on outlawing the use of atomic weapons in warfare. It would be naive to expect other nations to take such a plea seriously in view of our own lack of reticence in dropping the bomb when the war was on the very verge of being won without it.

Why, then, did we drop it? Or, assuming that the use of the bomb was justified, why did we not demonstrate its power in a test under the auspices of the UN, on the basis of which an ultimatum would be issued to Japan—transferring the burden of responsibility to the Japanese themselves?

In speculating upon possible answers to these questions, some facts available since the bombing may be helpful. We now know, for example, that Russia was scheduled to come into the war against Japan by August 8, 1945. Russia had agreed at Yalta to join the fight against Japan ninety days

Norman Cousins and Thomas K. Finletter, "A Beginning for Sanity," *The Saturday Review of Literature*, XXIV (June 15, 1946), 7–8. Reprinted by permission of *Saturday Review*.

after V-E day. Going after the knockout punch, we bombed Hiroshima on August 5, Nagasaki on August 7. Russia came into the war on August 8, as specified. Japan asked for surrender terms the same day.

Can it be that we were more anxious to prevent Russia from establishing a claim for full participation in the occupation against Japan than we were to think through the implications of unleashing atomic warfare? Whatever the answer, one thing seems likely: There was not enough time between July 16, when we knew at New Mexico that the bomb would work, and August 8, the Russian deadline date, for us to have set up the very complicated machinery of a test atomic bombing involving time-consuming problems of area preparations; invitations and arrangements for observers (the probability being that the transportation to the South Pacific would in itself exceed the time limit); issuance of an ultimatum and the conditions of fulfillment, even if a reply limit was set at only forty-eight hours or less—just to mention a few.

No; any test would have been impossible if the purpose was to knock Japan out before Russia came in—or at least before Russia could make anything other than a token of participation prior to a Japanese collapse.

It may be argued that this decision was justified, that it was a legitimate exercise of power politics in a rough-and-tumble world, that we thereby avoided a struggle for authority in Japan similar to what we have experienced in Germany and Italy, that unless we came out of the war with a decisive balance of power over Russia, we would be in no position to checkmate Russian expansion.

There is a dangerous plausibility here—a plausibility as inseparable from the war system of sovereign nations as armaments are from armaments races. It is the plausibility of power politics, of action leading to reaction, reaction leading to counter-reaction, and counter-reaction leading to war; of competitive systems of security rather than of workable world organization. It is a plausibility that rests on the flat assumption that war with Russia is inevitable, and that we should fight it at a time and under terms advantageous to us.

Such "plausibilities" are rejected by those who feel that the big job is to avert the next war, rather than to win it—even assuming that the next war will be worth winning, a somewhat dubious proposition. And they see no way to avert the next war other than through a world organization having the power to back up its decisions by law and relying upon preponderant force as needed. Such an organization would attempt to dispose of the fear-begetting-fear, provocation-begetting-provocation cycle; and to substitute in its place a central authority from which no member could withdraw or secede under any circumstances. It would automatically deprive potential aggressors of their traditional excuse for aggression—namely, their own encirclement and insecurity—and be strong enough to deal with them should a real threat arise.

The following selection shows the confusion and contradic-
tions in the American government over Russian partici-
pation in the Asiatic war.

FROM *The Forrestal Diaries*

TALKED WITH BYRNES [now at Potsdam as American Secretary of
State, having succeeded Mr. Stettinius on the conclusion of the San Francisco
Conference]. . . . Byrnes said he was most anxious to get the Japanese affair
over with before the Russians got in, with particular reference to Dairen and
Port Arthur. Once in there, he felt, it would not be easy to get them
out. . . .

Evidently on the question of Russian entry into the Pacific war the
wheel was now coming full circle. Forrestal was to get a further side-
light on this two years later at a reminiscent luncheon gathering at
which General Dwight D. Eisenhower was present. "When President
Truman came to Potsdam in the summer of 1945," Forrestal noted, "he
told Eisenhower he had as one of his primary objectives that of getting
Russia into the Japanese war. Eisenhower begged him at that time not to
assume that he had to give anything away to do this, that the Russians
were desperately anxious to get into the Eastern war and that in Eisenhower's opinion there was no question but that Japan was already thoroughly beaten. When the President told him at the end of the
Conference that he had achieved his objectives and was going home,
Eisenhower again remarked that he earnestly hoped the President had
not had to make any concessions to get them in."

Still later Forrestal recorded his own conclusion. In a note of June
23, 1947, he observed that the Russians would have to come into the
Marshall Plan; "they could no more afford to be out of it than they
could have afforded not to join in the war against Japan (fifty divisions
could not have kept them *out* of this war)." While Forrestal was mistaken about Soviet participation in the Marshall Plan, it does not follow
that his estimate as to the Pacific war was wrong.

Next day, a Sunday, Forrestal wandered through the ruins of Berlin
and was as deeply impressed by that staggering scene of destruction as
are all who have seen it. He also found that others did not share what
would seem to have been the President's rather optimistic mood about
the Russians.

Walter Millis, ed., with the collaboration of E. S. Duffield, *The Forrestal Diaries* (1951), pp.
78–9. Reprinted by permission of Princeton University.

*In 1946, the United States, which had a monopoly on the
production of atomic weapons, offered to share its knowledge and submit to United Nations control of atomic energy. The Baruch plan, which is described in the following
selection, was rejected by the Soviet Union.*

FROM *United States Proposals for the International Control of Atomic Energy*

STATEMENT BY BERNARD M. BARUCH, UNITED STATES REPRESENTATIVE TO THE ATOMIC ENERGY COMMISSION, JUNE 14, 1946

My Fellow Members of the United Nations Atomic Energy Commission, and
My Fellow Citizens of the World:

WE ARE HERE to make a choice between the quick and the dead.

That is our business.

Behind the black portent of the new atomic age lies a hope which, seized
upon with faith, can work our salvation. If we fail, then we have damned
every man to be the slave of Fear. Let us not deceive ourselves: We must
elect World Peace or World Destruction.

Science has torn from nature a secret so vast in its potentialities that our
minds cower from the terror it creates. Yet terror is not enough to inhibit the
use of the atomic bomb. The terror created by weapons has never stopped
man from employing them. For each new weapon a defense has been produced, in time. But now we face a condition in which adequate defense does
not exist.

Science, which gave us this dread power, shows that it *can* be made a
giant help to humanity, but science does *not* show us how to prevent its
baleful use. So we have been appointed to obviate that peril by finding a
meeting of the minds and the hearts of our peoples. Only in the will of
mankind lies the answer.

It is to express this will and make it effective that we have been
assembled. We must provide the mechanism to assure that atomic energy is
used for peaceful purposes and preclude its use in war. To that end, we must
provide immediate, swift, and sure punishment of those who violate the
agreements that are reached by the nations. Penalization is essential if peace

Senate Committee on Foreign Relations, *A Decade of American Foreign Policy: Basic Documents, 1941–1949* (1950), pp. 1079–81, 1082–7.

is to be more than a feverish interlude between wars. And, too, the United Nations can prescribe individual responsibility and punishment on the principles applied at Nürnberg by the Union of Soviet Socialist Republics, The United Kingdom, France, and the United States—a formula certain to benefit the world's future.

In this crisis, we represent not only our governments but, in a larger way, we represent the peoples of the world. We must remember that the peoples do not belong to the governments but that the governments belong to the peoples. We must answer their demands; we must answer the world's longing for peace and security.

In that desire the United States shares ardently and hopefully. The search of science for the absolute weapon has reached fruition in this country. But she stands ready to proscribe and destroy this instrument—to lift its use from death to life—if the world will join in a pact to that end.

In our success lies the promise of a new life, freed from the heart-stopping fears that now beset the world. The beginning of victory for the great ideals for which millions have bled and died lies in building a workable plan. Now we approach fulfilment of the aspirations of mankind. At the end of the road lies the fairer, better, surer life we crave and mean to have.

Only by a lasting peace are liberties and democracies strengthened and deepened. War is their enemy. And it will not do to believe that any of us can escape war's devastation. Victor, vanquished, and neutrals alike are affected physically, economically, and morally.

Against the degradation of war we can erect a safeguard. That is the guerdon for which we reach. Within the scope of the formula we outline here there will be found, to those who seek it, the essential elements of our purpose. Others will see only emptiness. Each of us carries his own mirror in which is reflected hope—or determined desperation—courage or cowardice.

There is a famine throughout the world today. It starves men's bodies. But there is a greater famine—the hunger of men's spirit. That starvation can be cured by the conquest of fear, and the substitution of hope, from which springs faith—faith in each other; faith that we want to work together toward salvation; and determination that those who threaten the peace and safety shall be punished.

The peoples of these democracies gathered here have a particular concern with our answer, for their peoples hate war. They will have a heavy exaction to make of those who fail to provide an escape. They are not afraid of an internationalism that protects; they are unwilling to be fobbed off by mouthings about narrow sovereignty, which is today's phrase for yesterday's isolation.

The basis of a sound foreign policy, in this new age, for all the nations here gathered, is that: anything that happens, no matter where or how, which menaces the peace of the world, or the economic stability concerns each and all of us.

That, roughly, may be said to be the central theme of the United Nations. It is with that thought we begin consideration of the most important subject that can engage mankind—life itself.

The United States proposes the creation of an International Atomic Development Authority, to which should be entrusted all phases of the development and use of atomic energy, starting with the raw material and including—

1. Managerial control or ownership of all atomic-energy activities potentially dangerous to world security.
2. Power to control, inspect, and license all other atomic activities.
3. The duty of fostering the beneficial uses of atomic energy.
4. Research and development responsibilities of an affirmative character intended to put the Authority in the forefront of atomic knowledge and thus to enable it to comprehend, and therefore to detect, misuse of atomic energy. To be effective the Authority must itself be the world's leader in the field of atomic knowledge and development and thus supplement its legal authority with the great power inherent in possession of leadership in knowledge.

I offer this as a basis for beginning our discussion.

But I think the peoples we serve would not believe—and without faith nothing counts—that a treaty, merely outlawing possession or use of the atomic bomb, constitutes effective fulfilment of the instructions to this Commission. Previous failures have been recorded in trying the method of simple renunciation, unsupported by effective guaranties of security and armament limitation. No one would have faith in that approach alone.

Now, if ever, is the time to act for the common good. Public opinion supports a world movement toward security. If I read the signs aright, the peoples want a program not composed merely of pious thoughts but of enforceable sanctions—an international law with teeth in it.

We of this nation, desirous of helping to bring peace to the world and realizing the heavy obligations upon us arising from our possession of the means of producing the bomb and from the fact that it is part of our armament, are prepared to make our full contribution toward effective control of atomic energy.

When an adequate system for control of atomic energy, including the renunciation of the bomb as a weapon, has been agreed upon and put into effective operation and condign punishments set up for violations of the rules of control which are to be stigmatized as international crimes, we propose that—

1. Manufacture of atomic bombs shall stop;
2. Existing bombs shall be disposed of pursuant to the terms of the treaty, and
3. The Authority shall be in possession of full information as to the know-how for the production of atomic energy.

Let me repeat, so as to avoid misunderstanding: my country is ready to make its full contribution toward the end we seek, subject of course, to our constitutional processes, and to an adequate system of control becoming fully effective, as we finally work it out.

Now as to violations: in the agreement, penalties of as serious a nature as the nations may wish and as immediate and certain in their execution as possible, should be fixed for:

1. Illegal possession or use of an atomic bomb;
2. Illegal possession, or separation, of atomic material suitable for use in an atomic bomb;
3. Seizure of any plant or other property belonging to or licensed by the Authority;
4. Wilful interference with the activities of the Authority;
5. Creation or operation of dangerous projects in a manner contrary to, or in the absence of, a license granted by the international control body.

It would be a deception, to which I am unwilling to lend myself, were I not to say to you and to our peoples, that the matter of punishment lies at the very heart of our present security system. It might as well be admitted, here and now, that the subject goes straight to the veto power contained in the Charter of the United Nations so far as it relates to the field of atomic energy. The Charter permits penalization only by concurrence of each of the five great powers—Union of Soviet Socialist Republics, the United Kingdom, China, France and the United States.

I want to make very plain that I am concerned here with the veto power only as it affects this particular problem. There must be no veto to protect those who violate their solemn agreements not to develop or use atomic energy for destructive purposes.

The bomb does not wait upon debate. To delay may be to die. The time between violation and preventive action or punishment would be all too short for extended discussion as to the course to be followed.

As matters now stand several years may be necessary for another country to produce a bomb, *de novo*. However, once the basic information is generally known, and the Authority has established producing plants for peaceful purposes in the several countries, an illegal seizure of such a plant might permit a malevolent nation to produce a bomb in 12 months, and if preceded by secret preparation and necessary facilities perhaps even in a much shorter time. The time required—the advance warning given of the possible use of a bomb—can only be generally estimated but obviously will depend upon many factors, including the success with which the Authority has been able to introduce elements of safety in the design of its plants and the degree to which illegal and secret preparation for the military use of atomic energy will have been eliminated. Presumably no nation would think of starting a war with only one bomb.

This shows how imperative speed is in detecting and penalizing violations.

The process of prevention and penalization—a problem of profound statecraft—is, as I read it, implicit in the Moscow statement, signed by the Union of Soviet Socialist Republics, the United States, and the United Kingdom a few months ago.

But before a country is ready to relinquish any winning weapons it must have more than words to reassure it. It must have a guarantee of safety, not only against the offenders in the atomic area but against the illegal users of other weapons—bacteriological, biological, gas—perhaps—why not?—against the war itself.

In the elimination of war lies our solution, for only then will nations cease to compete with one another in the production and use of dread "secret" weapons which are evaluated solely by their capacity to kill. This devilish program takes us back not merely to the Dark Ages, but from cosmos to chaos. If we succeed in finding a suitable way to control atomic weapons, it is reasonable to hope that we may also preclude the use of other weapons adaptable to mass destruction. When a man learns to say "A" he can, if he chooses, learn the rest of the alphabet, too.

Let this be anchored in our minds:

Peace is never long preserved by weight of metal or by an armament race. Peace can be made tranquil and secure only by understanding and agreement fortified by sanctions. We must embrace international cooperation or international disintegration.

Science has taught us how to put the atom to work. But to make it work for good instead of for evil lies in the domain dealing with the principles of human duty. We are now facing a problem more of ethics than of physics.

The solution will require apparent sacrifice in pride and in position, but better pain as the price of peace than death as the price of war.

I now submit the following measures as representing the fundamental features of a plan which would give effect to certain of the conclusions which I have epitomized.

1. *General.* The Authority should set up a thorough plan for control of the field of atomic energy, through various forms of ownership, dominion, licenses, operation, inspection, research and management by competent personnel. After this is provided for, there should be as little interference as may be with the economic plans and the present private, corporate and state relationships in the several countries involved.
2. *Raw Materials.* The Authority should have as one of its earliest purposes to obtain and maintain complete and accurate information on world supplies of uranium and thorium and to bring them under its dominion. The precise pattern of control for various types of deposits of such materials will have to depend upon the geological, mining, refining, and economic facts involved in different situations.

The Authority should conduct continuous surveys so that it will have the most complete knowledge of the world geology of uranium and thorium. Only after all current information on world sources of uranium and thorium is known to us all can equitable plans be made for their production, refining, and distribution.

3. *Primary Production Plants.* The Authority should exercise complete managerial control of the production of fissionable materials. This means that it should control and operate all plants producing fissionable materials in dangerous quantities and must own and control the product of these plants.

4. *Atomic Explosives.* The Authority should be given sole and exclusive right to conduct research in the field of atomic explosives. Research activities in the field of atomic explosives are essential in order that the Authority may keep in the forefront of knowledge in the field of atomic energy and fulfil the objective of preventing illicit manufacture of bombs. Only by maintaining its position as the best-informed agency will the Authority be able to determine the line between intrinsically dangerous and non-dangerous activities.

5. *Strategic Distribution of Activities and Materials.* The activities entrusted exclusively to the Authority because they are intrinsically dangerous to security should be distributed throughout the world. Similarly, stockpiles of raw materials and fissionable materials should not be centralized.

6. *Non-Dangerous Activities.* A function of the Authority should be promotion of the peacetime benefits of atomic energy.

Atomic research (except in explosives), the use of research reactors, the production of radioactive tracers by means of non-dangerous reactors, the use of such tracers, and to some extent the production of power should be open to nations and their citizens under reasonable licensing arrangements from the Authority. Denatured materials, whose use we know also requires suitable safeguards, should be furnished for such purposes by the Authority under lease or other arrangement. Denaturing seems to have been overestimated by the public as a safety measure.

7. *Definition of Dangerous and Non-Dangerous Activities.* Although a reasonable dividing line can be drawn between dangerous and non-dangerous activities, it is not hard and fast. Provision should, therefore, be made to assure constant reexamination of the questions and to permit revision of the dividing line as changing conditions and new discoveries may require.

8. *Operations of Dangerous Activities.* Any plant dealing with uranium or thorium after it once reaches the potential of dangerous use must be not only subject to the most rigorous and competent inspection by the Authority, but its actual operation shall be under the management, supervision, and control of the Authority.

9. *Inspection.* By assigning intrinsically dangerous activities exclusively to

the Authority, the difficulties of inspection are reduced. If the Authority is the only agency which may lawfully conduct dangerous activities, then visible operation by others than the Authority will constitute an unambiguous danger signal. Inspection will also occur in connection with the licensing functions of the Authority.

10. *Freedom of Access.* Adequate ingress and egress for all qualified representatives of the Authority must be assured. Many of the inspection activities of the Authority should grow out of, and be incidental to, its other functions. Important measures of inspection will be associated with the tight control of raw materials, for this is a keystone of the plan. The continuing activities of prospecting, survey, and research in relation to raw materials will be designed not only to serve the affirmative development functions of the Authority, but also to assure that no surreptitious operations are conducted in the raw materials field by nations or their citizens.

11. *Personnel.* The personnel of the Authority should be recruited on a basis of proven competence but also so far as possible on an international basis.

12. *Progress by Stages.* A primary step in the creation of the system of control is the setting forth, in comprehensive terms, of the functions, responsibilities, powers and limitations of the Authority. Once a Charter for the Authority has been adopted, the Authority and the system of control for which it will be responsible will require time to become fully organized and effective. The plan of control will, therefore, have to come into effect in successive stages. These should be specifically fixed in the Charter or means should be otherwise set forth in the Charter for transitions from one stage to another, as contemplated in the resolution of the United Nations Assembly which created this Commission.

13. *Disclosures.* In the deliberations of the United Nations Commission on Atomic Energy, the United States is prepared to make available the information essential to a reasonable understanding of the proposals which it advocates. Further disclosures must be dependent, in the interests of all, upon the effective ratification of the treaty. When the Authority is actually created, the United States will join the other nations in making available the further information essential to that organization for the performance of its functions. As the successive stages of international control are reached, the United States will be prepared to yield, to the extent required by each stage, national control of activities in this field to the Authority.

14. *International Control.* There will be questions about the extent of control to be allowed to national bodies, when the Authority is established. Purely national authorities for control and development of atomic energy should to the extent necessary for the effective operation of the Authority be subordinate to it. This is neither an endorsement nor a disapproval of

the creation of national authorities. The Commission should evolve a clear demarcation of the scope of duties and responsibilities of such national authorities.

And now I end. I have submitted an outline for present discussion. Our consideration will be broadened by the criticism of the United States proposals and by the plans of the other nations, which, it is to be hoped, will be submitted at their early convenience. I and my associates of the United States Delegation will make available to each member of this body books and pamphlets, including the Acheson–Lilienthal report, recently made by the United States Department of State, and the McMahon Committee Monograph No. 1 entitled "Essential Information on Atomic Energy" relating to the McMahon Bill recently passed by the United States Senate, which may prove of value in assessing the situation.

All of us are consecrated to making an end of gloom and hopelessness. It will not be an easy job. The way is long and thorny, but supremely worth traveling. All of us want to stand erect, with our faces to the sun, instead of being forced to burrow into the earth, like rats.

The pattern of salvation must be worked out by all for all.

The light at the end of the tunnel is dim, but our path seems to grow brighter as we actually begin our journey. We cannot yet light the way to the end. However, we hope the suggestions of my government will be illuminating.

Let us keep in mind the exhortation of Abraham Lincoln, whose words, uttered at a moment of shattering national peril, form a complete text for our deliberation. I quote, paraphrasing slightly:

"We cannot escape history. We of this meeting will be remembered in spite of ourselves. No personal significance or insignificance can spare one or another of us. The fiery trial through which we are passing will light us down in honor or dishonor to the latest generation.

"We say we are for Peace. The world will not forget that we say this. We know how to save Peace. The world knows that we do. We, even we here, hold the power and have the responsibility.

"We shall nobly save, or meanly lose, the last, best hope of earth. The way is plain, peaceful, generous, just—a way which, if followed, the world will forever applaud."

My thanks for your attention.

On March 5, 1946, Winston Churchill, in a speech at West-minster College in Fulton, Missouri, gave public recognition to the division that had arisen between the former allies.

FROM *Winston Churchill's Speech at Fulton*

EUROPE DIVIDED

A SHADOW HAS FALLEN upon the scenes so lately lighted by the Allied victory. Nobody knows what Soviet Russia and its Communist international organization intends to do in the immediate future, or what are the limits, if any, to their expansive and proselytizing tendencies. I have a strong admiration and regard for the valiant Russian people and for my war-time comrade, Marshal Stalin. There is sympathy and good will in Britain—and I doubt not here also—toward the peoples of all the Russias and a resolve to persevere through many differences and rebuffs in establishing lasting friendships. We understand the Russians need to be secure on her western frontiers from all renewal of German aggression. We welcome her to her rightful place among the leading nations of the world. Above all we welcome constant, frequent and growing contacts between the Russian people and our own people on both sides of the Atlantic. It is my duty, however, to place before you certain facts about the present position in Europe—I am sure I do not wish to, but it is my duty, I feel, to present them to you.

From Stettin in the Baltic to Triest in the Adriatic, an iron curtain has descended across the Continent. Behind that line lie all the capitals of the ancient states of central and eastern Europe. Warsaw, Berlin, Prague, Vienna, Budapest, Belgrade, Bucharest and Sofia, all these famous cities and the populations around them lie in the Soviet sphere and all are subject in one form or another, not only to Soviet influence but to a very high and increasing measure of control from Moscow. Athens alone, with its immortal glories, is free to decide its future at an election under British, American and French observation. The Russian-dominated Polish government has been encouraged to make enormous and wrongful inroads upon Germany, and mass expulsions of millions of Germans on a scale grievous and undreamed of are now taking place. The Communist parties, which were very small in all these eastern states of Europe, have been raised to pre-eminence and power far beyond their numbers and are seeking everywhere to obtain

Vital Speeches of the Day, XII (March 15, 1946), 331–2. Reprinted by permission of City News Publishing Co.

totalitarian control. Police governments are prevailing in nearly every case, and so far, except in Czechoslovakia, there is no true democracy. Turkey and Persia are both profoundly alarmed and disturbed at the claims which are made upon them and at the pressure being exerted by the Moscow government. An attempt is being made by the Russians in Berlin to build up a quasi-Communist party in their zone of occupied Germany by showing special favors to groups of Left-Wing German leaders. At the end of the fighting last June, the American and British armies withdrew westward, in accordance with an earlier agreement, to a depth at some points 150 miles on a front of nearly 400 miles to allow the Russians to occupy this vast expanse of territory which the western democracies had conquered. If now the Soviet government tries, by separate action, to build up a pro-Communist Germany in their areas this will cause new serious difficulties in the British and American zones, and will give the defeated Germans the power of putting themselves up to auction between the Soviets and western democracies. Whatever conclusions may be drawn from these facts—and facts they are—this is certainly not the liberated Europe we fought to build up. Nor is it one which contains the essentials of permanent peace.

The safety of the world, ladies and gentlemen, requires a new unity in Europe from which no nation should be permanently outcast.

It is impossible not to comprehend—twice we have seen them drawn by irresistible forces in time to secure the victory but only after frightful slaughter and devastation have occurred. Twice the United States has had to send millions of its young men to fight a war, but now war can find any nation between dusk and dawn. Surely we should work within the structure of the United Nations and in accordance with our charter. That is an open course of policy.

COMMUNIST FIFTH COLUMNS

In front of the iron curtain which lies across Europe are other causes for anxiety. In Italy the Communist party is seriously hampered by having to support the Communist trained Marshal Tito's claims to former Italian territory at the head of the Adriatic. Nevertheless the future of Italy hangs in the balance. Again one cannot imagine a regenerated Europe without a strong France. All my public life I have worked for a strong France and I never lost faith in her destiny, even in the darkest hours. I will not lose faith now. However, in a great number of countries, far from the Russian frontiers and throughout the world, Communist fifth columns are established and work in complete unity and absolute obedience to the directions they receive from the Communist center. Except in the British Commonwealth and in this United States, where Communism is in its infancy, the Communist parties or fifth columns constitute a growing challenge and peril to Christian civilization. These are somber facts for any one to have to recite on the morrow of a victory gained by so much splendid comradeship in arms and in the cause of freedom and democracy, and we should be most unwise not to face them squarely while time remains.

The outlook is also anxious in the Far East and especially in Manchuria. The agreement which was made at Yalta, to which I was a party, was extremely favorable to Soviet Russia, but it was made at a time when no one could say that the German war might not extend all through the summer and autumn of 1945 and when the Japanese war was expected to last for a further eighteen months from the end of the German war. In this country you are all so well informed about the Far East, and such devoted friends of China, that I do not need to expatiate on the situation there.

I have felt bound to portray the shadow which, alike in the West and in the East, falls upon the world. I was a minister at the time of the Versailles treaty and a close friend of Mr. Lloyd George. I did not myself agree with many things that were done, but I have a very vague impression in my mind of that situation, and I find it painful to contrast it with that which prevails now. In those days there were high hopes and unbounded confidence that the wars were over, and that the League of Nations would become all-powerful. I do not see or feel the same confidence or even the same hopes in the haggard world at this time.

WAR NOT INEVITABLE

On the other hand I repulse the idea that a new war is inevitable; still more that it is imminent. It is because I am so sure that our fortunes are in our own hands and that we hold the power to save the future, that I feel the duty to speak out now that I have an occasion to do so. I do not believe that Soviet Russia desires war. What they desire is the fruits of war and the indefinite expansion of their power and doctrines. But what we have to consider here today while time remains, is the permanent prevention of war and the establishment of conditions of freedom and democracy as rapidly as possible in all countries. Our difficulties and dangers will not be removed by closing our eyes to them. They will not be removed by mere waiting to see what happens; nor will they be relieved by a policy of appeasement. What is needed is a settlement and the longer this is delayed the more difficult it will be and the greater our dangers will become. From what I have seen of our Russian friends and allies during the war, I am convinced that there is nothing they admire so much as strength, and there is nothing for which they have less respect than for military weakness. For that reason the old doctrine of a balance of power is unsound. We cannot afford, if we can help it, to work on narrow margins, offering temptations to a trial of strength. If the western democracies stand together in strict adherence to the principles of the United Nations Charter, their influence for furthering these principles will be immense and no one is likely to molest them. If, however, they become divided or falter in their duty, and if these all-important years are allowed to slip away, then indeed catastrophe may overwhelm us all.

Last time I saw it all coming, and cried aloud to my fellow countrymen and to the world, but no one paid any attention. Up till the year 1933 or even 1935, Germany might have been saved from the awful fate which has overtaken her and we might all have been spared the miseries Hitler let loose upon mankind. There never was a war in all history easier to prevent by timely action than the one which has just desolated such great areas of the globe. It could have been prevented without the firing of a single shot, and Germany might be powerful, prosperous and honored today, but no one would listen and one by one we were all sucked into the awful whirlpool. We surely must not let that happen again. This can only be achieved by reaching now, in 1946, a good understanding on all points with Russia under the general authority of the United Nations Organization and by the maintenance of that good understanding through many peaceful years, by the world instrument, supported by the whole strength of the English-speaking world and all its connections.

Let no man underrate the abiding power of the British Empire and Commonwealth. Because you see the forty-six millions in our island harassed about their food supply, of which they grew only one half, even in war time, or because we have difficulty in restarting our industries and export trade after six years of passionate war effort, do not suppose that we shall not come through these dark years of privation as we have come through the glorious years of agony, or that half a century from now you will not see seventy or eighty millions of Britons spread about the world and united in defense of our traditions, our way of life and of the world causes we and you espouse. If the population of the English-speaking commonwealth be added to that of the United States, with all that such co-operation implies in the air, on the sea and in science and industry, there will be no quivering, precarious balance of power to offer its temptation to ambition or adventure. On the contrary, there will be an overwhelming assurance of security. If we adhere faithfully to the charter of the United Nations and walk forward in sedate and sober strength, seeking no one's land or treasure, or seeking to lay no arbitrary control on the thoughts of men, if all British moral and material forces and convictions are joined with your own in fraternal association, the highroads of the future will be clear, not only for us but for all, not only for our time but for a century to come.

In 1947 Britain informed the United States that she could no longer support the Greeks in their fight against a communist insurrection supported from the outside. On March 12 of that year President Truman went before Congress and asked for legislation to undertake the support of both

*Greece and Turkey, which was also in danger. The Tru-
man Doctrine marked a new step in American involvement
in world affairs.*

Message of the President to the Congress

Mr. President, Mr. Speaker, Members of the Congress of the United States:

THE GRAVITY OF THE SITUATION which confronts the world today
necessitates my appearance before a joint session of the Congress.

The foreign policy and the national security of this country are involved.

One aspect of the present situation, which I wish to present to you at this
time for your consideration and decision, concerns Greece and Turkey.

The United States has received from the Greek Government an urgent
appeal for financial and economic assistance. Preliminary reports from the
American Economic Mission now in Greece and reports from the American
Ambassador in Greece corroborate the statement of the Greek Government
that assistance is imperative if Greece is to survive as a free nation.

I do not believe that the American people and the Congress wish to turn
a deaf ear to the appeal of the Greek Government.

Greece is not a rich country. Lack of sufficient natural resources has
always forced the Greek people to work hard to make both ends met. Since
1940 this industrious and peace-loving country has suffered invasion, four
years of cruel enemy occupation, and bitter internal strife.

When forces of liberation entered Greece they found that the retreating
Germans had destroyed virtually all the railways, roads, port facilities, communications, and merchant marine. More than a thousand villages had been
burned. Eighty-five percent of the children were tubercular. Livestock, poultry, and draft animals had almost disappeared. Inflation had wiped out
practically all savings.

As a result of these tragic conditions, a militant minority, exploiting
human want and misery, was able to create political chaos which, until now,
has made economic recovery impossible.

Greece is today without funds to finance the importation of those goods
which are essential to bare subsistence. Under these circumstances the people
of Greece cannot make progress in solving their problems of reconstruction.
Greece is in desperate need of financial and economic assistance to enable it to

Senate Committee on Foreign Relations, *A Decade of American Foreign Policy: Basic Documents
1941–1949* (1950), pp. 1235–7.

resume purchases of food, clothing, fuel, and seeds. These are indispensable for the subsistence of its people and are obtainable only from abroad. Greece must have help to import the goods necessary to restore internal order and security so essential for economic and political recovery.

The Greek Government has also asked for the assistance of experienced American administrators, economists, and technicians to insure that the financial and other aid given to Greece shall be used effectively in creating a stable and self-sustaining economy and in improving its public administration.

The very existence of the Greek state is today threatened by the terrorist activities of several thousand armed men, led by Communists, who defy the Government's authority at a number of points, particularly along the northern boundaries. A commission appointed by the United Nations Security Council is at present investigating disturbed conditions in northern Greece and alleged border violations along the frontier between Greece on the one hand and Albania, Bulgaria, and Yugoslavia on the other.

Meanwhile, the Greek Government is unable to cope with the situation. The Greek Army is small and poorly equipped. It needs supplies and equipment if it is to restore authority to the Government throughout Greek territory.

Greece must have assistance if it is to become a self-supporting and self-respecting democracy.

The United States must supply that assistance. We have already extended to Greece certain types of relief and economic aid, but these are inadequate.

There is no other country to which democratic Greece can turn.

No other nation is willing and able to provide the necessary support for a democratic Greek Government.

The British Government, which has been helping Greece, can give no further financial or economic aid after March 31. Great Britain finds itself under the necessity of reducing or liquidating its commitments in several parts of the world, including Greece.

We have considered how the United Nations might assist in this crisis. But the situation is an urgent one requiring immediate action, and the United Nations and its related organizations are not in a position to extend help of the kind that is required.

It is important to note that the Greek Government has asked for our aid in utilizing effectively the financial and other assistance we may give to Greece, and in improving its public administration. It is of the utmost importance that we supervise the use of any funds made available to Greece, in such a manner that each dollar spent will count toward making Greece self-supporting, and will help to build an economy in which a healthy democracy can flourish.

No government is perfect. One of the chief virtues of a democracy, however, is that its defects are always visible and under democratic processes can be pointed out and corrected. The Government of Greece is not perfect. Nevertheless it represents 85 percent of the members of the Greek Parliament who were chosen in an election last year. Foreign observers, including 692 Americans, considered this election to be a fair expression of the views of the Greek people.

The Greek Government has been operating in an atmosphere of chaos and extremism. It has made mistakes. The extension of aid by this country does not mean that the United States condones everything that the Greek Government has done or will do. We have condemned in the past, and we condemn now, extremist measures of the right or the left. We have in the past advised tolerance, and we advise tolerance now.

Greece's neighbor, Turkey, also deserves our attention.

The future of Turkey as an independent and economically sound state is clearly no less important to the freedom-loving peoples of the world than the future of Greece. The circumstances in which Turkey finds itself today are considerably different from those of Greece. Turkey has been spared the disasters that have beset Greece. And during the war the United States and Great Britain furnished Turkey with material aid.

Nevertheless, Turkey now needs our support.

Since the war Turkey has sought additional financial assistance from Great Britain and the United States for the purpose of effecting that modernization necessary for the maintenance of its national integrity.

That integrity is essential to the preservation of order in the Middle East.

The British Government has informed us that, owing to its own difficulties, it can no longer extend financial or economic aid to Turkey.

As in the case of Greece, if Turkey is to have the assistance it needs, the United States must supply it. We are the only country able to provide that help.

I am fully aware of the broad implications involved if the United States extends assistance to Greece and Turkey, and I shall discuss these implications with you at this time.

One of the primary objectives of the foreign policy of the United States is the creation of conditions in which we and other nations will be able to work out a way of life free from coercion. This was a fundamental issue in the war with Germany and Japan. Our victory was won over countries which sought to impose their will, and their way of life, upon other nations.

To insure the peaceful development of nations, free from coercion, the United States has taken a leading part in establishing the United Nations. The United Nations is designed to make possible lasting freedom and independence for all its members. We shall not realize our objectives, however, unless we are willing to help free peoples to maintain their free institutions and their national integrity against aggressive movements that seek to impose upon them totalitarian regimes. This is no more than a frank recognition that totalitarian regimes imposed upon free peoples, by direct or indirect aggression, undermine the foundations of international peace and hence the security of the United States.

The peoples of a number of countries of the world have recently had totalitarian regimes forced upon them against their will. The Government of the United States has made frequent protests against coercion and intimidation, in violation of the Yalta agreement, in Poland, Rumania, and Bulgaria. I must also state that in a number of other countries there have been similar developments.

At the present moment in world history nearly every nation must choose between alternative ways of life. The choice is too often not a free one.

One way of life is based upon the will of the majority, and is distinguished by free institutions, representative government, free elections, guaranties, of individual liberty, freedom of speech and religion, and freedom from political oppression.

The second way of life is based upon the will of a minority forcibly imposed upon the majority. It relies upon terror and oppression, a controlled press and radio, fixed elections, and the suppression of personal freedoms.

I believe that it must be the policy of the United States to support free peoples who are resisting attempted subjugation by armed minorities or by outside pressures.

I believe that we must assist free peoples to work out their own destinies in their own way.

I believe that our help should be primarily through economic and financial aid which is essential to economic stability and orderly political processes.

The world is not static, and the *status quo* is not sacred. But we cannot allow changes in the *status quo* in violation of the Charter of the United Nations by such methods as coercion, or by such subterfuges as political infiltration. In helping free and independent nations to maintain their freedom, the United States will be giving effect to the principles of the Charter of the United Nations.

It is necessary only to glance at a map to realize that the survival and integrity of the Greek nation are of grave importance in a much wider situation. If Greece should fall under the control of an armed minority, the effect upon its neighbor, Turkey, would be immediate and serious. Confusion and disorder might well spread throughout the entire Middle East.

Moreover, the disappearance of Greece as an independent state would have a profound effect upon those countries in Europe whose peoples are struggling against great difficulties to maintain their freedoms and their independence while they repair the damages of war.

It would be an unspeakable tragedy if these countries, which have struggled so long against overwhelming odds, should lose that victory for which they sacrificed so much. Collapse of free institutions and loss of independence would be disastrous not only for them but for the world. Discouragement and possibly failure would quickly be the lot of neighboring peoples striving to maintain their freedom and independence.

Should we fail to aid Greece and Turkey in this fateful hour, the effect will be far-reaching to the West as well as to the East.

We must take immediate and resolute action.

I therefore ask the Congress to provide authority for assistance to Greece and Turkey in the amount of $400,000,000 for the period ending June 30, 1948. In requesting these funds, I have taken into consideration the maximum amount of relief assistance which would be furnished to Greece out of the $350,000,000 which I recently requested that the Congress authorize for the prevention of starvation and suffering in countries devastated by the war.

In addition to funds, I ask the Congress to authorize the detail of American civilian and military personnel to Greece and Turkey, at the request of those countries, to assist in the tasks of reconstruction, and for the purpose of supervising the use of such financial and material assistance as may be furnished. I recommend that authority also be provided for the instruction and training of selected Greek and Turkish personnel.

Finally, I ask that the Congress provide authority which will permit the speediest and most effective use, in terms of needed commodities, supplies, and equipment, of such funds as may be authorized.

If further funds, or further authority, should be needed for purposes indicated in this message, I shall not hesitate to bring the situation before the Congress. On this subject the Executive and Legislative branches of the Government must work together.

This is a serious course upon which we embark.

I would not recommend it except that the alternative is much more serious.

The United States contributed $341,000,000,000 toward winning World War II. This is an investment in world freedom and world peace.

The assistance that I am recommending for Greece and Turkey amounts to little more than one-tenth of one percent of this investment. It is only common sense that we should safeguard this investment and make sure that it was not in vain.

The seeds of totalitarian regimes are nurtured by misery and want. They spread and grow in the evil soil of poverty and strife. They reach their full growth when the hope of a people for a better life has died.

We must keep that hope alive.

The free peoples of the world look to us for support in maintaining their freedoms.

If we falter in our leadership, we may endanger the peace of the world— and we shall surely endanger the welfare of our own Nation.

Great responsibilities have been placed upon us by the swift movement of events.

I am confident that the Congress will face these responsibilities squarely.

The Russians did not fail to respond to the Truman Doctrine. The following editorial from Izvestia *presents their view.*

Editorial From Izvestia

ON MARCH 12, President Truman addressed a message to the U. S. Congress asking for 400 million dollars to be assigned for urgent aid to Greece and Turkey, and for authority to send to those countries American civil and military personnel, and to provide for the training by Americans by specially picked Greek and Turkish personnel.

Greece, said Truman, was in a desperate economic and political situation. Britain was no longer able to act as trustee for the Greeks. Turkey had requested speedy American aid. Turkey, unlike Greece, had not suffered from the Second World War, but she needed financial aid from Britain and from the U.S.A. in order to carry out that modernisation necessary for maintaining her national integrity. Since the British Government, on account of its own difficulties, was not capable of offering financial or other aid to the Turks, this aid must be furnished by the U.S.A.

Thus Congress was asked to do two "good deeds" at once—to save Greece from internal disorders and to pay for the cost of "modernising" Turkey.

The pathetic appeal of the Tsaldaris Government to the U.S.A. is clear evidence of the bankruptcy of the political regime in Greece. But the matter does not lie solely with the Greek Monarchists and their friends, now cracked up to American Congressmen as the direct descendents of the heroes of Thermopylae: it is well known that the real masters of Greece have been and are the British military authorities.

British troops have been on Greek territory since 1944. On Churchill's initiative, Britain took on herself the responsibility for "stabilising" political conditions in Greece. The British authorities did not confine themselves to perpetuating the rule of the reactionary, anti-democratic forces in Greece, making no scruple in supporting ex-collaborators with the Germans. The entire political and economic activities under a number of short-lived Greek Governments have been carried on under close British control and direction.

Today we can see the results of this policy—complete bankruptcy. British troops failed to bring peace and tranquillity to tormented Greece. The Greek people have been plunged into the abyss of new sufferings, of hunger and poverty. Civil war takes on ever fiercer forms.

Izvestia, March 13, 1947, in William A. Williams, *The Shaping of American Diplomacy* (1956), pp. 1003–5.

Was not the presence of foreign troops on Greek territory instrumental in bringing about this state of affairs? Does not Britain, who proclaimed herself the guardian of Greece, bear responsibility for the bankruptcy of her charge?

The American President's message completely glosses over these questions. The U.S.A. does not wish to criticise Britain, since she herself intends to follow the British example. Truman's statement makes it clear that the U.S.A. does not intend to deviate from the course of British policy in Greece. So one cannot expect better results.

The U. S. Government has no intention of acting in the Greek question as one might have expected a member of UNO, concerned about the fate of another member, to act. It is obvious that in Washington they do not wish to take into account the obligations assumed by the U. S. Government regarding UNO. Truman did not even consider it necessary to wait for the findings of the Security Council Commission specially sent to Greece to investigate the situation on the spot.

Truman, indeed, failed to reckon either with the international organisation or with the sovereignty of Greece. What will be left of Greek sovereignty when the "American military and civilian personnel" gets to work in Greece by means of the 250 million dollars brought into that country? The sovereignty and independence of Greece will be the first victims of such singular "defence."

The American arguments for assisting Turkey base themselves on the existence of a threat to the integrity of Turkish territory—though no-one and nothing actually threatens Turkey's integrity. This "assistance" is evidently aimed at putting this country also under U. S. control.

Some American commentators admit this quite openly. Walter Lippmann, for example, frankly points out in the *Herald Tribune* that an American alliance with Turkey would give the U.S.A. a strategic position, incomparably more advantageous than any other, from which power could be wielded over the Middle East.

Commenting on Truman's message to Congress, the *New York Times* proclaims the advent of "the age of American responsibility." Yet what is this responsibility but a smokescreen for expansion? The cry of saving Greece and Turkey from the expansion of the so-called "totalitarian states" is not new. Hitler used to refer to the Bolsheviks when he wanted to open the road for his own conquests. Now they want to take Greece and Turkey under their control, they raise a din about "totalitarian states." This seems all the more attractive since, in elbowing in itself, the U.S.A. is pushing non-totalitarian Britain out of yet another country or two.

We are now witnessing a fresh intrusion of the U.S.A. into the affairs of other states. American claims to leadership in international affairs grow parallel with the growing appetite of the American quarters concerned. But the American leaders, in the new historical circumstances, fail to reckon with the fact that the old methods of the colonisers and diehard politicians have out-lived their time and are doomed to failure. In this lies the chief weakness of Truman's message.

> *Aware that the threat of communist revolution was greatest where poverty existed, Secretary of State Marshall proposed a plan whereby the United States would help the European nations return to prosperity. Although the Iron Curtain countries were included in the Marshall Plan, Russian hostility prevented their participation.*

The European Recovery Program

REMARKS BY SECRETARY MARSHALL, JUNE 5, 1947

I NEED NOT TELL YOU GENTLEMEN that the world situation is very serious. That must be apparent to all intelligent people. I think one difficulty is that the problem is one of such enormous complexity that the very mass of facts presented to the public by press and radio make it exceedingly difficult for the man in the street to reach a clear appraisement of the situation. Furthermore, the people of this country are distant from the troubled areas of the earth and it is hard for them to comprehend the plight and consequent reactions of the long-suffering peoples, and the effect of those reactions on their governments in connection with our efforts to promote peace in the world.

In considering the requirements for the rehabilitation of Europe, the physical loss of life, the visible destruction of cities, factories, mines, and railroads was correctly estimated, but it has become obvious during recent months that this visible destruction was probably less serious than the dislocation of the entire fabric of European economy. For the past 10 years conditions have been highly abnormal. The feverish preparation for war and the more feverish maintenance of the war effort engulfed all aspects of national economies. Machinery has fallen into disrepair or is entirely obsolete. Under the arbitrary and destructive Nazi rule, virtually every possible enterprise was geared into the German war machine. Long-standing commercial ties, private institutions, banks, insurance companies, and shipping companies disappeared, through loss of capital, absorption through nationalization, or by simple destruction. In many countries, confidence in the local

Senate Committee on Foreign Relations, *A Decade of American Foreign Policy: Basic Documents, 1941–1949* (1950), pp. 1268–70.

currency has been severely shaken. The breakdown of the business structure of Europe during the war was complete. Recovery has been seriously retarded by the fact that two years after the close of hostilities a peace settlement with Germany and Austria has not been agreed upon. But even given a more prompt solution of these difficult problems, the rehabilitation of the economic structure of Europe quite evidently will require a much longer time and greater effort than had been foreseen.

There is a phase of this matter which is both interesting and serious. The farmer has always produced the foodstuffs to exchange with the city dweller for the other necessities of life. This division of labor is the basis of modern civilization. At the present time it is threatened with breakdown. The town and city industries are not producing adequate goods to exchange with the food-producing farmer. Raw materials and fuel are in short supply. Machinery is lacking or worn out. The farmer or the peasant cannot find the goods for sale which he desires to purchase. So the sale of his farm produce for money which he cannot use seems to him an unprofitable transaction. He, therefore, has withdrawn many fields from crop cultivation and is using them for grazing. He feeds more grain to stock and finds for himself and his family an ample supply of food, however short he may be on clothing and the other ordinary gadgets of civilization. Meanwhile people in the cities are short of food and fuel. So the governments are forced to use their foreign money and credits to procure these necessities abroad. This process exhausts funds which are urgently needed for reconstruction. Thus a very serious situation is rapidly developing which bodes no good for the world. The modern system of the division of labor upon which the exchange of products is based is in danger of breaking down.

The truth of the matter is that Europe's requirements for the next three or four years of foreign food and other essential products—principally from America—are so much greater than her present ability to pay that she must have substantial additional help or face economic, social, and political deterioration of a very grave character.

The remedy lies in breaking the vicious circle and restoring the confidence of the European people in the economic future of their own countries and of Europe as a whole. The manufacturer and the farmer throughout wide areas must be able and willing to exchange their products for currencies the continuing value of which is not open to question.

Aside from the demoralizing effect on the world at large and the possibilities of disturbances arising as a result of the desperation of the people concerned, the consequences to the economy of the United States should be apparent to all. It is logical that the United States should do whatever it is able to do to assist in the return of normal economic health in the world, without which there can be no political stability and no assured peace. Our policy is directed not against any country or doctrine but against hunger, poverty, desperation, and chaos. Its purpose should be the revival of a working economy in the world so as to permit the emergence of political and social conditions in which free institutions can exist. Such assistance, I am convinced, must not be on a piecemeal basis as various crises develop. Any assistance that this Government may render in the future should provide a cure rather than a mere palliative. Any government that is willing to assist in the task of recovery will find full cooperation, I am sure, on the part of the United States Government. Any government which maneuvers to block the recovery of other countries cannot expect help from us. Furthermore, governments, political parties, or groups which seek to perpetuate human misery in order to profit therefrom politically or otherwise will encounter the opposition of the United States.

It is already evident that, before the United States Government can proceed much further in its efforts to alleviate the situation and help start the European world on its way to recovery, there must be some agreement among the countries of Europe as to the requirements of the situation and the part those countries themselves will take in order to give proper effect to whatever action might be undertaken by this Government. It would be neither fitting nor efficacious for this Government to undertake to draw up unilaterally a program designed to place Europe on its feet economically. This is the business of the Europeans. The initiative, I think, must come from Europe. The role of this country should consist of friendly aid in the drafting of a European program and of later support of such a program so far as it may be practical for us to do so. The program should be a joint one, agreed to by a number, if not all, European nations.

An essential part of any successful action on the part of the United States is an understanding on the part of the people of America of the character of the problem and the remedies to be applied. Political passion and prejudice should have no part. With foresight, and a willingness on the part of our people to face up to the vast responsibility which history has clearly placed upon our country, the difficulties I have outlined can and will be overcome.

In February, 1948, democratic Czechoslovakia experienced a Communist coup d'état, which effectively made it a Russian satellite. The following correspondence between President Beneš and the Communist Party clearly indicates the course of events.

FROM *President Beneš' Correspondence with the Presidium of the Communist Party*

Letter from President Beneš to Presidium of the Communist Party

February 24, 1948

YOU SENT ME A LETTER on February 21 in which you express your attitude on a solution of the crisis and ask me to agree with it. Allow me to formulate my own attitude.

I feel fully the great responsibility of this fateful hour on our national and state life. From the beginning of this crisis I have been thinking about the situation as it was forming itself, putting these affairs of ours in connection with world affairs.

I am trying to see clearly not only the present situation but also the causes that led to it and the results that a decision can have. I am aware of the powerful forces through which the situation is being formed.

In a calm, matter of fact, impassionate and objective judgment of the situation I feel, through the common will of various groups of our citizens which turn their attention to me, that the will is expressed to maintain the peace and order and discipline voluntarily accepted to achieve a progressive and really socialist life.

How to achieve this goal? You know my sincerely democratic creed. I cannot but stay faithful to that creed even at this moment because democracy, according to my belief, is the only reliable and durable basis for a decent and dignified human life.

I insist on parliamentary democracy and parliamentary government as it limits democracy. I state I know very well it is necessary to social and economic content. I built my political work on these principles and cannot— without betraying myself—act otherwise.

The present crisis of democracy here too cannot be overcome but through democratic and parliamentary means. I thus do not overlook your

The Strategy and Tactics of World Communism, Supplement III, *The Coup d'Etat in Prague*, House of Representatives Committee on Foreign Affairs, National and International Movements, Subcommittee No. 5 Report (1948), pp. 25–7.

demands. I regard all our political parties associated in the National Front as bearers of political responsibility. We all accepted the principle of the National Front and this proved successful up to the recent time when the crisis began.

This crisis, however, in my opinion, does not deny the principle in itself. I am convinced that on this principle, even in the future, the necessary cooperation of all can be achieved. All disputes can be solved for the benefit of the national and common state of the Czechs and the Slovaks.

I therefore have been in negotiation with five political parties. I have listened to their views and some of them also have been put in writing. These are grave matters and I cannot ignore them.

Therefore, I again have to appeal to all to find a peaceful solution and new successful cooperation through parliamentary means and through the National Front.

That much for the formal side. As far as the personal side is concerned, it is clear to me, as I have said already, that the Prime Minister will be the chairman of the strongest party element, Gottwald.

Finally, on the factual side of this matter it is clear to me that socialism is a way of life desired by an overwhelming part of our nation. At the same time I believe that with socialism a certain measure of freedom and unity is possible and that these are vital principles to all in our national life.

Our nation has struggled for freedom almost throughout its history. History also has shown us where discord can lead.

I beg of you therefore to relive these facts and make them the starting point for our negotiations. Let us all together begin negotiations again for further durable cooperation and let us not allow prolongation of the split of the nation into two quarreling parts.

I believe that a reasonable agreement is possible because it is indispensable.

Reply by the Presidium of the Communist Party to Letter of President Beneš

February 25, 1948

The Presidium of the Central Committee of the Communist Party acknowledges your letter dated February 24 and states again that it cannot enter into negotiations with the present leadership of the National Socialist, People's and Slovak Democratic Parties because this would not conform to the interests of the unity of the people nor with the interests of further peaceful development of the republic.

Recent events indisputably proved that these three parties no longer represent the interests of the working people of the cities and countryside, that their leaders have betrayed the fundamental ideas of the people's democracy and National Front as they have been stated by the Kosice Government program and that they assumed the position of undermining the opposition.

This was shown again and again in the government, in the Constitutional National Assembly, in the press of these parties, and in actions that, with menacing levity, were organized by their central secretariats against the interests of the working people, against the security of the state, against the alliances of the republic, against state finance, against nationalized industry, against urgent agricultural reforms—in one word, against the whole constructive efforts of our people and against the very foundations, internal and external, of the security of the country.

These parties even got in touch with foreign circles hostile to our people's democratic order and our alliances, and in collaboration with these hostile foreign elements they attempted disruption of the present development of the republic.

This constantly increasing activity was crowned by an attempt to break up the government, an attempt that, as it was proved, should have been accompanied by actions aiming at a putsch.

Massive people's manifestations during the last few days clearly have shown our working people denounce, with complete unity and with indignation, the policy of these parties and ask the creation of a government in which all honest progressive patriots devoted to the republic and the people are represented.

Also among the members of the above-mentioned three parties an increasing amount of indignation can be seen. The members ask for a rebirth of their own parties and the National Front.

In conformity with this powerfully expressed will of the people, the Presidium of the Central Committee of the Communist Party approved the proposals of Premier Klement Gottwald according to which the government will be filled in with prominent representatives of all parties and also big nation-wide organizations.

We stress that a government filled in this way will present itself, with full agreement with the principles of parliamentary democracy, before the Constitutional National Assembly with its program and ask for its approval.

Being convinced that only such a highly constitutional and parliamentary process can guarantee the peaceful development of the republic and at the same time it corresponds to the ideas of a complete majority of the working people, the Presidium of the Central Committee hopes firmly after careful consideration that you will recognize the correctness of its conclusions and will agree with its proposals.

In 1949 the United States abandoned its traditional hostility toward entangling alliances and joined the North Atlantic Treaty Organization to counter Soviet pressure against

Western Europe. It was the decisive recognition that the Cold War was to be a lasting reality.

North Atlantic Treaty

THE PARTIES TO THIS TREATY reaffirm their faith in the purposes and principles of the Charter of the United Nations and their desire to live in peace with all peoples and all governments.

They are determined to safeguard the freedom, common heritage and civilization of their peoples, founded on the principles of democracy, individual liberty and the rule of law.

They seek to promote stability and well-being in the North Atlantic area.

They are resolved to unite their efforts for collective defense and for the preservation of peace and security.

They therefore agree to this North Atlantic Treaty:

ARTICLE I

The Parties undertake, as set forth in the Charter of the United Nations, to settle any international disputes in which they may be involved by peaceful means in such a manner that international peace and security, and justice, are not endangered, and to refrain in their international relations from the threat or use of force in any manner inconsistent with the purposes of the United Nations.

ARTICLE 2

The Parties will contribute toward the further development of peaceful and friendly international relations by strengthening their free institutions, by bringing about a better understanding of the principles upon which these institutions are founded, and by promoting conditions of stability and well-being. They will seek to eliminate conflict in their international economic policies and will encourage economic collaboration between any or all of them.

ARTICLE 3

In order more effectively to achieve the objectives of this Treaty, the Parties, separately and jointly, by means of continuous and effective self-help and mutual aid, will maintain and develop their individual and collective capacity to resist armed attack.

Senate Committee on Foreign Relations, *A Decade of American Foreign Policy: Basic Documents, 1941–1949* (1950), pp. 1328–31.

ARTICLE 4

The Parties will consult together whenever, in the opinion of any of them, the territorial integrity, political independence or security of any of the Parties is threatened.

ARTICLE 5

The Parties agree that an armed attack against one or more of them in Europe or North America shall be considered an attack against them all; and consequently they agree that, if such an armed attack occurs, each of them, in exercise of the right of individual or collective self-defense recognized by Article 51 of the Charter of the United Nations, will assist the Party or Parties so attacked by taking forthwith, individually and in concert with the other Parties, such action as it deems necessary, including the use of armed force, to restore and maintain the security of the North Atlantic area.

Any such armed attack and all measures taken as a result thereof shall immediately be reported to the Security Council. Such measures shall be terminated when the Security Council has taken the measures necessary to restore and maintain international peace and security.

ARTICLE 6

For the purpose of Article 5 an armed attack on one or more of the Parties is deemed to include an armed attack on the territory of any of the Parties in Europe or North America, on the Algerian departments of France, on the occupation forces of any Party in Europe, on the islands under the jurisdiction of any Party in the North Atlantic area north of the Tropic of Cancer or on the vessels or aircraft in this area of any of the Parties.

ARTICLE 7

This Treaty does not affect, and shall not be interpreted as affecting, in any way the rights and obligations under the Charter of the Parties which are members of the United Nations, or the primary responsibility of the Security Council for the maintenance of international peace and security.

ARTICLE 8

Each Party declares that none of the international engagements now in force between it and any other of the Parties or any third state is in conflict with the provisions of this Treaty, and undertakes not to enter into any international engagement in conflict with this Treaty.

ARTICLE 9

The Parties hereby established a council, on which each of them shall be represented, to consider matters concerning the implementation of this Treaty. The council shall be so organized as to be able to meet promptly at any time. The council shall set up such subsidiary bodies as may be necessary; in particular it shall establish immediately a defense committee which shall recommend measures for the implementation of Articles 3 and 5.

ARTICLE 10

The Parties may, by unanimous agreement, invite any other European state in a position to further the principles of this Treaty and to contribute to the security of the North Atlantic area to accede to this Treaty. Any state so invited may become a party to the Treaty by depositing its instrument of accession with the Government of the United States of America. The Government of the United States of America will inform each of the Parties of the deposit of each such instrument of accession.

ARTICLE 11

This Treaty shall be ratified and its provisions carried out by the Parties in accordance with their respective constitutional processes. The instruments of ratification shall be deposited as soon as possible with the Government of the United States of America, which will notify all the other signatories of each deposit. The Treaty shall enter into force between the states which have ratified it as soon as the ratifications of the majority of the signatories, including the ratifications of Belgium, Canada, France, Luxembourg, the Netherlands, the United Kingdom and the United States, have been deposited and shall come into effect with respect to other states on the date of the deposit of their ratifications.

ARTICLE 12

After the Treaty has been in force for ten years, or at any time thereafter, the Parties shall, if any of them so requests, consult together for the purpose of reviewing the Treaty, having regard for the factors then affecting peace and security in the North Atlantic area, including the development of universal as well as regional arrangements under the Charter of the United Nations for the maintenance of international peace and security.

ARTICLE 13

After the Treaty has been in force for twenty years, any Party may cease to be a party one year after its notice of denunciation has been given to the Government of the United States of America, which will inform the Governments of the other Parties of the deposit of each notice of denunciation.

ARTICLE 14

This Treaty, of which the English and French texts are equally authentic, shall be deposited in the archives of the Government of the United States of America. Duly certified copies thereof will be transmitted by that Government to the Governments of the other signatories.

In witness whereof, the undersigned plenipotentiaries have signed this Treaty.

Done at Washington, the fourth day of April, 1949.

For the Kingdom of Belgium:
P. H. Spaak
Silvercruys

For Canada:
Lester B. Pearson
H. H. Wrong

For the Kingdom of Denmark:
Gustav Rasmussen
Henrik Kauffmann

For France:
Schuman
H. Bonnet

For Iceland:
Bjarni Benediktsson
Thor Thors

For Italy:
Sforza
Alberto Tarchiani

For the Grand Duchy of Luxembourg:
Jos Bech
Hugues Le Gallais

For the Kingdom of the Netherlands:
Stikker
E. N. Van Kleffens

For the Kingdom of Norway:
Halvard M. Lange
Wilhelm Munthe Morgenstierne

For Portugal:
José Caeiro da Matta
Pedro Theotónio Pereira

For the United Kingdom of Great Britain and Northern Ireland:
Ernest Bevin
Oliver Franks

For the United States of America:
Dean Acheson

I certify that the foregoing is a true copy of the North Atlantic Treaty signed at Washington on April 4, 1949 in the English and French languages, the signed original of which is deposited in the archives of the Government of the United States of America.

In testimony whereof, I, Dean Acheson, Secretary of State of the United States of America, have hereunto caused the seal of the Department of State to be affixed and my name subscribed by the Authentication Officer of the said Department, at the city of Washington, in the District of Columbia, this fourth day of April, 1949.

DEAN ACHESON
Secretary of State
By M. P. CHAUVIN
Authentication Officer
Department of State

3 Russia's Responsibility

FROM *A Diplomatic History of the American People*
BY THOMAS A. BAILEY

> *We may well ask, "Why have they [the Soviets] deliberately acted for
> three long years so as to unite the free world against them?"*
>
> WINSTON CHURCHILL, 1949

UNFINISHED BUSINESS

URGENT PROBLEMS of an economic and humanitarian nature lay piled
on the tables of the diplomats when the war finally jarred to a close. "It is
now 11:59 on the clock of starvation," warned Herbert Hoover.

A temporary organization, the United Nations Relief and Rehabilitation
Administration (UNRRA), was launched late in 1943, when representatives
of forty-odd nations signed an agreement at the White House. Its primary
purpose was to help the liberated peoples of Europe and the Far East to get
back onto their feet. The uninvaded member nations were invited to contribute to the budget of UNRRA a small percentage of their incomes in 1943.
The United States, as the wealthiest participant, became the chief financial
backer and leader of this vast humanitarian enterprise. When the books were
closed in 1947, huge quantities of urgently needed food and other supplies
had been shipped to China and the nations of Europe, notably Poland, Italy,
Yugoslavia, Czechoslovakia, Greece, and Austria.

Hardly less clamorous was the problem of the several million Displaced
Persons (DP's), all of whom had been uprooted by the war and many of
whom dared not return to their Communist-enslaved homelands. The
American people were more generous in sending money to Europe than they
were in inviting the impoverished peoples of Europe to their shores. Painful
memories of unemployment during the Great Depression were still fresh.
Finally, in June, 1948, Congress made a belated beginning when it voted to
set aside quota restrictions and admit 205,000. The treatment of these DP's—
Delayed Pilgrims, someone has called them—was harshly criticized as over-

From *A Diplomatic History of the American People*, Seventh Edition, pp. 776–9, 790–1,
796–803, 807–9, by Thomas A. Bailey. Copyright © 1964 by Meredith Publishing Company.
Reprinted by permission of Appleton-Century-Crofts, Division of Meredith Publishing Company.

cautious, and the sifting process was widely condemned as discriminating against Catholics and Jews.

The settlement of lend-lease obligations, on the other hand, presented a far prettier picture than the prolonged wrangling over Allied debts after World War I. The total account at the end of World War II was approximately $50 billion, of which about $31 billion had gone to the British Empire and $11 billion to the Soviet Union. This staggering total was reduced some $10 billion by reverse-lend lease—that is, the supplying of goods or services for the United States at the other end. By late 1953, adjustments had been threshed out with all the major debtors, except the Soviet Union. As of that date, the settlement agreements had reduced the total to be paid to about $1 billion, which amounted to approximately three cents on the dollar.

The liquidation of the lend-lease account was both more generous and more realistic than that of the war-debt account following World War I. The original lend-lease agreements had stipulated that the ultimate terms should "promote mutually advantageous economic relations." Happily, this far-visioned formula was generally followed in making the necessary reductions.

THE COMMUNIST CHALLENGE

When the war ended with an atomic bang in 1945, the American people still retained a vast reservoir of good will toward their valiant Russian ally. He had saved their hides while saving his own. Not only were Americans counting on Soviet co-operation to create a warless world, but many of them favored lending Russia money and technical assistance to repair the ravages inflicted by the Nazi invader.

But the Kremlin brutally slapped aside the outstretched American hand, presumably because co-operation with the capitalistic West would retard the Communist revolution. The ideal of One World thus collided head on with the actuality of the Communist world. The resulting deadlock was the most momentous and terrifying single development of the postwar years.

By the summer of 1946, if not earlier, the various public opinion polls in the United States revealed disquieting conclusions. The American people did not regard Russia as a peace-loving nation, and they did not trust her to co-operate with the United Nations. Her dominance over her satellite neighbors, they felt, was prompted by aggressive rather than defensive designs, and they were convinced that the Kremlin was bent on enchaining the entire globe. Not only was another war probable within twenty-five years, most Americans believed, but the Russians were the most likely to start it.

The Soviets thus unwittingly engineered a psychological Pearl Harbor. Crying "capitalist encirclement," they were bolstering their armed forces while the democracies were demobilizing theirs. Within a few short months the aggressive tactics of Moscow had awakened the American people to the true nature of the Communist conspiracy. Thus forewarned and alerted, the

United States undertook to revamp its foreign policies and bolster its defenses in a determined effort not to be caught napping again.

THE BLAME FOR THE BREAK

Who was responsible for the shattered dream of One World? Apologists for Russia have insisted that the Soviets turned against America because America first turned against them. They further allege—the Myth of the Empty Chair—that if Roosevelt had not come to an untimely end, he would have been able to co-operate with the Kremlin.

The naked truth is that by mid-March, 1945—one month before the President's death—the Soviets were clearly taking over Poland and Romania as satellites in violation of their solemn pledges at Yalta. Roosevelt died knowing, or strongly suspecting, that he had failed in his gigantic gamble to wean Stalin away from his dangerous ideals by kind words and lend-lease largesse. The Russian leaders, although soft-pedaling Communist world revolution during the desperate days of World War II, had never really abandoned it. They had cleverly deceived the Americans, who in turn were in a mood to deceive themselves.

American military strategy, moreover, played directly into the hands of the Soviets. The forward-dashing American columns might have captured Berlin and Prague after costly fighting. But pursuant in part to arrangements made earlier with the Soviets, the Red Armies were allowed to enter these capitals as liberator-conquerors. The Americans kept their agreements, while hoping that the Russians, despite mounting evidence to the contrary, would keep theirs. The "liberating" Reds thus further entrenched themselves on the soil of the neighboring satellites.

Less defensible was the overhasty withdrawal of the American armies from Europe, and the consequent creation of a power vacuum into which the Soviets speedily moved. Short-sightedly assuming that victory is self-perpetuating, and that wars end with the shooting, the American public demanded a speedy dismantling of one of the most potent striking forces ever assembled. Roosevelt himself was privately committed to bringing the troops home at the earliest possible date. The men in uniform staged incredible "I Wanna Go Home" demonstrations, and they were backed to the hilt by lonesome wives, mothers, sweethearts, and children ("Bring-Daddy-Back-Home" clubs). As in 1918, the American fire department withdrew before the fire was completely out. Winston Churchill expressed the opinion in 1949 that only the existence of the atomic bomb, a temporary monopoly of the Americans, kept the Soviets from sweeping to the English channel.

The atomic bomb—a veritable apple of discord—aroused genuine fear in the Soviet Union. A tiny but vocal group of Americans, including ex-Governor Earle of Pennsylvania, was demanding a "preventive war" while the United States had this frightful new weapon and the Soviet Union did not.

The "rattling of the atomic bomb" became louder when American forces retained bomber bases within striking distance of Russia's industrial vitals, and undertook impressive naval demonstrations in the Mediterranean. Soviet suspicions deepened as Washington delayed or halted lend-lease shipments, and as the American public grew increasingly cold toward a proposed postwar loan of $6 billion.

THE IRON CURTAIN CLANGS DOWN

The oft-invaded Russians were determined to strengthen themselves against future foes by marshaling subservient satellite nations on their flanks. The descent of Moscow's "iron curtain" around the neighbors of the Soviet Union aroused the American people, more than anything else, to the nature of the Communist peril.

Soviet darkness gradually enshrouded Romania, Bulgaria, Albania, and Hungary, as Moscow-manipulated stooges took command. Washington, appealing to Stalin's unredeemed pledges at Yalta, lodged repeated protests with Moscow against coercion and intimidation. But in Soviet thinking security ranked higher than capitalistic conceptions of honor. Washington also made repeated representations to the satellites themselves—and with no greater success—against such offenses as the execution of political prisoners and the persecution of religious leaders.

Night likewise descended over Poland when a Soviet-dominated regime took control in 1945, also in defiance of Stalin's pledges at Yalta. After exasperating delays, the farcical "free and unfettered" election, also promised at Yalta, was held in 1947. The Communists polled about 90 per cent of the vote, although the American ambassador reported that in an honest election the opposition party would have won about 60 per cent of the votes. Washington's protests against the flouting of the Yalta pledges were wasted paper and ink.

Yugoslavia, a Communist satellite under the iron hand of Marshal Tito, presented special problems. The Yugoslavs reacted violently against America's opposition to their proposed grab of the Italian-Yugoslav city of Trieste, at the head of the Adriatic Sea. The internationalization of the city created a witches' cauldron, and numerous clashes ensued between the Yugoslav soldiers, on the one hand, and the American and British occupying troops, on the other.

The Western world breathed easier in 1948, when Tito parted company with Moscow, amid angry words. While still a Communist, he preferred his own local brand to that dictated by Moscow. Just as Roosevelt grasped the bloody hand of Stalin when he split with Hitler in 1941, so Truman grasped the bloody hand of Tito when he split with the Kremlin in 1948. In the hope of encouraging "Titoism" or independence among the other satellites of Moscow, the United States dispatched arms and supplies to Tito. In less than ten years these subventions amounted to about $2 billion, despite considerable opposition in America to underwriting any form of communism. As in the days of the Franco-American Alliance of 1778, a common danger was still making strange bedfellows.

> *Let us not be deceived—we are today in the midst of a cold war.*
>
> BERNARD BARUCH, April, 1947

THE TRUMAN DOCTRINE

The naked aggressions of Moscow had, by early 1947, swung American opinion around in favor of a "get-tough-with-Russia" policy. President Truman, aware of imminent Communist inroads and confident of strong public backing, prepared to take resolute action. As he privately remarked, "I'm tired of babying the Soviets."

The time for decision came in February, 1947. The overburdened British shocked Washington by announcing that they could no longer provide full-scale economic support for the "rightist" government of Greece. When they withdrew their assistance, the Communist guerrillas, who were receiving help from their Communist neighbors to the north, would no doubt seize control. Greece would then gravitate into the Soviet orbit. The position of Turkey, on which Moscow was exerting heavy pressure, would become untenable. The strategically vital eastern Mediterranean would presumably fall like a ripe pear into Communist hands, and the impact on the free world would be catastrophic.

President Truman, after hurried conferences with military and Congressional leaders, made a surprise appearance before Congress, on March 12, 1947, to present an epochal pronouncement. In solemn tones he described the plight of war-racked Greece, and then declared:

> One of the primary objectives of the foreign policy of the United States is the creation of conditions in which we and other nations will be able to work out a way of life free from coercion. . . . We shall not realize our objectives, however, unless we are willing to help free peoples to maintain their free institutions and their national integrity against aggressive movements that seek to impose upon them totalitarian regimes. [Applause.] This is no more than a frank recognition that totalitarian regimes imposed on free peoples, by direct or indirect aggression, undermine the foundations of international peace and hence the security of the United States.

Truman thereupon concluded that "it must be the policy of the United States to support free peoples who are resisting attempted subjugation by armed minorities or by outside pressures." With this goal in view, he requested an appropriation of $400 million for economic and military succor to Greece and Turkey. This, he conceded, was a "serious course," but the alternative to drifting was "much more serious. [Applause.]" The implication was clear that Congress had better expend a modest amount of the taxpayers' money than later expend the taxpayer himself. When Truman concluded, Congress arose as one man to applaud—except for one left-wing member.

CASH FOR "CONTAINMENT"

The Truman Doctrine was the major opening gun in what journalists called the "cold war"—a war waged by means other than shooting. It also inaugurated in a spectacular way the new policy of "containment" or the attempt to stem Soviet advances in vital spots. The public, though now willing to halt Russian aggression by risky measures, was momentarily stunned by the President's blast. But the feeling was general that while the "Truman Doctrine" was fraught with peril, a policy of dangerous do-nothingism was even more perilous. The only two major groups to express strong hostility were the left-wing "liberals," for whom Henry A. Wallace was a spokesman, and the old-line isolationists, for whom the *Chicago Tribune* was a leading mouthpiece.

Critics of the Truman Doctrine advanced numerous and weighty arguments. It would cost too much, for the initial appropriation would be but a drop in the bucket. It would create the bad precedent of sticking the national nose into the internal affairs of other nations. It would goad into war the Soviet Communists, who would not be fought with mere dollars. It would bypass the United Nations and weaken that organization at the very time when it was getting off to a wobbly start.

As far as the UN was concerned, Truman had clearly taken lone-hand action because of the inevitable delaying tactics of the Soviets. But he had gone so far out on the end of a limb that he could not be repudiated without weakening the United States in the eyes of the world at a critical hour. Senator Vandenberg of Michigan, who with a majority of his Republican colleagues continued to support a bipartisan foreign policy, helped to push through Congress a face-saving amendment. It stipulated that whenever the United Nations was prepared to take over the burden, the United States would lay it down.

After a windy debate of about two months, Congress approved the initial Truman Doctrine appropriation of $400 million on May 15, 1947. The vote, which reflected wide public support, was 67 to 23 in the Senate and 287 to 107 in the House.

The Truman Doctrine was of incalculable significance. It enabled the United States to seize the offensive in the "cold war" to "contain" communism. Although limited to Greece and Turkey, it was general in scope and led by direct steps to the vastly more important Marshall Plan and the North Atlantic Treaty Organization (NATO). It was a kind of lend-lease—this time against communism rather than fascism. It reversed the nonintervention principle of the original Monroe Doctrine, but like the Monroe Doctrine it aimed at long-range defense.

THE MARSHALL PLAN

Once the American people had accepted the principle of helping independent governments resist communism, they gradually perceived that stopgap aid for only Greece and Turkey was merely sending a boy on a man's errand. War-blasted Western Europe, further scourged by the icy winter of 1946–1947, was not making the necessary economic recovery. Local Communist groups were deliberately sabotaging progress by strikes and other incendiary tactics. If the chaos that was so favorable to communism should develop, the Communists would probably seize control of Italy and France. All Western Europe would then fall into their grip, and Moscow's influence would sweep to the English Channel.

Into the breach boldly stepped the Secretary of State, General Marshall. Speaking at the Harvard University commencement exercises, on June 5, 1947, he announced a policy that forthwith dwarfed the Truman Doctrine. He suggested that the nations of Europe get together, devise long-range plans for economic recovery, concentrate on self-help and mutual assistance, and present to Washington a specific statement of their needs. The United States would then support them with financial help "so far as it may be practical. . . ."

The Marshall speech did not at once make a great splash in the United States. It was not a clear-cut promise, and it put the burden of initiative squarely on Europe's shoulders. But gradually the American people perceived that the Marshall scheme was no unilateral Truman Doctrine aimed at military aid or temporary relief. It was an inclusive plan looking toward long-range rehabilitation.

The foreign ministers of France and Britain, recognizing the breathtaking implications of Marshall's overture, seized the initiative. They arranged for a meeting at Paris, to which the Soviet foreign minister, V. M. Molotov, was also invited. After a short but stormy stay, he finally walked out, thus spurning an enviable opportunity to tie up the Marshall Plan with obstructionism.

The British and French thereupon issued invitations for a general conference at Paris, to which twenty-two nations were invited—all Europe west of Russia except Fascist Spain. The eight nations under the shadow of the Kremlin declined, or were forced to spurn the "imperialist" plot, cooked up for "the enslavement of Europe." They were Albania, Bulgaria, Czechoslovakia, Finland, Hungary, Poland, Romania, and Yugoslavia. The sixteen that accepted were Austria, Belgium, Britain, Denmark, Eire, France, Greece, Iceland, Italy, Luxembourg, the Netherlands, Norway, Portugal, Sweden, Switzerland and Turkey. Representatives of these sixteen Marshall

Plan countries, meeting in Paris from July to September, 1947, finally wove their "shopping lists" of help desired from America into an integrated program.

One defiant answer of Moscow to the Marshall Plan was the nine-nation Communist Information Bureau (Cominform), announced on October 5, 1947. It was in effect a revival of the Old Comintern, which ostensibly had been disbanded in 1943. The new agency was openly designed to promote communism by sabotaging the economic recovery of Europe under the Marshall Plan. At the same time the Kremlin, through the counter Molotov Plan, would attempt to shackle its satellites together as an economie whole.

MARSHALING MARSHALL DOLLARS

The scene now shifted to Washington, where President Truman submitted his Marshall Plan estimates to Congress, in December, 1947. They embraced $17 billion for four-and-one-quarter years, with an initial outlay of $6.8 billion for the first fifteen months. The debate in Congress then began in earnest, and despite the urgent need for haste, consumed more than three precious months.

Advocates of the Marshall Plan, though appealing to simple humanitarianism, stressed the bread-and-butter argument that a prosperous Europe was essential for America's own prosperity. Industrial and agricultural groups, worried about their overseas markets, warmly seconded this view. But the necessity of halting Soviet communism was no doubt the compelling argument. The Marshall Plan was admittedly a calculated risk, but it was cheaper than war. If successful in redressing the European balance, it might head off a conflict that would be infinitely costly and destructive.

Critics of the Marshall scheme charged that it was just another "Operation Rathole." "Uncle Santa Claus" had already poured too much money into the pockets of ungrateful Europeans—about $12 billion in various loans and handouts since mid-1945. America had better make herself strong at home, conserve her resources, and help her own needy people. Otherwise she would offend the Soviets (who were already offended), divide Europe (which was already divided), and lay herself open to the Russian charge (which had already been made) of "dollar imperialism." The whole device, cried Henry A. Wallace, was a "Martial Plan."

The Kremlin unwittingly helped spur the languishing Marshall Plan appropriation through Congress. The Communist coup of February, 1948, in Czechoslovakia had a profound effect, especially the suicide of the beloved Foreign Minister Masaryk under circumstances that suggested foul play. Hardly less disturbing was Moscow's strong-arming of "Brave little" Finland into a distasteful alliance. These alarming developments not only increased enthusiasm for the Marshall Plan, but sped through Congress an unprecedented peacetime conscription law and an appropriation for a potent airforce.

The debate on Marshall aid at length ended. The legislators, who were unwilling to bind future Congresses by a long-term appropriation, finally voted $6.098 billion for various purposes during the first twelve months. The tacit understanding was that similar sums would be forthcoming through the next three years. This measure, after passing the House 329 to 74 and the Senate 69 to 19, was signed by Truman on April 3, 1948.

The Marshall Plan—officially known as the European Relief Program (ERP)—was approved just in time to influence the Italian election. The militant Communist Party, crying "Death to Truman" was threatening to seize control and undermine the position of the democracies in Europe. The Italian people, thus confronted with the choice between the concrete aid of the Marshall Plan and the pie-in-the-sky promises of communism, returned a smashing verdict against the Communists.

The Marshall Plan, which turned out to be a spectacular success, was an epochal step in both foreign policy and postwar recovery. This economic blood transfusion—altogether $10.25 billion in three years—took the Europeans off their backs and put them on their feet. It halted the westward surge of communism. It was one of the major steps in the evolution of the North Atlantic Treaty Organization (NATO). It was intervention of a sort—or counterintervention against the Communists—but intervention designed to create the economic and political conditions in which free men could make a free choice of government. Winston Churchill was not too far from the mark when he called the Marshall Plan "the most unsordid act in history." The money, to be sure, was given but it was given largely for what were deemed to be the best interests of the United States.

AIRLIFTS AND AIRWAVES

Berlin was perhaps the first critical area to suffer from Soviet resentment against the Marshall Plan. Moscow had long been disturbed by the success of the British, Americans, and French in unifying their German zones and in establishing currency reform. On June 24, 1948, therefore, the Soviets shut off all non-Russian traffic to Berlin, except by air. They evidently reasoned that America, Britain, and France, unable to supply the garrisons and populations in their sectors, would abandon the city. It would then become a rallying point for the Soviets in the unification of an all-Communist Germany.

President Truman, supported by the British, promptly and courageously refused to be run out of Berlin. In arriving at this decision, he correctly interpreted the mood of the American people. American and British airmen speedily inaugurated the Berlin airlift, through which they undertook the gigantic task of supplying not only their garrisons but the needs of some 2,500,000 people as well. "Operation Vittles," as it was called, at one time was flying in some 4500 tons of supplies a day, including coal—expensive coal.

The Berlin blockade backfired badly on Moscow. There were some ticklish scrapes with Russian fighter planes, and the peace of the world lay with the trigger fingers of Soviet airmen. But President Truman and his associates properly concluded that the Russians did not want to fight—otherwise they would have let war come then and there. The West gained in popularity with its fallen German foes, while the Soviets sank even lower. The Berlin airlift thus proved to be a stimulant to the formation of the West German Republic, and also an important step toward the North Atlantic Alliance. The Russians, pinched by a counterblockade of their zone by the West, finally agreed to end their blockade of Berlin in 1949, after about a year's trial.

Spectacular episodes meanwhile had further highlighted the pervasiveness of Soviet communism. The House Committee on Un-American Activities, which had been flushing out small-fry Communist conspirators, finally emerged with big game. It found evidence that in 1937–1938 Alger Hiss, then an official in the State Department, had betrayed important secrets to Soviet agents. After two sensational trials, Hiss was found guilty of perjury in 1950, and sentenced to a prison term of five years.

Such incidents induced the American people, despite a natural aversion to such methods, to try to match weapons with the Soviets on the propaganda front. When World War II had ended, an economy-minded Congress was giving niggardly support to an informational and cultural program, popularly known as the "Voice of America." It was designed to instruct other people in the American way of life, through radio and other agencies, and thus combat communism. As the wholesale propaganda activities of the Soviets became more blatant, and as the conviction deepened that the only way to bring the truth to the Russians and their satellites was by a short-wave radio, Congress pricked up its ears. Early in 1948 it put the "Voice of America" on a permanent basis with more adequate funds, although they were far short of what the Soviets were spending. The American short-wave radio program had serious defects, but its partial success was attested by persistent Soviet efforts to "jam" its broadcasts.

THE 12-POWER NORTH ATLANTIC PACT

The menace of Moscow elsewhere brought further noteworthy developments. In March, 1948, five nations of Western Europe—Britain, France, Belgium, the Netherlands, and Luxembourg—signed at Brussels a fifty-year defensive pact. By its terms they solemnly bound themselves to aid one another against an attack by an aggressor. The United States, as their chief economic underwriter and as a leader of the anti-Communist nations, was irresistibly drawn toward the new alliance.

Washington was in a receptive mood. In June, 1948, nearly three months after the birth of the Brussels pact, the United States Senate passed the Vandenberg resolution by the lopsided vote of 64 to 4. It affirmed American support for regional security pacts like the one recently adopted by the five European nations. With this green light plainly flashing, the State Department pressed negotiations to include the United States in the union. Moscow loudly proclaimed that Washington was weakening the United Nations (which the Soviets had already weakened), and was forming an aggressive bloc (which the Soviets had already formed by a network of treaties with their satellites). Regional security pacts conformed to both the letter and spirit of Article 51 of the UN Charter, and the proposed Atlantic alliance was clearly defensive rather than aggressive.

Representatives of twelve nations, with appropriate white-tie pageantry, finally met in Washington to sign the North Atlantic Treaty, on April 4, 1949. The charter members were the United States, Canada, Britain, France, Italy, Belgium, the Netherlands, Luxembourg, Norway, Denmark, Iceland, and Portugal. After paying their respects to the UN, they stipulated that an attack by an aggressor on one of them would be an attack on all of them. They further proclaimed that each of the other signatory nations, in the event of an assault on one member, would take "such action as it deems necessary," including "armed force." This pledge did not flatly commit the United States to war, or remove from Congress the war-declaring power. But it was a moral commitment to aid the victims of aggression for at least twenty years.

NONENTANGLEMENT BECOMES ENTANGLEMENT

The North Atlantic Pact was precedent-shattering. It was unquestionably a formal treaty of alliance, the first the United States had ever concluded in peacetime with a European power or powers. Yet such was the growing fear of the Soviet menace that this drastic departure from tradition met with widespread favor in America. The conviction was general that if World War III broke out, the republic would be sucked into it at the outset. The only sensible alternative seemed to be to attempt to avert it, as the United States had been unable or unwilling to do in 1914 and 1939, by serving notice on potential aggressors that they would have to reckon with America's might from the very outset. The loudest opposition to the alliance came from the last-ditch isolationists, from the Henry Wallaceites, and from the Communists. The leading Communist organ, the *New York Daily Worker,* branded the pact "International Murder, Inc."

The epochal North Atlantic Pact was approved by the Senate, in July, 1949, by a vote of 82 to 13. There was surprisingly little opposition. A few die-hard isolationists feared foreign entanglements, a loss of the war-declaring power of Congress, and commitments to heavy and dangerous defense expenditures. Opponents of the pact made a determined effort to relieve the United States of any obligation to rearm Western Europe, but such proposed amendments were beaten down by heavy majorities.

One presumed by-product of the North Atlantic Pact was the lifting of the Berlin blockade. Three weeks after the signing of the alliance the Soviets, in what may have been an attempt to head off American ratification, agreed tentatively to end the stoppage. The formal lifting came on May 12, 1949. The Soviets seemed less aggressive and self-assured, perhaps because of the success of the Marshall Plan, the Berlin airlift, and the Atlantic Treaty.

The threat of Russian communism had thus brought about a major revolution in American foreign policy within a few short years. The United States had reversed its Monroe Doctrine in relation to Greece by accepting the Truman Doctrine. It had forsaken nonintervention by promoting the Marshall Plan. It had tossed overboard the no-alliance tradition by signing the Atlantic Pact. It had adopted peacetime conscription and a wartime military budget. It had embarked upon all such departures with extreme reluctance but basically in response to the instinct of self-preservation. The new American policies—all defensive in their outlook—were actually authored more by the men in the Kremlin than by the men in Washington. The American people had hoped for a peaceful world after World War II, but the aggressions of the Soviets simply would not permit them to drop their guard.

4　A European View

FROM *A History of the Cold War* BY JOHN LUKACS

THE DIVISION OF EUROPE BECOMES RIGID
(TO 1949)

I

EVEN BEFORE THE END of the war Stalin alone of the Big Three remained in power. Because of the unexpected electoral victory of the British Labour Party, Churchill was replaced by Attlee during the closing days of the Potsdam Conference, where Truman had come to occupy Roosevelt's seat; soon thereafter General De Gaulle, disgusted with the new quagmire of French politics and parliaments, resigned and withdrew from public affairs. The conditions of defeated Germany and Italy were not yet auspicious for the emergence of important leaders; in China civil war was in development. Thus outside the Russian Empire the world suddenly seemed devoid of the impact of great personalities; but soon it became evident that Providence and political fortune had provided the English-speaking nations and, with them, the free world with two persons whose statesmanship proved adequate for halting the eventual spread of Russian Communist tyranny. Their integrity, bravery, and intelligence shine in retrospect through those murky years. They were Harry S. Truman and Ernest Bevin, the provincial Midwestern politician who through a stroke of fate became President of the United States and the erstwhile dock worker who became Foreign Secretary of Britain in 1945. They soon made a strong and confident impression. There were many reasons to believe that, unlike Roosevelt, the inexperienced Truman would let the State Department and its Secretaries determine the ultimate conduct of American foreign policy; but Truman, who, unlike his successor, knew from the first moment the historic traditions and necessity of strong presidential leadership, soon grasped the master wheel of the American ship of state with both hands. Meanwhile in Britain the somewhat colorless Prime Minister Attlee left to the Foreign Secretary the main task of insuring the continuity of British foreign policy in the best interests of the nation; and as early as in August 1945 Bevin's first speech in the House of Commons, direct and critical of Russian actions in Europe, dispelled the fears (or the hopes) of those who believed that the new Labour government would go to great lengths to accommodate the Russians.

Still, the United Kingdom, victorious in principle but impoverished in essence by the war, was no longer able to maintain her far-flung imperial and political commitments in all parts of the world. The British decision to grant full independence to India, Pakistan, Burma, and Palestine was made; from 1947 on, the British flag was hauled down in many places, while elsewhere the relationship of Britain with her colonial dependencies was newly reformed to the benefit of the latter in the name of the democratic principle. Yet none of these great transformations, including the dramatic birth of the Indian and Pakistani Republics on a vast subcontinent, and not even the birth of the State of Israel, had, as yet, an important bearing on the dreadful balance of the developing cold war. It was in Greece, the historic ally of Great Britain, that the turning point was reached.

2

By early 1947 President Truman and the American government finally concluded that the United States would not further acquiesce in the Communization—either by conquest, civil war, or subversion—of any portion of Europe or the Near East that lay outside the Russian imperial sphere in Eastern Europe. The so-called Truman Doctrine, the Marshall Plan, and the Containment Policy were the three principal instruments of this historic (though, in retrospect, hardly avoidable) decision.

In February 1947 the British government informed Washington that it could not alone sustain the armed struggle of the Greek state against the growing irregular tide of Communist guerrilla armies. Without hesitation Truman assumed the burden. His Message to Congress in March 1947 called for American military aid to a Greece and Turkey threatened by Russian pressure and eventual blackmail. After some debate congressional consent was given. Forthwith American military missions and abundant supplies were sent to these Eastern Mediterranean countries. In about a year the Greek Army defeated the Communist guerrillas everywhere. The prominence of American sea power in the Eastern Mediterranean, manifested by the Sixth Fleet, remained an important factor in world affairs ever since that time.

It was evident in 1945 that American statesmen were more responsive to economic than to political arguments when it came to the distressing problems of Europe. Predicated upon the belief that Communism would primarily prosper from economic chaos, fortified by strong inclinations of American common sense as well as by traditional American institutional generosity toward poverty and distress abroad, the so-called Marshall Plan was proposed in June 1947. The United States was willing to support, in the form of goods, gifts, and easy loans, the rebuilding of the war-torn economies of Britain and Europe. The aim of the Marshall Plan was the ultimate restoration of the balance in Europe by quickly getting the weakened nations of

Western Europe to their feet again; but its purposes were broader politically and even more generous economically, since Marshall Plan Aid was offered to Eastern Europe, including Russia, too. But Stalin refused to take it; indeed, he forced his westernmost ally, the still semi-democratic republic of Czechoslovakia, to reverse its original acceptance.

His purpose of dividing Europe was now clearer than ever before. Peace Treaties were already signed with former German allies, Italy, Hungary, Rumania, Finland; but except for a few unimportant details these amounted about to a confirmation of the respective Armistice instruments signed before; moreover, Russian forces were not withdrawn from Hungary, Rumania, or Poland, where they were to guard communication lines to East Germany and Eastern Austria, pending a German and Austrian Peace Treaty. About the latter the Council of Foreign Ministers were getting nowhere during interminable debates. Through a variety of methods the Russians took ruthless advantage of the subject condition of their captive European neighbors; and in 1947 Stalin speeded up the gradual Sovietization of his prospective satellites. With crudest methods, on occasion not shunning even the open involvement of Russian police organs, the representatives of the remaining democratic forces in Hungary, Rumania, Poland, Bulgaria, and East Germany were sometimes deported, at times imprisoned, on occasion silenced, and frequently chased into Western exile. In Yugoslavia and Albania, where no Russian troops were stationed, the police control of the Communist regimes was most complete. In some of the other satellites, particularly Hungary, the unpopularity and the occasional ineptitude of local Communist satraps were still an obstacle despite the power of their Russian masters. In June 1947 the semi-democratic government of Hungary had to be transformed by force; thereafter unabashed police tactics were the main instruments for insuring Russia's mastery in Eastern Europe.

Though, except for increasingly angry protests and for individual actions of personal rescue, the Western Powers did little to intervene, Stalin's brutalities in Eastern Europe deeply affected the free world. There was, therefore, not much argument about the wisdom of the American Policy of Containment—in essence a political expression of the purpose that motivated the so-called Truman Doctrine and the Marshall Plan—formulated by the thoughtful American diplomatist George F. Kennan and first indicated in 1947 in an article under the cipher "X" in the American magazine *Foreign Affairs*. Since Communism preaches a perpetual struggle against the non-Communist world, in certain historical situations this preaching may be rationalized into ruthless expansion unless it is met by the force of determined resistance. At least in Europe, it was now the supreme interest of the United States to prohibit the further overflow of Soviet influence beyond the already swollen limits of Stalin's new Russian Empire. This is the gist of the Policy of Containment. It sums up the events of the year 1947. It also suggests the principal direction of American world policy up to the present day.

3

By 1948 the leadership of Soviet Russia and of the United States over their respective halves of Europe (and also of Korea) was an accomplished fact. While Russian domination was welcomed by but a small minority of people in the eastern, American predominance was welcomed by most people in the western half of the continent, including Germany, where events were soon to test the measure of American determination. The American response to the Russian threat in Berlin was one of the finest American hours in the history of the cold war. A sense of relief and of Western Christian unity was diffused in the hearts of millions of Europeans. It was in 1948 that the term "cold war" became popular currency (I think the phrase was Walter Lippmann's). But it was also in 1948 that the term "West" acquired a new popular historical meaning: the cold wind of the Bolshevik threat from the steppes of Asia, instead of chilling the spirit into the mortal rigor of hopeless fear, suscitated significant new fires in the European spirit; and the unity of Western Christian civilization was first felt by thinking men in Europe and America together. In the American presidential election of 1948 (the first in a series of elections that were followed all over the free world with an interest that unconsciously reflected the knowledge that here the American people were choosing the leader of the West) foreign policy played no important part; and the unexpected victory of Harry Truman, no matter what its domestic electoral sources, assured the leadership of the free world of this vigorous personality for some years to come. In Western Europe the distressing aftermath of war and poverty still prevailed; but the spirit of people, especially of the young postwar generation, compared favorably with the radical and cynical mood of disillusionment that had followed the First World War. A genuine movement toward European Unity became current; together with constructive intellectual and religious tendencies, it was also manifest in politics through the broad emergence of Christian Democratic parties whose leadership was provided by the personal excellence of De Gasperi in Italy, Adenauer in Germany, Robert Schuman in France, Figl and Raab in Austria. Partly as a consequence of these developments and partly because of the blunders of Stalin's own brutalities, the Russians now suffered their first important setbacks in Europe.

Stalin's main blunders bear the names of Czechoslovakia, Yugoslavia, and Berlin: this order is chronological as well as one of ascending importance. In February 1948, nine years after the rapacious Hitler broke his word and incorporated the remains of a cowed Czech state, not knowing that his easy subjugation of Prague was an unnecessary act whose symbolic character galvanized resistance against him in the West, Stalin acted in a similar vein. The Czechoslovak Republic, whose pliant leaders had done everything not to arouse the ire or suspicion of their mastodon Russian neighbor, was not to be given the least opportunity to maintain certain traditional contacts with the West. Even without the pressure of Russian armies, a Communist *coup d'état*, dramatized by the following suicide of the Foreign Minister, Jan Masaryk, effectively transformed Czechoslovakia into an all-out Soviet satellite. The Western Powers were not willing to intervene; but at least they took immediate steps to close their ranks and proceed with military preparations. A Western European military and political Instrument was signed in Brussels in March 1948. American military preparations in Germany increased while the still existing gradual differences in the Eastern European captive nations were being reduced to uniformity through drastic measures that indicated impatience and worrisomeness on Stalin's part. But on 28 June 1948 a Communist bulletin brought to the world the surprising news of a break between Stalin and Tito.

Few events indicate clearer the Russian national and imperialist, as distinct from Communist, motives and ambitions of Stalin than the dark (and at times almost comic) story of Russian-Yugoslav misunderstandings. In no Eastern European country was there a native Communist Party stronger than in Yugoslavia; Tito was indeed the most radical of the Communist leaders. But he was a junior partner, not a satellite; he had won his civil war, if not wholly without Russian help, at least not as a carpetbagger suppliant following behind the mighty hordes of the advancing Russian armies. Frequently Stalin preferred submissive Russian agents to steadfast Communist leaders; he grew dissatisfied with Tito's Communist South Slav nationalism from 1945 onward. As often before in history, the crudity of Russian intervention alienated those who had been her best friends in the Balkans. When his Russian agents proved unequal to the task of upsetting Tito, Stalin pronounced Communist anathema upon Yugoslavia; but his subsequent threats only united the still considerably divided Yugoslav nation behind their audacious leader, whose prestige, in contrast to Stalin's, now began to rise throughout the world.

In line with his policy to eliminate the last Western islands within his monochrome East European Empire, Stalin began to put pressure on Berlin in the spring of 1948. It will be remembered that Berlin, like Vienna, was divided into four occupational zones where for symbolic purposes all four Allies were keeping garrisons, an arrangement made in 1944 and which indeed had precedents going back to the occupation of Paris after Napoleon's fall. Unlike Vienna, where a central Austrian government resided, Berlin was not the seat of a German government. In its eastern suburbs the Russians were setting up the rudiments of an East German satellite "administration," while the West German government, after some debate, made its home in Bonn in 1949. These arrangements consequent to the practical division of Germany were not yet advanced when in May 1948 the Russians began to suspend supplies and communications between West Berlin and the Western Zones of Germany. The object of this Blockade was the starving of West Berlin into submission. It was broken from the very beginning by the resoluteness of the population in concert with Allied military determination to stand fast. Along the official highway connecting Berlin with the Western

Zone, General Clark proposed to break through the Blockade with an American military column; but President Truman chose instead to depend on American ingenuity of material supply: the famous Berlin Air Lift was created. Throughout the dark autumn and winter days of 1948 a Berlin still largely in ruins drew hope and succor from the drone of American transport planes, piloted often by the same men who but a few years before cast bombs on that same city. Almost a hundred American, British, and French airmen gave their lives for the cause of freedom in Berlin. Their sacrifice was not in vain. The Russian bluff was called. In May 1949 the Russians lifted the "Blockade."

By that time, however, outside Berlin the division of Germany had begun to ossify. In Bonn in the West and in Berlin-Pankow in the East two rival German governments were installed. The Russians were beginning to give arms to their East German police and semi-military forces, while in the West the American military emphasis grew. In 1947–48 arrangements were made for American bombers to be installed on airfields in Britain. Increasing amounts of American military equipment were given to Western European nations. The permanent establishment of American forces in Europe was finally sealed by the instrument of the North Atlantic Treaty Organization, signed in March 1949. It was already foreseeable that unless important changes were to occur in the political relations of Moscow and Washington, at least a partial rearmament of West Germany by the United States and its allies would be but a matter of time.

Thus four years after the end of the Second World War within Russian Europe all resistance was crushed; but Russian and Communist expansion seemed to have come definitely to a halt. The Russification of Stalin's new Empire proceeded with its Communization; in 1949 a Russian Army Marshal was made Defense Minister of the Polish Republic, and the elimination of even proved and radical Communists who were not known Russian agents began in the rest of the satellite countries. Still, it was not Russian but American power that swayed the destinies of most of the world. The number and the extent of American—not of Russian—military, naval, and air bases were increasing. In Europe at least, Communism failed everywhere outside the iron curtain; strong American support insured the victory of the Christian Democrats in the important Italian elections of 1948. The European balance was becoming redressed—at the cost of the abandoned Eastern European nations, but at least altogether somewhat in favor of the West. In May 1949 Molotov, whose impregnable Soviet Russian conservatism was associated with a crucial decade of Russian history and expansion, left the Soviet Foreign Ministry; Stalin appointed Vishinsky in his place. This was at least a sign of his dissatisfaction with the way Russian foreign affairs were going.

Up to that time the United States had the atomic monopoly; but now in 1949 the Russians exploded their first atomic bomb—promptly monitored by

American atomic agencies under whose aegis the plans for the construction of a Hydrogen Bomb had already begun.

4

At this point, with the first phase of the cold war closing, we must look at the ideas guiding the course of the now inimical Giant Powers of the world. Both the Russian and the American peoples were told by their leaders that the Second World War brought no real peace, that they might have to gird themselves anew for the dangers of war. This was possible without drastic interference with the domestic prosperity of America; it was not possible in Russia, where the regimen of privations continued well after the war. While the American people, relentlessly reminded of their new international responsibilities, tended more and more in an internationalist direction, Stalin's Russia became more national and isolationist than it had ever been since the Communist Revolution. By 1949 the similarities between Stalin's regime and that of Tsar Nicholas I, for example, were so obvious that pages and pages from books such as the Marquis de Custine's description of his travels in the Russia of the 1840s would apply to Stalin's Russia in the 1940s; but Americans sought the key to Soviet conduct in dogma rather than in history, in the internationalist, revolutionary, and agnostic doctrines of "Leninist" Communism, rather than in the nationalist, isolationist, and orthodox features that were emerging under Stalin, whose xenophobic, puritan, anti-Semitic terror suggested a Tsar rather than any international Communist revolutionary figure, and whose exhortations of Russian national pride had deep roots in Russian history but no source at all in Marx. The American reaction, concentrating on the dangers of international Communism rather than on the historical features of Russian aggressiveness, was of course only in part due to the myopic American intellectual tendency of taking dogmas and abstractions unduly seriously. It was also motivated by a strong domestic undercurrent, a political anti-Communist reaction against the more and more obvious falseness of wartime radical and Russophile propaganda. It was the reaction against the illusions of an intellectual and political generation now on trial: and such shocking developments as the evidence of amateur espionage practiced by people like Alger Hiss, an able young top organization man of the New Deal generation, now revealed to have been at least a Communist sympathizer, were to carry this popular anti-Communist reaction far.

Thus we find a curious and corresponding duality in American and Russian political tendencies by 1949. On one hand, the Soviet Union was, more than ever, the mighty leader of international Communism; but in reality the tendency of her tyrannical ruler was more national than international, more Russian than Communist, more isolationist than revolutionary; for example, there were (and, to some extent, there still are) two iron curtains, one separating the satellites from the rest of Europe, the other separating Russia from her Sovietized satellites, and the latter was even thicker than the first. On one hand, the United States was committing herself only to the defense of certain Western European and marginal strategic territories against the eventual armed aggression of Russia; but in reality the tendency of this American policy was becoming ideological rather than political, and world-wide rather than limited to America's admittedly vast national and Allied interests; for example, the United States, even though she had written off Eastern Europe, assumed the role of a co-ordinating center of Eastern European émigré political and propaganda activities, while her military intelligence organs were already involved in an underhand struggle with their Soviet counterparts throughout the whole world.

For on a vital point American intentions and purposes were not entirely clear. We have seen that while, during and even after the war, the Anglo-American purpose was, broadly speaking, the reconstruction of Europe, the Russian purpose was the division of Europe; now Europe was torn asunder, and Containment and NATO were to keep any more portions from going. But there was an important difference between NATO and Containment that has remained obscured and unresolved until the present day. The original purpose of Containment—at least in Kennan's concept—was to build up Western Europe and commit the United States in her defense so that after a while Russia's rulers would see how their aggressive behavior was leading them nowhere. Thereafter the growth of a peacefully prosperous Europe would modify the unnatural division of the continent into Russian and American military spheres, so that ultimately a mutual reduction of the more extreme Russian and American commitments and of some of their most advanced outposts could follow. These were not insubstantial speculations. They rested on political and geographical realities. In 1949 there was still an important marginal area in the middle of Europe that was not yet fully ranged within either the Russian or the American military system (indeed, until 1951 the only line where NATO's territories bordered on Russia was the short stretch of the Russian-Norwegian frontier in the extreme North). Finland was under the Russian shadow, and the Russians insisted on binding Pacts with Finland; but Stalin told the Finns that their country could remain outside the Soviet political sphere if Sweden, across the Baltic, was to stay outside NATO and the American military sphere. In 1948 neither West Germany nor, of course, Switzerland and Austria, were part of NATO; the latter, a battleground of competing intelligence agencies, was, like Germany, divided between Eastern and Western Zones but, unlike Germany, not quite hopelessly: there was a central Austrian government sitting in Vienna, recognized by both Washington and Moscow. Further to the south neither Yugoslavia nor Greece nor Turkey belonged to NATO (the latter two were then included in 1951), while it is significant that the multiple military alliances that the Russians were tying among their satellite neighbors were not extended to Albania, the only geographically isolated member of the

Soviet group of states. Thus a motley but unbroken middle European zone separated the Russian and American spheres from the Arctic to the Aegean. This was the design of Kennan, who was the head of Policy Planning in the Department of State at the time; but this subtle and reasonable policy was soon superseded by the simple and military anti-Communist concept of NATO. Where the original purpose had been the ultimate dissolution of the division of Europe and Germany, NATO was to contribute to the hardening of that division into permanence. Absorbed by this newer purpose, the necessary imagination of American statesmanship began to falter; and we shall see how thereby the character of the American state and society began to develop in a centralized and military direction.

The question, therefore, arises whether American policy had understood Stalin's ambitions well enough. It was formulated at a time when Russia in Eastern Europe proceeded with shocking brutality. Around the edge of the new Russian Empire conditions were uncertain: the Red froth bubbled in northern Greece; France and Italy seemed withering in political and economic weakness. It was of the greatest importance to halt what was considered "the Red flood" before it could trickle and flow into Italy, France, Western Europe. But was this analysis sufficiently profound? There is no sufficient evidence that Stalin in 1947–48 had planned to advance into France and Italy or that he had even contemplated the imminent victory of the Communist Parties in those countries; indeed, the evidence points to the contrary. His actions were aimed at consolidating, in some cases with frantic haste, his imperial realms in Eastern Europe; and it is quite possible that the American preoccupation with Western Europe may have suited his purposes: for thus American attention was diverted from Eastern Europe.

Perhaps it would be well to put ourselves into Stalin's position in, say, 1947. He regarded Eastern Europe as his; he also felt somewhat justified in this possession. Russia had won the war against the German invaders. Her cities were devastated, her armies bled white; with age-old Russian suspicion, Stalin was prone to underestimate the Allied contribution to the victory over Germany. Russia had carried the main brunt of the war, while the United States, without wounds, emerged as the greatest and most powerful nation of the earth. It was the Americans, now in possession of the entire Western European pastry shop, who a few years before let him have his Eastern European cake with such unconcern; why couldn't he eat it, after all? Now Stalin did not particularly contest American power: he did not challenge America's sphere; did it not seem to him, however, that the Americans were beginning to challenge *his* sphere? Always he was willing enough to go along with sphere-of-interest arrangements; he, again like Russian diplomacy in the past, was a *quid pro quo* politician of sorts. When Churchill, at Potsdam, complained about Rumania. Stalin would retort that he fulfilled their bargain by not intervening in Greece; when Churchill or Truman insisted upon Poland, Stalin answered that Poland involved Russian interests while he had not the slightest concern with how the British protected theirs in Belgium or Holland. But Churchill, that cunning old British Capitalist Enemy of Communism, at least understood him on that point; the Americans did not. Stalin did not really compete with them over Western Europe; but why were they now, after the war, two years after Yalta, getting worked up about Eastern Europe, protesting loudly about imprisoned Cardinals? He did not really challenge what to him amounted to the American domination of Western Europe; the financial assistance which Moscow had furnished the Italian Communist Party, for example, was far less than what the Americans poured into Italy before the 1948 elections. Why, then, the American meddling in Eastern Europe? Had they not won enough in the war? All of the Pacific and the Atlantic basins, plus Western and Southern Europe? With his narrow Oriental eyes looking westward from the Byzantine windows of the Kremlin, Stalin may have reasoned thus.

Thus an amused historian may say that the first few years—and perhaps even the first decade—of the Russian-American crisis over Europe might have been due to a fundamental, mutual misunderstanding: Washington presupposing that the immediate Russian aim was to upset and conquer Western Europe, Moscow presupposing that the American aim was to upset and reconquer Eastern Europe—and that both presuppositions were wrong.

Thus a cynical historian may say that Moscow and Washington did not make out so badly, after all. True, in 1945 and thereafter a more intelligent and imaginative American policy could have prevented the Russian advance into the very middle of Europe and this spared much of the cost and the toil of the cold war; true, in 1945 and thereafter less crude and brutal Russian measures in Eastern Europe would not have provoked all of these countermeasures, including NATO, and Russian influence in Europe would not have been limited to the subject satellite capitals—but the cynic may say: so what? No cold war, no American dominion over one half, and no undisputed Russian dominion over the other half of Europe. No cold war, no rigid division of Europe—ah yes, a boon to Europe it may have been: but, if so, the Russians, for instance, would not be the masters of Hungary today, and the Americans would not be able to tie an armed Germany within their military system. Still, this imaginary cynic of a historian would not be entirely right—at least not yet. For, no matter how true is the maxim that one must want the consequences of what one wants, this maxim is seldom put into practice in the affairs of men and of nations; and it is especially true in democratic ages that the discrepancy between intentions and ultimate results is great, very great indeed.

What Is History—

Fact or Fancy?

CONTENTS

QUESTIONS FOR STUDY

1 *Is the study of history a "science"? If not, why not?*

2 *How does Butterfield differ in his approach to history from Robinson? From Acton? From Becker?*

3 *Ought the historian to make moral judgments about the past? Can he avoid doing so?*

4 *How far do you find the argument for relativism convincing?*

5 *Try to use Becker's theory of historical relativism to explain Marx's philosophy of history.*

6 *Does history have any use? If not, does it have any value?*

During the past 100 years men's ways of thinking about history have changed, just as their ways of thinking about science have. The great pioneers who laid the foundations of modern historical methodology in the nineteenth century could feel "assured of certain certainties." They believed that the past of the human race constituted a structure of fact that the historian could learn to understand through critical analysis of the surviving documents. Some held that scientific laws could be educed that would not only explain the past but would also predict the future. Some thought that a major part of the historian's task was to judge the men of past ages in the light of eternal moral principles. All were convinced of the objectivity of historical knowledge—the facts were objective; the laws were objective; the standards of moral judgment were objective.

In the twentieth century all these assumptions were challenged, and a theory of historical relativism grew up to complement the relativity of the physicists. The most recent movement of thought has been characterized by a mixture of confidence, humility, and common sense. Many contemporary historians claim less for their craft than did the great system builders of the nineteenth century, but they remain happily convinced of the validity of historical knowledge, within due limits, and of its enduring value as a way of understanding the human predicament.

1 The Science of History

Leopold von Ranke has been called the "father of modern historical scholarship." He was convinced that, if a historian studied the relevant documents with sufficient critical acumen, he could discover "what actually happened" in the past. The following extract is from his Histories of the Latin and Germanic Nations, *published in 1832.*

FROM *Histories of the Latin and Germanic Nations from 1494–1514* BY LEOPOLD VON RANKE

. . . THIS BOOK ATTEMPTS TO SEE these histories and the other, related histories of the Latin and Germanic nations in their unity. To history has been assigned the office of judging the past, of instructing the present for the benefit of future ages. To such high offices this work does not aspire: It wants only to show what actually happened (*wie es eigentlich gewesen*).

But whence the sources for such a new investigation? The basis of the present work, the sources of its material, are memoirs, diaries, letters, diplomatic reports, and original narratives of eyewitnesses; other writings were used only if they were immediately derived from the above mentioned or seemed to equal them because of some original information. These sources will be identified on every page; a second volume, to be published concurrently, will present the method of investigation and the critical conclusions.

Aim and subject mould the form of a book. The writing of history cannot be expected to possess the same free development of its subject which, in theory at least, is expected in a work of literature; I am not sure it was correct to ascribe this quality to the works of the great Greek and Roman masters.

The strict presentation of the facts, contingent and unattractive though they may be, is undoubtedly the supreme law. After this, it seems to me, comes the exposition of the unity and progress of events. Therefore, instead

Leopold von Ranke, *Histories of the Latin and Germanic Nations from 1494–1514*, translated by Fritz Stern in *The Varieties of History* (1956), pp. 55–8. Reprinted by permission of The World Publishing Company.

of starting as might have been expected with a general description of the political institutions of Europe—this would certainly have distracted, if not disrupted, our attention—I have preferred to discuss in detail each nation, each power, and each individual only when they assumed a preeminently active or dominant role. I have not been troubled by the fact that here and there they had to be mentioned beforehand, when their existence could not be ignored. In this way, we are better able to grasp the general line of their development, the direction they took, and the ideas by which they were motivated.

Finally what will be said of my treatment of particulars, which is such an essential part of the writing of history? Will it not often seem harsh, disconnected, colorless, and tiring? There are, of course, noble models both ancient and—be it remembered—modern; I have not dared to emulate them: theirs was a different world. A sublime ideal does exist: the event in its human intelligibility, its unity, and its diversity; this should be within one's reach. I know to what extent I have fallen short of my aim. One tries, one strives, but in the end it is not attained. Let none be disheartened by this! The most important thing is always what we deal with, as Jakobi says, humanity as it is, explicable or inexplicable: the life of the individual, of generations, and of nations, and at times the hand of God above them.

> *Henry Thomas Buckle held that the proper task of a historian was to discover general laws of historical development that were closely analogous to the laws of physical science.*

FROM *History of Civilization in England*

BY H. T. BUCKLE

OUR ACQUAINTANCE WITH HISTORY being so imperfect, while our materials are so numerous, it seems desirable that something should be done on a scale far larger than has hitherto been attempted, and that a strenuous effort should be made to bring up this great department of inquiry to a level with other departments, in order that we may maintain the balance and harmony of our knowledge. It is in this spirit that the present work has been conceived. To make the execution of it fully equal to the conception is impossible: still I hope to accomplish for the history of man something

Henry Thomas Buckle, *History of Civilization in England,* 2nd ed. (1858), pp. 5–8, 22–3, 29–31.

equivalent, or at all events analogous, to what has been effected by other inquirers for the different branches of natural science. In regard to nature, events apparently the most irregular and capricious have been explained, and have been shown to be in accordance with certain fixed and universal laws. This has been done because men of ability, and, above all, men of patient, untiring thought, have studied natural events with the view of discovering their regularity: and if human events were subjected to a similar treatment, we have every right to expect similar results. For it is clear that they who affirm that the facts of history are incapable of being generalized, take for granted the very question at issue. Indeed they do more than this. They not only assume what they cannot prove, but they assume what in the present state of knowledge is highly improbable. Whoever is at all acquainted with what has been done during the last two centuries, must be aware that every generation demonstrates some events to be regular and predictable, which the preceding generation had declared to be irregular and unpredictable: so that the marked tendency of advancing civilization is to strengthen our belief in the universality of order, of method, and of law. This being the case, it follows that if any facts, or class of facts, have not yet been reduced to order, we, so far from pronouncing them to be irreducible, should rather be guided by our experience of the past, and should admit the probability that what we now call inexplicable will at some future time be explained. This expectation of discovering regularity in the midst of confusion is so familiar to scientific men, that among the most eminent of them it becomes an article of faith: and if the same expectation is not generally found among historians, it must be ascribed partly to their being of inferior ability to the investigators of nature, and partly to the greater complexity of those social phenomena with which their studies are concerned.

Both these causes have retarded the creation of the science of history. The most celebrated historians are manifestly inferior to the most successful cultivators of physical science: no one having devoted himself to history who in point of intellect is at all to be compared with Kepler, Newton, or many others that might be named. And as to the greater complexity of the phenomena, the philosophic historian is opposed by difficulties far more formidable than is the student of nature; since, while on the one hand, his observations are more liable to those causes of error which arise from prejudice and passion, he, on the other hand, is unable to employ the great physical resource of experiment, by which we can often simplify even the most intricate problems in the external world.

It is not, therefore, surprising that the study of the movements of Man should be still in its infancy, as compared with the advanced state of the study of the movements of Nature. Indeed the difference between the progress of the two pursuits is so great, that while in physics the regularity of events, and the power of predicting them, are often taken for granted even in cases still unproved, a similar regularity is in history not only not taken for granted, but is actually denied. Hence it is that whoever wishes to raise history to a level with other branches of knowledge, is met by a preliminary obstacle; since he is told that in the affairs of men there is something mysterious and providential, which makes them impervious to our investigations, and which will always hide from us their future course. To this it might be sufficient to reply, that such an assertion is gratuitous; that it is by its nature incapable of proof; and that it is moreover opposed by the notorious fact that every where else increasing knowledge is accompanied by an increasing confidence in the uniformity with which, under the same circumstances, the same events must succeed each other. It will, however, be more satisfactory to probe the difficulty deeper, and inquire at once into the foundation of the common opinion that history must always remain in its present empirical state, and can never be raised to the rank of a science. We shall thus be led to one vast question, which indeed lies at the root of the whole subject, and is simply this: Are the actions of men, and therefore of societies, governed by fixed laws, or are they the result either of chance or of supernatural interference?

*   *   *

Of all offences, it might well be supposed that the crime of murder is one of the most arbitrary and irregular. . . . But now, how stands the fact? The fact is, that murder is committed with as much regularity, and bears as uniform a relation to certain known circumstances, as do the movements of the tides, and the rotations of the seasons. M. Quetelet, who has spent his life in collecting and methodizing the statistics of different countries, states, as the result of his laborious researches, that "in every thing which concerns crime, the same numbers re-occur with a constancy which cannot be mistaken: and that this is the case even with those crimes which seem quite independent of human foresight, such, for instance, as murders, which are generally committed after quarrels arising from circumstances apparently casual. Nevertheless, we know from experience that every year there not only take place nearly the same number of murders, but that even the instrument by which they are committed are employed in the same proportion." This was the language used in 1835 by confessedly the first statistician in Europe, and every subsequent investigation has confirmed its accuracy. For later inquiries have ascertained the extraordinary fact, that the uniform reproduction of crime is more clearly marked, and more capable of being predicted, than are the physical laws connected with the disease and destruction of our bodies.

*   *   *

Nor is it merely the crimes of men which are marked by this uniformity of sequence. Even the number of marriages annually contracted, is determined, not by the temper and wishes of individuals, but by large general facts, over which individuals can exercise no authority. It is now known that marriages bear a fixed and definite relation to the price of corn; and in England the experience of a century has proved that, instead of having any connexion with personal feelings, they are simply regulated by the average earnings of the great mass of the people, so that this immense social and religious institution is not only swayed, but is completely controlled, by the price of food and by the rate of wages. . . .

*   *   *

To those who have a steady conception of the regularity of events, and have firmly seized the great truth that the actions of men, being guided by their antecedents, are in reality never inconsistent, but, however capricious they may appear, only form part of one vast scheme of universal order, of which we in the present state of knowledge can barely see the outline,—to those who understand this, which is at once the key and the basis of history, the facts just adduced, so far from being strange, will be precisely what would have been expected, and ought long since to have been known. Indeed, the progress of inquiry is becoming so rapid and so earnest, that I entertain little doubt that before another century has elapsed, the chain of evidence will be complete, and it will be as rare to find an historian who denies the undeviating regularity of the moral world, as it now is to find a philosopher who denies the regularity of the material world.

> *The most famous attempt actually to construct a science of history in the nineteenth century was that of Karl Marx. The first extract given below is from a joint work of Marx and Engels published in 1846.*

FROM *The German Ideology*

BY KARL MARX AND FRIEDRICH ENGELS

MEN CAN BE DISTINGUISHED from animals by consciousness, by religion or anything else you like. They themselves begin to distinguish themselves from animals as soon as they begin to *produce* their means of subsistence, a step which is conditioned by their physical organization. By producing their means of subsistence men are indirectly producing their actual material life.

Karl Marx and Frederick Engels, *The German Ideology* (1947), pp. 7–9, 14–5, edited with an Introduction by R. Pascal. Reprinted by permission of International Publishers Co., Inc.

The way in which men produce their means of subsistence depends first of all on the nature of the actual means they find in existence and have to reproduce. This mode of production must not be considered simply as being the reproduction of the physical existence of the individuals. Rather it is a definite form of activity of these individuals, a definite form of expressing their life, a definite *mode of life* on their part. As individuals express their life, so they are. What they are, therefore, coincides with their production, both with *what* they produce and with *how* they produce. The nature of individuals thus depends on the material conditions determining their production.

This production only makes its appearance with the increase of population. In its turn this presupposes the intercourse of individuals with one another. The form of this intercourse is again determined by production.

The relations of different nations among themselves depend upon the extent to which each has developed its productive forces, the division of labour and internal intercourse. This statement is generally recognized. But not only the relation of one nation to others, but also the whole internal structure of the nation itself depends on the stage of development reached by its production and its internal and external intercourse. How far the productive forces of a nation are developed is shown most manifestly by the degree to which the division of labour has been carried. Each new productive force, in so far as it is not merely a quantitative extension of productive forces already known, (for instance the bringing into cultivation of fresh land), brings about a further development of the division of labour.

The division of labour inside a nation leads at first to the separation of industrial and commercial from agricultural labour, and hence to the separation of town and country and a clash of interests between them. Its further development leads to the separation of commercial from industrial labour. At the same time through the division of labour there develop further, inside these various branches, various divisions among the individuals co-operating in definite kinds of labour. The relative position of these individual groups is determined by the methods employed in agriculture, industry and commerce (patriarchalism, slavery, estates, classes). These same conditions are to be seen (given a more developed intercourse) in the relations of different nations to one another.

The various stages of development in the division of labour are just so many different forms of ownership; i.e., the existing stage in the division of labour determines also the relations of individuals to one another with reference to the material, instrument, and product of the labour. . . .

In direct contrast to German philosophy which descends from heaven to earth, here we ascend from earth to heaven. That is to say, we do not set out from what men say, imagine, conceive, nor from men as narrated, thought of, imagined, conceived, in order to arrive at men in the flesh. We set out from real, active men, and on the basis of their real life-process we demonstrate the development of the ideological reflexes and echoes of this life-process. The phantoms formed in the human brain are also, necessarily, sublimates of their material life-process, which is empirically verifiable and bound to material premises. Morality, religion, metaphysics, all the rest of ideology and their corresponding forms of consciousness, thus no longer retain the semblance of independence. They have no history, no development; but men, developing their material production and their material intercourse, alter, along with this their real existence, their thinking and the products of their thinking. Life is not determined by consciousness, but consciousness by life. In the first method of approach the starting-point is consciousness taken as the living individual; in the second it is the real living individuals themselves, as they are in actual life, and consciousness is considered solely as *their* consciousness.

The two following extracts are from works of Marx that appeared in 1859 and 1867.

FROM *Preface to A Contribution to the Critique of Political Economy* BY KARL MARX

IN THE SOCIAL PRODUCTION of their life, men enter into definite relations that are indispensable and independent of their will, relations of production which correspond to a definite stage of development of their material productive forces. The sum total of these relations of production constitutes the economic structure of society, the real foundation, on which rises a legal and political superstructure and to which correspond definite forms of social consciousness. The mode of production of material life conditions the social, political and intellectual life process in general. It is not the consciousness of men that determines their being, but, on the contrary, their social being that determines their consciousness. At a certain stage of their development, the material productive forces of society come in conflict with the existing relations of production, or—what is but a legal expression for the same thing—with the property relations within which they have been at work hitherto. From forms of development of the productive forces these relations turn into their fetters. Then begins an epoch of social revolution. With the change of the economic foundation the entire immense superstructure is more or less rapidly transformed. In considering such transformations a distinction should always be made between the material transfor-

---

Karl Marx, "Preface to A Contribution to the Critique of Political Economy," in *Karl Marx and Frederick Engels: Selected Works,* I (1951), 328–9. Reprinted by permission of International Publishers Co., Inc., and Lawrence and Wishart Ltd., London.

mation of the economic conditions of production, which can be determined with the precision of natural science, and the legal, political, religious, esthetic or philosophic—in short, ideological forms in which men become conscious of this conflict and fight it out. Just as our opinion of an individual is not based on what he thinks of himself, so can we not judge of such a period of transformation by its own consciousness; on the contrary, this consciousness must be explained rather from the contradictions of material life, from the existing conflict between the social productive forces and the relations of production. No social order ever perishes before all the productive forces for which there is room in it have developed; and new, higher relations of production never appear before the material conditions of their existence have matured in the womb of the old society itself. Therefore mankind always sets itself only such tasks as it can solve; since, looking at the matter more closely, it will always be found that the task itself arises only when the material conditions for its solution already exist or are at least in the process of formation. In broad outlines Asiatic, ancient, feudal, and modern bourgeois modes of production can be designated as progressive epochs in the economic formation of society. The bourgeois relations of production are the last antagonistic form of the social process of production —antagonistic not in the sense of individual antagonism, but of one arising from the social conditions of life of the individuals; at the same time the productive forces developing in the womb of bourgeois society create the material conditions for the solution of that antagonism. This social formation brings, therefore, the prehistory of human society to a close.

FROM *Capital* BY KARL MARX

AS SOON AS THIS PROCESS of transformation has sufficiently decomposed the old society from top to bottom, as soon as the labourers are turned into proletarians, their means of labour into capital, as soon as the capitalist mode of production stands on its own feet, then the further socialisation of labour and further transformation of the land and other means of production into socially exploited and, therefore, common means of production, as well as the further expropriation of private proprietors, takes a new form. That which is now to be expropriated is no longer the labourer working for himself, but the capitalist exploiting many labourers. This expropriation is accomplished by the action of the immanent laws of capitalistic production itself, by the centralisation of capital. One capitalist always kills many. Hand in hand with this centralisation, or this expropriation of many capitalists by

Karl Marx, *Capital* in *Karl Marx and Frederick Engels: Selected Works*, I (1951), 416-8. Reprinted by permission of Lawrence and Wishart Ltd., London.

few, develop, on an ever extending scale, the co-operative form of the labour-process, the conscious technical application of science, the methodical cultiva-tion of the soil, the transformation of the instruments of labour into instru-ments of labour only usable in common, the economising of all means of production by their use as the means of production of combined, socialised labour, the entanglement of all peoples in the net of the world market, and with this, the international character of the capitalistic régime. Along with the constantly diminishing number of the magnates of capital, who usurp and monopolise all advantages of this process of transformation, grows the mass of misery, oppression, slavery, degradation, exploitation; but with this too grows the revolt of the working-class, a class always increasing in numbers, and disciplined, united, organised by the very mechanism of the process of capitalist production itself. The monopoly of capital becomes a fetter upon the mode of production, which has sprung up and flourished along with, and under it. Centralisation of the means of production and socialisation of labour at last reach a point where they become incompatible with their capitalist integument. This integument is burst asunder. The knell of capitalist private property sounds. The expropriators are expropriated.

The capitalist mode of appropriation, the result of the capitalist mode of production, produces capitalist private property. This is the first negation of individual private property, as founded on the labour of the proprietor. But capitalist production begets, with the inexorability of a law of Nature, its own negation. It is the negation of negation. This does not re-establish private property for the producer, but gives him individual property based on the acquisitions of the capitalist era: i.e., on co-operation and the posses-sion in common of the land and of the means of production.

The transformation of scattered private property, arising from individ-ual labour, into capitalist private property is, naturally, a process, incompa-rably more protracted, violent, and difficult, than the transformation of capitalistic private property, already practically resting on socialised produc-tion, into socialised property. In the former case, we had the expropriation of the mass of the people by a few usurpers; in the latter, we have the expropriation of a few usurpers by the mass of the people.

2 The Historian as Judge

Lord Acton urged the historian to analyze his sources
scrupulously but not to stop there: He should proceed to sit
in judgment on the deeds of the past.

FROM *Inaugural Lecture on the Study of History*
BY J. E. E. ACTON

FOR OUR PURPOSE, the main thing to learn is not the art of accumulating material, but the sublimer art of investigating it, of discerning truth from falsehood and certainty from doubt. It is by solidity of criticism more than by the plenitude of erudition, that the study of history strengthens, and straightens, and extends the mind. And the accession of the critic in the place of the indefatigable compiler, of the artist in coloured narrative, the skilled limner of character, the persuasive advocate of good, or other, causes, amounts to a transfer of government, to a change of dynasty, in the historic realm. For the critic is one who, when he lights on an interesting statement, begins by suspecting it. He remains in suspense until he has subjected his authority to three operations. First, he asks whether he has read the passage as the author wrote it. For the transcriber, and the editor, and the official or officious censor on the top of the editor, have played strange tricks, and have much to answer for. And if they are not to blame, it may turn out that the author wrote his book twice over, that you can discover the first jet, the progressive variations, things added, and things struck out. Next is the question where the writer got his information. If from a previous writer, it can be ascertained, and the inquiry has to be repeated. If from unpublished papers, they must be traced, and when the fountain-head is reached, or the track disappears, the question of veracity arises. The responsible writer's character, his position, antecedents, and probable motives have to be examined into; and this is what, in a different and adapted sense of the word, may be called the higher criticism, in comparison with the servile and often mechanical work of pursuing statements to their root. For a historian has to be treated as a witness, and not believed unless his sincerity is established.

John Edward Emerich Acton, "Inaugural Lecture on the Study of History," in *Lectures on Modern History* (1906), pp. 15–6, 23–4, 26–8.

The maxim that a man must be presumed to be innocent until his guilt is proved, was not made for him.

*   *   *

I shall never again enjoy the opportunity of speaking my thoughts to such an audience as this, and on so privileged an occasion a lecturer may well be tempted to bethink himself whether he knows of any neglected truth, any cardinal proposition, that might serve as his selected epigraph, as a last signal, perhaps even as a target. I am not thinking of those shining precepts which are the registered property of every school; that is to say—Learn as much by writing as by reading; be not content with the best book; seek sidelights from the others; have no favourites; keep men and things apart; guard against the prestige of great names; see that your judgments are your own, and do not shrink from disagreement; no trusting without testing; be more severe to ideas than to actions; do not overlook the strength of the bad cause or the weakness of the good; never be surprised by the crumbling of an idol or the disclosure of a skeleton; judge talent at its best and character at its worst; suspect power more than vice, and study problems in preference to periods; for instance: the derivation of Luther, the scientific influence of Bacon, the predecessors of Adam Smith, the medieval masters of Rousseau, the consistency of Burke, the identity of the first Whig. Most of this, I suppose, is undisputed, and calls for no enlargement. But the weight of opinion is against me when I exhort you never to debase the moral currency or to lower the standard of rectitude, but to try others by the final maxim that governs your own lives, and to suffer no man and no cause to escape the undying penalty which history has the power to inflict on wrong. The plea in extenuation of guilt and mitigation of punishment is perpetual. At every step we are met by arguments which go to excuse, to palliate, to confound right and wrong, and reduce the just man to the level of the reprobate. The men who plot to baffle and resist us are, first of all, those who made history what it has become. They set up the principle that only a foolish Conservative judges the present time with the ideas of the past; that only a foolish Liberal judges the past with the ideas of the present.

The mission of that school was to make distant times, and especially the Middle Ages, then most distant of all, intelligible and acceptable to a society issuing from the eighteenth century. There were difficulties in the way; and among others this, that, in the first fervour of the Crusades the men who took the Cross, after receiving communion, heartily devoted the day to the extermination of Jews. To judge them by a fixed standard, to call them sacrilegious fanatics or furious hypocrites, was to yield a gratuitous victory to Voltaire. It became a rule of policy to praise the spirit when you could not defend the deed. So that we have no common code; our moral notions are always fluid; and you must consider the times, the class from which men sprang, the surrounding influences, the masters in their schools, the preachers in their pulpits, the movement they obscurely obeyed, and so on, until responsibility is merged in numbers, and not a culprit is left for execution. A murderer was no criminal if he followed local custom, if neighbours approved, if he was encouraged by official advisers or prompted by just authority, if he acted for the reason of state or the pure love of religion, or if he sheltered himself behind the complicity of the Law. The depression of morality was flagrant; but the motives were those which have enabled us to contemplate with distressing complacency the secret of unhallowed lives. The code that is greatly modified by time and place, will vary according to the cause. The amnesty is an artifice that enables us to make exceptions, to tamper with weights and measures, to deal unequal justice to friends and enemies.

It is associated with that philosophy which Cato attributes to the gods. For we have a theory which justifies Providence by the event, and holds nothing so deserving as success, to which there can be no victory in a bad cause; prescription and duration legitimate; and whatever exists is right and reasonable; and as God manifests His will by that which He tolerates, we must conform to the divine decree by living to shape the future after the ratified image of the past. Another theory, less confidently urged, regards History as our guide, as much by showing errors to evade as examples to pursue. It is suspicious of illusions in success, and, though there may be hope of ultimate triumph for what is true, if not by its own attraction, by the gradual exhaustion of error, it admits no corresponding promise for what is ethically right. It deems the canonisation of the historic past more perilous than ignorance or denial, because it would perpetuate the reign of sin and acknowledge the sovereignty of wrong, and conceives it the part of real greatness to know how to stand and fall alone, stemming, for a lifetime, the contemporary flood.

Ranke relates, without adornment, that William III ordered the extirpation of a Catholic clan, and scouts the faltering excuse of his defenders. But when he comes to the death and character of the international deliverer, Glencoe is forgotten, the imputation of murder drops, like a thing unworthy of notice. Johannes Mueller, a great Swiss celebrity, writes that the British Constitution occurred to somebody, perhaps to Halifax. This artless statement might not be approved by rigid lawyers as a faithful and felicitous indication of the manner of that mysterious growth of ages, from occult beginnings, that was never profaned by the invading wit of man; but it is less grotesque than it appears. Lord Halifax was the most original writer of political tracts in the pamphleteering crowd between Harrington and Bolingbroke; and in the Exclusion struggle he produced a scheme of limitations which, in substance, if not in form, foreshadowed the position of the monarchy in the later Hanoverian reigns. Although Halifax did not believe in the plot, he insisted that innocent victims should be sacrificed to content the multitude. Sir William Temple writes: "We only disagreed in one point, which was the leaving some priests to the law upon the accusation of being priests only, as the House of Commons had desired; which I thought wholly unjust. Upon this point Lord Halifax and I had so sharp a debate at Lord Sunderland's lodgings, that he told me, if I would not concur in points which were so necessary for the people's satisfaction, he would tell everybody I was a Papist. And upon his affirming that the plot must be handled as if it were true, whether it were so or no, in those points that were so generally believed." In spite of this accusing passage, Macaulay, who prefers Halifax to all the statesmen of his age, praises him for his mercy: "His dislike of extremes, and a forgiving and compassionate temper which seems to have been natural to him, preserved him from all participation in the worst crimes of his time."

If, in our uncertainty, we must often err, it may be sometimes better to risk excess in rigour than in indulgence, for then at least we do no injury by loss of principle. As Bayle has said, it is more probable that the secret motives of an indifferent action are bad than good; and this discouraging conclusion does not depend upon theology, for James Mozley supports the sceptic from the other flank, with all the artillery of Tractarian Oxford. "A Christian," he says, "is bound by his very creed to suspect evil, and cannot release himself. . . . He sees it where others do not; his instinct is divinely strengthened; his eye is supernaturally keen; he has a spiritual insight, and senses exercised to discern. . . . He owns the doctrine of original sin; that doctrine puts him necessarily on his guard against appearances, sustains his apprehension under perplexity, and prepares him for recognising anywhere what he knows to be everywhere." There is a popular saying of Madame de Staël, that we forgive whatever we really understand. The paradox has been judiciously pruned by her descendant, the Duke de Broglie, in the words: "Beware of too much explaining, lest we end by too much excusing." History, says Froude, does teach that right and wrong are real distinctions. Opinions alter, manners change, creeds rise and fall, but the moral law is written on the tablets of eternity. And if there are moments when we may resist the teaching of Froude, we have seldom the chance of resisting when he is supported by Mr. Goldwin Smith: "A sound historical morality will sanction strong measures in evil times; selfish ambition, treachery, murder, perjury, it will never sanction in the worst of times, for these are the things that make times evil.— Justice has been justice, mercy has been mercy, honour has been honour, good faith has been good faith, truthfulness has been truthfulness from the beginning." The doctrine that, as Sir Thomas Browne says, morality is not ambulatory, is expressed as follows by Burke, who, when true to himself, is the most intelligent of our instructors: "My principles enable me to form my judgment upon men and actions in history, just as they do in common life; and are not formed out of events and characters, either present or past. History is a preceptor of prudence, not of principles. The principles of true politics are those of morality enlarged; and I neither now do, nor ever will admit of any other."

3   *The Past and the Present*

In the early twentieth century a group of scholars in America wrote about the need for a "New History." They urged especially that the study of the past should be conducted in such a way as to illuminate the present and even to guide men's actions for the future.

FROM *The New History* BY J. H. ROBINSON

IN ITS AMPLEST MEANING History includes every trace and vestige of everything that man has done or thought since first he appeared on the earth. It may aspire to follow the fate of nations or it may depict the habits and emotions of the most obscure individual. Its sources of information extend from the rude flint hatchets of Chelles to this morning's newspaper. It is the vague and comprehensive science of past human affairs. We are within its bounds whether we decipher a mortgage on an Assyrian tile, estimate the value of the Diamond Necklace, or describe the over-short pastry to which Charles V was addicted to his undoing. The tragic reflections of Eli's daughter-in-law, when she learned of the discomfiture of her people at Ebenezer, are history; so are the provisions of Magna Charta, the origin of the doctrine of transubstantiation, the fall of Santiago, the difference between a black friar and a white friar, and the certified circulation of the *New York World* upon February 1 of the current year. Each fact has its interest and importance; all have been carefully recorded.

Now, when a writer opens and begins to peruse the thick, closely written volume of human experience, with a view of making an abstract of it for those who have no time to study the original work, he is immediately forced to ask himself what he shall select to present to his reader's attention. He finds that the great book from which he gains his information is grotesquely out of perspective, for it was compiled by many different hands, and by those widely separated in time and in sentiment—by Herodotus, Machiavelli, Eusebius, St. Simon, Otto of Freising, Pepys, St. Luke, the Duchess of Abrantès, Sallust, Cotton Mather. The portentously serious alternates with the lightest gossip. A dissipated courtier may be allotted a chapter and the destruction of a race be left unrecorded. It is clear that in treating history for the general reader the question of selection and proportion is momentous. Yet when we turn to our more popular treatises on the subject, the obvious and pressing need of picking and choosing, of selecting, reselecting, and selecting again, would seem to have escaped most writers. They appear to be the victims of tradition in dealing with the past. They exhibit but little appreciation of the vast resources upon which they might draw, and unconsciously follow, for the most part, an established routine in their selection of facts. When we consider the vast range of human interests, our histories furnish us with a sadly inadequate and misleading review of the past, and it might almost seem as if historians had joined in a conspiracy to foster a narrow and relatively unedifying conception of the true scope and intent of historical study. This is apparent if we examine any of the older standard outlines or handbooks from which a great part of the public has derived its notions of the past, either in school or later in life.

The following is an extract from a compendium much used until recently in schools and colleges: "Robert the Wise (of Anjou) (1309-1343), the successor of Charles II of Naples, and the champion of the Guelphs, could not extend his power over Sicily where Frederick II (1296–1337), the son of Peter of Aragon, reigned. Robert's granddaughter, Joan I, after a career of crime and misfortune, was strangled in prison by Charles Durazzo, the last male descendant of the house of Anjou in Lower Italy (1382), who seized on the government. Joan II, the last heir of Durazzo (1414–1435), first adopted Alfonso V, of Aragon, and then Louis III, of Anjou, and his brother, René. Alfonso, who inherited the crown of Sicily, united both kingdoms (1435), after a war with René and the Visconti of Milan."

This is not, as we might be tempted to suspect, a mere collection of data for contingent reference, no more intended to be read than a table of logarithms. It is a characteristic passage from the six pages which a distinguished scholar devoted to the Italy of Dante, Petrarch, and Lorenzo the Magnificent.

*   *   *

History is doubtless

> An orchard bearing several trees
> And fruits of different tastes.

It may please our fancy, gratify our serious or idle curiosity, test our memories, and, as Bolingbroke says, contribute to "a creditable kind of ignorance." But the one thing that it ought to do, and has not yet effectively done, is to help us to understand ourselves and our fellows and the problems and prospects of mankind. It is this most significant form of history's usefulness that has been most commonly neglected.

It is true that it has long been held that certain lessons could be derived from the past,—precedents for the statesman and the warrior, moral guidance and consoling instances of providential interference for the commonalty. But there is a growing suspicion, which has reached conviction in the minds of most modern historians, that this type of usefulness is purely illusory. The present writer is anxious to avoid any risk of being regarded as an advocate of these supposed advantages of historical study. Their value rests on the assumption that conditions remain sufficiently uniform to give precedents a perpetual value, while, as a matter of fact, conditions, at least in our own time, are so rapidly altering that for the most part it would be dangerous indeed to attempt to apply past experience to the solution of current problems. Moreover, we rarely have sufficient reliable information in regard to the supposed analogous situation in the past to enable us to apply it to present needs. Most of the appeals of inexpensive oratory to "what history teaches" belong to this class of assumed analogies which will not bear close scrutiny. When I speak of history enabling us to understand ourselves and the problems and prospects of mankind, I have something quite different in mind, which I will try to make plain by calling the reader's attention to the use that he makes of his own personal history.

We are almost entirely dependent upon our memory of our past thoughts and experiences for an understanding of the situation in which we find ourselves at any given moment. To take the nearest example, the reader will have to consult his own history to understand why his eyes are fixed upon this particular page. If he should fall into a sound sleep and be suddenly awakened, his memory might for the moment be paralyzed, and he would gaze in astonishment about the room, with no realization of his whereabouts. The fact that all the familiar objects about him presented themselves plainly to his view would not be sufficient to make him feel at home until his memory had come to his aid and enabled him to recall a certain portion of the past. The momentary suspension of memory's functions as one recovers from a fainting fit or emerges from the effects of an anaesthetic is sometimes so distressing as to amount to a sort of intellectual agony. In its normal state the mind selects automatically, from the almost infinite mass of memories, just those things in our past which make us feel at home in the present. It works so easily and efficiently that we are unconscious of what it is doing for us and of how dependent we are upon it. It supplies so promptly and so precisely what we need from the past in order to make the present intelligible that we are beguiled into the mistaken notion that the present is self-explanatory and quite able to take care of itself, and that the past is largely dead and irrelevant, except when we have to make a conscious effort to recall some elusive fact.

What we call history is not so different from our more intimate personal memories as at first sight it seems to be; for very many of the useful and essential elements in our recollections are not personal experiences at all, but include a multitude of things which we have been told or have read; and these play a very important part in our life. Should the reader of this page stop to reflect, he would perceive a long succession of historical antecedents leading up to his presence in a particular room, his ability to read the English language, his momentary freedom from pressing cares, and his inclination to center his attention upon a discussion of the nature and value of historical study. Were he not vaguely conscious of these historical antecedents, he would be in the bewildered condition spoken of above. Some of the memories necessary to save him from his bewilderment are parts of his own past experience, but many of them belong to the realm of history, namely, to what he has been told or what he has read of the past.

I could have no hope that this line of argument would make the slightest impression upon the reader, were he confined either to the immediate impressions of the moment, or to his personal experiences. It gives one something of a shock, indeed, to consider what a very small part of our guiding convictions are in any way connected with our personal experience. The date of our own birth is quite as strictly historical a fact as that of Artaphernes or of Innocent III; we are forced to a helpless reliance upon the evidence of others for both events.

So it comes about that our personal recollections insensibly merge into history in the ordinary sense of the word. History, from this point of view, may be regarded as an artificial extension and broadening of our memories and may be used to overcome the natural bewilderment of all unfamiliar situations. Could we suddenly be endowed with a Godlike and exhaustive knowledge of the whole history of mankind, far more complete than the combined knowledge of all the histories ever written, we should gain forthwith a Godlike appreciation of the world in which we live, and a Godlike insight into the evils which mankind now suffers, as well as into the most promising methods for alleviating them, *not because the past would furnish precedents of conduct, but because our conduct would be based upon a perfect comprehension of existing conditions founded upon a perfect knowledge of the past.* As yet we are not in a position to interrogate the past with a view to gaining light on great social, political, economic, religious, and educational questions in the manner in which we settle the personal problems which face us—for example, whether we should make such and such a visit or investment, or read such and such a book,—by unconsciously judging the situation in the light of our recollections. Historians have not as yet set themselves to furnish us with what lies behind our great contemporaneous task of human betterment. They have hitherto had other notions of their functions, and were they asked to furnish answers to the questions that a person *au courant* with the problems of the day would most naturally put to them, they would with one accord begin to make excuses. One would say that it had long been recognized that it was the historian's business to deal with kings, parliaments, constitutions, wars, treaties, and territorial changes; another would declare that recent history cannot be adequately written and that, therefore, we can never hope to bring the past into relation with the present, but must always leave a fitting interval between ourselves and the nearest point to which the historian should venture to extend his researches; a third will urge that to have a purpose in historical study is to endanger those principles of objectivity upon which all sound and scientific research must be based. So it comes about that our books are like very bad memories which insist upon recalling facts that have no assignable relation to our needs, and this is the reason why the practical value of history has so long been obscured.

In order to make still clearer our dependence upon history in dealing with the present, let the reader remember that we owe most of our institutions to a rather remote past, which alone can explain their origin. The conditions which produced the Holy Roman Apostolic Church, trial by jury, the Privy Council, the degree of LL.D., the Book of Common Prayer, "the liberal arts," were very different from those that exist to-day. Contemporaneous religious, educational, and legal ideals are not the immediate product of existing circumstances, but were developed in great part during periods when man knew far less than he now does. Curiously enough our habits of thought change much more slowly than our environment and are usually far in arrears. Our respect for a given institution or social convention may be purely traditional and have little relation to its value, as judged by existing conditions. We are, therefore, in constant danger of viewing present problems with obsolete emotions and of attempting to settle them by obsolete reasoning. This is one of the chief reasons why we are never by any means perfectly adjusted to our environment.

Our notions of a church and its proper function in society, of a capitalist, of a liberal education, of paying taxes, of Sunday observance, of poverty, of war, are determined only to a slight extent by what is happening to-day. The belief on which I was reared, that God ordained the observance of Sunday from the clouds of Sinai, is an anachronism which could not spontaneously have developed in the United States in the nineteenth century; nevertheless, it still continues to influence the conduct of many persons. We pay our taxes as grudgingly as if they were still the extortions of feudal barons or absolute monarchs for their personal gratification, although they are now a contribution to our common expenses fixed by our own representatives. Few have outgrown the emotions connected with war at a time when personal prowess played a much greater part than the Steel Trust. Conservative college presidents still feel obliged to defend the "liberal arts" and the "humanities" without any very clear understanding of how the task came to be imposed upon them. To do justice to the anachronisms in conservative economic and legal reasoning would require a whole volume.

Society is to-day engaged in a tremendous and unprecedented effort to better itself in manifold ways. Never has our knowledge of the world and of man been so great as it now is; never before has there been so much general good will and so much intelligent social activity as now prevails. The part that each of us can play in forwarding some phase of this reform will depend upon our understanding of existing conditions and opinion, and these can only be explained, as has been shown, by following more or less carefully the processes that produced them. We must develop historical-mindedness upon a far more generous scale than hitherto, for this will add a still deficient element in our intellectual equipment and will promote rational progress as nothing else can do. The present has hitherto been the willing victim of the past; the time has now come when it should turn on the past and exploit it in the interest of advance.

Herbert Butterfield was much more skeptical about the results that could be achieved by approaching the past with present-day considerations in mind.

FROM *The Whig Interpretation of History*

BY HERBERT BUTTERFIELD

THE PRIMARY ASSUMPTION of all attempts to understand the men of the past must be the belief that we can in some degree enter into minds that are unlike our own. If this belief were unfounded it would seem that men must be for ever locked away from one another, and all generations must be regarded as a world and a law unto themselves. If we were unable to enter in any way into the mind of a present-day Roman Catholic priest, for example, and similarly into the mind of an atheistical orator in Hyde Park, it is difficult to see how we could know anything of the still stranger men of the sixteenth century, or pretend to understand the process of history-making which has moulded us into the world of to-day. In reality the historian postulates that the world is in some sense always the same world and that even the men most dissimilar are never absolutely unlike. And though a sentence from Aquinas may fall so strangely upon modern ears that it becomes plausible to dismiss the man as a fool or a mind utterly and absolutely alien, I take it that to dismiss a man in this way is a method of blocking up the mind against him, and against something important in both human nature and its history; it is really the refusal to a historical personage of the effort of historical understanding. Precisely because of his unlikeness

Reprinted from *The Whig Interpretation of History* (1950), pp. 9–14, 16–8, 24–8, by Herbert Butterfield by permission of W. W. Norton & Company, Inc., and G. Bell & Sons Ltd., London. All Rights Reserved by W. W. Norton & Company, Inc.

to ourselves Aquinas is the more enticing subject for the historical imagination; for the chief aim of the historian is the elucidation of the unlikenesses between past and present and his chief function is to act in this way as the mediator between other generations and our own. It is not for him to stress and magnify the similarities between one age and another, and he is riding after a whole flock of misapprehensions if he goes to hunt for the present in the past. Rather it is his work to destroy those very analogies which we imagined to exist. When he shows us that Magna Carta is a feudal document in a feudal setting, with implications different from those we had taken for granted, he is disillusioning us concerning something in the past which we had assumed to be too like something in the present. That whole process of specialised research which has in so many fields revised the previously accepted whig interpretation of history, has set out bearings afresh in one period after another, by referring matters in this way to their context, and so discovering their unlikeness to the world of the present-day.

It is part and parcel of the whig interpretation of history that it studies the past with reference to the present; and though there may be a sense in which this is unobjectionable if its implications are carefully considered, and there may be a sense in which it is inescapable, it has often been an obstruction to historical understanding because it has been taken to mean the study of the past with direct and perpetual reference to the present. Through this system of immediate reference to the present-day, historical personages can easily and irresistibly be classed into the men who furthered progress and the men who tried to hinder it; so that a handy rule of thumb exists by which the historian can select and reject, and can make his points of emphasis. On this system the historian is bound to construe his function as demanding him to be vigilant for likenesses between past and present, instead of being vigilant for unlikenesses; so that he will find it easy to say that he has seen the present in the past, he will imagine that he has discovered a "root" or an "anticipation" of the 20th century, when in reality he is in a world of different connotations altogether, and he has merely tumbled upon what could be shown to be a misleading analogy. Working upon the same system the whig historian can draw lines through certain events, some such line as that which leads through Martin Luther and a long succession of whigs to modern liberty; and if he is not careful he begins to forget that this line is merely a mental trick of his; he comes to imagine that it represents something like a line of causation. The total result of this method is to impose a certain form upon the whole historical story, and to produce a scheme of general history which is bound to converge beautifully upon the present—all demonstrating throughout the ages the workings of an obvious principle of progress, of which the Protestants and whigs have been the perennial allies while Catholics and tories have perpetually formed obstruction. A caricature of this result is to be seen in a popular view that is still not quite eradicated: the view that the Middle Ages represented a period of darkness when man was kept tongue-tied by authority—a period against which the Renaissance was the reaction and the Reformation the great rebellion. It is illustrated to perfection in the argument of a man denouncing Roman Catholicism at a street corner, who said: "When the Pope ruled England them was called the Dark Ages."

The whig historian stands on the summit of the 20th century, and organises his scheme of history from the point of view of his own day; and he is a subtle man to overturn from his mountain-top where he can fortify himself with plausible argument. He can say that events take on their due proportions when observed through the lapse of time. He can say that events must be judged by their ultimate issues, which, since we can trace them no farther, we must at least follow down to the present. He can say that it is only in relation to the 20th century that one happening or another in the past has relevance or significance for us. He can use all the arguments that are so handy to men when discussion is dragged into the market place and philosophy is dethroned by common sense; so that it is no simple matter to demonstrate how the whig historian, from his mountain-top, sees the course of history only inverted and aslant. The fallacy lies in the fact that if the historian working on the 16th century keeps the 20th century in his mind, he makes direct reference across all the intervening period between Luther or the Popes and the world of our own day. And this immediate juxtaposition of past and present, though it makes everything easy and makes some inferences perilously obvious, is bound to lead to an over-simplification of the relations between events and a complete misapprehension of the relations between past and present.

*   *   *

There is an alternative line of assumption upon which the historian can base himself when he comes to his study of the past; and it is the one upon which he does seem more or less consciously to act and to direct his mind when he is engaged upon a piece of research. On this view he comes to his labours conscious of the fact that he is trying to understand the past for the sake of the past, and though it is true that he can never entirely abstract himself from his own age, it is none the less certain that this consciousness of his purpose is a very different one from that of the whig historian, who tells himself that he is studying the past for the sake of the present. Real historical understanding is not achieved by the subordination of the past to the present, but rather by our making the past our present and attempting to see life with the eyes of another century than our own. It is not reached by assuming that our own age is the absolute to which Luther and Calvin and their generation are only relative; it is only reached by fully accepting the fact that their generation was as valid as our generation, their issues as momentous as our issues and their day as full and as vital to them as our day is to us. The twentieth century which has its own hairs to split may have little patience with Arius and Athanasius who burdened the world with a quarrel about a diphthong, but the historian has not achieved historical understanding, has not reached that kind of understanding in which the mind can find rest, until he has seen that that diphthong was bound to be the most urgent matter in the universe to those people. It is when the emphasis is laid in this way upon the historian's attempt to understand the past, that it becomes clear how much he is concerned to elucidate the unlikenesses between past and present. Instead of being moved to indignation by something in the past which at first seems alien and perhaps even wicked to our own day, instead of leaving it in the outer darkness, he makes the effort to bring this thing into the context where it is natural, and he elucidates the matter by showing its relation to other things which we do understand. Whereas the man who keeps his eye on the present tends to ask some such question as, How did religious liberty arise? while the whig historian by a subtle organisation of his sympathies tends to read it as the question, To whom must we be grateful for our religious liberty? the historian who is engaged upon studying the 16th century at close hand is more likely to find himself asking why men in those days were so given to persecution. This is in a special sense the historian's question for it is a question about the past rather than about the present, and in answering it the historian is on his own ground and is making the kind of contribution which he is most fitted to make. It is in this sense that he is always forgiving sins by the mere fact that he is finding out why they happened. The things which are most alien to ourselves are the very object of his exposition. And until he has shown why men persecuted in the 16th century one may doubt whether he is competent to discuss the further question of how religious liberty has come down to the 20th.

* * *

The whig method of approach is closely connected with the question of the abridgment of history; for both the method and the kind of history that results from it would be impossible if all the facts were told in all their fullness. The theory that is behind the whig interpretation—the theory that we study the past for the sake of the present—is one that is really introduced for the purpose of facilitating the abridgment of history; and its effect is to provide us with a handy rule of thumb by which we can easily discover what was important in the past, for the simple reason that, by definition, we mean what is important "from our point of view." No one could mistake the aptness of this theory for a school of writers who might show the least inclination to undervalue one side of the historical story; and indeed there would be no point in holding it if it were not for the fact that it serves to simplify the study of history by providing an excuse for leaving things out. The theory is important because it provides us in the long run with a path through the complexity of history; it really gives us a short cut through that maze of interactions by which the past was turned into our present; it helps us to circumvent the real problem of historical study. If we can exclude certain things on the ground that they have no direct bearing on the present, we have removed the most troublesome elements in the complexity and the crooked is made straight. There is no doubt that the application of this principle must produce in history a bias in favour of the whigs and must fall unfavourably on Catholics and tories. Whig history in other words is not a genuine abridgment, for it is really based upon what is an implicit principle of selection. The adoption of this principle and this method commits us to a certain organisation of the whole historical story. A very different case arises when the historian, examining the 16th century, sets out to discover the things which were important to that age itself or were influential at that time. And if we could imagine a general survey of the centuries which should be an abridgment of all the works of historical research, and if we were then to compare this with a survey of the whole period which was compiled on the whig principle, that is to say, "from the point of view of the present," we should not only find that the complications had been greatly over-simplified in the whig version, but we should find the story recast and the most important valuations amended; in other words we should find an abridged history which tells a different story altogether. According to the consistency with which we have applied the principle of direct reference to the present, we are driven to that version of history which is called the whig interpretation.

Seeing Protestant fighting Catholic in the 16th century we remember our own feelings concerning liberty in the 20th, and we keep before our eyes the relative positions of Catholic and Protestant to-day. There is open to us a whole range of concealed inference based upon this mental juxtaposition of the 16th century with the present; and, even before we have examined the subject closely, our story will have assumed its general shape; Protestants will be seen to have been fighting for the future, while it will be obvious that the Catholics were fighting for the past. Given this original bias we can follow a technical procedure that is bound to confirm and imprison us in it; for when we come, say, to examine Martin Luther more closely, we have a magnet that can draw out of history the very things that we go to look for, and by a hundred quotations torn from their context and robbed of their relevance to a particular historical conjuncture we can prove that there is an analogy between the ideas of Luther and the world of the present day, we can see in Luther a foreshadowing of the present. History is subtle lore and it may lock us in the longest argument in a circle that one can imagine. It matters very much how we start upon our labours—whether for example we take the Protestants of the 16th century as men who were fighting to bring about our modern world, while the Catholics were struggling to keep the mediaeval, or whether we take the whole present as the child of the whole past and see rather the modern world emerging from the clash of both Catholic and Protestant. If we use the present as our perpetual touchstone, we can easily divide the men of the 16th century into progressive and reactionary; but we are likely to beg fewer questions, and we are better able to discover the way in which the past was turned into our present, if we adopt the outlook of the 16th century upon itself, or if we view the process of events as it appears to us when we look at the movements of our own generation; and in this case we shall tend to see not so much progressive fighting reactionary but rather two parties differing on the question of what the next step in progress is to be. Instead of seeing the modern world emerge as the victory of the children of light over the children of darkness in any generation, it is at least better to see it emerge as the result of a clash of wills, a result which often neither party wanted or even dreamed of, a result which indeed in some cases both parties would equally have hated, but a result for the achievement of which the existence of both and the clash of both were necessary.

4   Historical Relativism

Carl L. Becker, in a famous presidential address delivered to the American Historical Association, argued that every historian was so inescapably conditioned by the age in which he lived that he could never hope to establish permanently valid interpretations of the past. Historical truth was relative—it would always "vary with the time and place of the observer."

Everyman His Own Historian[1]   BY CARL L. BECKER

I

ONCE UPON A TIME, long long ago, I learned how to reduce a fraction to its lowest terms. Whether I could still perform that operation is uncertain; but the discipline involved in early training had its uses, since it taught me that in order to understand the essential nature of anything it is well to strip it of all superficial and irrelevant accretions—in short, to reduce it to its lowest terms. That operation I now venture, with some apprehension and all due apologies, to perform on the subject of history.

I ought first of all to explain that when I use the term history I mean knowledge of history. No doubt throughout all past time there actually occurred a series of events which, whether we know what it was or not, constitutes history in some ultimate sense. Nevertheless, much the greater part of these events we can know nothing about, not even that they occurred; many of them we can know only imperfectly; and even the few events that we think we know for sure we can never be absolutely certain of, since we can never revive them, never observe or test them directly. The event itself once occurred, but as an actual event it has disappeared; so that in dealing with it the only objective reality we can observe or test is some material trace which the event has left—usually a written document. With

[1] Presidential Address delivered before the American Historical Association at Minneapolis, December 29, 1931.

these traces of vanished events, these documents, we must be content since they are all we have; from them we infer what the event was, we affirm that it is a fact that the event was so and so. We do not say "Lincoln is assassinated"; we say "it is a fact that Lincoln was assassinated." The event *was,* but is no longer; it is only the affirmed fact about the event that *is,* that persists, and will persist until we discover that our affirmation is wrong or inadequate. Let us then admit that there are two histories: the actual series of events that once occurred; and the ideal series that we affirm and hold in memory. The first is absolute and unchanged—it was what it was whatever we do or say about it; the second is relative, always changing in response to the increase or refinement of knowledge. The two series correspond more or less, it is our aim to make the correspondence as exact as possible; but the actual series of events exists for us only in terms of the ideal series which we affirm and hold in memory. This is why I am forced to identify history with knowledge of history. For all practical purposes history is, for us and for the time being, what we know it to be.

It is history in this sense that I wish to reduce to its lowest terms. In order to do that I need a very simple definition. I once read that "History is the knowledge of events that have occurred in the past." That is a simple definition, but not simple enough. It contains three words that require examination. The first is knowledge. Knowledge is a formidable word. I always think of knowledge as something that is stored up in the *Encyclopaedia Britannica* or the *Summa Theologica;* something difficult to acquire, something at all events that I have not. Resenting a definition that denies me the title of historian, I therefore ask what is most essential to knowledge. Well, memory, I should think (and I mean memory in the broad sense, the memory of events inferred as well as the memory of events observed); other things are necessary too, but memory is fundamental: without memory no knowledge. So our definition becomes, "History is the memory of events that have occurred in the past." But events—the word carries an implication of something grand, like the taking of the Bastille or the Spanish-American War. An occurrence need not be spectacular to be an event. If I drive a motor car down the crooked streets of Ithaca, that is an event—something done; if the traffic cop bawls me out, that is an event—something said; if I have evil thoughts of him for so doing, that is an event—something thought. In truth anything done, said, or thought is an event, important or not as may turn out. But since we do not ordinarily speak without thinking, at least in some rudimentary way, and since the psychologists tell us that we can not think without speaking, or at least not without having anticipatory vibrations in the larynx, we may well combine thought events and speech events under one term; and so our definition becomes, "History is the memory of things said and done in the past." But the past—the word is both misleading and unnecessary: misleading, because the past, used in connection with history, seems to imply the distant past, as if history ceased before we were born; unnecessary, because after all everything said or done is already in the past as soon as it is said or done. Therefore I will omit that word, and our definition becomes, "History is the memory of things said and done." This is a definition that reduces history to its lowest terms, and yet includes everything that is essential to understanding what it really is.

If the essence of history is the memory of things said and done, then it is obvious that every normal person, Mr. Everyman, knows some history. Of course we do what we can to conceal this invidious truth. Assuming a professional manner, we say that so and so knows no history, when we mean no more than that he failed to pass the examinations set for a higher degree; and simple-minded persons, undergraduates and others, taken in by academic classifications of knowledge, think they know no history because they have never taken a course in history in college, or have never read Gibbon's *Decline and Fall of the Roman Empire*. No doubt the academic convention has its uses, but it is one of the superficial accretions that must be stripped off if we would understand history reduced to its lowest terms. Mr. Everyman, as well as you and I, remembers things said and done, and must do so at every waking moment. Suppose Mr. Everyman to have awakened this morning unable to remember anything said or done. He would be a lost soul indeed. This has happened, this sudden loss of all historical knowledge. But normally it does not happen. Normally the memory of Mr. Everyman, when he awakens in the morning, reaches out into the country of the past and of distant places and instantaneously recreates his little world of endeavor, pulls together as it were things said and done in his yesterdays, and coördinates them with his present perceptions and with things to be said and done in his to-morrows. Without this historical knowledge, this memory of things said and done, his to-day would be aimless and his to-morrow without significance.

Since we are concerned with history in its lowest terms, we will suppose that Mr. Everyman is not a professor of history, but just an ordinary citizen without excess knowledge. Not having a lecture to prepare, his memory of things said and done, when he awakened this morning, presumably did not drag into consciousness any events connected with the Liman von Sanders mission or the Pseudo-Isidorian Decretals; it presumably dragged into consciousness an image of things said and done yesterday in the office, the highly significant fact that General Motors had dropped three points, a conference arranged for ten o'clock in the morning, a promise to play nine holes at four-thirty in the afternoon, and other historical events of similar import. Mr. Everyman knows more history than this, but at the moment of awakening this is sufficient: memory of things said and done, history functioning, at seven-thirty in the morning, in its very lowest terms, has effectively oriented Mr. Everyman in his little world of endeavor.

Yet not quite effectively after all perhaps; for unaided memory is notoriously fickle; and it may happen that Mr. Everyman, as he drinks his coffee, is uneasily aware of something said or done that he fails now to recall. A common enough occurrence, as we all know to our sorrow—this remembering, not the historical event, but only that there was an event which we ought to remember but can not. This is Mr. Everyman's difficulty, a bit of history lies dead and inert in the sources, unable to do any work for Mr. Everyman because his memory refuses to bring it alive in consciousness. What then does Mr. Everyman do? He does what any historian would do: he does a bit of historical research in the sources. From his little Private Record Office (I mean his vest pocket) he takes a book in MS, volume XXXV it may be, and turns to page 23, and there he reads: "December 29, pay Smith's coal bill, 20 tons, \$1017.20." Instantaneously a series of historical events comes to life in Mr. Everyman's mind. He has an image of himself ordering twenty tons of coal from Smith last summer, of Smith's wagons driving up to his house, and of the precious coal sliding dustily through the cellar window. Historical events, these are, not so important as the forging of the Isidorian Decretals, but still important to Mr. Everyman: historical events which he was not present to observe, but which, by an artificial extension of memory, he can form a clear picture of, because he has done a little original research in the manuscripts preserved in his Private Record Office.

The picture Mr. Everyman forms of Smith's wagons delivering the coal at his house is a picture of things said and done in the past. But it does not stand alone, it is not a pure antiquarian image to be enjoyed for its own sake; on the contrary, it is associated with a picture of things to be said and done in the future; so that throughout the day Mr. Everyman intermittently holds in mind, together with a picture of Smith's coal wagons, a picture of himself going at four o'clock in the afternoon to Smith's office in order to pay his bill. At four o'clock Mr. Everyman is accordingly at Smith's office. "I wish to pay that coal bill," he says. Smith looks dubious and disappointed, takes down a ledger (or a filing case), does a bit of original research in his Private Record Office, and announces: "You don't owe me any money, Mr. Everyman. You ordered the coal here all right, but I didn't have the kind you wanted, and so turned the order over to Brown. It was Brown delivered your coal: he's the man you owe." Whereupon Mr. Everyman goes to Brown's office; and Brown takes down a ledger, does a bit of original research in his Private Record Office, which happily confirms the researches of Smith; and Mr. Everyman pays his bill, and in the evening, after returning from the Country Club, makes a further search in another collection of documents, where, sure enough, he finds a bill from Brown, properly drawn, for twenty tons of stove coal, \$1017.20. The research is now completed. Since his mind rests satisfied, Mr. Everyman has found the explanation of the series of events that concerned him.

Mr. Everyman would be astonished to learn that he is an historian, yet it is obvious, isn't it, that he has performed all the essential operations involved in historical research. Needing or wanting to do something (which happened to be, not to deliver a lecture or write a book, but to pay a bill; and this is what misleads him and us as to what he is really doing), the first step was to recall things said and done. Unaided memory proving inadequate, a further step was essential—the examination of certain documents in order to discover the necessary but as yet unknown facts. Unhappily the documents were found to give conflicting reports, so that a critical comparison of the texts had to be instituted in order to eliminate error. All this having been satisfactorily accomplished, Mr. Everyman is ready for the final operation— the formation in his mind, by an artificial extension of memory, of a picture, a definitive picture let us hope, of a selected series of historical events—of himself ordering coal from Smith, of Smith turning the order over to Brown, and of Brown delivering the coal at his house. In the light of this picture Mr. Everyman could, and did, pay his bill. If Mr. Everyman had undertaken these researches in order to write a book instead of to pay a bill, no one would think of denying that he was an historian.

II

I have tried to reduce history to its lowest terms, first by defining it as the memory of things said and done, second by showing concretely how the memory of things said and done is essential to the performance of the simplest acts of daily life. I wish now to note the more general implications of Mr. Everyman's activities. In the realm of affairs Mr. Everyman has been paying his coal bill; in the realm of consciousness he has been doing that fundamental thing which enables man alone to have, properly speaking, a history: he has been reenforcing and enriching his immediate perceptions to the end that he may live in a world of semblance more spacious and satisfying than is to be found within the narrow confines of the fleeting present moment.

We are apt to think of the past as dead, the future as nonexistent, the present alone as real; and prematurely wise or disillusioned counselors have urged us to burn always with "a hard, gemlike flame" in order to give "the highest quality to the moments as they pass, and simply for those moments' sake." This no doubt is what the glowworm does; but I think that man, who alone is properly aware that the present moment passes, can for that very reason make no good use of the present moment simply for its own sake. Strictly speaking, the present doesn't exist for us, or is at best no more than an infinitesimal point in time, gone before we can note it as present. Nevertheless, we must have a present; and so we create one by robbing the past, by holding on to the most recent events and pretending that they all belong to our immediate perceptions. If, for example, I raise my arm, the total event is a series of occurrences of which the first are past before the last have taken place; and yet you perceive it as a single movement executed in one present instant. This telescoping of successive events into a single instant philosophers call the "specious present." Doubtless they would assign rather narrow limits to the specious present; but I will willfully make a free use of it, and say that we can extend the specious present as much as we like. In common speech we do so: we speak of the "present hour," the "present year," the "present generation." Perhaps all living creatures have a specious present; but man has this superiority, as Pascal says, that he is aware of himself and the universe, can as it were hold himself at arm's length and with some measure of objectivity watch himself and his fellows functioning in the world during a brief span of allotted years. Of all the creatures, man alone has a specious present that may be deliberately and purposefully enlarged and diversified and enriched.

The extent to which the specious present may thus be enlarged and enriched will depend upon knowledge, the artificial extension of memory, the memory of things said and done in the past and distant places. But not upon knowledge alone; rather upon knowledge directed by purpose. The specious present is an unstable pattern of thought, incessantly changing in response to our immediate perceptions and the purposes that arise therefrom. At any given moment each one of us (professional historian no less than Mr. Everyman) weaves into this unstable pattern such actual or artificial memories as may be necessary to orient us in our little world of endeavor. But to be oriented in our little world of endeavor we must be prepared for what is coming to us (the payment of a coal bill, the delivery of a presidential address, the establishment of a League of Nations, or whatever); and to be prepared for what is coming to us it is necessary, not only to recall certain past events, but to anticipate (note I do not say predict) the future. Thus from the specious present, which always includes more or less of the past, the future refuses to be excluded; and the more of the past we drag into the specious present, the more an hypothetical, patterned future is likely to crowd into it also. Which comes first, which is cause and which effect, whether our memories construct a pattern of past events at the behest of our desires and hopes, or whether our desires and hopes spring from a pattern of past events imposed upon us by experience and knowledge, I shall not attempt to say. What I suspect is that memory of past and anticipation of future events work together, go hand in hand as it were in a friendly way, without disputing over priority and leadership.

At all events they go together, so that in a very real sense it is impossible to divorce history from life: Mr. Everyman can not do what he needs or desires to do without recalling past events; he can not recall past events without in some subtle fashion relating them to what he needs or desires to do. This is the natural function of history, of history reduced to its lowest terms, of history conceived as the memory of things said and done: memory of things said and done (whether in our immediate yesterdays or in the long past of mankind), running hand in hand with the anticipation of things to be said and done, enables us, each to the extent of his knowledge and imagination, to be intelligent, to push back the narrow confines of the fleeting present moment so that what we are doing may be judged in the light of what we have done and what we hope to do. In this sense all *living* history, as Croce says, is contemporaneous: in so far as we think the past (and otherwise the past, however fully related in documents, is nothing to us) it becomes an integral and living part of our present world of semblance.

It must then be obvious that living history, the ideal series of events that we affirm and hold in memory, since it is so intimately associated with what we are doing and with what we hope to do, can not be precisely the same for all at any given time, or the same for one generation as for another. History in this sense can not be reduced to a verifiable set of statistics or formulated in terms of universally valid mathematical formulas. It is rather an imaginative creation, a personal possession which each one of us, Mr. Everyman, fashions out of his individual experience, adapts to his practical or emotional needs, and adorns as well as may be to suit his aesthetic tastes. In thus creating his own history, there are, nevertheless, limits which Mr. Everyman may not overstep without incurring penalties. The limits are set by his fellows. If Mr. Everyman lived quite alone in an unconditioned world he would be free to affirm and hold in memory any ideal series of events that struck his fancy, and thus create a world of semblance quite in accord with the heart's desire. Unfortunately, Mr. Everyman has to live in a world of Browns and Smiths; a sad experience, which has taught him the expediency of recalling certain events with much exactness. In all the immediately practical affairs of life Mr. Everyman is a good historian, as expert, in conducting the researches necessary for paying his coal bill, as need be. His expertness comes partly from long practice, but chiefly from the circumstance that his researches are prescribed and guided by very definite and practical objects which concern him intimately. The problem of what documents to consult, what facts to select, troubles Mr. Everyman not at all. Since he is not writing a book on "Some Aspects of the Coal Industry Objectively Considered," it does not occur to him to collect all the facts and let them speak for themselves. Wishing merely to pay his coal bill, he selects only such facts as may be relevant; and not wishing to pay it twice, he is sufficiently aware, without ever having read Bernheim's *Lehrbuch,* that the relevant facts must be clearly established by the testimony of independent witnesses not self-deceived. He does not know, or need to know, that his personal interest in the performance is a disturbing bias which will prevent him from learning the whole truth or arriving at ultimate causes. Mr. Everyman does not wish to learn the whole truth or to arrive at ultimate causes. He wishes to pay his coal bill. That is to say, he wishes to adjust himself to a practical situation, and on that low pragmatic level he is a good historian precisely because he is not disinterested: he will solve his problems, if he does solve them, by virtue of his intelligence and not by virtue of his indifference.

Nevertheless, Mr. Everyman does not live by bread alone; and on all proper occasions his memory of things said and done, easily enlarging his specious present beyond the narrow circle of daily affairs, will, must inevitably, in mere compensation for the intolerable dullness and vexation of the fleeting present moment, fashion for him a more spacious world than that of the immediately practical. He can readily recall the days of his youth, the places he has lived in, the ventures he has made, the adventures he has had—all the crowded events of a lifetime; and beyond and around this central pattern of personally experienced events, there will be embroidered a more dimly seen pattern of artificial memories, memories of things reputed to have been said and done in past times which he has not known, in distant places which he has not seen. This outer pattern of remembered events that encloses and completes the central pattern of his personal experience, Mr. Everyman has woven, he could not tell you how, out of the most diverse threads of information, picked up in the most casual way, from the most unrelated sources—from things learned at home and in school, from knowledge gained in business or profession, from newspapers glanced at, from books (yes, even history books) read or heard of, from remembered scraps of newsreels or educational films or *ex cathedra* utterances of presidents and kings, from fifteen-minute discourses on the history of civilization broadcast by the courtesy (it may be) of Pepsodent, the Bulova Watch Company, or the Shepard Stores in Boston. Daily and hourly, from a thousand unnoted sources, there is lodged in Mr. Everyman's mind a mass of unrelated and related information and misinformation, of impressions and images, out of which he somehow manages, undeliberately for the most part, to fashion a history, a patterned picture of remembered things said and done in past times and distant places. It is not possible, it is not essential, that this picture should be complete or completely true: it is essential that it should be useful to Mr. Everyman; and that it may be useful to him he will hold in memory, of all the things he might hold in memory, those things only which can be related with some reasonable degree of relevance and harmony to his idea of himself and of what he is doing in the world and what he hopes to do.

In constructing this more remote and far-flung pattern of remembered things, Mr. Everyman works with something of the freedom of a creative artist; the history which he imaginatively recreates as an artificial extension of his personal experience will inevitably be an engaging blend of fact and fancy, a mythical adaptation of that which actually happened. In part it will be true, in part false; as a whole perhaps neither true nor false, but only the most convenient form of error. Not that Mr. Everyman wishes or intends to deceive himself or others. Mr. Everyman has a wholesome respect for cold, hard facts, never suspecting how malleable they are, how easy it is to coax and cajole them; but he necessarily takes the facts as they come to him, and is enamored of those that seem best suited to his interests or promise most in the way of emotional satisfaction. The exact truth of remembered events he has in any case no time, and no need, to curiously question or meticulously verify. No doubt he can, if he be an American, call up an image of the signing of the Declaration of Independence in 1776 as readily as he can call up an image of Smith's coal wagons creaking up the hill last summer. He suspects the one image no more than the other; but the signing of the Declaration, touching not his practical interests, calls for no careful historical research on his part. He may perhaps, without knowing why, affirm and hold in memory that the Declaration was signed by the members of the Continental Congress on the fourth of July. It is a vivid and sufficient image which Mr. Everyman may hold to the end of his days without incurring penalties. Neither Brown nor Smith has any interest in setting him right; nor will any court ever send him a summons for failing to recall that the Declaration, "being engrossed and compared at the table, was signed by the members" on the second of August. As an actual event, the signing of the Declaration was what it was; as a remembered event it will be, for Mr. Everyman, what Mr. Everyman contrives to make it: will have for him significance and magic, much or little or none at all, as it fits well or ill into his little world of interests and aspirations and emotional comforts.

III

What then of us, historians by profession? What have we to do with Mr. Everyman, or he with us? More, I venture to believe, than we are apt to think. For each of us is Mr. Everyman too. Each of us is subject to the limitations of time and place; and for each of us, no less than for the Browns and Smiths of the world, the pattern of remembered things said and done will be woven, safeguard the process how we may, at the behest of circumstance and purpose.

True it is that although each of us is Mr. Everyman, each is something more than his own historian. Mr. Everyman, being but an informal historian, is under no bond to remember what is irrelevant to his personal affairs. But we are historians by profession. Our profession, less intimately bound up with the practical activities, is to be directly concerned with the ideal series of events that is only of casual or occasional import to others; it is our business in life to be ever preoccupied with that far-flung pattern of artificial memories that encloses and completes the central pattern of individual experience. We are Mr. Everybody's historian as well as our own, since our histories serve the double purpose, which written histories have always served, of keeping alive the recollection of memorable men and events. We are thus of that ancient and honorable company of wise men of the tribe, of bards and story-tellers and minstrels, of soothsayers and priests, to whom in successive ages has been entrusted the keeping of the useful myths. Let not the harmless, necessary word "myth" put us out of countenance. In the history of history a myth is a once valid but now discarded version of the human story, as our now valid versions will in due course be relegated to the category of discarded myths. With our predecessors, the bards and story-tellers and priests, we have therefore this in common: that it is our function, as it was theirs, not to create, but to preserve and perpetuate the social tradition; to harmonize, as well as ignorance and prejudice permit, the actual and the remembered series of events; to enlarge and enrich the specious present common to us all to the end that "society" (the tribe, the nation, or all mankind) may judge of what it is doing in the light of what it has done and what it hopes to do.

History as the artificial extension of the social memory (and I willingly concede that there are other appropriate ways of apprehending human experience) is an art of long standing, necessarily so since it springs instinctively from the impulse to enlarge the range of immediate experience; and however camouflaged by the disfiguring jargon of science, it is still in essence what it has always been. History in this sense is story, in aim always a true story; a story that employs all the devices of literary art (statement and generalization, narration and description, comparison and comment and analogy) to present the succession of events in the life of man, and from the succession of events thus presented to derive a satisfactory meaning. The history written by historians, like the history informally fashioned by Mr. Everyman, is thus a convenient blend of truth and fancy, of what we commonly distinguish as "fact" and "interpretation." In primitive times, when tradition is orally transmitted, bards and story-tellers frankly embroider or improvise the facts to heighten the dramatic import of the story. With the use of written records, history, gradually differentiated from fiction, is understood as the story of events that actually occurred; and with the increase and refinement of knowledge the historian recognizes that his first duty is to be sure of his facts, let their meaning be what it may. Nevertheless, in every age history is taken to be a story of actual events from which a significant meaning may be derived; and in every age the illusion is that the present version is valid because the related facts are true, whereas former versions are invalid because based upon inaccurate or inadequate facts.

Never was this conviction more impressively displayed than in our own time—that age of erudition in which we live, or from which we are perhaps just emerging. Finding the course of history littered with the *débris* of exploded philosophies, the historians of the last century, unwilling to be forever duped, turned away (as they fondly hoped) from "interpretation" to the rigorous examination of the factual event, just as it occurred. Perfecting the technique of investigation, they laboriously collected and edited the sources of information, and with incredible persistence and ingenuity ran illusive error to earth, letting the significance of the Middle Ages wait until it was certainly known "whether Charles the Fat was at Ingelheim or Lustnau on July 1, 887," shedding their "life-blood," in many a hard fought battle, "for the sublime truths of Sac and Soc." I have no quarrel with this so great concern with hoti's business. One of the first duties of man is not to be duped, to be aware of his world; and to derive the significance of human experience from events that never occurred is surely an enterprise of doubtful value. To establish the facts is always in order, and is indeed the first duty of the historian; but to suppose that the facts, once established in all their fullness, will "speak for themselves" is an illusion. It was perhaps peculiarly the illusion of those historians of the last century who found some special magic in the word "scientific." The scientific historian, it seems, was one who set forth the facts without injecting any extraneous meaning into them. He was the objective man whom Nietzsche described—"a mirror: accustomed to prostration before something that wants to be known, . . . he waits until something comes, and then expands himself sensitively, so that even the light footsteps and gliding past of spiritual things may not be lost in his surface and film." [2] "It is not I who speak, but history which speaks through me," was Fustel's reproof to applauding students. "If a certain philosophy emerges from this scientific history, it must be permitted to emerge naturally, of its own accord, all but independently of the will of the historian." [3] Thus the scientific historian deliberately renounced philosophy only to submit to it without being aware. His philosophy was just this, that by not taking thought a cubit would be added to his stature. With no other preconception than the will to know, the historian would reflect in his surface and film the "order of events throughout past times in all places"; so that, in the fullness of time, when innumerable patient expert scholars, by "exhausting the sources," should have reflected without refracting the truth of all the facts, the definitive and impregnable meaning of human experience would emerge of its own accord to enlighten and emancipate mankind. Hoping to find something without looking for it, expecting to obtain final answers to life's riddle by resolutely refusing to ask questions—it was surely the most romantic species of realism yet invented, the oddest attempt ever made to get something for nothing!

That mood is passing. The fullness of time is not yet, overmuch learning proves a weariness to the flesh, and a younger generation that knows not Von Ranke is eager to believe that Fustel's counsel, if one of perfection, is equally one of futility. Even the most disinterested historian has at least one preconception, which is the fixed idea that he has none. The facts of history are already set forth, implicitly, in the sources; and the historian who could restate without reshaping them would, by submerging and suffocating the mind in diffuse existence, accomplish the superfluous task of depriving human experience of all significance. Left to themselves, the facts do not speak; left to themselves they do not exist, not really, since for all practical purposes there is no fact until some one affirms it. The least the historian can do with any historical fact is to select and affirm it. To select and affirm even the simplest complex of facts is to give them a certain place in a certain pattern of ideas, and this alone is sufficient to give them a special meaning. However "hard" or "cold" they may be, historical facts are after all not material substances which, like bricks or scantlings, possess definite shape and clear, persistent outline. To set forth historical facts is not comparable to dumping a barrow of bricks. A brick retains its form and pressure wherever placed; but the form and substance of historical facts, having a negotiable existence only in literary discourse, vary with the words employed to convey

[2] *Beyond Good and Evil*, p. 140.
[3] Quoted in *English Historical Review*, V. 1.

them. Since history is not part of the external material world, but an imaginative reconstruction of vanished events, its form and substance are inseparable: in the realm of literary discourse substance, being an idea, *is* form; and form, conveying the idea, *is* substance. It is thus not the undiscriminated fact, but the perceiving mind of the historian that speaks: the special meaning which the facts are made to convey emerges from the substance-form which the historian employs to recreate imaginatively a series of events not present to perception.

In constructing this substance-form of vanished events, the historian, like Mr. Everyman, like the bards and story-tellers of an earlier time, will be conditioned by the specious present in which alone he can be aware of his world. Being neither omniscient nor omnipresent, the historian is not the same person always and everywhere; and for him, as for Mr. Everyman, the form and significance of remembered events, like the extension and velocity of physical objects, will vary with the time and place of the observer. After fifty years we can clearly see that it was not history which spoke through Fustel, but Fustel who spoke through history. We see less clearly perhaps that the voice of Fustel was the voice, amplified and freed from static as one may say, of Mr. Everyman; what the admiring students applauded on that famous occasion was neither history nor Fustel, but a deftly colored pattern of selected events which Fustel fashioned, all the more skillfully for not being aware of doing so, in the service of Mr. Everyman's emotional needs— the emotional satisfaction, so essential to Frenchmen at that time, of perceiving that French institutions were not of German origin. And so it must always be. Played upon by all the diverse, unnoted influences of his own time, the historian will elicit history out of documents by the same principle, however more consciously and expertly applied, that Mr. Everyman employs to breed legends out of remembered episodes and oral tradition.

Berate him as we will for not reading our books, Mr. Everyman is stronger than we are, and sooner or later we must adapt our knowledge to his necessities. Otherwise he will leave us to our own devices, leave us it may be to cultivate a species of dry professional arrogance growing out of the thin soil of antiquarian research. Such research, valuable not in itself but for some ulterior purpose, will be of little import except in so far as it is transmuted into common knowledge. The history that lies inert in unread books does no work in the world. The history that does work in the world, the history that influences the course of history, is living history, that pattern of remembered events, whether true or false, that enlarges and enriches the collective specious present, the specious present of Mr. Everyman. It is for this reason that the history of history is a record of the "new history" that in every age rises to confound and supplant the old. It should be a relief to us to renounce omniscience, to recognize that every generation, our own included, will, must inevitably, understand the past and anticipate the future in the light of its own restricted experience, must inevitably play on the dead whatever tricks it finds necessary for its own peace of mind. The appropriate trick for any

age is not a malicious invention designed to take anyone in, but an unconscious and necessary effort on the part of "society" to understand what it is
doing in the light of what it has done and what it hopes to do. We,
historians by profession, share in this necessary effort. But we do not impose
our version of the human story on Mr. Everyman; in the end it is rather Mr.
Everyman who imposes his version on us—compelling us, in an age of
political revolution, to see that history is past politics, in an age of social stress
and conflict to search for the economic interpretation. If we remain too long
recalcitrant Mr. Everyman will ignore us, shelving our recondite works
behind glass doors rarely opened. Our proper function is not to repeat the
past but to make use of it, to correct and rationalize for common use Mr.
Everyman's mythological adaptation of what actually happened. We are
surely under bond to be as honest and as intelligent as human frailty
permits; but the secret of our success in the long run is in conforming to the
temper of Mr. Everyman, which we seem to guide only because we are so
sure, eventually, to follow it.

Neither the value nor the dignity of history need suffer by regarding it
as a foreshortened and incomplete representation of the reality that once was,
an unstable pattern of remembered things redesigned and newly colored to
suit the convenience of those who make use of it. Nor need our labors be the
less highly prized because our task is limited, our contributions of incidental
and temporary significance. History is an indispensable even though not the
highest form of intellectual endeavor, since it makes, as Santayana says, a gift
of "great interests . . . to the heart. A barbarian is no less subject to the past
than is the civic man who knows what the past is and means to be loyal to it;
but the barbarian, for want of a transpersonal memory, crawls among
superstitions which he cannot understand or revoke and among people
whom he may hate or love, but whom he can never think of raising to a
higher plane, to the level of a purer happiness. The whole dignity of human
endeavor is thus bound up with historic issues, and as conscience needs to be
controlled by experience if it is to become rational, so personal experience
itself needs to be enlarged ideally if the failures and successes it reports are to
touch impersonal interests." [4]

I do not present this view of history as one that is stable and must
prevail. Whatever validity it may claim, it is certain, on its own premises, to
be supplanted; for its premises, imposed upon us by the climate of opinion in
which we live and think, predispose us to regard all things, and all principles
of things, as no more than "inconstant modes or fashions," as but the
"concurrence, renewed from moment to moment, of forces parting sooner or
later on their way." It is the limitation of the genetic approach to human
experience that it must be content to transform problems since it can never
solve them. However accurately we may determine the "facts" of history, the
facts themselves and our interpretations of them, and our interpretation of

[4] *The Life of Reason*, V. 68.

our own interpretations, will be seen in a different perspective or a less vivid light as mankind moves into the unknown future. Regarded historically, as a process of becoming, man and his world can obviously be understood only tentatively, since it is by definition something still in the making, something as yet unfinished. Unfortunately for the "permanent contribution" and the universally valid philosophy, time passes; time, the enemy of man as the Greeks thought; to-morrow and to-morrow and to-morrow creeps in this petty pace, and all our yesterdays diminish and grow dim: so that, in the lengthening perspective of the centuries, even the most striking events (the Declaration of Independence, the French Revolution, the Great War itself; like the Diet of Worms before them, like the signing of the Magna Carta and the coronation of Charlemagne and the crossing of the Rubicon and the battle of Marathon) must inevitably, for posterity, fade away into pale replicas of the original picture, for each succeeding generation losing, as they recede into a more distant past, some significance that once was noted in them, some quality of enchantment that once was theirs.

5 Reappraisals of the Problem

*If all our judgments about the past are necessarily condi-
tioned by our experience of the present (Becker) and if
judgments of this sort are obviously unsound (Butterfield),
it might seem that the study of history is at best a futile
occupation. The fact that it continues to attract fine minds
suggests that there is more to be said.*

*Isaiah Berlin has argued that it is indeed possible to
make objective judgments about the past and has attacked
the relativist theory on logical grounds.*

FROM *Historical Inevitability* BY ISAIAH BERLIN

WHEN EVERYTHING HAS BEEN SAID in favor of attributing responsibility for character and action to natural and institutional causes; when
everything possible has been done to correct blind or over-simple interpretations of conduct which fix too much blame on individuals and their free acts;
when, in fact, there is strong evidence to show that it was difficult or
impossible for men to do otherwise than they did, given their material
environment or education or the influence upon them of various "social
pressures"; when every relevant psychological and sociological consideration
has been taken into account, every impersonal factor given due weight; after
"hegemonist," nationalist, and other historical heresies have been exposed
and refuted; after every effort has been made to induce history to aspire, so
far as it can without open absurdity, after the pure condition of a science;
after all these severities, we continue to praise and to blame. We blame others
as we blame ourselves; and the more we know, the more, it may be, we are
disposed to blame. Certainly it will surprise us to be told that the better we
understand our own actions—our own motives and the circumstances surrounding them—the freer from self-blame we shall inevitably feel. The
contrary is surely often true. The more deeply we investigate the course of

Isaiah Berlin, *Historical Inevitability* (1954), pp. 58–62. Published by Oxford University Press
under the auspices of the London School of Economics and Political Science, London.

our own conduct, the more blameworthy our behavior may seem to us to be, the more remorse we may be disposed to feel; and if this holds for ourselves, it is not reasonable to expect us necessarily, and in all cases, to withhold it from others. Our situations may differ from theirs, but not always so widely as to make all comparisons unfair. We ourselves may be accused unjustly, and so become acutely sensitive to the dangers of unjustly blaming others. But because blame can be unjust and the temptation to utter it very strong, it does not follow that it is never just; and because judgments can be based on ignorance, can spring from violent, or perverse, or silly, or shallow, or unfair notions, it does not follow that the opposites of these qualities do not exist at all; that we are mysteriously doomed to a degree of relativism and subjectivism in history, from which we are no less mysteriously free, or at any rate more free, in our normal daily thought and transactions with one another. Indeed, the major fallacy of this position must by now be too obvious to need pointing out. We are told that we are creatures of nature or environment, or of history, and that this colors our temperament, our judgments, our principles. Every judgment is relative, every evaluation subjective, made what and as it is by the interplay of the factors of its own time and place, individual or collective. But relative to what? Subjective in contrast with what? Involved in some ephemeral pattern as opposed to what conceivable, presumably timeless, independence of such distorting factors? Relative terms (especially pejoratives) need correlatives, or else they turn out to be without meaning themselves, mere gibes, propagandist phrases designed to throw discredit, and not to describe or analyze. We know what we mean by disparaging a judgment or a method as subjective or biased—we mean that proper methods of weighing evidence have been too far ignored: or that what are normally called facts have been overlooked or suppressed or perverted; or that evidence normally accepted as sufficient to account for the acts of one individual or society is, for no good reason, ignored in some other case similar in all relevant respects; or that canons of interpretation are arbitrarily altered from case to case, that is, without consistency or principle; or that we have reasons for thinking that the historian in question wished to establish certain conclusions for reasons other than those justified by the evidence according to canons of valid inference accepted as normal in his day or in ours, and that this has blinded him to the criteria and methods normal in his field for verifying facts and proving conclusions; or all, or any, of these together; or other considerations like them. These are the kinds of ways in which superficiality is, in practice, distinguished from depth, bias from objectivity, perversion of facts from honesty, stupidity from perspicacity, passion and confusion from detachment and lucidity. And if we grasp these rules correctly, we are fully justified in denouncing breaches of them on the part of anyone; why should we not? But, it may be objected, what of words such as we have used so liberally above—"valid," "normal," "proper," "relevant," "perverted," "suppression of facts," "interpretation"—what do they signify? Is the meaning and use of these crucial terms so very fixed and unambiguous? May not that which is thought relevant or convincing in one generation be regarded as irrelevant in the next? What are unquestioned facts to one historian may, often enough, seem merely a suspicious piece of theorizing to another. This is indeed so. Rules for the weighing of evidence do change. The accepted data of one age seem to its remote successors shot through with metaphysical presuppositions so queer as to be scarcely intelligible. All objectivity, we shall again be told, is subjective, is what it is relatively to its own time and place; all veracity, reliability, all the insights and gifts of an intellectually fertile period are such only relatively to their own "climate of opinion"; nothing is eternal, everything flows. Yet frequently as this kind of thing has been said, and plausible as it may seem it remains in this context mere rhetoric. We do distinguish facts, not indeed from the valuations which enter into their very texture, but from interpretations of them; the borderline may not be distinct, but if I say that Stalin is dead and General Franco still alive, my statement may be accurate or mistaken, but nobody in his senses could, as words are used, take me to be advancing a theory or an interpretation. But if I say that Stalin exterminated a great many peasant proprietors because in his infancy he had been swaddled by his nurse, and that this made him aggressive, while General Franco has not done so because he did not go through this kind of experience, no one but a very naive student of the social sciences would take me to be claiming to assert a fact, and that, no matter how many times I begin my sentences with the words "It is a fact." And I shall not readily believe you if you tell me that for Thucydides (or even for some Sumerian scribe) no fundamental distinction existed between relatively "hard" facts and relatively "disputable" interpretations. The borderline has, no doubt, always been wide and vague; it may be a shifting frontier, more distinct in some terrains than in others, but unless we know where, within certain limits, it lies, we fail to understand descriptive language altogether. The modes of thought of the ancients or of any cultures remote from our own are comprehensible to us only in the degree to which we share some, at any rate, of their basic categories; and the distinction between fact and theory is basic among these. I may dispute whether a given historian is profound or shallow, objective in his methods and impartial in his judgments, or borne on the wings of some obsessive hypothesis or overpowering emotion: but what I mean by these contrasted terms will not be utterly different for those who disagree with me, else there would be no argument; and will not, if I can claim to decipher texts at all correctly, be so widely different in different cultures and times and places as to make all communication systematically misleading and delusive. "Objective," "true," "fair," are words of large content, their uses are many, their edges often blurred. Ambiguities and confusions are always possible and often dangerous. Nevertheless such terms do possess meanings, which may, indeed, be fluid, but stay within limits recognized by normal usage, and refer to standards commonly accepted by those who work in relevant fields; and that not merely within one generation or society, but across large stretches of time and space. The mere claim that these crucial terms, these concepts or categories or standards, change in meaning or application, is to assume that such changes can to some degree be traced by methods which themselves are *pro tanto* not held liable to such change; for if these change in their turn, then, *ex hypothesi,* they do so in no way discoverable by us. And if not discoverable, then not discountable, and therefore of no use as a stick with which to beat us for our alleged subjectiveness or relativity, our delusions of grandeur and permanence, of the absoluteness of our standards in a world of ceaseless change.

> *J. H. Hexter has explained how the historian—even though he is formed by his own "day"—can still hope to attain to a true understanding of the past.*

FROM *The Historian and His Day* BY J. H. HEXTER

THE PRESENT-MINDED CONTEND that in writing history no historian can free himself of his total experience and that that experience is inextricably involved not only in the limits of knowledge but also in the passions, prejudices, assumptions and prepossessions, in the events, crises and tensions of his own day. Therefore those passions, prejudices, assumptions, prepossessions, events, crises and tensions of the historian's own day inevitably permeate what he writes about the past. This is the crucial allegation of the present-minded, and if it is wholly correct, the issue must be settled in their favor and the history-minded pack up their apodictic and categorical-imperative baggage and depart in silence. Frequently discussions of this crucial issue have got bogged down because the history-minded keep trying to prove that the historian can counteract the influence of his own day, while the present-minded keep saying that this is utterly impossible. And of course on this question the latter are quite right. A historian has no day but his own, so what is he going to counteract it with? He is in the situation of Archimedes who could find no fulcrum for the lever with which to move the Earth. Clearly if the historian is to be history-minded rather than present-minded he must find the means of being so in his own day, not outside it. And thus at last we come up against the crucial question—what *is* the historian's own day?

As soon as we put the question this way we realize that there is no ideal

Reprinted from *Reappraisals in History* (1962), pp. 5–13, by J. H. Hexter by permission of Northwestern University Press and Longmans, Green & Co., Ltd., Harlow, England.

Historian's Day; there are many days, all different, and each with a particular historian attached to it. Now since in actuality there is no such thing as
The Historian's Day, no one can be qualified to say what it actually consists
of. Indeed, although I know a good number of individual historians on
terms of greater or less intimacy, I would feel ill-qualified to describe with
certainty what any of their days are. There is, however, one historian about
whose day I can speak with assurance. For I myself am a historian at least in
the technical sense of the word; I have possessed for a considerable time the
parchment inscribed with the appropriate phrases to indicate that I have
served my apprenticeship and am out of my indentures. So I will describe as
briefly as I can my own day. I do so out of no appetite for self-revelation or
self-expression, but simply because the subject is germane to our inquiry and
because it is the one matter on which I happen to be the world's leading
authority. Let us then hurry through this dreary journal.

I rise early and have breakfast. While eating, I glance through the
morning paper and read the editorial page. I then go to the college that
employs me and teach for two to four hours five days a week. Most of the
time the subject matter I deal with in class is cobwebbed with age. Three
fourths of it dates back from a century and a quarter to three millennia; all
of it happened at least thirty years ago. Then comes lunch with a few of my
colleagues. Conversation at lunch ranges widely through professional shop-
talk, politics, high and ghostly matters like religion, the nature of art or the
universe, and the problems of child rearing, and finally academic scuttlebutt.
At present there is considerable discussion of the peculiar incongruence
between the social importance of the academic and his economic reward.
This topic has the merit of revealing the profound like-mindedness, tran-
scending all occasional conflicts, of our little community. From lunch to
bedtime my day is grimly uniform. There are of course occasional and casual
variations—preparation of the ancient material above mentioned for the next
day's classes, a ride in the country with the family, a committee meeting at
college, a movie, a play, a novel, or a book by some self-anointed Deep
Thinker. Still by and large from one in the afternoon to midnight, with time
out for dinner and domestic matters, I read things written between 1450 and
1650 or books written by historians on the basis of things written between
1450 and 1650. I vary the routine on certain days by writing about what I
have read on the other days. On Saturdays and in the summer I start my
reading or writing at nine instead of noon. It is only fair to add that most
days I turn on a news broadcast or two at dinnertime, and that I spend an
hour or two with the Sunday paper.

Now I am sure that many people will consider so many days so spent to
be a frightful waste of precious time; and indeed, as most of the days of most
men, it does seem a bit trivial. Be that as it may, it remains one historian's
own day. It is his own day in the only sense in which that phrase can be used
without its being pretentious, pompous and meaningless. For a man's own
days are not everything that happens in the world while he lives and

breathes. As I write, portentous and momentous things are no doubt being done in Peiping, Teheran, Bonn, and Jakarta. But these things are no part of my day; they are outside of my experience, and though one or two of them may faintly impinge on my consciousness tomorrow via the headlines in the morning paper, that is probably as far as they will get. At best they are likely to remain fluttering fragments on the fringe of my experience, not well-ordered parts of it. I must insist emphatically that the history I write is, as the present-minded say, intimately connected with my own day and inextricably linked with my own experience; but I must insist with even stronger emphasis that my day is not someone else's day, or the ideal Day of Contemporary Man; it is just the way I happen to dispose of twenty-four hours. By the same token the experience that is inextricably linked to any history I may happen to write is not the ideal Experience of Twentieth-Century Man in World Chaos, but just the way I happen to put in my time over the series of my days.

Now it may seem immodest or perhaps simply fantastic to take days spent as are mine—days so little attuned to the great harmonies, discords and issues of the present—and hold them up for contemplation. Yet I will dare to suggest that in this historian's own humdrum days there is one peculiarity that merits thought. The peculiarity lies in the curious relation that days so squandered seem to establish between the present and a rather remote sector of the past. I do not pretend that I am wholly unconcerned by the larger public issues and catastrophes of the present; nor am I without opinions on a large number of contemporary issues. On some of them I am vigorously dogmatic as, indeed, are most of the historians I know. Yet my knowledge about such issues, although occasionally fairly extensive, tends to be haphazard, vague, unsystematic and disorderly. And the brute fact of the matter is that even if I had the inclination, I do not have the time to straighten that knowledge out except at the cost of alterations in the ordering of my days that I am not in the least inclined to undertake.

So for a small part of my day I live under a comfortable rule of bland intellectual irresponsibility vis-à-vis the Great Issues of the Contemporary World, a rule that permits me to go off half-cocked with only slight and occasional compunction. But during most of my day—that portion of it that I spend in dealing with the Great and Not-So-Great Issues of the World between 1450 and 1650—I live under an altogether different rule. The commandments of that rule are:

1. Do not go off half-cocked.
2. Get the story straight.
3. Keep prejudices about present-day issues out of this area.

The commandments are counsels of perfection, but they are not merely that; they are enforced by sanctions, both external and internal. The serried array of historical trade journals equipped with extensive book-review columns provides the most powerful external sanction. The columns are often at the disposal of cantankerous cranks ever ready to expose to obloquy "pamphleteers" who think that Clio is an "easy bought mistress bound to suit her ways to the intellectual appetites of the current customer."[1] On more than one occasion I have been a cantankerous crank. When I write about the period between 1450 and 1650 I am well aware of a desire to give unto others no occasion to do unto me as I have done unto some of them.

The reviewing host seems largely to have lined up with the history-minded. This seems to be a consequence of their training. Whatever the theoretical biases of their individual members, the better departments of graduate study in history do not encourage those undergoing their novitiate to resolve research problems by reference to current ideological conflicts. Consequently most of us have been conditioned to feel that it is not quite proper to characterize John Pym as a liberal, or Thomas More as a socialist, or Niccolò Machiavelli as a proto-Fascist, and we tend to regard this sort of characterization as at best a risky pedagogic device. Not only the characterization but the thought process that leads to it lie under a psychological ban; and thus to the external sanction of the review columns is added the internal sanction of the still small voice that keeps saying, "One really shouldn't do it that way."[2]

The austere rule we live under as historians has some curious consequences. In my case one of the consequences is that my knowledge of the period around the sixteenth century in Europe is of a rather different order than my knowledge about current happenings. Those preponderant segments of my own day spent in the discussion, investigation and contemplation of that remote era may not be profitably spent but at least they are spent in an orderly, systematic, purposeful way. The contrast can be pointed up by a few details. I have never read the Social Security Act, but I have read the Elizabethan Poor Law in all its successive versions and moreover I have made some study of its application. I have never read the work of a single existentialist but I have read Calvin's *Institutes of the Christian Religion* from cover to cover. I know practically nothing for sure about the relation of the institutions of higher education in America to the social structure, but I know a fair bit about the relation between the two in France, England and the Netherlands in the fifteenth and sixteenth centuries. I have never studied the Economic Reports to the President that would enable me to appraise the state of the American nation in the 1950s, but I have studied closely the *Discourse of the Commonwealth of England* and derived from it some reasonably coherent notions about the condition of England in the 1550s. Now the consequence of all this is inevitable. Instead of the passions,

---

[1] *American Historical Review*, 51 (1946), 487.
[2] I do not for a moment intend to imply that current dilemmas have not suggested *problems* for historical investigation. It is obvious that such dilemmas are among the numerous and entirely legitimate points of origin of historical study. The actual issue, however, has nothing to do with the point of origin of historical studies, but with the mode of treatment of historical problems.

prejudices, assumptions and prepossessions, the events, crises and tensions of the present dominating my view of the past, *it is the other way about.* The passions, prejudices, assumptions and prepossessions, the events, crises and tensions of early modern Europe to a very considerable extent lend precision to my rather haphazard notions about the present. I make sense of present-day welfare-state policy by thinking of it in connection with the "commonwealth" policies of Elizabeth. I do the like with respect to the contemporary struggle for power and conflict of ideologies by throwing on them such light as I find in the Catholic-Calvinist struggle of the sixteenth century.

Teaching makes me aware of the peculiarities of my perspective. The days of my students are very different from mine. They have spent little time indeed in contemplating the events of the sixteenth century. So when I tell them that the Christian Humanists, in their optimistic aspiration to reform the world by means of education, were rather like our own progressive educators, I help them understand the Christian Humanists. But my teaching strategy moves in the opposite direction from my own intellectual experience. The comparison first suggested itself to me as a means for understanding not Christian Humanism but progressive education. There is no need to labor this point. After all, ordinarily the process of thought is from the better known to the worse known, and my knowledge of the sixteenth century is a good bit more precise than my knowledge of the twentieth. Perhaps there is nothing to be said for this peculiar way of thinking; it may be altogether silly; but in the immediate context I am not obliged to defend it. I present it simply as one of those brute facts of life dear to the heart of the present-minded. It is in fact one way that one historian's day affects his judgment.

In the controversy that provided the starting point of this rambling essay, the essential question is sometimes posed with respect to the relation of the historian to his own *day*. In other instances it is posed with respect to his relation to his own *time*. Having discovered how idiosyncratic was the day of one historian we may inquire whether his time is also peculiar. The answer is, "Yes, his time *is* a bit odd." And here it is possible to take a welcome leave of the first person singular. For, although my day is peculiar to me, my time, as a historian, is like the time of other historians.

For our purposes the crucial fact about the ordinary time of all men, even of historians in their personal as against their professional capacity, is that in no man's time is he *really* sure what is going to happen next. This is true, obviously, not only of men of the present time but also of all men of all past times. Of course there are large routine areas of existence in which we can make pretty good guesses; and if this were not so, life would be unbearable. Thus, my guess, five evenings a week in term time, that I will be getting up the following morning to teach classes at my place of employment provides me with a useful operating rule; yet it has been wrong occasionally, and will be wrong again. With respect to many matters more important, all is uncertain. Will there be war or peace next year? Will my children turn out well or ill? Will I be alive or dead thirty years hence? three years hence? tomorrow?

The saddest words of tongue or pen may be, "It might have been." The most human are, "If I had only known." But it is precisely characteristic of the historian that he does know. He is really sure what is going to happen next, not in his time as a pilgrim here below, but in his own time as a historian. The public servant Conyers Read, for example, when he worked high in the councils of the Office of Strategic Services did not know what the outcome of the maneuvers he helped plan would be. But for all the years from 1568 during which he painstakingly investigated the public career of Francis Walsingham, the eminent Tudor historian Conyers Read knew that the Spanish Armada would come against England and that the diplomatic maneuvers of Mr. Secretary Walsingham would assist in its defeat. Somewhat inaccurately we might say that while man's time ordinarily is oriented to the future, the historian's time is oriented to the past. It might be better to say that while men are ordinarily trying to connect the present with a future that is to be, the historian connects his present with a future that has already been.

The professional historian does not have a monopoly of his peculiar time, or rather, as Carl Becker once put it, every man is on occasion his own historian. But the historian alone lives systematically in the historian's own time. And from what we have been saying it is clear that this time has a unique dimension. Each man in his own time tries to discover the motives and the causes of the actions of those people he has to deal with; and the historian does the like with varying degrees of success. But, as other men do not and cannot, the historian knows something of the results of the acts of those he deals with: this is the unique dimension of the historian's time. If, in saying that the historian cannot escape his own time, the present-minded meant this peculiarly historical time—which they do not—they would be on solid ground. For the circumstances are rare indeed in which the historian has no notion whatever of the outcome of the events with which he is dealing. The very fact that he is a historian and that he has interested himself in a particular set of events fairly assures that at the outset he will have some knowledge of what happened afterward.

This knowledge makes it impossible for the historian to do merely what the history-minded say he should do—consider the past in its own terms, and envisage events as the men who lived through them did. Surely he should try to do that; just as certainly he must do more than that simply because he knows about those events what none of the men contemporary with them knew; he knows what their consequences were. To see the events surrounding the obscure monk Luther as Leo X saw them—as another "monks' quarrel" and a possible danger to the perquisites of the Curia—may help us understand the peculiar inefficacy of Papal policy at the time; but that does not preclude the historian from seeing the same events as the decisive step towards the final breach of the religious unity of Western Civilization. We may be quite sure however that nobody at the time, not even Luther himself, saw those events that way. The historian who resolutely refused to use the insight that his own peculiar time gave him would not be superior to his fellows; he would be merely foolish, betraying a singular failure to grasp what history is. For history is a becoming, an ongoing, and it is to be understood not only in terms of what comes before but also of what comes after.

What conclusions can we draw from our cursory examination of the historian's own time and his own day? What of the necessity, alleged by the present-minded, of rewriting history anew each generation? In some respects the estimate is over-generous, in one respect too niggardly. The necessity will in part be a function of the lapsed time between the events written about and the present. The history of the Treaty of Versailles of 1919 may indeed need to be written over a number of times in the next few generations as its consequences more completely unfold. But this is not true of the Treaty of Madrid of 1527. Its consequences for better or worse pretty well finished their unfolding a good while back. The need for rewriting history is also a function of the increase in actual data on the thing to be written about. Obviously any general estimate of the rate of increase of such data would be meaningless. History also must be rewritten as the relevant and usable knowledge about man, about his ways and his waywardness, increases. Here again there has been a tendency to exaggerate the speed with which that knowledge is increasing. The hosannahs that have greeted many master ideas about man during the past fifty years seem more often than not to be a reflection of an urge toward secular salvation in a shaky world rather than a precise estimate of the cognitive value of the ideas in question. Frequently such master ideas have turned out to be plain old notions in new fancy dress, or simply wrong. Perhaps the imperative, felt by the present-minded, to rewrite history every generation is less the fruit of a real necessity than of their own attempts to write it always in conformity with the latest intellectual mode. A little less haste might mean a little more speed. For the person engaged in the operation it is all too easy to mistake for progress a process that only involves skipping from recent to current errors.

If, instead of asking how often history *must* or ought to be rewritten we ask how often it *will* be rewritten, the answer is that it will be rewritten, as it always has been, from day to day. This is so because the rewriting of history is inescapably what each working historian in fact does in his own day. That is precisely how he puts in his time. We seek new data. We re-examine old data to discover in them relations and connections that our honored predecessors may have missed. On these data we seek to bring to bear whatever may seem enlightening and relevant out of our own day. And what may be relevant is as wide as the full range of our own daily experience, intellectual, aesthetic, political, social, personal. Some current event may, of course, afford a historian an understanding of what men meant five hundred years ago when they said that a prince must rule through *amour et crémeur,* love and fear. But then so might his perusal of a socio-psychological investigation into the ambivalence of authority in Papua. So might his reading of Shakespeare's *Richard II*. And so might his relations with his own children.

For each historian brings to the rewriting of history the full range of the remembered experience of his own days, that unique array that he alone possesses and is. For some historians that sector of their experience which impinges on the Great Crisis of the Contemporary World sets up the vibrations that attune them to the part of the past that is the object of their professional attention. Some of us, however, vibrate less readily to those crises. We feel our way toward the goals of our historic quest by lines of experience having precious little to do with the Great Crises of the Contemporary World. He would be bold indeed who would insist that all historians should follow one and the same line of experience in their quest, or who would venture to say what this single line is that all should follow. He would not only be bold; he would almost certainly be wrong. History thrives in measure as the experience of each historian differs from that of his fellows. It is indeed the wide and varied range of experience covered by all the days of all historians that makes the rewriting of history—not in each generation but for each historian—at once necessary and inevitable.

One of the great historians of the twentieth century, Marc Bloch, held that knowledge about the past and knowledge about the present are mutually complementary and that both kinds of knowledge are essential for an understanding of the modern world. He wrote the following lines while working as a Resistance leader in France during World War II. The Nazis shot him in 1944.

FROM *The Historian's Craft* BY MARC BLOCH

[*Some scholars hold—B.T.*] that contemporary society is perfectly susceptible of scientific investigation. But they admit this only to reserve its study for branches of learning quite distinct from that which has the past for its object. They analyze, and they claim, for example, to understand the contemporary economic system on the basis of observations limited to a few decades. In a word, they consider the epoch in which we live as separated from its predecessors by contrasts so clear as to be self-explanatory. Such is

Marc Bloch, *The Historian's Craft*, pp. 38–47, translated by Peter Putnam. Copyright 1953 by Alfred A. Knopf, Inc.

also the instinctive attitude of a great many of the merely curious. The history of the remoter periods attracts them only as an innocuous intellectual luxury. On one hand, a small group of antiquarians taking a ghoulish delight in unwrapping the winding-sheets of the dead gods; on the other, sociologists, economists, and publicists, the only explorers of the living.

UNDERSTANDING THE PRESENT BY THE PAST

Under close scrutiny the prerogative of self-intelligibility thus attributed to present time is found to be based upon a set of strange postulates.

In the first place, it supposes that, within a generation or two, human affairs have undergone a change which is not merely rapid, but total, so that no institution of long standing, no traditional form of conduct, could have escaped the revolutions of the laboratory and the factory. It overlooks the force of inertia peculiar to so many social creations.

Man spends his time devising techniques of which he afterwards remains a more or less willing prisoner. What traveler in northern France has not been struck by the strange pattern of the fields? For centuries, changes in ownership have modified the original design; yet, even today, the sight of these inordinately long and narrow strips, dividing the arable land into a prodigious number of pieces, is something which baffles the scientific agriculturalist. The waste of effort which such a disposition entails and the problems which it imposes upon the cultivators are undeniable. How are we to account for it? Certain impatient publicists have replied: "By the Civil Code and its inevitable effects. Change the laws on inheritance and the evil will be removed." Had they known history better, or had they further questioned a peasant mentality shaped by centuries of experience, they would not have thought the cure so simple. Indeed, this pattern dates back to origins so distant that no scholar has yet succeeded in accounting for it satisfactorily. The settlers in the era of the dolmens have more to do with it than the lawyers of the First Empire. Perpetuating itself, as it were, of necessity, for want of correction, this ignorance of the past not only confuses contemporary science, but confounds contemporary action.

A society that could be completely molded by its immediately preceding period would have to have a structure so malleable as to be virtually invertebrate. It would also have to be a society in which communication between generations was conducted, so to speak, in "Indian file"—the children having contact with their ancestors only through the mediation of their parents.

Now, this is not true. It is not true even when the communication is purely oral. Take our villages, for example. Because working conditions keep the mother and father away almost all day, the young children are brought up chiefly by their grandparents. Consequently, with the molding of each new mind, there is a backward step, joining the most malleable to the most inflexible mentality, while skipping that generation which is the sponsor of change. There is small room for doubt that this is the source of that traditionalism inherent in so many peasant societies. The instance is particularly clear, but it is far from unique. Because the natural antagonism between age groups is always intensified between neighboring generations, more than one youth has learned at least as much from the aged as from those in their prime.

Still more strongly, between even widely scattered generations, the written word vastly facilitates those transfers of thought which supply the true continuity of a civilization. Take Luther, Calvin, Loyola, certainly men from another time—from the sixteenth century, in fact. The first duty of the historian who would understand and explain them will be to return them to their milieu, where they are immersed in the mental climate of their time and faced by problems of conscience rather different from our own. But who would dare to say that the understanding of the Protestant or the Catholic Reformation, several centuries removed, is not far more important for a proper grasp of the world today than a great many other movements of thought or feeling, which are certainly more recent, yet more ephemeral?

In a word, the fallacy is clear, and it is only necessary to formulate it in order to destroy it. It represents the course of human evolution as a series of short, violent jerks, no one of which exceeds the space of a few lifetimes. Observation proves, on the contrary, that the mighty convulsions of that vast, continuing development are perfectly capable of extending from the beginning of time to the present. What would we think of a geophysicist who, satisfied with having computed their remoteness to a fraction of an inch, would then conclude that the influence of the moon upon the earth is far greater than that of the sun? Neither in outer space, nor in time, can the potency of a force be measured by the single dimension of distance.

Finally, what of those things past which seem to have lost all authority over the present—faiths which have vanished without a trace, social forms which have miscarried, techniques which have perished? Would anyone think that, even among these, there is nothing useful for his understanding? That would be to forget that there is no true understanding without a certain range of comparison; provided, of course, that that comparison is based upon differing and, at the same time, related realities. One could scarcely deny that such is here the case.

Certainly, we no longer consider today, as Machiavelli wrote, and as Hume or Bonald thought, that there is, in time, "at least something which is changeless: that is man." We have learned that man, too, has changed a great deal in his mind and, no less certainly, in the most delicate organs of his body. How should it be otherwise? His mental climate has been greatly altered; and to no less an extent, so, too, have his hygiene and his diet. However, there must be a permanent foundation in human nature and in human society, or the very names of man or society become meaningless. How, then, are we to believe that we understand these men, if we study them only in their reactions to circumstances peculiar to a moment? It would be an inadequate test of them, even for that particular moment. A great many potentialities, which might at any instant emerge from conceal-ment, a great many more or less unconscious drives behind individual or collective attitudes, would remain in the shadows. In a unique case the specific elements cannot be differentiated; hence an interpretation cannot be made.

UNDERSTANDING THE PAST BY THE PRESENT

This solidarity of the ages is so effective that the lines of connection work both ways. Misunderstanding of the present is the inevitable consequence of ignorance of the past. But a man may wear himself out just as fruitlessly in seeking to understand the past, if he is totally ignorant of the present. There is an anecdote which I have already recounted elsewhere: I had gone with Henri Pirenne to Stockholm; we had scarcely arrived, when he said to me: "What shall we go to see first? It seems that there is a new city hall here. Let's start there." Then, as if to ward off my surprise, he added: "If I were an antiquarian, I would have eyes only for old stuff, but I am a historian. Therefore, I love life." This faculty of understanding the living is, in very truth, the master quality of the historian. Despite their occasional frigidity of style, the greatest of our number have all possessed it. Fustel or Maitland, in their austere way, had it as much as Michelet. And, perhaps, it originates as a gift from the fairies, quite inaccessible to anyone who has not found it in his cradle. That does not lessen the obligation to exercise and develop it con-stantly. How? How better than by the example of Henri Pirenne—by keeping in constant touch with the present day?

For here, in the present, is immediately perceptible that vibrance of human life which only a great effort of the imagination can restore to the old texts. I have many times read, and I have often narrated, accounts of wars and battles. Did I truly know, in the full sense of that word, did I know from within, before I myself had suffered the terrible, sickening reality, what it meant for an army to be encircled, what it meant for a people to meet defeat? Before I myself had breathed the joy of victory in the summer and autumn of 1918 (and, although, alas! its perfume will not again be quite the same, I yearn to fill my lungs with it a second time) did I truly know all that was inherent in that beautiful word? In the last analysis, whether con-sciously or no, it is always by borrowing from our daily experiences and by shading them, where necessary, with new tints that we derive the elements which help us to restore the past. The very names we use to describe ancient ideas or vanished forms of social organization would be quite meaningless if we had not known living men. The value of these merely instinctive impressions will be increased a hundredfold if they are replaced by a ready and critical observation. A great mathematician would not, I suppose, be less great because blind to the world in which he lives. But the scholar who has no inclination to observe the men, the things, or the events around him will perhaps deserve the title, as Pirenne put it, of a useful antiquarian. He would be wise to renounce all claims to that of a historian.

Moreover, the cultivation of historical sensitivity is not always all that is involved. It may happen, in a given line, that the knowledge of the present bears even more immediately upon the understanding of the past.

It would be a grievous error, indeed, to think that the order which historians adopt for their inquiries must necessarily correspond to the sequence of events. Even though they restore its true direction afterwards, they have often benefited at the outset by reading history, as Maitland said, "backwards." For the natural progression of all research is from the best (or least badly) understood to the most obscure. Certainly, it is far from true that the light of documentation grows ever brighter as we pass down the corridor of the ages. For example, we are much less well-informed on the tenth century of our era than on the epoch of Caesar or Augustus. In the majority of cases however, the nearest periods correspond better with the zones of relative clarity. We must add that, in proceeding mechanically from early to late, there is always the risk of wasting time in tracking down the beginning or causes of phenomena which, in the event, may turn out to be somewhat imaginary. The most illustrious among us have occasionally made strange mistakes through having neglected to pursue a prudently retrogressive method whenever and wherever it was indicated. Fustel de Coulanges devoted himself to the "origins" of feudal institutions of which he had formed, I fear, only a rather confused picture, and to the beginnings of a serfdom which, misled by secondhand descriptions, he conceived in entirely false colors.

Now, more often than is generally supposed, it happens that, in order to find daylight, the historian may have to pursue his subject right up to the present. In certain of its fundamental features, our rural landscape, as has been previously mentioned, dates from a very remote epoch. However, in order to interpret the rare documents which permit us to fathom its misty beginnings, in order to ask the right questions, even in order to know what we were talking about, it was necessary to fulfill a primary condition: that of observing and analyzing our present landscape. For it alone furnished those comprehensive vistas without which it was impossible to begin. Not, indeed, that there could be any question of imposing this forever-static picture, just as it is, at each stage of the journey upstream to the headwaters of the past. Here, as elsewhere, it is change which the historian is seeking to grasp. But in the film which he is examining, only the last picture remains quite clear. In order to reconstruct the faded features of the others, it behooves him first to unwind the spool in the opposite direction from that in which the pictures were taken.

There is, then, just one science of men in time. It requires us to join the study of the dead and the living. What shall we call it? I have already explained why the ancient name, "history," seemed to me the best. It is the most comprehensive, the least exclusive, the most electric with stirring reminders of a more than age-old endeavor. In proposing to extend history right down to the present (contrary to certain prejudices which are not so old as history itself), I have no desire to expand the claims of my own profession. Life is too short, and science too vast, to permit even the greatest genius a total experience of humanity. Some men will always specialize in the present, as others do in the Stone Age or in Egyptology. We simply ask both to bear in mind that historical research will tolerate no autarchy. Isolated, each will understand only by halves, even within his own field of study; for the only true history, which can advance only through mutual aid, is universal history.

A Note on the Type

This book is set in Granjon, a type named in compliment to Robert Granjon, type-cutter and printer—Antwerp, Lyons, Rome, Paris—active from 1523 to 1590. The boldest and most original designer of his time, he was one of the first to practice the trade of type-founder apart from that of printer.

This type face was designed by George W. Jones, who based his drawings on a type used by Claude Garamond (1510–1561) in his beautiful French books, and more closely resembles Garamond's own than do any of the various modern types that bear his name.

This book was designed by Betty Anderson. It was composed, printed, and bound by Kingsport Press, Inc., Kingsport, Tennessee.

B